Onward and Upward

Guide for Getting Through New York Divorce & Family Law Issues

Compiled and Edited by

Cari B. Rincker, Esq.

ISBN-13: 978-0-692-55654-2
ISBN-10: 0692556540

"This publication is designed to provide general information prepared by professionals in regard to the subject matter covered. It is sold with the understanding that the publisher is not engaged in rendering legal, accounting or other professional service. Although prepared by professionals, the publication should not be utilized as a substitute for a professional service in specific situations. If legal advice or other expert assistance is required, the service of a professional should be sought."

(From a Declaration of Principles jointly adopted by a Committee of the American Bar Association and a Committee of Publishers)

Original sources of authority should be consulted by attorneys or other professionals dealing with specific legal matters.

This book is designed for people living in the State of New York or otherwise subject to New York family and matrimonial law. This book is **not a substitute for individual legal or professional advice** tailored to individual facts and circumstances. No **attorney-client relationship** is intended or established by reading this material between the reader and the authors. Readers should confer with an attorney and the appropriate state or federal agency to ascertain the current status of the law.

Every effort has been made to include up-to-date information; however, the law is not static and is constantly changing. Research and background materials were completed in Fall 2015. If you believe there are any inaccuracies in the law printed in this book, please email the editor and coordinator Cari B. Rincker, Esq. at cari@rinckerlaw.com noting the page number and paragraph. Every effort will be made to update this book in subsequent versions.

DEDICATION

To my parents, who have given me both roots and wings. After four decades together, they are role models to me on what a loving partnership looks like.

- Cari B. Rincker, Esq.

INTRODUCTION

By Cari B. Rincker, Esq.

Not only does this book cover ***a myriad of New York family and matrimonial law issues***, it also provides information on the variety of ***resources and professionals*** available to help people through various transitions in their life – getting married, having children, separating from a partner, going through a divorce, and moving on after a divorce and separation and becoming a better version of oneself. This book is a ***unique compilation*** offering invaluable information and diverse viewpoints on this subject matter.

The authors themselves have a ***variety of experiences***, backgrounds, and education. Each of the authors of this book cares deeply about people going through various family and matrimonial issues and wants the reader to go through life "***Onward and Upward***" through whatever comes his or her way. As people, we cannot fully control what happens to us – but we can control how we react to it to move to the next chapter in our lives. A divorce or separation is simply a transition to a new phase.

This book is ***not intended to give legal advice***; readers should seek the guidance of licensed professionals to best help guide them. This resource is aimed to give a general overview of New York family and matrimonial law and practical information to help guide the reader to the professionals available to them. No matter the situation – whether you are cohabitating with a long term partner, getting married, having children, or going through a divorce or separation – there is something in this book for you.

TABLE OF CONTENTS

ACKNOWLEDGMENTS

Proofreaders: Ruth Kornegay-Baez + Karen Laifer, Esq.
Book Cover Design: Ranch House Designs, Inc.

PART I: PROCESSES

SECTION A: COURTS

CHAPTER 1

FAMILY COURT VS. SUPREME COURT

By Nicole Trivlis, Esq.

For many types of family matters, a party seeking the assistance of a court to determine an issue usually has the option of filing their case in the ***New York Supreme Court*** or the ***New York Family Court***. Both state courts are located in each county in New York. Although both of these courts may have the power to hear and determine your matter, choosing the proper venue to file your matter will depend on a number of factors. These factors include, but are not limited to, the nature of your matter and your financial resources.

Background

Supreme Court

The New York Supreme Court was established in 1691 through legislation adopted by the New York Assembly and is governed by the ***New York State Civil Practice Law and Rules***, commonly known as the "CPLR." The Supreme Court is a ***court of general jurisdiction***, meaning it has the authority to hear all types of cases, including divorces and many family law disputes. There are 62 Supreme Courts in New York State, one in each county with each respective Supreme Court having jurisdiction over the local courts and matters filed in their particular county. The name Supreme Court arose due to the Court's authority over the local courts in the county. Despite its name, the Supreme Court is not the highest court in New York State. The highest court in ***New York State is the Court of Appeals***.

Family Court

The New York State Family Court was created in 1962 through an amendment to the New York State Constitution. See New York Constitution Article VI, § 13. There is at least one Family Court located in each county in New York State, and, commonly, there is more than one courthouse in each county. Unlike the Supreme Court, the Family Court is a ***court of limited jurisdiction*** as it only has the power to hear matters authorized by the Family Court Act. The Family Court Act is composed of twelve articles that set forth the procedures the Family Court is to follow when deciding cases. The Family Court has jurisdiction to hear and determine the following matters:

1. Juvenile Delinquency Cases

Article 3 of the Family Court Act grants the Family Court authority to hear juvenile delinquency cases. A juvenile delinquency proceeding is brought by an agency against a child under the age of 16. In this proceeding, the agency alleges that the child committed acts that if committed by an adult, would constitute criminal conduct under the ***New York Penal Code***. When the Family Court makes a determination on the juvenile delinquency proceeding, the child may be placed on probation, placed in a group home or facility, or released to his or her parents. For more information on juvenile delinquency cases, read Chapter 12 by Ronna Gordon-Galchus and Frank M. Galchus.

2. Spousal and Child Support Cases

Article 4 of the Family Court Act authorizes the Family Court to hear spousal and child support cases. Although Article 4 of the Family Court Act grants the Family Court original jurisdiction over proceedings for the ***support of dependents***, Article VI, § 13(b)(4) of the ***New York State Constitution*** limits this power to support issues that are not related to a marital separation, divorce, annulment of marriage, or dissolution of marriage. Wendy Harris writes more about Spousal Maintenance in Part III Section B while Deborah Kaminetzky goes into great detail on child support in Chapter 11.

3. Paternity Cases

Article 5 of the Family Court Act grants the Family Court jurisdiction in proceedings to establish paternity. If a couple is married, the husband is ***automatically presumed to be the father*** of the child born during the parties' marriage. For circumstances where a couple is not married, the mother and father must sign an ***Acknowledgement of Paternity***, or obtain an ***Order of Filiation*** prior to paternity being legally established. If either party refuses to sign the Acknowledgement of Paternity, a proceeding may be initiated. For more information on paternity cases, read Chapter 14 authored by Ravi Cattry.

4. Custody and Visitation Cases

Article 6 of the Family Court Act grants the Family Court jurisdiction to determine ***temporary or permanent custody and visitation*** of a minor in an action for divorce, separation, or annulment with the same powers as the Supreme Court. The Supreme Court may refer a custody issue to the Family Court, even if it is in the context of a matrimonial action that the Supreme Court has jurisdiction over, such as an action for a divorce. See New York Family Court Act § 467(a) and § 652(a).

Regardless of a referral of custody from the Supreme Court, the Family Court has jurisdiction to make a determination on an application to enforce an award of custody and visitation made by the Supreme Court.[1] Upon a showing of a subsequent change of circumstances, they also have the power to make a determination on an application to modify a custody and visitation judgment or order issued by the Supreme Court. See New York Family Court Act § 652(a). Bonnie Mohr and Cari Rincker delve into more detail on custody and visitation issues in Chapter 10.

---

1 However, if the order of judgment from the Supreme Court has provided that it may be enforced or modified only in the Supreme Court, the Family Court is precluded from making a determination on these applications. See New York Family Court Act § 652(b).

5. Persons in Need of Supervision (PINS) Cases

Article 7 of the Family Court Act authorizes the Family Court to hear PINS cases, which is a proceeding ***brought by a parent or guardian***, ***person injured by the child***, or by an authorized ***agency***, against a child that alleges the parent is unable to control the child. The Family Court has the authority to determine if the child is in need of supervision or treatment. Kymberly Robinson writes briefly on PINS cases in Chapter 15.

6. Family Offenses (Orders of Protection)

Article 8 of the Family Court Act authorizes the Family Court to hear proceedings filed by a party seeking an order of protection. In order for the Court to have jurisdiction, the parties must be related by ***blood or marriage, formerly married, unrelated but have a child together, or have an intimate relationship with each other***. The Family Court has the authority to issue an order of protection for: disorderly conduct, harassment, aggravated harassment, menacing, reckless endangerment, assault or attempted assault, stalking, or criminal mischief. Joseph Nivin goes into more detail on Family Offenses in Section IV(A).

7. Conciliation Proceedings

Article 9 of the Family Court Act grants the Family Court jurisdiction over conciliation proceedings, or a proceeding brought by a party seeking assistance with reconciliation in their marriage. The Family Court has very limited authority with these types of proceedings. They have the power to conduct information conferences and refer the parties to ***voluntary social and religious organizations*** for counseling. Ravi Cattry speaks briefly on these proceedings in Section IV(B).

8. Child Protective Proceedings

Article 10 of the Family Court Act authorizes an agency to commence a proceeding against parents to have the Family Court determine whether they have ***neglected or abused their child(ren)***.

If a determination is made that the parent has neglected or abused their child(ren), the agency ***may remove*** the child(ren) from the home and place them in foster care. Joseph Nivin goes into more detail on child protective proceedings in Chapter 13.

Concurrent Jurisdiction Between Family Court and Supreme Court

As a court of general jurisdiction, the Supreme Court has concurrent jurisdiction over most matters the Family Court has jurisdiction to hear and determine pursuant to the Family Court Act.[2] Given that the ***Family Court's power is limited***, and it is only able to preside over those matters set forth in the Family Court Act, it does not have concurrent jurisdiction over most matters the Supreme Court has the power to hear and determine. For example, the Family Court does not have jurisdiction to hear divorce cases. Only the ***Supreme Court*** can determine a ***divorce proceeding***. Additionally, the Family Court does not have jurisdiction to hear matters to determine the property rights of spouses, such as, awarding exclusive use and possession of the marital residence, or directing a former spouse to turn over property to enforce support provisions, unless the Supreme Court authorizes this power by referring the matter to the Family Court. See New York Family Court Act § 466.

The Family Court also does not have the power to refer a matter to the Supreme Court. If a petition is filed in the Family Court prior to the filing of a divorce action, the Supreme Court may consolidate the petition with the divorce action. Consolidation of your matter is in the discretion of the Supreme Court judge who will make a determination based upon the factors of your case, such as, how far along your matter is in Family Court and the nature of your Family Court proceeding.

Type of Case	Family Court	Supreme Court
Child Support	Unmarried or Married	Married
Spousal Support	Unmarried or Married	Married
Paternity	All	
Child Custody	Unmarried or Married	Married

2 The Supreme Court does not determine PINS matters or Juvenile Delinquency matters. Additionally, if the parties are not married at the time action is filed, the action must be filed in the Family Court.

Child Visitation	Unmarried or Married	Married
Family Offenses	Unmarried or Married	Married
Conciliation Proceeding	All	
Persons in Need of Supervision	All	
Juvenile Delinquency	All	
Divorce/Annulment		All

Choosing the Court

For matters that either court has jurisdiction to hear and determine, the party or agency filing the proceeding has a ***choice of venue***. Choosing which court to file your matter may depend on how quickly each particular court can hear your case, whether you have retained an attorney to assist you in your matter, and the fees associated with commencing a lawsuit in either court.

> When someone is unrepresented by counsel, the courts will say that person is "*pro se*."

To commence an action in the Supreme Court and have an index number assigned to your case, you must pay a ***filing fee*** of $210. To have a judge assigned to your matter, you must then file a ***Request for Judicial Intervention***, and, in most cases, pay an additional filing fee of $95. When you file a matter in the Supreme Court, it is called an action and the parties are referred to as a ***plaintiff and defendant***. The procedural aspects of the Supreme Court make it difficult to proceed without an attorney, and often the retention of one is necessary, and sometimes mandatory.

Although ***retaining an attorney is recommended***, Family Court is friendlier to unrepresented litigants. Unlike the Supreme Court, a case filed in the Family Court may be filed for ***free***. The Family Court provides standard forms for most of the petitions heard before the Court. A matter filed in the Family Court is called a ***proceeding,*** and the parties are referred to as the ***petitioner and the respondent***. Depending on the type of your case, your matter will be heard by a **Judge, Support Magistrate, Court Attorney Referee or Judicial Hearing Officer**. As soon as a case is filed, your case will automatically be assigned to one of the foregoing and placed on the court's calendar.

The cost of hiring an attorney to represent you in your matter will vary. Hiring a private lawyer is often costly due to the multiple court appearances that may be necessary if you are proceeding within the court system. Resolving a matter often takes ***several appearances***, with each appearance typically lasting at least two hours. If you are unable to afford an attorney to represent you, one may be available through legal aid or the 18B panel available in Family Court and Supreme Court. Attorneys appointed through 18B are more frequently appointed in Family Court. If you believe you are experiencing a financial hardship and may qualify for assistance, you should advise the Court at your first appearance and they will instruct you of the procedure for applying for assistance.

Judge: Judges decide any legal questions that arise during the proceedings, and determine the outcome of cases.

Support Magistrate: Support magistrates oversee child and spousal support and paternity cases and determine the outcome of cases by issuing orders of support and filiation. The support magistrate orders can be appealed to a Family Court judge.

Court Referee: A court referee is an attorney who hears cases and reports their recommendations to a Family Court judge. The parties may agree to have the referee hear and determine the outcome of their case.

Judicial Hearing Officer (JHO): A JHO is a former or retired judge appointed for a one-year term. A JHO hears contested paternity proceedings, custody and visitation proceedings and family offenses matters. A JHO will hear a case and report their recommendations to a Family Court judge who will determine the outcome of the case.

Conclusion

When you have a choice of venue, prior to filing your matter, it is important to educate yourself on your local courts and consult with an attorney who can guide you to make the right decision on the best venue for your matter to be heard. The complexity of your matter, your financial resources, and the timeframe for when each court is able to hear your matter are all important factors to be considered and evaluated prior to filing your matter.

Nicole Trivlis, Esq.

Nicole Trivlis began her legal career in matrimonial law as a paralegal upon her graduation from the Catholic University of America (BA - 2004). She is a graduate of Pace University School of Law (JD - 2008). Nicole is currently an associate with the Silva Thomas PC law firm (www.silvathomas.com) in New York, New York where she focuses her practice on matrimonial law. Nicole is admitted to practice law in New York, Connecticut, the District of Columbia, the Southern District of New York, and the Eastern District of New York. She has represented high-net worth individuals in contested and uncontested matrimonial actions, paternity proceedings, and custody matters. Nicole has negotiated and drafted various prenuptial, postnuptial, settlement, and separation agreements.

Nicole also has significant experience with national and international courts. While in law school, she interned for Trial Chambers III at the International Criminal Tribunal for the Former Yugoslavia in The Hague, The Netherlands and The United States Court of International Trade. Additionally, she was a student attorney for John Jay Legal Services Immigration Justice Clinic at Pace Law School where she actively represented immigration clients before the Immigration Courts.

Following her graduation from law school, Nicole gained extensive experience with the New York State Courts and the Federal Courts as an attorney in private practice in New York and as a legal consultant for private and government agencies in Washington, D.C. Nicole is an active member of the New York Women's Bar Association, and was the Chair of the New Lawyer's Section of the Westchester County Bar Association (2010-2012) and was elected to the Board of Directors of the Putnam County Bar Association (2011-2012). Nicole has been instrumental in organizing several CLE programs and events through her active participation in these professional associations.

SECTION A: COURTS

CHAPTER 2

INTEGRATED DOMESTIC VIOLENCE UNIT

By Ravi Cattry, Esq.

Traditionally, a family that had issues of domestic violence comingled with issues of matrimonial law or family law would have to appear in various courts and in front of multiple judges in order to resolve all of these issues. The family members would be required to go to Criminal Court or Family Court for domestic violence issues, Family Court for custody and visitation issues, and Supreme Court for matrimonial issues. Such separation in otherwise connected issues led to a great deal of time spent in court and inconsistency by judges in making decisions due to lack of information about what was happening in other matters in other courts regarding the same family.

History of IDV

In 2003, New York announced the expansion of ***Integrated Domestic Violence Courts*** ("IDV Courts" or "IDV"), whose purpose was to bring all cases involving domestic violence plus any other matrimonial or family law issues in front of one judge. New York State calls this the "one family – one judge" model and there are over 40 IDV Courts located in each of the twelve Judicial Districts in New York. This concept of judicial economy helps make the process more efficient and cost effective, not only for the courts, but also for the clients in helping reduce legal fees.

IDV Court judges are trained to be able to hear criminal, matrimonial, and family law cases, which allows them to make informed decisions in each aspect of the law for each particular family. The aim of this court is to improve safety for victims of domestic abuse and make offenders more accountable while cutting down on time spent in reaching these decisions. The courts also help reduce the confusion that can be caused by multiple orders from multiple courts that may contradict each other.

The IDV Process

A case ends up in the IDV Court through an administrative order issued by contributing courts, attorneys, law enforcement, victim advocates, or other community providers. The presiding judge in the IDV Court will review the cases and will make the ultimate decision of whether or not to transfer all of the cases to IDV Court.

A judge in IDV Court will work with the prosecutor to resolve domestic violence issues including issuing orders of protection for any and all victims, mandating counseling for the offender, sentencing offenders to jail time or any other punishment that is appropriate, and order payment of restitution, if such is required in the case. At the same time, the IDV judge can preside over a divorce case, taking into account the issues that come up in the domestic violence case. Further, the same judge can decide on issues that would appear in front of a judge in Family Court and decide what would be in the best interest of the children and all other parties while considering issues arising in the other two cases before him or her. In terms of clerical issues, all of these issues are considered separate cases, but in terms of adjudication, the judge will consider information from all cases in deciding on courses of action in any case. The order in which the cases are adjudicated depends on the judge, but in general most judges address criminal cases first, then family law issues followed by matrimonial issues.

Benefits of IDV Court

IDV Courts allow for more oversight of offenders because now one judge is in charge of coordinating among the justice system and various social service agencies. The judge can keep a close eye on the offender and can act swiftly in situations of non-compliance to any mandated orders by the IDV Court. The IDV Court can also coordinate services for victims, such as counseling, housing, and job training. Having all of these issues before one judge makes the communication between the courts and social service agencies faster and more efficient.

Additionally, IDV Courts allow multiple stakeholders to each have their voices heard in making these decisions, such as the prosecutor, defense attorney, family court attorney, and law guardians.

One judge presiding over all of the various issues allows for a facilitation of conversation between all individuals to decide on courses of action that are best for all parties involved. It also provides the judge with all of the information necessary to make whole decisions that do not confuse parties or give them contradictory orders.

Ravi Cattry, Esq.

Ravi Cattry is an associate attorney and is licensed to practice in New York and New Jersey and admitted into the Eastern and Southern District Courts of New York. She completed a Bachelor of Science at Fordham University in Manhattan where she was a double major in psychology and economics. She received a Juris Doctor from Pace University School of Law in White Plains, New York.

Before joining Rincker Law, PLLC, Ravi worked at a general practice firm located in Kew Gardens, New York. While working there her practice areas included landlord and tenant disputes, matrimonial and family law issues, commercial law, and immigration law. Ravi also worked with a boutique law firm specializing in bankruptcy law in Manhattan. During law school she interned with the Integrated Domestic Violence Court in White Plains, New York, where she assisted in handling divorce cases intertwined with domestic violence cases.

Ravi is fluent in Hindi and Punjabi, and conversational in Spanish. In her free time Ravi enjoys reading, watching movies, playing tennis, and keeping up with her favorite soccer teams.

SECTION B: DISPUTE RESOLUTION

CHAPTER 3

CHOOSING THE BEST PROCESS: DO I NEGOTIATE OR LITIGATE?

By Daniel Clement, Esq.

If divorce were a game, there would be no winners, at least in economic terms. Everyone loses; familial relationships are destroyed, whatever marital wealth was acquired is split, and legal bills are incurred. This Chapter provides a broad overview of the negotiation and litigation processes in divorce.

Overview of Processes

The income that used to support a single household during the marriage has to support ***two post-divorce homes***. The economy of scale of an intact household is lost; whereas there was formerly one set of household and related expenses, now there are two – e.g., there are now two refrigerators to stock, two rent or mortgage payments, and two sets of utility bills. Whether as a result of certainty that the post-divorce dollars have to go farther or because of the psychological need to "win," the divorce process could easily spiral into a vicious money grab. After all, every dollar a spouse gets in the divorce is one less for the other.

Often the outcome of the divorce, its expense, and the agitation suffered are presaged by the method of dispute resolution selected. While there are many routes to any given destination, the route selected sometimes defines the adventure. This is particularly true in the case of divorce, where, for instance, the issues of divorce can be resolved through ***negotiation***, ***litigation,*** or even ***mediation***.

The process of dispute resolution selected is directly related to the amount of control in the outcome and the level of vitriol. For instance, where the parties are most antagonistic in a hotly contested case that is litigated in court, the parties surrender virtually all control in the outcome to the judge who will decide the parties' fates. Conversely, parties, who can ***manage their antagonism*** and can communicate, may attempt to negotiate, with or without the help of their lawyers, and find a creative resolution that addresses all their needs, wants, and concerns.

A ***negotiated settlement*** permits parties to maintain almost complete control over their divorce settlement on the most acceptable terms. Of course, where there are claims of domestic violence or the parties are in an abusive or coercive relationship, negotiations may not be a viable alternative to litigation.

Significantly, embarking on a course of action at the outset of a divorce does not foreclose a complete reversal of process, tactics, strategy, or goals. An ***aggressive litigation position*** could drive the other party into negotiating a resolution perceived as untenable at the start of the process. On the other hand, a party entrenched in a negotiating position, unwilling to bend, could force the other party to litigate, forcing a judge to be the final arbiter of their dispute.

There is no universal answer to the questions, "***What divorce process is best for me? Should I negotiate or litigate?***" That decision is facts and circumstances dependent. For instance, when there is an emergent situation (e.g., a spouse is threatening to relocate with the children a great distance from the martial home without the other spouse's consent, a spouse is transferring money from the joint bank account, or is leaving one person unable to support his or herself) then that person needs ***immediate court intervention***. There is no time to negotiate or mediate. The facts dictate that person should immediately go to court.

On the other hand, other issues, like fixing the buy-out price of the marital home, may be an easier issue to resolve through an arms-length negotiation. They do not require a person to immediately see a judge.

In any event, for someone to make an informed decision how to proceed in connection with his/her divorce, that person needs to understand how a divorce is resolved in both litigation and negotiation. More information on Alternative Dispute Resolution ("ADR") methods including mediation, collaborate law, neutral evaluation and arbitration are found in Chapter 4 a through d, respectively.

The Litigated Divorce in New York

Commencing the Divorce or Annulment

A divorce or annulment is a lawsuit: there is a plaintiff and a defendant. The ***Summons*** is the first legal paper filed in court; it is the filing of the summons and purchasing the index number that commences the matrimonial action in Supreme Court. Though there is a Family Court in New York, it does not have the jurisdiction to hear divorces-only the Supreme Court has the power to grant a divorce.

In New York in order to commence an action dissolving a marriage, whether it be divorce, annulment or declaring a marriage void, the plaintiff must file either a ***Summons with Notice*** or a ***Summons and a Verified Complaint***.

The Summons with Notice (or the Verified Complaint) details the type of action being brought, i.e., divorce or annulment, and the legal ground. Since New York is now a no-fault state, the summons for divorce will now typically claim that the marriage has irretrievably broken down (i.e., the "no fault ground). More information on the grounds for annulment and divorce are found in Chapters 27 and 28, respectively. The summons could also demand ***equitable distribution*** of the marital assets, custody of the children, payment of maintenance and child support, an award of counsel fees, and even the right for the wife to resume using a maiden name.

The summons with notice (or verified complaint) must also be served with the "***Notice of Entry Automatic Orders***" and the ***Notice of Continuing Health Insurance***. The automatic stays prevent both parties from transferring assets, terminating insurance policies or changing beneficiary designations during the divorce. The forms are available online via the courts at https://www.nycourts.gov/divorce/forms_instructions/Notice.pdf.

The summons in a divorce must be personally served upon the defendant in the matrimonial action. This is best accomplished when service is made by a professional process server. The plaintiff cannot personally serve the defendant.

After the defendant is served and "***appears***" in the action (i.e., filing a ***Notice of Appearance***), the plaintiff serves the Verified Complaint (if that person had not done so already). The complaint contains basic information such as the names and addresses of the parties, the date and location of the marriage, health insurance information, and the names and birthdates of the children of the marriage.

The Verified Complaint will also allege the facts that support the plaintiff's grounds or legal basis for the divorce. Since New York adopted no-fault divorce in 2010, it is common for the complaint to allege that the marriage has irretrievably broken down with no hope of reconciliation for at least six months before the divorce was commenced. However, the complaint may also state a fault-ground (e.g., adultery, cruel and inhuman treatment) that may require specific allegations supporting that ground.

> A complaint or answer in a divorce is "verified"- the plaintiff or defendant states under oath that the statements are true.

Once the defendant receives the Verified Complaint then the defendant will file a Verified Answer, responding to the allegations in the complaint. The defendant may also file a counterclaim containing the defendant's grounds for the divorce. Someone may wish to counterclaim if he or she is seeking different relief than what is set-forth in the Verified Complaint.

Statement of Net Worth

Early in the divorce process, the parties will be asked to fill out a ***Statement of Net Worth***. This comprehensive document contains all the information that will be used to work out the financial issues in the divorce including equitable distribution, child support, and maintenance. It is ***critically important*** to fill out the statement truthfully and carefully. This form is available online at https://www.nycourts.gov/forms/matrimonial/networth.pdf.

> A helpful tip for variable expenses is to look at the last three or six months and average these expenses.

The net worth statement will detail information about the parties' income, their individual or joint assets (e.g., real property, cash, vehicles, investment accounts, business interests) and individual or joint liabilities (e.g., credit card debt, car loans, and mortgages. All expenses will need to be enumerated –

> Discrepancies in monthly expenses and monthly income should be brought to the lawyer's attention.

from big ticket items like monthly mortgage payment and utility bills to much smaller expenses like magazine subscriptions and haircuts.

The statement of net worth will be the ***jumping off point*** for all the money issues in a case. All of the information you provide will be carefully scrutinized by the other party, his or her lawyer, and the judge hearing the case.

The parties, under penalties of perjury, swear to the truth of the information in his or her net worth statement. A person should not be tempted to overstate expenses or understate income on his or her statement of net worth, especially if you feel your spouse is being unreasonable; doing so can destroy your credibility, and that can have a critical bearing on the rest of the case.

Completing the statement of net worth can seem overwhelming. Avoid the temptation to estimate items or include the costs not yet purchased. The extensive discovery process during the litigation may bring out inconsistencies in the statement of net worth. These inconsistencies hurt a party's credibility. A Statement of Net Worth should not be casually completed as it may be the most important document in the divorce.

The Preliminary Conference

In New York, the ***first court appearance*** in a divorce case is generally the Preliminary Conference, commonly called the "PC." Some states refer to this initial appearance as a case management conference. The New York court rules mandate that the parties be present for every court appearance, including the PC.

One of the primary purposes of the preliminary conference is to identify both the resolved and unresolved issues in the divorce. Once an issue has been identified as "resolved" in the preliminary conference order, it cannot be litigated. For examples, the parties may agree to child custody, waiver of spousal maintenance, grounds, etc.

During the conference, both parties have the opportunity to provide the judge with their "version" or theory of the case. If child custody is involved, an attorney for the child may be appointed to represent the interests of the children. The court also may order the parties to be interviewed by a forensic evaluator (i.e., a mental health professional) who will prepare a comprehensive written evaluation detailing the family history, exploring the family dynamics, and identifying their psychological issues. This detailed study, paid for by the parties, will assist the court in determining custody.

When there are issues over equitable distribution, and particularly when the value of assets are in dispute, the court may appoint an expert to appraise the value of the marital property. Values can be determined for the marital home, a party's interest in a business, a pension, or any other asset acquired during the marriage.

Finally, at the preliminary conference, the judge will fix a ***timetable*** in which the case is to be trial ready. The court will set a deadline for the parties to complete discovery and schedule compliance conferences to ensure that its deadlines are obeyed.

Sometimes, contested divorce cases can be settled at the Preliminary Conference, particularly if the judge or court attorney takes an active role in the conference, i.e., he or she will mediate disputes or foreshadow a ruling. If the case is resolved at the preliminary conference or during the discovery phase of the divorce, this conference may be the only time that person will need to appear in court.

Motions

The other way someone may find his or herself in court in a matrimonial action is if one party makes a motion. A motion is a ***formal written request*** made by one of the parties for an order requiring or preventing the other party from doing something. A court decides a motion in an order.

The most common initial motion in a divorce action in New York is a motion for ***pendente lite*** relief (Latin for "while the matter is pending"). A common motion for ***pendente lite*** relief requests temporary maintenance, interim child support, and an interim award of attorneys' fees. Other common motions include requests for temporary custody of children, an order of protection when there are issues of domestic violence, or for contempt of court, when prior court orders have been disobeyed.

To decide the ***pendente lite*** applications, the court relies on affidavits and memorandum of law ("briefs") submitted by the parties. The court will scrutinize the parties' statements of net worth. The amount of temporary maintenance and child support may be determined by application of statutory guidelines. More information on child support and spousal maintenance are in Chapter 11 and Section III(B), respectively.

Unless the parties are able to settle the motion on their own, the Court decides a motion in an Order. If a party believes that the judge erred, then that person may take an appeal to the Appellate Division. However, when it comes to appeals of temporary child support or maintenance, the Courts often rules that that best remedy of an inappropriate support award is a ***prompt trial***.

Like any other court order, if a party fails to obey a ***pendente lite*** order and pay the required temporary payments, he/she risks being found in contempt of court.

Discovery

Knowledge is power, particularly when it comes to divorce. A party can only make wise and informed decisions about settlement when he or she has access to all the facts. A party can only prove and disprove facts at trial if he or she has competent evidence.

So, how do you find out how much an asset is worth, what your spouse's income is, or how much money is really in the bank account? While some spouses may feel comfortable relying on the information provided by the other spouse, many people prefer to learn these and other facts for themselves; that is what happens during discovery.

In discovery, the divorcing spouses and their attorneys attempt to learn all the financial facts in the divorce by exchanging information. Financial documents and records and other information exchanges can all be part of the discovery process.

Some of the tools most commonly used during discovery include:

1. Demands for Discovery and Inspection

This discovery device is used to require your spouse to produce a laundry list of records including bank statements, check registers, investment account statements, credit card bills, income tax returns, and pay stubs. Computer hard drives and records from social media sites may be required to be produced. Virtually nothing is off limits.

> The discoverable time period is from the date of the marriage to the date forward; however, the demands are usually restricted to a three year or five year period.

2. Interrogatories

Interrogatories are written questions that the other party has to answer under oath in written form. Additional demands for discovery can be made along with the interrogatories.

3. Depositions

At a deposition (a/k/a "Examination Before Trial" or "EBT"), parties are questioned under oath about relevant issues. A stenographic record is made of the testimony that reflects the exact words spoken. In some cases, depositions are videotaped. Later, during the trial, if the testimony given during the trial varies from the deposition testimony, the witness can be impeached, using his/her own words to attack his/her credibility.

4. Demand for Authorizations

If one party makes a claim about employment status or a medical condition, the other party can demand that the spouse give the other person authorizations allowing third parties to provide that person with the spouse's confidential records. For instance, if the spouse claims he or she is unable to work because of a medical disability, authorizations could be demanded to obtain the relevant medical records and doctors' reports.

5. Appraisals

In an appraisal, an expert is called upon to provide dollar values for specific assets. Assets that can be valued include your home, artwork, pensions, businesses, professional licenses, and even educational degrees.

Court Conferences

Throughout the discovery process, which can take months, the court will keep the parties on a short leash. The parties (and their lawyers) will have to appear in court at various "Compliance Conferences" to ensure that discovery deadlines are being complied with and no issues have arisen. Each time the parties are in court, the judge will attempt to resolve issues. While not every issue is resolvable, in almost every case, some are.

The court will almost never miss an opportunity to, at least attempt to, resolve an issue. An agreement resolving an issue is noted in an agreement called a "Stipulation." The hope is that ***little by little***, issue by issue, all the disputes are resolved until the entire divorce action can be settled in a comprehensive Stipulation of Settlement.

Thanks to movies like *Kramer vs. Kramer* and *The War of the Roses*, many people are familiar only with the concept of divorce being fought in a courtroom. Some divorcing couples can work out their divorce through ***negotiations*** aided by their attorneys.

If all the issues of the divorce have been resolved, the parties can proceed to judgment as an ***uncontested divorce*** (or "settled contested divorce"). For those couples who can hammer out an agreement without protracted litigation, the benefits can be significant. Studies have shown that divorces resolved through negotiations typically involve less stress and achieve more satisfactory results than those that are litigated. Why? Because the parties involved in the divorce better understand the circumstances surrounding their case than the judge, who has a fleeting interest in the case. The parties are best-positioned to find a fair and workable resolution to their issues.

The good news is that most divorces that begin as contested settle at some point before trial. If the divorce is settled on a day the parties are in court, the judge may allocute the settlement and ask the parties a series of questions to ensure that the agreement was the result of ***fair negotiations***. For example, the judge will ask:

- if the agreement was procured with the assistance of counsel;
- that the parties are satisfied with his or her counsel;
- that the parties read and understood the agreement;
- that the agreement was not procured by coercion;
- that no promises were made that are not contained in the agreement; and
- that the parties are competent to enter into the agreement.

The Trial

If some or all of the issues remain unresolved by the time discovery is completed, then the court sets the matter for trial. All the work and preparation that take place during the earlier stages of divorce culminate at the trial. The legal theories and strategies are applied to the facts; all the evidence is presented to a judge in the form of testimony for a final ruling on all the unresolved issues.

If a trial is necessary in a divorce case, not every issue need be tried. Many issues are worked out during the pretrial process, and only those issues that have not been resolved need to be tried. For example, there could be an agreement on child custody and visitation, but not on child support and maintenance. In that case, the trial would be limited to those two unresolved issues. In other cases, there may be agreement on how some assets are equitably distributed, but not others.

There is no jury; the judge decides all unresolved custody and financial issues. During the trial, evidence will be presented through ***testimony***. The plaintiff presents his or her case first, followed by the defendant. Every witness may be ***cross-examined*** by the other side.

Once the trial is concluded, the judge will issue a decision. That decision will be final unless one party files an appeal. A person cannot file an appeal just because he or she does not agree with the judge's decision; an appeal can only be filed if there was an error of law (i.e., the judge misapplied a law) or an error of fact (i.e., the facts did not support the ruling).

Negotiations

The hallmark of a "good" negotiated divorce settlement is that ***no one is completely satisfied with the result***. Both parties feel that they gave too much. In other words, no one feels that they "won," but each one knows they did not lose. The settlement is structured around the parties' actual needs and desires. By giving a little, the parties are both able to find some common ground and resolve whatever differences they may have.

For instance, in a case involving child custody and access, both mom and dad may want to maximize their time with a child. Where, for instance, mom works particular evenings during the week, dad can have parenting time on those nights and both parents save on the cost of child care.

In another example, one person may want $5,000 a month in maintenance after a long term marriage dissolves, but that person's real concern is making a $2,500 mortgage payment. The other spouse can barely afford $3,000, and certainly not the $5,000 sought by the other spouse. Perhaps a compromise can be reached where the payor can pay the some amount of maintenance sufficient to pay the mortgagte and some household expenses, so the children will not be uprooted, by taking advantge of the tax deductbility of the maintenance payment.

Divorce negotiations know no time or place constraints. A drop-off or pick-up of the children could result in a conversation with a spouse wherein the parenting time schedule is resolved. Absent an order of protection, there is no reason why parties could not attempt to engage in direct discussions ever.

Direct communication, as long as it is not coercive or threatening, may be desirable between the parties. In most cases, particularly litigated cases, all communications are between attorneys. A divorcing party speaks to his or her lawyer, the lawyer speaks to the opposing counsel, who then speaks to the other spouse. Both attorneys speak to the judge.

Do you remember the ***game of telephone***? A group lines up and someone whispers something into the first person's ear, who tells the secret to the second person and the process continues down the line. How did that work out?

The last person's version seldom resembled what was really said. Every person added his or her little spin until it failed to resemble what was originally said. Why should a divorce negotiation be any different?

This is why judges, when they have the parties and attorneys in court at a conference or to argue a motion, never fail to attempt to resolve some aspect of the divorce. There is no time when a negotiation cannot take place. The negotiations can be formal – i.e., a scheduled meeting with the two parties and their attorneys or they can be informal- a call between the attorneys.

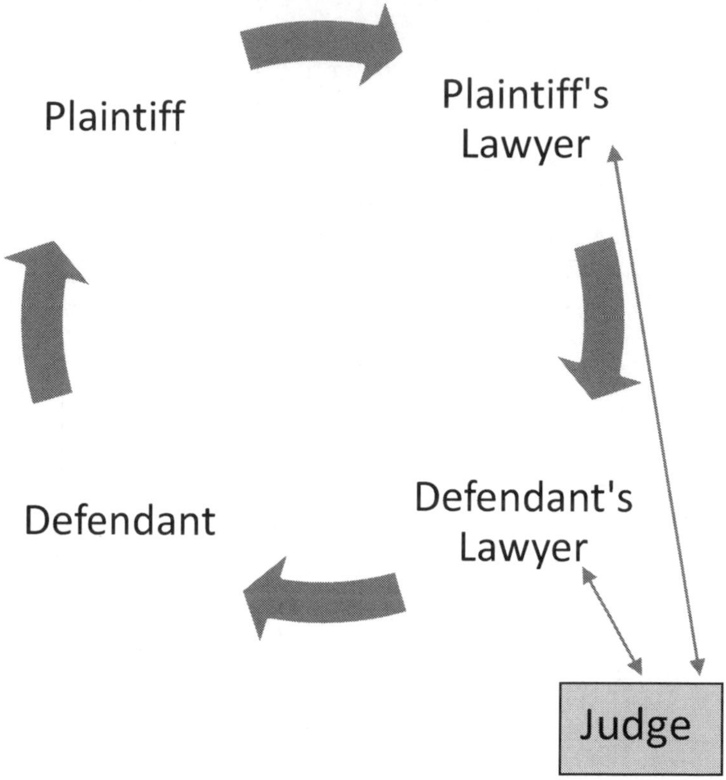

Oftentimes, an agreement on one issue leads to further agreement- ***movement begets movement***. A common technique used in a "***four-way meeting***" is to start with an issue where everyone can agree. The agreement on the issue is noted and then the next issue is presented. When resistance is hit, after a bit of discussion, the issue should be tabled, and the next issue addressed until all the easily resolvable issues have been settled. Then, circle back, hitting the previously unresolved issues; positions soften and, slowly, these issues on which the parties were previously deadlocked, are now ripe for resolution.

> A "four-way" is with both lawyers and both parties present for a settlement conference.

It is important that everyone be present at the four-way negotiation – not in the physical way, but ***truly engaged***. The linear lawyer-centric communication that exists in litigation cannot exist. The parties themselves must be involved, ready to explain why he or she is asking for something or, conversely, rejecting a proposal.

Conclusion

Litigation and negotiation are not mutually exclusive as divorce resolution techniques. They can co-exist. The truth is that most divorces that ***start out as contested cases*** are resolved through some negotiated settlement. It also clear that a negotiated settlement leads to more satisfaction in the result, which is not surprising as the parties can retain some degree of control over both the process and its outcome.

While litigation and negotiation provide the ***procedural structure*** to the divorce, neither will overcome unfavorable facts or existing law. For instance, New York requires that the settlement agreements address the issue of child support when there are children of the marriage. Absent facts and circumstances to support a position, a non-custodial parent will always pay something in the way of child support.

Both litigation and negotiation provide the processes, the procedural means by which to resolve substantive issues. Which is best? A person going through a divorce should discuss these options with his or her matrimonial attorney.

Daniel Clement, Esq.

Daniel Clement is a dedicated, hands-on New York divorce and family law attorney with more than 25 years' experience. He takes a pragmatic, individualized and realistic approach to helping his clients through the often thorny path of divorce.

Daniel graduated from Brooklyn Law School and the State University of New York at Albany. He is a member of the New York City Bar Assoc., and has served as a member of the Matrimonial Committee. He has also worked as an Arbitrator in the Small Claims Court of the City of New York.

In addition to practicing, Daniel has extensively written and lectured on a range of family law issues. Daniel writes and maintains a blog, the New York Divorce Report, which explores current topics in New York family law and matrimonial practice.

For more information about Daniel and his practice, visit clementlaw.com.

SECTION B: DISPUTE RESOLUTION

CHAPTER 4

ALTERNATIVE DISPUTE RESOLUTION

SUBPART A: MEDIATION

By Cari B. Rincker, Esq.

Mediation is oftentimes an overlooked and misunderstood dispute resolution device. Mediation can be one of the more ***effective, cost-efficient*** mechanisms to come to an agreement. Mediation is a voluntary process giving the participants control over the result.

What is Mediation?

Mediation vs. Arbitration

Mediation is oftentimes confused with ***arbitration***. In mediation, a mediator acts as a neutral third party to help the parties reach an amicable resolution. Put simply, a mediator helps facilitate a conversation between the parties. A mediator is not a judge or a jury and does not make a decision for the parties. However, in some instances, mediators can provide general information to the parties regarding the law. To the contrary, an arbitrator acts like a judge making a decision for the parties. This is an important distinction because parties often look to the mediator to make the decision; however, that is not the role of the mediator.

Mediation vs. Conciliation

Some mediators focus on reconciliation, or "***conciliation***." But most do not. If someone hopes to reconcile with his or her spouse or ex-boyfriend or girlfriend, mediation may not be the right choice. There are, however, conciliation professionals that may help the parties take strides towards reconciliation.

What Can Be Mediated?

In the family and matrimonial law context, nearly every type of dispute can utilize mediation in one form or another. To explain, mediation can be utilized in the following scenarios:

- Prenuptial/post-nuptial agreements
- Child support
- Spousal maintenance
- Child custody and visitation (*i.e.*, a parenting plan)
- Equitable distribution in the divorce context
- Pet ownership/custody disputes
- Family business (*e.g.*, between spouses, parents and children)
- Communication issues between family members
- Fee disputes between clients and attorneys or other professionals

> For example, if there is a ***Temporary Order of Protection***, the parties may wish to be present in the mediation with their respective lawyers.

In most circumstances, mediators will not mediate cases with ***domestic violence allegations*** or orders of protections; however, in some instances mediation can still be an effective settlement device so that safety issues and the ***imbalance of power*** is properly addressed.

When Does Mediation Take Place?

Mediation can take place at ***anytime, anywhere***. It can take place at any stage during the litigation process or it can take place before the parties have gone to court. In some cases, parties may try mediation and then later decide to litigate their dispute. However, parties can then come back and try mediation again once the parties have gained more information.

In Person vs. Virtual Mediation

> Mediation is always the most effective in person; however, sometimes life or finances do not allow for the parties to be in the same geographic location.

Most mediation is done in person, with parties in the same room. In some cases, the parties caucus with the mediator privately (i.e., without the other person present) for equal amounts of time. However, there are some mediators who can conduct "***virtual mediation***" via Skype (or other video conferencing tool). This can be particularly helpful when the parties live geographically distant where it might be cost prohibitive to meet in person during mediation.

Confidentiality

No matter the form of mediation, everything that is said during the session is always confidential. Not only is the mediator required the keep the information learned private but the parties cannot use the information learned during mediation later in court. Some mediators even destroy notes after the mediation period has concluded.

Overview of Mediation Process

Initial Consultation

It is recommended that parties considering a mediation first have an initial consultation with the mediator. This initial consultation can be via the ***telephone or in-person***. The parties may choose to have the initial consultation together or separately.

> Typically parties split the costs of mediation equally (50/50); however, parties can have other agreements. Payment for the mediator can and should be agreed to during the consultation period.

During this stage, the mediator oftentimes will have the parties sign a confidentiality agreement, explaining that everything stated during the consultation or subsequent mediation sessions will be confidential. The mediator will then describe the mediation ***process and fees***. He/she may have the parties sign an initial consultation agreement and go through a client intake form with the parties.

Importantly, this is the opportunity for the parties and the mediator to get to know each other. The clients should ask questions about the mediator's experience and the mediation process. Similarly, the mediator will try to get a feel for the dispute and the issues that need to be mediated.

Mediation Period

This is the meat and potatoes of the mediation process. Mediation sessions last for ***approximately two hours*** (can vary with mediators). Some mediators send written debriefs to clients after mediation sessions while others do not. Importantly, the mediator cannot give the parties legal advice (even if he or she is a lawyer); therefore, it is recommended that the parties have their own consulting lawyer during this period to ask him or her questions.

When ***financial disclosure*** is an issue (e.g., spousal/child support, equitable distribution, prenuptial agreement), the parties can agree during this period on what will be exchanged and by what method. For example, in the divorce mediation context, the parties could voluntarily decide to complete and exchange a Statement of Net Worth along with two years of financial statements. Parties may decide to get certain properties appraised. In mediation, the parties (and the mediator) make the rules instead of the court.

> Parties in a divorce may agree upon a real estate appraiser or art appraiser during this period. Payment of the appraisals can be mediated as well.

How ***many mediation sessions*** are required? This depends on a myriad of issues. Are children involved? Are there complex financial issues? How are the parties communicating? Oftentimes, parties have to work through various emotional issues before certain financial issues can be decided. Every person and each couple during the mediation process moves at their own pace. Some couples might be able to resolve a narrow issue concerning parenting time in one mediation session where another pair of parents might require five plus sessions to come to a final resolution.

The time between mediation sessions can vary significantly. The parties can go at their own pace. In some instances, parties have "homework" after mediation session and need a few weeks to work on collecting the required information for the next mediation session. In other cases, parties don't want to lose momentum and need only a few days before their next session. In others, parties might want to take a month or two between sessions to spend time negotiating on their own and seeing how temporary arrangements are working. Again, the parties have the control on the timing instead of a courthouse.

Agreement or Memorandum of Understanding

The hope, but not always the ultimate goal of mediation, is to have terms for a final agreement. If the mediator is an attorney, he or she may offer to draft the final settlement agreement, parenting plan, or prenuptial/postnuptial agreement; however, it is important for the parties to then take the mediator-drafted agreement to their individual lawyers to review. Alternatively, the mediator can draft a ***Memorandum of Understanding*** ("MOU") that the parties can then take to their individual attorneys – one of which will memorialize it into a formal document.

That being said, in some cases, parties do not wish (or need) a written agreement. For example, perhaps two parents are having a dispute about summer vacation and summer camp. They come to an oral agreement during the mediation session and don't wish to amend their parenting plan (or custody and visitation agreement) or put this agreement in writing because they wish to address this issue each year as it arises.

Executing and Filing Necessary Documents

The final stage during the mediation process is to ***execute and file*** (if appropriate) any documents with the court. The mediator may no longer be involved in this stage. The parties may be working directly with their individual attorneys.

Choosing a Mediator

In closing, it is important to choose the right mediator for you and your particular dispute. Mediators vary in experience, language proficiency, subject matter expertise, style, fees, communication, and level of involvement. For example, some mediators are able to ***speak fluently*** in different languages or have knowledge in certain family law disputes (e.g., animal ownership disputes). Some mediators do "virtual mediation" while others do not. It is important to be thorough during the consultation process to get an honest understanding of the process.

Referrals may be the most effective method in locating a qualified mediator in a particular area. People seeking mediators should ***request***

referrals from his or her attorney or other professionals (e.g., accountant, financial advisor). If you are unable to get a quality lead through referrals sources, then professional mediation associations throughout the State of New York may be contacted (e.g., New York State Council on Divorce Mediation, Family & Divorce Mediation Council of Greater New York). Various bar associations throughout the state also offer referral programs (e.g., New York State Bar Association, Association for the Bar for the City of New York, New York County Lawyers Association).

Additionally, every county in New York has its own ***Community Dispute Resolution Center*** ("CDRC") that can mediate some limited areas of family law disputes. A list of programs is available at https://www.nycourts.gov/ip/adr/ProgramList.shtml. There are also other community organizations that offer mediation services for various family law disputes. More information on those programs can be found in Chapter 4.

Conclusion

Most family law disputes can be mediated. Unless there is an emergency that needs to be quickly addressed by a courthouse or a substantial imbalance in power, most couples can benefit from having a neutral third party ***facilitate a discussion between them***. When two companies go to war in a courthouse, it is unlikely that those two companies will ever have a working relationship again. Similarly, if two parents go to war in a courtroom, it is difficult for the two people to have a working co-parenting relationship afterwards.

Mediation can heal communication problems and preserve family relationships. Even if parties do not have children together, it makes sound economic sense to mediate issues with a qualified professional. When people step into a courtroom, they are putting their own lives at the mercy of a judge who barely knows them. Isn't it better for someone to have more control over his or her own life?

Cari B. Rincker, Esq.

Cari Rincker is the principal attorney at Rincker Law, PLLC, a national law practice focusing on "Food, Farm & Family." She is licensed to practice law in New York, New Jersey, Connecticut, Illinois and Washington, D.C. Cari was named as a Rising Star for Metro New York in 2015 by "Super Lawyers" and is an award-winning blogger. Cari is involved in several professional organizations including the Association for the Bar of the City of New York's Matrimonial Law Committee.

In addition to her litigation practice, Cari is also a trained mediator for divorces, child custody and visitation, and commercial disputes. She was also an adjunct professor at New York University, College of Steinhardt (2013-2014), where she taught an undergraduate food law class.

On the food and agriculture side of her practice, Cari is the Chair of the American Bar Association, General Practice, Solo & Small Firm Division's Agriculture Law Committee and won the 2014 Excellence in Agriculture Law Award by the American Agriculture Law Association.

Cari is a distinguished alumni from Lake Land College in Mattoon, Illinois and Texas A & M University. Before attending law school at Pace University School of Law in White Plains, New York, Cari obtained a Master of Science from the University of Illinois. Cari's practice is family-centered and counsels clients on a myriad of family law and matrimonial law issues.

For more information about Rincker Law, PLLC, visit www.rinckerlaw.com. You can also follow Cari on Twitter @CariRincker @RinckerLaw and Instagram.

SECTION B: DISPUTE RESOLUTION

CHAPTER 4

ALTERNATIVE DISPUTE RESOLUTION

SUBPART B: COLLABORATIVE DIVORCE

By Andrea Vacca, Esq.

Collaborative law is a process that can help a couple come to a negotiated settlement of their family law matter without ever stepping into a courtroom. It helps families creatively resolve issues with the guidance of professionals.

Collaborative law is based on ***four main principles***:

1. The parties agree in writing that they and their collaborative lawyers will not go to court.
2. Both parties commit to an honest and open exchange of documents and information.
3. Neither party, nor their attorney, will make threats or seek to force an agreement under duress.
4. Each option for settlement takes into account the highest interests and goals of both parties and their children.

Throughout the negotiations, each party will have an attorney by his or her side and the focus will be kept on each party's interests and goals while searching for a solution that works for both of them. This is in contrast to many litigated cases where the focus is on each party's positions and demands being made. Litigation sets up parties for a win/lose outcome. Collaborative law is focused on finding a win/win. The process is less adversarial than litigation because, at the commencement of the case, the attorneys and clients are signing what is known as a ***Participation Agreement***, which states, among other things, that conflict will be kept to a minimum, threats will not be made and all relevant information will be disclosed.

By keeping ***conflict to a minimum***, the process is able to move forward in a more ***productive manner***. Time isn't wasted in court and there are no depositions or trial. All negotiations are taking place around a conference table with both parties and their attorneys present.

One of the major benefits of the collaborative process is that the parties stay in control of the issues to be resolved, rather than handing that control over to their attorneys or a judge.

Litigation by nature focuses on where the parties disagree and it is the litigation attorney's job to prove that one party's position is right and the other's is wrong. Collaborative law focuses on where the parties can find common ground. By focusing on each party's true interests (rather than positions), collaborative attorneys are able to help the clients to find creative solutions that can work for both of them.

How the Collaborative Process Actually Works

Each party will retain his or her own independent family/matrimonial attorney who has been trained in the collaborative process. The attorneys will jointly recommend other collaborative professionals such as financial professionals, divorce coaches and/or child specialists as part of the team. All negotiations are conducted in highly structured, face-to-face meetings between the couple, the attorneys and/or the other team professionals. Each meeting will be based upon a written agenda that the parties and professionals have agreed upon. Each meeting will be followed up with minutes that accurately reflect what was discussed and agreed to at the meeting and what tasks need to be completed before the next meeting.

The Benefits of the Collaborative Process

There are many benefits to the collaborative divorce process. Here are a few of them:

1. **The parties remain in control** – Decision-making is directly in the hands of the parties rather than in the hands of a judge. No one will be imposing a "one-size-fits-all" solution upon them and their family.

2. **It's better for the children** – Children are given a voice in the process because their needs and interests are kept in the forefront of negotiations, yet they are kept out of

the conflict. This helps to alleviate potential trauma that can potentially last for generations.

3. **The process is confidential** – The family's issues and financial concerns will be kept private and out of court.

4. **The process is focused on solving problems and reaching an agreement** – Each client's needs, interests concerns and goals will be recognized and considered.

5. **The focus is kept on the future** – The collaborative process is not only concerned with the immediate problems that a couple may be facing. Instead, the goal is to find solutions that work in the long term.

The Role of Professionals in the Collaborative Process

Role of Lawyers

During the process, the attorney will help the client ***gather necessary information*** and will provide the client with information about his or her ***rights, responsibilities and options***. The attorney will also help the client get clear on his or her true interests and goals so that any negotiated settlement will meet those goals. In collaborative meetings, the attorney will encourage and empower the client to speak about what he or she needs and will be there to advocate for those needs whenever necessary. Ultimately, negotiations in the collaborative process will address all of the issues that need to be resolved including child custody and parenting arrangements, child support, spousal support, distribution of property, and any other issue that is important to that specific family. If the parties are unable to reach an agreement in the collaborative process on all of the necessary issues and they decide that they need to have a judge make decisions for them, they will retain litigation attorneys for that purpose.

Role of the Other Professionals

Experienced collaborative attorneys know that working with other collaborative professionals can assist the couple to arrive at an agreement that best meets the immediate and long term needs of the family. These other collaborative professionals include (but are not limited to):

- ***Divorce coaches***, who assist the parties to develop better communication tools so they can understand their spouse and can be better understood when expressing their own interest and needs. Coaches also help the parties manage all of the difficult emotions that arise during the divorce process.
- ***Child specialists***, who give the children a "voice" in the process. Child specialists work with parents to assist them in creating a parenting plan that meets the children's best interests.
- ***Financial specialists***, who gather and analyze financial information and assist the clients in making informed decisions about finances.

The Role of the Law in the Collaborative Process

The law is often openly discussed throughout the collaborative process. The law surrounding child custody and parenting time, child support, spousal maintenance and equitable distribution will all be explained to the clients. If the attorneys have differences of opinion about what may happen if the parties asked a judge to make decisions for them, they will talk openly about that fact in a 4-way meeting with both parties present. Unlike in a litigated matter, the parties can choose ***how or even whether, to apply the law*** to their particular matter.

Questions to Ask a Collaborative Attorney

For a person who is considering a collaborative divorce, here are a few questions to ask a collaborative lawyer during the consultation:

1. **Are you concerned about whether my spouse gets what he or she wants out of this divorce?**

This question will help you determine whether an attorney understands the difference between collaboration and cooperation. ***Collaboration*** is about making sure that both your goals and the other person's goals are met, even if the goals aren't the same. This is a lot more difficult than simply ***cooperating***, which is about two people working together for mutual benefit toward common goals. Not many couples have common goals at the end of a marriage. One may want to stay in the marital home and the other wants to sell it. One may want equal parenting time with the children and the other may want to be the primary parent. Collaboration allows agreements to be made even when the parties' goals are this disparate.

2. **Do you believe that people who are in conflict can negotiate without drawing lines in the sand and using threats and coercion to get what they want?**

An attorney trained in collaborative law will answer "Yes" and will explain the difference between a ***position and an interest***. Maintaining a position means insisting on a specific outcome. That's the "line in the sand." Negotiating with interests in mind is being open to different outcomes that can meet that underlying interest.

Collaborative lawyers will encourage their clients to articulate interests rather than take positions. This opens up options and may clear a path to an outcome that may meet both parties' individual goals.

3. **Are you comfortable using other professionals as part of our divorce team?**

You want to know that your attorney has had positive experiences working with different divorce professionals including the divorce coaches, child specialists and financial professionals discussed above.

Attorneys with a collaborative mindset will give you examples of how their other clients have ***reaped the benefits*** of having one or more of these specialized professionals on their team, and how their divorces generally ran more smoothly as a result.

4. **Do you belong to any collaborative practice groups? Have you taken any advanced collaborative training courses?**

By determining whether the attorney is a member in a ***collaborative practice group***, a person will know whether an attorney is someone committed to working in the collaborative law process and receiving ongoing training, or whether they simply took a ***basic 3-day training*** course for the purpose of adding "collaborative lawyer" to their resume.

Knowing that the attorney is committed to the collaborative mindset is essential to the success of the process. The above questions will enable people going through a divorce identify committed collaborative attorneys so the process will move forward in a positive manner.

Andrea Vacca, Esq.

Andrea Vacca is the founder of Vacca Law and Mediation, a law firm in Manhattan that focuses exclusively on non-adversarial divorce and family law matters. Ms. Vacca regularly lectures and writes on the topics of collaborative law, mediation, and topics related to non-adversarial family law. She blogs at www.creativeresolutionsblog.com.

After practicing traditional litigation-focused family law for many years, Andrea became certified as a family and divorce mediator and later as a collaborative divorce attorney. Andrea's firm now works only with clients who want to keep their divorces out of court and want their prenuptial and postnuptial agreements negotiated in a non-adversarial manner. Andrea uses collaborative and cooperative divorce processes as well as mediation to achieve these goals.

She serves as Vice President of the New York Women's Bar Association; Secretary of the New York Association of Collaborative Professionals; is on the Editorial Board of Matrimonial Strategist; on the Advisory Council of FamilyKind; is a member of the Family and Divorce Mediation Council of Greater New York; a member of New York County Lawyers; and a member of the New York State Bar Association. Andrea received her B.A. in Journalism from SUNY College at Buffalo and her J.D. from Albany Law School of Union University. She also has a certificate in Positive Psychology.

SECTION B: DISPUTE RESOLUTION

CHAPTER 4

ALTERNATIVE DISPUTE RESOLUTION

SUBPART C: NEUTRAL EVALUATION

By Briana Denney, Esq.

Neutral evaluation is, as the name suggests, evaluation of a case by a ***neutral third party***. In the context of matrimonial and family law disputes, neutral evaluators are attorneys with expertise in matrimonial and family law.

When It Should Be Used

The neutral evaluator ***hears from both sides***, ***reviews any relevant evidence***, and ***evaluates the strengths and weaknesses*** of each party's position. In addition, he or she will provide an opinion as to the likely outcome if the case were to go to trial. This opinion is formed based on the neutral evaluator's expertise in the area, considering the facts and documents that will be presented by each party, or his/her attorney, to the court. Because this is an informal, non-binding opinion, the ***cost of neutral evaluation is substantially less*** than preparing for and going to trial. Neutral evaluation can be used in an attempt to resolve the entire matter or to resolve discrete issues.

Like all other forms of ***Alternative Dispute Resolution*** ("ADR"), neutral evaluation is *not* appropriate in cases involving child abuse or neglect, domestic violence, or a severe power imbalance between the parties. For neutral evaluation to be effective, the parties must be present during the case presentations, the resulting discussion(s), and the rendering of the neutral evaluator's opinion. Victims of domestic violence would likely be very uncomfortable sitting across the table from an abusive spouse. Also, unlike the court which has security in the form of court officers, neutral evaluation occurs at private law offices.

The neutral evaluation process can be used at ***any time prior to a case going to trial***. Therefore, it can be used before a case even goes into court, immediately before trial or at any time between. It is often-said that using neutral evaluation as early in a case as possible is the best time to use the process so that neither party is entrenched in his or her positions. However, the key to using neutral evaluation is that it can and should only be used once all of the relevant information is discovered and exchanged.

Discovery

In order to provide an opinion about a likely trial result, the neutral evaluator must be able to ***review the proof each party*** intends to provide to establish his or her position. For instance, in a case in which real estate or businesses are at issue, neutral evaluation would be appropriate only after the real estate or businesses have been valued. In a case in which a party is claiming separate property credits towards real estate or other assets, neutral evaluation would be appropriate only after all relevant documents are exchanged and, possibly, after depositions are completed. Because resolution of one area of a divorce case often depends on resolution of other areas, often it is not until the case is marked ready for trial that a case is ready for neutral evaluation. As an example, the amount of funds a party is awarded as and for property distribution can impact whether, and how much, maintenance is awarded and, in turn, how much child support is awarded. Therefore, in order to resolve all of these issues, all of the ***documentation, appraisals and other discovery*** regarding all of the financial issues will need to be completed prior to neutral evaluation being used.

Neutral evaluation can be used for resolution of any issues within the context of a divorce case. For instance, neutral evaluation could be used for particular issues or the entirety of the case. However, as already stated, since so many issues and outcomes are inter-dependent, it is often most effective if all of the financial issues and/or all the custody and visitation issues are accessible to the neutral evaluator prior to evaluation.

Focus on Financial Issues

On a related note, if the neutral evaluator is acting within the strictest definition of the role (as discussed in more detail below) and providing an opinion as to what may well happen if the case goes to trial, it is often ***financial issues*** which are most effectively brought before and resolved by the neutral evaluator. Custody and visitation are subjects in which the assigned judge has an enormous amount of discretion in making awards. With the same set of facts, one judge could come to a conclusion that is quite different from another judge. While custody and visitation are subjects which can and should be resolved in alternative dispute resolution if and when possible, neutral evaluation may not be the best process to use.

Procedures

Unlike mediation (which has ethical standards and models) and litigation (which is governed by hundreds of local and statewide rules of procedure and evidence), there are no standards or rules for the process of neutral evaluation. Therefore, prior to engaging in neutral evaluation, it is imperative that the attorneys and the neutral evaluator address and ***agree upon the procedure and the "rules"*** of the process, which should be recited in the neutral evaluator's retainer agreement.

A helpful resource for procedure is the ***Neutral Evaluation Program of the New York County Supreme Court***, which is a matrimonial-specific neutral evaluation program. The protocol is available online at https://www.nycourts.gov/courts/1jd/supctmanh/Matrimonial_NEP_menu.shtml. This New York County program is offered to litigants ***free of charge for a 3-hour session***. Thereafter, the neutral evaluator may charge his or her hourly rate. The parties must agree on how additional charges will be divided between them. Often, the most equitable way to divide such charges is pro rata, based on each party's income. Even when there is a substantial income differential, it is important that each party contribute to some percentage of the cost so that each party has a financial stake in continuing the process.

The protocols related to the neutral evaluation program are set forth below. For those parties who are not eligible for the New York County program (because their case is not within New York County or not yet in court), suggestions for private neutral evaluation for each step are made below the program protocols:

> Neutral evaluation is a form of ***settlement discussion*** and, as such, statements made during the process cannot be used as evidence at trial. The neutral evaluator cannot be called as a witness, nor can the parties or their attorneys disclose, at trial or otherwise, information from the session(s).

1. The judge or special referee issues an order of reference for neutral evaluation with the specific subject matter or issues that is before the neutral evaluator. The parties must agree to use the neutral evaluation process. All communications related to neutral valuation are ***confidential***.

   The parties and the attorneys agree to use neutral evaluation.

2. A ***neutral evaluation coordinator*** receives the order and randomly selects 3 names from a roster of approved neutral evaluators. The 3 names are emailed to the party's attorneys. If the attorneys cannot agree on a neutral evaluator, each side can object to one of the proposed evaluators and the remaining evaluator is appointed. If there is a conflict with the remaining neutral evaluator, counsel shall notify the coordinator who shall select an additional 3 neutral evaluators from the panel.

   The attorneys should select a reputable, experienced matrimonial attorney in the geographic area who will agree to act as a neutral evaluator. If the attorneys or parties cannot agree on one person, each of the neutral evaluators selected shall agree on a neutral evaluator to use. The retainer for the neutral evaluator should specify that all communications related to neutral evaluation are confidential.

3. The parties and attorneys are required **to appear before the selected neutral evaluator** within 45 days of the evaluator being confirmed. The neutral evaluator shall select a date, no less than 5 days prior to the neutral evaluation, in which the parties shall simultaneously submit to each other and the neutral evaluator, a Statement of Net Worth and a concise, 2 page summary of the issues, relevant facts, and applicable law, if any. The neutral evaluator may request limited, additional information if he or she believes it will add to the evaluation.

The retainer for the neutral evaluator shall also list the specific protocols that will be followed including, but not limited to, the documents each party is to provide prior to the session(s).

4. At the neutral evaluation, the neutral evaluator hears abbreviated case presentations, and reviews any documents related to the case which are required in order to make an informed opinion. The neutral evaluator provides a **non-binding assessment** of the merits of each party's case and the likely outcome as to what will happen if the case were to proceed to trial. The neutral evaluator can provide settlement assistance at the parties' request.

> "**Non-binding**" means that it is voluntary on the parties to accept the decision of the neutral evaluation.

Again, the retainer for the neutral evaluator should address the role of the neutral evaluator: is it to provide an oral opinion about the likely outcome? Is it to provide a written opinion about the likely outcome?

As described above, the neutral evaluation process is ***far less formal than a court hearing*** or trial. Therefore, not only does it save time and money, it may also permit parties a sense of greater direct participation in their own case. It should be noted, however, that the neutral evaluator has no judicial power or authority. Therefore, any recommendation or opinion is not binding upon the parties and is not enforceable in court. It is simply a process that will provide such an opinion and it is then up to the parties – or their attorneys – to draft and sign an agreement.

To summarize, neutral evaluation can be a very useful process in resolving matrimonial disputes, ***especially with financial issues***. It can only be used when the parties agree to use it and have all the information they need to support their positions. While the neutral evaluator's opinion is not binding, it serves as a neutral opinion from a professional with expertise in the area about what will likely happen if the case were to go to trial based upon the same arguments and evidence that would be presented to the court.

Briana Denney, Esq.

Briana Denney, a partner in the law firm of Newman & Denney P.C., represents clients in all aspects of matrimonial and family law matters, including prenuptial and postnuptial agreements, divorce, child custody and visitation, and enforcement of divorce agreements and judgments. Prior to private practice, she was a court attorney for Justice Rosalyn Richer. Briana is an active member of several bar associations and committees. She grew up in Arizona and attended the University of Arizona, where she earned her B.A. in Psychology with honors. She moved from Boston to attend the City University of New York where she earned her J.D. For more information about Briana and Newman & Denney P.C., visit www.newmandenney.com.

SECTION B: DISPUTE RESOLUTION

CHAPTER 4

ALTERNATIVE DISPUTE RESOLUTION

SUBPART D: ARBITRATION

By Kymberly A. Robinson, Esq.

Arbitration is another form of ***Alternative Dispute Resolution*** ("ADR"). Albeit rare, arbitration can be a more expedited and cost effective method for resolving economic issues in a divorce than litigation. Put simply, arbitration is less formal than a trial in New York Supreme Court and can be more emotionally healthy for everyone involved. See Glauber v. Glauber, 192 A.D.2d 94 (2nd Dept., 1993).

Importantly, mediation is not for every couple. Some divorcing couples need ***someone else to make a decision for them*** based on the law and facts. Oftentimes, people are involved in litigation because they want "their day in court" to feel heard. Arbitration is like an informal trial before a neutral third party allowing each side to "tell their story" and make his or her argument with the evidence they have. Like a judge, an arbitrator issues a decision for the parties.

What Issues Can Be Arbitrated?

In matrimonial law, arbitration is used with economic issues including equitable distribution, spousal maintenance and child support. See e.g., Sperling v. Sperling, 26 A.D.2d 827 (2nd Dept., 1966) (where arbitration of child support increase dispute was appropriate). For this reason, agreements must "***expressly and unequivocally***" specify which issues will be arbitrated and those that are not covered are not required to be arbitrated. See Bowmer v. Bowmer, 50 N.Y.2d 288, 293-294 (N.Y. 1980) (emphasis added). Arbitration of custody of minor children ***is not permitted*** in New York for public policy reasons. See Glauber v. Glauber, 192 A.D.2d 94 (2nd Dept., 1993). DRL § 70 and §

240 leave decisions on child custody and visitation to the courts.

Please note that arbitrators are obligated to determine child support in accordance with ***Child Support Standards Act*** ("CSSA") guidelines. If the arbitrator deviates from the CSSA, then the arbitration award may be vacated. See Hirsch v. Hirsch, 4 A.D.3d 451 (2nd Dept., 2004); and Frieden v. Frieden, 22 A.D.3d 634 (2nd Dept., 2005). More information on child support and the CSSA is found in Chapter 11 authored by Deborah Kaminetzky.

The Arbitration Process

"Binding" or "Non-Binding"?

Unlike mediators, arbitrators ***act like a judge*** and ***make a decision*** for the parties. Said arbitration can be ***binding*** (a final decision that the parties agree to uphold) or ***non-binding*** (the parties do not have to agree to follow a non-binding arbitration decision). Some prenuptial agreements include an arbitration clause stating that the parties will use binding arbitration. From a practical standpoint, most arbitration done in the matrimonial arena is binding. Binding arbitration is final and can only be appealed upon limited circumstances.

Picking the Arbitrator

The arbitrator does ***not have to be a judge or a lawyer***, but is oftentimes a retired judge or an experienced matrimonial attorney. Some religious divorcing couples choose a ***rabbi***, priest, or religious leader for arbitration. Like mediation or early neutral evaluation, the parties should choose a ***mutually agreed upon arbitrator***. This autonomy is a major advantage of all forms of ADR. In the court system, divorcing couples are at the mercy of whatever matrimonial judge was assigned to their case.

Suggested questions to ask an arbitrator during the interview/consultation process:

1. Where were you trained?
2. How many divorces have you arbitrated?
3. If the arbitrator is a retired judge, does this person have the mindset of expedition and economy? What is his/her suggested timeline?
4. What is arbitrator's schedule over the next several months?
5. What rules/procedures does the arbitrator follow? (Request a copy if available.)

Here are a couple of places to find matrimonial arbitrators in New York:

- New York Academy of Mediators and Arbitrators at http://www.nymediators.org
- The Arbitrator Regional Directory at http://arbitrators.regionaldirectory.us/new-york.htm

Divorcing couples should find a trained arbitrator with experience in matrimonial and family law.

Arbitrator May Screen for Domestic Violence

In mediation, a mediator will not take a case where there are allegations of domestic violence. Similarly, due to the nature of ADR, an arbitrator must screen for domestic violence before engaging with the couple in arbitration. To do this, the arbitrator will likely interview each person separately and pay special attention to any indication of domestic violence. In the alternative, a psychologist, social worker, or other mental health professional may screen the couple.

Entering into an Arbitration Agreement

> An ***arbitration agreement*** is different than a ***retainer agreement*** because it goes into more detail about the arbitration process and timelines. However, like a retainer agreement, an arbitration agreement will also set forth the fees to be charged, the method of payment, the services provided, and services excluded.

After picking an arbitrator, couples enter into an arbitration agreement. In this agreement the parties agree to submit to the arbitrator to resolve their issues. These can be used to stay a court action pending arbitration. Once arbitration is in process, the arbitrator takes an oath to hear and decide the issues ***faithfully and fairly***. See CPLR § 7506(a).

Preliminary Procedure

> ***Pro Rata:*** If the arbitrator costs \$300/hour and Spouse A makes \$100,000/year and Spouse B makes \$50,000/year, they might agree that spouse A pays \$200/hour and Spouse B pays \$100/hour.

Even before the arbitration begins, both parties and the arbitrator can decide ***upon what rules and timelines to follow***. Arbitrators are paid by the parties, so the issue of who will pay for the arbitrator should be resolved before the arbitration begins. Most commonly, the parties split the cost 50/50; however, this can be negotiated (e.g., pro rata or some other agreed upon formula).

The arbitration hearing is scheduled at an agreed upon time and location. Please note that the arbitration does not have to take place in New York for the arbitrator to follow New York law. For example, if one person lives in New York and the other lives in Pennsylvania, the arbitration hearing may take place in New Jersey so it is mutually convenient (or inconvenient). In matrimonial litigation, parties have little control on when the trial will take place. Similar to a hearing in a court or a trial, the arbitrator must notify the parties of the ***time, date, and place*** of the arbitration. <u>See</u> § CPLR 7506(b).

Arbitration Rules

Arbitrators are not bound by the rules of evidence; however, more relaxed rules of evidence are usually followed by the parties, attorneys and arbitrator. This structure makes it easier for the attorneys and arbitrators. That said, arbitration will eliminate typical litigation formalities.

Regardless if legal rules and procedures are followed, the arbitrator is obligated to treat the parties ***fairly and equitably***. Either party may request a copy of the rules/guidelines when interviewing an arbitrator. Arbitration can use rules or protocols to the extent that they promote fairness and equality in the arbitration process.

Discovery Procedure

Parties to an arbitration agreement can use all discovery methods used in litigation (including depositions, interrogatories, discovery and inspection of documents, subpoenas). Oftentimes, parties and counsel involved in arbitration agree to a more expedited discovery schedule and limit discovery in scope and time to reduce costs.

The Arbitration

In arbitration, the neutral arbitrator conducts a mini-trial in which he or she hears arguments, listens to testimony from both sides and is presented with evidence from both spouses in the manner in which each wants to present it. The arbitrator can make both legal and factual determinations on the remaining economic issues for the divorce; he or she will then issue a ***written opinion*** to the parties.

Religious Tribunals

In the ***Jewish Orthodox community***, many couples use ***rabbinical tribunals***, commonly referred to as a "***beth din***" to resolve their disputes, since it is against Jewish law to sue a fellow Jew. The ***Beth Din of America*** ("BDA") is currently the most substantial network of Jewish "courts" in the United States. Additionally, there are specific qualifications for obtaining a Jewish divorce (a "***get***"). A majority of decisions in the New York courts discuss these ***rabbinical tribunals*** and arbitrating in the Jewish Orthodox community is a highly specialized field that is beyond the purview of this chapter. More information on Jewish divorces is discussed in Deborah Kaminetzky's Chapter 31.

> A **get** is a Jewish divorce document under Jewish religious law which is presented by a husband to his wife to permit her to marry another man so that the laws of adultery no longer apply.

Other religions also commonly use religious tribunals to settle their issues through arbitration. In Christianity, disputes may be resolved by the rules of Christian Conciliation. Christian disputes are arbitrated by the ***Peacemaking Ministries*** and its affiliate, the ***Institute for Christian Conciliation*** ("ICC"). Muslims may use a religious tribunal to arbitrate disputes; these tribunals are made up of ***panels derived from local mosques***.

Vacating a "Binding" Arbitration Decision

Grounds for vacating a ***binding arbitration decision*** are set forth in CPLR § 7511 and are similar to defenses for enforcement of a contract, including ***fraud, duress, or overreaching***. See Silber v. Silber, 204 A.D.2d 527 (2nd Dept., 1994); and Lieberman v. Lieberman, 149 Misc.2d 983 (Sup. Ct. Kings Co., 1991) (the ***threat of Sirov***, which subjects the recipient to shame, scorn, and ridicule in the Jewish religion did not constitute duress). The standard of proof for these are a ***preponderance of the evidence***. One way a decision can be overturned is where a spouse lied about his or her financial assets to the detriment of the parties' children.

A binding arbitration decision can also be vacated due to the ***arbitrator's misconduct***, ***undisclosed conflict of interest*** on the part of the arbitrator, the arbitrator not following the rules set in the beginning of the arbitration, or the arbitrator exceeding the scope of his or her powers.

Entering an Arbitration Award in Court

Once arbitration is completely concluded and the spouses are both satisfied, an arbitration award must be made in court ***by motion***, and will be ***confirmed*** unless there is a ***motion to modify or vacate*** within one year. See CPLR § 7510. Finally, a judgment shall be entered upon the ***confirmation of an award***. See CPLR § 7514.

Kymberly A. Robinson, Esq.

Kymberly is an associate attorney with Rincker Law, PLLC. She is admitted to practice law in New York and Florida. She attended Union College in Schenectady, New York for her undergraduate studies, where she graduated with high honors as a psychology major. She then obtained her J.D. from Pace University School of Law in White Plains, New York and, subsequently, her L.L.M. (with a concentration in family law) from the Benjamin N. Cardozo School of Law in Manhattan. Kymberly entered the field of matrimonial and family law as a way to couple her interest in psychology and personal relationships with her legal education.

More information on Rincker Law, PLLC can be found at www.rinckerlaw.com.

SECTION C: PRACTICAL TIPS

CHAPTER 5

CHOOSING THE RIGHT PROFESSIONAL FOR YOU

By Maxine S. Broderick, Esq.

Selecting a matrimonial or family law attorney is a daunting task, but the professional a prospective client chooses can save time, money and unnecessary emotional distress in the long term. Choosing an attorney is similar to choosing a doctor or an accountant. The same qualities a prospective patient or client might look for in a doctor or accountant are those that should be sought in a family or matrimonial attorney.

Qualities to Look For

Experience Matters

The most important aspect of choosing an attorney is finding a professional with requisite experience. Although all licensed New York attorneys are permitted to engage in family and matrimonial practice, not all are qualified to do so. Therefore, as a general guideline, it is best to retain an attorney who specifically concentrates in this practice area.

As in all areas of law, matrimonial and family law can be very ***technical and complex***, especially when substantial assets are to be divided. Even an attorney who has practiced for 35 years does not know everything there is to know as matrimonial and family case law changes literally every day. Therefore, a prospective client would do best to bypass general practitioners and focus on finding a competent attorney who concentrates in this area.

The easiest way to determine an attorney's experience level is simple – ASK. In addition to inquiring how many years an attorney has practiced matrimonial and family law, ask how many divorce or custody disputes the attorney has handled. For the tech savvy, it is possible to research independently the number of cases an attorney has engaged in with respect to matrimonial and family law. It is also prudent to inquire if an attorney has the skills to take a matter to trial if needed. Lastly, find out how many cases an attorney is handling at once. A stellar attorney who has no time to return telephone calls or reply to e-mail promptly will leave a new client sorely disappointed.

Be wary of any practitioner who is not forthright about his or her experience or who becomes defensive when certain questions are raised. If the attorney is well-qualified, he or she will welcome the opportunity to highlight his/her accomplishments.

Temperament

A quality many prospective clients overlook in considering which attorney should handle their case is ***overall attitude***. Like all professionals, attorneys have differing personality types and work styles. Selecting the right attorney might mean the difference between being ensnared in a protracted legal battle that costs $50,000 and an expeditious process that meets client needs while keeping fees relatively low.

Many aspects of a divorce are rather straight-forward. For example, in a circumstance where both spouses are well-educated and generate equal income, spousal support or "alimony" is unnecessary in most cases. However, an emotionally-charged issue such as which parent should have primary physical custody of a child is highly sensitive and may require litigation. Litigation typically requires extensive research, drafting of voluminous legal documents and numerous court appearances. An attorney who takes a collaborative, ***cool-headed approach*** to negotiating a child custody arrangement can achieve as good an outcome as an attorney who is hot-tempered and insists upon the resolution of minor disputes to be determined through extensive litigation.

Each time an attorney files a motion or makes a court appearance, he or she is billing a client from $250 to $600 an hour. Bear in mind that oftentimes issues can be resolved by several telephone conferences between attorneys.

If a prospective client is seeking an attorney known for being "***a pitbull***," there are countless attorneys inclined to argue tirelessly every detail of a case, no matter how small. However, that client should be prepared for a hefty legal bill, and may not receive any added benefit in the disposition of the case. Further, some judges do not care for this style of litigation.

Another notion prospective clients should keep in mind is that they may have to reveal personal, and often ***embarrassing details***, about his or her home life to a virtual stranger. Discussing what led to the breakdown of a marriage, sexual infidelity or emotional abuse is never easy. On that basis, a prospective client should select an attorney who will take what is disclosed seriously, and who is easy to relate to and non-judgmental. A client should avoid an attorney who may be at the top of the profession, yet comes off as cold and not invested in the welfare of the family.

On that basis, a prospective client should select an attorney with whom he or she feels at ease and with whom sensitive matters can be discussed, i.e., ***someone a client can trust***. The last thing a client should do in a contentious matrimonial or family law matter is withhold information from an attorney because the client is uncomfortable. If a client does not leave an initial consultation feeling a sense of comfort and ease, there is nothing to obligate the client to return to that attorney's office.

Office Hours and Location

In choosing an attorney, a prospective client should consider whether an attorney can ***accommodate their work, school or family schedule***. If a client is a full-time day student, the client may opt to work with an attorney who offers extended, evening or weekend hours. In the midst of a matrimonial or family law matter, a client may need to meet with his or her attorney numerous times. If the attorney's office hours are inconvenient or it would take the client 3 hours of travel to meet with the attorney, then this mismatch may slow down or harm a case.

Billing Practices

Before signing a retainer agreement or remitting money to an attorney, a client should be very clear about billing practices. It should be clear whether the attorney accepts legal fees in installments. It should also be clear whether the attorney bills for travel time and expenses related to court appearances. A prospective client should also know if a paralegal will be doing the bulk of the work, and if so, that paralegal's billable rate. This is information that an attorney, or his or her staff, should be pleased to communicate if a potential client poses such questions.

Many clients are surprised to learn that attorney fees are set according to an attorney's level of experience and reputation. There is no governing body that sets fees for attorneys. Therefore, attorneys are permitted to charge what he or she would like to for legal services – within reason.

According to the rules of ***professional conduct***, New York attorneys are required to provide matrimonial clients a ***written retainer agreement*** and a statement concerning ***client rights and responsibilities***. Carefully reviewing these documents and asking questions is the best way to avoid "sticker shock" when a client receives an invoice from his or her attorney.

There are attorneys who bill clients for speaking to colleagues about a case. For example, if a junior attorney bills his or her time at $250 an hour and seeks guidance from a senior partner who charges $600 an hour, a client could be responsible for paying both attorneys for the same 30-minute period. The take away is that a client should read the retainer thoroughly and not be afraid to ask questions.

Professional Discipline

Believe it or not, some attorneys do not always do the right thing. For that reason, each region of New York State maintains a ***grievance and disciplinary*** committee. If an attorney's conduct is outside of the defined standards of matrimonial or family law practice, sooner or later these folks are going to hear about it and conduct an investigation. If allegations are serious enough, and are substantiated, that attorney is subject to disciplinary action that becomes public. A prospective client can contact the state or local bar association to check if an attorney has a record of professional misconduct.

Most attorneys do not have a negative record, so prospective clients should not be overly focused on this. The types of violations that can be problematic for attorneys are not returning unused retainer payments, neglecting telephone calls, or far more serious transgressions like theft.

Academics

While where an attorney attended law school or what his or her grades were can be an indicator that a person is particularly bright, it does not guarantee that the attorney is competent in matrimonial or family law. Prospective clients should not be blinded by lofty credentials. However, it is fair game to inquire where the attorney attended law school and received his or her undergraduate degree.

Reputation

Finally, a prospective client will want to select an attorney with a good reputation. And that does not mean an attorney who is well-liked by his or her colleagues for performance on the golf course. A client seeking a matrimonial or family attorney should select a practitioner who is respected by others in the profession and in the community. An attorney with a great reputation and good professional relationships can save a client in legal fees. If an attorney is known to judges and court personnel that attorney might be able to move matters along more quickly than another. That is not to imply that certain attorneys receive preferential treatment, but when an attorney knows all of the right people to call and is viewed favorably, it can expedite a case which ultimately saves the client money.

A prospective client may inquire about an attorney's reputation by asking other attorneys how that attorney is generally regarded in the legal community. Clients should also do a bit of independent research to determine if an attorney is an active member of professional organizations, bar association committees, civic associations or alumni clubs. This is often an indicator that the attorney is known, and well-regarded by his or her peers, especially if they are a committee chairperson or executive board member. An attorney with a great reputation will often be published in scholarly journals or legal newspapers. Such an attorney is also likely to lecture other attorneys or teach at the university or law school level.

Happy hunting.

Maxine S. Broderick, Esq.

A lifelong resident of Long Island, New York, Ms. Broderick concentrates her practice on matrimonial and family law. She is experienced in handling uncontested and contested divorces, legal separation, child support, child custody, visitation, spousal support, orders of protection and modification of Family Court orders.

Committed to community service, Ms. Broderick has provided pro bono legal assistance to low income New Yorkers with respect to personal bankruptcy, uncontested and contested divorces, consumer debt, foreclosure prevention and housing disputes.

Ms. Broderick was named an "Access to Justice Champion" by the Nassau County Bar Association for pro bono service in 2013, was the recipient of an Outstanding Service certificate from the Nassau County Coalition Against Domestic Violence (NCCADV) in 2012, and was recognized by the New York State Courts Access to Justice Program for outstanding work and dedicated service in the uncontested divorce Volunteer Lawyers Program in 2010.

She is a member of the New York State Bar Association, the Association of Black Women Attorneys (ABWA), the Nassau County Bar Association, the Nassau County Women's Bar Association, the Hempstead Branch of the NAACP and is President-elect of the Amistad Long Island Black Bar Association.

Ms. Broderick is a proud graduate of Sacred Heart Academy in Hempstead, New York, earned a bachelor degree from Fordham University and a juris doctor from Brooklyn Law School in 2003.

She is admitted to practice law in New York State, The United States District Court, Eastern District of New York (EDNY), The United States District Court, Southern District of New York (SDNY), and was admitted to The U.S. Supreme Court in 2014. For more information about Ms. Broderick's practice, visit www.brodericklawny.com.

SECTION C: PRACTICAL TIPS

CHAPTER 6

COMMUNITY RESOURCES FOR THE DIVORCING AND SEPARATING FAMILIES

By Lesley Ann Friedland, Esq. and Stefany Schaefer

A ***family shift*** is the inevitable result of separation and divorce. For children, the shift can be traumatic. The popular assumption is that children are harmed because their parents live in separate homes. However, the big risk factor for children is their exposure to ***conflict and hostility*** between their parents, not their physical living situation. For that reason, parents are responsible for helping their children transition with the least emotional harm. This is not an easy task considering the fact that parents themselves are under tremendous stress.

Even though divorce and separation affect a large portion of our society, ***supportive services*** are not readily available for the family. Most people on the divorce journey may consult an attorney or possibly a therapist. The divorce attorney usually focuses on the financial well-being of the client and the amount of parenting time that the client will have with the children. The therapist may work only with the information provided by the parents and speculation regarding how the parents believe the children feel. Both the therapist and lawyer are two resources that are client driven and often do not focus on the overall picture. There is no one size fits all solution, but there are ***community resources*** that can help families along the way.

Role of Community Organizations in Family Conflict

Education and community support are a key benefit for parents who are contemplating divorce or separation. Most people get a lot of help and information while planning their wedding, choosing their careers or selecting a place to live – so why wouldn't we gather information as to best handle our divorce and separation. Parents need answers to questions like:

- What will the legal process entail?
- How might their children react?
- How can the family survive this transition that touches every aspect of their lives?

Parents are entitled to learn how to co-parent in a way that is emotionally and physically safe for them and in their child's best interest. Certain countries, like Australia, have fully embraced the concept that the government owes a duty of help to separating families. They make information and support for the transitioning family readily available. Here in New York there are some resources that support the separating family, however it is often incumbent upon you to seek them out.

New York State Parent Education and Awareness Program

To start with, parents should know about the ***New York State Parent Education and Awareness Program*** for the separating and divorcing family. The primary goal of this program is to teach parents different ways they can reduce the stress of family changes and protect their children from the negative effects of ongoing parental conflict in order to foster and promote their children's healthy adjustment and development. People can self-refer to classes, or a judge may order them to take one. A couple does not attend class at the same time as one another and each parent may attend classes sponsored by different providers. Even though parents are often strapped for time during this difficult period in their lives, attending a NYS certified class is time well spent to learn your legal options and how to help yourself and children during this crucial period. In addition, jurists often appreciate a parent's effort to seek and obtain help. At ***FamilyKind***, classes are taught by a lawyer and a mental health professional, however, no legal advice or therapy is provided. Professionals ***teach strategies and coping skills*** to help the family take healthy steps toward the new family configuration. To find a NYS certified class in your neighborhood, visit https://www.nycourts.gov/ip/parent-ed/ (last visited September 6, 2015).

Programs for Children

Parents may also avail themselves of programming designed specifically for children. Not many programs for children are available in New York City, and classes are not certified by New York State, yet they can be very helpful to the ***transitioning family***. The programming for children helps reassure them that their family configuration may change, but the love that their parents feel for them is forever. Stand-alone classes for children ages 7-12 and teens are offered by ***FamilyKind***, and after school programming is available in various schools around the country provided by ***Banana Splits*** (http://www.bananasplitsresourcecenter.org). ***Institute for Psychoanalytic Training and Research*** ("IPTAR") provides therapeutic services for children and adolescents on a sliding fee scale (https://iptar.org/iptar-clinical-center/mental-health-counseling/ (last visited September 6, 2015).

Legal Information for Families Today ("LIFT") is a great resource created to enhance access to justice for children and families by providing legal information, community education, and compassionate guidance. LIFT has information tables in all five of the NYC Family Courts and further information about their services (many free of charge) may be found on their website: http://www.liftonline.org/ei-sites.html (last visited September 6, 2015).

Mediation

Divorce mediation benefits couples who are separating or considering separation. This service allows people to reduce the financial and emotional cost of divorce and to expedite the process. The mediator is a trained neutral professional who allows the parties to ***express their feelings*** and helps participants to be heard in a safe space. Through mediation, clients are guided to ***identify their***

interests rather than locking into a position. This process can result in minimizing anger and maximizing cooperation among the parties. Parents often do not mediate with their attorney present, but may do so if desired. Although mediation is an excellent resource, the service may not be appropriate for all couples. At intake, couples are screened for domestic violence, substance abuse, and mental illness to assess if the parties can safely engage with each other in a neutral environment. Also, even though the total financial and emotional cost of a mediated divorce is often far less expensive than a litigated divorce, the bill can still be significant. More information on the mediation process is found in Chapter 4a by Cari Rincker.

There are numerous community organizations through the State of New York that offer mediation and other supportive programs. For example, ***Ackerman Institute for Families*** in Manhattan provides divorce and family mediation on a limited basis, and they also have a vast number of supportive therapeutic programs for the family available on a sliding fee scale. For more information on its divorce mediation program visit https://www.ackerman.org/divorce-mediation/. Another organization, ***New York Legal Assistance Group*** ("NYLAG") in the Financial District of Manhattan provides free and sliding scale divorce mediation and legal services to low-income New Yorkers. The mediators at NYLAG address financial and parenting time issues. (http://nylag.org/units/the-mediation-project). NYLAG also has a list of consulting attorneys that work on a sliding scale basis. ***FamilyKind*** on the Upper West Side of Manhattan provides divorce and family conflict mediation services to residents of New York City, Long Island, Westchester and New Jersey on a sliding fee scale (http://www.familykind.org/families/mediation-parent-coordination/ [last visited September 6, 2015]).

Community Dispute Resolution Centers ("CDRC")

Are you interested in mediation services but are financially strapped? The ***New York State Court System*** partners with local non-profits known as ***Community Dispute Resolution Centers*** ("CDRCs") to provide alternative dispute resolution services, including mediation, to people in need. The CDRCs can be of help to families with parenting and school issues, but some do not handle the financial matters that often accompany divorce and separation. CDRCs are located around New York State and provide mediation either free of charge or at a low cost.

In New York City, the ***New York PEACE Institute*** ("NYPI") serves Kings and New York Counties, ***New York Center for Interpersonal Development*** ("NYCID") serves Richmond County and ***Community Mediation Services*** ("CMS") works with people in Queens. For a complete list of centers in NYS, services provided and fees charged: https://www.nycourts.gov/ip/adr/ProgramList.shtml (last visited September 6, 2015).

Supervised Visitation

When there is an allegation of either domestic violence or one parent not providing a safe environment for the child possibly due to the use of alcohol or drugs, a request may be made to the court for the visitation or access to be supervised. Supervised visitation or access may be conducted by an agency such as ***The Society for Prevention of Cruelty to Children*** ("NYSPCC") http://www.nyspcc.org/our-work/therapeutic-supervised-visitation-program/ or ***Safe Horizons*** http://www.safehorizon.org/page/court-programs-73.html (last visited September 6, 2015). These organizations provide a safe and clean site for visits to take place so a family can move forward. The supervisors may also prepare a report that can be furnished to the court to establish whether unsupervised visitation/access would be safe for the child.

Communication Skills

Improving communication skills should be an important goal of separating parents because after all, once a couple has a child, they are linked together for the child's entire life. The actual separation or divorce is only one step in the continuum of being parents. ***GoodTalk4Parents*** is a program that charges fees on a sliding scale and is customized for couples who need help establishing skills for productive and effective co-parenting communication that is free from conflict. More information on this particular program can be accessed online at http://www.familykind.org/families/goodtalk4parents/. The program emphasizes healthy communication so that parents can better share and manage the exchange of important information about their children, such as education, extra-curricular activities, medical appointments, discipline, and behavior. These communication skills can come in handy especially when a child has special ***medical or***

emotional needs so that each parent can be assured that the child's needs are being met in each household.

Parenting Skills

Because ***kids do not come with instructions***, whether you are an intact family or one in transition, help and support is needed. This may be even truer when children transition from one home to another and children and parents are developing new ways to cope with their new family configuration. ***Ackerman Institute for the Family*** has an on-line parenting guide with useful information: http://ackerman.org/wp-content/uploads/2014/01/Family-Matters.pdf. Supportive in person classes for parents are also available to ease the way. One such program provided by ***FamilyKind***, Systematic Training for Effective Parenting, is evidence based and nationally recognized (http://www.familykind.org/step-systematic-training-for-effective-parenting/ [last visited September 6, 2015]).

Parent Coordination

Parenting Coordination is a pivotal service that helps couples in high conflict cases learn to co-parent. The experienced parenting coordinator aids the parents in resolving a wide range of issues from discussing parenting time to addressing life-changing decisions such as relocation. Depending on the circumstances, parenting coordinators may work with the parents together or each parent separately. Parenting coordinators can even be charged by the court, after a case is concluded, with making decisions for the parents when the couple reaches an impasse. ***FamilyKind***, and other community organizations, make Parenting Coordinators available to parents on a sliding fee scale. For more information on parent coordination, review Chapter 24 by Paul Hymowitz.

Workshops for Blended Families

With the reconfiguration of families, re-coupling and blended families are very common. Being a step parent is wonderful, but not without its challenges. Even in the best of situations, there are adjustments that need to be made — physically, financially, and emotionally. The divorce rate for ***blended families*** is even higher than the divorce rate for first-time marriages. Workshops given by certified step parent coaches can provide support for these newly established families. The ***Step Family Foundation*** provides supportive services to the new family configuration (http://www.stepfamily.org/coaches-and-counselors-in-usa.html#New York). ***FamilyKind*** also provides classes for blended families at a reduced fee (http://www.familykind.org/families/workshops/ [last visited September 6, 2015]).

Group Meetings/ Meetups

Some community organizations offer some form of a separation and divorce "meetup" group in which members share their experience and concerns about the divorce and separation process. The discussions may be facilitated by professionals who cover a wide range of topics including approaching the divorce topic with children, successful parenting during divorce, and life after separation or divorce. The charge for meetups is often minimal.

Other Services & Resources

Finally, there are several organizations that provide support for the divorcing family including The ***Jewish Board of Family and Children's Services*** ("JBFCS") (http://www.jbfcs.org/programs-services/jewish-community-services-2/support-programs-single-parentsdivorced/#.VeTRBWDtuFI) and the ***Ackerman Institute*** (https://www.ackerman.org [last visited September 6, 2015]). Likewise, the Internet contains resources in the form of articles, podcasts, blogs written by professionals, client testimonials, and most importantly, a ***Children's Bill of Rights***, a reminder to help parents focus on what it most important: the wellbeing of their children.

Final Thoughts

Although the family shift can seem difficult at times, there are resources in the community that can be of help to you. Strong, safe communication between parents helps them maintain a durable structure for children allowing both parents to provide the consistency and discipline needed for children to thrive in their newly established environment. Research shows that all things being equal, a child needs the involvement of both parents to adapt to the new family configuration. It is incumbent upon you to reach out (whether or not your ex does) and avail yourself of the available resources. And always remember, there is a ***light at the end of the tunnel.***

Lesley Ann Friedland, Esq.

Lesley Ann Friedland is FamilyKind's Executive Director. Prior to her work at FamilyKind, Ms. Friedland was employed by the New York State Family Court for over 25 years as a Court Attorney Referee hearing cases concerning visitation, custody, neglect, abuse and domestic violence and as a Court Attorney assisting Judges. While at the Family Court, Ms. Friedland also oversaw the Kings County NYS Certified Parent Education Program and also served as the Court liaison to the Mediation program. There Ms. Friedland realized the benefits these services held for families in transition. Unfortunately, in 2008/9 both programs along with other valuable resources were no longer funded. Knowing that supportive services were vital to the health of transitioning families, in 2012 Ms. Friedland left her job and founded FamilyKind, a 501(C) (3) public charity. With the support of accomplished and altruistic mediators, parenting coordinators, lawyers and educators, FamilyKind seeks to fulfill two missions: provide high quality services for divorcing and separating families without regard to their financial resources and to change the way our society views the transitioning family. Friedland graduated with a BA from Sarah Lawrence College and a JD from Antioch School of Law.

Stefany Schaefer

Stefany Schaefer assists with special projects at FamilyKind and also serves as the FamilyKind Meetup Group organizer. She has worked with children and families in a variety of roles including private tutor, nanny, and a Court Appointed Special Advocate. Through her work, she has gained experience in family dynamics, family court proceedings in abuse and neglect cases, child development, and family conflict. Ms. Schaefer earned her B.A. in Forensic Psychology and Certificate in Dispute Resolution from John Jay College of Criminal Justice. She is committed to continue to empower families both through her work with FamilyKind and with her aspiration to pursue a career in family law.

SECTION C: PRACTICAL TIPS

CHAPTER 7

STRATEGIES FOR A LOWER LEGAL BILL

. . . because the divorce should not cost more than the wedding . . .

By Bonnie L. Mohr, Esq.

In order to save money on a divorce action, a person should use his or her attorney intelligently. These tips and strategies will help make the most use of an attorney's time.

Do not use an attorney as a therapist.

Your spouse cheated on you. You saw it on Facebook.

In the grand scheme of the divorce action or a family law dispute, the affair and other "not fair" facts play only minimum importance. The focus of the court and the goal in a divorce action requires the financial untangling of a marriage. If a person constantly complains to his or her attorney about the cheating or the unfair credit card debts, that person still pays for his or her attorney's time and shifts the attorney's focus away from the divorce action and onto the client's emotional pain.

In a family law dispute, the issues may be more limited as the parties were typically never married, but the focus should still be on the resolution instead of the faults or "bad parenting" of the other parent.

Along those lines, an attorney's time should be utilized to settle the divorce or family law action, not punish the spouse (or ex) with extensive and expensive litigation.

Do not use an attorney as a legal assistant or paralegal.

> The statement of net worth is a comprehensive financial document detailing case facts, your income, expenses, assets and liabilities. Attorneys are required to certify the accuracy of this very important document.

During the litigated divorce action, court rules require the parties to exchange (at least) three years of financial documents and a statement of net worth. Even if a divorce is not litigated, the attorneys may still require the exchange of the statement of net worth and financial documents for a certain time period.

Needless to say, the preparation of an accurate statement of net worth is a time-consuming endeavor for the attorney and the individual. The attorney needs to review this document with the individual and certify the accuracy of its contents. To save the attorney's time (and lower the bill), the client should prepare the statement of net worth to the best of his or her ability. This task requires tracking down one's:

- ***expenses*** (particularly monthly expenses such as phone bills, utilities, rents and mortgages);
- ***assets*** (e.g., bank accounts and balances, vehicles, real estate); and
- ***liabilities*** (e.g., mortgage balances, credit card balances).

Additionally, the parties can do their attorney (and themselves) a favor by providing his or her attorney with organized copies of the required financial documents. If the attorney has to organize the documents the individual provided or repeatedly ask the individual for the documents he or she did not provide, then the attorney can (and should) bill the party for this extra time.

Do not use an attorney as a copy center.

When a family or matrimonial attorney asks for documents, the client should provide the attorney with organized copies of the documents. If the client gives the attorney original documents, then the attorney will likely bill the client for the time to make office copies of those documents and the cost of the copies.

Clients can also save their attorney time and their own money by providing the documents in PDF format for the document exchange or providing multiple hard copies for the attorney. Discuss this with the attorney first.

Do not use an attorney as a messenger.

During the course of the divorce action, the parties are separating on both a ***short-term basis*** and a ***long-term basis***. Attorneys prefer to focus on the long-term separation and division of the marital assets such as the house, the retirement accounts and the bank accounts. In the interim, the parties should make sure the mortgage, rent or shared expenses are paid on time. Where possible, a client should have these conversations with his or her spouse and not through the attorney. It is an incredible waste of time and money to spend attorney time arguing about a cable bill.

When it comes to the exchange of children, oftentimes the attorney becomes a messenger. For example, attorneys become the "go between" in conversations about when and where the exchange of the children will take place and the protocol if someone is running late. The client can save money in attorneys' fees if he or she can speak directly with his/her spouse about the children.

> Give a man a fish and you feed him for a day; teach a man to fish and you feed him for a lifetime.
> - Chinese Proverb

Not surprisingly, many of the issues between parents have more to do with the (lack of) ***communication*** and ***parenting style*** than legal issues. The attorney is only available for these types of communications for as long as the divorce action is pending. Do use attorneys (or other professionals discussed here in this book) for counsel on effective ways to communicate with a spouse for future interactions.

As a caveat to this section, if there is (alleged) domestic violence or an overly controlling spouse, the parties *should be* communicating through the attorneys.

Use an attorney as a counselor at law.

A counselor at law is an ***advisor***. Clients should use a licensed family or matrimonial lawyer to advise them on the pending case. Attorneys can advise clients in different ways, such as answering questions on the applicable law, discussing legal strategy (e.g., whether to file a motion, have a trial) or discussing settlement options (e.g., timing, settlement terms, strategy).

An attorney should also advise a client on the pros and cons of available resources. For instance, there are times where a parenting coordinator is the better resource for resolving parenting time conflicts.

Do use an attorney as a strategist.

"A strategist is a person with responsibility for the formulation and implementation of a strategy. Strategy generally involves setting goals, determining actions to achieve the goals, and mobilizing resources to execute the actions. A strategy describes how the ends (goals) will be achieved by the means" (Wikipedia – definition of strategist).

During a divorce action, work with an attorney to set goals and determine how to achieve those goals. The most basic tools available to attorneys include mediation, arbitration, negotiation and litigation. Before meeting with an attorney, consider the "wants" or goals to achieve in a divorce action and then discuss with the attorney. Goals can be anything from a quick-as-possible divorce, half the pension, or custody of the children.

Even though a client and attorney may have developed goals and a legal strategy from the onset of the action, the goals and strategy are ***subject to change*** at any given moment. This is especially the case if a motion is won or lost, the players (or their behavior) has changed, or the goals have shifted. The family and matrimonial lawyer should be used as a strategist throughout the process.

Do use an attorney for critical document review.

The parties should use their family and matrimonial law attorney to review the:

- statement of net worth,
- legal documents such as motions and pleadings,
- settlement proposals,
- financial documents,
- professionally prepared reports such as home appraisals and any other documents produced during discovery.

The parties should support their attorney through the review of these documents by answering questions and providing any missing pieces of information to the extent that they can. The parties can also assist their attorney by going through these documents themselves and alerting their attorney to any red flags or financial inconsistencies.

Do use an attorney to negotiate a settlement.

Litigation is extremely expensive. Unless someone has a high net worth or qualifies for free legal services (either by income or circumstances), both parties to a divorce action will be paying legal fees for probably two attorneys from assets it has taken those parties years to accumulate. That said, it will save parties to a divorce significant moneys in attorneys' fees and litigation expenses if parties can negotiate a divorce action with attorneys, the court, or a mediator. Clients should trust their attorney on the timing of settlement negotiations.

Bonnie L. Mohr, Esq.

Bonnie L. Mohr, managing member of the Law Offices of Bonnie L. Mohr, PLLC, started the firm in 2008 to create a practice that educates and guides clients through life-altering and stressful family situations utilizing a comprehensive, holistic and strategic approach.

The firm's practice focuses on matrimonial law including contested and uncontested divorces, prenuptial and postnuptial agreements, and post-judgment enforcements. Bonnie also practices in the family courts on such matters as child support, parenting time (custody and visitation), paternity and family offense matters.

Bonnie L. Mohr is licensed to practice law in the states of New York (2004), New Jersey (2004), and Pennsylvania (2008). She is also licensed to practice in the district courts of the Eastern District of New York, the Southern District of New York and the District of New Jersey.

Bonnie's memberships include the matrimonial and family law committees for the Women's Bar Association, New York County Lawyer's Association and New York State Bar Association. Bonnie is also a member of the New York City Bar Association, where she was leader of the matrimonial mentoring circle.

SECTION C: PRACTICAL TIPS

CHAPTER 8

SOCIAL MEDIA AND DIVORCE

By Ravi Cattry, Esq.

Modern day technologies allow people to communicate in real time and through means that allow a wide array of people to view the information that is being shared. This information, shared via ***social media websites***, such as Facebook, Twitter, LinkedIn, Instagram, YouTube, and Tumblr, can play a major role in matrimonial cases both in terms of being used as evidence in a divorce and other repercussions post final decree of a divorce, such as consequences of sharing confidential information of divorce settlements.

Social Media as Evidence in Divorce Case

New York courts have held that social media is discoverable because privacy is not at issue, the information is generally relevant to the divorce case, and there is no violation of privilege.[3] There is no expectation of privacy on social media websites because the main purpose of these websites is to be able to share information with others. Even if you have a locked profile where others have to send a request to view the posts, you are still sharing information that is meant for more than just your eyes and thus there is no reasonable expectation of privacy.

During the discovery stage of a divorce, the court *may* order a party to turn over usernames and passwords to social media websites, or print out the entirety of the profile from inception up to the current day. Alternatively, it is possible that information be produced via

[3] Loporcaro v. City of New York, No. 100406/10, 2012 WL 1231021 (N.Y. Sup. Ct. 04/09/2012).

subpoenas. Any information received from these websites may then be used in the divorce proceeding as evidence for or against the spouse. The requests for the type of information that is wanted should relevant to issues with the divorce. Courts oftentimes strike down requests for being overbroad.

The information may be collected from social media websites, as well as applications on cell phones. This includes information from apps for ***online dating***, such as Tinder, OkCupid, Happn, and Grindr, ***messaging apps***, such as WhatsApp, Viber, and Snapchat, ***location apps***, such as Foursquare, which keep record of places a person has been and where they have "checked in," and applications used for ***professional connections***, such as LinkedIn. A party may be able to get pictures, videos, messages, and posts from any and all of these websites and applications.

Courts have yet to rule on whether or not attorneys may send Facebook friend requests to opposing parties, but the New York City Bar Ethics Committee have addressed how attorneys should behave in terms of looking at social media profiles of opposing parties. The Ethics Committee concluded that an attorney ***or his agent*** may use his real name and profile to send friend requests to *unrepresented* opposing parties in order to gain information without having to disclose the reason for making the request. However, ***creating fake names and fake profiles*** to seek access to a party's information is strictly prohibited by the New York Rules of Professional Conduct.

Protecting Information Posted on Social Media

Since information posted on social media can be used in divorce proceedings as evidence, it is crucial for a party in a matrimonial litigation to consider his or her social media use and history. As mentioned before, locking the profile, so that only certain people see it, does not make information private or insulate it from matrimonial litigation. However, unfriending acrimonious ex-relationships and their friends may help. If a spouse cannot access the Facebook wall or Twitter feed of a party without permission from the court it may limit him or her in the information that can be collected; after all, motion practice is expensive and not always immediately rewarding. That said, this doesn't protect someone when a spouse has taken screenshots of social media interactions or postings before the spouse was "unfriended."

Depending on timing, parties in divorce litigation should refrain from deleting information posted on social media accounts because a court may consider that destruction of evidence. If a court finds that a party deliberately deleted, manipulated, or refused to hand over information regarding their social media accounts to avoid complying with court orders or in anticipation of discovery orders, the court may impose sanctions. For example, in a case in Virginia, a party that deleted a Facebook account in order to resist turning over information had an adverse jury inference instruction imposed and the party and the attorney were ordered to pay reasonable attorneys' fees for ***spoliation***.[4] Talk to your lawyer before deleting social media accounts or information/photographs.

> **Spoliation**. The intentional, reckless, or negligent withholding, hiding, altering or destroying of evidence relevant to a legal proceeding. Deleting an unflattering picture might fall in this category if the picture could be relevant to the legal proceeding at hand.

While information that has already been posted usually cannot be deleted or edited, once a divorce proceeding starts parties ***should refrain from posting or sharing*** information that has to do with the proceedings themselves or any other information that might be used as evidence in the divorce. Divorce proceedings can be difficult, so parties can feel the need to vent their feelings on social media, but sharing details about how difficult the opposing party is being or specifics of a divorce settlement may lead to issues of those posts becoming evidence in the proceeding as well as an issue of breaking attorney-client privilege.

[4] Lester v. Allied Concrete Co., No. CL08-150, CL09-223 (Va. Cir. Ct. 09/01/2011).

All information shared between a party and his or her attorney is considered privileged and an opposing party is not entitled to learn what was discussed. However, if a party shares details of his or her conversation ***with an attorney on social media*** publically or private message with third parties, it may allow the opposing party to not only use that information in the divorce case, but also learn other conversations because that information is no longer privileged.

In regards to ***attorney-client privilege***, it is also important to ensure that any communication between an attorney and a client is done from a computer or phone that is solely belonging to the client and ***not shared with others***. It is also important to restrict all communications with attorneys to private emails that are password protected. If divorcing spouses are ***sharing email addresses or social media accounts***, those should also be immediately ceased in favor of individual email addresses and if necessary, their own social media accounts.

Top Ten Things You Should Know About Social Media If You Are Involved in Divorce Litigation

1. Your social media account may be used against you.
2. Do not delete your social media accounts or content without consulting your attorney.
3. Do not post about your matrimonial or family law dispute.
4. Never post comments on social media relating to conversations with your attorney.
5. Keep social media posts positive, putting you and your family in good light.
6. Unfriending your spouse and/or their friends at outset of the legal proceeding may prevent social media from being used against you.
7. Do not contact your attorney from computers or email addresses that are shared with others, including social media messaging accounts.
8. Use individual social media accounts and email addresses instead of shared accounts.
9. Do not create fake profiles in order to gain access to a spouse's social media accounts.
10. Encourage friends and other family members to refrain from posting information about the legal proceedings and comments or pictures that may disparage your spouse.

Ravi Cattry, Esq.

Ravi Cattry is an associate attorney at Rincker Law, PLLC and is licensed to practice in New York and New Jersey and admitted into the Eastern and Southern District Courts of New York. She completed a Bachelor of Science at Fordham University in Manhattan where she was a double major in psychology and economics. She received a Juris Doctor from Pace University School of Law in White Plains, New York.

Before joining Rincker Law, PLLC, Ravi worked at a general practice firm located in Kew Gardens, New York. While working there her practice areas included landlord and tenant disputes, matrimonial and family law issues, commercial law, and immigration law. Ravi also worked with a boutique law firm specializing in bankruptcy law in Manhattan. During law school she interned with the Integrated Domestic Violence Court in White Plains, New York, where she assisted in handling divorce cases intertwined with domestic violence cases.

Ravi is fluent in Hindi and Punjabi, and conversational in Spanish. In her free time Ravi enjoys reading, watching movies, playing tennis, and keeping up with her favorite soccer teams. For more information about Rincker Law, PLLC, visit www.rinckerlaw.com.

SECTION C: PRACTICAL TIPS

CHAPTER 9

COURTROOM DECORUM

By Ravi Cattry, Esq.

Appearing in court comes as a part of a matrimonial or family case, and being in court comes with certain (mostly unwritten) rules that should be followed. These rules concern how to dress in court and how to behave in court. Remembering the three Ps will help parties meet the rules required for court: parties should be **P**roperly dressed, **P**olite, and **P**unctual.

Dressing for Court

The way a person dresses in court ***reflects his or her attitude*** about the case and the respect he or she has towards the judge and the legal progress in general. Court is in session during all seasons and dressing appropriately for all of these months is important. The rule for dressing for court is to be conservative. The clothes chosen to wear to court should always be ***clean, without any tears or rips***, should not have any bold prints or writing, and show a minimal amount of skin.

For men who are dressing for court, it is not necessary to go out and buy a suit. It is not even necessary to wear a suit. Men should wear a full-sleeved collar shirt that is buttoned completely. A ***tie is not necessary***, but should be worn whenever possible. The only bottoms acceptable for court are pants. No matter how hot it is outside, shorts are never appropriate for court. Additionally, jeans and cargo pants are not acceptable for court. Sneakers, sandals, and any type of shoe that shows toes or heels should not be worn to court. Similar to wearing clean clothes, shoes should also be clean and devoid of bold graphics, designs, or words. Make sure that all clothes are also as wrinkle-free as possible.

For women, it is not necessary to wear a suit either. Nor is it necessary to wear a skirt or a dress to court, if a party finds it uncomfortable. If a party does choose to wear a dress or skirt to court, the length should reach the knees. Anything shorter than that is inappropriate for a courtroom. Similar to the rules for men, women should also only wear clothes that are clean, wrinkle-free, ***without bold prints***, designs, or writing on them. Women should wear tops that do not show cleavage. A suit jacket is not necessary, but if shoulders are bared, a sweater is appropriate. Women should wear closed-toe shoes. Heels are not necessary.

Additionally, jewelry or accessories that make too much noise should be left at home as some courts and judges may find them a distraction. For example, electronic watches that beep or bracelets that bang against each other and make noise should not be worn to court.

During the winter months, be sure to ***remove jackets***, scarves, winter hats, etc. before entering the courtroom. Hats are never appropriate in the courtroom and should be removed before entering. It can often be chilly in the courtroom itself so a sweater may come in handy even in the summer months.

Behavior in the Court

Decorum in the court can be more important than a person's dress in court. The most important rule is to always be ***courteous to all people*** involved in the litigation including the judge, court personnel, the opposing side, and a party's own attorney and co-parties/family members. While in court, ***remain quiet*** while other cases are in front of the judge. When a party's case is called, he or she should refrain from making comments about what is happening in the proceedings or reacting to what is happening in the courtroom either positively or negatively. Parties should also refrain from talking directly to the other party. If the judge asks questions, parties should stand when answering and only direct answers to the judge.

Those in court should ***turn off their cell phones*** before they enter the courtroom. Food and drink is not allowed inside and should be finished before entering. Parties should also refrain from chewing gum in courtrooms because it can be noisy and can also make it difficult to understand what is being said.

Always ***arrive on time*** for your court date. It is advisable that parties arrive before their appointed time to allow them time to address any issues and questions with their attorney. If a party is late, he or she should try to be as quiet as possible when entering the courtroom to avoid disturbing ongoing proceedings.

Ravi Cattry, Esq.

Ravi Cattry is an associate attorney at Rincker Law, PLLC and is licensed to practice in New York and New Jersey and admitted into the Eastern and Southern District Courts of New York. She completed a Bachelor of Science at Fordham University in Manhattan where she was a double major in psychology and economics. She received a Juris Doctor from Pace University School of Law in White Plains, New York.

Before joining Rincker Law, PLLC, Ravi worked at a general practice firm located in Kew Gardens, New York. While working there her practice areas included landlord and tenant disputes, matrimonial and family law issues, commercial law, and immigration law. Ravi also worked with a boutique law firm specializing in bankruptcy law in Manhattan. During law school she interned with the Integrated Domestic Violence Court in White Plains, New York, where she assisted in handling divorce cases intertwined with domestic violence cases.

Ravi is fluent in Hindi and Punjabi, and conversational in Spanish. In her free time Ravi enjoys reading, watching movies, playing tennis, and keeping up with her favorite soccer teams. For more information about Rincker Law, PLLC, visit www.rinckerlaw.com.

PART II: CHILDREN

SECTION A: TYPES OF PROCEEDINGS

CHAPTER 10

CHILD CUSTODY, VISITATION AND PARENTING TIME

By Cari B. Rincker, Esq. and Bonnie L. Mohr, Esq.

Absent reasons otherwise, the courts presume that children are best served by meaningful access to both parents. Starting with this premise, parents should work together, with their attorneys as necessary, to create a schedule for their child's access to both parents. If the parents cannot agree to the terms of this schedule, even with the help of attorneys, the court will create the schedule for the parents. As the courts so eloquently put it: ***do you really want a stranger making these decisions?***

These are the key questions that must be answered:

(1) Who will the child live with primarily?
(2) How will major decisions be made?
(3) What is the parenting time/access schedule?

As simple as these questions may seem, these are difficult questions to answer when you consider the parents' protective love of their child and concern about the other parent's ability to parent, the schedules of the parents and the child, the different parenting styles, the duration of the schedule, the tension between the parents and the need for the access schedule to accommodate the child's development and growth. Parents fail to realize that at some point the child will want to spend all of his or her time with friends.

Custody

Determinations of custody are based on the "***best interest of the child***." See DRL § 70; DRL § 240; see Eschbach v. Eschbach, 56 N.Y.2d 167 (N.Y. 1982); see Welsh v. Lewis, 292 A.D.2d 536 (2nd Dept., 2002) (emphasis added). These factors include, *inter alia*:

(1) The parent who has been the primary caretaker;
(2) The age and health of the parties;
(2) The need for stability and continuity in the child's life;
(3) The relative financial ability of each parent;
(4) The quality of home environment and the parental guidance each parent provides;
(5) The ability of each parent to provide for the child's emotional and intellectual development;
(6) The relative fitness of each parent;
(7) The length of time the present custodial arrangement has been in effect; and
(8) The desires of the child.

These factors are established by case law in New York and are not contained in a specific rule of law. Courts are given ***broad deference*** with the interpretation of these factors. The court looks at the ***totality of the circumstances***.

New York's jurisdiction over child custody is codified in DRL § 76. Most commonly, jurisdiction is based on New York being the home state of the child. In other words, the child has resided (and has been domiciled) in New York for ***at least six (6) months*** before the commencement of a custody proceeding. See DRL § 76 (a). If New York does not have ***personal jurisdiction*** over the child, a court cannot make any determinations of custody.

> The word "***domiciled***" means the place of primary residence, such as where you file a tax return or enroll the child in school. You can have many residences or places where you live (think vacation home or long summer visits), but only one primary residence or domicile. On the other hand, ***personal jurisdiction*** is a court's jurisdiction or reach over a person. For the court to have jurisdiction over a child, the child must have been domiciled in the state for at least six months. If personal jurisdiction is the issue, it is because the parties disagree which state is the child's home state for the last six months.

Oftentimes, people say they want "custody" – "***full custody***" or "***shared custody***." But the term "custody" is often misunderstood.

In New York, there are two types:

(1) **Physical (or residential) custody** – who the child lives with *primarily*; and

(2) **Legal custody** – decision-making.

Physical Custody

As noted above, the term "***physical custody***" or "***residential custody***" is who the child(ren) live with *primarily* (i.e., over 50% of the time by looking at overnight stays and "waking hours"). There are two main options with physical custody:

(1) **Primary Physical Custody with Visitation to the non-custodial parent** – Primary physical custody to one parent while giving the other parent reasonable visitation/parenting time; or

(2) **Joint Physical Custody** – Equal parenting time to both parents.

In determining who will be the custodial parent, the court looks at the "best interest of the child" factors. Courts in New York will not typically grant joint physical custody (or "shared physical custody") unless both parties consent, because courts in New York typically favor the child(ren) having one primary "home" for stability.

As you can imagine, joint custody is complicated for logistical reasons. Often joint custody arrangements turn into primary physical custody situations upon a modification simply because the joint custody is impractical and does not work for the parties. For example, in a relocation case where there was originally joint physical custody, the court modified custody to award the father primary physical custody based on the mother's request to relocate to Connecticut (while the father had continuously resided in Saratoga, New York). See Dickerson v. Robenstein, 68 A.D.3d 1179 (3rd Dept., 2009). Joint physical custody is most typically applied to cases where the parents live in the same locality and it is easy to transport the child back and forth between the parent's homes.

> **An example clause for day-to-day decisions in a parenting agreement might read as follows:** "Each Parent will make day-to-day decisions regarding the care and control of the Children during the time they are caring for the Children. This includes any emergency decisions affecting the health or safety of the Children and routine decisions regarding bedtime, homework, health care, and day-to-day school, religious, social and athletic activities customary for a child of his/her age and maturity, and the general rules of conduct, such as prohibited activities, curfews, and household obligations shall be made by the Parent with whom the minor Children are then residing. The Parties shall cooperate and establish a mutually agreeable policy regarding such day-to-day decisions, but the primary responsibility for routine decisions shall rest with the Parent with whom the Children are then staying."

Legal Custody

Legal custody refers to the parent or parents that have decision-making authority over "***major decisions***" regarding the child, such as non-emergency medical care, religion, education, and extracurricular activities. When you think of the phrase "legal custody," replace it with the phrase "decision-making" (e.g., sole decision-making or joint decision-making). Please note that "***day-to-day***" decisions are made with the parent who has parenting time during that period (e.g., when to brush teeth, when to do homework, when to go to sleep, what clothes to wear, etc.).

Here are the various choices with legal custody:

(1) Legal custody to one parent;

(2) Legal custody to one parent requiring good faith consultation with the other parent;

(3) Joint legal custody with the custodial parent having the "tie-breaking" in the case of an impasse;

(4) Joint legal custody with some way of determining how an impasse will be handled, such as:

a. Having a third party be consulted before the "tie-break" can be made or have the third party make the decision (e.g., general doctor for nonemergency health, school advisor for education);

b. Either consulting with a ***parent coordinator*** before a "tie-break" can be made or have the parent coordinator make the decision for the parents like an arbitrator; or

c. Use of ***mediation*** before a "tie-break" can be made; and,

d. ***Spheres of Influence*** – each parent has decision-making authority for a different area of the child's life such as medical decisions, religion, education or extracurricular activities. With the spheres of influence, the parent with the decision-making authority may have an obligation to consult with the other parent before making that final decision in their sphere of influence (e.g., Father to have "tie-break" on health and education and Mother to have "tie-break" on religion and extra-curricular activities); and,

(5) **True joint legal custody requiring mutual consent.**

The phrase "***joint custody***" refers to joint legal custody and is only awarded where the parents can cooperate and make "decisions" together (and communicate with each other in a meaningful way to make those decisions). See e.g., Braiman v. Braiman, 44 N.Y.2d 584 (N.Y. 1978). Because the parents must have a good relationship, courts in New York require consent by both parents. Courts have this position because they feel that parents must be able to get along with each other in order to make decisions together. Therefore, courts usually do not recommend joint legal custody if the parents have an acrimonious relationship or have had a history of domestic violence or family offenses requiring an order of protection. Courts are increasingly recommending spheres of influence so that each parent is meaningfully involved in the decision-making process in their child's life.

Special Issues on Custody

Splitting Siblings

The courts prefer to keep siblings together for stability, companionship and close family ties. "Young brothers and sisters need each other's strengths and association in their everyday and often common experiences, and to separate them, unnecessarily, is likely to be traumatic and harmful." Obey v. Degling, 37 N.Y.2d 768 (1975). However, the courts will order split custody if it's in the best interest of each child to live with a different parent. See Matter of Bilodeau v. Bilodeau, 161 AD2d 906 (3rd Dept 1990).

Consider splitting the children in separate households if the children are exceptionally abusive and combative with each other, one of the children has mental health problems that negatively impact the other child or the children have special bonds with different parents and prefer to live in different households.

If the children are in different households, the parents must consider the frequency and duration of sibling visitation. For example, the children may live with different parents during the week, but live with the same parent during the weekend.

More on "Nesting"

A "nesting" situation requires ***three households*** – the mother, the father and the child. While the mother and the father live in their own homes, they rotate between the "child's" home to exercise their parenting time. This allows the child to maintain a stable home environment and the parents do all the shifting between their respective homes and the child's home.

Nesting has several complications. The parents must agree on a parenting schedule with the child, the parents must agree on house rules and the parents must maintain multiple households.

A Few Other Considerations

Information Sharing

Most parenting plans include a provision requiring the parents to share information about the child(ren) with such information as:

> **"Parenting plans"** or **"custody and visitation agreements"** are the same thing. If a couple is going through a divorce, then provisions relating to custody and visitation can be included in the divorce settlement agreement.

- medical records
- psychological records
- law enforcement records
- school report cards
- school progress reports
- school event calendar (e.g., school play, parent-teacher conferences)
- extra-curricular activities calendar (e.g., baseball game schedule or dance recitals).

Some parents decide to keep a shared calendar (e.g., Google calendar) with the child's schedule to keep the other parent more easily informed. Most schools duplicate information for each parent.

Mutual Respect

Parenting plans should include a provision requiring the parents to ***respect one another and his/her relationship with the child***. It will also require that the parents not disparage (ridicule, discredit, mock, demean, denounce or derogate) the other parent. When parents speak poorly of the other parent, it can negatively affect the relationship between both parents and the child. Courts take disparagement of the other parent seriously. Along those same lines, children should not be aware of the details of the court dispute between the parents and should not be given access to court pleadings.

Mutual respect extends to respecting the other parent's time and being on time for drop-offs and pick-ups. Mutual respect extends to giving the other parent advance notice of when you cannot exercise parenting time. As the custodial parent, this gives the non-custodial parent an opportunity for additional parenting time. As the non-custodial parent, this means the custodial parent may need to obtain child-care if you are not exercising your parenting time. Mutual respect means acknowledging that there will be parenting disputes that have nothing to do with the divorce or your dislike for each other and everything to do with parenting decisions. Mutual respect means making decisions that benefit your child even at your expense.

Communication Between Parents

There should be a mechanism in place for the parents to communicate with one another about the care and welfare of the child. If an order of protection is in place, courts can consider a "carve-out" for communication about the child (e.g., text message and email only). Parents should consider a clause requiring that communication to the other parent about the child or child support be with the parent directly (or via a third party when there is an order of protection) – such communication should never be via the child. This is called "triangulation" and can have deleterious effects on the child who is "caught in the middle."

Visitation & Parenting Time

The courts believe that a child should have meaningful access to both parents regardless of their skill as a parent. The meaningful access to the non-custodial parent is referred to as visitation or parenting time. Parents must keep in mind that they will have different parenting styles, different methods of discipline and different standards. This means that the other parent may let the child stay up late watching "inappropriate" movies, feed the child "junk" food and return the child in "dirty" clothes.

Visitation & parenting time starts with a basic parenting schedule, a holiday schedule and a summer schedule. Visitation is easier for everyone if the parents work together for smooth exchanges of the child from one parent to the other, maintain similar rules in both households and communicate with each other – and not through the child – about the child or the child's schedule.

Basic Parenting Schedule

Parents should decide on a "basic parenting time schedule" that the parents will conduct in a regular week. Parents should consider what is reasonable taking into consideration the location of the parent's home, the parent's schedule and the child's schedule.

If the parents do not live near each other, the parenting schedule deviates from regular short-term access such as every other weekend to less regular, long-term access such as school vacations and a month during the summer.

If one parent has primary physical custody then the parents should decide the best visitation schedule to help foster a positive relationship between the non-custodial parent and the child. For example, the non-custodial parent might have parenting time every other weekend from Friday afterschool to Sunday night and every Wednesday night. Here is what that schedule might look like in a 4 week interval:

	M	T	W	R	F	S	S
Wk1			NCP* 3pm to overnight	NCP take child to school at 8am	NCP 3pm-overnight	NCP - all day/ night	NCP until 6pm. CP** to pick up from NCP
Wk2					NCP 3pm-overnight	NCP - all day/ night	NCP until 6pm. CP to pick up from NCP
Wk3			NCP 3pm to overnight	NCP take child to school at 8am	NCP 3pm-overnight	NCP - all day/ night	NCP until 6pm. CP to pick up from NCP
Wk4					NCP 3pm-overnight	NCP - all day/ night	NCP until 6pm. CP to pick up from NCP

*Non-Custodial Parent ("NCP")
**Custodial Parent ("CP")

Mid-week parenting time is only realistic when the parents live in the same proximity geographically.

In the ***above illustration***, the custodial parent is picking up the child from the non-custodial parent's home. This is negotiable and can be flip-flopped. Alternatively, parents might decide on a mutually convenient "***drop-off and pick-up location***" or the exchange takes place by dropping off and picking the child from school.

Tip: Before you call a babysitter, call the non-custodial parent. The non-custodial parent is free child-care.

There is ***no "rule"*** when it comes to a basic parenting time. Parents ***can think creatively*** when determining a workable plan. For example, perhaps the non-custodial parent can pick the child up from school each day; after a few hours of parenting time, that parent can deliver to child to the custodial parent's home. This afterschool visitation might be in addition to weekend time.

If the parents decide on a "joint physical custody arrangement" then the parents might alternate weeks (i.e., Monday thru Sunday). Alternatively, the parents might use a 2 day/5 day schedule where the child would be with one parent for two days (Monday and Tuesday), then the other parent for 2 days (Wednesday and Thursday), and alternate weekends (Friday, Saturday and Sunday. An example 2 day/5 day schedule might look like this on a four-week interval:

	M	**T**	**W**	**R**	**F**	**S**	**S**
Week 1	Dad[5]	Dad	Mom	Mom	Dad	Dad	Dad
Week 2	Dad	Dad	Mom	Mom	Mom	Mom	Mom
Week 3	Dad	Dad	Mom	Mom	Dad	Dad	Dad
Week 4	Dad	Dad	Mom	Mom	Mom	Mom	Mom

[5] Mom and Dad are used here for illustrative purposes only. The family may have two Moms or two Dads.

This 2/5 schedule works well with the drop-off and pick-up occurring at the school. The parent with the weekend parenting time is responsible for picking the child up from school on Friday afternoon and getting the child to school on time on Monday morning.

> *Tip:* Facilitate exchanges by using the child's school. For example, the non-custodial could pick-up the child after school on Friday and return the child to school on Monday morning. This avoids a potentially awkward exchange for the parents and frees up the custodial parent's Friday afternoon and Sunday evening. This also works for mid-week overnight visits.

The key is to create a schedule that best accommodates everyone's schedules, is predictable for scheduling appointments and activities and offers a degree of flexibility.

Holiday Schedule

After deciding the "basic parenting time schedule", parents should then decide how they want to handle holidays. Holidays include the following:

- School holidays/ National holidays (e.g., Columbus Day, Memorial Day)
- Religious holidays (e.g., Easter)
- Other holidays (e.g., Halloween)
- Birthdays (parents and children)
- Father's Day and Mother's Day

Parents should make a list of all applicable holidays in which the parents want to celebrate with the child (or have additional parenting time if the child is out of school) and decide what they would like to do for each holiday. For example, with some holidays, the parents may elect to alternate years while with other holidays, perhaps only one parent will have parenting time (e.g., one parent is Christian and the other parent is Jewish and each observes different religious holidays).

An example holiday schedule may look like this[6]:

Holiday	Odd-Numbered Years	Even-Numbered Years
Columbus Day	Mother	Father
Halloween	Father from 5pm to 9pm	Mother from 5pm to 9pm
Mother's Birthday (November 7th)	Mother from 6pm to 8pm (if school night), otherwise, all day/night	Mother from 6pm to 8pm (if school night), otherwise, all day/night
Thanksgiving	Father	Mother
Christmas Eve	Mother	Father
Christmas Day	Father	Mother
New Year's Eve	Mother	Father
New Year's Day	Mother	Father
Martin Luther King (MLK) Day	Father	Mother
Father's Birthday (Feb. 10th)	Father from 6pm to 8pm (if school night), otherwise, all day/night	Father from 6pm to 8pm (if school night), otherwise, all day/night
President's Day	Mother	Father
Easter	Father	Mother

[6] This example is with a Mother and a Father. The authors recognize that there may be two mothers or two fathers in some families.

Mother's Day	Mother	Mother
Memorial Day	Father	Mother
Father's Day	Father	Father
Fourth of July	Mother	Father
Labor Day	Father	Mother

The parents may select to also alternate time with the child(ren) on birthdays so have a schedule when both parents can celebrate with the child(ren) on or around his/her birthday.

> *Tip*: Structure the exchange time to accommodate celebration of the holiday, traffic or plane fares. For example, you want a parenting plan that avoids forcing a parent to fly with a child during peak airline fares or will require an exchange during rush hour traffic if it can be avoided.

School Breaks

Schools in New York typically have four (4) school breaks: Thanksgiving/Fall Break, Christmas/Winter Break, President's Day/Mid-Winter Break, and Easter/Spring Break. When drafting a parenting plan, parents should be cognizant on what was agreed to with the holiday schedule. Here is an example schedule (for illustrative purposes):

School Break	Time	Even Years	Odd Years
Mid-Winter Recess (President's Day Week)	7 consecutive days	Father	Mother
Spring Recess (Easter Break)	7 (out of 10) consecutive days	Mother	Father

Thanksgiving Recess	Close of School Wednesday until Sunday evening	Father	Mother
Winter Recess (Christmas Break)	7 consecutive days	Mother (except for Christmas Eve & New Year's Eve)	Father (except for Christmas Eve & New Year's Eve)

As an alternative, parents may wish to share each break equally (i.e. one parent would have the first four and half days of the spring break and other parent would have the second four and a half days) so both parents would have extended parenting time during the school break.

Summer Break

When crafting a parenting plan, parents should consider parenting time during the summer with both parents in light of the summer camp or extra-curricular activity schedule of the children. For example, the parents might elect to split summer vacation equally (50/50) or give the non-custodial parent two consecutive weeks of vacation with the child(ren).

Supervised Visitation

The New York Court of Appeals has held that absent any threat to the child's wellbeing, those people who have visitation rights have the right to unsupervised visitation with his or her child. Weiss v. Weiss, 52 N.Y.2d 170 (1981); Nancy M. v. Brian M., 227 A.D.2d 404 (1996); Twersky v. Twersky, 103 A.D.2d 775 (1984). For the court to order supervised visitation, there must be a finding that the unsupervised visitation is adverse to the child's best interest. Courts consider the following factors, among others, in deciding whether to order supervised visitation:

(1) ***Mental illness*** if, due to the mental condition, it would cause potential harm to the child if the visits were

unsupervised;

(2) ***Substance abuse***, if it causes the parent to act in a way that could be injurious to the child if visits were unsupervised;

(3) ***Sexual behavior*** (for example if the parent might engage with a romantic partner in front of the child and adversely affect the child) during unsupervised visits; and

(4) ***Threats of abduction***.

Grandparent Visitation

Grandparent visitation is not automatic in New York. There is an assumption that the grandparent will have visitation with their grandchild through the grandchild's parent. There is also a presumption that a fit parents acts in the best interest of their child. This means the courts will give great weight to the parent's decision about their child's visitation and access to the child's grandparents. See Troxel v. Granville, 530 U.S. 57 (2000).

There are circumstances when the grandparent can obtain a court order for visitation with the grandchild. First, the grandparent has to prove a right to be heard in the court. To prove the right to be heard in court, the grandparent must show their child (the child's mother or father) is deceased or show an extraordinary circumstance that justifies the court's involvement. Second, the grandparent then has to prove that it is in the best interest of the child to have court ordered visitation with the grandparent.

Sibling Visitation

Siblings have a statutory right to visitation with each other. This is true whether the relationship be of ***full-blood siblings*** or ***half-blood siblings***. There is a two-part analysis for evaluating sibling visitation. First, standing – or the right to be heard – has to be established. Second, the court must determine whether the visitation is in the best interest of the child(ren). See Fitzpatrick v. Youngs, 186 Misc.2d 344, 346 (2000).

DRL § 71 states that "where circumstances show that conditions exist in which equity would see fit to intervene, a brother or sister or, if he or she be a minor, a proper person on his or her behalf, whether by half or whole blood, may apply to the supreme court by commencing a special proceeding for visitation rights for such brother or sister in respect to such child." The issue of standing was central in the case of Noonan v. Noonan, 145 Misc.2d 638 (1989). In that case, a mother petitioned on behalf of her three children for visitation with the children of their father's previous marriage. The court held that the half-blood siblings had standing to seek visitation, but that the petitioner's daughter from a previous marriage (with no blood relation to the children at issue) did not have standing. Thus, visitation was awarded to only the two half-blood siblings.

Once standing is established, the court considers various factors to decide if visitation is in the ***best interest of the child*** and, if so, under what conditions. See E.S. v. P.D., 8 N.Y.3d 150 (2007). It is unclear whether that standard applies solely to the child(ren) with whom visitation is sought, but case law gives preference to the best interest of them over the siblings seeking visitation. The best interest standard is at the discretion of the court. For example, if the best interest of the child(ren) to be visited is sacrificed by serving the best interest of the children seeking visitation, the court might question the validity of the petition in the first place. Factors given the most weight by the court include prior relationships with siblings, the reason visitation with the siblings stopped after a divorce, the future benefit of having a relationship with the siblings, the opinion and recommendation of the attorneys for the children, and the preferences of the children expressed during in camera interview. Whether the children had a relationship with each other and how strong that relationship was before the parents broke up is a huge consideration. Where there is no familial bond among half-siblings, visitation is usually denied, as it was in the case of In re Justin H., 215 A.D.2d 180 (1995).

In Isabel R. v. Meghan Mc., 23 Misc. 3d 1102(A) (2009), visitation was granted with a specific visitation schedule. In that case, the mother, on behalf of her children, M. and J., petitioned the court for visitation with their half-sister, O., respondent's child. Ruben R. was the father of all three children and not a party to the action. While Ruben and respondent were married, M. and J. would frequently go over to their father and respondent's home to spend time with their younger sister. The children frequently had sleep-overs, played at each other's homes, and referred to each other as "brother" and "sister." O. was very familiar with petitioner and petitioner even babysat for O. on occasion. When Ruben and respondent ended their marriage, petitioner tried to work out a schedule with respondent for the children to continue their relationship. Respondent subsequently re-married and had another child. She was not interested in O. having a relationship with M. and J. and wanted O. to be fully immersed in her new family with respondent's new husband and baby. Respondent was also concerned that if O. were to see M. and J., petitioner might let them see the father as well, who was previously denied visitation with O. After in camera interviews with the children who expressed their desire to maintain a relationship with each other and consulting with the attorneys for the children, the court determined that the children might have visitation with their sister, O., and set forth a detailed schedule of visitation.

> **A Few Special Considerations**
>
> ***Frequency:***
> Carefully consider how much access you want with your child. When the child is with you, the other parent should have the same access. For example, if you want daily phone calls, the other parent will want daily phone calls. This may be disruptive to your lives.
>
> ***Age-Appropriate:***
> Also, communication with your child should be age-appropriate. Small children typically do not want to talk on the phone for any length of time. Teenagers, may not want to spend any time on the phone and can only be reached by text message.
>
> ***Duration:***
> It's important to have a meaningful communication with your child. However, your child has a busy life. While you may want a half-hour Skype session, the child may not have a half-hour to spend on Skype between school, bed-time, homework, dinner and after-school activities.

Electronic Communication

In this electronic age, parents can craft an agreement allowing the parent to have meaningful communication with the child(ren) using electronic methods (*i.e.*, ***Parenting 2.0!***) including:

- Telephone (*e.g.*, to the other parent's phone or the child's phone)
- Video-conferencing (*e.g.*, FaceTime, Skype)
- Text messaging (*e.g.*, WhatsApp, Viber)
- Social media (*e.g.*, Facebook, Instagram, Twitter, Snapchat)
- Electronic mail (*i.e.*, "e-mail").

In some cases, parents might decide on a specific period of time when the other parent can call and talk to the child(ren) (e.g., from 6pm to 7pm). In most situations, this electronic communication should be for a reasonable period of time in light of the child's age and without interruption or monitoring from the other parent.

Travel

The Courts have found travel to be in the best interest of the child. Consequently, a parent should not unreasonably withhold consent for the child to travel with the other parent. If the non-traveling parent unreasonably withholds consent then the court can override the non-traveling parent's objection to the travel. See Matter of Arroyo v. Agosta, 2010 NY Slip Op 08566, 78 AD3d 938 (2nd Dep't 2010).

Common language in a parenting plan requires advance notice of travel, the exchange of travel itineraries, including flight information, and contact information at the travel site such as hotel name and phone number. The more stringent agreements require proof of return airline tickets.

The parents need to decide when the travel requirements apply. Is notice of the travel itinerary necessary for international travel only? Or is the itinerary also necessary for national travel within the United States?

The parents also need a system for obtaining travel consent letters, requesting the child's passport for travel and redefining the manner and frequency of communications with the child. For national travel, it is still easy to make a phone call. For international travel, the parents may need to postpone daily phone calls and agree to Skype every other day.

Modification

To modify custody or parenting time, there must be a ***substantial change in circumstances*** such that a modification is necessary to ensure the continued best interest and welfare of the child. The parent asking for the modification must demonstrate to the court that a hearing should be held. In other words, the parent asking for the change in custody or parenting time must demonstrate enough facts in the court papers to show that a hearing should be had. The hearing is to determine if there really is a substantial change in circumstances and the change in custody or parenting time is better for the child. If the parent cannot show the court a substantial change in circumstances in the papers, the court has the right not to hold the hearing.

Cari B. Rincker, Esq.

Cari Rincker is the principal attorney at Rincker Law, PLLC, a national law practice focusing on "Food, Farm & Family." She is licensed to practice law in New York, New Jersey, Connecticut, Illinois and Washington, D.C. Cari was named as a Rising Star for Metro New York in 2015 by "Super Lawyers" and is an award-winning blogger. Cari is involved in several professional organizations including the Association for the Bar of the City of New York's Matrimonial Law Committee.

In addition to her litigation practice, Cari is also a trained mediator for divorces, child custody and visitation, and commercial disputes. She was also an adjunct professor at New York University, College of Steinhardt (2013-2014), where she taught an undergraduate food law class.

Cari is a distinguished alumni from Lake Land College in Mattoon, Illinois and Texas A & M University. Before attending law school at Pace University School of Law in White Plains, New York, Cari obtained a Master of Science from the University of Illinois. Cari's practice is family-centered and counsels clients on a myriad of family law and matrimonial law issues.

For more information about Rincker Law, PLLC, visit www.rinckerlaw.com.

Bonnie L. Mohr, Esq.

Bonnie L. Mohr, managing member of the Law Offices of Bonnie L. Mohr, PLLC, started the firm in 2008 to create a practice that educates and guides clients through life-altering and stressful family situations utilizing a comprehensive, holistic and strategic approach.

The firm's practice focuses on matrimonial law including contested and uncontested divorces, prenuptial and postnuptial agreements, and post-judgment enforcements. Bonnie also practices in the family courts on such matters as child support, parenting time (custody and visitation), paternity and family offense matters.

Bonnie L. Mohr is licensed to practice law in the states of New York (2004), New Jersey (2004), and Pennsylvania (2008). She is also licensed to practice in the district courts of the Eastern District of New York, the Southern District of New York and the District of New Jersey.

Bonnie's memberships include the matrimonial and family law committees for the Women's Bar Association, New York County Lawyer's Association and New York State Bar Association. Bonnie is also a member of the New York City Bar Association, where she was leader of the matrimonial mentoring circle. For more information about Bonnie's practice, visit www.mohresq.com.

SECTION A: TYPES OF PROCEEDINGS

CHAPTER 11

CHILD SUPPORT

Deborah E. Kaminetzky, Esq.

In New York State child support is mandated by the ***Child Support Standards Act*** ("CSSA"). New York differs from many other states in that child support is required until age 21 rather than age 18. This Chapter breaks down the CSSA and common child support issues.

The Formula

Both parents incomes, whether married or not, are taken into account when figuring out how much child support is necessary. The CSSA has a formula for figuring out the amount of ***basic support***; extras for the child, known as "***add-ons***" are usually proportional according to each parent's income (i.e., "***pro rata***"). It is very important to understand that each case is individual and that parents may have very good reasons for ***deviating from the calculation*** or opting out altogether. Generally the courts will go along with ***non-CSSA formula arrangements*** if the parents knowingly waive the CSSA calculation, the terms are reasonable, and there is evidence that the child will receive adequate support. Examples of this are when lump sum payments are given or the custodial parent receives the deed to the marital home in exchange for lowered or nonexistent child support payments.

CSSA Calculation

Step 1: Calculating the Income for Child Support Purposes

Income for child support purposes is calculated as follows:

Gross Income[7]
(Less) - Social Security
(Less) - Medicare
(Less) - Local Taxes[8]
(Less) - Other Deductions[9]

Net Income for Child Support

This is done for each parent. Let's use the following two examples with Family A and Family B, using estimated figures:[10]

Family A:

1. ***Custodial parent's gross income*** is $27,500. After subtracting social security (approximately $2,000) and Medicare (approximately $500), his/her income for child support purposes is $25,000. Local taxes were not subtracted here because he/she resides in Nassau County, New York.

2. ***The non-custodial parent's gross income*** is $85,000. After subtracting social security (approximately $6,000), Medicare

[7] This includes all taxable income such as wages, dividends, investment income, pension/retirement income, stipends, unemployment insurance benefits, cash benefits for workers compensation, disability, social security and veterans' benefits.

[8] New York City and Yonkers

[9] Other deductions include, but are not limited to, alimony or maintenance payments, child support paid to other children the parent is obligated to support, public assistance, and unreimbursed business expenses that do not reduce personal expenditure. More information on deductions can be found on the UD-8 or available at http://www.nycourts.gov/divorce/forms_instructions/ud-8.pdf (last visited August 12, 2015). http://www.nycourts.gov/divorce/forms_instructions/ud-8.pdf (last visited August 12, 2015).

[10] These are estimates and used for illustrative purposes only. These calculations are not intended to give tax advice to the reader.

(approximately $1,000), and local taxes because he/she resides in Queens County, New York (approximately $3,000), then his/her income for child support purposes is $75,000.

Family B:

1. ***Custodial parent's gross income*** is $88,000. After subtracting social security (approximately $6,000) and Medicare (approximately $2,000), his/her income for child support purposes is $80,000. Local taxes were not subtracted here because he/she resides in Dutchess County, New York.

2. ***The non-custodial parent's gross income*** is $215,000. After subtracting social security (approximately $8,000), Medicare (approximately $4,000), and local taxes because he/she resides in Yonkers, New York (approximately $3,000), then his/her income for child support purposes is $200,000.

Step 2: Look at the Combined Parental Income

The next step is to combine the parental incomes (not the gross incomes – the income calculated for child support purposes). The cap for basic child support is $141,000.00 of combined parental income. After the cap, the court applies a number of factors memorialized below.

For Family A, the combined parental income is $100,000, below the "cap." For Family B, however, the combined parental income is $280,000.

Step 3: What Percentage Applies Based on Number of Children?

Basic child support is 17% for one child, 25% for two children, 29% for three children, 31% for four children and 35% for five or more children.

Family A has 1 child, so 17% applies.

Family B has 3 children, so 29% applies.

Step 4: What is the Combined Support Obligation?

Next, apply the percentage in Step 3 up to the cap of $141,000.

Therefore, for Family A, the Combined Support Obligation is 17% of $100,000, or $17,000.
For Family B, the Combined Support Obligation is 29% of $141,000 or $40,890.

Step 5: Look at the Pro-Rata Percentages

To calculate the pro rata percentages, one parent's income is divided by the combined parental income.

Family A:

Custodial Parent - $25,000/$100,000 = 25%
Noncustodial Parent - $75,000/$100,000 = 75%

Family B:

Custodial Parent - $80,000/$280,000 = 29%
Noncustodial Parent - $200,000/$280,000 = 71%

Step 6: Calculate the Basic Child Support

Noncustodial Parent will pay his/her pro rata share (Step 5) of the Combined Support Obligation (Step 6) to the custodial parent. The custodial parent pays their proportional share of support by providing food, clothing and shelter to the child/children and does not have to account to the non-custodial parent.

Family A: 75% of $17,000, which would be $12,750 or $1062.50 per month or $245.19 per week.

Family B: 71% of $40,890, which would be $29,031.90 or $2,419.33 per month or $558.31 per week.

Add-Ons

Add-ons are paid for proportionally by each parent according to his/her income. Mandatory add-ons include:

- Child care (so that the custodial parent can work or go to school)
- Health insurance
- Unreimbursed medical expenses

It is discretionary on the court for extra-curricular activities to be an add-on expense. The parties can also agree to this add-on. The same pro-rata percentages used in Step 5 will be used here. Parents can elect to do a monthly or weekly reconciliation of add-on expenditures for reimbursement.

Upward or Downward Deviation

There are ten factors a court will use if it determines that the formula will result in an "***unjust or inappropriate***" amount of child support. Parties may also agree to such a deviation in their agreement by waiving the formula and stating what the reason for the deviation is. The factors are:

1. The ***financial resources*** of the parents and the child. For instance, if one parent, in addition to his/her income, also has substantial assets that may be a consideration.
2. The ***physical and emotional health*** of the child. For instance, a "special needs" child may need more than the amount in the formula.
3. The ***standard of living*** the child would have enjoyed but for the divorce. For instance, if the non-custodial parent makes significantly more than the cap on the formula the court has the discretion to award more basic child support. A good example of this would be Family B in our example above.
4. The ***tax consequences*** to the parents.
5. The ***non-monetary contributions*** the parents will make toward the child.
6. The ***educational*** needs of the parents.

7. The fact that one parent's income is ***substantially less*** than the other's.
8. The amount of money the non-custodial parent needs to ***support other children*** not of the marriage. This applies when there is an already existing court order of support. The court will also take into consideration whether anyone else is responsible for the support of the other children.
9. Extraordinary costs of ***visitation*** of the non-custodial parent.
10. Any other factor the court considers relevant.

Miscellaneous Issues

Support Collection Unit

You can elect to have your child support paid to you through what is known as ***Support Collections Unit*** ("SCU"). The unit either arranges with the payor's employer to collect the court ordered amount of child support, or in cases where there is no employer, the payer can pay directly to the unit. The unit will also from time to time perform a search on the payor to determine if there is an asset from which to collect any arrears on child support, meaning the payor is behind on his/her support payments.

Special Income Issues

The court can also consider as income items such as familial help with bills, ***fringe benefits*** from work, etc. The court can also "***impute***" income to an individual who claims not to have money by assessing the lifestyle, type of car driven, vacations taken, etc. The court can even order child support from a one-time occurrence such as inheritance or lottery winnings.

Modification

Child support orders can be modified. For a divorce prior to October 13, 2010 a child support order can be modified by a showing that there has been a ***change in circumstance*** in either of the parent's incomes. For cases after that date, there is a different standard – there can still be a change in circumstances, or if ***three years*** have passed, or if there has been a change of ***fifteen percent*** up or down of either of the parent's incomes. If the order is over two years old and the money is being collected by a local support collections unit a ***cost of living adjustment*** ("COLA") hearing may be held to determine if the amount of child support is correct.

Self-Support Reserve

For parents with very low incomes (after deductions), there is a "***self support reserve***" where if they make less than the adequate amount, currently $15,890, the amount of support is set at a minimum of $25 per week. Contrary to popular belief, ***bankruptcy*** does not relieve someone of a child support obligation.

Child Support When Parents Share Joint Physical Custody

There is a common misconception that if the parents have true joint custody, whereby the child lives with each parent the same amount of time, no basic child support must be paid. The Courts have found that even in this scenario one parent must be the ***custodial parent for child support purposes*** especially if there is a disparity in incomes. Normally the parent with the ***higher income*** will pay support to the parent with the lower income and add-ons will be split proportionately.

Private School

Courts in New York will rule that a non-custodial parent must contribute toward private school if they determine that the child's needs are best met by that school, the child has attended the school and his/her life would be disrupted by a change, and for several other reasons. The court will also take into account whether the noncustodial parent will suffer financially by having to pay for the private school. Parents can, however, agree in a stipulation that they will or will not pay for such things. They also can agree to pay up until a certain amount or a percentage or take into account whether scholarship is available.

College

Parents are generally not obligated to pay for college. Should they choose to pay for college, the non-custodial parent can receive a ***dollar for dollar credit*** toward their child support obligation for any monies expended on room and board at college for their child. Many parents choose to include in their agreement that they are willing to pay for college up to what is known as a SUNY (***State University of New York***) or CUNY (***City University of New York***) cap. This means that they will pay their proportionate share of what it would cost for the child to attend a SUNY or CUNY school. Contrary to popular belief, this does not limit the child to one of those schools. Should the child be admitted to an Ivy League college for instance, the non-custodial parent would still be obligated to pay his/her share (of what a SUNY or CUNY would have cost) and perhaps the child would qualify for aid or a loan to make up the difference.

Emancipation

Child support will end upon emancipation of the child. ***Emancipation*** in New York is at ***age 21*** unlike many other states where the age of emancipation is 18. Furthermore, if the child is a full time college student then it may be ***extended until age 22*** to help ensure that the child has an appropriate amount of support through college.

There are several "emancipation events" such as, ***marriage*** – whether void (such as marriage to someone already married) or voidable (such as where one or both parties to the marriage are below the age of consent), entry into the armed forces, working ***full time*** (not at a temporary or summer job) and moving out of the home of the residential parent. College is not considered an emancipation event. Should a couple agree in their negotiated agreement or stipulation of settlement the non-custodial parent may get a dollar for dollar credit against child support for the ***room and board portion*** of college.

Deborah E. Kaminetzky, Esq.

Deborah E. Kaminetzky is the founding member of Kaminetzky & Associates, P.C. located in Cedarhurst, New York. Prior to starting the firm Deborah worked at a Long Island firm where she learned the practice of Matrimonial and Family law. Deborah has also worked at the New York Department of Consumer Affairs where she was responsible for prosecuting unlicensed home improvement contractors and negotiating settlements for consumers. Prior to practicing law, Ms. Kaminetzky served on the Architectural Control Committee of a Home Owners Association in Boca Raton while living in Florida, and was the president of a commercial property management corporation in the New York Metro area.

Ms. Kaminetzky is a member of the American Bar Association (General Practice, Solo and Small firm Division and Law Practice Management Sections), New York State Bar Association (Estate, Family Law and General Practice Sections), Nassau County Bar Association (where she serves as Chair of the Technology and Practice Management Committee, and is active in the Community Relations and Education Committee, Women in the Law committees and General and Solo Committee) Great Neck Lawyers Association, and The Nassau County Women's Bar Association.

Ms. Kaminetzky was recently appointed to the Committee on Law Practice Management of the New York State Bar Association. Ms. Kaminetzky serves on the Board of Directors of the Yashar Attorney and Judges Chapter of Hadassah as a Vice President, and was their Woman of the Year 2012. Deborah graduated from New York Law School in 1991 and the University of Michigan, Ann Arbor in 1986.

Ms. Kaminetzky was admitted to the First Department in 1991 and the United States Supreme Court Bar in February of 2015.

Deborah is on the Matrimonial fee dispute arbitration panel for Nassau County. She expanded her alternative dispute resolution practice by completing a Mediation certificate program in December of 2013 from The New York Peace Institute.

Ms. Kaminetzky has spoken to various groups on topics including matrimonial law, technology and social media use, and disaster preparedness for business including cybersecurity.

For more information about Ms. Kaminetzky and her practice, visit www.kaminetzkylaw.com.

SECTION A: TYPES OF PROCEEDINGS

CHAPTER 12

JUVENILE DELINQUENCY

By Ronna Gordon-Galchus, Esq. and Frank M. Galchus, Esq.

If a 10 year old gets into a fight at school, he or she may not only be sent to the principal's office, but can also face prosecution in court. This Chapter gives an overview of juvenile delinquency actions in New York Family Court.

Family Court v. Criminal Court

If a child is arrested, depending on his or her age and the type of crime alleged, the case may be brought to Family Court. There are many differences between prosecution in ***Family Court*** and ***Criminal Court***. In some instances in Family Court, a child's case may be eligible for diversion, and after a referral to the ***Department of Probation***, may not be brought before a judge. Instead, the child may be monitored by the probation department for a period of time and be offered services or ***counseling***. In Family Court, a child can be charged with a ***misdemeanor***, a ***felony***, or a ***designated felony***.

> **Misdemeanor** – a criminal act for which a juvenile can be placed for an initial period of up to 12 months. Examples are simple assault and petit larceny.
>
> **Felony** – criminal act for which a juvenile can be placed for an initial period of up to 18 months. Examples are most robberies and burglaries.
>
> **Designated Felony** – extremely serious crimes such as murder, arson, and kidnapping.

In Criminal Court, someone charged with a crime is called a ***defendant***. In Family Court, he or she is called a ***respondent***. In Criminal Court a defendant can be released ***on his own recognizance*** or be held in jail until bail is posted. ***Family Court does not set bail.*** Either the child is released to a parent or guardian's custody or remanded to a detention facility. And also unlike Criminal Court, all trials are heard ***before a judge only***, not a jury (i.e., a bench trial).

In a juvenile delinquency case, Section 300 of the Family Court Act ("FCA") is the controlling law. If a child is arrested, ***probable cause*** must exist for the arrest to be lawful. Although there are procedural differences between the prosecution of children and adults, the same standard of law applies. If a child is placed into police custody and is remanded by the court, the child is entitled to a probable cause hearing within a few days. What this actually means is that the prosecution must present a certain degree of evidence to demonstrate that the arrest was lawful. This is usually done by ***witness testimony***. At a probable cause hearing, there should be a full opportunity for the juvenile's lawyer to cross-examine the witness and show that probable cause did not exist. If the lawyer is successful, then the case should be dismissed. If the court rules that there was probable cause, then the case would be held over for trial.

Jurisdiction

It is important to know that although a juvenile may be a young teenager, ***certain types of crimes*** such as murder, rape, and robbery can be prosecuted in adult Criminal Court, and not Family Court. In those situations the teen will be prosecuted in adult court and sentenced as a juvenile offender.

A juvenile delinquent is someone who is ***over the age of seven and less than sixteen years old, who has committed an act that would constitute a crime if it had been committed by an adult***. Although there have been recent proposals to increase the age of criminal responsibility to 18 years of age, New York still remains one of two states that prosecutes 16 and 17 years olds in adult court.

Pre-Trial Hearings

1. *Wade*[11] Hearing

As in adult court, ***pre-trial suppression hearings*** also exist for the juvenile. A *Wade* hearing is a type of pretrial procedure which determines if the juvenile was subjected to unnecessarily suggestive identification procedures. If the respondent was placed into a lineup, show-up, or some other type of identification procedure, a hearing would determine if that procedure was too suggestive. An example would be the respondent in a lineup being the only individual in a bright colored shirt while the "fillers" are wearing dark clothing. Another example would be a witness making an identification of the respondent who is surrounded by uniform police officers and is handcuffed. In these examples, the out of court identification procedures should be suppressed because the circumstances surrounding the identification were very ***suggestive and prejudicial***. This would mean that at the actual fact-finding, testimony about the suppressed procedure would not be allowed.

2. *Mapp*[12] Hearing

A *Mapp* hearing is another example of a pretrial hearing. If the respondent is alleged to have contraband in his or her possession, a hearing should be held to determine the ***lawfulness*** of the police stop and any subsequent search of the respondent and his immediate area. If a police officer failed to have enough information to stop and search the child, all property recovered must be suppressed, and not permitted to be used at a trial.

---

[11] U.S. v. Wade, 388 U.S. 218 (1967).

[12] Mapp v. Ohio, 367 U.S. 643 (1960).

3. ***Huntley***[13] **Hearing**

Often juveniles are questioned by the police and statements are taken from them. A very big difference between the interrogation of a child and that of an adult by the police is the environment where the questioning is done. All questioning of juveniles by the police must be done in a ***special room*** designated as a juvenile room, and must be done in the ***presence of a parent or guardian***. As with adults, a statement or confession from a juvenile can never be the product of the threat of force or undue pressure. The pretrial hearing to suppress a statement is called a *Huntley* hearing.

The Fact-Finding Hearing

A trial is called a fact-finding hearing, and as in a criminal proceeding against an adult, the prosecution must prove its case ***beyond a reasonable doubt***. This burden is never shifted and rests solely on the prosecution. The prosecution must call at least one witness, who can then be cross- examined by the respondent's lawyer. A respondent can present witnesses but is never required to call witnesses, and if he or she chooses, can testify on his/her own behalf. A ***respondent is never required to testify*** nor can it be held against him or her if he/she chooses not to testify. In fact, quite often it may not be in a respondent's best interest to testify. Remember, the burden of proof always remains with the prosecution. The major difference between trials in Family Court and those in adult court is the lack of a jury in Family Court. A respondent who goes to trial will have his or her case heard and decided before a single judge. The judge is the trier of fact and also makes the order of disposition if there is a finding against the respondent. In adult court, the selection of a fair and impartial jury is an integral part of the proceedings. This is not the situation in a juvenile delinquency case which gets prosecuted in Family Court.

A finding against a juvenile, either after fact-finding or by a respondent's admission, even though it involves conduct that would be considered criminal if committed by an adult, does not give that juvenile a ***criminal record***.

---

[13] People v. Huntley, 15 NY2d 72 (1965).

The Dispositional Hearing

If the Court makes a finding against a respondent, then a dispositional hearing will be held to determine the ***outcome of the case***. At a hearing, witnesses may be called to testify, documents submitted into evidence, and the respondent may also make a statement, but is not required to. The Department of Probation submits an ***investigatory report*** and the respondent may be ordered to have a ***mental health evaluation***. After the dispositional hearing, the court enters an order of disposition.

This disposition could range from the matter being dismissed to the respondent being removed from his/her home and being put in a ***restrictive placement***. Of course the level of crime which the respondent was found to have committed can have relevance in the type of disposition. For example, if a respondent was found to have committed a designated felony and inflicted serious physical injury upon a person who is 62 years of age or older, the court shall order a restrictive placement. However, in most cases, the court shall consider the needs and ***best interests of the respondent*** as well as the need for the ***protection of the community***. The court must also consider if it is contrary to the best interests of the respondent to remain in his or her home, or for the community. The dispositional aspect of a juvenile delinquency case will often attempt to find a way for the respondent to get assistance, counseling, and services.

Plea Bargaining

Similar to adult court, plea bargaining is also present in Family Court juvenile delinquency proceedings. Often a respondent may not desire to go to trial, and would rather ***settle the matter*** prior to a fact finding hearing. Depending on the quality of the evidence which is against the respondent, it may be wiser for a respondent to make an ***admission to the court***.

Often the prosecution will offer the respondent the opportunity to make an admission to a lesser charge. This could mean making an admission to a misdemeanor instead of a felony, or to a non-designated felony from a designated felony. However, unlike adult court where plea bargaining usually results in knowing what the ultimate sentence will be at the time the plea is entered into, the disposition in a respondent's case is usually left open and largely depends on the reports which come back from the Department of Probation, Mental Health, and other agencies. Respondents can be placed on probation, given ***conditional discharges***, or placed away from their home. Respondents' placements can also be extended after a hearing has been conducted.

It is of extreme importance that a respondent avoid two designated felony findings, because that would eliminate the opportunity for a teenager prosecuted in adult court to be granted youthful offender treatment. Youthful offender treatment is not considered a conviction, even though a defendant has pleaded guilty. However, there could be certain circumstances in Family Court that could be of consequence if a teenage is facing charges in adult court later on down the road.

Attorney for Respondent

All respondents in Family Court are entitled to an attorney. A parent or guardian may be well-advised to retain an attorney if possible before the child's first court appearance, since important matters such as the child's liberty during the prosecution will be decided then. If a respondent appears in court without an attorney, generally, a ***financial inquiry will be conducted*** to determine if the child qualifies for appointed counsel, or if an attorney must be hired.

A respondent's attorney is held to the same high standard of representation as an attorney for a criminal defendant. The attorney's role is to ***zealously represent the child***, and to be guided by the ***child's wishes***, not those of a parent or guardian. This is so whether or not the parent or guardian has hired the attorney or the attorney has been appointed by the court. The attorney must first advise the child as to the consequences of going to trial or making an admission. Whether the child wants to make an admission or proceed to a fact-finding, the attorney in the end must follow the direction of the client, even if this is against the parent or guardian's wishes.

The attorney for a child is bound by the attorney/client privilege, and cannot divulge any information which is a product of this relationship. The attorney must inform the child about the merits of the case against him or her, as well as the possible outcomes and dispositions. In the end, it is the child charged with juvenile delinquency who decides whether or not to fight the case.

Ronna Gordon-Galchus, Esq.

Ronna Gordon-Galchus has been practicing law for more than 25 years. She began her career as an attorney with the Criminal Defense Division of the Legal Aid Society representing indigent individuals charged with crimes. Throughout the years she has devoted her practice to representing people facing various levels of felonies and misdemeanors and has tried numerous jury and non-jury trials. A large part of her practice is dedicated to those who are involved with cases in Family Court, including representing juveniles who have been arrested and charged with delinquency. She has also have authored numerous appellate briefs and has argued both in the Appellate Division and the New York State Court of Appeals.

Frank Galchus, Esq.

Frank Galchus began his legal career more than 30 years ago with the Criminal Defense Division of the Legal Aid Society. Since then he has represented clients in criminal matters and family matters in Criminal Court, Supreme Court, and Family Court. His Family Court representation includes children who have been arrested and are facing charges in Family Court.

SECTION A: TYPES OF PROCEEDINGS

CHAPTER 13

CHILD PROTECTIVE PROCEEDINGS

By Joseph Nivin, Esq.

A ***child protective proceeding*** is one of the most difficult experiences that a person can have. These proceedings commence when a parent, or a person acting as a parent, faces accusations of ***child abuse or neglect***. The purpose of this Chapter is to help people who face these allegations to know their rights, and to have the best possible outcome at the conclusion of the case.

The Beginning Stages

The Purpose of a Child Protective Proceeding

When an agency files a child protective proceeding, the purpose is to obtain court orders which interfere with the respondents' parental rights. The agency may seek removal of the children from the home, supervision by a child protective agency, orders of protection, and/or orders for completion of services.

Child protective proceedings begin with allegations that the children are victims of ***abuse*** and/or ***neglect***. Neglect is also known as ***maltreatment***.

Commencement of the Investigation

Child protective investigations begin with a call to the ***State Central Register of Child Abuse and Maltreatment*** ("SCR"), also known as the "Hotline." The function of the SCR is to receive calls regarding suspected child abuse and maltreatment. The SCR will relay the call to the local child protective agency. If the child or children live in New York City, then the local child protective agency is the ***Administration for Children's Services*** ("ACS").

Definitions

Child protective proceedings can be filed against the children's parents or ***persons legally responsible***. A "person legally responsible" ("PLR") includes the child's "custodian, guardian, or any other person responsible for the child's care at the relevant time."[14] When a court determines whether the respondent is a PLR, it determines whether the respondent functioned as a parent substitute.

"Abuse" fits into two categories: ***physical abuse*** and ***sexual abuse***.

- Acts of **physical abuse** are acts or omissions causing the child physical injury which can lead to death, long-term impairment, or disfigurement. Physical abuse can also mean placing the child in danger of such injury.
- ***Sexual abuse*** is where the child's parent or person legally responsible commits a criminal sexual offense against the child, or allows such an offense to be committed.

Neglect can include (1) failure to provide adequate food, clothing, shelter, education, or medical care, (2) excessive corporal punishment, (3) repeated illegal drug use, (4) repeated and excessive alcohol abuse, (5) any other acts or omissions that require the aid of the court, and/or (6) abandonment of the child.

"Neglect" has been interpreted to include domestic violence in the presence of the child or children. However, a person cannot be found to have abused or neglected the child simply by being the *victim* of domestic violence. Additionally, a parent or PLR cannot be prosecuted simply for drug or alcohol abuse if he or she is "regularly and voluntarily" participating in a treatment program, unless the drug or alcohol abuse by itself caused harm or risk of harm to the child or children.

---

[14] N.Y. Family Court § 1012(g).

The Investigation

Upon receiving the call, the local child protective agency will assign the investigation to a caseworker. The caseworker will speak with the source of the report, and will also visit the home of the family. The worker will speak with the parents, and any other people who are accused of abuse and neglect, such as stepparents. The caseworker will speak with the children as well. The caseworker may also speak with the children's medical professionals, teachers, and anyone else who may have information about the allegations.

> If the people who are accused of abuse or neglect are being investigated by the police, and/or have already been arrested, then they should not speak about the allegations to the caseworker, or to anybody, except for their attorneys. Statements to the caseworker can be used in the prosecution of the criminal action.

The caseworker will have sixty (60) days to complete the investigation. The investigation can either be concluded as ***indicated*** or ***unfounded***. If the investigation is concluded as ***indicated***, that means that there is ***some credible evidence*** of abuse or maltreatment. If the investigation is concluded as **unfounded,** that means that there is ***no credible evidence*** of abuse or maltreatment.

Parents will receive a notification of whether the report is indicated or unfounded. Indicated determinations can be challenged at a ***fair hearing***.

What Happens When the Subjects of the Report Deny Access to the Caseworker?

The social services agency has remedies in cases where its caseworkers are denied access to the children, and/or to the home of the children.

Where there is ***reasonable cause to suspect that a child or children's life or health may be in danger,*** the social services agency can seek an order that ***the child or children be produced for an interview and for observation of the children's condition***, outside of the presence of the parents or other persons legally responsible. In order to seek such an order, the social services agency will have to prove that: (1) a report was made, (2) the investigator has either been unable to locate the child or has been denied access to the child sufficient to determine the child's safety, and (3) the investigator has advised the parent or persons legally responsible that the investigator may seek such a court order.

Where there is ***probable cause to believe that an abused or neglected child may be found on the premises,*** the social services agency may seek an order authorizing entry to the home and/or conduct a ***home visit*** to evaluate the home environment, if (1) a report has been made, (2) the investigator has been denied access to the home of the child, and (3) the investigator has advised the parent or persons legally responsible that the investigator may seek such a court order.

Steps that the Agency May Take Where There are Safety Concerns

Where there are concerns about the safety of the children, the agency will likely call the parents or other persons legally responsible into the agency offices for a conference. At the conference, agency staff may discuss services to address the safety concerns, such as parenting skills classes, homemaking services, and drug treatment programs. Where the agency deems it necessary, it may file a petition in the Family Court to seek court orders to protect the children. This chapter will focus on those cases where the agency files a petition in court, known as an ***Article Ten*** petition.

Child Protective Procedure

Who May File

An Article Ten petition may be filed by a child protective agency, or by a "person on the court's direction."[15]

Removal Prior to the Filing of the Petition

The child protective agency has the authority to remove the child or children prior to the filing of a petition. However, where possible, the agency has to file a petition ***prior to removal.*** If the removal takes

[15] N.Y. Family Court Act § 1032.

place ***prior to the filing of the petition***, then the agency must file a petition with the court no later than the next court day.

The agency can file a petition which seeks only the removal of a child, but does not allege abuse or neglect. The agency can do so either before or after the removal. However, the agency must file a petition alleging abuse or neglect within three court days, unless the child is returned to the place where the child was residing, or "for good cause shown."[16]

Initial Appearance

When the agency seeks court intervention, it will file a petition with the court, which includes the allegations of abuse and neglect. The caseworker will generally tell the parent and/or person legally responsible, also known as the ***respondent***, to come to court on that date.

The ***initial appearance*** will take place on the day that the petition is filed. At that appearance, the agency will make applications regarding the **status** of the child or children. The ***status*** may include:

(1) **Remand**, which is temporary placement into foster care, or

(2) **Parole**, also known as ***temporary release***, to a parent or suitable relative, under the supervision of the local social services agency.

Where the agency seeks a removal of the child, the agency will have to prove that: (1) the child is at ***imminent risk*** if he or she remains in the care of his or her parent or person legally responsible, and (2) that it would be ***contrary to the child's welfare and best interests*** to remain in the care of his or her parent or person legally responsible.

The agency will have to argue that it either made ***reasonable efforts*** to eliminate the need for removal, or that ***reasonable efforts were not appropriate*** given the circumstances. Even if the court finds that that no reasonable efforts were made, and such actions were appropriate under the circumstances, it can still issue a removal order if it finds that the child would be at imminent risk in the care of the respondents. The reasonable efforts issue only affects whether the agency receives federal funding for the child's care.

The agency may also seek a ***temporary order of protection***, which may include an order that the respondent stay away from the child, an order excluding a respondent from the child's home, an order

---

[16] N.Y. Family Court Act §§ 1022(b) and 1026(c).

that a respondent not be alone with the child, an order that the respondent not have contact with the child if under the influence of drugs or alcohol, an order that the respondent not use corporal punishment, an order that the respondent not leave the child alone and unsupervised, and/or an order that the respondent not interfere with the care and custody of the child's caregiver.

If the respondent does not appear at the initial appearance, then the court will order that the respondent be served with a summons and the petition. The court will then schedule a date for ***return of service*** for the respondent to appear.

If the child is removed from the care of a parent, or if a parent is excluded from the child's home, then the parents should request that the court order visitation, even if it is supervised visitation. In most cases, where a child is removed, the visits will start out supervised.

If a child is placed in foster care, then the respondents have the right to request that the agency explore relatives and/or family friends as potential foster parents. These are known as ***kinship resources***. The parents should provide contact information to the caseworker about potential kinship resources, including addresses, telephone numbers, and dates of birth. This will permit the agency to conduct **clearances**, to assess whether the proposed resources are appropriate.

Assignment of Counsel

Respondents in Article Ten proceedings have the right to be represented by counsel. If the respondents meet certain income guidelines, then the court may appoint counsel at the public expense. All children who are the subjects of Article Ten proceedings are assigned attorneys, regardless of the age of the children.

Derivative Abuse and Neglect

A major source of confusion for respondents in child protective proceedings is the concept of ***derivative abuse and neglect.*** In cases where there is more than one child in the home, the agency will generally file petitions alleging that all of the children are abused and/or neglected. The agency is also likely to file petitions on behalf of all of the respondents' children, even children who do not live in the same home.

Where the agency alleges that a child is ***derivatively abused*** or ***derivatively neglected***, the agency is alleging that the child is in danger of being abused and/or neglected because of the abuse or neglect of another child, often called the ***target child***. The argument that is most commonly used by the agency is that the abuse and/or neglect of the target child showed such an impaired level of parental judgment that it placed any child in the respondent's care at risk of abuse and/or neglect. At a trial, it is ultimately in the discretion of the court whether to accept such an argument from the agency.

1027 and 1028 Hearings

At the initial appearance, if the agency is seeking a removal of any of the children from the respondent's home, and the respondent is present, then he or she is entitled to a "***1027 hearing***." Some courts have held that respondents are entitled to a 1027 hearing even when the agency is simply asking to place the children temporarily in the home of the other parent.

> 1027 and 1028 are sections of the statute.

At a 1027 hearing, the agency has to prove that the children would be at ***imminent risk*** in the care of the respondent. The agency will likely call the caseworker to testify. The respondent's attorney and the attorney for the children will have the opportunity to ask questions of the caseworker, in what is called ***cross-examination***. The respondent will also have the right to testify.

In determining whether to grant the agency's application for a removal, the court has to balance the risk that the child would face if it remained in the care of the respondent against the ***harm that removal might bring***. Furthermore, the court has to weigh whether the risk can be mitigated by ***reasonable efforts to avoid removal***, or a ***temporary order of protection*** short of removal.

A "***1028 hearing***" takes place after the court has already granted the agency's application for removal. At a 1028 hearing, the respondent is asking for the children to be returned. The standards, and the procedure, for a 1028 hearing are identical to those for a 1027 hearing. Respondents often seek 1028 hearings at return of service. Even where the respondent has appeared at the initial appearance, respondents' attorneys will often counsel their clients to consent to the removal there, and then seek a 1028 hearing. While the downside is obvious (the child will be out of the respondents' care for at least a few days), the advantage is that the respondents' attorneys will have more time to prepare. At a 1027 hearing, the respondent's attorney has to proceed immediately to a hearing, often having no information whatsoever about the case. At a 1028 hearing, the respondent's attorney will be able to get **discovery** from the agency, specifically any records regarding the investigation. The attorney will also be able to meet with the respondent, and learn the respondent's version of events. Importantly, the respondent is entitled to a 1028 hearing within ***three business days***.

Another consideration for respondents, when deciding whether to request either a 1027 or 1028 hearing, is that the respondent is only entitled to one such hearing prior to ***disposition***, except "for good cause shown." As a result, if the respondent plans to complete services, then the respondent may choose not to request a hearing until those services are complete. For example, if the respondent is engaged in, or plans to enter, a drug treatment program, the respondent may not request a hearing until that program is completed. Otherwise, the respondent may lose his or her opportunity to have such a hearing when he or she has clean time, and has completed the program.

The rules of evidence are much less strict at 1027 and 1028 hearings than they are in other legal proceedings. Specifically, the witnesses at these hearings can testify to ***hearsay***, meaning that any witnesses, including the caseworker and the respondent, can tell the court about things that other people told them. As a result, the caseworker can testify to what the child's teacher, doctor, etc. said during the investigation.

1061 Hearings

> 1061 is also a section in the statute. Lawyers and judges often refer to specific hearings based on section number or court case name.

A respondent who wishes to challenge an order short of removal is entitled to a "***1061 hearing***." An example would be where the parents live together, the child remains with the mother, and an order is issued excluding the father from the home. In that case, the father would have the right to seek a 1061 hearing.

Here are a few key points:

- The court is unlikely to grant a 1061 hearing on an expedited basis. Therefore, the respondent is likely to wait several months for a 1061 hearing.
- The standard in a 1061 hearing is whether there is "good cause" for the order being challenged.

Conferences

The court will hold a series of conferences, which include a ***preliminary conference***, a ***compliance conference***, and a ***settlement conference***. At conferences, the parties and their attorneys will not see the judge, but rather see an attorney who works for the judge, called a ***court attorney*** or a ***law secretary***. It is often frustrating to litigants to come to court hoping for something to change, only to walk out of the courthouse with a new adjourn date, without seeing the judge.

1. Preliminary Conference

At the preliminary conference, the agency will discuss the ***service plan*** for both the respondents and the child or children. The service plan includes interventions designed to eliminate the risk factors which led to the case. The plan may include parenting skills classes, anger management classes, domestic violence classes, individual therapy, and a drug treatment program. The service plan for the children may include early intervention services for young children, or individual therapy for older children. The attorneys will also discuss the progress of visitation.

The attorneys will establish a schedule for ***discovery***, where the agency turns over its records to the attorneys. The attorneys will discuss whether any ***motions*** need to be filed prior to trial. These motions include requests to the court for orders releasing medical information, such as medical and/or psychiatric records, which the agency hopes to present to the court in support of its case.

2. Compliance Conference

The next court date will be for a ***compliance conference***, where the court will ensure that the agency complied with the discovery schedule, the respondents are engaged in services, and visitation is taking place as ordered.

3. Settlement Conference

> From a practical standpoint, settlement discussions will usually take place throughout the process and not reserved only for the settlement conference.

At a ***settlement conference***, the attorneys will discuss whether settlement of the case is possible, or whether the case has to proceed to trial. The various settlement options are discussed below.

Alternatives to Trial

There are several ways to avoid a trial in a child protective proceeding. The first option is an ***admission***. If the respondent makes an admission, then he or she will admit in open court to one or more of the acts of abuse or neglect that is alleged in the petition. This option is not recommended for respondents who have active criminal cases based upon the same allegations as the child protective proceedings. Admissions, like anything else taking place in open court, are recorded. The admission can be used against the respondent in the criminal proceeding.

The next option is called a ***1051(a)***, or a ***submission to the court's jurisdiction***. Where a respondent "takes a 1051(a)," the respondent is neither admitting nor denying the allegations, but is simply consenting to the entry of a court order stating that he or she abused or neglected the children.

Both an admission and a 1051(a) give the court the authority to issue court orders against the respondents, which will be further discussed below. *The effect of an admission or submission is the same as if the case went to trial, and the agency won.*

If all parties agree, including the agency and the attorney for the child, then the court can issue an ***adjournment in contemplation of dismissal***, more commonly known as an "**ACD**." An ACD *cannot* be issued over the objection of the agency or the attorney for the child. Where the court issues an ACD, then the court will issue orders that the respondents comply with certain conditions of behavior for a fixed period of time. These may include, for example, orders that the respondents not engage in any corporal punishment, orders that the respondents complete a parenting skills class, or orders that the child's home be maintained in a safe and sanitary condition. At the conclusion of the period of the ACD, unless the agency files a petition alleging that the respondents violated the orders, then the case will be dismissed. However, if the court finds that the respondent violated the terms of the ACD, then the case will be placed back on the court's calendar, usually for trial.

Once the period of the ACD expires, then the respondent should write a letter to the State Central Register, with the ACD order attached, requesting that the report of the indicated case be ***expunged and sealed***, or removed from its records.

The agency will not agree to an ACD where the child is removed from the care of the respondents, unless the child has been returned to their care.

The Trial

If there is no resolution, then the case will go to **trial**, also known as the **fact finding hearing**. At the trial, the agency will have to prove its allegations of child abuse and/or neglect. Additionally, if a respondent who is a non-parent argues that he or she is not a PLR, then the agency will have to prove that the respondent is in fact a PLR.

The agency will present witnesses and evidence. The agency will almost always call the caseworker to testify. Other witnesses may include police officers involved in the case, doctors, teachers, and/or people close to the family who allegedly have information about the acts of abuse or neglect. Evidence may include, for example, medical records, police reports, and/or photographs. The agency's witnesses will be cross-examined by the attorneys for the respondents and the attorney for the children.

At the conclusion of the agency's case, the attorneys for the respondents can ask that the petition be dismissed for the agency's failure to present a ***prima facie case***. When that application is made, the respondents' attorneys argue that even if everything that was said was true, it is not enough for a finding of abuse and/or neglect.

If the court grants the application of the respondents' attorneys, then the entire case will be dismissed. If the application is denied, then the respondents will have the opportunity to present a case.

The respondents themselves will usually testify. The respondents may also call other witnesses, such as relatives and family friends who can testify regarding the respondents' version of events. Most attorneys will counsel the respondents not to testify if they have an active criminal case, as their testimony in Family Court can be used against them in their criminal cases. The attorney for the children may also present a case, but this rarely happens.

At the conclusion of the testimony and evidence, the court will have to decide whether the agency proved its case by a standard called a ***preponderance of the evidence***. That means that the court has to decide whether more than half of the credible evidence showed that the children were abused and/or neglected.

If the court determines that the agency failed to prove its case, then the petition will be dismissed, and all court orders will be vacated. If the petition is dismissed, then the respondent should write a letter to the ***State Central Register*** ("SCR"), with the dismissal order enclosed, requesting that the report of the indicated case be expunged and sealed. The court can also dismiss the case on the basis that ***the aid of the court is no longer required***, meaning that the court's involvement is no longer needed to protect the child. This is commonly known as a **1051(c)**.

If the court determines that the agency proved its case, then there will be an ***order of fact finding*** stating that the children were abused and/or neglected by the respondents. This is called *a* ***finding of abuse*** or a ***finding of neglect***.

Special Rules of Evidence in Child Protective Proceedings

In child protective proceedings, the statements by the children are ***admissible***. That means that witnesses can testify regarding the children's statements, even though they would normally be hearsay.
In order for the children's statements to be sufficient to prove abuse and/or neglect, there must be ***corroboration***. Therefore, the agency cannot simply present the statements of ***one child***, and rest its case. Rather, the agency must present evidence "***tending to support the reliability of the previous statements***."[17]

Courts have held that where more than one child makes statements tending to support the reliability of the other's statements, the corroboration requirement is satisfied. This is called ***cross-corroboration***. For example, if one child tells the caseworker that the mother beat him regularly with a belt, and the other child says that he witnessed it, then the children's statements will usually be held to cross-corroborate each other.

---

[17] N.Y. Family Court Act § 1046(a)(vi).

If the agency presents a child's statements regarding abuse and/or neglect, and the statements are sufficiently corroborated, that does not mean that the agency automatically wins the trial. Rather, it means that the burden shifts to the respondents to oppose the agency's case in order to avoid an abuse or neglect finding.

Disposition

Reports

After a finding of abuse or neglect, the case proceeds to **disposition**. Disposition is akin to sentencing in a criminal case. Prior to disposition, the court will usually order an **Investigation and Report**, known as an "**I and R**". An "I and R" is an investigation by the agency, in which a caseworker speaks with the respondents, any foster parents, foster care agency caseworkers, close friends and relatives who are involved in the child's life, the children's pediatricians, and the children's teachers. The "I and R" will contain the agency's recommendations for dispositional orders, most importantly whether the children should remain in, or return to, the home that they resided in at the time that the case was filed.

The court may also order a forensic report, known as an "**FET**," which is a mental health evaluation by a court-appointed professional. In some cases, such as cases where there was a finding of sexual abuse, FETs are mandatory.

The Court's Options

At disposition, the court's options are as follows:

1) **Placement** in foster care, for a period of up to twelve months;
2) **Release** to a parent, person legally responsible, or other suitable relative, which may be under the agency's supervision, for a period of up to twelve months;
3) **Suspension of judgment**, which directs the respondents to comply with certain orders, such as maintenance of the home in a safe and sanitary condition, abstinence from drugs and alcohol, no use of corporal punishment, etc.;
4) **An order of custody**, if there is a pending custody petition; or
5) **An order of protection**.

If the court issues a ***suspended judgment***, and there is no allegation that the respondent violated the order, then the respondent can request, at the time that the suspended judgment expires, that the petition be dismissed as if the case went to trial and the respondent won.

Orders of protection are usually issued in conjunction with other orders. They generally last for the same amount of time as those orders. For example, the court can issue an order releasing the children to the care of the mother with twelve months of supervision, with an order of protection that the mother refrain from using corporal punishment. That order of protection will usually also be for twelve months.

The court can issue orders of protection lasting ***until the child's eighteenth birthday*** against people who are ***no longer members of the child's household*** and ***are not related by blood or marriage to a member of the child's household***. Those orders are usually against an ex-paramour of the child's parent who lived with the child at the time that the petition was filed, and who no longer lives there.

Cases Where the Parents' Rights Can Be Terminated at Disposition

In cases involving ***severe or repeated abuse***, the court may terminate the parental rights of the respondent at disposition. In order for this to be an option, the court has to find that at fact finding, the agency proved severe or repeated abuse by ***clear and convincing evidence***.

> "**Clear and convincing evidence**" is a higher standard of proof than the usual "**preponderance of the evidence**" standard; however, it is less than "**beyond all reasonable doubt**," which is used in criminal proceedings.

Severe abuse is defined as:

(1) Abuse resulting from **reckless or intentional acts** which show a **depraved indifference to human life**, resulting in **serious physical injury** to the child, or
(2) Felony sex offenses committed against the child, or knowingly allowing these offenses to be committed, or
(3) A conviction for **murder** or **manslaughter,** or **criminal solicitation, facilitation,** or **conspiracy** to commit those

crimes, where the victim or the intended victim was the child, a sibling of the child, or another parent of the child[18], or

(4) A conviction of **felony assault,** or **attempted felony assault** against the child, if the child was under eleven years old at the time of the acts.

Repeated abuse is defined as:

(1) A finding of physical abuse, where, in the last five years, the parent has been found to have physically abused a child or committed a felony sex offense against a child, or
(2) A finding of felony sexual abuse, where the parent has, in the last five years, been found to have physically abused a child or committed another felony sex offense against a child.

The prior finding of felony sexual abuse may be from a child protective proceeding in Family Court, or from a criminal conviction.

Where the court terminates parental rights based upon a finding of severe or repeated abuse, the court must find that the agency has made ***diligent efforts to encourage or strengthen the parental relationship***, unless the court finds that reasonable efforts are not required. Reasonable efforts would <u>only</u> be required if the court finds that they:

- would be in the best interests of the child,
- are not contrary to the health and safety of the child, and
- would likely result in the reunification of the parent and the child in the foreseeable future.

<u>Post-Dispositional Proceedings</u>

Permanency Hearings

Wherever a child remains out of the respondents' home for a period of at least **eight months**, the court has to hold permanency hearings. At a permanency hearing, the court has to determine: (1) a **goal** for the child to achieve permanency, (2) whether the agency made **reasonable efforts** to achieve permanency for the child, and (3)

[18] It is a defense that the parent who was killed committed acts of abuse against the convicted parent, or against the child or another child of the parent, and the abuse was a factor in causing the homicide.

whether the child should remain placed outside of the home of his or her parents.

The permanency goal may be: (1) return to parent, (2) placement for adoption, (3) referral for legal guardianship, (4) permanent placement with a fit and willing relative, or (5) placement in another planned permanent living arrangement, commonly referred to as "**APPLA**." APPLA is generally reserved for ***teenage children***, where the goal is for them to live independently in the foreseeable future.

Unless the child is already home with the parents on a trial basis, known as a ***trial discharge***, the court will generally continue placement until the conclusion of the next permanency hearing. If the child is on trial discharge, and it is progressing without significant issues, then the court will likely issue an order authorizing a final discharge, or release of the child out of placement, with ten days' notice to the court and all counsel. Once ***final discharge*** takes place, the court will no longer be involved with the family and there will be no further court proceedings. The first permanency hearing must take place eight months after the removal of the child. Thereafter, the permanency hearings must take place every six months or until permanency is achieved.

Extensions of Supervision

Where the court has ordered that the child be released to a parent or other suitable person under agency supervision, the agency may ask for an extension of supervision, if the agency believes that it needs more time to supervise the family than the order provided. The court will have to determine whether there is good cause to extend supervision. This generally takes place where the respondent still has to complete services, or where the issues which brought the case to the attention of the court still continue.

Collateral Consequences of a Finding of Abuse or Neglect

The most severe, and immediate consequence, of a finding of abuse or neglect is that it gives the court the authority to place a child in foster care.

Where a child is placed in foster care, and remains in foster care for ***fifteen out of the most recent twenty-two months,*** then the agency may be required by law to file a petition to ***terminate the parental rights*** of the respondents, in order to free the child for adoption by someone else. If the child is in foster care for fifteen out of the most recent twenty-two months, the only circumstances where the agency would not be required to file such a petition would be if: (1) the permanency goal is one other than adoption, (2) the child is at least fourteen years old, and would not consent to adoption, (3) there are no grounds for a petition to terminate parental rights, or (4) there is another child protective proceeding involving the child, and the appropriate goal is return to parent.

After a finding of abuse or neglect, there will be a record of the finding on file with the ***New York Statewide Central Register of Child Abuse and Maltreatment*** ("SCR") until the respondent's youngest child turns twenty-eight (28) years old. The record will affect the respondent in any future custody cases in Family or Supreme Court. Additionally, it will negatively affect any application that the respondent makes to become a foster or adoptive parent. Furthermore, if the respondent applies for employment in a child care field, including but not limited to employment as a teacher or child care worker, then the record will negatively affect the application.

Discharge from Foster Care and Other Out-Of-Home Placement

Trial and Final Discharge

When a child first goes home from foster care, it will be on a ***trial discharge***. Where a child is on trial discharge, the child is still legally in foster care, but resides with the parent. The agency can generally do a trial discharge at any time after disposition without a court order. However, the court has the authority to order that the child not be trial discharged without a court order. The agency can take a child from trial discharge back into placement without a court order. This is commonly known as "**failing the trial discharge**."

Where a trial discharge succeeds, then it will end in ***final discharge***, which means that the child is released completely from foster care. The agency cannot do a final discharge without court order.

Custody or Guardianship

Another person, such as a ***non-respondent parent*** or other suitable relative, may file for custody or guardianship of a child during a child protective proceeding. Custody or guardianship petitions will not be heard until disposition. If the court grants custody or guardianship at disposition, then it ends the court's authority to continue hearing the case, and there will be no supervision over the family.

If the custody or guardianship petitions are disputed, then the court will hold a hearing on the petition, which will also function as the dispositional hearing.

There is also ***kinship guardianship***, commonly known as "**kin-gap**." The kin-gap program allows kinship foster parents to receive public funds to serve as permanent guardians for the children without adopting them. As a result, the respondent parents do not lose their legal status as parents. In order for the court to entertain an application for kinship guardianship, the agency has to approve it.

Adoption

Prior to the child being adopted, there either needs to be a ***surrender***, or a ***termination of parental rights***.

A parent may sign a ***conditional surrender***, where the surrender is signed but under certain conditions. Those conditions usually include adoption by a specific relative, the right to receive photographs of the child, and the right to contact the child on special occasions. After signing the surrender, the parent will no longer be the child's legal parent, and the child will be freed for adoption, consistent with the terms of the conditional surrender.

A parent may also sign a surrender, even an ***unconditional surrender***, in order to avoid a termination of parental rights. Orders terminating parental rights are admissible as proof of abuse or neglect of future children. Additionally, if parents who have had their rights terminated have children removed from them in the future, the agency may <u>not</u> be required to make reasonable efforts to achieve reunification with those children.

Terminations of parental rights may be based upon:

(1) **Abandonment**, which is failure to have contact with, or support a child financially, for six consecutive months;

(2) **Permanent neglect,** which is failure for **one year** or **fifteen out of the most recent twenty-two months** to maintain contact with, or to plan for the future of the child, notwithstanding the agency's diligent efforts;
(3) **Mental illness or mental retardation**, to the extent that the child would be in danger of being neglected for the foreseeable future if placed in the care of the respondent; or
(4) **Severe or repeated abuse**.

Those grounds for termination of parental rights must be proven by "clear and convincing evidence."

If the court issues an order terminating the respondent's parental rights, then the respondent is no longer the child's legal parent, and the child may be adopted without the respondent's consent.

Independent Living

When a child in foster care turns eighteen years old, then his or her consent to remain in foster care is required. If the youth decides not to consent, then he or she does not remain in foster care.

Youth ***age out*** of foster care when they turn twenty-one. However, the agency may file for an ***exception to policy*** to allow them to remain in foster after the age of twenty-one, usually if the youth is in school and the agency wishes to continue to support the youth financially.

Advice for Respondents

Below are several pieces of advice that most attorneys representing respondents in child protective proceedings give to their clients.

- **Do not talk to the caseworker about the allegations in the petition.** Any statements that you make to the caseworker can be used against the parent in future hearings. The parent can and should talk to the caseworker about services and about visitation, but not about the allegations.

- **Complete your services.** Many people believe that the court will ultimately determine that they did not commit any acts of abuse or neglect, and that therefore, they do not need to complete services. However, child protective cases tend to go on for a long time, and if the children are removed from the home, the court will *not* usually grant liberal visitation without participation in services. The court will also *not* return children to their parents' care if they are not participating in services. More importantly, with respect to a cause of action for a termination of parental rights, the "clock" starts when the child is removed, not when a finding of abuse or neglect is entered. Therefore, if a child is removed in September 2015, the parent does not enter services, and the child remains in foster care, then the agency can file a petition to terminate the parent's rights in September 2016, no matter when, or if, the respondent has been found to have committed any acts of abuse or neglect.

- **Visit the children if they are removed from your care.** Many people are reluctant to visit their children, because it is humiliating to visit under the supervision of a caseworker, and it is very difficult to leave after the visit. However, respondents virtually never get their children back if they are not visiting. Also, failure to maintain contact with the children is likely to lead to termination of parental rights.

- **Maintain as good of a relationship with your caseworkers as possible.** This may be the hardest piece of advice for people to follow, but the respondent's experience in Family Court will be much easier if he or she has a decent relationship with the caseworker. While it should not be the case, the agency is far less likely to consent to the return of children to respondents when the caseworkers have a bad relationship with them. It is true that the court can issue orders returning children over the agency's objection, but the road to reunification is far easier, and much faster, if it is on the agency's consent.

Conclusion

The child protective part in Family Court deals with some of the most difficult, and some of the most important, questions that a court has to face. It has to balance the protection of children with questions of due process, and the interests that children have in growing up with their parents.

A parent's experience in the child protective system is painful and humiliating. A parent finds his/her parental judgment questioned by strangers. However, a parent's journey through Family Court can be a valuable obstacle to overcome. Parents can tackle the issues which led them into the system, and break the cycle of child abuse and neglect. As a result, they can give their children, and their children's children, the opportunity for a better life and a better future.

Joseph Nivin, Esq.

Joseph Nivin is a solo practitioner at The Law Offices of Joseph H. Nivin, P.C., a law firm focusing on family and matrimonial law, with offices in Jamaica, Queens and in Manhattan. He graduated from Brooklyn Law School in 2007, and received his undergraduate degree at the University of Pennsylvania in 2004. Prior to opening his practice, Mr. Nivin was an agency attorney at the Administration for Children's Services of the City of New York, where he represented the New York City government in child abuse and neglect proceedings. Mr. Nivin is a member of the New York State Bar Association, the New York City Bar Association, the Queens County Bar Association, and the Brandeis Association of Queens County. He serves on the Queens County Bar Association Juvenile Justice Committee and on the Committee on Lawyer Assistance. Mr. Nivin is a member of the Assigned Counsel/Attorneys for Children Panel for the Second Judicial Department, and is certified to represent indigent litigants, as well as children, in Family Court proceedings at both the trial and appellate levels. He was selected as a 2015 Rising Star in Super Lawyers magazine. More information regarding Mr. Nivin's office is available on the web at www.nivinlaw.com.

SECTION A: TYPES OF PROCEEDINGS

CHAPTER 14

PATERNITY

By Ravi Cattry, Esq.

Mary is pregnant and the father of her baby is Frank. They are currently living together in New York State, but are not married. When Mary goes into labor, they both head to the hospital where Mary gives birth to a baby boy named Casey. After the birth, Mary and Frank are approached by a hospital staff member to discuss with them the options of how to establish paternity for Casey to name Frank his father.

As the hospital staff member explains to Mary and Frank, in New York State, a child born to unwed parents is only considered the legal child of the mother and not the father. In order for the biological father to be legally recognized as the father of the child, he must establish paternity in one of two manners: (1) with the filing of an Acknowledgement of Paternity form or (2) by starting a paternity petition and having an order of filiation entered in court.

Acknowledging paternity is important for all parties involved. Once a father acknowledges a child as his, he has the right to establish custody and visitation rights. His name will also be added to the child's birth certificate. The mother benefits because she can then seek child support from the father. The child benefits by knowing who his or her father is, receiving healthcare that is available through the father, access to the father's medical history and genetic information, and other financial benefits, such as a ***right to an inheritance***, social security benefits, and veterans benefits.

Acknowledgment of Paternity ("AOP")

Mary and Frank's first option is to complete a form called an Acknowledgement of Paternity ("AOP"). You can view the AOP online at https://www.childsupport.ny.gov/pdfs/4418nyc.pdf. An

AOP is a form available only to unwed parents and is to be completed by the biological mother and biological father. If the mother was married at any time during the pregnancy or at the time of birth, the AOP is not available for her and the biological father to complete. The one exception to this rule is if the biological mother and biological father marry each other after the birth of the child. If that occurs, the AOP option is still available to them. Minors, those under the age of 18, can also complete an AOP form to acknowledge paternity of the biological father.

In Mary and Frank's case they are unwed and Mary was not married during any part of the pregnancy nor at the time of birth, therefore they can complete this form.

Procedure

In New York State, the AOP form can be completed at any time up to and through the child turning 21 years of age. After the birth of the child, the AOP can be signed either at the hospital or at a social services office.

Most hospitals in New York have trained staff members who are prepared to walk the parents of a child through the procedure of completing the form and also to answer any questions that might arise during this process.

The AOP form, LDS-4418, is two pages long and asks for information regarding the mother, the biological father, and the child. The mother and father must fill in their full names, address, birthdates, and social security number. For the child, the form requests information regarding the child's full name, date of birth, and place of birth. If the parents wish to change the last name of the child from what appears on the birth certificate, that change can also be made on this form.

After the mother and father complete the form, they must each have two witnesses sign the form. The witnesses cannot be related to either the mother or father. Additionally, this form is only available to the biological mother and biological father of the child. No other family member, such as the grandparents of the child, or any other person may complete the form or have any influence on it.

Once completed, either the hospital or someone at the social services office will sign off on the form and file it. The form is filed with the registrar of the district where the birth certificate was filed and a certified copy of the AOP will be mailed to the parents. For births in hospitals located outside of New York City, the AOP will also be filed with the State Department of Health. For all births in New York State, the AOP will be filed with the Putative Father Registry. The Putative Father Registry is a record of the names and addresses of all persons who sign the AOP or who the court determines to be the father of the child of an unwed mother.

The AOP must be voluntarily signed by both parents of the child and only signed if there is no doubt about the paternity of the child. If there is any question of the paternity the mother and father should refrain from signing the AOP and seek a DNA test to confirm paternity. The hospital staff member will have information about the procedure for a DNA test to determine paternity.

Effect of Signing an AOP

Upon receiving a copy of the certified AOP, the paternity of the child is confirmed. The mother may seek child support from the biological father now, and the father may seek custody and visitation of the child. The child can now receive healthcare through the father and financial benefits, such as social security benefits and inheritance rights.

All of the information provided in the AOP and listed in the Putative Father Registry is confidential. The information will only be released with a court order showing good cause.

In Mary and Frank's case, after the hospital employee discusses the legal ramifications with both of them regarding acknowledging paternity, and there are no questions regarding the paternity of Casey, they can voluntarily sign the AOP form. This completes all of the requirements for acknowledging paternity in New York State for unwed parents.

Vacating the AOP

Once an AOP is signed, it is possible to withdraw it. Either parent may withdraw the AOP by filing a petition to vacate with the family court. The location of the court is determined by which county the parents live in. If the parents reside in separate counties, the motion to vacate can be filed in either. If the parents live in the same county, the motion to vacate must be filed in that county.

The procedure for vacation of an acknowledgement of paternity depends on whether or not the parents were minors at the time of signing the AOP.

If the parent is 18 years of age or older at the time of signing the AOP, the petition to vacate can be filed either (1) within 60 days of the date of signing the AOP or (2) within 60 days of the date on which an answer to a petition is required relating to the child and in which the parent is a party, whichever is earlier.

If the parent is under 18 years of age at the time the AOP is signed, the petition to vacate may be filed the earlier of the following: (1) within 60 days after that parent's 18th birthday or (2) within 60 days of the date on which an answer to a petition is required relating to the child and in which the parent is a party provided that the parent was advised at any such proceeding of the right to file a petition to vacate.

Once the time to file the petition to vacate has passed, either parent may only challenge the AOP in court if it was signed based on fraud, duress, or mistake of material fact. The petitioner bears the burden of proof.

If the parent filing the petition to vacate has successfully challenged the AOP, the court will ***order genetic testing*** to determine the child's father. If the father who completed the AOP is determined to be the child's father, the court will make a finding of paternity and enter an order of filiation that states that he is the father. If the genetic testing confirms that he is not the father, the AOP will be vacated. The court will also provide a copy of this finding to the registrar of the district where the AOP was filed and to the Putative Father Registry. Additionally, if the party is receiving child support services, a copy will be provided to the child support enforcement unit.

Order of Filiation

Now suppose one of two of these scenarios occurs: (1) Mary is pregnant with Frank's baby, but Frank denies paternity or (2) Mary is pregnant with Frank's baby, but is married to Harry. In the first instance, Frank is unwilling to sign the AOP and in the second case, Mary and Frank cannot sign the AOP because she is married to someone else. In both of these cases, Mary's only option for acknowledging Frank as the father of her child, Casey, is by filing a petition in Family Court to get an order of filiation.

An order of filiation is a court order that declares a man as the legal father of a child. This option is available if a party denies paternity of the child, or if the mother was married at any time during the pregnancy or at the time of birth to someone other than the biological father, or if the parties choose to not sign an Acknowledgement of Paternity form.

Procedure

The paternity petition can be filed by the child's mother, a man who believes he is the father of the child, the child, the child's legal guardian, or if the child is receiving public assistance, the Department of Social Services. The Department of Social Services can also include in the petition an order of support.

The paternity petition can be filed by the mother while she is pregnant, unlike the AOP, which can only be signed upon the birth of the child, or up until the child is 21 years of age and supporting him or herself. A paternity petition can be filed after the child turns 21 if the father has admitted to being the father in writing or has been paying child support.

The paternity petition is filed in Family Court and the county is determined by the addresses of where the parties live.

The party filing the petition is called the petitioner and the other parent/party is called the respondent. In the situation where Frank is ***denying paternity*** and Mary files the petition, Mary is the petitioner and Frank is the respondent. Once the petition is filed in Family Court, the petitioner must serve a copy of the petition and a summons upon the respondent. These papers must be served by someone over the age of 18 and someone who is not a party to the petition. An affidavit of service must be completed by the person who serves the papers as proof of service. The papers must be served at least eight days before the next court date.

If the mother was married to someone who is not the father of the child either during the pregnancy or at the time of birth, that person must be served with a copy of the petition in order to make him aware of the case. This occurs because in New York the husband of the mother is assumed to be the father of her child. If this is untrue and a petition is filed to have the biological father acknowledge paternity, the husband must have a chance to appear in court and be heard on the matter of paternity. In the situation where Mary is married to Harry but Frank is the actual father of her baby, Harry is assumed to be the father of Casey solely because he was married to Casey's mother, Mary, during the pregnancy and at the time of Casey's birth. Therefore when either Mary or Frank files a petition to determine paternity, Harry must be included as a respondent, so that he has a chance to be heard on this matter.

On the day that the parties are supposed to appear in court, the petitioner should bring a copy of the child's birth certificate with him or her. Once in court, one of two things can happen: (1) an order of filiation can be entered upon consent or (2) a hearing can be conducted in order to determine paternity.

An order of filiation entered upon consent is when both the mother and the father of the child agree that the man involved in the petition is indeed the biological father. If an order of filiation is entered upon consent, it is very difficult to vacate it, so all parties involved must be sure that paternity is correct before they agree to it.

If when Mary and Frank appear in court, and Harry is not an existing party, Frank decides to acknowledge the paternity of Casey, then an order of filiation upon consent can be entered by the court.

If an order of filiation upon consent does not occur and the man in the petition denies being the biological father, the Support Magistrate will order blood or DNA tests of both parties and the child. The parties will be given a date and place to appear for the tests and the case will be adjourned to another date. The payment for the results is the responsibility of the mother, but if the alleged father is determined to be the biological father then he will pay the laboratory fees. The results of the tests will be sent directly to the court and will be explained to all parties at the next court date.

If after the explanation of the results by the court the man involved in this case is the father and he still denies paternity, the case is rescheduled for a hearing. At the hearing, both parties may testify, call witnesses, and offer the results of the blood or DNA tests into evidence. If petitioner submits sufficient proof then an order of filiation will be entered. If the proof is not sufficient, the case will be dismissed.

Mother's Husband as a Party to Filiation Proceeding

In the situation where the mother's husband was also a party to the petition, the court will first make a ruling concerning the relationship of the husband to the child. If the court finds that the husband is not the biological father, then the petition against the alleged father will continue. The procedure for the petition against the alleged father will follow the same course as if there was no husband in the situation.

Effect of an Order of Filiation

Similar to the AOP, the order of filiation will be filed with the registrar of the district where the birth certificate was filed and if the child was born in a hospital outside of New York City, with the Department of Health of New York. In cases of all births in New York State, the order of filiation will also be filed with the Putative Father Registry. Also similar to the AOP, the order of filiation gives the mother, father, and the child the same rights as they would have had if an AOP had been completed.

It is very important for parties to attend the court dates because failure to do so may result in a default judgment against the non-appearing party. If the petitioner fails to appear, a default judgment will be entered where paternity is not acknowledged because the petitioner bears the burden of proof in proving paternity. If the respondent fails to appear, a default judgment in favor of paternity may be entered because the respondent is not there to raise any defenses.

Vacation of Order of Filiation

Similar to vacating a completed AOP, an order of filiation may also be vacated. However, vacation of such an acknowledgement is more difficult than vacating the AOP within 60 days of signing the form.

In order to vacate an order of filiation, a petition must be filed in Family Court. In this petition, the person looking to vacate the order of filiation bears the burden of showing why the order of filiation should be set aside. Under New York law, a judgment or order from the court can only be set aside under limited circumstances. The circumstances under which courts have vacated an order of filiation include fraud, misrepresentation, or other misconduct by the adverse party, or lack of jurisdiction by the court that rendered the decision.

In instances where it would be appear that the order of filiation should be vacated because it meets one of the reasons set above, the court may still deny the petition to vacate if it finds that the vacating would not be in the best interest of the child. New York courts have held that if a relationship has developed between the father and child or if the child has come to rely on the father due to spending extensive time with him or the father paying for basic necessities for the child, the petitioner may be estopped from vacating order of filiation because breaking that relationship is not in the best interest of the child. ***Estoppel*** is the legal term used to say that the court will prevent something from happening. Courts have had such holdings even in cases where there were knowing misrepresentations about paternity by one party.

> **Estoppel**. A court may refuse to vacate a paternity petition if a man held himself out to be the father of a child (despite knowing that he was not the biological father) by paying for the education of the child, for medical care, and spending time with the child. The purpose of this refusal to vacate is that the child has come to rely on this father financially and emotionally even though there is no biological connection and it is in the best interest of the child to maintain that connection. The father is stopped from denying that the child is his.

The court is also unlikely to vacate an order of filiation just because the parents are having difficulties in reaching agreement regarding custody and child support. A petition to vacate an order of filiation cannot be used to deny a father or child rights just because the parents cannot agree on other subjects unrelated to paternity.

Other Issues Arising in Paternity Cases

The discussion thus far regarding paternity cases has only been about instances where a heterosexual couple was having their own biological child, both parents were legal residents of the United States, and the alleged father was alive. There are many cases, especially in New York where the population is extremely diverse, where the procedures and explanations stated above are not enough to address their situation.

Immigration issues

New York has a very diverse population, which includes a large immigrant population. Sometimes these residents of New York State do not have legal residence here. The lack of that status often prevents them from seeking information or following procedures due to their fear of revealing their legal status in the United States.

The Acknowledgement of Paternity form asks for the Social Security Number ("SSN") for both the father and the mother of the child. The sight of that might create a fear in the parent or parents who do not have one. However, in New York you do not need to complete that section in order to properly acknowledge paternity. Even if the SSN is left blank on the form, these parents will be able to receive the same benefits of acknowledging paternity that the parents who have valid SSNs do. There is no need for either parent to reveal his or her immigration status, residency, or citizenship in the AOP in order to complete the form or if a petition for an order of filiation is filed.

Surrogates

For some couples and families having children is not always possible without help of a third party. In certain instances, the couple may need the help of a surrogate. There are many types of surrogacies and each type has a separate standard for how paternity is established. New York, in general, views any contract for a surrogacy against public policy and will refuse to enforce them. However, once the child is born, there are ways to establish the intended parents as the actual parents of the child.

In the case where an unmarried surrogate is carrying the genetic child of a married couple, meaning that the wife's egg was fertilized by the husband's sperm, New York law does not require the signing of an AOP or an order of filiation. The child is considered to be the child of the husband and wife and not the surrogate.

Where the surrogate is carrying a child that is only the genetic child of one of the intended parents, there is a two-step process. If one of the intended parents is the sperm donor, he may sign an AOP with the surrogate, provided that the surrogate was unmarried during the pregnancy and at the time of birth. If the surrogate was married at any point, an order of filiation may be filed by the genetic parent. Once paternity is established, either through the signing of the AOP or through an order of filiation, the surrogate will relinquish custody and all parental rights to the child, which then allows the non-genetic parent to adopt the child. If the mother's egg was used in the surrogacy, paternity is not established, there is only an adoption proceeding that occurs.

In the case where neither intended parent is genetically related to the child, a full adoption proceeding must occur.

In many states pre-birth parentage orders are entered by courts to establish who the parents will be once the child is born. In New York State, such orders are considered against public policy. However, New York does recognize pre-birth parentage orders that are from a state that recognizes them. For example, if a New York couple went to California in order to have a child via a surrogate and got a pre-birth order from California listing them as the parents of the unborn child, a New York court would uphold that order because California courts find these orders valid.

Same Sex Couples

A topic that is related to surrogacy is the issue of same sex parents and paternity. If a same sex couple is having a child where only one of the intended parents is genetically linked to the child, the best way to get the other intended parent legal rights is through second parent adoption. This would involve the surrogate relinquishing custody and all parental rights in order for the non-genetic parent to adopt the child.

In the case where a lesbian couple is having a child where the woman carrying is the genetic parent and the sperm donor is anonymous, adoption is generally not necessary for married couples, but is most likely going to be necessary for unmarried couples. However, for same sex fathers, where one is genetically related to the child, a second parent adoption most likely would have to occur for the father who is not genetically related.

Order of Filiation After the Death of the Father

Previously in order to establish paternity New York required that the father be living in order to draw blood or do a cheek swab to collect DNA and compare it to the child. Since then science and technology have made great advancements, which allow DNA samples to be taken from more than just a living body, and New York courts have started to acknowledge these methods as valid.

Recently in Queens County Family Court, a court allowed a petitioner in a paternity suit to use the decedent father's frozen blood samples in order to establish paternity.[19] However, this new precedent was only allowed because the deceased father had openly and notoriously held himself out to be the father of the child in question. The decision from Queens County Family Court emphasized that this is an important factor in using DNA from sources other than a living body in order to establish paternity. A New York court did deny a petition by a mother to exhume the body of the alleged father in order to get a DNA sample and establish paternity because there was no showing that the alleged father had made any acknowledgement of paternity. The law and courts are still behind in terms of addressing advancements in DNA technology in reference to paternity, but with new methods that can be used to prove paternity these issues will need to be addressed in the near future.

Jurisdiction

The choice of court in which to file paternity petitions is based on the county in which the parents are living. Where the parents are living in the same county, knowing where to file the petition is a simple decision. If the parents live in the same state but different counties, the petition can be filed in either county. While this can be difficult because it may require one of the parties to do more traveling, being in the same state helps in terms of which law applies. However, difficulties arise when parents are located in separate states.

> **Full Faith and Credit**. Under the Constitution, Article IV, Section I, each state must recognize legislative acts, public records, and judicial decisions of other states within the United States. The purpose of the clause is to ensure that a judicial decision in one state cannot be ignored by the court of another state.
>
> For example, a New York court enters a child support order where the father has to pay a certain amount to the mother for child care. The father later moves to Florida where he stops paying. A Florida court can enter a judgment against the father for the missed payments based on the child support order from the New York court based on the Full Faith and Credit clause.

[19] Anne R. v. Francis C., 167 Misc. 2d 343, 634 N.Y.S.2d 399 (Fam. Ct. Queens County 1995).

The issue of which state to file the petition in becomes more difficult because separate states means significant travel for one of the parties. A bigger issue that can arise is which state's law to apply. Generally, the state in which the petition is filed is one of the options for which state's law might apply. However, this might not be the case if the child was born in another state, or conceived in another state, or if the state in which the petition is filed does not have significant connections with the child or either of the parents (such as living in the state long enough to establish residency, giving the courts of that state jurisdiction over the issue of paternity).

Another jurisdictional issue that can arise is whether an order of filiation from one state will be upheld in another state. Generally, full faith and credit is given to all final judgments from one state in another state. However, if there is any question about the validity of the judgment a court in another state may refuse to give ***full faith and credit*** to the order of filiation. Recently, a court in Michigan refused to give full faith and credit to an order of filiation entered in New York because the petitioner, the alleged father in that case, had failed to include the husband of the mother of the child as a necessary party in the determining of paternity.

Ravi Cattry, Esq.

Ravi Cattry is an associate attorney and is licensed to practice in New York and New Jersey and admitted into the Eastern and Southern District Courts of New York. She completed a Bachelor of Science at Fordham University in Manhattan where she was a double major in psychology and economics. She received a Juris Doctor from Pace University School of Law in White Plains, New York.

Before joining Rincker Law, PLLC, Ravi worked at a general practice firm located in Kew Gardens, New York. While working there her practice areas included landlord and tenant disputes, matrimonial and family law issues, commercial law, and immigration law. Ravi also worked with a boutique law firm specializing in bankruptcy law in Manhattan. During law school she interned with the Integrated Domestic Violence Court in White Plains, New York, where she assisted in handling divorce cases intertwined with domestic violence cases.

Ravi is fluent in Hindi and Punjabi, and conversational in Spanish. In her free time Ravi enjoys reading, watching movies, playing tennis, and keeping up with her favorite soccer teams. For more information about Rincker Law, PLLC, visit www.rinckerlaw.com.

SECTION A: TYPES OF PROCEEDINGS

CHAPTER 15

PERSONS IN NEED OF SUPERVISION

By Kymberly A. Robinson, Esq.

PINS is an acronym for "***persons in need of supervision***." These are children under the age of 18 whose parents or guardians have ***lost control of the child*** to the point that the child is ***skipping school***, behaving in ***dangerous ways***, and/or being ***habitually disobedient***. It usually is not a single-incident occurrence. See Matter of Robert Z., 214 A.D.2d 203 (3rd Dept., 1995).

Until 2002, PINS only applied to children under the age of 16.

Background

According to the Family Court Act ("FCA"), PINS are children who are "***incorrigible, ungovernable or habitually disobedient*** and beyond the lawful control of a parent or other person legally responsible for such child's care." See FCA § 712(a) (emphasis added). For example, someone in need of supervision is someone who has a ***history of running away***, using marijuana, ***gang involvement***, missing curfew, and/or school truancy.

Truancy is a term to describe the act of "skipping" or absenteeism from school.

Children and teens who are living in a home with constant fighting among family members and homes where they feel unaccepted or rejected are at higher risk for bad behavior and running away from home.

In a study published by the Vera Institute of Justice in March 2002 available at http://www.vera.org/sites/default/files/resources/downloads/159_243.pdf (last visited July 21, 2015), ***truancy*** was the most common allegation in a PINS petition. As one can imagine, the majority of these children are in their mid-teens.

Special Considerations

Runaway Children

Running away is a special situation. A child who has run away can be a nightmare for a parent for several reasons. First, the parent will wonder if he or she did something to "make" the child run away. Second, the parent will be concerned for the child's safety. Unlike with adults, if a child runs away, the parent or guardian can ask the court to issue a warrant. To do this, the parent must file a PINS petition (discussed below) requesting the warrant.

After the judge issues the warrant, the ***police will look for the runaway child***. When the police find the child, he or she will be brought to court immediately and a decision will be made as to whether that child can be ***safely returned to his or her home***. Usually the family will then be referred to some sort of ***family services professional or agency***. Different counties have their own protocols and requirements, (such as first filing a missing person's report), time frame, etc., so it is important to check the court's website for the specific county in which one lives.

PINS Proceedings

PINS proceedings, the process by which a person is placed under supervision of the court, are under the jurisdiction of Article 7 of the FCA. Except for appeals, there are never court fees in family court matters.

Diversion Programs

In lieu of a PINS proceeding, some New York City cases may be settled through the ***Family Assessment Program*** run through the ***Administration for Children's Services*** and ***NYC Department of Probation*** available at

http://www.nyc.gov/html/acs/html/support_families/family_assessment_program.shtml (last visited August 4, 2015). Each county has its own set of guidelines for PINS cases in terms of what steps towards resolving the issues should be taken. Each county throughout New York State stresses the importance of ***immediate access to services*** to resolve any behavior issues with minors and their parents or guardians. It is advisable to visit the website for the family court in the specific county in which a family lives to see what courts will require before bringing the matter into a courtroom. These programs and PINS proceedings in general are designed to keep children ***out of the juvenile justice system*** in the future.

> Bad behavior is sometimes a sign of mental illness. That is why meeting with a ***mental health professional*** is highly recommended at the first sign of "acting out."

Similarly, many jurisdictions have a similar diversion program, which means a department responsible for attempting to remedy the child's behavior by working with the family and a team of professionals to prevent the family from having to enter the court system. One example of a diversion program is the ***Family & Children's Diversion Program*** in Long Island. The website for this organization is http://www.familyandchildrens.org/pins-diversion/ (last visited August 4, 2015).

Initiating the Process

This process is initiated by filing a PINS Petition. A PINS Petition can be filed by either parent or other guardian, peace or police officer, person injured by the minor, or a school or other authorized agency. This PINS Petition, along with a summons, must be personally served upon the child and his or her parent, notifying them to appear in family court on a specific date and time. The Petition will include a description of the ***dangerous behavior*** and a request that the court find the child ***in need of supervision***.

The Process

At court, the person who filed the petition will testify about the child's behavior. In a PINS proceeding, the child will be represented by an attorney, who may be ***assigned or hired privately***. The court will eventually need to hear more evidence and ***hear from the child***. A ***probable cause hearing*** may be ordered when the court needs to decide if the ***child needs to stay somewhere else*** pending the fact-finding hearing, especially when the court is concerned that the child might not appear for the fact-finding hearing. Such a place could be in a foster environment, with another relative, or in a non-secure facility.

After the ***fact-finding hearing***, the judge will decide if the child committed acts described in the petition that are dangerous. The court may use a mental health evaluator or request a report from the probation department of the child's behavior, home life, and school life (including attendance at school). The judge will also set a dispositional hearing date if it is concluded that the child committed acts alleged in the petition.

At the ***dispositional hearing***, the judge will decide whether the child is in need of supervision. The order from the dispositional hearing will specifically include where the child will reside for the next ***18 months or less***, and what services, if any, the child will receive. The order can do a few things:

> If the child is ***placed outside of the parents' or guardians' home***, that person may be financially responsible for the child. For this reason, ***a child support case*** may be initiated against the parent or guardian.

- Give the child a *suspended judgment*. In other words, the court offers a list of things the child must do or must not do. If the child complies, the case can be dismissed;

- Put the child on probation. This is similar to probation in other instances in that the child must regularly meet with his or her probation officer and follow certain rules;

- Place the child in a group home, with a foster family, or other non-secure facility. This is more common where there is tension between the child and the parents or guardian and returning home is not a great option;

- Restitution. If the child is at least 10 years old, the judge can order the child to pay for any damage done to someone's property, or require the child to perform community service; or

- Adjourn the case for up to six months. If everything is fine during that period, the case will probably dismissed.

If the judge finds that the person is ***not in need of supervision***, he or she may dismiss the case entirely.

Relation to Juvenile Delinquency Cases

The court can substitute a PINS finding in lieu of a juvenile delinquency finding. Such a case was Matter of Derrick C., 137 Misc.2d 124 (Fam. Ct. Richmond Co., 1987) where the court substituted the delinquency petition for a finding that the boy was in need of supervision. In this case an 11 year old child committed an act which, if done by an adult, would constitute the crime of criminal trespass in the third degree, a class B misdemeanor. It was the first juvenile delinquency proceeding ever commenced against this boy, who was emotionally neglected by his mother who was a depressed and a chronic victim of domestic violence, which was witnessed by the boy. According to a report, while at a diagnostic treatment center for 6 months, the boy presented in a "warm, charming manner" being seen as "very verbal, articulate, (and) clearly intelligent" at 126. He was ultimately placed in a residential facility for 12 more months. Thus, in

> To clarify, PINS is not the same as juvenile delinquency. Unlike in a juvenile delinquency proceeding, it does not create a criminal record and, as stated above, the child cannot be put in a secure or locked facility as a result of a PINS case. See FCA § 702(2).

> Sometimes a PINS case can materialize into a parental abuse and neglect case, which is a child protective proceeding.

this case, treating the boy as a PINS was more appropriate so long as "the right of the community to protection would not be compromised thereby" at 126.

Violations

If the child ***violates the court's order***, the person who originally filed the PINS petition can file a ***violation petition***. The court may then hold a new ***dispositional hearing***. At this hearing the judge can change the order and order anything it could have from the onset. In some cases, the child may be ***adjudicated a juvenile delinquent*** and become subject to placement in a secure facility.

In re Daniel I., 57 A.D.3d 666 (2nd Dept., 2008) is an interesting case. Although a PINS violation can turn into a juvenile delinquency matter, sometimes a violation of a PINS order is more proof why the child is in continuing need of supervision. In the case of Daniel I., the child was adjudicated a PINS and required to wear an ***electronic monitoring device***, which he then ***broke and violated his curfew***. The Appellate Court held that the "Family Court may not 'bootstrap' a PINS adjudication onto one alleging juvenile delinquency by charging a PINS who absconds from a non-secure facility with conduct that, if committed by an adult, would constitute escape" at 667. See also, In re Gabriela A., 103 A.D.888 (2nd Dept., 2013) (where eloping from non-secure facility is consistent with being in need of supervision). That court further stressed that the actions which constituted the violation are the exact actions that call for a child being adjudicated a PINS in the first place.

Kymberly A. Robinson, Esq.

Kymberly is an associate attorney with Rincker Law, PLLC. Kymberly is admitted to practice law in New York and Florida. She attended Union College in Schenectady, New York for her undergraduate studies, where she graduated with high honors as a psychology major. She then obtained her J.D. from Pace University School of Law in White Plains, New York and, subsequently, her L.L.M. (with a concentration in family law) from the Benjamin N. Cardozo School of Law in Manhattan. Kymberly entered the field of matrimonial and family law as a way to couple her interest in psychology and personal relationships with her legal education.

SECTION A: TYPES OF PROCEEDINGS

CHAPTER 16

ADOPTION

By Denise E. Seidelman, Esq. and Nina E. Rumbold, Esq.

There are many different types of adoptions ranging from the adoption of a child ***unknown to a parent*** at the initiation of the adoption process to the adoption of a child already in the home through a ***step or second parent adoption***. Some children join their adoptive family shortly after birth while others are adopted after having spent years in the foster care system. When it comes to the adoption of a newborn, adoptive parents have ***several choices***. They can pursue their adoption through a New York State authorized adoption agency or they can pursue an independent adoption with the guidance of an attorney. While there are some opportunities to adopt internationally, most U.S. adoptions involve children residing in the United States. No one method of adoption is "best" because there are advantages and disadvantages to each. Also, as with everything in life, there is no one adoption experience. For some, the process feels almost effortless, while for others, there are many more challenges along the way. Regardless of what path a person chooses, becoming educated on the legal and emotional aspects of adoption and working with dedicated and ethical professionals is critical.

> The ***form of adoption*** is a critical first step. A person should meet with an adoption professional at the outset of the process.

The purpose of this chapter is to provide a concise summary of the various methods of adoption. Since all adoptions are highly regulated by the state, it's critical for people interested in adoption to consult with an attorney or experienced adoption professional at the outset. The importance of this cannot be overstated since the failure to comply with the technical adoption requirements can have profound consequences. Consultation with an adoption professional can also assist you to determine which method of adoption is best suited to your particular needs and desires. For example, if a person is open to adopting an older child, adoption through the ***foster care system*** may be the best choice; whereas if a person is hoping to adopt a newborn, that person will likely want to pursue either a private agency or private placement adoption. An adoption professional can advise you on the steps you must take to meet the legal requirements necessary to bring a child into you family through adoption. There are also adoptive parent support groups such as the ***Adoptive Parents Committee*** ("APC"), with chapters throughout the state, which offer educational workshops on all aspects of the adoption process and also serve as a resource for referrals to adoption professionals.

Methods of Adoption

Private Placement Adoption

Private placement adoption is accomplished when a birth parent places a child directly with adoptive parent(s) ***without an agency acting as an intermediary***. Private placement adoption is also referred to as "***Independent Placement***." As the name suggests, the parties to the adoption have located each other independently and determined that they wish to make an adoption plan together. Adoptive parents and birth parents learn of each other in many ways, including:

- connections through family and friends;
- networking through social media or the internet; and
- placing print advertisements in newspapers.

Birth parents and adoptive parents exchange information to determine if they are a good "match." Although information is exchanged, ***confidentiality can still be maintained***; last names, addresses and identifying information are only disclosed as desired. The assistance of an attorney, with expertise in the area of private placement adoption, is highly recommended and often required in this type of adoption. Private Placement adoption is attractive because it ***avoids the cost of an agency fee***, and can sometimes happen very quickly and inexpensively. However, since the adoptive parent(s) can incur costs during the adoption search, those expenses serve to diminish the cost difference between private placement and agency adoptions. From the birth parent(s)' perspective, the ability to control the process of selecting the adoptive parent(s) for their expected child allows them to ***feel more empowered*** to plan for their child rather than relying on the intervention of an agency.

Some legal steps are required before a person begins to search for a child. New York law requires hopeful adoptive parents to be certified by a court as "qualified" to adopt before they can take custody of a child for the purpose of adoption. In order to be qualified to adopt, that person must petition either the Family Court or Surrogate's Court in the county where that person resides for an Order Certifying that person as a ***Qualified Adoptive Parent(s)***. A ***home study report***, prepared by a "***disinterested person***," must be submitted to the court together with your petition. A "disinterested person" may be either an agency authorized by New York State or a private individual (most typically a licensed certified social worker) whom the court deems sufficiently qualified to determine the adoptive parent's suitability to adopt. If the home study preparer is an authorized agency, the home study report will include a ***criminal history report*** and ***child abuse clearances*** as well as recent medical statements, letters of reference, and other documents demonstrating that the adoptive parent has the emotional, financial, and physical ability to adopt a child. If the home study is prepared by a private social worker or counselor, the court will obtain the required criminal and child abuse clearances.

While the legal process is unfolding, it is a good idea for interested parents to create an "***adoption profile***" which serves as a way for the person to introduce him or herself to a parent considering placing his or her child for adoption. Many adoptive parents display their profiles on adoption websites, advertise in newspapers, and send out bulk networking letters (typically by e-mail) to extended family and friends. All of these activities should be undertaken in consultation with an attorney to insure that they are legal, effective, and that the person's need for privacy is adequately protected.

Most private placement adoptions are ***planned in advance*** of the adoptive child's birth. Typically, after adoptive parents make the initial connection with an expectant parent(s), there is a period of time during which the adoptive parent(s) and potential birth parent(s) get to know one another. This communication takes place either through e-mail or by phone but, depending on the circumstances, the parties can also choose to meet in person. It is advisable for the adoptive parent(s) to immediately inform their attorney that they are in communication with a potential birth parent so that the attorney can advise them and alert them to any potential risks. Once the adoptive parent(s) and the potential birth parent(s) choose to pursue an adoption plan, the potential birth parent(s) should be represented by ***independent legal counsel***. The adoptive parent(s) are usually responsible to pay for the birth parent(s)' legal expenses. The birth parent(s)' attorney can counsel them regarding the legal aspects of the process to insure that their decision to place their child for adoption is knowing and voluntary. The attorney will also explore whether there are any legal impediments to the adoption plan. At that point, the adoptive parent(s)' attorney should undertake to obtain all available ***pre-natal records*** as well as a social/medical history from the potential birth parent(s). The adoptive parent(s)' attorney and the birth parent(s)' attorney should communicate directly to review all aspects of the adoption plan with the goal of insuring that the plan is legally secure and meets the needs of the child and of the adoptive and birth parents.

Once the adoptive parent(s) and the expectant parent(s) have made an ***emotional commitment*** to one another, the attorneys jump into full gear to insure that all ***legal requirements*** are fulfilled. Since adoption expenses are highly regulated by the court, adoptive parent(s) should never give anything of value to the expectant parent without first speaking to their attorney to insure the payment is legally permissible. As harsh or unfair as it sounds, any money paid to an expectant parent is completely "at risk" since an expectant parent would never be legally compelled to reimburse the adoptive parent(s)' funds paid to her, or on her behalf, during the pregnancy.

After the baby is born, the expectant parent(s)' attorney will meet with them – typically at the hospital – to determine whether they still wish to proceed with the adoption. If so, the placing parent(s) will execute the legal consent documents. If the birth parent(s) sign ***New York consent*** documents, s/he has the ability to revoke that consent for a period of time after signing unless the consent was signed before the court. Despite the applicable revocation period, the adoptive parent(s) take the child home once the consent has been signed unless the child is born or resides outside of New York State. In that circumstance, the ***Interstate Compact on the Placement of Children*** ("ICPC") requires that the adoptive parent(s) stay in the state where the child was born or resides until the ICPC offices in New York and in the child's state determine that the paperwork fully complies with legal requirements.

Once the child is in the adoptive home, the adoptive parent(s) file a petition with the court requesting that the court issue an order declaring them the legal parents of the child. The court will meticulously scrutinize all legal documents to insure compliance with state law. The court will also review a "***post placement home study report***" describing the child's adjustment in the adoptive home. If the adoptive parent(s) and child are adjusting well, and the paperwork is in order, the court will issue an Order terminating the rights of the child's biological parents and declaring the adoptive parent(s) the legal parents of the child. The court will then notify the vital records office in the state where the child was born of the adoption and direct that they issue a ***new birth certificate*** naming the adoptive parent(s) the legal parents of the child and giving the child the name selected by the adoptive parent(s).

Private Agency Adoption

Private agency adoption involves an agency that has been ***authorized by the state*** to act as an intermediary between adoptive parents seeking a child and expectant parents who are considering adoption as a plan for their child. New York State residents can only work with agencies authorized by the State of New York regardless of whether the agency is licensed by the state where the agency is located. Private agencies engage in outreach and education programs to assist both adoptive and birth parents. Typically, the agency has ***waiting adoptive parents*** who have been screened and approved by the agency that can be matched with birth parents seeking adoptive parents for their child. As with private placement adoption, identifying information can be shared or kept confidential as desired by the parties. Private agency adoption is attractive because the agency does the "work" of matching adoptive and birth parents and because the agency is a built in "support system" for all of the parties. Since agencies ***charge a fee for these services***, which is higher than the fee typically charged by an attorney in a private placement adoption, some adoptive parents choose the private placement route in an effort to reduce costs.

When selecting a New York State authorized agency, adoptive parents need to understand the agency's fee structure. Private adoption agencies vary widely in terms of their total fee, the structure of the payments, the services included in the agency fee, and their adoptive parent qualification requirements. For example, some agencies may discourage or even decline to work with adoptive parents based on their ***age, marital status, or sexual orientation***. The agency's specific policies may also impact such things as: the amount of information you receive prior to the placement, whether you can meet the birth parent(s) prior to making a financial commitment, and your ability to make a choice on the issue of post placement contact. Every person is entitled to feel respected and emotionally supported by the agency throughout the adoption process. Every person interested in a private agency adoption should speak to a number of different agencies, and ask for references, prior to signing on with the agency.

Just as the court determines the adoptive parent(s)' qualification to adopt in a private placement adoption, the agency determines the adoptive parent(s)' ***qualification in an agency adoption***. This involves the preparation of a home study report, obtaining criminal and child abuse clearance, and obtaining documentation to insure that the adoptive parents are medically and financially capable of parenting a child. The agency should also provide the adoptive parents with education regarding the emotional aspects of the adoption process.

Once the adoptive parent(s) have been approved by the agency, the agency will work to match them with a parent(s) making an adoption plan for their child. The agency should make an effort to obtain a ***medical/social history*** from the biological parents of the adoptive child. The agency will also attempt to obtain the child's pre-natal records. The agency caseworker should provide the biological parents with needed adoption related services, including counseling. Since the agency is charged with overseeing the adoption process, the agency caseworker will meet with the expectant mother to determine her financial needs during her pregnancy. In most agencies, those expenses are ***passed on to the adoptive parents***, although the agency will disburse those expenses from the adoptive parent(s)' escrow account maintained by the agency. Any monies paid to the birth mother during her pregnancy are "at risk" since the birth mother would never be compelled to reimburse the adoptive parents those expenses in the event she decides not to place her child for adoption.

Once the child is born, the ***agency representative will meet the birth parent(s)*** – typically at the hospital – to reconfirm the parent(s)' intention to place the child for adoption. If the birth parent wishes to proceed with the adoption, s/he will sign a surrender document transferring his or her parental rights to the agency. While the agency is the legal guardian of the child, the agency transfers physical custody to the adoptive parent(s). The birth parent has a period of time, after signing the surrender, when s/he can revoke the surrender and seek the return of the child. Where the child is born in a state different from the adoptive parent(s)', the adoptive parent(s) are not permitted to bring the child home until they receive permission from the ***Interstate Compact on the Placement of Children***.

After the adoptive child goes home with the adoptive parent(s), the agency supervises the placement for a period long enough for the agency to determine whether finalizing the adoption is in the best interest of the child. Once the agency makes that decision, which is typically between ***three (3) to six (6) months*** after the placement, the agency will notify the adoptive parent(s) that they are prepared to consent to the adoption. At this point the adoptive parent(s) retain an attorney for the purpose of petitioning the court to approve the adoption, terminate the birth parents' parental rights and declare the adoptive parent(s) to be the legal parents of the child. As in any adoption, the court will scrutinize the legal documents to insure compliance with state adoption requirements. After the ***Order of Adoption*** is signed by the Judge, the state where the baby is born will amend the birth certificate to name the adoptive parent(s) as "parents" and to give the child the name selected by the adoptive parent(s).

Public Agency Adoptions

A public agency adoption involves a child whose ***guardianship*** has been committed by a Family Court to the care of a local commissioner of social services. While a biological parent can voluntarily surrender his or her parental rights to a social service agency, most children are in foster care because they have been ***involuntarily removed from their parents*** based on an allegation of abuse or neglect. While some children may be returned to their parents, after their parents demonstrate their ability to care for them, it is often the case that the parents' parental rights are involuntarily terminated by the court. Once the birth parents' rights are terminated, the child is legally "***freed for adoption***." Unfortunately many children who have been freed for adoption remain in temporary foster homes while they are waiting to be adopted by their "forever family." Many people choose to pursue a public agency adoption out of a sense of public service and the desire to provide love and support to an older child who would otherwise not have a family. For others, a public agency adoption is attractive because there is virtually no cost to the adoptive parents and the parents may even be eligible to receive an adoption subsidy if the child is considered to have "special needs" or is deemed "hard to place."

Others do not feel that a public agency adoption is the right choice for them either because they are hoping to adopt a newborn or because they do not feel prepared to adopt an older child who may have special needs.

A public agency adoption can be initiated through your County ***Department of Social Services***. Before being accepted as an adoptive parent, there is a need to participate in parenting training classes and to complete a detailed home study report. The adoptive training is designed to help adoptive parents: (1) understand adoption, (2) know their strengths, (3) decide if they are ready to adopt, (4) provide skills and knowledge needed for adoption and (5) understand the kind of child that would best fit their parenting style.

While there are occasions where adoptive parents may take custody of a child who has not yet been freed for adoption, adoptive parents should only do so with the understanding that the child may be returned to his or her biological parent by the court. Where the child has already been freed for adoption, the adoptive parents can take custody secure in the knowledge that they will be able to adopt unless they are deemed unsuitable by the court.

As mentioned above, adoptive parents are ***not required to pay any fees*** in connection with a public agency adoption and they may be eligible to receive an adoption subsidy. Many children are also entitled to ongoing medical or mental health services provided at no cost to the family.

International Adoption, Re-Adoption and Registration of Foreign Adoptions

International adoption is the legal process through which a citizen or habitual resident of one country adopts a child from a different country utilizing the legal system of the country where the child resides. Since April of 2008, when the United States implemented the ***Hague Adoption Convention***, all adoptions between habitual residents of the United States and residents of another country which has signed the convention, must comply with Hague adoption requirements. The list of countries which have signed the convention may be found online at http://adoption.state.gov/hague_convention/countries.php. In fact, the United States State Department website contains a wealth of information on the international adoption process.

In any international adoption, adoptive parents must satisfy the requirements of the country of the adoptive child's origin as well as the requirements of the ***United States Citizenship and Immigration Services*** ("USCIS"). Countries vary significantly with regard to the age of children waiting to be adopted and the quality of the medical care provided to those children. There is also considerable variation among countries with respect to the required characteristics of adoptive parents as they relate to the adoptive parents' age, marital status, and health history.

For most people, the first step in the international adoption process is the selection of an international adoption agency. If the country you will be adopting from has signed the Hague Adoption Convention, you are only permitted to work with a Hague accredited adoption agency.

The benefit of the international adoption process is that the child is already freed for adoption and there is no risk that the birth parents will seek to reclaim custody of the child. Many adoptive parents also find it emotionally rewarding to know that they'll be providing a home to a child who would otherwise be living in very difficult circumstances. The challenge today is that many countries have closed their adoption programs with the United States. The United States State Department has also discontinued the adoption of children from some countries due to concerns regarding the integrity of the adoption process. Adoptive parents seeking to adopt internationally are required to jump through quite a number of hoops that can make the process time consuming and costly. Finally, because most countries require the adoptive parents to spend time with the child prior to the approval of the adoption, the adoptive parents must be prepared to spend some time in the child's country of origin prior to bringing their child home.

Re-Adoption

Re-Adoption is the legal process whereby a state court in the United States, with jurisdiction over adoption matters, enters an ***Order of Adoption*** in favor of adoptive parents who previously adopted their child in a jurisdiction outside of the United States.

If the adoptive child entered the United States on an ***IR-4 or IH-4 Visa***, the child will not be eligible for automatic United States citizenship unless the adoptive parent(s) obtain an Order of Re-adoption before the child's 18th birthday. Once the child is re-adopted, the parent can obtain a State issued Certificate of Birth Data. The adoptive parents may also change the child's name as part of the re-adoption process.

Although adoptive parents are not legally required to re-adopt an internationally adopted child who entered the United States on an ***IR-3 visa***, they may wish to obtain an Order from their state court which recognizes the foreign judgment. The simple process of registering the foreign adoption will enable you to obtain a Judgment of Adoption from your state's court which must be accepted by all other courts in the United States. This may be helpful to those families adopting from non-Hague countries where it may be more difficult to obtain a replacement Judgment and also ensures that the adoption will be legally recognized throughout the United States. The child's name may also be changed as part of the registration of foreign adoption process.

Step Parent Adoption

When the legal or biological parent of a child marries or re-marries, the parent's spouse may adopt his or her child without terminating the rights of the consenting spouse. A step parent adoption may be accomplished where the child's other biological parent, (who is not petitioning for the adoption) either ***consents to the adoption*** or where the court concludes that the other biological parent has no legally recognized parental relationship with the child.

Step parent adoptions are also recommended in situations where a child, conceived through donor insemination, is born to a lesbian couple even if the spouse is already named as parent on the child's birth certificate. While the non-gestating mother is unlikely to be a genetic parent of the child, New York will name her as a parent on the child's birth certificate based on a gender neutral application of the marital presumption. Despite being on the birth certificate, the non-gestating mother should obtain an Order of Adoption through a step parent adoption in order to protect the non-genetic mother's legal relationship to the child in the event her parentage is challenged either in the context of a divorce or in a state which does not apply the marital presumption in a gender neutral fashion.

Unfortunately, even in the case of a step parent, the adoptive parent must fulfill almost all of the legal requirements imposed on families adopting a child from a stranger. In short, ***a home study report, child abuse and criminal clearances, and medical***

affidavits and letters of reference must still be submitted to the court in a step parent adoption.

Second Parent Adoption

A ***Second Parent Adoption*** is a legal procedure which allows someone to adopt the child of his or her "intimate partner" (who is not their spouse) without terminating the rights of the consenting parent. A second parent adoption may be necessary because one partner is the biological parent of the child, one partner previously adopted the child, or one partner was previously declared to be a legal parent pursuant to a surrogacy agreement. For whatever reason, second parent adoptions secure the parental relationship of each parent to the child. For the most part, second parent adoptions proceed in the same manner as a step parent adoption. The distinction is that the adoptive parent is not married to the legal parent.

Denise E. Seidelman, Esq.

Denise Seidelman is a partner in Rumbold & Seidelman, LLP, a firm devoted exclusively to adoption and reproductive law since 1996. Denise's practice includes the full gamut of adoption services ranging from private placement and agency adoptions to step and second parent adoptions. She also provides legal counsel to those building their families through egg, sperm, and embryo donation as well as those needing the assistance of a gestational surrogate. She is actively involved in the legislative effort to reform New York law so that those building their families with the assistance of reproductive technology will be recognized under New York law. Denise is licensed to practice law in New York and New Jersey. She is on the Board of Path2Parenthood, a Fellow of the American Academy of Adoption Attorneys, the American Academy of Assisted Reproductive

Technology Attorneys, and a member of the National LGBT Bar Association Family Law Institute. Denise has lectured frequently on the legal aspects of the adoption process and on reproductive law before the New York State and New York City Bar Associations as well as before the New York Judicial Institute. Denise is a graduate of the University of Pennsylvania and the Washington College of Law. She was admitted to practice in New York in 1980 and in New Jersey in 2006. She began her legal career as a trial attorney for the Criminal Defense Division of the New York City Legal Aid Society. For more information visit www.adoptionlawny.com.

Nina E. Rumbold, Esq.

Nina E. Rumbold, Esq., is a Partner in the firm of Rumbold & Seidelman, LLP, practicing exclusively in the areas of adoption and reproductive law. Ms. Rumbold is a fellow of the American Academy of Adoption Attorneys, the American Academy of Assisted Reproductive Technology Attorneys and a member of the National LGBT Bar Association Family Law Institute. She received her Juris Doctor degree from New York University Law School and is admitted to practice in New York and New Jersey. Ms. Rumbold has lectured on Adoption Law and Reproductive Law as a member of the faculties of the ABA Family Law Section, Practicing Law Institute, the New York Judicial Institute, and the New York City Bar Center for Continuing Legal Education. She is the past President of New York Attorneys for Adoption and Family Formation (NYAAFF), an organization of New York attorneys that advocates for legislative reform in the areas of adoption and reproductive law. She is also a regular speaker at the Adoptive Parents Committee annual conference. For more information, visit www.adoptionlawny.com.

SECTION B: COURT ISSUES

CHAPTER 17

FORENSIC EVALUATIONS

By Veronica Escobar, Esq.

When parents come to court and file petitions regarding a conflict in matters of custody or visitation (i.e. "parenting time"), it is already evident that they have interpersonal issues, which have made it difficult, if not impossible, for them to come to a decision or compromise regarding the rearing of their child(ren). This chapter discusses the use and applicability of forensic evaluators in child custody and parenting time disputes.

When Forensic Evaluations are Utilized

Once parents have commenced the litigation process, they oftentimes realize a few things – among them are:

1) The court process ***runs your life***, not the other way around;
2) Litigation can take ***a long time*** to resolve;
3) The court process can be ***very unpleasant***; and
4) The parents are better off being adults and ***reaching a compromise***.

With the assistance and counsel of their attorneys, parties can and do often reach an amicable resolution – always with the best interest of the child(ren) at the forefront.

Unfortunately, there are instances wherein the court confronts a matter where one or both parents have engaged in behavior or exhibit certain patterns that raise concerns or "***red flags***" regarding his or her fitness as a parent. Among these "red flags" may be the following, including but not limited to:

- substance abuse,
- alcoholism,
- history of mental illness,

- perpetration of domestic violence,
- parental neglect and/or abandonment,
- parental interference and parental alienation (for more information on these issues see Chapter 21).

Also, at times, one or more of the children could present with behavior that is concerning to the court and raises questions of ***parental fitness*** and whether a change in custody is warranted.

Requesting a Forensic Evaluation

> An OTSC is a considered more of an "emergency motion" in New York. The OTSC has a faster return date to court; a Notice of Motion requires a return a date at least 14 days prior to it being filed in the Court.

It is in these circumstances that a forensic evaluation ***may be requested***. Depending on the judge or referee, a verbal application may be made. More commonly, the request for the evaluation is made via a written motion, an ***Order to Show Cause*** ("OTSC") or ***Notice of Motion***.

The motion itself not only contains ***factual allegations*** regarding the need for a forensic evaluation but is also accompanied by supporting ***"case law"*** – past court decisions, usually from the Appellate Division or Court of Appeals (the highest court in New York State) that support the arguments being made in favor of the forensic evaluation.

Opposing counsel, the attorney who did not request the forensic evaluation, should file a ***written response in opposition to the motion*** for a forensic evaluation – if they oppose the application. However, he or she may be in favor it, and may also file a cross-motion (i.e., his or her own written motion) for forensics with their specific supporting arguments and case law. The ***Attorney for the Child*** is also encouraged to file a written response regarding their position on the request for the forensic evaluation, if he or she was not the attorney who filed the original motion requesting it. When the motion "returns" to court, the judge will oftentimes issue a written decision, either approving or denying the request for the forensic evaluation and citing the reasons as well as any supporting case law.

Of note, the court itself may order a forensic evaluation without counsel formally requesting it if the parties' actions or behaviors are of such a concern that the court requires it as a part of making an ultimate determination.

What is a Forensic Evaluation?

Plainly put, it is a psychological evaluation conducted by a ***psychologist***. The terms "***psychologist, evaluator, forensic evaluator***" will be used interchangeably in this chapter. To break it down: the parents and child(ren) are interviewed separately in three separate sessions (normally) for a minimum of an hour each time. Furthermore, there are ***verbal and written psychological tests*** administered. The child(ren) are also observed with both parents in separate sessions.

In addition to the parents and child(ren), others can also be interviewed for the purpose of the evaluation as "***collateral sources***." These individuals include, but are not limited to other relatives, teachers, and therapeutic service providers. These interviews, however, are ***not extensive*** and are oftentimes conducted ***telephonically***, but they can be in person. The parents are also encouraged to provide ***relevant documentation***, another type of collateral source, including but not limited to:

- police reports,
- a child's report card or other educational materials, and
- medical or psychiatric records to the evaluator.

The evaluator determines the importance or "weight" they give these sources of information.

Based on the answers provided during the interviews, interpretation of the psychological data, clinical observations made, and review of documents, the forensic evaluator ***drafts a thorough report*** memorializing the above and offers his or her opinion on each parent's psychological state and any diagnoses, as well as that of the child(ren). Included in his or her opinion, the forensic evaluator could highlight current or potential problems, as well as recommendations for therapeutic intervention.

The most important piece of the evaluation, particularly for the attorneys involved, is the psychologist's ***recommendation regarding custody and parenting time***. They guide the attorney in discussions with his or her client, as well as in discussions with the other attorneys involved in the litigation. While the evaluation and its accompanying recommendations are not the controlling or decisive factor for the judge or referee presiding over the matter, the evaluation can be quite persuasive, particularly because no one else involved in the proceedings possesses the education and expertise of the psychologist.

How the Forensic Evaluation is Utilized

Review by Attorneys and the Parents

Once the court and the attorneys receive the evaluation, it is ***available for review*** by the parents. The attorney maintains a copy with his or her file and is prohibited from sharing it with others; the client is never allowed a personal copy. The reason for the latter is quite simple: a forensic evaluation is a "***court document***," authorized by a signed court order and therefore belongs in the court file. However, the document itself has not become a part of the "***court record***," in that it has ***not been entered into evidence*** and cannot be discussed on the record (in the presence of the referee or judge) or in any type of motion practice. A forensic evaluation becomes a part of the court record when it is entered into evidence at the ***trial stage***. The evaluation document is entered into evidence through the verbal testimony of the forensic psychologist at trial. The referee or judge will not read the document until after this occurs.

Trial

If the court matter cannot be resolved and must go to trial for ***a judicial determination***, then the forensic evaluator is typically the first witness called to testify. The court (i.e., referee or judge) may call the psychologist as the "court's witness." If the forensic evaluation is in favor of one parent over the other, the attorney for that parent will usually call the evaluator as his or her witness.

If the evaluation is in favor of one parent, then the attorney for that parent will ask questions during the direct examination that tend to highlight and support the evaluator's process and his or her observations and recommendations, and to highlight the relative unfitness of the other parent. If the evaluation was unfavorable to a parent, then his or her attorney will attempt to discredit the report itself and the evaluator during examination. The Attorney for the Child's questioning may either seek to support or affirm the evaluation – this ***depends on the position of the child client*** or if the child lacks decision-making capacity (under the age of seven or having certain developmental disabilities) the attorney substituting the child's judgment with his or her own.

Conclusion

Lastly, forensic evaluations should only be requested ***when warranted***. Amongst the family law and matrimonial bar, there has been a trend towards over-requesting forensic evaluations as a means to ***resolve conflict***. The courts do not look upon this favorably as these evaluations should be reserved for the most alarming and concerning of cases. Parents will inevitably disagree in some custody and visitation disputes and engage in ***immature and vengeful*** behavior. Sometimes, a parent may even lie to get his or her way, which is never right. These combative behaviors alone are not necessarily worthy of a forensic evaluation.

Forensic evaluations are ***time-consuming*** and can extend the time a court matter remains active from one to two years, which prolongs the parties' time in court. The evaluations are also ***quite expensive***. These evaluations are either paid for by the parents, or by the taxpayers if the parents are indigent (i.e., low income). If necessary, a trial will determine who the fitter custodial parent is.

Ultimately, a forensic evaluation can be an invaluable tool in matters where the ***child's emotional, psychological and physical safety*** may be compromised. It is a guide for attorneys in providing informed counsel to their clients and provides the bench with additional information to make a thoughtful and reasoned decision that places the child's best interest at the forefront.

Veronica Escobar, Esq.

Veronica Escobar is the Principal and Founder of The Law Offices of Veronica Escobar, a practice focusing exclusively in the areas of Elder Law, Special Needs Planning and Trusts and Estates, as well as Family Law. Prior to forming her own law practice, Veronica worked as an attorney representing the City of New York, Administration for Children's Services (ACS) in child abuse and neglect matters (commonly referred to as an "Article 10") ranging from educational neglect to serious forms of abuse.

Veronica is admitted to practice in the State of New York. She is also admitted to practice before the U.S. District Courts for the Eastern and Southern

Districts of New York and the United States Supreme Court. She graduated summa cum laude from Fordham College at Rose Hill, Fordham University, where she was also elected to Phi Beta Kappa, with a degree in American Studies and a minor in Latin American/Latino Studies. She also received her law degree from Fordham, where she was a Notes and Articles Editor of the Fordham International Law Journal.

Currently, she is the Co-Chair of the Diversity Committee of the Elder Law and Special Needs Section of the New York State Bar, a member of the Elder Law and Special Needs and Trusts and Estates Sections of the New York State Bar Association, and is a Deputy Regional President for the Hispanic National Bar Association (HNBA) New York Region. She is an adjunct member of the Legal Problems of the Aging Committee and a past member of The Family Court and Family Law Committee at the New York City Bar.

She is also an avid reader of everything, a music lover, concertgoer, museum fan, and burgeoning world traveler, as well as an information sponge.

To learn more about Veronica, you can connect to her website www.veronicaescobarlaw.com, or on Facebook at www.facebook.com/VeronicaEscobarLawNewYork.

SECTION B: COURT ISSUES

CHAPTER 18

ROLE OF THE ATTORNEY FOR THE CHILDREN

By Veronica Escobar, Esq.

In life, ***conflicts between parents*** will sometimes draw in their child(ren). It is never healthy or appropriate to involve a child in adult situations or issues; and this is definitely the case in a court proceeding. A courthouse is not a place for a child and the conflict should remain ***between the parents*** and within the confines of the building. It *should* but it oftentimes does not and since the child is at the center of the conflict, he or she should have legal representation to be his or her voice in the proceedings – without ever having to enter a courtroom or face a judge.

Applicability

> Attorney for the Child was previously referred to as a Law Guardian.

The ***Attorney for the Child*** was created to address the need for a child to have "meaningful" or "effective" representation in matters that directly affect their lives and relationship to their parents. The Attorney for the Child represents the child(ren) in exactly the same way they would represent an adult client, providing (among other things):

- effective counseling,
- advocacy,
- maintaining the attorney/client privilege,
- maintaining confidentiality,
- preserving the child(ren)'s privacy,

- filing written motions (when necessary),
- opposing motions (if appropriate),
- actively participating in hearings or trials, and
- entering settlement negotiations.

The Attorney for the Child

1. The Assigned Counsel Panel (The Office of Attorneys for Children)

The Attorney for the Child is often a member of an ***attorney panel***, which has been designated by the Appellate Division. There are four Appellate Divisions in the State of New York and each county has an attorney panel. The attorneys on this panel are in private practice and ***certified to represent children*** in child neglect and abuse, juvenile delinquency, termination of parental rights, custody and visitation, family offense and guardianship matters within the Family Court.

These same attorneys may also represent children in ***matrimonial matters*** in Supreme Court and both parents pay his or her retainer. A "***private pay***" Attorney for the Child is also available in Family Court from the aforementioned attorney panel, when both parents appear with retained counsel. In this instance, the presumption is that the parents can both bear the cost of paying Attorney for the Child's legal fees; this presumption may be rebutted with ***financial documentation***. In that case the attorney will be assigned to represent the child.

2. The Legal Aid Society and Institutional Providers

Attorneys who work with ***The Legal Aid Society*** ("LAS"), ***Juvenile Rights Practice*** ("JRP") are regularly assigned to represent children in child abuse and neglect and juvenile delinquency proceedings, ***unless LAS has represented*** the parent in an adult civil or criminal matter. In that instance, LAS is unable to accept assignment. If there is a subsequent custody/visitation, family offense or guardianship proceeding, the attorney from the JRP will represent the child in that matter as well. This also applies for other Attorneys for Children; to the extent possible their representation of the child will continue if the parents return to court in the future. There are also other non-profits, referred to as "Institutional Providers" in the State of New York that contract with the City of New York or State to represent children in these matters; these providers often differ by county.

The Attorney for the Child: The Attorney-Client Relationship

An Attorney for the Child represents any child, from ***newborn to the age of seventeen***. The Attorney for the Child can also represent a ***group of siblings***; in other words, the Attorney for the Child can have more than one child client. However, if the children's stated interests differ from one another and the attorney feels he or she cannot adequately represent them, that attorney may move the court (i.e., make a motion) to be relieved of representing one or more of the children and another attorney or attorneys is assigned to represent them in his/her stead. The original Attorney for the Child may continue to represent one of the children or can be relieved of representing all of them.

The Attorney for the Child must provide what practitioners call "***straight advocacy***" for a child ***seven years and older***. Straight advocacy means the attorney must represent the child's stated position and wishes, regardless if the attorney agrees with them or not. The attorney, as a counselor at law, has a duty to not only explain his or her role as an attorney to the child but how the decisions the child makes can affect his or her life now and into the future. The child, however, is the one who makes the decision and guides the attorney's representation.

Obviously, the type and content of the conversation had by the attorney with the child is directly correlated to the child's ***age, maturity and level of understanding***. In other words, you can have a more sophisticated conversation with a sixteen-year-old than you can a ten-year-old. However, the conversation and any necessary subsequent conversations must be had between the attorney and his or her client.

When the child is ***under the age of seven***, the Attorney for the Child may "substitute" the child's judgment with their own *if* they find that the child lacks "sufficient capacity," is not capable of making a "***reasoned decision***," and/or if the decision they are making places them at "substantial risk" of imminent serious harm.

If the Attorney for the Child believes that an older client's (i.e., a client over the age of seven) stated position places them at substantial risk of harm or if they suffer from diminished capacity, the attorney may deviate from the child's position – but only if ***absolutely necessary*** – and advocate a position as close to the child's position as possible while at the same time protecting them from imminent danger. The attorney-client relationship continues and the Attorney for the Child should continue to counsel the client.

The expectation is that the Attorney for the Child can effectively address the needs of his or her client and also assist in bridging the gap between the parents and his or her respective interests. A child has a voice and an effective Attorney for the Child ***can allow it to be heard.***

Veronica Escobar, Esq.

Veronica Escobar is the Principal and Founder of The Law Offices of Veronica Escobar, a practice focusing exclusively in the areas of Elder Law, Special Needs Planning and Trusts and Estates. Prior to forming her own law practice, Veronica worked as an attorney representing the City of New York, Administration for Children's Services (ACS) in child abuse and neglect matters (commonly referred to as an "Article 10") ranging from educational neglect to serious forms of abuse.

Veronica is admitted to practice in the State of New York. She is also admitted to practice before the U.S. District Courts for the Eastern and Southern Districts of New York and the United States Supreme Court. She graduated summa cum laude from Fordham College at Rose Hill, Fordham University, where she was also elected to Phi Beta Kappa, with a degree in American Studies and a minor in Latin American/Latino Studies. She also received her law degree from Fordham, where she was a Notes and Articles Editor of the Fordham International Law Journal.

Currently, she is the Co-Chair of the Diversity Committee of the Elder Law and Special Needs Section of the New York State Bar, a member of the Elder Law and Special Needs and Trusts and Estates Sections of the New York State Bar Association, and is a Deputy Regional President for the Hispanic National Bar Association (HNBA) New York Region. She is a past member of the Legal Problems of the Aging and the Family Court and Family Law Committees of the New York City Bar.

She is also an avid reader of everything, a music lover, concertgoer, museum fan, and burgeoning world traveler, as well as an information sponge.

To learn more about Veronica, you can connect to her website www.veronicaescobarlaw.com, on Twitter @EscobarLawNY or on Facebook at www.facebook.com/VeronicaEscobarLawNewYork.

SECTION C: SPECIAL CONSIDERATIONS

CHAPTER 19

EMANCIPATION

By Maxine S. Broderick, Esq.

For purposes of child support, one parent is designated the "custodial" parent and the other the "non-custodial" parent. This is so even when the parties have joint custody of the child. The "custodial parent," as explained in Chapter 10, is typically the parent with whom the child resides a ***greater portion of time***. For child support, the non-custodial parent is required to pay child support (and "add-ons") to the custodial parent until the child is ***emancipated***. More information on child support is in Chapter 11.

> As noted in Chapter 11, child support "add-ons" include health insurance, unreimbursed medical expenses, reasonable child care expenses, and reasonable educational expenses. Payment for extra-curricular activities may be required at the court's discretion.

New York Law on Emancipation

In New York children are considered minors, for child support purposes, until the age of 21. In addition to the age ceiling, there are other circumstances in which a child is deemed "emancipated." Emancipation means that the child is considered to be independent in many respects, and thus the non-custodial parent is no longer required by law to provide child support. This Chapter discusses the "events" that trigger emancipation.

It is essential to understand that emancipation is not automatic in New York. The parent seeking relief from a child support obligation must first seek the court's permission. Here are a few events that trigger emancipation under New York law:

Full-Time Employment

> It is important to note that a child can **become emancipated for a period of time** and subsequently **become un-emancipated again**. For example, a child may enlist in the military at age 18 and be discharged at age 20 and move back in with the custodial parent. As a result, the non-custodial parent's financial obligation would resume until the child reaches 21.

A child becomes emancipated when he or she undertakes full-time, permanent employment. Often high school and college students maintain full-time jobs during summer break to pay for incidentals. Although employment is full-time, it is considered to be temporary for the purposes of providing child support. Full-time employment that implicates emancipation occurs when a child over the age of 16 works 30 or more hours a week, and pays for most of his/her own expenses, even if living with a parent.

Marriage

When a child marries they are no longer the financial responsibility of either parent. Generally speaking, spouses are responsible for each other's basic needs and financial well-being and basic needs. Therefore, when a child marries, the non-custodial parent is relieved of paying child support. Another consideration is that married people typically establish residences away from their parents, and this too triggers emancipation.

Establishes Own Residence

As stated above, once a child moves out of the parental home and establishes his or her own, permanent residence away from home, they become emancipated. It is important to note that living in a college dormitory or going to summer camp, or any other temporary change in housing does not qualify. In the event that a child returns to live with either parent before age 21, unemancipation can be revived, and child support payment may resume.

Military Service

When a child enlists in the military, they are effectively emancipated. Similar to what occurs when a child marries, the shift in financial responsibility moves from the parents to the government or agency enlisting the child. The military is financially responsible for the basic needs of the child until he or she discharged. In the event that a child is discharged before the age of 21 and returns to the parental home, unemancipaton can be revived, and child support payment may resume.

Death

In the unfortunate event that a child passes away before the age of 21, the non-custodial parent is no longer responsible for providing child support. Keep in mind that the death of a child does not relieve the non-custodial parent from paying medical expenses up to the time of the child's untimely passing.

Emancipation by Agreement

Parents can re-define emancipation by written agreement. While parents may not remove their financial responsibility for a child under age 21, they can extend it. For instance, parents may decide that emancipation will occur when the child turns 23 years of age or finishes an undergraduate degree, whichever happens first. While parents may negotiate such agreements, the terms are always subject to approval by a court so the terms must be in the best interests of the child.

Final Thoughts

Above are the limited set of circumstances in which a non-custodial parent may be relieved of their obligation to pay child support; however, this relief is <u>never</u> automatic. A parent must receive permission from the court before suspending child support payments. If the parent engages in "self-help," and stops paying child support without an order terminating support, that parent will accrue child support arrears and is subject to punitive measures from a driver's license or passport being revoked up to incarceration. Please also note that in some cases, due to the child's health or medical condition, the court may determine that emancipation is delayed. Additionally, if an emancipation event has occurred, a child can be ***re-emancipated*** provided there is another significant change in circumstances.

As you can see, the law with emancipation is not clear-cut. Both payors and payees should discuss these various trigger events with their family lawyer to better understand the financial obligations of child support.

Maxine S. Broderick, Esq.

A lifelong resident of Long Island, New York, Ms. Broderick concentrates her practice on matrimonial and family law. She is experienced in handling uncontested and contested divorces, legal separation, child support, child custody, visitation, spousal support, orders of protection and modification of Family Court orders.

Committed to community service, Ms. Broderick has provided pro bono legal assistance to low income New Yorkers with respect to personal bankruptcy, uncontested and contested divorces, consumer debt, foreclosure prevention and housing disputes.

Ms. Broderick was named an "Access to Justice Champion" by the Nassau County Bar Association for pro bono service in 2013, was the recipient of an Outstanding Service certificate from the Nassau County Coalition Against Domestic Violence (NCCADV) in 2012, and was recognized by the New York State Courts Access to Justice Program for outstanding work and dedicated service in the uncontested divorce Volunteer Lawyers Program in 2010.

She is a member of the New York State Bar Association, the Association of Black Women Attorneys (ABWA), the Nassau County Bar Association, the Nassau County Women's Bar Association, the Hempstead Branch of the NAACP and is President-elect of the Amistad Long Island Black Bar Association.

Ms. Broderick is a proud graduate of Sacred Heart Academy in Hempstead, New York, earned a bachelor degree from Fordham University and a juris doctor from Brooklyn Law School in 2003.

She is admitted to practice law in New York State, The United States District Court, Eastern District of New York (EDNY), The United States District Court, Southern District of New York (SDNY), and was admitted to The U.S. Supreme Court in 2014. For more information about Ms. Broderick's practice, visit www.brodericklawny.com.

SECTION C: SPECIAL CONSIDERATIONS

CHAPTER 20

RELOCATION

By Veronica Escobar, Esq.

Moving – all of us have done it at least once in our lives. We move alone, or as part of a family unit. We move away to pursue an education, a new job, to be closer to family, for our health and sometimes, for love. It can be stressful, exciting, and maybe just a tad frightening and overwhelming. Eventually, we settle in, adjust, and make our new surroundings home.

Separation and divorce split a once intact family unit; however, the family ties remain and this connection can never be broken. But forming part of this type of a family brings challenges, many of which have already been spoken about in other parts of this book. One of them is the subject of ***physical relocation*** of the custodial parent with the child(ren).

Petition for Relocation

The custodial parent is either the person who has ***de facto physical custody*** of the child, without any court order, or the parent who has physical custody pursuant to a court order and perhaps was also awarded sole legal custody of the child(ren).

If the parent has de facto custody of the child(ren), then he or she will need to file petitions for legal and physical custody and relocation contemporaneously. If the non-custodial parent objects to the de facto custodial parent's petition for custody, this will add a potential wrinkle to the petition to relocate. However, this wrinkle will be addressed here.

If the parent has legal and physical custody of the child(ren) pursuant to a court order and if the issue of relocation was not addressed in the Stipulation of Settlement, he or she will need to file a

petition for relocation. Having custody pursuant to a court order does not mean the court will approve a request to relocate.

Stipulations of Settlement may address relocation in one of two ways:

- It can fix the ***geographic limits*** of a custodial parent's potential future move, known among practitioners as the "***radius clause***" (e.g. they cannot move more than 50 miles from New York City; they cannot move outside of New York State); or
- It can direct that the custodial parent ***obtain the express written permission*** of the non-custodial parent to relocate and if this is not obtained, a directive to file a petition for relocation.

The latter scenario is more common.

Why Do Custodial Parents Wish to Relocate?

For the same reasons other people do, but these reasons alone will not always be sufficient for a court to permit a move of the child(ren). Why? Because the child(ren) have another parent whose relationship with them will be directly impacted by a move. And that is pretty compelling.

After the Filing of the Petition

Once a relocation petition has been filed in court, one of two things can happen:

- The parents reach a settlement that will permit the petitioning parent to move with the child(ren) but also allow the non custodial parent to maintain a relationship with the children; or
- The petition will go trial.

Settlement

A settlement will depend on a few factors and the following is not an exhaustive list but they are the most common: 1) the distance (miles) from the original home state to the relocation state; 2) the non-custodial parent's lifestyle, including his or her job schedule; 3) the non-custodial parent's financial situation; 4) the age(s) of the child(ren) and; 5) the child(ren)'s academic/school calendar.

Typically, the parent allowed to relocate ***will bear the cost of transporting the child(ren)*** to spend parenting time with the other parent since he/she petitioned for the move, although the parents will sometimes agree to split the travel fees.

Depending on the above factors, which again are not exhaustive, it is quite common for the non custodial parent to be given ample parenting time with the child(ren), and this includes some or all of the school year recesses (breaks) as well as half of or the entire summer recess. The latter depends on the distance between the non-custodial parent and the child(ren) as there may be even more frequent parenting time if the distance is not as great. The custodial parent should acknowledge the ***impact of the move on the left behind parent*** and, in a way, compensate him or her with a fair or equitable amount of parenting time, if this is something the non-custodial parent's lifestyle and resources can accommodate.

Trial

If there is no meeting of the minds and the parents are trial bound, then the "best interests of the child" standard now plays the most important role in determining whether the court will permit the petitioning parent to move with the child(ren).

Best Interest of the Child

The "best interests" standard has been discussed elsewhere in this book, and is what practitioners refer to as a "catch all" phrase in that there is no exhaustive list of factors regarding "best interests of the child." The court will look at the "***totality of the circumstances***" – the whole picture – in order to make a determination. It really depends on the particular family; however, there are prevalent factors that are usually taken into consideration:

1) Economic opportunities for the petitioning parent;
2) Financial necessity of the petitioning parent;
3) Remarriage;
4) Health of the parent or child;
5) Educational needs of the parent or child;
6) The non-custodial parent's level of involvement in the child(ren)'s lives; and
7) The child(ren)'s preference.

In the end, the child's best interests, and not necessarily each parent's, are paramount.

The Factors

1. Economic opportunities

The custodial parent may have an opportunity for professional advancement or higher wages in another state that would confer ***financial and quality of life benefits*** to the child(ren). The circumstances surrounding this opportunity will be examined, and this could also include family and emotional support. Again, economic opportunities are not decisive and it is weighed against other factors. Different courts have taken similar circumstances and ruled differently.

2. Financial Necessity

The custodial parent may be struggling to financially maintain him or herself in this state and could possibly have employment opportunities outside of New York City or New York State that would allow him or her to pursue his/her economic betterment. The court will likely look at whether the custodial parent made a ***"serious" effort*** to secure better employment opportunities within New York City or State. In cases where the court has held that the parent did not make a serious effort to secure employment within New York State, the relocation has been denied.

For example, accepting employment in California not because he or she was unable to find employment in New York but because he or she wanted to live in California is not a sufficient basis for relocation. Again, the court will look at other factors, including but not limited to, the financial circumstances during the marriage or partnership with the non-custodial parent, available family support, and in cases where there is solely economic betterment, whether the non-acceptance of new employment could jeopardize the current employment and whether the latter is sufficient to meet their financial needs. However, ***true economic necessity*** is a persuasive factor.

3. Remarriage

It is possible that the petitioning parent's ***subsequent marriage*** or remarriage may affect their ability to remain in the state, in that the spouse may have economic or professional opportunities offered to him or her that will improve the family's quality of life – and this extends to the child(ren). However, this factor must be examined along with all other factors and circumstances and is case specific.

4. **Health or educational needs of the parent or child**

If the health of the parent or child is at issue, the court is more likely to be ***sympathetic***; however, educational needs present more of a challenge as a justification for relocation.

5. **The non-custodial parent's level of involvement in the child(ren)'s life**

If the non-custodial parent has been afforded generous parenting time and has utilized it and been an active participant in the child's formation, the court will consider this as a factor against relocation. The opposite is also true; if a non-custodial parent has been a marginal figure in the child's life, by choice, this would be a factor in favor of relocation. If a non-custodial parent has ***exhibited inappropriate conduct*** (and this is determined on a case by case basis) this would also be a factor in favor of approving relocation.

6. **The child(ren)'s preference**

The court will consider a child's preference but it is hardly ever a determinative factor and is likely to be scrutinized and examined alongside other factors.

Radius Clauses

Radius clauses were previously mentioned as part of a Stipulation of Settlement; however these clauses can also be upheld or modified at trial. Even if the parents had previously agreed to certain terms or restrictions within the "radius clause," a court may or may not give it weight during a subsequent trial to request relocation. Also, the absence of a "radius clause" in a Stipulation of Settlement should not be construed to mean that a custodial parent could relocate without permission, that a non-custodial parent would not object to a subsequent relocation, or that the court would approve or deny it.

If the Relocation Request is Granted

If the request is granted, the court will fashion a parenting time schedule that will compensate the non custodial parent for the loss of access they will incur as a result of the child(ren)'s move. And as mentioned previously, the court may direct that the custodial parent bear the cost of travel expenses for the child(ren).

Moving is not a decision that should be taken lightly. Just as in life, every decision made should be done with thoughtfulness and maturity – and these principles are equally applicable here. The bond between parent and child is arguably the strongest bond that human beings can form. Care should be taken to preserve that bond, even if there is a physical distance that separates a child from his or her parent.

Veronica Escobar, Esq.

Veronica Escobar is the Principal and Founder of The Law Offices of Veronica Escobar, a practice focusing exclusively in the areas of Elder Law, Special Needs Planning and Trusts and Estates. Prior to forming her own law practice, Veronica worked as an attorney representing the City of New York, Administration for Children's Services (ACS) in child abuse and neglect matters (commonly referred to as an "Article 10") ranging from educational neglect to serious forms of abuse.

Veronica is admitted to practice in the State of New York. She is also admitted to practice before the U.S. District Courts for the Eastern and Southern Districts of New York and the United States Supreme Court. She graduated summa cum laude from Fordham College at Rose Hill, Fordham University, where she was also elected to Phi Beta Kappa, with a degree in American Studies and a minor in Latin American/Latino Studies. She also received her law degree from Fordham, where she was a Notes and Articles Editor of the Fordham International Law Journal.

Currently, she is the Co-Chair of the Diversity Committee of the Elder Law and Special Needs Section of the New York State Bar, a member of the Elder Law and Special Needs and Trusts and Estates Sections of the New York State Bar Association, and is a Deputy Regional President for the Hispanic National Bar Association (HNBA) New York Region. She is a past member of the Legal Problems of the Aging and the Family Court and Family Law Committees of the New York City Bar.

She is also an avid reader of everything, a music lover, concertgoer, museum fan, and burgeoning world traveler, as well as an information sponge.

SECTION C: SPECIAL CONSIDERATIONS

CHAPTER 21

PARENTAL INTERFERENCE AND PARENTAL ALIENATION

By Veronica Escobar, Esq.

As the Neil Sedaka song says, "Breaking up is hard to do." And it is even more difficult when people have children together, because even if the romantic or marital relationship comes to an end, their role as parents will last for a lifetime. Here is where parents can make a choice: put their children's needs ahead of their own and assume the co-parent role or be selfish and set up his or her children for heartbreak and failure.

Interpersonal relationships are never black and white because ***human beings are complex***. People oftentimes make their lives more complicated than it needs to be, especially when they hold on to hurt, anger, resentment, misunderstandings and unpleasant memories against an ex romantic partner or spouse. And sometimes, we go out of our way to hurt one another – and that is never the answer.

Children are the product of two people – their parents, with whom they share DNA, physical characteristics as well as personality traits. Children must learn to love themselves. If, a parent goes out of his or her way to hurt the child's other parent, to exclude the parent from the child's life, or worse, turn that child against the other parent to the point that the child excludes him or her from their life, then that parent is destroying the child.

There are two concepts that family law practitioners confront in some of their cases and they are ***parental interference*** and ***parental alienation***. The public tends to conflate the two, however they are distinct from one another – but parental interference if gone unchecked by the non-custodial parent, not brought to the court's attention, and without therapeutic intervention, can overtime lead to parental alienation. At that point, unfortunately, it may be too late to repair the child-parent relationship.

Parental Interference

Broadly speaking, parental interference is when one parent, typically the custodial parent (either de facto or pursuant to a court order), takes steps to interfere in the relationship between the child and non-custodial parent. The types of behaviors can range from (and this is not an exhaustive list):

1) preventing parental access to the child(ren);
2) not making the child(ren) available for parenting time;
3) "forgetting" about scheduled parenting time;
4) scheduling activities for the child(ren) during the other parent's time;
5) scheduling vacations with the child without informing the other parent and that interfere with his parenting time
6) not making the child available for telephonic contact;
7) interrupting telephonic contact by terminating the phone call or distracting the child while he or she is on the phone;
8) not informing or consulting with the non-custodial parent on medical or educational issues;
9) not notifying the other parent regarding emergencies involving the child(ren); and
10) making disparaging comments about the other parent to the child or in the child's presence and allowing the child to be present when others make disparaging comments.

How can one remedy parental interference? By bringing court action, either a ***petition for visitation*** (if there is no formal court order in existence) or if there is an existing court order outline parenting time, a Petition for a Violation of an Order of Visitation. If the parental interference is ongoing, while the matter is in litigation, the attorney for the offended parent may bring a Petition for Violation of an Order on behalf of the client. If the client is self-represented (*pro se*), he or she may file the same Violation Petition.

The parent accused of parental interference may either admit the violation(s) or if he or she denies it, then the petition is set down for a hearing. If the court determines there is a violation of the parenting time order, they can modify the order by allowing the non-custodial parent more parenting time (thus reducing the custodial parent's time) or providing "make up" parenting time. The remedies depend on the particular circumstances and allegations.

Now, if the parental interference is pervasive and serious, it may compel the non-custodial parent to file for a ***modification of the current custody order***. A tell-tale sign is when these behaviors begin to affect the child personally, emotionally, academically and in their relationship with the other parent. Elsewhere in this book, the standard to modify custody was discussed; depending on the allegations and circumstances, instances of parental interference may lead to a transfer of custody because a custodial parent's inability to respect the other parent can and does raise serious concerns about their fitness as a custodial parent.

Parental Alienation Syndrome

Parental alienation, sometimes referred to as "Parental Alienation Syndrome," often starts out with elements of parental interference, but over time becomes much more insidious; it is the process wherein the custodial parent grooms the child to "turn" against the other parent and thus alienating the child from that parent. The process takes time, but the results are devastating to the non-custodial parent and the child's long-term psychological, physical and emotional well-being. Oftentimes, it may take years to reverse the damage – if the relationship can ever be repaired.

This Chapter cannot begin to give parental alienation the in depth treatment it requires but will address some of the "red flags" that can assist in identifying it, hopefully, early on. The hallmark of parental alienation is the ***child's refusal to see or speak to the other parent***. Oftentimes, there is no reason given other than "I do not want to."

When a jurist is confronted with this, they will often (hopefully) go against the child's wishes and impose parenting time and frequently in a therapeutic setting. The court will also admonish the custodial parent to encourage parenting time and to promote a relationship between the child and the non-custodial parent. It is hoped that the therapeutic intervention can repair the rift.

Another "red flag" is where the child seems to be emulating the custodial parent's "voice" in that it is apparent the child has been heavily influenced or coached by the parent as to what to say and feel. Eventually the custodial parent's "voice" becomes the child's and he or she adopts the viewpoint and feelings of the custodial parent without being able to explain why they feel the way they do. The child is aligned with the custodial parent, going as far as to mock the non-custodial parent – among other negative behaviors.

In serious cases where alienation is suspected, not only is therapeutic intervention ordered but a forensic evaluation will likely be conducted in order to obtain a clearer picture of the family, a diagnosis, if possible, as well as observations and recommendations – and the latter may include transferring custody from the alienating parent to the alienated parent. The transfer of custody is not without pitfalls, mainly that it could worsen the alienated parent's relationship with the child(ren) and bring some emotional trauma, but it is almost always the most appropriate remedy – otherwise the parent-child relationship is certain to be destroyed and the child(ren's) future relationships with others (like peers, romantic interests, extended family, and employers and employees) at risk of serious impairment.

Yes, human beings are imperfect and sometimes irrational. Most parents are flawed and make mistakes but often, with time and reflection, they can make amends and move forward as co-parents leaving the past behind. In the unfortunate scenarios where selfishness and anger override compassion for the children and the other parent, it is imperative to be vigilant and to take decisive action.

Veronica Escobar, Esq.

Veronica Escobar is the Principal and Founder of The Law Offices of Veronica Escobar, a practice focusing exclusively in the areas of Elder Law, Special Needs Planning and Trusts and Estates. Prior to forming her own law practice, Veronica worked as an attorney representing the City of New York, Administration for Children's Services (ACS) in child abuse and neglect matters (commonly referred to as an "Article 10") ranging from educational neglect to serious forms of abuse.

Veronica is admitted to practice in the State of New York. She is also admitted to practice before the U.S. District Courts for the Eastern and Southern Districts of New York and the United States Supreme Court. She graduated summa cum laude from Fordham College at Rose Hill, Fordham University, where she was also elected to Phi Beta Kappa, with a degree in American Studies and a minor in Latin American/Latino Studies. She also received her law degree from Fordham, where she was a Notes and Articles Editor of the Fordham International Law Journal.

SECTION C: SPECIAL CONSIDERATIONS

CHAPTER 22

DOMESTIC AND INTERNATIONAL PARENTAL CHILD ABUCTION - KIDNAPPING

By Ann Marquez, Esq. & Donna Manvich, MA, JD

Parental Child Abduction otherwise known as ***Parental Kidnapping*** occurs when a taking parent deprives a left behind parent of his or her legal right to custody or visitation by *illegally* taking the child so that the other parent is not able to have parenting time with the child. Custody jurisdiction and child abduction laws have been enacted to ensure that a parent will not gain any legal or practical advantage by taking the child to a new state or country at the expense of the child and/or of the left behind parent when there are orders of custody/visitation in place.

A parent seeking to relocate with the child should go to family court ***where the child currently resides*** and file for relocation, ***prior to moving to a different state*** or country with the child. The parent or family member should never resort to ***self-help*** by taking the child away on their own. If the parent or family member with custodial or visitation rights removes the child in contravention of the left behind parent's rights, then the left behind parent should seek immediate court intervention, as time is of the essence.

Each case of parental child abduction has its own ***unique set of circumstances***. The reasons a parent or family member may illegally remove a child are as varied as the parties themselves, however, below are some of the more common reasons for parental abduction:

- To punish or hurt the other parent.
- To force continued interaction with the left-behind parent.
- Because the abducting parent is in fear of losing custody or visitation rights and does not trust the legal system to treat him or her fairly.

- There is a direct threat to the child's safety and the abducting parent believes the child should be removed from a parent who is perceived to molest, abuse, or neglect the child.

General Warning Signs

Several common warning signs may indicate that a parent or family member is planning to abduct a child. It is important to remember that any of these warning signs do not in and of themselves mean that a child is about to be abducted and conversely, the absence of any of the below does not mean that a child will not be abducted. However, a parent who suspects that a child may be taken should be mindful of these warning signs and seek assistance of an attorney for possible court intervention as well as intervention by law enforcement agencies. There are ***preemptive steps*** that should be taken if it appears that a parental child abduction is highly plausible. A person should consult an attorney, law enforcement agency, the ***National Center for Missing and Exploited Children*** ("NCMEC") or ***U.S. Department of State-Office of Children's Issues*** (International Abduction) for help if he or she believes a child is about to be taken and any of the following occur:

- The taking parent is planning to quit or has already ***quit a job***.
- The taking parent is preparing to sell or already has ***sold a home***.
- The taking parent is closing or has ***closed bank accounts***.
- The taking parent is ***applying for passports*** for him or herself and/or the child.
- The taking parent is attempting to obtain the ***child's school or medical records***.
- The taking parent has ***threatened abduction*** or has actually abducted the child in the past. Any direct threat of a child abduction should *always* be taken seriously.
- The taking parent is suspected of abuse, and these suspicions are supported by family and friends who confirm that the ***child is in danger***.
- The taking parent has ***dual citizenship***.

- The taking parent has family or other forms of close social support in another state/country and has ***no strong ties to the child's home state***.
- The taking parent has ***no employment and/or financial ties*** to the state where the child is located.
- The taking parent's ***immigration status*** affecting his or her rights to remain in this country is in jeopardy.
- There is a history of ***marital instability***, lack of cooperation with the other parent, domestic violence, or child abuse.
- The taking parent has a ***criminal record***.
- The taking parent has a history of ***non-compliance*** with court orders.

Parental Child Abduction State Laws: Criminal and Civil

Background

Prior to 1968, state courts could exercise jurisdiction over a child custody case based either on a ***child's presence*** in that state or any ***significant connection*** that the child or any of the parties might have to a state. It should come as no surprise that oftentimes two different states claimed jurisdiction over a single child custody case. Moreover, courts freely modified sister-state's orders because the question of whether the ***Full Faith and Credit*** clause of the U.S. Constitution was actually applied to custody decrees had never been settled. There was no common and consistent way to determine which state had proper jurisdiction to decide the matter. This legal climate fostered both child abduction and *forum shopping*. Because parents with physical possession of a child could choose the forum that would likely decide custody in their favor, parents had an incentive to abduct children and take them to a location that would be more favorable towards them. Although abducting parents benefited under this system, their "seize and run" tactics exacted a heavy toll on the children involved as well as on the left behind parent. In addition, the judicial systems of the states were often bogged down as multiple states often heard custody cases regarding the same children. Given the interstate nature of the problem, some form of federal intervention was necessary.

In 1968 the ***Uniform Child Custody Jurisdiction Act*** ("UCCJA") was enacted. The UCCJA sought to regulate not only which court had jurisdiction to make and modify custody and visitation determinations, but also sought to define the all-important interstate effect such determinations were to be given in sister states. Unfortunately, the UCCJA still allowed for confusion between the states as to which one obtained jurisdiction over a child custody matter. Primarily the confusion under this Act was the result again of *jurisdictional* concerns. The ***bifurcated issue*** of jurisdiction being granted to the state where the child resided and/or where there was significant contact with the state had still not been settled.

Today, numerous laws are in place for the protection of children at risk in parental abduction cases; these laws are designed to promote uniformity for jurisdictional issues and deter forum shopping. Both criminal and civil laws were enacted to prevent abduction across state lines within the United States. The most important and current of these are under the ***Parental Kidnapping Prevention Act*** ("PKPA") and the ***Uniform Child Custody Jurisdiction and Enforcement Act*** ("UCCJEA") and its legislative mirror in New York, under ***N.Y. Domestic Relations Law***, at § 75 et seq. (DRL §§75-78).

The PKPA often works in ***concert with state laws***, such as state adoptions of the UCCJEA, in order to facilitate the return of a child who has been taken illegally. All 50 states and all U.S. territories follow the UCCJEA in some form. The custody provisions in the federal law correspond to those that have been adopted by the different states.

In New York, the UCCJEA is mirrored by N.Y. Dom. Rel. Law § 75, et seq. In its introduction the New York Legislature writes:

> This article may be cited as the 'uniform child custody jurisdiction and enforcement act',...It is the intent of the legislature in enacting this article to provide an effective mechanism to obtain and enforce orders of custody and visitation across state lines and to do so in a manner that ensures that the safety of the children is paramount and that victims of domestic violence and child abuse are protected. It is further the intent of the legislature that this article be construed so

> as to ensure that custody and visitation by perpetrators of domestic violence or homicide of a parent, legal custodian, legal guardian, sibling, half-sibling or step-sibling of a child is restricted…

Thus, one sees that the meaning of the UCCJEA is mirrored in New York statutory law.

It is important to keep in mind that the UCCJEA is not a substantive custody statute. In other words, it ***does not dictate standards*** for establishing or modifying child custody orders and visitation decisions. Those decisions must be determined by the state court between the parents under the laws of the child's home state. It is only *after* a custody order and visitation determination is made that the protections under the UCCJEA apply if the child is removed in breach of a parent's custodial or visitation rights. Further, the UCCJEA never applies to child support cases.

The Parental Kidnapping Prevention Act of 1980 (PKPA)

Providing for civil remedies, this Federal Act gives jurisdictional priority to the child's home State in parental abduction cases where conflicts arise between two states. It extends the ***Federal Fugitive Felon Act*** to cases in which a child has been taken out of a state where that act constitutes a felony, thus enabling the FBI to investigate.

In an attempt to address the confusion and close existing gaps in order to bring greater uniformity to interstate child custody issues, Congress in 1980 enacted ***The Parental Kidnapping Prevention Act*** ("PKPA"), (28 U.S.C.A. § 1738A [Supp. 1993]). The PKPA granted full faith and credit to custody and visitation determinations made by sister states who had original jurisdiction over the custody matter unless the original state no longer had, or declined to exercise, jurisdiction. In addition, the PKPA deferred to the "***exclusive, continuing jurisdiction***" of the decree state as long as that state exercised jurisdiction consistently with the PKPA when it made its determination, had jurisdiction under its own law, and remained the residence of the child or any contestant.

> "**Contestant**" is defined as a person, including a parent, who claims a right to custody or visitation with respect to a child.

Further, the PKPA sought to ensure that contestants, any parent whose parental rights had not been terminated, and any person who had physical custody of the child was provided reasonable notice and opportunity to be heard in court. Importantly, the PKPA prioritized ***home state jurisdiction*** in ***initial custody cases*** by applying the ***Full Faith and Credit Clause*** of the U.S. Constitution so that each state would have to abide by the custody decisions made by another state's court. This was an improvement over the UCCJA which allowed that two states could have simultaneous jurisdiction over a dispute when one was the home state and the other had significant connection jurisdiction. A significant connection to a state is, among other things, where a parent resides in a state or where the child has been removed to the state and now resides there. Under the PKPA, a child's home state has jurisdiction when immediately preceding the time involved, the child lived with his parents, a parent, or a person acting as parent, for at least ***six consecutive months*** within the state. If a child ***is less than six months old***, the state in which the child lived from birth with any of such persons was considered the home state. Any period of temporary absence from the child's home state is usually counted as part of the six-month or other period. This is intended to limit jurisdiction in initial custody cases solely to the child's home state by preventing a significant connection state from exercising jurisdiction over a matter when the child, who is the subject of the proceeding, has a home state.

One readily can see the importance of going to court to have a valid custody order in place when parents separate or divorce and there are children involved. Without an order from the court, there is simply nothing that has been violated and little or no recourse for the left behind parent. The presumption is that both parents have equal rights to their children when an agreement is not filed with the court. The existence of a custody order that has been violated sets in motion the ability of law enforcement and the courts to retrieve the child and gives law enforcement the power to access the ***Federal Parent Locator Service*** for purposes of identifying the whereabouts of a child who has been abducted by a parent.

The Uniform Child Custody Jurisdiction and Enforcement Act (UCCJEA)

The Uniform Child Custody Jurisdiction and Enforcement Act, adopted unanimously by the ***National Conference of Commissioners on Uniform State Laws*** in 1997 and approved by the American Bar Association in 1998, amends UCCJA to bring it into conformity with the Parental Kidnapping Prevention Act. UCCJEA also clarifies jurisdictional provisions of UCCJA that courts have interpreted inconsistently across the country.

UCCJEA and its Implementation

The ***Uniform Child Custody Jurisdiction and Enforcement Act*** ("UCCJEA") is the most recent federal law designed to deter interstate parental kidnapping and promote uniform jurisdiction and enforcement provisions in interstate child custody and visitation cases. The UCCJEA is a federal law that was approved in 1997 by the ***National Conference of Commissioners on Uniform State Laws*** ("NCCUSL") as a replacement for its 1968 ***Uniform Child Custody Jurisdiction Act*** ("UCCJA"). The UCCJEA governs state courts' ***jurisdiction*** to make and modify "***child custody determinations***," a term that expressly includes custody and visitation orders. The UCCJEA supports the PKPA position where any state that is not the "***home state***" of the subject child or children will defer to the "home state," if there is one, in taking jurisdiction over a child custody dispute.

The UCCJEA also ensures the ***continuing exclusive jurisdiction of the child's home state***. In other words, if a state once takes jurisdiction over a child custody dispute, it retains jurisdiction so long as the child or the parent bringing the action remains in the home state.

Temporary Emergency Jurisdiction

In addition, the UCCJEA added an important explication of jurisdiction in emergency situations regarding the abuse of a child and/or parent or the neglect of a child. In such a case, the state that is not a home state may exercise temporary emergency jurisdiction if the ***child's safety is at risk***, pursuant to the UCCJEA. Temporary emergency jurisdiction is limited in that the state is exercising jurisdiction only for the limited purpose of securing the child's safety, and then there is a transfer of the proceeding back to the home state, or if there is none, to a state with another ground for jurisdiction, once the danger has passed.

New York DRL § 76 specifies when New York may ***exercise emergency jurisdiction*** in an initial custody proceeding and provides, in part, "there is substantial evidence before this court to continue emergency jurisdiction to assess the child's safety in the care and custody of the parent." Such temporary emergency jurisdiction can be exercised when a child is present within a state and is abandoned, mistreated or abused. In any of these instances, the state where the child is currently located may take emergency temporary jurisdiction over the child to ensure the child's safety. Additionally, ***threats to siblings or a parent*** may also trigger the granting of emergency jurisdiction in order to ensure their safety as well.

<u>**Domestic Violence**</u>

Unlike its predecessors, the UCCJEA included key concerns regarding domestic violence victims who must litigate child custody interstate. Under the UCCJEA, protection against disclosure of a victim's address may be instituted, emergency jurisdiction may be granted in cases where a parent or sibling is at risk, and courts are required to consider family abuse in their "***inconvenient forum***" analysis. This change widened the scope of the statutory law protecting children, siblings, and their parents.

Additional Statutory Resources

1. <u>**The Missing Children's Act of 1982 (28 U.S.C. § 534(a))**</u> – This Act requires the ***Federal Bureau of Investigation*** ("FBI") to enter descriptive information on missing children into the ***National Crime Information Center*** ("NCIC") database, a computer database with information on missing persons that can be accessed by law enforcement agencies nationwide.

2. <u>**The National Child Search Assistance Act of 1990 (42 U.S.C. § 5780)**</u> – This Act requires that state and local law enforcement agencies immediately enter information on

missing children younger than 18 into the NCIC database and prohibits such agencies from maintaining ***any waiting period*** prior to taking a report of a missing child.

3. **The Missing Children's Assistance Act (42 U.S.C. §§ 5771 et seq.)** – Enacted in 1984 and reauthorized in 1988, 1992, and 1999, this Act resulted in the establishment of the National Center for Missing and Exploited Children. NCMEC serves as a national resource center on missing children, providing support to criminal justice system personnel and aggrieved parents as they seek to identify and recover missing children, including those who have been abducted by a parent. It operates a toll-free hotline, provides technical assistance to law enforcement personnel in the field, and educates the public and others on relevant issues.

For a comprehensive summary of state criminal custodial interference laws, refer to the compilation of "Parental Kidnapping Statutes" located on the website of the ***National District Attorneys Association*** at www.ndaa.org.

Enforcement of the Laws

Without a court ordered custody decision, parental kidnapping in the eyes of the law may not be legitimate. Parents are viewed as having equal rights to the child and either can go wherever and whenever they choose with their child if there is no order in place stating otherwise. With that being said, if one parent removes the child ***to an unknown location*** in order to deny the custody or visitation rights of the other parent, even when there is no standing custody order in place, it may be considered parental kidnapping based on the taking parent's determination to thwart the custody and/or visitation rights of the left behind parent. In addition, if the parent moves with the child to another location ***without notifying the left behind parent*** it is considered parental kidnapping, even if there is no custody or visitation order in place.

The UCCJEA and N.Y. DRL §75 et seq. add ***enforcement provisions*** to the jurisdictional provisions under the law. States are required to enforce custody or visitation orders from sister states that are in substantial conformity with the UCCJEA. An order from a state that has continuing exclusive jurisdiction, therefore, will be enforced in any other state or territory within the United States.

A ***Writ of Habeas Corpus*** petition can be filed by the left behind parent seeking a court order mandating the taking parent to produce the child in court. In addition, the left behind parent can file a petition alleging violation of the court's custody/visitation order along with the writ of habeas corpus, which may allow the court to utilize local law enforcement agencies in order to locate and return the subject child or children.

However, if the child, sibling or parent is in imminent danger of abuse, then the following expedited procedure is in place. If there is ***danger to a child*** or if it appears that the child will be illegally removed from the enforcing jurisdiction, a petition may be filed for a warrant to take immediate physical custody of the child together with a petition for an expedited proceeding.

Under *NY DRL § 77-j*, for obtaining a warrant to take physical custody of child, the law in New York mirrors the UCCJEA and provides that:

1. Upon the filing of a petition seeking enforcement of a child custody determination, the Petitioner, (left behind parent) may file a ***verified application*** for the issuance of a warrant to take physical custody of the child if the child is at imminent risk of suffering serious physical harm or of removal from this state.

2. If the court, upon the testimony of the petitioner or other witness, finds that the child is likely to suffer ***imminent serious physical harm*** or to be removed from this state, it may issue a warrant to take physical custody of the child. Except in extraordinary circumstances, the petition must be heard on the next court day after the warrant is executed. Any adjournment for extraordinary circumstances shall be for not more than ***three court days***.

3. A warrant to take ***physical custody*** of a child must:
   (a) Recite the facts upon which a conclusion of imminent ***serious physical harm*** or removal from the jurisdiction is based;
   (b) Direct law enforcement officers to take physical custody of the child immediately and

deliver the child to the petitioner or, where necessary, to act jointly with the local ***child protective service*** to take immediate steps to protect the child; and
(c) Provide for the placement of the child pending final relief.

4. The respondent must then be ***served*** with the petition, warrant, and order immediately after the child is taken into physical custody.

5. A warrant to take physical custody of a child is enforceable throughout this state. If the court finds, on the basis of the testimony of the petitioner or other witness, that a less intrusive remedy is not effective, it may authorize law enforcement officers to enter private property in order to execute the warrant and take physical custody of the child. If required by ***exigent circumstances*** of the case and necessary to the protection of the child, the court may authorize law enforcement officers to make a forcible entry at any hour.

If the warrant issues, law enforcement officers will serve the warrant and obtain physical custody of the child. Upon receiving a verified petition, the court orders the party who has taken the child to submit to an immediate hearing (the next judicial day unless impossible) for enforcement. The court may rule with respect to enforcement at the hearing, although there are provisions to allow for extended hearing and standards to contest enforcement. This ***emergency remedy*** operates much like a writ of habeas corpus, in which the body subject to the writ (in this case the child) must be presented immediately to the court.

Once the court determines jurisdiction over the matter of the child's custody and visitation the other party has to be provided with notice. When a person is outside this state, notice may be given in any manner prescribed by the law of this state for ***service of process***.

In New York, the court requires *proof of service* in the manner prescribed by the laws of N.Y. Generally, this is done by personal service, which is a means by which a party to a lawsuit receives notice of a court action, and is typically accomplished by handing the notice and other legal documents in person to the taking parent. Many jurisdictions allow additional methods of service. If, after ***due diligence***, attempts to find the other parent have failed and personal service of notice is impossible, then the court may allow service of notice by ***substitute service***, including but not limited to, a publication in specified newspapers. The UCCJEA also gives prosecutors the power to enforce custody or visitation orders, and the law gives law enforcement officers the power to try to locate a child under instructions from prosecutors.

Regardless of the reason why a child goes missing, federal law requires law enforcement agencies to respond in a rapid and specific way. Federal law prohibits law enforcement agencies from establishing or maintaining any sort of waiting period before accepting a missing child report (42 U.S.C. § 5780). Federal law also requires law enforcement agencies to enter the missing child's information into the FBI's ***National Crime Information Center*** ("NCIC") database and the state law enforcement system database (42 U.S.C. § 5780). The ***Adam Walsh Child Protection and Safety Act of 2006*** ("Adam Walsh Act"), Pub. L. No. 109-248 mandates law enforcement to make an entry of information about missing and abducted children into the ***National Crime Information Center*** (NCIC) within two hours of receipt of the report.

The ***Enforcement Provisions*** of Article 3 of the UCCJEA contain the following:

- Temporary enforcement of visitation determinations.
- Creates an interstate registration process for out-of-state custody determinations.
- Establishes a procedure for ***speedy interstate enforcement*** of custody and visitation determinations.
- Authorizes ***issuance of warrants*** directing law enforcement to pick up children at risk of being harmed or removed from the state.
- Authorizes public officials to assist in the civil enforcement of custody determinations.

Steps To Take in the Event of a Parental Abduction

If the child has been the victim of parental kidnapping the ***National Center for Missing & Exploited Children*** lists the following actions the left behind parent should take immediately:

1. Call or go to the local law enforcement agency and file a missing person report.

2. Report the child missing to the ***National Center for Missing & Exploited Children*** (NCMEC) by calling toll-free at 1-800-THE-LOST (1-800-843-5678) and visit NCMEC's website at www.missingkids.com. Complete its "***Missing Person Report for an Abducted Child***." Bring it along when going to the local law enforcement agency.

3. Ask law enforcement to enter information about the child into the FBI's NCIC. Federal law requires law enforcement to enter each missing child case into NCIC within two hours after the receipt of the initial report. If law enforcement does not immediately act, cite the relevant sections of the applicable laws and show it to them – ***Missing Children Act***, ***National Child Search Assistance Act***, and ***Adam Walsh Child Protection and Safety Act of 2006***. To obtain copies of the statutes contact the NCMEC. Bring the copies with you when meeting with law enforcement authorities and make them aware of the law. Law enforcement will decide if the circumstances of a child's disappearance meet the protocol for activation of an ***America's Missing: Broadcast Emergency Response ("AMBER") Alert*** and/or other community notification.

4. Verify law enforcement has made the NCIC entry. If it is not possible to get this information from the ***local law enforcement agency***, call NCMEC toll free at 1-800-THE-LOST (1-800-843-5678) and ask them to check NCIC to see if the child is listed. NCMEC can confirm NCIC entries but is not authorized to make them.

5. If law enforcement does not enter information about the child into NCIC, the ***missing child clearinghouse*** may be able to help by contacting the law enforcement agency about the case. Contact NCMEC for additional information.

6. Ask local FBI office to enter information about the child into NCIC. The Missing Children Act authorizes the FBI to make such entries. Contact information for the FBI is available in the local telephone book and at www.fbi.gov.

From the home page click on the "***Your Local FBI Office***" link.

7. File a ***petition for custody*** if an order is not currently in place. Consider hiring a lawyer for assistance. A temporary custody order is usually enough to get help from law enforcement authorities at least until the child is located.

8. File a ***missing person report*** and enter the child's description into NCIC. Keep in mind that a court can issue a custody order even if the child has been abducted from the home state jurisdiction or taken outside of the country and there was never a legal marriage between the child's parents. If the abductor's whereabouts are unknown, a parent can serve the abductor by publication or alternative service with permission of the court. Time is of the essence in a child abduction situation – the sooner a person acts the more likely the abductor will be prevented from getting a valid custody determination from another jurisdiction or country.

9. Obtain additional copies of applicable child custody and visitation orders from the court. It is important to have two or three ***certified copies*** available to show or give to law enforcement and other agencies.

10. Consider asking law enforcement or the prosecutor to ***file criminal charges*** against the abductor. Weigh the pros and cons of such action by discussing it with an attorney or the district attorney's office. A parent should be prepared to press charges after the child is returned.

11. If the prosecutor charges the abductor with a felony, law enforcement authorities should promptly enter the felony warrant into NCIC. NCIC files for the ***child and abductor*** should always be cross-referenced. Ask law enforcement or NCMEC to verify these NCIC entries have been made.

International Parental Child Abduction

When a taking parent abducts a child by illegally removing the child from their habitual residence to a foreign country, thereby depriving the left behind parent of a parental role in the child's life, it is considered an ***international parental child abduction***. The ***Hague Convention on the Civil Aspects of International Child Abduction*** ("Hague Convention") is a treaty with member countries called signatory countries.

The Hague Convention is a ***multilateral treaty***, which seeks to protect children from the harmful effects of abduction and retention across international boundaries by providing a procedure for the child's *prompt* return to their prior habitual residence. It serves to ***simplify and expedite the return process*** when children have been abducted internationally. The United States ratified the Hague on Oct. 25, 1980, T.I.A.S. No. 11,670 and it took effect in the United States in 1988 following enactment of the ***International Child Abduction Remedies Act***. It must be ***emphasized*** that the remedies available under the Hague Convention treaty can only be implemented between signatory countries. In other words, if the child is abducted to a foreign country that is not a "***signatory member***" of the Hague, then the left behind parent does not have the available remedies of the treaty between countries under the Hague. The petitioning parent seeking the recovery of an abducted child by another parent may be more difficult if the country the child is taken to is not a signatory to the Hague. (See below for further suggestions.)

Pursuant to the Convention, Art.3: the ***removal or the retention*** of a child is to be considered "wrongful" when it is in breach of the custody rights of another person when those custodial rights were actually being exercised at the time of the removal, or would have been exercised but for the removal.

The United States and Foreign Country pursuant to the Hague Convention

Here, in the United States, the ***International Child Abduction Remedies Act*** ("ICARA") (42 U.S.C. §§ 11601-11610) is a federal statute designed to provide procedures to implement the Hague

Convention ***authorizing state and federal courts*** to hear cases under this treaty when a child has been unlawfully brought into or retained in the United States.

In 1993, the United States passed a federal statute making it a ***federal crime*** (*i.e.*, a felony) to remove or attempt to remove a child younger than 16 years old from the U.S. or to retain a child who is in the U.S., with the intent to obstruct the lawful exercise of the parental rights of the other parent. Congress has clarified, through the ***Extradition Treaties Interpretation Act*** of 1998, that U.S. authorities shall interpret the term "kidnapping" to include parental kidnapping in any criminal extradition treaty to which the United States is a party. By doing so, the spectrum of international kidnapping and possible remedies was importantly broadened to include the taking of a child by a parent.

In determining jurisdiction in a Hague case when there is a custody order from a foreign country and that order is presented in the United States for recognition and enforcement, the ICARA provides jurisdiction to implement the Hague here in the U.S. Under ICARA, "the courts of the States and the United States district courts shall have concurrent original jurisdiction of actions arising under the Convention." Further, custody orders from foreign countries will be treated like those from sister states in the U.S. and therefore will be given full faith and credit.

The Hague Convention applies to cases where a child ***under the age of sixteen*** (16) years has been removed from his or her ***habitual residence*** in ***breach of rights of custody*** of a petitioner, which the petitioner had been exercising at the time of the *wrongful* removal or *wrongful* retention of the child. The removal or the retention of a child is to be considered "wrongful" if the act is in breach of the custody rights of another person when those custodial rights were actually being exercised at the time of the removal, or would have been exercised but for the removal of the child from his or her habitual residence. The *only relevant point* in time for determining habitual residence is the habitual residence of the child immediately before the removal or retention of the child. One of the Convention's main purposes is to provide for a 'prompt' return, to restore the factual *status quo*, and prevent an abducting parent from gaining any advantage over the non-abducting parent. A court considering a ***Hague-ICARA petition*** has jurisdiction to decide the merits only of the wrongful removal claim, not of any underlying custody or support dispute. The Hague Convention is intended to restore the pre-abduction status quo and to prevent parents from crossing borders in search of a more sympathetic court.

The Hague Convention is administered and implemented by the ***Central Authority*** established in each signatory country, to assist in the location and recovery of the children utilizing Hague Convention channels. If the Central Authority, which receives an application as referred to in Article 8 of the Convention, has reason to believe that the child is in another Contracting State, it *shall directly and without delay transmit the application* to the Central Authority of that Contracting State. The Judicial or administrative authority of the contracting State is then supposed to reach a decision within six (6) weeks from the date of the commencement of the proceeding. If this has not happened within that timeframe, then the requesting state or the applicant has the right to request a statement of the reasons for the delay. It is detrimental to the child and to the left behind parent to hinder the return of the child by allowing delays. Thus, the Central Authority of the country the child has been taken to is mandated under the Convention to ensure their *prompt* assistance for the return of the abducted child. In other words, the Hague convention allows its signatory members to communicate directly with one another regarding a parentally abducted child through each country's Central Authority which is established specifically for this purpose.

From 1995 to April 2008, ***National Center for Missing and Exploited Children*** fulfilled the functions of the U.S. Central Authority under the Hague Convention on "incoming cases" in which a parent abducts a child into the U.S. from a treaty partner country. Today, the U.S. Department of State assumes primary responsibility over incoming Hague Convention abduction cases, as of April 2008.

If the foreign country the child has been taken into is a signatory of the Hague convention there are certain affirmative defenses that may be asserted by the abducting parent that will prevent the return of the child to his or her state of habitual residence.

Under ICARA, the "taking parent" who opposes the return of the child has the burden of establishing the following:

1. By the ***preponderance of the evidence***, the Respondent must prove the following affirmative defenses:
    - the well-settled defense;
    - person consented or subsequently acquiesced defense;
    - mature child defense.

2. By ***clear and convincing evidence***, the Respondent must prove the following affirmative defenses:
    - grave risk defense; and
    - violation of fundamental principles of human rights/freedoms defense.

See Convention, art. 13; 42 U.S.C. 11603 (e)(2).

Affirmative Defenses

Here are a few *affirmative defenses* that a "taking parent" can raise:

1. **The Child is Well Settled in His/Her New Home**

Under the Convention, "(w)here a child has been wrongfully removed or retained at the date of the commencement of the proceedings before the judicial or administrative authority of the Contracting State where the child is, ***a period of less than one year*** has elapsed from the date of the wrongful removal or retention, the authority concerned ***shall order*** the return of the child forthwith…" Convention, art. 12. The one-year limitation runs from the date the wrongful removal or retention occurred. The date of a wrongful removal is usually a simple matter, since one presumes that a parent with custody rights will know when those custody rights were violated.

However, if the child has lived in the foreign country ***for more than one year***, then it is possible for the abducting parent to assert the defense that the child is ***well settled*** in their new home and his or her removal would harm the child at this point in time because the child is now acclimated to new surroundings and is enmeshed and strongly connected to a new life.

This ***one-year period of time*** emphasizes that time is of the essence for the left behind parent, who must act *fast* by seeking legal assistance for a Hague petition and contacting a Central Authority for the recovery of the abducted child.

Unlike domestic parental abduction, even where the taking parent removed the child, secreted the child's whereabouts from the left behind parent and is in a foreign country where it has taken over one year to discover the child's whereabouts, the taking parent may still raise the affirmative defense that the child is now well settled in his or her new home.

The Hague Convention does not define "well settled" or state how this defense is to be proven, but confers ***discretionary power on the court*** to determine whether or not the defense justifies refusing to repatriate the child. Importantly, such a defense does not compel the district court to allow the child to remain with the abducting parent. Each case has different particulars and each is left to the determination and discretion of the court.

The courts, however, do recognize various factors in determining whether or not a child has become well settled: the age of the child; the stability of the child's residence in the new environment; whether the child attends school or day care consistently; whether the child attends church or other religious institutions regularly; the stability of the abducting parent's employment; and whether the child has friends and relatives in their new home. In addition, the court must also consider evidence concerning the child's contacts with and other ties to his or her state of habitual residence. It should be noted that these factors are neither mandatory nor exclusive.

As stated above, the treaty's primary aim is to deter family members from removing children to jurisdictions more favorable for their custody claims in order to obtain a right of custody from the authorities of the country to which the child has been taken. In addition, the aim of the treaty is to secure the prompt return of children wrongfully removed to or retained in any ***Contracting State*** and to ensure that rights of custody and access under the law of one Contracting State are consistently respected in the other Contracting States. Unless the child has significant emotional and physical connections demonstrating security, stability, and permanence in his or her new environment, he or she should not be considered well settled no matter what length of time has transpired. The Hague Convention permits the court to consider the ***totality of the circumstances*** regarding a child's welfare when determining if that child is indeed well settled in his or her new environment. Given the Convention's underlying goals, nothing less than *substantial* evidence of the child's significant connections to the new country is intended to suffice to meet the respondent's burden of proof. To successfully invoke the well settled exception, the respondent must show by substantial evidence that the child is in fact so settled in his/her new environment that a return would be disruptive with likely harmful effects.

2. The Child will Suffer a Grave Risk of Harm if Returned to His/Her Habitual Residence

Pursuant to Article 13(b) of the Convention, a court may refuse to return a child if it finds that there is a grave risk that his or her return would expose the child to ***physical or psychological harm*** or otherwise place the child in an intolerable situation. The taking parent bears the burden of proof by clear and convincing evidence.

The Hague Convention, art. 13(b)'s exception for ***grave harm*** to the child is not license for a court in the abducted-to country to speculate on where the child would be happiest. Instead, the term "grave" means "**more than a serious risk**." The situation contemplated by Article 13(b) would include sending a child back to a war zone, or where famine and disease are prevalent. It would also include cases of serious abuse or neglect of the child in his or her habitual residence when the court in the country of habitual residence, for whatever reason, is incapable or unwilling to give the child adequate protection.

3. Mature Child Defense: The Child Objects To Being Returned

Under Article 13, the Convention also recognizes that a ***child may object*** to being returned to his or her ***habitual residence***. The judicial or administrative authority may refuse to order the return of the child if it finds that the child objects to being returned and has attained an age and degree of maturity at which it is appropriate to take account of his or her views. The party opposing the child's return must prove this defense by a ***preponderance of the evidence***.

Pursuant to Article 13, a child's objection to return simply is not tantamount to "the wishes of the child." While the wishes or desires of a child may be appropriate for a court to consider in a custody case, they are not relevant in a Hague return case. First, the court assesses whether the child is ***sufficiently mature***. Then, the court must determine if the child should be ***returned despite his or her objection***. Factors may exist that counterbalance the objections of a mature child. A court should consider those factors and exercise its discretion in light of all available evidence or against the child's wishes. A child's objection to being returned may be accorded little if any weight if the court believes that the child's decision is the product of the abductor's ***undue influence***.

Steps to Take in a Hague Convention-International Parental Child Abduction

1. Call ***U.S. Department of State's Office of Children's Issues*** toll-free at 1-888-407-4747 or by dialing directly at 202-736-9090 for advice about what to do.

2. Call the ***National Center for Missing & Exploited Children*** toll free at 1-800-THE-LOST (1-800-843-5678). It also offers guidance in instances of international child abduction by a parent.

3. If the child has been taken to another country that is a member of the ***Hague Convention***, then contact the ***U.S. State Department's Office of Children's Issues*** ("OCI") without delay to start the process of filing an "application for return" under the Hague Convention. Contact the Office of Children's Issues toll-free at 1-888-407-4747 or by dialing directly at 202-736-9090. The application is transmitted from the OCI – this country's "central authority" for such cases – to the foreign country's central authority, and is then heard in the foreign country's courts in the locality where the child has been taken. This requires the left behind parent to ***file a Hague petition*** in a foreign country's court for the recovery of the abducted child. A completed Hague application with the Central Authority only is not sufficient. Remember, a Hague petition must also be filed.[20]

4. If the parent does not have a ***passport***, then the parent should apply for one immediately in the event that he/she has to travel outside of the United States to recover the child. Visit the U.S. Department of State's website at www.travel.state.gov, and click on the "Apply for a Passport" link.

---

[20] For additional legal resources: contact the governing central authority or access the Directory of the International Academy of Matrimonial Lawyers for legal help in the country where the child has been taken. Also, many countries provide free Legal Aid lawyers for Hague Convention petitioners.

5. If the child is in the process of being abducted internationally by the other parent or family member, contact the ***U.S. Department of State's Office of Children's Issues*** toll-free at 1-888-407-4747 or by dialing directly at 202-736-9090 for advice about what to do. Also call NCMEC toll free at 1-800-THE-LOST (1-800-843-5678) and contact the FBI. Contact information for the FBI is available in your local telephone book and at www.fbi.gov. From the home page click on the "Your Local FBI Office" link. Ask to speak to the ***FBI's Crimes Against Children Coordinator***. The FBI has jurisdiction to investigate violations of the federal ***International Parental Kidnapping Crime Act*** ("IPKCA").

6. If an international abduction is in progress, urge law enforcement to ***immediately contact*** the U.S. ***National Central Bureau*** (USNCB)-INTERPOL for help in intercepting the abductor. USNCB-INTERPOL does not respond to requests directly from parents. Law enforcement authorities handling international parental-kidnapping cases should contact USNCB-INTERPOL at 202-616-9000 for assistance. Additional information is available at www.usdoj.gov/usncb. Law enforcement agencies may contact USNCBINTERPOL directly or through the INTERPOL State Liaison Office. Additionally, law enforcement agencies in the United States may contact USNCB-INTERPOL directly through NLETS and The International Justice and Public Safety Network, at DCINTER00.

7. Parents concerned about an abduction in progress should also immediately contact NCMEC and OCI. Transportation carriers the abductor may use such as airlines, train and bus companies; and local law enforcement and ***Immigration and Customs Enforcement*** ("ICE") officials at airports and other transportation facilities the abductor may use, should be put on notice of the imminent abduction and request help in preventing the child's removal from the country. Provide a photograph of the child and suspected abductor if available.

8. Contact the local missing child clearinghouse and any local nonprofit, missing children's ***not-for-Profit (or "nonprofit") organizations***, ("NPO") for whatever assistance they may

provide. Referrals to NPOs are available from the ***Association of Missing and Exploited Children's Organizations Inc.*** ("AMECO") by calling toll-free at 1-877-263-2620, dialing directly at 703-838-8379, or visiting www.amecoinc.org.

When a Child is Kidnapped by a Parent and taken to a Non-Hague Foreign Country

The left behind parent has fewer options than if the child were taken to a country participating under Hague. There is no central authority to contact if the child is taken to a non-signatory state. It is strongly suggested that the left behind parent seek legal consultation/services from an attorney.

Additional Steps to Take

1. Contact the ***National Center for Missing and Exploited Children*** ("NCMEC") by calling them at 1-800-THE-LOST (1-800-843-5678) for resources regarding both domestic and international kidnapping.

2. If a parent has a reason to believe the child was taken to a particular country, he or she should contact that ***country's embassy*** without delay and ask them what recourse he or she has under their laws. Check online at www.embassy.org for the embassy's contact information. Whether or not a custody order from the United States is recognized in a foreign country is up to that country. An embassy may help a parent secure legal representation in a foreign country where the child has been taken.

3. If a child is taken to an ***INTERPOL member country***, a parent should consult with law-enforcement authorities in the country from which the child was taken. Ask law enforcement for assistance with an ***INTERPOL Missing Child (Yellow) Notice***. INTERPOL notices are international requests for cooperation or alerts, allowing police in the member countries to share critical crime related information. In addition, INTERPOL has a less formal

request for cooperation and alert mechanism known as a "diffusion." A diffusion may be used to request the arrest of an individual or additional information in relation to a police investigation. Keep in mind that INTERPOL does not respond to a parent's direct request for help. A law enforcement agency will have to request their intervention.

4. ***Contact the FBI.*** The FBI has offices around the globe. These offices – called ***legal attachés*** or legats – are located in the U.S. embassies in the foreign country. FBI authority in parental kidnapping cases stems from the Fugitive Felon Act as part of Title 18, United States Code, § 1073–UFAP. Although this statute most commonly applies to ***fugitives who flee interstate and/or internationally***, Congress has specifically declared that the statute is also applicable in cases involving interstate or international parental kidnapping. Because many fugitives flee with their own children, the statute serves as an effective means for the FBI to help local and state law enforcement arrest these fugitives. In order for the FBI to assist with a UFAP arrest warrant, the following criteria must be met:

   - There must be ***probable cause*** to believe the abducting parent has fled interstate or internationally to avoid prosecution or confinement.

   - State authorities must have an ***outstanding warrant*** for the abductor's arrest charging him/her with a felony under the laws of the state from which the fugitive flees.

   - State authorities must agree to ***extradite and prosecute*** that fugitive from anywhere in the U.S. if the subject is apprehended by the FBI.

   - The local prosecuting attorney or police agency should make a ***written request*** for FBI assistance.

   - The U.S. Attorney must authorize the ***filing of a complaint***, and the federal arrest process must be outstanding before the investigation is instituted.

Be Prepared – Be Proactive

Parents should be prepared in the event of a parental kidnapping. It will be easier to help law enforcement agencies, courts, and the attorney if the parent has measures in place that will save time and reduce the likelihood that the child will be removed from his or her habitual residence. The ***National Center for Missing and Exploited Children*** together with the ***Department of Justice*** ("DOJ") and the ABA list the following important steps to take *before* a child is abducted. What appears below is not an exhaustive list as set out by these agencies. For a complete listing, it is suggested that the National Center for Missing and Exploited Children be accessed on line at www.missingkids.com.

1. Parents should ***take pictures*** of their child often. Parents should be sure to take profile shots as well as front poses. It may be a good idea for parents to take videos of the child frequently. A photograph of the other parent may also be helpful in the event of an abduction.

2. Parents should keep a complete ***written description*** of their child. This should include hair and eye color, height, weight, date of birth, birthmarks, other unique physical attributes and other features such as glasses, contact lenses, braces, piercings, and tattoos.

3. Parents should keep their child's ***Social Security number*** ("SSN") with them. Internal Revenue Service rules require all children older than 1 year of age to have a SSN.

4. Parents should have his/her child ***fingerprinted***. Most law enforcement agencies provide this service at no charge, but it does not keep the child's prints on file. Parents will be given the only fingerprint card for safekeeping.

5. Parents should teach their child his or her ***full name*** and how to ***use the telephone***. Parents should make sure the child knows his/her complete telephone number including area code. If the child is old enough to remember more

than one number, the parent should teach the child his/her office, cellular, and/or other numbers. Parents should let the child know that he or she will always accept a ***collect call*** from the child and demonstrate how to make a collect call. Additionally, parents should show their child how to dial the ***operator and "911"*** for help and demonstrate what to say.

6. Parents should notify ***schools, daycare centers, and babysitters*** of custody orders. Certified copies of the custody order should be placed in a child's school files and copies should be given to teachers, daycare personnel, and babysitters. If there is a risk of abduction by the noncustodial parent, inform all individuals who care for your child about that risk and give them a photograph of the noncustodial parent if you have one. The custodial parent should ask to be immediately alerted if the noncustodial parent makes any unscheduled visits, and instruct the facility not to allow the child to leave the property with the noncustodial parent without the other parent's permission. The best protection is to have a provision in a parent's custody order ***prohibiting unauthorized pick-up*** of the child by the noncustodial parent from schools, daycare centers, and babysitters. Even without such a provision though, a child should be released only to the parent entitled to custody. It is important to keep school authorities, daycare personnel, and babysitters aware of any changes in the custody or visitation arrangements. The custodial parent must also realize if the noncustodial parent is ***violent or threatening***, school and daycare officials as well as babysitters may have no alternative but to release the child to that parent in order to prevent immediate injury to the child or other children in the area.

7. A parent should ***ask the child's school and/or caretakers*** to immediately notify law enforcement in the event of an abduction. A copy of the custody order should be immediately given to law enforcement responding to the call. Custodial parents should notify school officials, daycare personnel, and babysitters if their children are going

to be absent and ask to be immediately notified if their children do not arrive on schedule. A few jurisdictions require school officials to verify student absences, but custodial parents need to be sure all people who normally care for their children know the situation and the possibility of abduction. *Time is critical in abduction cases. If a child is abducted on the way to school, daycare, or the babysitter, it is extremely important for the custodial parent to be immediately notified so a search for the child and abductor can immediately begin.*

8. Keep ***lists of information.*** Make a list of the noncustodial parent's address, telephone numbers, SSN or citizen-identification numbers, passport number(s), driver's license number, credit-card numbers, bank-account numbers, and date and place of birth. The same information should be gathered for relatives and friends who might help the abductor carry out an abduction.

9. File or ***register the custody decree*** in the court where the noncustodial parent lives. Filing or registering the order puts the court on notice that a custody determination already exists. A valid order is entitled to enforcement and cannot be modified except as specified in the PKPA and consistent state laws.

10. ***Flag passport applications.*** A parent who is concerned a child may be taken to another country without his or her consent can request the child's name be placed in the U.S. Department of State's Children's Passport Issuance Alert Program. To make use of this program a parent or attorney should provide the child's full name, date and place of birth, telephone number, and a copy of the relevant custody orders to the Office of Children's Issues, U.S. Department of State 1-888-407-4747 or call direct to 202-736-9090, fax 202-736-9132. This form is available at www.travel.state.gov. From the home page click on the "Children & Family" link. Under the "***International Parental Child Abduction***" heading click on the "Guarding against & responding to parental child abduction" link. Then respectively click on the "A-Z Index of Topics" and "***Form – Request Entry into the***

Children's Passport Alert Program" links. The requesting parent should be notified when a passport application is received for his or her child. If the U.S. Department of State has a court order on file providing for joint or sole custody to the requesting parent or restricting the child's travel, a passport should not be issued.

The harmful effects of a child's wrongful removal or retention away from his or her habitual residence has prompted lawmakers both ***nationally and internationally*** to consider children as independent from their parents, with their own rights and requirements. The struggle to combat domestic and international parental child abduction is reflected in the legislation that has been touched upon in this chapter, legislation that is inspired by the desire to protect children. While the aim of the legislation is clear, it would be undeniably more efficient and better for the child if parents were inspired by the same desire to protect their children from the trauma of a parental abduction.

References

The Criminal Justice System's Response to Parental Abduction, Kathi L. Grasso, Andrea J. Sedlak, Janet L. Chiancone, Frances Gragg, Dana Schultz, and Joseph F. Ryan, Juvenile Justice Bulletin, (December 2001), https://www.ncjrs.gov/pdffiles1/ojjdp/186160.pdf.

Explanatory Report on the 1980 Hague Child Abduction Convention, by Elisa Perez-Vera, 1982, HCCH Publications, available at http://www.hcch.net/upload/expl28.pdf.

Family Abduction Prevention and Response, 2009 Sixth Edition, Revised by Patricia M. Hoff, Esquire, National Center for Missing & Exploited Children®, available at http://www.missingkids.com/en_US/publications/NC75.pdf.

The Federal Bureau of Investigation (The F.B.I.), Violent Crimes Against Children, Family Child Abductions, Options Under the Law, https://www.fbi.gov/about-us/investigate/vc_majorthefts/cac/family-abductions.

International Parental Child Abduction, U.S. Department of State, Bureau of Consular Affairs, Preventing Abductions, http://travel.state.gov/content/childabduction/english/preventing.html.html.

Polly Klaas Foundation, Guidelines For Recovery Of Missing Children Family/Parental Abductions, http://www.pollyklaas.org/yourchild/prntsug4.pdf.

Preventing International Child Abduction in Divorce, Vol. 28 No. 3, By Jeremy D. Morley, American Bar Association, GP Solo, April/May 2011 available at http://www.americanbar.org/publications/gp_solo/2011/april_may/parental_tug-of-warpreventinginternationalchildabduction.html.

Ann Marquez, Esq.

Ann Marquez, Esq. is admitted to practice law in the State of New York, as well as the United States District Courts for the Eastern and Southern Districts of New York. Ms. Marquez is a passionate advocate of a child's best interests and possesses extensive experience advocating issues relating to child welfare (child abuse, neglect) international parental child abduction, and all custody/visitation matters. Ms. Marquez is on the attorney list of the US Department of State for cases involving international parental child abductions under the Hague Convention.

Ms. Marquez began her career as an agency attorney for the City of New York's Child Protective Services, representing the agency in over 1500 various child welfare proceedings. As a result, she gained significant insight into the "best interests" of the child, and now dedicates her practice to the advocacy of children and parents in domestic and international cases.

Ms. Marquez represented the prevailing party in a complex case of international parental child abduction in federal district court that distinguished a recent U.S. Supreme Court ruling. See Buenaver v. Vasquez (In re R.V.B), 13-CV-4354 (E.D.N.Y. 2014).

Donna Manvich MA, JD

Donna Manvich holds a J.D. from Touro Law Center and a master's degree in Philosophy from SUNY Stony Brook. She is president of Jurissistance Inc., a company dedicated to legal research and writing. Ms. Manvich is also passionate in her advocacy regarding such matters as International Parental Child Abduction and children's rights. Her collaboration by way of support with Ms. Marquez is a natural fit and the two have worked together for many years.

SECTION D: PROFESSIONALS

CHAPTER 23

PARENTING COACHES

By Susan Nason

Parenting, in ***the best of times***, is challenging. When a person has decided to divorce, everything in his or her life becomes more complicated, including parenting. The stakes seem higher, and, unless the soon to be ex-spouses are united in their parenting, they've each now lost both their spouse and ***parenting teammate***.

This is an Emotional Time

This time is fraught with ***high emotions***, melt downs, tantrums, crying, retreating and acting out. On the upside, this is a perfect time to bond with one's child(ren). ***Acknowledge feelings***, offer choices, set limits. Keep in mind that acknowledging a child's feelings does not mean that one is agreeing with them. What it does mean is that one is ***validating their feelings***, willing to hear them out about how angry, sad, scared they are. Children need to know that their ***strong emotions*** won't scare their parent away, or make their parent angry at them.

Telling Your Children About Divorce or Separation

Telling child(ren) about divorce or separation from the other parent is never easy. It is normal to feel uneasy about when to tell them, what to tell them, how to tell them and who should tell them. The answers to these questions largely depends on the age of the child(ren).

When to Tell Them

Ideally, the divorcing couple should try to tell their child(ren) at a *mutually convenient time* for all. For the child(ren) who are over 3, one might say something like, "Jonny, Mary, your Dad and I need to talk to you about something important to all of us. Do you have time now, or do you want to meet at 4pm on Saturday?" Before this discussion, try to imagine what their reactions will be and be prepared to answer the children's questions as fully and honestly as possible.

What to Tell Them

When it's time to sit down to talk, for children who are 4 and over, let them know that both parents put a lot of *effort into making the marriage work*, but have decided that by divorcing <u>everyone</u> in the family will have a chance at a better life. If the child(ren) are old enough to understand, say to them that both Mommy and Daddy decided it's best to live apart and that *no one is to blame* for this decision. Furthermore, it would be helpful to acknowledge that this will be a *hard time* (transition) for everyone and both parents will be available to help them through any feelings they may have.

> The conversation might start by one parent saying something like, "We have sad news to share with you. We have decided to get a divorce. We've both put a lot of thought into this, it's no one's fault; no one is to blame. We want you to know that you can come to either of us to discuss whatever you need to discuss. We are working out how and where we will live now that Daddy and Mommy won't be living together anymore."

Priorities for Certain Age Groups

Toddlers

Toddlers, by their very nature, are beginners at everything. Family life for them is all about routines – and those routines are changing constantly with time, growth, maturity and shifting seasons. At this age a child is more likely to take the change in the family structure in stride (even though they will miss the non-custodial parent dearly). Once a consistent parenting schedule is established, toddlers will quickly settle into their new routine. In a sense, divorce is not as unsettling to toddlers because it's the only life they have known.

Children Ages 4 to 8

Children ages four to eight will feel the split ***more intensely*** then toddlers. Since they are older and have more life experience than toddlers, they will develop ***coping skills*** to handle the change in their living arrangements. When speaking to children 4 to 8 years of age, it is important to tell them that both parents love them and will be taking care of them and listening to them whenever with them.

Though it isn't always possible to know ***where both parents will be living*** during the separation period and after the divorce, the children should be aware of the parent's plan and goals. What will the parenting time schedule look like? Will parents both be living in the same neighborhood? Will the parents be making decisions about the child(ren) jointly or separately?

Children Ages 9 to 12

Children ages nine through pre-teens are shifting their focus from the immediate family to their peers. They may act blasé about your news, but they will be feeling off-balance – possibly confused and scared. As with younger children, it is important to keep in mind that *one's behavior* will set the tone for how well children ages 9 to 12 will *cope with this drastic change.*

This age group is likely to have many questions about the ***impacts on their life***. Parents should be honest with children 9 through 12. Parents should reassure them that the parents have both given this a lot of thought and planning, especially planning for their comfort, safety and a continuation of their current lifestyle as much as possible.

Children this age might begin to ***take sides with one of the parents***, defending that parent from any real or perceived attacks from the other parent. Some children begin to ***feel guilty*** that they prefer one of their parents to the other. Parents should clearly communicate to the child(ren) that both parents are still involved and are still Mom and Dad. Parents should resist the temptation to disparage the other parent in front of or with the child. This can have deleterious effects on the child.

Teens and Young Adults

Teens and young adults probably ***saw it coming***. They will likely experience the whole gamut of emotions: ***fear, confusion, deep sadness***. The children may even be relieved for the separation if they observed a lot of fighting and bickering. Parents might hear: **"Why didn't you do this years ago?!"**

> One important thing to keep in mind for children of any age is that your spouse is still your child's parent. Research shows that children from divorced homes who do well had parents who kept any fighting and bickering, name calling or drama well under control. It is critical to reaffirm to your child(ren) and to yourself that your child's mental health is your priority.

The loss for this age range is ***hard for them to accept***. After all, a two-parent household is the only life they have known. Parents should be especially gentle with young adults: they are often themselves just starting to think more concretely about what it ***means to fall in love***, commit to someone and get married. To see a marriage fall apart might be an unwelcome eye-opener to them.

Emotional Conversations

Children will likely have a significant degree of emotion during this time. It's not atypical for a child to blame the parent for "ruining their life." Parents should acknowledge the child's feeling during this time instead of getting defensive. Parents should avoid giving a logical explanation about why the children should feel differently. A parent's conversation might go like this:

Parents Should Acknowledge Their Own Emotions Too

During these times, parents should not only be gentle with the children but also gentle with themselves. Parents oftentimes forget that they too are going through a life altering experience. Parents may be emotionally raw themselves. Thus, parents should not only acknowledge their children's feelings but their own. Parents should seek help if and when needed.

Child: I hate you, you are ruining my life!

Parent: Wow, you are having very strong feelings about this. And you are very angry at me. This is a very sad time, isn't it?

Child: Yeah, I am angry at you. Why couldn't you two stay married?

Parent: You're wondering about that. Why do you think?

Child: Because you fought all the time? Because I was bad and you don't want to live with me all the time anymore? Because you don't love each other anymore?

Parent: You noticed that we fought often. Yes, we did. And you are concerned that the times you didn't behave how we wanted you to is why we are getting divorced. I can assure you that that's not the reason. We are getting divorced because we know everyone will be better off if we do, we know that we can't live together anymore. This is a hard time for all of us. I'm glad you and I can talk about what's on your mind. We are going to try to make sure that as many of your needs that we can meet are met. We are still both your parents and we love you very much. This divorce is about Daddy and Mommy, not about anything you did.

Susan Nason

Susan Nason was trained by her aunt, author Adele Faber and co-author Elaine Mazlish and has been a facilitator of their "How To Talk So Kids Will Listen, How To Listen So Kids Will Talk" and "Siblings Without Rivalry" workshops for over 35 years. She recently retired from her position as Assistant to the Director of The First Presbyterian Church Nursery School where she worked for 35 years; her position included working with parents as the school's Parent Educator and working with teachers to facilitate a harmonious atmosphere in their classrooms. Susan has a thriving domestic and international Parent Counseling practice specializing in exploring conscious parenting employing therapeutic, spiritual and practical approaches to the challenges of raising children. Susan teaches concrete and effective communication skills to parents of children of all ages.

She has facilitated workshops at the Ackerman Institute for the Family, Seleni Institute, All Souls Church School, The Brick Church School, First Presbyterian Church Nursery School, Barrow Street Nursery School, Rockefeller Children's School, Ross Global Academy, Girl's Prep, Chelsea Day, Bowery Babes and Beit Rabban. She conducts teacher trainings in and around the Tri-state area. She has been a speaker for the Parents' League, the Junior League, Hudson River Park Mama's, Bowery Babes and other organizations and schools.

Most importantly, she brings her love and compassion of being a proud mother and ecstatic grandmother to her work with parents and children.

SECTION D: PROFESSIONALS

CHAPTER 24

PARENT COORDINATION

By Paul Hymowitz, PhD

Over several decades, our society has evolved into one of primarily ***two wage earning spouses*** with increased sharing of childcare responsibilities in the context of a ***higher rate of divorce***. In the past, custody would be typically awarded to one parent, usually the mother, and collaborative parenting arrangements would occur only when the adults were getting along. In recent years, the courts have been more likely, by official policy or judicial fiat, to have a presumption of joint custodial responsibilities in many cases, and thus more high-conflict parents are sharing caretaking involvement. This has had the unintended consequence of increased litigation and revolving door high-conflict family cases that never resolve.

Alternate dispute resolution (ADR) approaches have long been seen as having advantages over the adversarial process, especially for the well-being of children. However, processes like mediation are generally most efficacious with relatively low-conflict cases. It was therefore urgent to offer litigious, higher-conflict families an ADR process better suited to their needs. In this context, the idea of ***parenting coordination*** ("PC") was developed in the 1990s and formalized by a national organization, ***Association for Family and Conciliation Courts*** ("AFCC"), in 2004. The PC process would be rather narrowly focused on assisting parents, particularly those with intractable conflict, with implementing and complying with their parenting plan or court ordered custodial arrangements.

The PC process is expressly ***not therapy*** with a goal of improving family dynamics, but rather it is closer to case management with a goal of "***parallel parenting***" and disengagement between the parties. Unlike mediation, which is aimed at negotiation and compromise between the interests of the involved adults, the PC process is child centered and typically may involve an ***arbitration component*** guided by the professional's knowledge of the child's needs. With many states mandating their own guidelines for the PC process and other states without guidelines, the exact parameters of the process remain somewhat ill defined. However, two essentials of PC work, at least from the point of view of AFCC guidelines, are first, that the process will be ***transparent to the court*** and thus the family's confidentiality will be only partially protected, and second, the professional will serve an ***arbitrating or tie-breaking function*** in the face of an unresolvable issue between the parties.

What are the Qualifications of the Parenting Coordinator?

Although there are no state licensures, AFCC has promulgated guidelines for the qualifications of a parenting coordinator, and those seeking such a service should establish that the basic criteria have been met by the provider. The PC provider should have a professional background and be licensed in the mental health or legal field. The professional should then have specialized training and be certified as a mediator and as a parenting coordinator. Both parents should meet the parenting coordinator, together or individually, to determine if the fit is a good one.

Whom is the PC Process Intended For?

The participants in the PC process will generally be parents with shared or joint custody. The cases will usually be of a high-conflict nature or at least such that co-parenting is achieved only with court intervention. The individuals will need to be able to afford private fees, which are typically not covered by insurance. However, some professionals will offer ***sliding scale or negotiated rates***; additionally, the PC concept is to provide as-needed help so ideally the charges would be situational and not constant. Some cases, such as those involving domestic violence or severe mental illness, will not be appropriate for a PC process. However, unlike mediation, wherein a significant power imbalance between the couple or noteworthy personality disorder traits in one or both parties may militate against reaching a settlement, the PC process assumes the presence of such negative factors.

What Constitutes the Parenting Coordination Process?

The AFCC guidelines concerning the PC process can be distilled into five basic tasks. The professional gathers information, reviews documents, and speaks to other professionals, educators and extended family members in order to have a basic assessment of the case. The professional provides education concerning the special needs and developmental issues of the subject child(ren). Case coordination is an essential component of the process so that all professionals involved with the family are working together to help optimize the parenting. ***Conflict management*** will be needed to adjudicate between the feuding parties, helping them achieve a workable compromise. Finally, decision making on the part of the PC may be the only alternative when the parties reach intractable conflict or when the child's interests are not being sufficiently considered.

A case vignette may help exemplify the kinds of issues the PC process confronts:

> An Asian man and American woman divorced when their son was five years old and having considerable gender confusion if not outright "gender identity disorder," a condition where the child rejects his/her given gender. The boy's intolerance of things male was particularly disturbing for his father, the product of a traditional, patriarchal culture, intensifying conflicts with the far more liberal-minded mother, who seemed to be tolerant of, if not gratified by, her son's artistic and one might say, feminine inclinations. The couple separated, fought over all the parenting arrangements and eventually went through a court ordered evaluation, which ended in a joint custody plan. The boy was in therapy with a very experienced expert on gender identity, but the therapist had become somewhat polarized between the parents and in opposition to the father.

Enter the parenting coordinator who initially had to assess the situation, meeting with and establishing rapport with each parent, speaking with the therapist and reviewing documents, particularly the ***lengthy forensic evaluation***. Parenting education then followed, marked by reassurance with the mother that her ex was a trustworthy parent who would not abuse their son, while the father was encouraged to support the boy's therapy and recognize that the therapist had his child's best interests in mind in gently fostering his male identity. Each parent was also apprised of the importance of ***minimizing conflict***, and tolerating his/her counterpart, despite their vastly different styles and values.

This PC intervention illustrates the importance of case management in that there were instances where both parties' lawyers were involved in conference calls with the mental health coordinator to forestall possible court intervention, (as had previously occurred with regard to the father's inadequate apartment, a studio with room for only one bed, which was rightly objected to by the mother of the child who was now approaching his mid-elementary school years). ***Conflict management***, involving dispute resolution, is also a necessary component of all PC processes. In this case, for instance, a semi-annual meeting with both parents typically entailed the invoking of "enlightened self-interest," a concept coined by Christine Coates of AFCC, to refer to negotiating from the vantage point of giving up something to get something in return, as, in this instance, in showing some flexibility of scheduling to accommodate travel plans and flights, which was of benefit to each parent.

Final Thoughts

In summary, parenting coordination is a relatively new and novel alternate dispute resolution approach to primarily high-conflict families who would otherwise be mired in intractable litigation. Whether the PC process can be effective with such families on a wide scale is uncertain. The support of the courts and of state guidelines varies across the country, and this limits the scope and authority of the PC professional.

Paul Hymowitz, Ph.D.

Paul Hymowitz, Ph.D. has been practicing psychology for over 30 years. Specializing in divorce and custody work, he previously co-edited one book on the matter, entitled *A Handbook of Divorce and Custody*.

Paul Hymowitz is on the faculties of New York Medical College, Yeshiva University and IPTAR (Institute for Psychoanalytic Training and Research). For more information, visit paulhymowitzphd.com.

PART III: MARITAL DISSOLUTION

SECTION A: THE PATH FOR SEPARATION

CHAPTER 25

MOVING OUT

By Ravi Cattry, Esq.

The first instinct when going through a divorce can often be to move out of the marital home to ***reduce the tension*** of getting divorced. However, some fear that moving out may negatively impact them in the divorce by giving the other spouse the fault-ground of physical abandonment in the divorce. This Chapter focuses on "moving out."

Avoiding "Abandonment" Ground

In way of background, Domestic Relations Law Section 170 defines ***abandonment*** as an act by one spouse for one year or more, which can be either ***physical or constructive***. ***Physical abandonment*** is moving out of the marital home in a manner that meets the elements stated to the right, whereas constructive abandonment can occur when one spouse locks the other out of the marital home, the actions of one spouse make it impossible to live together, or lack of sexual relations. For more information on grounds for divorce, see Chapter 28 by Cari Rincker and Kymberly Robinson.

> **Elements for Physical Abandonment**
>
> (1) Voluntary separation of one spouse from another
> (2) An intent not to resume cohabitation
> (3) Lack of consent of the other spouse
> (4) No justification

In 2011, New York State introduced no fault divorce where the reason for divorce can be irretrievable breakdown of the marital relationship rather than a specific fault. Most courts prefer to handle divorce as "no fault" rather than fault and the trend is that most divorces are filed as no fault. That said, even if the grounds for divorce are no fault, moving out of the marital home may create the fault ground of "physical abandonment" if it is done ***without consent*** of the other spouse. The issue of "fault" can be applicable with equitable distribution. More information on equitable distribution is found in Chapter 30. A simple "move out" letter (discussed below) can memorialize that the move-out was done with the consent of the other party.

Effects of Moving Out of the Marital Residence

Besides (potentially) creating the fault-ground of abandonment, there are other effects on moving out of the marital residence. Here are a few:

Finances

Moving out can affect finances, ownership of items in the marital home, and child support. Finances are a major consideration while moving out because the spouse moving out may still be responsible for paying the mortgage and other bills. If the home is in the name of both spouses, the spouse moving out is still legally obligated to pay for costs of maintaining the marital home. Moving out does not absolve that spouse of those duties. This can then make moving out more expensive because the moving out spouse is responsible for costs of the marital home as well as costs of living in a new place while divorce proceedings are ongoing.

Exclusive Occupancy Over the Marital Home

Another issue that may arise by moving out is that the party that remains in the home may be awarded exclusive occupancy over the marital home while the divorce proceedings are ongoing. This is called ***pendente lite*** (or temporary) ***exclusive occupancy***. Upon motion, the court can award exclusive occupancy of the marital home under two circumstances:

- upon a showing that a spouse's presence has caused domestic strife and that spouse has established an alternative residence or
- upon showing that exclusive occupancy is necessary to protect safety of persons or property.

Therefore, if a party chooses to move, even with permission, he or she may be limited access to the marital home if a *pendente lite* motion is made. After the divorce is finalized, the court can give permanent exclusive occupancy to one party, which may or may not be affected by moving out during the divorce action.

Equitable Division of Personal Property

Moving out can also have an ***effect on ownership*** of items that are in the marital home, such as art, furniture, appliances, and personal effects from a practical standpoint rather than a legal one. Even after moving out, both spouses are entitled to rights regarding marital property. Realistically though, moving out means that the party residing in the home has all of the control over the property. It can be difficult for a spouse to take all of his or her property when he or she moves out of the house; therefore, leaving that property in the house may be the only option. When a divorce commences, protective orders are put in place to prevent one party from disposing of assets without consent of the other party, which will protect assets if one party were to move out of the house. This, however, does not always stop a spouse from disposing of or harming assets.

Children

Another issue created by moving out is ***child custody***. Moving out may affect a party's right to be a custodial parent, as courts generally prefer to maintain status quo. Moving out and not spending enough time with children may impact how child custody and visitation are decided later in divorce proceedings. More information on child custody and visitation is found in Chapter 10 by Cari Rincker and Bonnie Mohr. Importantly, depending on where the leaving spouse stays during the divorce case, there might not be enough room to have children stay overnight, which can also impact decisions on child custody.

The "Move-Out" Agreement or Letter

Before one spouse decides to move out of the marital residence, unless there is an emergency, it is important that spouses discuss the above issues. Spouses should make decisions on payment of bills – who will pay what bills and when. They should also discuss allowing the moving out spouse to have access to the marital home in order to have access to belongings left behind or spend time with the children in the marital home. Child custody should also be discussed, including issues such as picking children up from school, after school activities, spending time with children in general, and any major holidays or birthdays that might arise during the ongoing divorce proceedings.

These items can be put into an informal writing just so that both parties are clear on who has what responsibilities. A lawyer can also help in creating a document that can serve as a temporary agreement while divorce proceedings are finalized. If it is not possible to stay in the marital home during a divorce, the above issues should be considered before making the decision to move out.

If a spouse does decide to move out, a move-out letter can be written and signed by both parties declaring that the spouse leaving is doing so ***with the permission*** of the other spouse and this move should not be considered physical abandonment. This type of letter is not usually necessary during a divorce proceeding, but it can be used to make a party more comfortable about moving out to reduce stress of the divorce. This letter can be informal and can be signed by each spouse. The letter does not need to be notarized, but it can be if the parties choose to do so. An attorney can also help with the drafting of the letter.

Ravi Cattry, Esq.

Ravi Cattry is an associate attorney at Rincker Law, PLLC and is licensed to practice in New York and New Jersey and admitted into the Eastern and Southern District Courts of New York. She completed a Bachelor of Science at Fordham University in Manhattan where she was a double major in psychology and economics. She received a Juris Doctor from Pace University School of Law in White Plains, New York.

For more information about Rincker Law, PLLC visit www.rinckerlaw.com.

SECTION A: THE PATH FOR SEPARATION

CHAPTER 26

DIVORCE PATHS: THE UNCONTESTED VS. CONTESTED DIVORCE

By Sheera Gefen, Esq.

Often when one hears the word "divorce," various thoughts and images come to mind: a couple with ***high tensions and emotions***, a judge making decisions that affect the lives of parents and children, large amounts of money spent on attorney fees…the list goes on and on. Fortunately, when couples agree on the major issues involved in their divorce, (including parenting and economic issues), they ***can avoid the many taxing variables*** that would normally appear in a contested matrimonial action. Thus, the path of the uncontested divorce is most certainly a preferable one, if spouses can manage to communicate and negotiate amicably among themselves or through the help of their attorneys and/or mediators.

What is an "Uncontested Divorce"?

There are ***two types of uncontested divorces*** in New York State:

1) A divorce whereby both spouses agree to a resolution of all outstanding issues involved in their case (i.e. custody and visitation, child support, maintenance, and equitable distribution);

2) A "***default" divorce*** wherein a spouse fails to "appear" (respond) after the initial summons is served upon him or her.

Uncontested divorces are usually (but not always) "simple," less costly, and faster to complete in that they do not require as much time and effort to finalize as those that are contested. Importantly, they ***do not necessitate appearances*** in court before a judge. The simplest uncontested divorce occurs when the divorcing couple has no children, no requests for any maintenance, and no property or debts to be divided. In this situation, some parties choose not to hire their own attorneys and instead file the necessary papers with the court themselves, or ***pro se***. This is ***not recommended***, as unrepresented parties often ***make mistakes*** that can delay the process. Additionally, unrepresented parties may be unaware of their legal rights.

When the parties have children – especially minor children – issues of custody, parenting time, child support and educational expenses arise and need to be addressed in a written agreement known as a "stipulation of settlement" or "stipulation." If the parents (usually through the help of their attorneys) arrive at a written settlement, it is submitted to the court's "uncontested calendar" along with other documents that a judge reviews before signing the final Judgment of Divorce that incorporates the terms of the stipulation.

Similarly, when the parties have additional issues in their divorce that have been negotiated and agreed upon – such as those regarding property and debt distribution and spousal maintenance, the terms are laid out in their comprehensive written stipulation and eventually incorporated into their Judgment of Divorce.

The New York State Uniform Court System website (www.nycourts.gov) has a list, along with attachments, of the ***uncontested divorce forms*** that are filed with the court. Such forms include but are not limited to the Plaintiff's and Defendant's Affidavits, the Child Support Worksheet (if applicable) and the Sworn Statement of Removal of Barriers to Remarriage (applicable if the parties married in a religious ceremony).

Once the appropriate paperwork is submitted to the court, the time frame for waiting for a signed Judgment of Divorce varies according to the county in which the documents have been filed. Some counties have a quicker turn-around than others (for example, New York County is faster than other counties in New York City) – though time spans also depend on how busy the judges and clerks are at a particular period.

Although a divorce case may begin as uncontested, it is important to keep in mind that it can always turn into a "contested action," if court intervention is required for any reason.

What is a "Contested Divorce"?

Put simply, a "contested divorce" ensues once one party decides that he/she wants court intervention. When this occurs, a ***Request for Judicial Intervention*** ("**RJI**") is filed by either of the parties and a date is scheduled for a Preliminary Conference before an assigned judge. Although an RJI must be filed no later than 45 days from the service of the summons, in reality it is often filed days or weeks thereafter.

Preliminary Conference (the "PC")

The Preliminary Conference is the ***first court appearance*** in a matrimonial action. At this appearance, the parties and their attorneys indicate the issues in the divorce that have been resolved. Additionally, they provide the judge and his or her court attorney the opportunity to obtain an overview and understanding of the unresolved issues in the case. Both parties are required to prepare, sign, exchange and file "Statements of Net Worth" no later than 10 days prior to the date of the Preliminary Conference. The reality in practice, however, is that Statements of Net Worth are most often exchanged and filed at the Preliminary Conference itself or soon thereafter. A ***Statement of Net Worth*** is a sworn document, signed in the presence of a notary public, which discloses all financial information in detail such as assets, liabilities, income and expenses. It should include supporting documentation, such as copies of W-2 earning statements, tax returns, and paystubs.

The Preliminary Conference also sets forth a discovery schedule in a formal "***Preliminary Conference Order***" signed by a judge, in which both sides have deadlines to request and exchange certain financial documentation. ***Deposition dates*** are often scheduled at this time. Additionally, neutral experts such as pension appraisers and real estate appraisers are often appointed by the court during this conference, if not reserved for later on in the process. If custody or parenting time (visitation) is in dispute, a law guardian, also known as an "attorney for the child(ren)" may be appointed as well. ***Forensic custody experts*** (such as neutral psychologists) are most usually appointed months later at future court conferences (although it is possible for the court to appoint them at the PC).

Compliance Conference ("CC")

As the name denotes, the Compliance Conference is an appearance in court wherein the parties report on the ***status of discovery*** and inform the judge whether or not the Preliminary Conference order has been complied with. Depending on the nature of the case and what is at issue, as well as the preference of a particular judge, deadlines may be extended to provide each party with more time to complete the discovery process. One or more compliance conferences may take place before the Pre-trial Conference is scheduled.

Pre-Trial Conference

The Pre-trial conference serves as a ***last attempt*** for the court to assess whether the parties may settle their case and prevent a trial. Trials are costly, time-consuming and risky – in that neither party has a crystal ball that can accurately predict how the judge will determine the finality of the case. Therefore, it behooves the parties to work even harder at settling their case, if they have reached this phase.

If the case is still not settled by this time, ***last minute discovery matters*** are brought to the court's attention and the attorneys for the parties have an opportunity to raise additional concerns they may have with aspects of their divorce to the judge. Deadlines for the exchange and filing of pre-trial documents may be set at this time, if they have not been established already. Those documents may include proposed parenting plans, statements of proposed dispositions, witness lists and updated Statements of Net Worth.

Trial

A trial takes place as a last resort – when both parties fail to reach an agreement that finalizes the issues outstanding in their divorce. A Note of Issue is filed before the trial takes place, indicating that discovery has been completed. At trial, the parties bring forth their witnesses to testify in court and admit exhibits in an effort to convince the judge that their position is the one that should prevail when it comes time to deciding how the matters in conflict should be resolved.

Sometimes a judge will hear testimony pertaining to custody and parenting time only and refer the financial issues to a "Special Referee" who will "hear and report" his or her recommendations. Alternatively, if the parties consent, the Special Referee may "hear and determine" the outcome of the issues referred to him or her.

After the completion of trial, judges will often request that each party submit a "***Post-Trial Memorandum***" that outlines the facts and the application of the law to the case and that provides a summation of the particular party's personal position on the issues in the divorce. After reviewing the transcripts and post-trial memos, the judge will render a written decision and will grant a Judgement of Divorce incorporating the terms of the judge's decision.

Some Special Considerations

Motions

During a contested divorce proceeding, either side may file a "motion." A motion is a formal written application or request to a judge to render an order for a particular desired outcome. There are various types of motions that may be brought before a judge throughout the litigation of a contested divorce action. Some motions are referred to as "***Orders to Show Cause.***" Those differ in their procedure, (for example Orders to Show Cause have to be served onto the opposing side according to the specific direction of the court, while Notices of Motions may be served by mail, unless otherwise ordered by the court), and in the time frames in which they are heard before a judge. Orders to Show Cause are usually heard quicker than Notices of Motion, but are otherwise substantively similar in that they each make formal applications to the judge.

A common motion that is often heard at the date of the Preliminary Conference is a motion for "***pendente lite***" relief. "*Pendente Lite*" is Latin for "pending litigation." Hence, it is made in the midst of the litigation requesting such relief as temporary custody, temporary child support and/or temporary spousal support, and exclusive possession of the marital residence. A common motion that is heard at the Compliance Conference phase is a motion to compel discovery.

Alternative Dispute Resolution ("ADR")

Because the litigation of a divorce action is a financially and emotionally burdensome endeavor, some spouses may be great candidates for alternative means of resolving their disputes, such as through the use of a mediator or collaborative lawyers. Both processes are non-adversarial in nature and rely on the cooperation and respect of both parties and their voluntary exchange of financial information. The processes are meant to be quicker, less costly, less tension-inducing and a more individualized way of reaching a satisfying outcome. There are several chapters in this book dedicated to ADR. You may read Chapters 4 a-d, on mediation, collaborative law, neutral evaluation and arbitration for more information.

Sheera Gefen, Esq.

Sheera Gefen, Esq. graduated *phi beta kappa*, *magna cum laud*, with a B.A. in psychology from Barnard College, Columbia University and earned her J.D. from Fordham Law School. She has been a practicing attorney for 14 years and has gained expertise exclusively in matrimonial law for most of her career, working for District Council 37's Municipal Employees Legal Services. She has extensive experience representing clients in custody, child support, maintenance and equitable distribution matters as well as resolving disputes pertaining to the distribution of governmental and ERISA pensions. For the past 10 years, Sheera has been an instructor of Business Law at Touro College. Her research on the psychological implications of procedural justice has been presented at various psychology and law conferences including the European Conference on Psychology and Law in Krakow, Poland, the annual meeting of the International Congress of Applied Psychology in San Francisco, CA, and the annual meeting of the American Psychological Society in Washington, D.C. She often appears as a guest-lecturer at universities, speaking on topics related to the interplay between psychology and law. Sheera is also a Certified Divorce Mediator and a member of the Academy of Professional Family Mediators. She resides with her husband and children in Long Island, NY.

SECTION B: SPOUSAL MAINTENANCE

By Wendy A. Harris, Esq.

"***Maintenance***" is the term used in New York to refer to money paid by one spouse to the other for a period time. It may be paid both during the ***pendency of the divorce*** (i.e., ***temporary maintenance***) and after a final judgment of divorce (i.e., durational or permanent maintenance).

> The term maintenance is sometimes used interchangeably with the terms "**alimony**" or "**spousal support**" but the term alimony is reserved in the limited cases in New York when permanent maintenance is awarded.

This maintenance payment is separate and distinct from payments for child support, discussed in more detail in Chapter 11. Spousal maintenance is usually paid directly to the spouse for the purpose of helping that spouse become financially independent after a divorce (i.e., "***rehabilitative maintenance***").

Recent Changes in Maintenance Law

As of the date this book was drafted, the maintenance law is applied as set forth currently in Domestic Relations Law ("DRL") § 236 Part B; however, new legislation was passed by the New York State Legislature in July 2015, and was signed into law by Governor Cuomo on September 25, 2015, that changes certain important aspects of the maintenance law under § 236. These changes take effect 30 days (temporary maintenance) and 120 days (durational maintenance) after Governor Cuomo's signing. This Chapter discusses both the ***current law***, and the ***new standard***, the balance of which will apply after ***January 25, 2016***, about one (1) month after this book was published.

This Chapter further discusses the factors a court will consider in reaching a maintenance award on a temporary and post-divorce basis. Note, however, that the parties are often in the best position to understand their economic relationship, and that court disputes regarding maintenance can be expensive and the results sometimes uncertain. It is, therefore, often in the best interests of the parties that they reach an agreement through negotiation or mediation regarding maintenance to be paid. In addition, if the parties have signed a pre or post-nuptial agreement or separation agreement, the terms of maintenance may have already been considered and dealt with prior to reaching judicial involvement. For more information on prenuptial and postnuptial agreements, please review Section V(B) by Sabra Sasson. If the parties do reach an agreement regarding maintenance at any time, each party must indicate in that agreement the he or she understands the maintenance laws, and the factors a court would have considered.

Temporary Maintenance

> **"Income"** of the parties for maintenance is (1) income as defined under the Child Support Standards Act, (see Chapter 11), plus (2) any income from property that is subject to equitable distribution. DRL § 236B (5-a)(b)(4). Maintenance is deducted from the paying party's income for calculation of child support.

Temporary Maintenance, also known as "*pendente lite*" maintenance, is support that is available to the party earning less money (the "less monied spouse") during the time between the filing of the divorce action and the final judgment of divorce. If the parties do not jointly reach an agreement regarding maintenance, the court determines the presumptive amount of temporary maintenance to be paid and by whom by applying a statutory mathematical formula to the parties' respective incomes. Temporary maintenance terminates upon the issuance of the final award of maintenance in a judgment of divorce or the death of either party, whichever occurs first.

The formula to determine ***presumptive temporary maintenance*** was established in 2010 as part of a larger overhaul of New York's divorce laws and applies to actions filed after October 12, 2010. The legislature established the ***formulaic guideline*** to provide parties with more predictability and consistency in maintenance awards, and the adopted formula is meant to arrive at an amount to cover the less monied spouse's basic living expenses, including housing costs.[21]

In application, the formula has had mixed success, sometimes resulting in inequitable awards. See, e.g., Scott M. v. Ilona, 915 N.Y.S.2d 834 (J. Sunshine) (2nd Dept. 2011). In the Scott M. case, the more monied spouse, after payment of presumptive temporary maintenance and child support, would have had $39,000 available annually, and the less monied spouse would have had $78,000 annually. In that case, the

[21] Khaira v. Khaira, 93 A.D.3d 194, 200 (1st Dept. 2012).

judge was permitted to deviate from the presumptive amount because, after a consideration of numerous factors, the award was determined to be "unjust or inappropriate." Id. See also DRL § 236(B)(5-a)(e)(1). As always, the parties may also reach an agreement to deviate from the presumptive amount through negotiation.

In July 2015, the legislature voted to revise the formula for presumptive temporary maintenance to address concerns in its application. Those changes take effect for cases filed after October 25, 2015, and are discussed later on in this Chapter.

The Statutory Formula

To determine temporary maintenance, the court is required to undertake two calculations:

(a) Formula 1: 30% of the higher income [up to $543,000] (minus) 20% of the lower income

(b) Formula 2: 40% of the combined income (minus) 100% of the lower income

The presumptive temporary maintenance amount is the lower amount of the two calculations.

EXAMPLE #1:

In the case where one party earns $120,000, and the other party earns $40,000, the formula would apply as follows:

[30% of $120,000 = $36,000] minus [20% of $40,000 = $8000] = ($36,000 - $8,000) = **$28,000**

[40% of $160,000 (combined income of $120,000+$40,000) = $64,000] minus [100% of $40,000 (lower income)] = ($64,000 - $40,000) = **$24,000**

The presumptive amount of temporary maintenance is the lesser of the two calculations, which is $24,000 annually, or $2,000 per month, during the pendency of the divorce.

Two-Thirds of Income. Temporary maintenance is available under this statutory formula, *only* when one spouse's income is less than ***two-thirds of the other spouse's income***. DRL § 236B(5-a). This limitation exists because, in applying the above formula, if one party earns more than two-thirds of the other's income, then the resulting presumptive amount would be zero or a negative number. So, for example, if one spouse makes $120,000, the other spouse cannot make more than $80,000 for temporary maintenance to be available by formulaic calculation; however it may be available based on a court's decision to deviate from the formula (see below).

EXAMPLE #2

In the case where one party earns $120,000, and the other party earns $80,000, the formula would apply as follows:

[30% of $120,000 = $36,000] minus [20% of $80,000 = $16,000] = ($36,000 - $16,000) = **$20,000**

[40% of $200,000 (combined income of $120,000+$80,000) = [$80,000]] minus [100% of $80,000 (lower income)] = ($80,000 - $80,000) = **$0**

The lower amount of the two is zero, and thus no formulaic maintenance is available. Note that if the less moneyed spouse earns more than $80,000, the result of the second formula would be a negative number.

<u>Low-Income Adjustment</u>. There is a low-income adjustment available to the paying party, if the payment of the presumptive maintenance award would ***reduce his or her income*** below 135% of poverty income (referred to as the "***self-support reserve***"). The self-support reserve in 2015 is $15,890. In these circumstances, the court will recalculate the payment by taking the paying party's income minus the self-support reserve. The party will then pay the difference between his or her income and the self-support reserve. If the paying party's income is less than the reserve, no maintenance payment would be required.

EXAMPLE #3

In the case where one party earns $21,000, and the other party earns $0 the formula and low-income adjustment would apply as follows:

[30% of $21,000 = $6300] minus [20% of $0 = $0] = ($6300 - $0) = **$6300**

[40% of $21,000 (combined income of $21,000+$0) = [$8400]] minus [100% of $0 (lower income)] = ($8400- $0) = **$8400**

The presumptive amount of temporary maintenance is the lesser of the two calculations, which is $6300 annually, or $525 per month, during the pendency of the divorce. However, in this case, paying the presumptive amount would place the payor's income at less than the self-support reserve:

$21,000 (minus) $6300 = $14,700. Therefore the low-income adjustment would apply as follows:

$21,000 (income of payor) minus $15,890 (self-support reserve) = $5,110.

The paying party's maintenance payment would be adjusted to $5,110 annually or $425.83 each month, so that he or she is not living below the self-support reserve.

The New York Courts provide guiding worksheets and an online calculator to assist a party in calculating temporary maintenance under the formula at http://www.nycourts.gov/Divorce/TMG-Worksheet.pdf (last visited on September 4, 2015) and http://www.nycourts.gov/Divorce/calculator.pdf (last visited on September 4, 2015). However, it is recommended that a party consult with an attorney if he or she has any concerns about paying or receiving temporary maintenance.

Amounts Above the Income Cap

Currently, income subject to the statutory formula is capped at $543,000, and after October 25, 2015, will be capped at $175,000. However, the court "shall determine" whether any ***additional presumptive temporary*** maintenance is warranted based on the portion of income above the applicable cap. See DRL § 236B (5-a)(c)(2)(A). In making this determination, the court takes into consideration such factors as the financial needs of the parties and their current standard of living, each party's earning capacity, the parties' conduct, the parties' other financial and family responsibilities, and tax consequences.

The specific ***nineteen factors*** considered by the court are set forth in DRL § 236B(5-a)(c)(2) and are:

- the ***length of the marriage***;
- the ***substantial differences*** in the incomes of the parties;
- the ***standard of living*** of the parties established during the marriage;
- the ***age and health*** of the parties;
- the ***present and future earning*** capacity of the parties;
- the need of one party to incur ***education or training*** expenses;
- the ***wasteful dissipation*** of marital property;

- the ***transfer or encumbrance*** made in contemplation of a matrimonial action without fair consideration;
- the existence and duration of a ***pre-marital joint household*** or a pre-divorce separate household;
- acts by one party against another that have inhibited or continue to ***inhibit a party***'s earning capacity or ability to obtain meaningful employment;
- the availability and cost of ***medical insurance*** for the parties;
- the care of the ***children or stepchildren***, disabled adult children or stepchildren, elderly parents or in-laws that has inhibited or continues to inhibit a party's earning capacity or ability to obtain meaningful employment;
- the inability of one party to obtain ***meaningful employment*** due to age or absence from the workforce;
- the need to pay for ***exceptional additional expenses*** for the child or children, including, but not limited to, schooling, day care, and medical treatment;
- the ***tax consequences*** to each party;
- ***marital property*** subject to distribution pursuant to subdivision five of this part;
- the ***reduced or lost earning capacity*** of the party seeking temporary maintenance as a result of having foregone or delayed education, training, employment or career opportunities during the marriage; and
- the ***contributions and services*** of the party seeking temporary maintenance as a spouse, parent, wage earner and homemaker and to the career or career potential of the other party.
- ***any other factor*** which the court shall expressly find to be just and proper.

In reaching a determination regarding including income above cap, a court must set forth the factors considered and the reasons for its decision to provide maintenance based on income in excess of the cap.

EXAMPLE #4

In the case where one party earns $1,000,000, and the other party earns $150,000 the formula would apply as follows:

[30% of $543,000 (the income cap) = $162,900] minus [20% of $150,000 = $30,000] = ($162,900 - $30,000) = **$132,900**

[40% of $693,000 (combined income of $543,000+$150,000) = $277,000] minus [100% of $150,000 (lower income)] = ($277,000- $150,000) = **$127,000**

The presumptive amount of temporary maintenance is the lesser of the two calculations, which is $127,000 annually, or $10,583 per month, during the pendency of the divorce. However, in this case, the court also must consider the nineteen factors discussed above to determine if the less monied spouse should receive additional maintenance based upon the $427,000 in income above the statutory cap.

In a 2011 New York Supreme Court[22] case, the court increased a presumptive temporary maintenance award of $12,500 to $17,500 per month where one party (the husband) earned well in excess of $1 million, and the other party (the wife) was currently unemployed (although due to an ongoing drug addiction). The court found that "some additional amount of maintenance [was] appropriate" based on the husband's income above the cap, after considering, among other factors, the duration of the marriage, the standard of living, and the health and earning potentials of the spouses. Specifically, the court noted the that the parties had been married for 17 years, the substantial difference in the parties' income, the high standard of living enjoyed by the parties during the marriage, the wife's poor health and the husband's good health, and the husband's "excellent" future earning capacity and the "unclear" earning capacity of the wife.

Deviating From the Formula

It is ***presumed*** that the amount calculated under the temporary maintenance formula, plus any additional guideline amount of maintenance based on income above the income cap is the correct and appropriate amount of temporary maintenance (hence, the term "***presumptive temporary maintenance guidelines***"). However, a court may deviate from the presumptive amount upon a finding that the guidelines result in an "***unjust or inappropriate*** amount." See DRL § 236B (5-a)(e). This finding could result in the presumptive amount going up or going down. The court must appropriately support and explain the reason for the deviation in a written opinion. Khaira, 93 A.D.3d at 201.

To determine whether a deviation is appropriate, a court analyzes ***seventeen*** of the same factors discussed above, excluding only

[22] H.K. v. J.K., 32 Misc.3d 1226A (Sup. Ct. N.Y., June 27, 2011).

the first two listed (the length of the marriage and the substantial differences in the incomes of the parties) from its consideration.

Although not an exhaustive list, some examples of reasons for deviation include:

- **Attributed Income**. The New York Supreme Court in Rockland County found that the application of the formula, which resulted in a presumptive amount of zero, was unjust and inappropriate because the wife's "income" was money attributed to her from her husband's business on her tax return. The money was earned by the business, and not paid to the wife in the traditional sense. In that case, the court increased the temporary maintenance paid by the husband to the wife from zero to $2000 per month. C.K. v. M.K., 31 Misc. 3d 937, 923 N.Y.S.2d 817 (N.Y. Sup. Ct. 2011).

- **Child Support Obligations**. The New York Supreme Court in Kings County found that a presumptive award of $3,097 each month to be paid by the husband was unjust and inappropriate because of two factors: (i) the pre-divorce joint household of the parties; and (ii) the child care expense obligation of the husband. The court also noted that the shift in resources from the husband to the wife resulted in a substantial reduction in resources for the husband. While the resource shift was not in itself a basis for deviating from the formula, the court took it into account when considering other factors justifying deviation and decreased the monthly maintenance payments. Scott M., 915 N.Y.S.2d 834.

- **Payment of Household Expenses**. The New York Supreme Court in Nassau County found that the presumptive amount of temporary maintenance was unjust and inappropriate because it did not take into account the fact that the payor spouse (the husband) was required to pay all of the carrying costs of the marital home. Under the statutory formula the husband would be required to pay $12,358 each month in maintenance *in addition to* carrying costs of $7,274. The court reasoned that in the existing circumstances the amount paid in carrying costs was no longer available income for maintenance calculation purposes. The "blind application" of the statutory formula would therefore be unjust and inappropriate, and the court lowered the monthly maintenance payments from $12,358 to $10,922 each month. D.R.C. v. A.C., 32 Misc. 3d 293, N.Y.S.2d 496 (N.Y. Sup. Ct. 2011).

- **Difficulty in Ascertaining Payor's or Payee's Income**. The New York Supreme Court in Kings County found that it was appropriate to deviate from the presumptive temporary maintenance amount, where the husband had failed to provide an accurate account of his income. The court reasoned that it could not calculate the presumptively correct sum in light of the husband's lack of candor and inconsistent financial affidavits. The court under those circumstances found that it was "an appropriate situation for the Court, under the authority in DRL § 236B(5-a)(g), to deviate from awarding a presumptively correct sum of temporary support under the guidelines and to award maintenance based on the needs of the payee or the standard of living of the parties prior to commencement of the divorce action." Salman v. Salman, 37 Misc. 3d 1210(A), 1210A (N.Y. Sup. Ct. 2012).

- **Look to Pendente Lite Standard if Award Would be "Unjust and Inappropriate."** In the each of the examples discussed above, the court applied the seventeen factors set forth in the statute to reason that the presumptive maintenance payment would be unjust and inappropriate and therefore deviation was appropriate. In those circumstances, the court may look to the pre-2010 *pendente lite* standard for maintenance, which includes the needs of the payee and the parties' prior standard of living to determine the appropriate amount. See, e.g., J.V. v. G.V., 939 N.Y.S.2d 740 (N.Y. Sup. Ct. 2011); McCarthy v. McCarthy, 156 A.D.2d 346 (2d Dept. 1989).

On the other hand, the New York Supreme Court in New York County denied both the husband's and wife's requests to deviate from the presumptive amount, where (1) the husband had sufficient income to pay the presumptive award and still maintain the marital assets and meet his and the parties' child's expenses, and (2) the presumptive amount was sufficient to meet the wife's needs in accordance with the parties' lifestyle. However, the court did take note of the significant temporary maintenance award, and require the wife to be responsible for her own expenses, including her household expenses (utilities, internet, telephone, etc.), nanny expenses for when the parties' child stayed with her, and her unreimbursed medical and therapy expenses. See H.K. v. J.K., 32 Misc.3d 1226A (Sup. Ct. N.Y., June 27, 2011).

Voluntary Agreement to Deviate

Parties may also always jointly reach an agreement on their own to deviate from the presumptive amount. In any such agreement containing a deviation, the parties must state in writing that they have been advised of and understand the presumptive award each would pay or receive, respectively, and the reason for the deviation. See DRL § 236B(5-a). This requirement is to ensure that said modification is done knowingly.

Maintenance Following the Judgment of Divorce

Until January 25, 2016, the formula discussed above only applies to temporary maintenance calculations and does not apply to post-divorce maintenance, which is *currently* left to a judge's discretion (or the parties' agreement). Courts do not routinely use the presumptive amount of temporary maintenance as the amount for post-divorce maintenance, instead relying on the factors set forth in DRL § 236B(6) after financial disclosures between the parties and an opportunity for factual development by the parties and the court.

Early in each case, both parties must fully disclose their financial net worth by filing a "***Statement of Net Worth***" with the court together with their most recent year's tax returns and W-2s. Parties may also have an ***opportunity for discovery*** (i.e., an opportunity to request financial information from the other party and from third parties such as banks and employers) and depositions (i.e., an opportunity to ask another party questions while that party is under oath) to determine all assets and income earned by the other spouse. If both parties have been involved in the finances during the marriage, there may be little need for discovery with respect to the other spouse's income. However, in certain circumstances, discovery may be necessary if one spouse has not been forthcoming about or has not shared financial information with the other spouse during the marriage.

Once financial disclosures and discovery are complete, the parties may be able to reach an agreement with respect to the ***appropriate level and duration of maintenance***. If the parties are unable to agree, the court will hold a trial to determine the financial status of the parties, whether post-divorce maintenance is appropriate, and the amount and duration of that maintenance.

Maintenance Factors

Post-divorce maintenance is awarded after a fact gathering trial and is based on a court's consideration of the twenty factors set forth in DRL § 236B(6). These factors are:

- the ***income and property*** of both parties including marital property equitably distributed;
- the ***length*** of the marriage;
- the ***age and health*** of both parties;
- the present and future ***earning capacity*** of both parties;
- the need of one party to incur ***education or training*** expenses;
- the existence and duration of a pre-marital ***joint household*** or a pre-divorce separate household;
- acts by one party against another that have ***inhibited*** or continue to inhibit a party's earning capacity or ability to obtain meaningful employment (for example domestic violence).
- the ability of the party seeking maintenance to become ***self-supporting***;
- reduced or lost lifetime earning capacity of the party seeking maintenance as a result of having foregone or ***delayed education***, training, employment, or career opportunities during the marriage;
- the ***presence of children*** of the marriage in the respective homes of the parties;
- the ***care of the children*** or stepchildren, disabled adult children or stepchildren, elderly parents or in-laws that has inhibited or continues to inhibit a party's earning capacity;
- the ***inability*** of one party to obtain meaningful employment due to age or absence from the workforce;
- the need to pay for ***exceptional additional expenses*** for the child/children, including but not limited to, schooling, day care, and medical treatment;
- the ***tax consequences*** to each party;
- the ***equitable distribution*** of marital property;

- ***contributions and services*** of the party seeking maintenance as a spouse, parent, wage earner and homemaker, and to the career or career potential of the other party;
- the ***wasteful dissipation*** of marital property by either spouse;
- the ***transfer or encumbrance*** made in contemplation of a matrimonial action without fair consideration;
- the ***loss of health insurance*** benefits upon dissolution of the marriage, and the availability and cost of medical insurance for the parties; and
- ***any other factor*** which the court shall expressly find to be just and proper.

The amount of post-judgment maintenance is ***discretionary*** and different judges may emphasize certain factors over others. Note that many of these factors are similar to the factors used to determine deviations of or increases in temporary maintenance.

Duration of Maintenance

After the court decides, or the parties agree on, the amount of maintenance to be paid, the duration – that is, how long a party will receive it – is determined. Maintenance can be either "***durational***," meaning it lasts for a fixed time period and then ends, or "***non-durational***," meaning that it will be paid for the supported party's lifetime (a/k/a "permanent maintenance" or "alimony"). Non-durational maintenance is rare in New York and it typically exists only in special circumstances where one party is older or ill, or ill equipped to become self-supporting during his or her lifetime.[23]

In reaching a decision on duration, courts typically consider the time that it will take the receiving spouse "to ***obtain training to become financially independent***, or to allow the dependent spouse to restore his or her earning power to a previous level." Michelle S., 683 N.Y.S.2d 89 (emphasis added). The amount of time this will take is dependent on the facts of each case and is difficult to predict. Some

---

[23] When the dependent spouse is unlikely to become completely self-supporting, durational limits on maintenance are inappropriate. Lifetime maintenance may be awarded when the dependent spouse is incapable of future self-support, has no skills or training, or is mentally or physically ill. Michelle S. v. Charles S., 683 N.Y.S.2d 89 (1st Dept. 1999).

general guidelines are listed below, but there is no hard and fast rule on duration applied by the courts.

1. **Length of marriage**: Typically, the longer marriage, the longer the duration of maintenance payments. This factor may be more important if one party stayed home during the marriage to support the family at home.

2. **Reduced or lost lifetime earning capacity**: The court may also consider lengthening the duration of maintenance when the receiving party stayed home to raise the parties' children, or took time off from his or her career to support the other spouse, therefore delaying his or her own professional development.

3. **Acts inhibiting a spouse's earning capacity or ability to work**: Courts may consider domestic violence and the toll it had on the abused spouse's ability to work or to obtain an education. For example, in one particularly egregious case, the husband refused to allow his wife to learn English, to leave the house without his permission or to work outside the home. The court found that a longer duration of maintenance was appropriate given that the husband's conduct was designed to prevent his wife from being self supporting. See G.K. v L.K., 932 N.Y.S.2d 420, 420 (N.Y. Sup. Ct. 2010).

4. **Need of one party to incur education or training expenses**: The duration of maintenance may be limited if one party needs only a specified period of time to receive education or training that will lead to employment and self sufficiency.

Courts view maintenance as "temporary support" that is not meant to last forever. Therefore, the receiving party should always be planning for his or her financial future and anticipating becoming self-supporting, if possible. Certain coaches can be an invaluable resource in helping people transition to becoming self-sufficient. For more information on life coaches and financial organizers, review both Chapter 37 and 39, respectively.

Tax Implications of Maintenance

Maintenance (including temporary maintenance) is a ***tax deduction*** for the paying spouse, and ***taxable income*** to the receiving party. Before reaching an agreement on the amount of maintenance, each party should check with an accountant to ensure that he or she understands the tax implications of making or receiving maintenance payments. A court deciding on the amount of maintenance may also consider the tax consequences to each party. If a party has concerns about the effect of a payment, that party should work with his or her attorney to raise the issue with the court.

Parties may also want to review IRS Publication 504 ("Divorced and Separated Individuals"), available at http://www.irs.gov/pub/irs-pdf/p504.pdf (last visited September 4, 2015).

Termination and Modifications

There are statutory rules for the termination of spousal support. First, maintenance payments ordered by the court ***must terminate*** upon:

- remarriage; or
- death.

See DRL § 236B(1)(a); DRL § 248. Furthermore, a court ***may*** terminate or modify spousal maintenance upon one of the following:

- Modification by a court due to a ***substantial change in circumstances*** (DRL § 236B(9)); or
- Application and proof that the receiving spouse is (i) ***habitually living with another person*** and (ii) holding him or herself out as that person's spouse[24] (DRL § 248).

[24] DRL § 248 specifically refers to modification if a former husband can demonstrate that his former "wife" is living with another "man." Although rarely explicitly clarified, one court has found that the provision must be applied in "a gender-neutral manner" in order to preserve its constitutionality in light of the Supreme Court's decision in Orr v. Orr, 440 U.S. 268 (1979). See, e.g., Wood v. Wood, 104 Misc. 2d 109, 111, 428 N.Y.S.2d 136, 137 (N.Y. Fam. Ct. 1980). The provision would also presumably now apply to a former spouse of the same sex, holding out another person as his or her spouse. § 248 has been modified in the new legislation discussed in Part C, below, to be gender neutral.

As for the cohabitation instance, New York courts have routinely clarified that "holding out" oneself as married is strictly interpreted, and must be more than a romantic relationship. It must result from some "assertive conduct" by the former spouse such as using the other person's surname, or signing documents as husband and wife. Bliss v. Bliss, 66 NY2d 382 (1985) (ex-wife lived with man for 14 years, but court found there was no proof that former wife and man were holding themselves out as husband and wife). But see, Sanseri v. Sanseri, 2015 N.Y. Misc. LEXIS 1296, *49, 2015 NY Slip Op 25128 (N.Y. Sup. Ct. April 6, 2015) ("In 2015, the facts of shared intra-couple economy - shared residences, a shared bedroom, shared bank accounts, shared child responsibilities, shared travel, shared activities, shared socializing – are the equivalent of 'holding out' as a married couple").

In an agreement the parties can ***determine the circumstances*** in which maintenance may or shall terminate. For instance, maintenance may terminate on a date agreed to by the parties, or upon the occurrence of a change in circumstances agreed to by the parties, such as a specified decrease or increase in the level of income earned by one party or the other. Parties are cautioned not to tie the termination of maintenance to a child reaching the age of emancipation (within 6 months) or the payments may be reclassified as child support, which is not tax deductible and can have unintended tax implications. See I.R.C. § 71(c)(2) (IRS will treat the amount of a payment that is tied to "contingencies involving child" such as "the child attaining a specified age, marrying, dying, leaving school, or a similar contingency," as child support); See also Johnson v. Commissioner of Internal Revenue, T.C. Memo-2014-67, 2014 Tax Ct. LEXIS 63 (2014).

A ***modification of a maintenance*** award may be permitted if a party can demonstrate (i) a "substantial change in circumstances" (if the award is set out in a court order), or (ii) that an "extreme hardship" would result if payments are not modified (if the maintenance is set out in a separation agreement). See DRL § 236(B)(9)(b)(1). If there are genuine facts in dispute, a court will ***conduct a hearing*** to decide whether the facts support a modification based on a substantial change in circumstances or an extreme hardship.

If a paying party seeks a ***downward modification*** based on a "***substantial change in circumstances***" the court determines how substantial the change is by comparing the paying party's financial circumstances at the time of the motion for modification with the circumstances that existed at the time of the original maintenance award. Examples of a substantial change in circumstances that could warrant a modification include:

- an ***illness*** that prevents the paying party from working or increases unreimbursed medical expenses,
- the ***loss of employment***, or
- a ***decrease in salary*** that is not the result of the party's actions or fault.

The ***burden*** of showing a substantial change in circumstances rests on the party seeking a reduction. The court will hold a hearing to ensure that the party seeking to lower his or her maintenance payments has not become underemployed or unemployed intentionally or voluntarily for the purpose of decreasing payments. If the court believes that a party is attempting to avoid maintenance payments, the court may order the party to pay based on potential earning capacity.

A receiving party may also seek an ***upward modification*** based on a substantial change in circumstances, or an inability to be self-supporting. See DRL § 236B(9). For example, a court might increase the amount of maintenance payments the supported party receives if a long-term illness decreases that party's ability to work, but increases his or her health care expenses.[25] However, if the party seeking upward modification is responsible for his or her financial change in circumstances, the court is unlikely to permit an increase. For example, a court denied an increase where the party requesting the upward modification voluntarily left a job due to illness, but failed to obtain treatment that would have permitted her to work.[26]

The "***extreme hardship***" standard that applies to modifications of maintenance agreed to in a separation agreement is a stricter standard than substantial change in circumstances. Whether a party would experience an extreme hardship without a modification is a fact of specific inquiry. There is limited case law defining what constitutes an extreme hardship but at least some New York courts have found extreme hardship to mean that a party is almost lacking resources or shelter.

Maintenance Following Enactment of New Law

As of the publication of this Chapter, both houses of the ***New York State Legislature*** passed legislation, with overwhelming support,

---

[25] Bischoff v. Bischoff, 553 N.Y.S.2d 102, 103 (1st Dept. 1990).

[26] Zacchia v. Zacchia, 168 A.D.2d 677, 678 (2nd Dept. 1990).

significantly revising the maintenance provisions of New York Domestic Relations Law. That legislation was signed by Governor Cuomo on September 25, 2015. After signature by the Governor, the provisions related to temporary maintenance will take effect ***30 days*** after the bill was signed ***– October 25, 2015*** – and the provisions related to post-judgment maintenance will take effect ***120 days*** after the bill was signed into law ***– January 25, 2016.***

The new law resulted from concerns over the application of the current temporary maintenance formula, which appeared to many to result in an inequitable shift of income from one party to the other without regard for the need of the receiving party or the parties' standard of living prior to filing for divorce. In addition, because the temporary formula currently did not apply to post-divorce maintenance awards, the parties still ***lacked predictability and consistency.***

The new law works to address these issues. The relevant changes are listed below.

1. One of the most significant changes to the law is that a ***statutory guidelines formula*** for presumptive maintenance now applies to ***both temporary and post-divorce maintenance.*** This change will result in more predictability and consistency in maintenance awards.

2. The ***income cap*** used for the maintenance formula will be lowered from $543,000 to ***$175,000*** for both temporary and post-divorce maintenance awards. The cap will be recalculated every two years using the consumer price index.

3. The court will continue to have ***discretion*** to award maintenance on income ***over the cap*** or to ***deviate from the guidelines*** if the award would be unjust or inappropriate. (See "Deviating From the Formula" above for a discussion of the factors considered for deviation)

4. In determining temporary maintenance, the court now has the discretion to ***allocate responsibility*** between the parties for payments of family expenses (such as mortgage or carrying charges) while the divorce action is pending.

5. Temporary maintenance would now terminate ***no later than*** the death of either party or entry of the judgment of divorce.

This revision means that that a court has discretion to limit the duration of temporary maintenance if, for example, the parties were married for only a short time (6 months) but the divorce is pending for a long period of time (e.g., 1 year).

6. The law has been revised to include ***two separate mathematical calculations*** for maintenance, taking into consideration whether the party paying maintenance is also paying child support.

   a. **<u>Calculation #1</u>**: If child support is payable **by** the party paying maintenance, then the court:

      (i) Subtracts 25% of the maintenance payee's income from 20% of the maintenance payor's income;

      (ii) Multiplies the sum of the maintenance payor's income and the maintenance payee's income by 40% and subtracts the maintenance payee's income from the result; and

      (iii) The lower of the two amounts will be the guideline amount of maintenance.

EXAMPLE #6

In the case where the party paying maintenance and child support earns $120,000, and the party receiving payments earns $40,000 the formula applies as follows:

[20% of 120,000 = $24,000] minus [25% of $40,000 = $10,000] = ($24,000 – $10,000) = **$14,000**

[40% of $160,000 (combined income of $120,000+$40,000) = $64,000] minus [100% of $40,000 (lower income)] = ($64,000 - $40,000) = **$24,000**

The presumptive amount of maintenance is the lesser of the two calculations, which is $14,000 annually, or $1,167 per month.

This new formula results in significant savings for the non-custodial parent who is also paying child support.

   b. **<u>Calculation #2</u>**: If child support is payable **to** the party paying maintenance or there is **no** child support, then there is no change to the current formula and the court:

(i) Subtracts 20% of the maintenance payee's income from 30% of the maintenance payor's income;

(ii) Multiplies the sum of the maintenance payor's income and the maintenance payee's income by 40% and subtracts the maintenance payee's income from the result; and

(iii) The ***lower of the two amounts*** will be the guideline amount of maintenance.

EXAMPLE #7

In the case where the party paying maintenance and receiving child support earns $120,000, and the party receiving maintenance and paying child support earns $40,000 the formula applies as follows:

[30% of $120,000 = $36,000] minus [20% of $40,000 = $8000] = ($36,000 - $8,000) = **$28,000**

[40% of $160,000 (combined income of $120,000+$40,000) = $64,000] minus [100% of $40,000 (lower income)] = ($64,000 - $40,000) = **$24,000**

The presumptive amount of maintenance is the lesser of the two calculations, which is $24,000 annually, or $2,000 per month.

Under the new law, maintenance is calculated ***before child support***. When child support is calculated it now takes into account the maintenance paid by the non-custodial parent, subtracting the maintenance to be paid from the income of the payor and adding the maintenance received to the income of the payee.

Income for *post divorce maintenance* also now includes income from income-producing property that is conveyed to a party under equitable distribution.

7. The new law provides advisory guidelines with respect to the ***duration*** of post –divorce maintenance awards based on the ***length of the marriage***. For example, for marriages between 0 and 15 years, it is suggested the court provide maintenance for a duration that is 15-30% of the length of the marriage; for marriages of more than 15 and up to 20 years, maintenance would be 30% to 40% of the length of the marriage; and for

marriages of more than 20 years, maintenance would be for 35% to 50% of the length of the marriage. The guidelines are ***advisory*** and a court would still be able to award a longer duration or non-durational, post-divorce maintenance in an appropriate case. In addition, the law provides that in determining the duration of maintenance, a court is required to consider anticipated retirement assets, benefits, and retirement eligibility age.

8. The new law provides new factors for the court to consider in post-divorce maintenance, including termination of child support and income or imputed income on assets being equitably distributed.

9. Retirement, either full or partial, provides grounds for modification of a post-divorce maintenance award, if it results in a substantial drop in income.

Importantly, the law will have ***no retroactive effect***, and will only apply to cases filed after its effective date. A party may, therefore, want to consult with his or her lawyer to determine whether it would be beneficial to wait to file for divorce until after the effective date, or whether a sooner filing date may benefit the party.

Wendy A. Harris, Esq.

Wendy Harris is the founding member of Wendy Harris Law, PLLC, a law firm dedicated to providing quality services to individuals, families, and small businesses. Wendy has over 14 years of experience representing a diverse range of clients in civil litigations, regulatory investigations, estate planning, and matrimonial and family law matters.

After receiving her JD, cum laude, from Cornell Law School, Wendy began her legal career clerking for Judge Kollar-Kotelly and Judge Oberdorfer, both of the United States District Court for the District of Columbia.

Wendy is a member of the New York Bar, and is admitted to practice before both federal and state courts in New York. For more information about Wendy's practice, visit www.wendyharrislaw.com.

SECTION C: GROUNDS

CHAPTER 27

GROUNDS FOR ANNULMENT

By Deborah E. Kaminetzky, Esq.

Before the enactment of New York's no fault divorce, people who were married only a short time and had no children might have considered annulment rather than divorce proceedings. Now that New York allows divorce based on irretrievable breakdown of the marriage, annulment in New York tends to be more complicated than divorce. Annulment, however, may be preferred for religious reasons.

The Grounds

Just like New York has specific grounds for divorce, annulment also has specific grounds. The grounds are:

1. Failure of a party to have reached the ***age of consent***;
2. ***Lack of understanding*** such as being mentally retarded or mentally ill;
3. ***Physical incapacity*** to consummate the marriage;
4. Consent obtained by ***force, duress, or fraud***; and
5. ***Incurable mental illness*** for five years or more.

More information on grounds for divorce is found in Chapter 28 by Kymberly Robinson and Cari Rincker.

Third Party Affidavit/Testimony

Unlike divorce based on irretrievable breakdown, an annulment requires evidence and ***corroboration of that evidence***. That means that even if both parties agree and can testify that one of the grounds has been met, the court will require a ***third party witness*** (or affidavit).

As an example, if two people agree and are willing to testify that one party made it clear prior to marriage that they wished to have children and the other party agreed but then refused after the marriage (i.e., ***fraudulent inducement***), not only would both parties have to either testify or sign affidavits regarding those facts but they would need a third party to sign an affidavit or testify that they heard those conversations.

This is a much harder thing to accomplish than what is required for no fault divorce, as all that is required for no fault is testimony that the marriage is irretrievably broken with no third party evidence. With annulment, not only does there have to be a third party witness, but they have to agree to get involved by signing a sworn statement or testifying in court. Not everyone is willing to be involved in such personal matters.

Additional Documents to Be Filed

The ***auxiliary documents*** required in an annulment are similar to those required in a no fault divorce so there is no savings in time, effort or cost to accomplish an annulment with the exception of a stipulation of settlement. A ***stipulation of settlement*** which settles all matrimonial issues between the parties in a divorce is not necessarily required in an annulment; however, it is recommended in some situations. Once the paperwork is submitted, it still takes several months for the judgment of annulment to be signed (time period varies depending on the county).

It is recommended to include a waiver of estate rights in an annulment agreement. In case one party passes away in the interim, a waiver of estate guarantees that the other party does not benefit from the decedent's estate; they are, after all, agreeing to an action which ends their marriage. In addition, sometimes there are financial issues between the parties, even though they agree on ending the marriage, and those usually need to be worked out in writing.

The annulment procedure is unfortunately more complex than a no fault divorce. However, it may be preferable for religious, legal, or personal reasons.

Deborah E. Kaminetzky, Esq.

Deborah E. Kaminetzky is the founding member of Kaminetzky & Associates, P.C. located in Cedarhurst, New York. Prior to starting the firm Deborah worked at a Long Island firm where she learned the practice of Matrimonial and Family law. Deborah has also worked at the New York Department of Consumer Affairs where she was responsible for prosecuting unlicensed home improvement contractors and negotiating settlements for consumers. Prior to practicing law, Ms. Kaminetzky served on the Architectural Control Committee of a Home Owners Association in Boca Raton while living in Florida, and was the president of a commercial property management corporation in the New York Metro area.

Ms. Kaminetzky is a member of the American Bar Association (General Practice, Solo and Small firm Division and Law Practice Management Sections), New York State Bar Association (Estate, Family Law and General Practice Sections), Nassau County Bar Association (where she serves as Chair of the Technology and Practice Management Committee, and is active in the Community Relations and Education Committee, Women in the Law committees and General and Solo Committee) Great Neck Lawyers Association, and The Nassau County Women's Bar Association.

Ms. Kaminetzky was recently appointed to the Committee on Law Practice Management of the New York State Bar Association. Ms. Kaminetzky serves on the Board of Directors of the Yashar Attorney and Judges Chapter of Hadassah as a Vice President, and was their Woman of the Year 2012. Deborah graduated from New York Law School in 1991 and the University of Michigan, Ann Arbor in 1986.

Ms. Kaminetzky was admitted to the First Department in 1991 and the United States Supreme Court Bar in February of 2015.

Deborah is on the Matrimonial fee dispute arbitration panel for Nassau County. She expanded her alternative dispute resolution practice by completing a Mediation certificate program in December of 2013 from The New York Peace Institute.

Ms. Kaminetzky has spoken to various groups on topics including matrimonial law, technology and social media use, and disaster preparedness for business including cybersecurity.

For more information about Ms. Kaminetzky and her practice, visit www.kaminetzkylaw.com.

SECTION C: GROUNDS

CHAPTER 28

GROUNDS FOR DIVORCE

By Cari B. Rincker, Esq. & Kymberly A. Robinson, Esq.

New York is and has always been a grounds state for divorce. In other words, to get a divorce in New York, you must have a "ground." Prior to 2010, the only "no fault" ground for divorce was when a couple lived separate and apart pursuant to a separation agreement. On October 12, 2010, a second "no fault" ground was added – "irretrievable breakdown." New York also has the following six fault-based grounds for divorce under the New York Domestic Relations Law ("DRL"):

1) ***Cruel and Inhuman Treatment*** – DRL § 170(1);
2) ***Abandonment*** (actual or constructive) – DRL § 170(2);
3) ***Imprisonment*** for three years or more – DRL § 170(3); and,
4) ***Adultery*** – DRL § 170(4).

This chapter will first discuss the "fault" grounds and then move into the "no-fault" grounds for divorce. The relevance of "grounds" will be discussed at the end of the chapter.

Fault Grounds

Cruel and Inhuman Treatment

To establish cruel and inhuman treatment, the plaintiff must establish a ***course of conduct*** by the defendant "which so endangers the physical or mental well-being of the plaintiff as to render it unsafe or improper for the plaintiff to cohabitate with the defendant." DRL § 170(1). In other words, a plaintiff must show ***more than mere incompatibility***. A course of conduct requires a ***series of instances***, not just one singular event. See Milone v. Milone, 698 N.Y.S.2d 173 (2nd Dept., 1999). However, the interpretation of this varies with the ***duration of the marriage***.

Typically, the ***longer the marriage the more proof is required*** to prove cruel and inhuman treatment, unless the couple spent little time physically living together in same household. See e.g. Brady v. Brady, 486 N.Y.S.2d 891 (1985) (stating that "conduct must be viewed in ***context of the entire marriage***, including duration . . .") (emphasis added). In Soto v. Soto, 216 A.D.2d 455 (2nd Dept., 1995) for example, the court stated that "[i]n view of the short duration of the marriage, the verbal abuse, both public and private, and physical harassment of the husband by the wife cruel and inhuman treatment was proven." The reason for this is that in a long-term marriage people fight, people go through hard times, and it is possible that someone might lose their cool more than once and in an inappropriate manner. In a short term marriage, the risk is lower merely because of the short passage of time.

Bearing in mind the duration of the marriage, the ***frequency of the incidences***, and the seriousness of the misconduct, the types of conduct that might be included as cruel and inhuman treatment under DRL § 170(1) include, but are not limited to:

- Physical abuse/violence;
- Verbal/emotional abuse;
- Threats of violence;
- Sexual infidelity and/or telling spouse about adultery whether or not it actually occurred;
- False accusations of infidelity;
- Drug and/or alcohol abuse;
- Compulsive gambling;
- Surveillance and/or wiretapping;
- Lure and attraction of a paramour; and
- Denial of sexual relations in addition to other misconduct.

On the other hand, the types of conduct that are not viewed as cruel and inhuman include, but are not limited to:

- Incompatibility;
- Acrimonious or strained marital relationship;
- Loveless or "dead" marriage (DRL § 170(7) is for this);
- Irreconcilable differences (again, DRL § 170(7) is for this);
- Isolated acts of violence (particularly in longer term marriage);
- Public embarrassment; and

- Fiscal irresponsibility and/or manipulation.

It seems appropriate to mention here that some people suffer from alcoholism, substance abuse, and/or mental illness(es). While these are not alone enough for establishing cruel and inhuman treatment, if these addictions and/or mental illness(es) cause a spouse to become abusive and in turn cause the other spouse to fear for his or her safety, cruel and inhuman treatment can be alleged. See Wenzel v. Wenzel, 122 Misc.2d 1001 (Sup. Ct. Suffolk Co., 1984). In sum, due to so many different variables, the court will consider each case's specific facts and circumstances in determining whether cruel and inhuman treatment exists.

As a last note on cruel and inhuman treatment, there is a ***five-year statute of limitations*** for pleading cruel and inhuman treatment. See I.S. v. R.S., 499 N.Y.S.2d 106 (2nd Dept., 1986). That means, one cannot plead this ground if there has been no cruel and inhuman treatment in the five years immediately preceding the filing for divorce.

Abandonment

There are two types of abandonment in New York: (i) ***actual (physical) abandonment*** and (ii) ***constructive abandonment***. Abandonment, either actual or constructive, must have occurred be for at least one year pursuant to DRL § 170(2) in order to allege it as a ground for divorce.

Actual (Physical) Abandonment

Actual (physical) abandonment occurs when a spouse's physical departure from the marital residence is:

- unjustified,
- voluntary,
- without consent, and
- with an intention to not return to the marital home.

> It is possible for a couple to have a "***dual divorce***" with both parties divorcing the other person.

Each of these elements must be satisfied. For instance, it is not actual abandonment to leave the marital residence if one fears for his/her safety. Furthermore, abandonment ***cannot be mutual***. In other words, where both spouses want a divorce based on abandonment, the "mutuality" of the abandonment negates an essential element of this ground. Spouses cannot abandon each other and then plead abandonment.

Actual abandonment can be established where ***one spouse locks out the other spouse*** for more than one year. See, e.g. Schine v. Schine, 31 N.Y.2d 113 (1972). It may also be established if one spouses ***refuses to relocate*** with the other spouse. See, e.g. Bazant v. Bazant, 439 N.Y.S.2d 521 (4th Dept., 1981). "***Social abandonment***" does not arise to the level of actual abandonment, as harsh as that may sound. See, e.g. Davis v. Davis, 71 A.D.3d 13 (2nd Dept., 2009) (where husband had refused to engage in social interaction with wife by refusing to celebrate with her or acknowledge Valentine's Day, Christmas, Thanksgiving, and wife's birthday, by refusing to eat meals together, by refusing to attend family functions or accompany wife to movies, shopping, restaurants, and church services, by leaving her once at hospital emergency room, by removing wife's belongings from marital bedroom, and by otherwise ignoring her).

If you are contemplating a divorce and either want to move out, or your spouse asks you to move out, you want to make sure you are not "abandoning" your spouse, so you should seek a simple move-out letter from an attorney which will document that the spouse does not seek to abandon the other, but is moving out pending the divorce.

Constructive Abandonment

Constructive abandonment occurs when there is an ***unjustified failure or refusal of one spouse to engage in sexual relations*** for one year or more. ***A single refusal*** to engage in sexual relations is insufficient. See Silver v. Silver, 677 N.Y.S.2d 593 (2nd Dept., 1998). Additionally, the plaintiff must have ***repeatedly requested*** a resumption of sexual relations. See Chase v. Chase, 618 N.Y.S.2d 94 (2nd Dept., 1994). Similarly, it has been held that the refusal to engage in any ***social companionship*** or interaction for more than one year may be considered constructive abandonment as well. See, e.g. C.P. v. G.P., 800 N.Y.S.2d 343 (Sup. Ct. Nassau Co., 2005) (where the husband refused to eat a meal with wife, participate in birthdays, attend weddings, attend holiday parties, and sporadically refused to sleep in marital bedroom). Although this case seems to have similar facts to the Davis case, it is different because this one is dealing with constructive abandonment, not actual abandonment. Keep in mind that these are only case examples and while some things are statutorily based, different courts can interpret similar facts, but reach different results.

Let's look at an example for constructive abandonment for a little twist on this ground: What happens if a couple is having trouble in their marriage and they stop having sex, which prompts one to file for divorce based on constructive abandonment? After the divorce action is commenced, they try to fix their relationship and resume a sexual relationship; however, it fails. In Haymes v. Haymes, 252 A.D.2d 439, 440 (1st Dept., 1998) the Court held that, considering the totality of the circumstances (and specifically the unsuccessfulness of the reconciliation attempt), even though the parties had a brief (six week) "interlude of cohabitation and sexual relations" the plaintiff could still assert a claim of constructive abandonment. Thus, a brief fling with your ex will not vitiate this ground.

Imprisonment

To plead this ground for divorce, the imprisonment must have occurred for ***three consecutive years during the marriage***. Imprisonment means ***actual confinement*** (in a prison, jail, detainment center, correctional facility, or correctional mental facility), not probation or being "out on bail." See Pergolizzi v. Pergolizzi, 301 N.Y.S.2d 366 (N.Y. Sup. Ct. Kings Co., 1969). In cases where the conviction is reversed, if it was reversed after the spouse served three or more consecutive years, a divorce may still be granted on this ground. On the other hand, if the ***conviction was reversed*** before any time in confinement is served, a plaintiff cannot plead this ground. However, where no prison or confinement time is served because the sentence is suspended or the offender is placed on probation, there is in fact no "confinement" and, hence, no basis for divorce on the grounds of imprisonment. See Colascione v. Colascione, 57 Misc. 2d 199 (Sup. Ct. Nassau Co, 1968). A divorce based on imprisonment has a five year statute of limitations. Thus, one cannot plead this ground if his or her spouse has been released over five years ago.

Adultery

Adultery under DRL § 170(4) includes ***sexual intercourse***, ***oral sex***, ***anal sex***, sex with an animal or dead human body during the marriage, but not necessarily prior to the commencement of a divorce. See Dougherty v. Dougherty, 680 N.Y.S.2d 759 (3rd Dept., 1998). Adultery does not include kissing, fondling, sexting, or online sexual relationships. See Hunter v. Hunter, 614 N.Y.S.2d 784 (3rd Dept., 1994). To bring a cause of action of divorce base upon adultery, there must ***be more than one singular act of adultery***. See Salomon v. Salomon, 423 N.Y.S.2d 605 (Sup. Ct. Suffolk Co., 1979). It is also required that the plaintiff must not procure/arrange the infidelity. See Santoro v. Santoro, 56 N.Y.S.2d 539 (2nd Dept., 1945). Such an incident would mean buying a prostitute for your spouse and then claiming he or she committed adultery. The law also requires that you provide evidence of the adultery from a third party, such as a private investigator. This is one reason why divorces based on the ground of adultery can be highly emotional and expensive.

Defenses to adultery include ***forgiveness, condonation or consent*** of the non-adulterating spouse, and recrimination (if both parties commit adultery they cancel each other out). This does not mean, however, that there might not be another fault-based ground for divorce.

The statute of limitations for this ground is ***five years after the discovery of infidelity***. Therefore, if a spouse learned of the infidelity in 2000 and does not file for divorce until 2007 then he or she cannot plead this ground.

Although many people are not aware of this, adultery is still a crime in New York as a ***Class B misdemeanor*** and subject to a two-year statute of limitation. See Penal Law 255.17. However, these are rarely prosecuted.

No-Fault Grounds

New York has two "no-fault" grounds for divorce: (1) living separate and apart pursuant to a separation agreement or judgment and (2) irretrievable breakdown. Each are discussed below.

Living Separate and Apart Pursuant to a Separation Agreement or Judgment

Merely deciding to live apart is not a ground for divorce; however, living separate and apart pursuant to a separation decree or judgment, or separation agreement is a ground. For this ground to apply the parties must have been living separate and apart ***for one year after the entry of a decree of judgment, or after the signing of an agreement***. After the one year period has elapsed, either spouse may file for a divorce. Importantly, the divorce is not automatic – one of the parties must "ask" for the divorce after the legal separation.

- **Separation Agreements.** Separation agreements must be signed by both parties before a Notary Public, set forth terms and conditions by which the parties will live, and be filed with the County Clerk where the parties reside. It is recommended that each side be represented by separate counsel.

- **Judgment of Separation.** A separation judgment can be obtained by filing an action for separation (as compared to an action for divorce). The court then sets the terms and conditions for the separation.

A Judgement of Separation is typically sought when an agreement cannot be reached or if the parties want to revoke the judgment if "satisfactory evidence of their reconciliation" is submitted to the court. See DRL § 203. Importantly, a judgment of separation does not distribute marital property like a divorce does. See Valade v. Valade, 261 A.D.2d 881 (4th Dept., 1999). The only way to end a marriage is by divorce, at which point marital property will be distributed pursuant to equitable distribution law.

Irretrievable Breakdown

The New York Domestic Relations Law does not define "irretrievable breakdown", but Black's Law Dictionary defines "irreconcilable differences" as "persistent and unresolvable disagreements between spouses, leading to the breakdown of the marriage." This ground only requires one party to state under oath that the marriage has been irretrievably broken for six months or more prior to the commencement of the divorce. See DRL § 170(7). Many couples like this ground for divorce because the court no longer has to assign blame to one party.

So what if one party doesn't think their marriage is irretrievably broken? Unfortunately, the party has very little power to stop the divorce from happening. There is no defense to this ground. See L.A.B. v. B.B., 44 Misc.3d 1209(A) (Sup.Ct. Westchester Co., 2014) citing D.R.C. v. A.C., 32 Misc.3d 293, 306 (Sup. Ct. Nassau Co., 2011). For example, the parties can be living together and have had sex within the six month period and still have this ground for divorce. Sexual intercourse and or cohabitation are unrelated issues.

> In Alvarado v. Alvarado, 45 Misc.3d 412 (Sup. Ct. Richmond Co., 2014), for example, Husband's sworn statements on at least three occasions that parties' marriage was irretrievably broken down for at least six months were held to be sufficient to establish grounds for divorce. Accordingly, the Wife was judicially estopped in divorce action from claiming there was a question of fact regarding the grounds for divorce. Similarly, in GT. v. A.T., 43 Misc.3d 500 (Sup. Ct. Suffolk Co., 2014) the Court held that where the plaintiff swore under oath that the grounds for divorce was the irretrievable breakdown of the marriage for at least six months, the defendant could not testify to the state of their marriage at trial in an effort to try to overcome this fact.

The Relevance of "Fault"

There are two types of marital fault: (i) *economic* and (ii) *non-economic*. Economic fault includes "dissipation or secreting of assets, or other conduct which unfairly prevents the court from making an equitable distribution of marital property." Blickstein v. Blickstein, 99 A.D.2d 287, 293 (2nd Dept., 1984). Economic fault is absolutely considered in equitable distribution under DRL 236(B)(5)(a).

Incidentally, some fault-based grounds for divorce can have economic ramifications. Such a case would be in an adultery situation where a spouse is spending copious amounts of money on prostitutes or on a paramour. This type of situation is considered economic fault. The adulterous behavior is not what is at issue for equitable distribution, but the dissipation of assets is. In addition to affecting equitable distribution, economic fault can also affect maintenance and child support.

Generally, courts do not financially punish one party due to non-economic marital fault. However, if they do, marital fault is considered under the "just and proper" equitable distribution factor if the behavior is "egregious," meaning it "shocks the conscience of the court." There are three reasons behind this limitation on using marital fault to punish a spouse in equitable distribution, which are summarized in the O'Brien decision: "because marital fault is inconsistent with the underlying assumption that a marriage is in part an economic partnership and upon its dissolution the parties are entitled to a fair share of the marital estate, because fault will usually be difficult to assign and because introduction of the issue may involve the courts in time-consuming procedural

> ***Equitable distribution factors*** are outlined in DRL § 236 B(5)(a) and includes: (1) the income and property of each party at the time of marriage; (2) the duration of the marriage and the age and health of both parties; (3) the need of a custodial parent to occupy or own the marital residence and to use or own its household effects; (4) the loss of inheritance and pension rights upon dissolution of the marriage as of the date of dissolution; (5) the loss of health insurance benefits upon dissolution of the marriage; (6) any award of maintenance under subdivision six of this party; (7) any equitable claim to, interest in, or direct or indirect contribution made to the acquisition of such marital property by the party not having title, including joint efforts or expenditures and contributions and services as a spouse, parent, wage earner and homemaker, and to the career or career potential of the other party; (8) the liquid or non-liquid character of all marital property; (9) the probable future financial circumstances of each party; (10) the impossibility or difficulty of evaluating any component asset or any interest in a business, corporation or profession, and the economic desirability of retaining such asset or interest intact and free from any claim or interference by the other party; (11) the tax consequences to each party; (12) the ***wasteful dissipation of assets*** by either spouse; (13) any transfer or encumbrance made in contemplation of a matrimonial action without fair consideration; and, (14) ***any other factor which the court*** shall expressly find to be just and proper.

maneuvers relating to collateral issues." O'Brien v. O'Brien, 66 N.Y.2d 576 (1985) (internal citations omitted).

Examples of egregious marital fault include patterns of ***extreme domestic violence***. See Havell v. Islam, 301 A.D.2d 338 (1st Dept., 2002) (where the husband broke the lock to the wife's bedroom where she slept separately from him, sat in a chair for over an hour at the foot of her bed waiting for her to wake up on the morning of one of their daughter's birthday with a barbell and yellow gloves, and severely beat her while she screamed through the whole thing waking their three young daughters who had to hold him back until help arrived). It also includes attempted murder of one spouse by the other. See Brancoveanu v. Brancoveanu, 145 A.D.2d 395, 398 (2nd Dept., 1988) (where the court held that it would be a "great injustice" for the husband to be awarded a portion of his wife's dental practice when he engaged someone to murder her); and Wenzel v. Wenzel (where husband attacked wife with a knife and stabbed her repeatedly).

Many people do not want to assign fault to one party for ***social, professional, and/or religious reasons***. This is one of the reasons non-fault based grounds for divorce exist. Socially and professionally defendants could worry that a finding of fault will reflect negatively on them if someone finds out, such as their children, employer, or a future love interest. However, divorce records are sealed for 99 years in New York. From a religious standpoint, adultery may be a violation of a religious tenet. Marital fault, namely cruel and inhuman treatment, may effect immigration issues.

Although fault-based grounds versus non-fault based grounds for divorce may have very little effect on the end result of the divorce, grounds are important because an action for divorce can be dismissed if the grounds for divorce are not properly pleaded. Fault grounds may, however, play a part in equitable distribution and may be pleaded for personal reasons, as discussed above.

Cari B. Rincker, Esq.

Cari Rincker is the principal attorney at Rincker Law, PLLC, a national law practice focusing on "Food, Farm & Family." She is licensed to practice law in New York, New Jersey, Connecticut, Illinois and Washington, D.C. Cari was named as a Rising Star for Metro New York in 2015 by "Super Lawyers" and is an award-winning blogger. Cari is involved in several professional organizations including the Association for the Bar of the City of New York's Matrimonial Law Committee. Cari's practice is family-centered and counsels clients on a myriad of family law and matrimonial law issues.

Cari is active on social media. You can follow her on Twitter @CariRincker and Instagram. She also authors a "Food, Farm & Family" blog.

Kymberly A. Robinson, Esq.

Kymberly A. Robinson is an associate attorney at Rincker Law, PLLC and is admitted to practice law in New York and Florida. She attended Union College in Schenectady, New York for her undergraduate studies, where she graduated with high honors as a psychology major. She then obtained her J.D. from Pace University School of Law in White Plains, New York and, subsequently, her L.L.M. (with a concentration in family law) from the Benjamin N. Cardozo School of Law in Manhattan. Kymberly entered the field of matrimonial and family law as a way to couple her interest in psychology and personal relationships with her legal education.

For more information on Rincker Law, PLLC, visit www.rinckerlaw.com.

SECTION D: PROPERTY DIVISION

CHAPTER 29

IDENTIFICATION OF SEPARATE & MARITAL PROPERTY

By Sheera Gefen Esq.

The ***division of property*** plays an important role in the divorce process. Though at times this can be straightforward, the distribution of assets in a divorce is often a complex undertaking when trying to juggle the facts and circumstances of a specific case with the applicable laws of New York State.

The laws pertaining to the equitable distribution of assets and liabilities were codified in the state's statutory Domestic Relations Law ("DRL") Section 236 (B) on July 19, 1980. Since that time, there has been much discussion on its contents by judges who have interpreted, clarified and sometimes expanded the rules pertaining to the ***equitable distribution of property***. Case law, therefore, has also become very relevant in determining how property is divided between spouses.

Financial Disclosure

Under the DRL, each party in a divorce has a mandatory obligation to provide ***full financial disclosure*** of his and her assets, regardless of whether or not the asset was obtained or accrued during the marriage, and without regard to who has title of the asset. To ensure full financial disclosure, the law requires that each spouse lists his and her assets and liabilities on a comprehensive document entitled a "***Statement of Net Worth***."

- **Assets**: An asset may include, but is not limited to: cash, bank accounts, stocks, bonds, business interests, real estate, cars, jewelry, artwork, antiques, furniture, and retirement accounts. Assets may also be intangible – such as a license or degree earned during the marriage that enhances the earning capacity of a spouse or intellectual property (e.g., trademarks, copyrights, and patents).

- **Liability**: A liability can include a mortgage, note, credit card debt, car loan, personal loans, etc.

Money owed to people or businesses (i.e., "accounts receivables") are also included on the Statement of Net Worth. Courts require that each Statement of Net Worth be accompanied by recent ***tax documents*** (i.e., W-2 and tax return) as well as a current paystub.

Identification of Property

Once the Statements of Net Worth are signed, notarized and exchanged between the spouses, the next step is to determine which property is deemed "marital" versus which property is deemed "separate." This determination is crucial before negotiating and deciding how the property will be divided between the spouses; unless otherwise agreed by the spouses, marital property will eventually be split fairly while title to separate property will remain with its owner.

Put differently, all property in a marriage will ***fit into one of three buckets***. Each person has his or her own separate property bucket and together they have a marital property bucket. In ***each bucket*** there are both assets and liabilities.

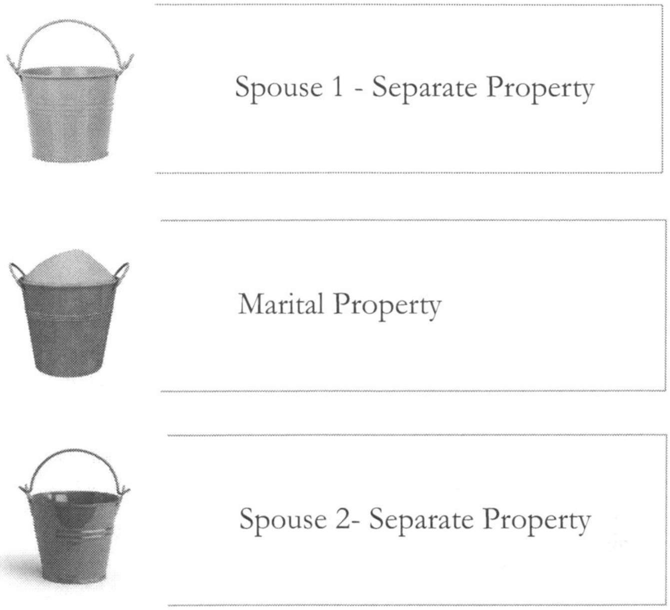

Identification of Marital and Separate Property

What is Marital Property?

Marital property is defined as all assets that were ***acquired during the marriage***, (i.e., before the signing of a separation agreement or commencement of a divorce action), by either or both spouses, regardless of the form in which title is held. For example, a house, a car, furniture, and jewelry that were purchased during the marriage would be considered marital property. Similarly, a bank account and a 401(k) retirement account that was opened during the marriage and that had contributions during the marriage, would be considered marital property. Because these assets are marital, they are subject to be divided between the parties in a divorce.

What is Separate Property?

In contrast to marital property, DRL Section 236 B(1)(d) defines separate property as the following:

(1) property acquired before marriage or property ***acquired by bequest***, devise, or descent, or gift from a party other than the spouse;

(2) compensation for ***personal injuries*** (with limited exceptions);

(3) property acquired in ***exchange*** for or the increase in value of separate property, except to the extent that such appreciation is due in part to the contributions or efforts of the other spouse; and,

(4) property described as separate property by ***written agreement*** of the parties.

In addition to the statutory list above, there may be other types of "separate" property, such as property acquired after the commencement of the divorce action that will be discussed in further detail below.

A Few Special Considerations

Pre-Marital Property

As the New York State statute dictates, property acquired by one spouse before marriage is deemed "separate property." Co-habitation between the parties (or even forming a domestic partnership) before marriage **does not make property acquired during that time** "marital." Since the starting point for assessing the distribution of property for equitable distribution purposes is the actual date of the marriage, it is often quite simple to determine which assets were acquired before that specific date.

> Suppose David and Janet were married on September 23, 2006. A few weeks after their wedding ceremony, they opened a joint checking and joint savings bank account in both of their names at Chase Bank in Manhattan. At the same time, they each opened his and her own individual savings accounts at the same bank. Years later, David commenced a divorce action against Janet and during the discovery period claimed that his individual savings account, titled in his name only, was his to keep after the divorce, as it was his own separate property. However, during the discovery process, bank records were obtained, and it was noted that the account held in David's name only was actually opened after the marriage. Hence Janet had a valid claim to it as well, as it was deemed "marital" as opposed to "pre-marital" or "separate" property.

At other times it may be difficult to remember the exact time that an asset was acquired and even more difficult to prove a claim of separate property if there is no record of its purchase. In the absence of proof that certain property was obtained by one spouse before the marriage, courts have to rely on the testimony of the parties. Due to this, some couples choose to identify and delineate their "pre-marital" property that is important to them in a ***prenuptial agreement*** so that there is no debate and confusion later on, in the event of a divorce. For more information on prenuptial agreements, please read Section V(B) by Sabra Sasson.

A gift from one prospective spouse (before marriage) to the other spouse is considered the separate property of the recipient. An engagement ring, however, is a "gift in contemplation of marriage." If the engagement is called off, then ownership reverts back to the giver. Once the couple gets married, then the engagement ring is the separate property of the recipient. In this instance, the engagement ring's value will not be subject to equitable distribution in a divorce (no matter the length of the marriage).

Inheritances and Gifts

When one spouse obtains an inheritance and/or a gift from someone *other* than the other spouse, the property is deemed separate and remains with its recipient. This concept seems fairly simple on its face, but can get tricky when one spouse argues that an inheritance or gift was meant for *both* spouses.

When it comes to settling a claim regarding an inheritance, the solution is oftentimes simple: the parties exchange a copy of the deceased's ***Last Will and Testament*** and read the intention of the bequest. However, gifts are not as easy to deal with when trying to figure out whether the gift was intended for one or both spouses. Anecdotal evidence and the credibility of each party may end up being the only factors that a judge is forced to take into consideration in reaching a determination as to whether a specific gift should be deemed marital or separate.

Unless a prenuptial or postnuptial agreement says otherwise, gifts between spouses are marital. Unless otherwise agreed, wedding gifts are presumed intended for both spouses in honor of their marriage, and are therefore considered marital.

Personal Injury Compensation

Some portions of a personal injury award are considered marital while others are separate. To illustrate, compensation for ***lost wages*** is marital and subject to equitable distribution. However, ***punitive damages*** and money awarded to a ***spouse for pain and suffering*** are identified as separate property and will not be divided between the parties in a divorce. It is worth noting that although parts of a personal injury award may be deemed "separate" as mentioned above, the receipt of such money may still influence other aspects of a divorce. For example, the amount of money that a spouse received for pain and suffering after the settlement of a claim may affect his or her claim for, or against, maintenance in a divorce.

Property Acquired with Separate Property

If property is acquired in exchange for separate property, it is deemed "separate." For example, during his marriage, Robert used $100,000 of his inheritance money ("separate property") to buy his dream car in his own name. Based on the rule above, the car – and therefore its value – would not be subject to equitable distribution upon Robert's divorce.

However, ***exceptions to this rule do exist***. For instance, if Robert added his wife Nancy to the title of the purchased vehicle during the marriage, Nancy could make a claim that the addition of her name to the title is evidence of a "gift" from Robert to Nancy and the asset has been re-classified or "transmuted" from "separate" to "marital." Thus, Nancy would potentially have a right to claim equitable distribution of its value.

Similarly, if Robert used the $100,000 towards an already existing marital asset, (such as towards a lump sum payment on a mortgage of a marital residence), Nancy could argue that the separate property was "co-mingled" with marital property and therefore she has a valid entitlement to some of the $100,000, despite the fact that it was originally considered a separate inherited asset. On the other hand, if the separate money that was co-mingled could be traced to its original source, it might keep its "separate" identity and Robert may receive a credit for his separate property.

As one can surmise from the examples above, it is important to emphasize that when issues of commingling and alleged ***transmutation*** of assets arise, the resulting analysis and outcomes of claims are not always uniform and they vary on a case by case basis.

Increases in Value of Separate Property

The general rule in New York State is that when the value of a separate property increases, then that increase in value remains separate property. However, lawyers for the non-titled spouse may argue that this increase in value should be considered a "marital" asset when the enhanced value was the result of a spouse's "contributions" or "efforts."

Suppose that Ted owns a vacation home in upstate New York that he purchased for $90,000 five years before his marriage to Susan. Because Ted bought the property before marriage, it is presumed to be identified as his separate property.

However, suppose now that while Ted remodeled the home himself by building an extra bedroom and bathroom, Susan was the homemaker who took care of the parties' three children. This is an example of Susan's indirect "contributions" to the enhanced value of the home, (i.e., if Susan herself had remodeled the property, then those contributions would be considered "direct"). Now that the value of the enhancements on the property has increased by an extra $45,000 due to Ted AND Susan's contributions, this increase in value may be classified as "marital' and subject to equitable distribution. On the other hand, if no contributions or enhancements to the property were made and the property's value merely increased due to "market forces," then the increases in value would remain Ted's separate property.

Written Agreements

As stated earlier in this Chapter, some couples contemplate the reality that their marriage could possibly end in divorce, and therefore choose to enter into a "pre-nuptial agreement" or "pre-nup" in order to avoid disputes that may arise down the road. Among other things, a pre-nup can identify each spouse's separate property and can provide that each spouse shall waive and relinquish any and all claims, interest and rights to the other's separate property, as well as to the appreciation thereof, in the event of a divorce. More information on prenuptial agreements can be found in Section V(B).

If a couple does not sign a pre-nup before marriage, but wishes to sign a contract during the marriage that has the same effect of a pre-nup, it can be done as well. This written contract is referred to as a "***post-nuptial agreement***" or "post-nup" and is enforceable in a divorce if the terms are reasonable and properly executed. For example, suppose Rachel wishes to start her own interior design company during her marriage to Carlos. She and Carlos can contractually agree in a written post-nup that Carlos will not be entitled to any interest in Rachel's business in the event of a divorce. More information on post-nuptial agreements can be found in Section V(B).

Property Acquired After the Commencement of a Divorce

It is clear from case law and practice that when property is acquired by a spouse ***after a divorce*** action was commenced, it is presumed to be the separate property of the spouse who acquired it. The initiation of a divorce action occurs when the plaintiff, (the party who files for divorce), purchases an index number with the county clerk (not when one party says that he/she wants a divorce). However, if the non-titled spouse can prove that the post-commencement asset was purchased with ***marital funds***, the asset's identity will be marital and subject to equitable distribution.

Burden of Proof

It is important to remember that there is a legal presumption that any and all property acquired during the marriage and before the execution of a Separation Agreement (or Settlement Agreement) or commencement of a divorce action is marital and therefore subject to equitable distribution. However, if a spouse makes a claim that property acquired during the "marital" time frame is actually "separate," then it is that spouse who made such a claim who has the burden to prove that claim. The standard of proof in civil court is by the "***preponderance of the evidence***," which means that it is more likely than not.

Changes in the Law

The laws pertaining to divorce in New York State change and evolve over time. The state's politicians amend old laws and pass new ones, while judges make decisions that vary from prior precedent. Thus, both the legislature and the court are ***powerful influences*** on the outcome of a couple's divorce. It is therefore especially important for matrimonial attorneys to stay on top of the latest developments in the law so that they can effectively represent their clients. Similarly, in most cases, it is important for the parties going through a divorce to be represented by an attorney knowledgeable in matrimonial law to best advise them of their rights.

Sheera Gefen, Esq.

Sheera Gefen, Esq. graduated *phi beta kappa*, *magna cum laud*, with a B.A. in psychology from Barnard College, Columbia University and earned her J.D. from Fordham Law School. She has been a practicing attorney for 14 years and has gained expertise exclusively in matrimonial law for most of her career, working for District Council 37's Municipal Employees Legal Services. She has extensive experience representing clients in custody, child support, maintenance and equitable distribution matters as well as resolving disputes pertaining to the distribution of governmental and ERISA pensions. For the past 10 years, Sheera has been an instructor of Business Law at Touro College. Her research on the psychological implications of procedural justice has been presented at various psychology and law conferences including the European Conference on Psychology and Law in Krakow, Poland, the annual meeting of the International Congress of Applied Psychology in San Francisco, CA, and the annual meeting of the American Psychological Society in Washington, D.C. She often appears as a guest-lecturer at universities, speaking on topics related to the interplay between psychology and law. Sheera is also a Certified Divorce Mediator and a member of the Academy of Professional Family Mediators. She resides with her husband and children in Long Island, NY.

SECTION D: PROPERTY DIVISION

CHAPTER 30

EQUITABLE DIVISION OF MARITAL PROPERTY

SUBPART A: OVERVIEW

By Ravi Cattry, Esq.

In New York State, the division of property during divorce is governed by Domestic Relations Law ("DRL") Section § 236(B). This law lists ***thirteen factors*** that courts consider in determining how property should be divided.

(1) The ***income and property*** of each party at the time of marriage, and at the time of the commencement of the action;

(2) The ***duration of the parties' marriage*** and the age and health of both parties;

(3) The need of either party to ***occupy or own the marital residence*** and the use and ownership of its household effects;

(4) The ***loss of either party of inheritance*** and pension rights upon dissolution of the marriage as of the date of dissolution;

(5) Any ***award of maintenance*** under Domestic Relations Law Section 236(B)(6);

(6) Any ***equitable claim*** to, interest in, or direct or indirect contribution made to the acquisition of marital property by the party not having title, including joint efforts or expenditures and contributions and services as a spouse, parent, wage earner and homemaker, and to the career or career potential of the other party;

(7) The ***liquid or non-liquid character*** of all marital property;

(8) The ***probable future financial circumstances*** of each party;

(9) The ***impossibility or difficulty of evaluating*** any component asset or any interest in a business, corporation or profession, and the economic desirability of retaining such asset or interest intact and free from any claim or interference by any other party;

(10) The ***tax consequences*** of each party;

(11) The ***wasteful dissipation*** of marital property by either party;

(12) Any ***transfer or encumbrance*** made in contemplation of a matrimonial action without fair consideration; and

(13) Any other factor which the parties expressly find just and proper.

The court does not need to consider all factors listed in the statute nor is any one factor given more importance or weight than another. This section of the book focuses on specific equitable distribution issues; however, this Chapter will briefly describe these thirteen factors.

The 13 Factors

Factor 1

The ***income and property*** *of each party at the time of marriage, and at the time of the commencement of the action.*

Under this factor, the court will take a look at each party's income and holdings at the time the marriage started and compare it to the date the divorce action was commenced. The court looks to determine how each party has fared in the acquisition of property and how each ***party's income has changed*** during the course of the marriage. If one party's income has decreased significantly in order to maintain the household and due to parental duties, that factor will be taken into consideration for distribution of property.

Factor 2

The ***duration of the parties' marriage*** *and the age and health of both parties.*

This factor is used to determine the ***future earning capacities*** of the parties. There are no specific rules that the court follows in regards to longer vs. shorter marriages, but it often happens that parties in a longer marriage will have property distributed more equally whereas in a shorter marriage the court will try to separate the property as much as possible to leave each party in the position that he or she was in before the marriage. Additionally, the health of each party will have an impact on ability to earn a living after the divorce and support him or herself, which may increase the distribution award to a spouse with poorer health.

Factor 3

The need of either party to occupy or own the ***marital residence*** *and the use and ownership of its household effects.*

This factor is important to determine for the spouse with parental custody of the children. The court will look to see if having one party remain in the martial home is in the best interests of the children and whether the party is financially able to afford living in the home. This includes taking into consideration whether ***moving and uprooting children*** from their home could cause emotional or psychological issues as well as whether the party could afford a similar home that would result in more savings. The court may also look at the value of the home and what debt is associated with it.

Factor 4

The ***loss of either party of inheritance*** *and pension rights upon dissolution of the marriage as of the date of dissolution.*

After a divorce, a spouse will no longer be entitled to any inheritance that he or she would have received after the death of his or her spouse, including any separate property that belonged solely to the spouse. The court will determine how much of a loss occurs by losing this right, which in turn can have an effect on the distribution award.

Similarly, a divorced spouse will no longer have a right to the pension rights or retirement benefits of his or her ex-spouse. However, a spouse will be able to have a distribution of any pension rights and retirement benefits that accrued during the marriage.

Factor 5

Any ***award of maintenance*** *under Domestic Relations Law Section 236(B)(6).*

The amount a spouse receives in maintenance, or alimony, will also be considered in determining how other property is distributed. For example, a party may be given more property during equitable distribution in lieu of maintenance, or because a party receives maintenance he or she may be awarded less in equitable distribution. More information on spousal maintenance is in Section III(B) by Wendy Harris.

Factor 6

Any ***equitable claim*** *to, interest in, or direct or indirect contribution made to the acquisition of marital property by the party not having title, including joint efforts or expenditures and contributions and services as a spouse, parent, wage earner and homemaker, and to the career or career potential of the other party.*

This factor requires the court to look at what contributions each party made, together and separately, by the non-titled spouse in the acquisition of property that is in the name of only one spouse. The court also considers the contributions of one spouse in the ***furtherance of the career*** of another spouse. Therefore, the court will consider things like one spouse maintaining the home and raising children allowing the other spouse to engage in gainful employment in order to acquire property. This factor allows a court to distribute property regardless of whose name it is titled in.

Factor 7

The ***liquid or non-liquid character*** *of all marital property.*

Once the court identifies all of the assets and whether property is considered separate or marital, it will determine whether each asset is liquid, meaning it has a certain cash value, or whether the property cannot be easily turned into cash or a ***cash equivalent***. For assets that cannot be easily liquidated in order to divide the value between the parties, the court may order the party holding that asset to pay a cash equivalent to the other party to compensate for the non-liquid asset.

Factor 8

The ***probable future financial circumstances*** *of each party.*

The court will look as well to the ***education, training, previous employment experience***, current employment, prospect of future employment, and ability to become ***self-supporting*** in determining equitable distribution. A spouse that did not work during the course of the marriage may be given a higher distribution award to compensate for difficulty in obtaining employment after being out of the work force for a lengthy time. However, if both spouses worked during the course of marriage and future prospects are similar, the court is unlikely to give one party a disproportionate award. This factor tends to be very fact specific to each case.

Factor 9

The ***impossibility or difficulty of evaluating*** *any component asset or any interest in a business, corporation or profession, and the economic desirability of retaining such asset or interest intact and free from any claim or interference by any other party.*

Similar to factor seven, there may be certain property, such as licenses, professional practices, closely held corporations, and other business entities, which from a practical and policy standpoint would be best if they were not divided. Therefore, in lieu of dividing such assets, a court may choose to provide the other spouse with cash value of those assets or other property that would satisfy a spouse's interest in that asset.

Factor 10

*The **tax consequences** of each party.*

The court must be made aware of any tax consequences that can occur because of the transfer of property from one spouse to another. This may require the help of a tax expert who can assist counsel and the court in determining how equitable distribution may affect each party. The court can be relieved of its duty to take this factor into consideration if parties fail to provide the court with clear and competent evidence regarding tax liabilities.

Factor 11

*The **wasteful dissipation** of marital property by either party.*

Whether a spouse mismanaged marital assets or appropriated them for personal use when they were set out for other purposes is a fact based finding. If a court finds that such wasteful dissipation occurred, the party doing the wasting may be required to give the other party property or cash in the value of what was appropriated.

Factor 12

*Any **transfer or encumbrance** made in contemplation of a matrimonial action without fair consideration.*

Similarly to the above factor, this factor takes into consideration transfers by one party in attempt to defraud the other party of interest in the property that was transferred. The Supreme Court may not have power over the third party to whom the defrauding spouse transferred an asset, but the court can take the value of the asset transferred and include it in the distribution award.

Factor 13

*Any other factor which the parties expressly find **just and proper**.*

This is a catch all, which allows the court to take into consideration any other factor that is not specifically named in this statute, but may be relevant in determining the distribution awards. Courts have previously taken into consideration a ***party's conduct*** during litigation, such as delay tactics, interfering with discovery attempts by either the party or his or her attorney, and a party's lack of credibility,[27] or fault-grounds. Factors relating to marital fault are ***not*** considered in determining distribution awards.

Ravi Cattry, Esq.

Ravi Cattry is an associate attorney and is licensed to practice in New York and New Jersey and admitted into the Eastern and Southern District Courts of New York. She completed a Bachelor of Science at Fordham University in Manhattan where she was a double major in psychology and economics. She received a Juris Doctor from Pace University School of Law in White Plains, New York.

Before joining Rincker Law, PLLC, Ravi worked at a general practice firm located in Kew Gardens, New York. While working there her practice areas included landlord and tenant disputes, matrimonial and family law issues, commercial law, and immigration law. Ravi also worked with a boutique law firm specializing in bankruptcy law in Manhattan. During law school she interned with the Integrated Domestic Violence Court in White Plains, New York, where she assisted in handling divorce cases intertwined with domestic violence cases.

Ravi is fluent in Hindi and Punjabi, and conversational in Spanish. In her free time Ravi enjoys reading, watching movies, playing tennis, and keeping up with her favorite soccer teams. For more information about Rincker Law, PLLC, visit www.rinckerlaw.com.

---

[27] Wilbur v. Wilbur, 116 AD2d 953 (3rd Dept., 1986).

SECTION D: PROPERTY DIVISION

CHAPTER 30

EQUITABLE DIVISION OF MARITAL PROPERTY

SUBPART B: HOUSEHOLD EFFECTS

By Kymberly A. Robinson, Esq.

As discussed in Chapter 29, property in New York is either classified as marital or separate property. Then, only the marital property is subject to equitable distribution. This Chapter will focus on the equitable distribution of household effects (such as furniture, pictures, memorabilia, etc.).

Tips for Division of Household Effects

Clothing and Personal Effects

When couples are separating, it is a good idea for the spouse leaving the marital residence to set aside his or her clothing and personal effects or take them as soon as possible. If the spouse is leaving clothing and personal effects to pick up at a later date, it is a good idea to make a list of the items boxed up, their location, and label the boxes themselves.

If there is an order of protection then the spouse leaving the marital residence may not be able to gain reentry in the near future. Similarly, in more contentious divorces, clothing and personal effects are in danger of being accidentally "thrown out" if the spouse does not take his or her belongings upon moving out. It is never a good idea to throw away or sell a spouse's personal effects without his or her permission. If a divorce has been commenced then the automatic orders will prohibit the disposal or assignment of personal property.

Clothing and personal effects can sometimes be of great value, which can complicate matters. For example, think of the divorcing couple where the husband collected Rolex watches or the wife has an extensive collection of Chanel handbags. In those rare cases, clothing and personal effects are important in property distribution because of their high value. In these cases, the clothing and personal effects should be valued before being distributed to one spouse or the other.

However, let common sense prevail with the division of personal effects. These items can easily be divided by the parties themselves, avoiding the need to engage a lawyer in hours of battling over your favorite pair of jeans. It makes sense that the husband would want his clothing and that the wife would want her clothing.

Furniture & Appliances

In dividing up furniture and appliances, it is a good idea to use post-its on larger items, such as the furniture. Each spouse can have a color post-it assigned to him or her. Furthermore, each spouse should make a list with the items he or she would like to take after the divorce. Sometimes it is also a good idea to take pictures of certain items, which may be helpful for the hard-to-describe items.

In some cases, furniture and appliances may have significant value. In such circumstances, the parties may wish to consider an appraisal. In most circumstances, furniture and appliances have limited value.

Separating couples should again use common sense when dividing furniture and appliances. For example, if one spouse is a gourmet chef and the other has never even turned on the stove, it makes sense that the stand-alone Kitchenmaid mixer should go to the spouse who cooks. As another example, if one spouse is moving into an apartment and the other is staying in the house, the moving spouse probably should not take a 10 person dining table.

Sometimes both spouses do not see the value in certain items or do not have a need for them. One should not underestimate an item that does not appeal to that person's taste, but can be sold at a tag sale for instance to someone who would appreciate it and pay good money in return. Thus, if neither spouse wants certain items, they can agree to hold a tag sale together and split the proceeds 50/50. This is a great way to make some extra money and get rid of items that neither spouse wants. For instance, both spouses might want to start new after the divorce and not want the same casual china set that the family ate breakfast on together each morning, in his or her new life. This could be a great thing to sell at a tag sale, and enable each spouse to separately then go out and buy his or her new casual china set.

Valuables & Collectibles

Many times people come into a marriage with items and buy similar items during the marriage to expand upon their collection. In this case, spouses should not forget that anything bought prior to the marriage or received via gift or inheritance is separate property. Separate property was discussed in greater detail in Chapter 30. Valuables and collectibles that are of significant monetary value should likely be appraised.

Photographs

Often times, photographs and videos are items both parties want to take after the divorce. Luckily, unlike with items such as houses, credit card points, and cars, some personal property can easily and relatively cheaply, be replicated. For example, many videos and pictures now are saved electronically. These would be easy for both spouses to retain. They simply would exchange memory cards or email files to each other. Older pictures are not quite as quick to transfer, but can be done as well.

Several photography stores specialize in duplicating original photographs or videos. In some cases, couples fight over old wedding pictures with family members when they could have the album replicated and they could both retain a copy. For younger couples, the photographer or wedding videographer might have an electronic copy stored somewhere as well. Courts especially dislike getting involved in disputes such as photographs because there is no way to assign a financial value.

Mementos

Probably one of the hardest things for a parent to compromise on and divide during a divorce are things that the children made. This can be especially difficult if one parent wanted the marriage to work and the other has moved on. For birthdays, Mother's day, and Father's day, it would be easy to divide the children's artwork. However, it would be more difficult for other things such as the children's first finger paintings or family portraits. Dividing these items during a divorce can be extremely emotional and takes a lot of compromise if one is an emotional person and sad about the divorce. However, there are services available that might be able to help both parents with these types of disputes. For example, a video or photo album could be created with images of the parting mementos; alternatively, some might even be recreated with a 3-D printer.

Important Documentation

It is important for both parties to have copies of financial information such as tax returns. The same is true for the children's birth certificates and passports. In these cases, copies and scans can be made and exchanged between the parties. Since only one person can keep the original it should be the person who has primary residential custody of the children. It is also possible to obtain certified copies of birth certifies. The more organized a couple is from the beginning of the marriage, the easier and faster it will be to locate any and all important documents that each should have access to after the divorce.

Examples of Court Cases

Property division can become outrageous. Below are some examples that serve as a warning to divorcing couples.

One humorous example is a 1999 case from Las Vegas, Nevada dealing with a beanie baby collection worth \$2,500 - \$5,000. In that case, the judge ordered the couple, Mr. and Mrs. Mountain (in the middle of the courtroom floor) to lay out all of the beanie babies and they were divided between them under the judge's supervision one by one.

In another outrageous example, in Michigan, an Oakland County Circuit Court Family Judge, Cheryl Matthews, was presented with the Scullys, who were fighting over their dogs' semen to be used for artificial insemination. In that case, each spouse claimed ownership over the semen produced by three Bullmastiffs (two of which were by then deceased). The couple made money from dog breeding so this was a valuable asset to them. In the end, the case was referred to a civil court because it was determined to have dealt with a contract dispute over distribution of the dogs and breeding requirements for the American Kennel Club.

Final Thoughts

The most important advice to take away from this Chapter is that being organized, making lists, staying open-minded, and being practical will make the division of personal property quicker and cheaper for divorcing couples.

Kymberly A. Robinson, Esq.

Kymberly is an associate attorney with Rincker Law, PLLC and is admitted to practice law in New York and Florida. She attended Union College in Schenectady, New York for her undergraduate studies, where she graduated with high honors as a psychology major. She then obtained her J.D. from Pace University School of Law in White Plains, New York and, subsequently, her L.L.M. (with a concentration in family law) from the Benjamin N. Cardozo School of Law in Manhattan. Kymberly entered the field of matrimonial and family law as a way to couple her interest in psychology and personal relationships with her legal education.

Before joining Rincker Law, PLLC, Kymberly was an associate at boutique matrimonial law firms in Westchester County, Manhattan, and Florida. She was also a volunteer at the New York County Access to Justice Program-Uncontested Divorce Clinic where she assisted self-represented litigants in the divorce process. During law school Kymberly also participated in two legal clinics: one at the Pace Women's Justice Center, where she represented clients in obtaining orders of protection and another at the Brooklyn Family Defense Project, where she assisted in defending families in child abuse and neglect proceedings.

Kymberly likes to spend her free time with her family and also enjoys working out, cooking healthy meals, and getting together with friends. She lives in Westchester County, New York with her husband and daughter.

For more information about Rincker Law, PLLC, visit www.rinckerlaw.com.

SECTION D: PROPERTY DIVISION

CHAPTER 30

EQUITABLE DIVISION OF MARITAL PROPERTY

SUBPART C: REAL ESTATE

Sabra R. Sasson, Esq.[28]

When getting divorced, after all of the assets are identified, often the largest asset to be addressed and considered by the couple during divorce is the marital residence, and as such requires the most consideration. If the couple has other real estate, additional questions and consideration is to be given.

Real estate law can be complicated and confusing. This Chapter will focus upon the most common types of real estate that couples may have when going through divorce – ***marital residence*** such as a single family house, a ***residential cooperative apartment unit***, or a ***residential condominium*** unit. For some couples, additional expertise may be needed to discuss and consider other forms of real estate such as ***commercial property***, or if there is a substantial real estate portfolio (for example if one or both of the spouses are real estate developers or speculators) and in those instances more inquiry may be necessary which goes beyond the scope of this chapter.

Identify Real Property and its Characteristics

Assuming that the parties do not have a prenuptial or post nuptial agreement in place at the time of divorce, real property in both joint and individual names should be identified. Sometimes property can be owned with others as well and that means that the parties may

---

28 Portions of this Chapter were originally published in an article titled "Real Estate Concepts for Divorce and Family Mediators" in the New York State Council on Divorce Mediation's THE REPORT Vol. 2014, No 2 at 17-23. Used with permission from the New York State Council on Divorce Mediation in November 2015.

not own 100% of the property, and in order to distribute this property, they may need the consent and signatures of people outside of their relationship.

Once the real estate is identified, then the following characteristics must be evaluated:

- how title is held,
- date of acquisition,
- location of the property,
- type,
- use, and
- source of funds used to acquire the property.

Identify each piece of real estate by its address. ***Farm and other rural property*** could have other identifiers.

Who is Named on the Title?

This question can be easily answered by examining the title documents which is the ***deed*** for a house or a condominium unit. The title documents for a cooperative apartment unit is the ***Stock Certificate*** and the ***Proprietary Lease***. Also take note of any qualifiers after the name of the owners, such as "***tenants in common***" or "***joint tenants***" or "***tenants by the entireties***" or "***joint tenants with rights of survivorship.***"

Other Characteristics

The following should be kept in mind for the other real property characteristics:

- **Date of acquisition** is the date when the party or parties acquired ownership of the property and that will usually be the same date as the date on the title document.
- **Type**: Identify whether the property is vacant land, residential or commercial property.
- **Use**: Was the property used as a primary residence, secondary or vacation home, or investment purposes?
- What was the **purchase price** of the property at the time the property was acquired?

As for the ***source of funds***, how was the property acquired? Ordinarily, property is purchased with cash and/or financing. Identify how much was cash and how much was financed. What is the source of the cash use to acquire the property? Were the funds used from pre-marital funds, wedding or other gifts, inheritance, or marital funds? This is also a good time to inquire about other ***additional encumbrances*** such as a line of credit or any personal judgments or tax liens. If someone is unsure, then a title or lien search can identify such liens.

Is the Property Marital or Pre-Marital?

> Please keep in mind that a **civil union** is not the same thing as a marriage; thus, if a couple had a civil union for two years prior to getting married, and one party purchased a brownstone during those two years of a civil union then the brownstone is premarital.

This question can be answered by determining whether the property was acquired before marriage by looking at the ***date of acquisition*** and the ***date of marriage***. If it is determined that the property is pre-marital – i.e., it was purchased by one or both spouses prior to the marriage date – then the property is a ***pre-marital asset***.

In this instance, the portion of the purchase price that was paid prior to marriage is ***not subject to equitable division***. So, if there is no mortgage against the property, then the full value of the property is premarital and stays with the party who purchased it prior to marriage. However, if there is a mortgage lien against the property then this raises questions as to whether the asset lost its character as "separate" property and transmuted into marital, subject to equitable distribution. And, if any ***improvements were made*** during the marriage, questions about the source of funds used to make such improvements and the effect on the value of the property are to be considered.

Who is Moving?

Generally speaking, if the property is ***separate property*** and owned by one spouse, then the other spouse will typically move out of the property within a certain period of time and secure his/her own housing arrangements. On the other hand, if the property is marital property, whether or not title is held in both spouses' names, then the next topic of discussion will be whether either of them intend to still occupy the residence, and discussions regarding the current value of the property and the sum to be paid to buy out the other party ensue. The parties may also want to take into consideration any improvements that may have been made during or prior to marriage and consider how it may have affected the value of the property.

If the property was ***purchased during the marriage***, then regardless of who is named on the title, the property is marital property, subject to any interest of any other party whose name may be on the title.

> Example: There was a couple who was married and shortly after the marriage, the couple decided to purchase a house. For various reasons, the Husband and the Husband's mother purchased the home and the deed did not have the wife's name on the title. This couple did not have a prenuptial agreement. The house was determined to be marital property since it was purchased during the marriage. The couple agreed to return the contribution made by the Husband's mother to her and the balance of the value of the house was divided between them.

So what do you do with property that was acquired during the marriage? Will you sell the property and divide the proceeds? Does one party want to keep the property? Or are there children and the couple wants to delay a sale of the property until the children grow older and move out of the home? Or is there some other consideration such as market changes?

More to Decide On

Once a divorcing couple decides what they wish to do with the property, then they must consider the liens, encumbrances and the money used for the down-payment. Was the down payment that was used to make the purchase taken from separate funds or from marital funds?

> Another example involves a young couple who purchased a home shortly after marriage. They did not have children between them. A few months after they closed, they decided to end their marriage. Neither of them wanted to keep the house. After many discussions, the couple decided to sell the house, pay off the mortgage and divide the proceeds between them. However, they had spent a lot of money on landscaping and they used funds from the husband's retirement account and because they owned the house for a short period of time there would be ordinary gains tax to pay. The couple agreed to pay the balance of the landscaping bill from the sale proceeds and divide the balance between them. The husband could use his portion to reimburse his retirement plan for the loan that he made to acquire the house.

The next step is to evaluate the value of property. Was it recently acquired or was it purchased a while ago and the value may have changed? Divorcing couples may choose to hire a ***real estate broker*** or a ***real estate appraiser*** to value the property or rely upon various real estate websites (www.propertyshark.com or www.zillow.com or other sites) for valuation. Real estate is a complicated area and requires thought and consideration and conversations to determine the outcome.

Even when two people agree upon the plan of what to do with the property, who will be responsible for the ***carrying costs*** (e.g., real estate taxes, maintenance, common charges, utilities, landscaping etc.) and any ***future repairs*** or improvements in the interim? And who can claim the mortgage tax deduction for ***mortgage interest***?

Other Considerations

Down-Payment

Where a property was acquired by the divorcing couple during their marriage, the property is likely to be considered a marital asset and the equitable distribution rules would apply. However, if it is determined that the source of the down-payment was from pre-marital assets of one of the spouses, then the couple can decide to ***refund the down-payment amount*** that was paid by that spouse and then divide the remainder of the net sale proceeds (after closing costs such as mortgage payoff, transfer taxes, attorney's fees, etc.) between them. But what will they do if there is not enough proceeds after paying the mortgage and closing costs to refund the full amount of the down-payment that was paid? Instead, the couple can look to ***pro rata*** **value** of what each of them contributed to make the down-payment.

- For instance, if each of them contributed ***one half of the down-payment***, then the proceeds would be divided in half between them even though the amount they each receive will be less than what they each had put into the property.
- If they had ***contributed unevenly***, such that one spouse contributed 20% of the down- payment and the other spouse contributed 80%, then the proceeds would be divided *pro rata*, in proportion to each of their contributions.

> A couple purchased a home after marriage and one spouse contributed $75,000 toward their $100,000 down-payment and the other spouse contributed $25,000. A few years later they decide to divorce and they agree that it is best to sell the house, repay their down-payment, and divide the proceeds equally. If the proceeds from the sale of the house, after paying off the mortgage, broker commissions, legal fees and other closing costs, exceed $100,000 then they can return the $75,000 to one spouse and the $25,000 to the other spouse, and divide the balance between them. However, if the sale proceeds after expenses is less than $100,000, then dividing the proceeds pro rata, 75% to one spouse and 25% to the other, would be a fair solution.

What if one spouse paid 100% of the down-payment and the other spouse paid all of the mortgage payments? In this instance, what would be a fair distribution of the sale proceeds?

Repairs and Improvements

Were repairs and improvements factored into the value of the property or will the cost be refunded to the party who paid for them? This issue should be unquestionably discussed with the equitable distribution of real estate

Utilities

Will the parties seek to refund utility costs? Or co-op maintenance? Or condo common charges? While many couples who divorce through mediation have considered the impact of improvements and discussed the possibility of reimbursing those expenses, fully or partially, most couples have decided to disregard such considerations for co-op maintenance and utilities.

Tax Considerations

Will ***capital gains*** tax apply? If so, then how will it be reported and paid? There are no income tax consequences on transfers of property between spouses, or former spouses if incident to a divorce. If the property is sold, the parties may be entitled to a ***tax exclusion*** up to $250,000 on an individual income return or up to $500,000 on a joint income tax return where certain requirements are met. Depending upon where the property is located there may be an additional city transfer tax to be paid in addition to the NYS transfer tax that is due for any real estate sale in New York. And, if the property was an investment property (i.e. it was a rental) there may be eligibility to defer any tax due on the gain from a sale of the property if the rules governing 1031 exchanges are followed precisely.

Final Thoughts

While some of these issues may not be applicable to every situation, if these issues are not considered and discussed, they can become a problem and create conflict later which can lead to more cost and expense, for any unresolved issues. Divorcing individuals are encouraged to take the time to consider these issues because it will save them time and money later.

Sabra R. Sasson, Esq.

Sabra R. Sasson is an attorney and mediator practicing in New York City. She is the founder and Principal of Sabra Law Group, PLLC, a mediation and law practice in midtown Manhattan that offers legal and mediation services to its clients. Sabra handles the legal aspects of major transitions – buying or selling property, planning for marriage or getting divorced – and protects her clients' interests so they can focus on their evolution into this new life change. She employs her skills and experience to help her clients focus on life post-divorce and guide them through the process to get there. For couples embarking on marriage, she helps them protect accumulated assets and create a plan for building assets, wealth and valuables in the future.

Sabra graduated from Brandeis University in 1995 with a Bachelor's in Mathematics and minor in Education, whereafter she enrolled in law school and graduated from Hofstra University School of Law in 1998 with her Juris Doctorate. She sat for the bar exam in three states and was thereafter admitted to practice law in New York, New Jersey and Connecticut, and has been practicing law ever since.

Sabra is currently writing a book to guide and empower couples through the process of "uncoupling," THE HARMONIOUS DIVORCE: THE FOUR STEP PROCESS TO UNCOUPLING. She is also the author of a chapter in the best-selling book SUCCESS FROM THE HEART. Connect with her at www.sabralawgroup.com.

SECTION D: PROPERTY DIVISION

CHAPTER 30

EQUITABLE DIVISION OF MARITAL PROPERTY

SUBPART D: BUSINESSES

By Kymberly A. Robinson, Esq.

Any property that is acquired by either spouse during the marriage (with limited exceptions) is marital property, ***including business interests***. Furthermore, separate property that increases in value during the marriage can be considered marital property under certain circumstances. In cases of a business or professional practice, the spouse seeking an interest in a business or professional practice must demonstrate that he/she made a substantial contribution to the title-holding spouse's acquisition of the license and/or degree or the business interest. If the business is marital property, it will be distributed equitably.

Distributing the Business

Case Illustrations

Here are two examples of how a business interest was distributed upon divorce:

(1) Rich-Wolfe v. Wolfe, 83 A.D.3d 1359 (3d Dept., 2011) – In this case, the wife received a value of 50% of the parties' construction and demolition businesses since she contributed a ***great amount to the success*** of that business and worked ***full time*** for the business. She was the office manager and bookkeeper. Even the husband agreed that she made

"***substantial direct and indirect contributions***" to the marital estate.

(2) Scher v. Scher, 2012 N.Y. Slip Op 502 (2d Dept., 2012) – In this case, the husband had incorporated a business three years before the marriage. The wife was awarded 20% of the appreciated value of a business because she made ***direct contributions*** to the business as its bookkeeper for seven years, and indirect contributions as homemaker and occasional caretaker of one of the husband's children from a prior marriage, enabling the husband to expand the business.

Court's Discretion

The trial court has much discretion as to when to value a business. See La Barre v. La Barre, 251 A.D.3d 1008 (4th Dept., 1998). Generally, assets which appreciate passively, through market forces, are often valued as of the date of trial, while assets which appreciate actively, through contribution of the parties, are often valued as of the date of the commencement of the action. Needless to say that when the value of an ***asset fluctuates greatly***, the date of valuation can become a highly contested issue. Once a valuation date is chosen, a value must be assignment to the asset. A professional should perform a valuation of the business, if and when necessary.

Valuing the Business

The purpose of valuing a business is so that a ***fair market value*** can be established. Everything from tangible items (such as computers, trucks, machinery, and equipment) to intangible items (such as customer lists, trademarks, and goodwill) has value. Without a fair market value, it would be difficult to distribute the asset (the business). In valuing a business, there needs to be an assessment of the ***type of business***, ***tangible assets*** of the business (i.e. furniture, cash register, etc.), ***earning capacity*** of the business, and ***good will*** (i.e. reputation of the business, ownership of a brand or trade name, and the record of successful operation over an extended period of time).

Methods for Valuation

One way to do this is by using a forensic accountant, but there are several other ways as well. Let us take a look at the different ways a business can be valued and for what type of business each method would work best:

1. **The Book Value/Adjusted Book Value Method**: This method is oftentimes referred to as the "***Adjusted Method***." It looks at the corporate books and takes the assets (usually the original cost of the business) minus the liabilities. The Adjusted Method also takes into account depreciation (normal "wear and tear" on the business) and the market value of the inventory of the business. This method is particularly useful when the business owns ***income producing assets*** (e.g., securities). The downfall of this method is that is does not account for intangible assets, so the true value may be off.[29]

2. **The Earnings or Market Method**: This is sometimes referred to as the "Income Approach." It is based on the market value or earning capacity of the business. One would need to determine what an ***outside person would pay*** for the business (i.e., the Fair Market Value), while considering the earning capacity of it. This would work best where there is a recent offer for the business. This is a popular valuation method for small businesses.[30]

> For instance, Kyle owns a bagel store. Recently, the man that runs the coffee shop next door offered to buy the business for $1.5 million. Kyle rejected the offer though. $1.5 million would be a good number to use to assign a value to his bagel business.

3. **Excess Earnings Method**: This method determines the fair market value by adding tangible assets and goodwill. This method

[29] See Drohan v. Drohan, 193 A.D.2d 1070 (4th Dept., 1993) where the court used a combination of methods, including the book value method to value husband's insurance agency.
[30] See Myers v. Myers, 255 A.D.2d 711 (3rd Dept., 1998) for an example where the court shows why family business, closely held corporations *lack* marketability and, thus, why that valuation would not work for this type of business.

is good for a business that has an emphasis on the personnel, such as a professional or service-type of business rather than a store.[31]

> Lucy owns a massage parlor in a small spa-retreat town. She has made a name for herself by having a large variety of essential oils that she offers to use on each client during the massage free of charge. (She then has a gift shop where clients can purchase these oils or oils that she has created by mixing one or more together). Lucy is especially known for her personal essential oils creations that she makes by mixing certain scents together. Her shop is often featured in local visitor guides and recommended by the locals to people visiting the town. The excess earnings method would able to account for the goodwill of Lucy's massage business.

4. **Capitalization of Earnings Method**: This method takes the business's past earnings and attempts to calculate what future earnings would be. Then these assumed future earnings are converted to a present day value. This could be useful for many types of businesses, except for relatively new ones for obvious reasons. This seems to be the most versatile method.[32]

> Brody has owned a bookstore for 10 years. Even with the emergence of the Kindle and other electronic readers, his customers have remained loyal. His earnings have been fairly consistent for the past 6 years. It would be relatively easy to guess Brody's earnings in the next year to come.

5. **Liquidation Method**: This takes all of the assets and asks: what is the money one could get for the assets if forced to sell in a short time (liquidating the assets)? This is best for businesses where things can easily be converted to liquid (like real estate). This might be a good method for valuing restaurants.

> Wendy owns a diner. She owns the building, the kitchen equipment, machinery, the furniture, the fixtures, the cash register, etc. These assets can easily be assigned a value. She makes a list of all of her assets including the value of the building and totals the amount. This would be an example of the liquidation method.

---

[31] See Douglas v. Douglas, 281 A.D.2d 709 (3rd Dept., 2001) for an example of the court using the excess earnings method in valuating the husband's law practice.

[32] See Siegel v. Siegel, 132 A.D.2d 247 (2nd Dept., 1987) for an example of the court using the capitalization of earnings method in valuing two closely held corporations (in the carpet and rug industry).

These different methods are applied to different types of businesses and circumstances. There is no one-size-fits-all business valuation method.

Case Illustrations

Whether there is a formal business valuation or not, it is clearly established law that courts have the discretion in how to value a business. Specifically, "the determination of the value of business interest is a function properly within the fact-finding power of the court." Daddino v. Daddino, 37 A.D.3d 518 (2nd Dept., 2007). In that case, the court itself valued the business interest of the husband, relying on the yearly valuations that were made pursuant to the company's shareholders' agreement. Similarly stated by the same court in another case, "There is no uniform method of fixing value of an ongoing business for equitable distribution purposes and valuation is properly within the fact-finding power of the trial court." Miness v. Miness, 229 A.D.2d 520 (2nd Dept., 1996).

> In Gaglio v. Molnar-Gaglio, 300 A.D.2d 934 (3rd Dept., 2002), the husband was an antique dealer. Shortly after the marriage, the couple went into the antique dealing business together and formed a corporation. The wife did not receive a salary for her work but accompanied her husband to antique shows and had access to the corporate books. Eventually the wife gave up her role in the business to care for the parties' child. Shortly thereafter, the husband formed a new corporation (and the former business' assets were depleted by withdrawal by both parties). Upon the divorce, the parties needed to value the business. After the business valuations by two experts, it was apparent that the wife's and husband's experts determined vastly different values. This was due to the fact that the husband's expert merely looked at the corporate books, while the wife's expert based his valuation on a discretionary cash flow analysis (an analysis looking to what cash is going directly to the business owner) after determining that the husband seriously under-reported his cash flow. In the end, the court used the wife's expert and valued the business higher to reflect all of the unreported income the husband was receiving.

Let us look at how the court valued a deli business in the case of Ruggiero v. Ruggiero, 2013 N.Y. Slip Op 31955(U) (Sup. Ct. Suffolk County, July 29, 2013). The court used the Income Approach to determine the fair value of Zan's Deli. The expert for the estate calculated the value of the business "by computing the present value of future benefits to be received by the shareholders, typically in the form of cash flow." This is similar to the ***Capitalization of Earnings Method***.

When there is a largely cash business, valuation can be challenging. Although a cash business can be a scary thought to the non-owner spouse who fears he or she will be disadvantaged through the valuation of the business, courts are able to account for this lack of reported income. The following case is a good example of how courts do that:

Not Dividing the Asset

If all of these methods fail, DRL § 236B(5)(d)(9) provides that the court ***may keep the asset intact*** (not divide it) and use other assets to ***offset the award*** of a business in full to one spouse. This is most common for divorces involving a small business because valuation methods and division would not make sense for a small amount of value. This way the spouses get an equitable share of the marital estate, but a business can be retained by one spouse only.

Business Valuations

Where couples want to see the value of the asset for purposes of settling their property division disputes, a value assessment is performed by a Certified Public Accountant ("CPA") that specializes in business valuations. The value assessment is not admissible in court, but is useful in negotiations. A ***formal business valuation*** would be necessary if the matter was going to be in court, and this formal business valuation costs a lot more than a value assessment. Rates for a value assessment typical are around $2,500 in New York City and Long Island. For a formal business valuation, one could expect to pay anywhere from $7,500 to $15,000 in New York City and Long Island. Please note that these figures do not include the professional's travel expenses and court time should he/she be required to testify.

With small businesses (any business earning under $1,000,000 per year excluding the owner's benefits-such as salary, any write-offs, etc.) valuations are usually performed by analyzing the business's financial records for the past 3-5 years and determining for how much a similar business would sell. This is similar to Method #2, above. It is important to use an experienced business valuator since he/she has knowledge of the fair market value of similar companies and knowledge of the "industry enterprise value."

When one hires a business valuator for a value assessment, one can expect to pay half of the fee upfront and the other half upon delivery of a report by the professional. The client might also sign a one page agreement acknowledging that the valuation will reflect the ***most probably selling price*** ("MPSP") and that the valuation is not a guarantee of the true value of the business, especially where there is suspected unreported income. Once the fee is paid, it will usually take between 4-6 weeks for a report to be sent.

Unfortunately, in a small business, an owner may be able to hide income or assets through the business. The most common situation of this is when the owner lives vicariously through the business and uses the business account as his or her personal account. This can make valuation challenging. In these situations, one might also hire a forensic accountant who is experienced in finding unreported income.[33]

Kymberly A. Robinson, Esq.

Kymberly is an associate attorney with Rincker Law, PLLC and is admitted to practice law in New York and Florida. She attended Union College in Schenectady, New York for her undergraduate studies, where she graduated with high honors as a psychology major. She then obtained her J.D. from Pace University School of Law in White Plains, New York and, subsequently, her L.L.M. (with a concentration in family law) from the Benjamin N. Cardozo School of Law in Manhattan. Kymberly entered the field of matrimonial and family law as a way to couple her interest in psychology and personal relationships with her legal education.

Kymberly likes to spend her free time with her family and also enjoys working out, cooking healthy meals, and getting together with friends. She lives in Westchester County, New York with her husband and daughter.

For more information about Rincker Law, PLLC, visit www.rinckerlaw.com.

[33] The information in this "Business Valuations" section was partially obtained through an interview with Anthony Citrolo, CPA, of Strategic Merger and Acquisition Advisors & NY Business Brokerage with offices in Manhattan and Long Island. He is a Certified Merger and Acquisition Advisor (CMAA) and a Certified Business Intermediary (CBI).

SECTION D: PROPERTY DIVISION

CHAPTER 30

EQUITABLE DIVISION OF MARITAL PROPERTY

SUBPART E: RETIREMENT ASSETS

By Karen Greenberg, Esq.

Pensions and all other retirement benefits accrued during the marriage constitute marital property subject to equitable distribution. Calculation of the "marital" portion is measured from the date of the marriage to the date of the commencement of the divorce. Any part of the pension/retirement asset which accrued before the date of the marriage, is separate property and not subject to equitable distribution. While the equitable distribution of retirement assets is subject to the same general considerations as any other asset, because of the unique character of these assets, there are additional state and federal laws and regulations that may be applicable. Further, a large body of case law has evolved pertaining to the distribution of pensions and other retirement assets. And to make matters even more complicated, the laws that apply depend on the particular type of pension/asset it is – whether the retirement plan is a ***defined benefit plan*** or a ***defined contribution plan***, the rules of the particular retirement plan, whether it is a governmental plan or a private plan, and which particular governmental plan it is – e.g. Federal, New York City, or Military.

General Principles of Pensions and Retirement Benefits

First and foremost, almost all pensions and retirement benefits are subject to Federal and/or State "*anti-alienation*" statutes. This means that pensions and retirement benefits cannot be assigned, transferred or garnished except by means of a special court order which is only for the enforcement of support, or to effectuate the division of property in a divorce. This type of special court order is called a ***Domestic Relations Order*** *("DRO")* or ***Qualified Domestic Relations Order*** *("QDRO").* When a DRO has been deemed "qualified" by the Retirement Plan, *i.e.* after the Plan has determined it meets the statutory and the plan's own requirements, the DRO becomes a QDRO. For the sake of simplicity in this chapter, these orders will always be termed "QDROs."

Thus, if American Express sues and gets a judgment of $10,000.00 against someone who defaults on paying his/her credit card bill, Amex can satisfy that judgment by seizing the money from the person's bank account or by garnishing the person's wages. However, no part of that individual's ***deferred compensation account***, or any other retirement account, can be taken by Amex to pay the judgment even if there are no other assets. Further, Amex cannot enforce the judgment against that person's monthly pension payment, even if the pension is the only source of income. These retirement assets and income cannot be touched by ordinary creditors due to ***anti-alienation statutes***. By contrast, for example, if the Wife is found entitled to a $10,000.00 distributive award for equitable distribution of marital property, the court can issue a QDRO which will order the retirement plan to pay $10,000.00 from the former husband's retirement account (*e.g.*, a 401K account) directly to the Wife. Alternatively, the court can issue a QDRO which will direct the Husband's pension plan to pay directly to the Wife, a certain amount from each and every pension payment that the Husband is entitled to receive in the future, until the sum of $10,000.00 has been paid.

> The matrimonial attorney will either prepare the QDRO herself, or hire an outside company to prepare the QDRO. After it has been prepared in conformance with the plan's requirements, the attorney will submit the QDRO to the court for signing, and have the signed QDRO served upon the retirement plan administrator.

A QDRO is a very ***powerful and complex instrument***; it must meet both the particular plan's requirements as well as statutory requirements. A QDRO is most often used to divide the retirement asset itself in the process of equitable distribution. The QDRO must conform to the settlement agreement of the parties in all respects, or the decision of the court if there is a trial.

Vesting

Both ***vested*** and ***non-vested*** pensions/retirement benefits (meaning vesting status as of the date of commencement of the divorce action) are subject to equitable distribution.

- **<u>In a pension plan</u>**, "vesting" means that the employee has worked a sufficient number of years, so that s/he will absolutely be entitled to the pension benefit in the future once the age/work requirements are met.
- **<u>For a defined contribution plan</u>**, an employee's contributions (as opposed to an employer's contributions) are 100% vested immediately. The time for vesting of the employer's contributions, depends upon the terms of the particular plan.

Contributions

It does not matter whether the employee spouse has made ***actual out-of-pocket*** contributions to the pension/retirement plan. There is ***no distinction*** between contributions made by the employee, the employer, or a union on behalf of the employee. The portion of the asset attributable to the period of the spouse's employment under the plan during the marriage, is always marital property. It is therefore subject to equitable distribution.

Social Security

Social Security benefits are not subject to equitable distribution by the court in a divorce action. However, under the Social Security Law if the parties ***have been married at least 10 years*** at the time of the judgment of divorce, then a spouse can collect social security under the ex-spouse's account, rather than on his/her own account, if that yields a greater monthly benefit. Generally, if one-half of the ex-spouses' ***accrued social security benefit*** is greater than the social security benefit based upon the individual's own work record, then social security benefits would be paid under the ex-spouse's account. However, there is no reduction in the ex-spouse's actual social security monthly benefit, for payment made to a former spouse. The Social Security fund bears the additional "cost." This ***10-year rule*** is a particularly important consideration in the timing of a divorce, if one spouse has a sparse work history.

Veterans Administration Benefits

> The requisite 10 year period is calculated from the date of the marriage, to the date the judgment of divorce is ***signed***.

Veterans Administration ("VA") ***disability benefits*** do not represent deferred compensation, and are not subject to equitable distribution. The ***Federal Uniformed Former Spouses' Protection Act*** prohibits a state court in a matrimonial action from distributing VA disability benefits. In contrast, military pensions are subject to equitable distribution.

Disability Pensions

Disability pensions are subject to equitable distribution only to the extent of the portion of the pension that relates to deferred compensation (i.e. the portion that is equivalent to the normal pension that has accrued based upon employment). The portion of the disability pension that relates to compensation for personal injury is deemed to be separate property and not subject to equitable distribution. This issue most often arises in the context of retirement based upon "***accidental disability***" or "***line of duty***" disability pensions for police officers, firefighters, EMT workers and certain other government employees. It is very important that any marital settlement agreement and the ensuing QDRO, be very carefully prepared to account for the possibility of the employee retiring under a ***disability pension*** rather than a ***normal retirement pension***.

Obtaining Information on Retirement Assets

Many people are not aware of all of their retirement assets. This might be especially true in a long marriage, where a pension may have accrued decades before the commencement of the divorce action, stemming from long past employment. Therefore, it is crucial to ascertain what plans each spouse was covered by at any time during the marriage, including union plans, employment plans, IRAs, and self-administered plans from a business. Due to this, the matrimonial attorney may ask ***for a detailed work history of each party***, as well as union memberships and self-employment, to aid in ferreting out retirement assets. In order to get information about any pension or retirement asset, the employee-spouse ("***Participant***") must execute a specific authorization in front of a Notary Public, permitting the retirement plan to disclose all records and information pertaining to the plan. If the spouse or the plan is uncooperative, records can also be obtained by a ***subpoena***. Useful information is also available online at www.freeerisa.com for current and past retirement plans maintained by private employers.

> A **subpoena** is a document issued by an attorney or a judge that is directed to a particular retirement plan. The subpoena can order the plan to provide all documents pertaining to a party's retirement asset(s).

Type of Retirement Assets

The distribution of a retirement asset in a divorce, whether pursuant to a settlement agreement or after trial by the court, may be dependent upon what type of retirement asset it is. There are two major categories:

- Defined Benefit vs. Defined Contribution Plans
- Governmental vs. Private Plans (ERISA-covered Plans).

Defined Benefit vs. Defined Contribution Plans

A ***defined benefit plan*** is what one commonly thinks of as a "**pension.**" There is a formula, which defines how the retirement benefit is calculated. The formula is often based upon average or final salary and length of service. This is a rapidly vanishing breed of retirement benefit, as all the risk for future payment, is with the employer. The actual amount the employee contributes to the pension, bears little or no relation to the monthly pension at retirement. Monthly pension payments are usually ***paid beginning at a specific retirement age***, or reduced benefits may be paid at an "***early retirement age***." There are no individual accounts for each employee, except sometimes there is an account based upon the employee's individual contributions. In the private sector, to minimize the expense and to spread the risk to the employee, many employers have converted their ***defined benefit plans*** to defined contribution plans, or ***cash balance plans***. A cash balance plan is a hybrid, but is generally treated as a defined benefit plan in a divorce.

> For example, the annual pension benefit at the time of retirement may be equal to the number of years of service x final salary x 2 %. So if one spouse was a teacher, and worked for 25 years, and had a salary of $90,000.00 at the time of retirement, his/her annual pension would be 25 x $90,000.00 x 2% or $45,000.00 per year.

> Some examples of <u>**Defined Benefit Plans**</u> are:
> - New York State and Local Employees Retirement System
> - N.Y.C. Police Pension Fund
> - U.S. Federal Employees Retirement System
> - 1199 National Pension Fund
> - AFSCME Employees Pension Plan
> - Consolidated Edison Retirement Plan

A ***defined contribution plan*** is one where there is ***an actual individual account*** for the employee. Contributions to the plan account for an employee may be made solely by the

> Some examples of <u>**Defined Contribution Plans**</u> are:
> - N.Y.C. Deferred Compensation Plan (457 Plan)
> - Federal Thrift Savings Plan
> - 401K or 403(b) Plans; Incentive Savings Plans
> - Profit Sharing Plans
> - Employee Stock Purchase Plans
> - Consolidated Edison Thrift Savings Plans

employer or a union, or by the employee, or by both. The benefit at retirement is the total amount in the retirement account at that time. The value of the account will be determined by the amount of contributions, plus the interest and investment earnings (or losses) that have accrued. Although at the time of retirement, the plan may have an option (or it may be mandatory) to "annuitize" the payments, which means converting the account into actuarially equivalent life-time monthly payments, the plan is still a defined contribution plan.

There are also ***Individual Retirement Arrangement*** plans ("IRAs") Keogh Plans, and SEP ("***self-employment plans***") which fall under the category of ***defined contribution plans***. IRAs usually do not need QDROs to divide them.

Governmental vs. Private Plans (ERISA-covered Plans)

After categorizing a plan as a defined benefit or a defined contribution plan, it must then be determined whether it is a ***governmental plan*** or a ***private plan***. Most private retirement plans, including most union plans, are covered by a federal law called ***Employees Retirement Income Security Act*** ("**ERISA**," sounds like "uh-reh-sa"). All government plans, whether local, state, federal or military, are not covered by ERISA. The distinction is important, and goes to the former spouse's rights – i.e., how and when the retirement benefit can be paid to the non-employee former spouse, tax consequences, and what can or should be included in the marital settlement agreement, and the type of QDRO needed to divide it.

Distributing Retirement Assets

There are basically two methods for distributing retirement assets. For the sake of simplicity, in the discussion of distribution of retirement assets to follow, a ***defined benefit plan*** will be termed a "**pension**" and a ***defined contribution plan*** account will be termed a "**retirement account**," regardless of what particular kind of defined contribution plan it is.

The first method of distribution is by ***immediate offset*** of one spouse's pension or retirement account against the other spouse's pension or retirement account in whole or part; or as an offset in whole or part against another marital asset; and/***or for a lump sum cash***

distributive award. The second method is ***distribution*** of the future pension payments or the retirement account ***by QDRO.*** Many matrimonial judges and attorneys will say, "Let's QDRO (pronouncing it "quadro") the pension," or "Let's Majauskas the pension." If there are no other marital assets or if the value of the retirement asset greatly exceeds the other marital assets, then distribution ***must*** be done by the QDRO method.

Immediate Offset or Cash Buy-Out

In accordance with the general principles of equitable distribution that all marital assets must be valued, the pension/retirement account must be given a "present value" if an immediate distribution or offset against another retirement or non-retirement asset is desired. Valuation is determined as of the date of commencement of the divorce action.

For ***valuation of a retirement account*** (*i.e.* a defined contribution plan), if the account was accrued entirely during the marriage, then the ***present value*** is the amount in the account on the date closest to the commencement of the action date. This value is readily obtained from the participant-spouse's account records.

If the member-spouse started in the plan before the marriage, then the amount in the account on the date of the marriage (plus or minus investment earnings or losses on that amount) is separate property. ***The separate property amount must be deducted*** from the present account value, to determine the value of the marital share. This calculation of the marital share can be very complicated. Some retirement plans will perform the calculation for the member, and some will not. Sometimes the two parties and their attorneys will do an approximation of the amount to deduct in order to arrive at the marital amount. To be done precisely, every quarterly statement from the date of marriage to the date of commencement of the divorce action is necessary and an ***expert may be hired*** to perform the calculation of the value of the marital share of the account.

If there are ***loans*** outstanding, an agreement will be made by the parties and their attorneys, or the court will decide, whether the loan amount should be considered in determining the value of the retirement account for equitable distribution purposes. It all depends upon the particular circumstances and facts. In general, if the loan proceeds were used for marital purposes, then the account value is properly reduced by the outstanding loan. But if the participant took a loan from his retirement account of $10,000.00 to buy his girlfriend a car, then that $10,000.00 would be " added back" in determining the account value for purposes of equitable distribution.

> John and Mary have been married for 25 years and their children are grown. For the entire time of their marriage, John has been a N.Y.C. police officer. He does not wish to retire yet, although he could. Mary has been working for three years and just joined her pension plan. They bought their jointly owned two-family residence soon after they got married. The mortgage balance of $50,000 will be paid off in five years. The fair market value of the house has been appraised at $650,000. After deducting the mortgage balance, the value of the house for equitable distribution purposes is $600,000. John's Police Pension has been appraised at $700,000. Mary really wants to keep the house as a place for her children (and future grandchildren) to gather. She also feels the rental income will be a good source of income for her future. John very much wants to keep his whole pension. They decide to settle the distribution of these assets, by Mary getting sole title to the house, and John keeping his entire pension.

For pensions, valuation is more complex. The pension will have to be "***appraised***" by an **expert** to determine the present value of the marital share on the date of commencement of the divorce. If the case is being litigated, the pension appraiser will be appointed by the court. The appraiser will need to have the participant-spouse's pension records, and complete information about the pension plan. Then he will calculate the yearly pension amount that the participant has accrued, as of the date of commencement of the action, using the formula for the particular pension plan. In the simplest terms, the present value of a pension can be thought of as what it would cost in present dollars, at the interest rate prevailing on the valuation date, to purchase an annuity that would pay the accrued pension benefit, beginning at the normal retirement age, for the rest of the participant-spouse's life. The closer to retirement age, the larger the pension value. The appraiser, after determining the value, then applies the "***couverture fraction***" to determine the value of the marital portion. So for instance, if the value of the pension is calculated to be $200,000, and the participant-spouse has been in the pension plan for 20 years, and married for only the past 5 years, the couverture fraction would be 5 years divided by 20 years, or one-fourth. Therefore the value of the marital share of the pension is one-fourth of $200,000 or $50,000. Now that the value of the marital share of the pension and/or retirement account has been valued, it may be distributed.

While at first blush, it seems that John still owes Mary $100,000, a factor to consider is that all of John's future pension payments will be taxable, whereas if the house were sold now and the proceeds divided, there would be no income tax due. Therefore, the parties and their attorneys effectively "reduced" the value of the pension by $100,000 (approximately 14%) to at least partially account for the taxes that will be due on the pension payments, making the values of the pension and the house equal. This is called "***tax impacting***."

Distribution by QDRO

For distribution by QDRO, the spouse who has the pension or retirement benefit is always called the "***Participant***," and the other spouse is always called the "***Alternate Payee***" if it is a private (ERISA) plan. *If it is a government plan*, the spouses may be referred to in the same way, or sometimes as the "***member***" and the "***former spouse.***" The terms "member spouse" and "former spouse" will be used in the following discussion for both governmental and private (ERISA) plans. All payments from a pension plan or other retirement plan made under a QDRO, are taxable to the recipient of the monies.

1. Distribution of Retirement Accounts by QDRO

For distribution of retirement accounts (*i.e.* defined contribution plans), the share awarded to the former spouse, will be either a ***percentage of the account value*** as of the commencement date of the divorce action, ***or a specific dollar amount***. While usually in long-term marriages, the percentage awarded is 50%, it does not have to be. If the member spouse was in the plan before the marriage, then the pre-marital (separate property) part of the account will be excluded. Similarly, how loans will be treated, will be agreed upon or determined by the court. The marital share of the retirement account is calculated the same way whether it is a governmental plan or an ERISA (private) plan.

Then the parties or the court must decide whether the former spouse's share should be ***adjusted by gains or losses***, up to the date of segregation (pursuant to the QDRO) of the former spouse's share. The parties can agree instead that it will be a ***sum certain*** to be paid, without any increase or decrease for market forces.

Generally, it is the obligation of the former spouse, who will be receiving the benefits from the member's retirement account, to make sure the QDRO is prepared and submitted to the court for the judge's signature. Upon receipt of the QDRO, the retirement plan administrator will review it to make sure it is ***qualified*** under the law and its own plan. If the QDRO is qualified, the plan must follow the terms exactly, because it is a court order. The plan will segregate the former spouse's share in a separate account.

Depending upon the particular retirement plan involved, the former spouse may have the option to leave the funds with the plan in his/her own retirement account. If the former spouse leaves the funds in the plan, s/he can then direct how the funds will be invested based upon the investment options available. For all intents and purposes, the former spouse then becomes a "member" of the retirement plan. The former spouse can designate a beneficiary in the event of his/her death, and can choose the forms available for payment in the future when s/he wants to start withdrawals.

If leaving the funds in the plan is not an option under the terms of the plan, or if the former spouse wishes to withdraw some or all of the funds, the entire ***amount received by the former spouse is taxable***. However, taxes can be deferred by rolling the monies received into a ***rollover IRA*** set up especially to receive it, or into another retirement account. Keep in mind that if the former spouse is younger than 59 ½ years old, there will be an additional income tax penalty of 10% of the amount withdrawn. But note, if it is an ***ERISA-covered private retirement account, the additional 10% penalty does not apply*** to withdrawals directly from the account. Although the penalty is waived in this one instance, taxes will still be due on the amount withdrawn (unless rolled over).

2. Distribution of Pensions by QDRO

The distribution of a pension by the QDRO method is different because it is unknown at the time of the divorce, how many more years the member spouse will work in employment covered by the pension plan. Therefore the percentage of the monthly pension at the time of retirement which is "marital," is likewise unknown. Thus it cannot be stated as a fixed percentage in the divorce agreement or the court order. The pension accrued *both before the date of marriage*, and *after the commencement of the divorce action*, must be excluded as ***separate property.*** The NY Court of Appeals in 1984 in the case of **Majauskas v. Majauskas** (61 NY2d 481, 474 NYS2d 699 (Ct. Apps. 1984) devised a formula to calculate what part of the future pension payment is marital, and therefore subject to equitable distribution. The ***Majausaks formula*** defines the ***marital fraction*** (also called "***couverture fraction***") as "A" divided by "B."

> "A" is equal to **the number of months of credited service** that the member spouse had in the pension plan during the marriage (i.e. from the date of the marriage to the date of commencement of the divorce action) and "B" is equal to the **total number of months** of credited service that the member-spouse has in the pension plan at the time of his/her retirement.

- "A" is a ***known or ascertainable number.***
- "B" is an ***unknown number*** (unless the member spouse has already retired at the time of commencement of the divorce action). B includes all the months of pre-marital, marital and post-marital coverage in the pension plan.

As with division by method one, ***the percentage of the marital share*** to be awarded to the former spouse is set forth by the parties in their agreement, or determined by the court. Assuming that it is 50%, the agreement will provide, and the QDRO will direct, that the pension plan pay directly to the former spouse, at the time of the member's retirement: 50% of each pension payment ***multiplied by the fraction A/B*** ("the Majauskas fraction").

While the fraction is stated above using months, in an actual case it would be in whatever unit that particular pension plan uses in crediting service, be it "years," "days," "hours," "pension credits," or "points." So, for instance, a QDRO addressed to a military reserve pension, must be spelled out as "points."

Under distribution of a ***governmental pension*** by QDRO using the Majauskas formula, a former spouse's share is directly related to the member-spouse's pension. The former spouse can only collect "if, as and when" the member collects. The former spouse's monthly share is "***carved out***" of the member spouse's share of the future pension payments, or it can be said the former spouse has a "shared interest" in the member spouse's pension.

In sharp contrast to governmental plans, in ***private (ERISA) pension plans*** only, the former spouse is permitted by federal law to collect his/her share independently of when the member spouse collects his/her pension. The former spouse can begin receiving his/her pension share at any time ***after the earliest date permissible*** under the terms of the plan for the member spouse to retire. The former spouse's share will be reduced to account for her earlier collection of a pension, so that it is actuarially equivalent. This is called a "***separate interest***" as distinguished from the "shared interest" or "carve-out" under a governmental plan. The former spouse will receive her share for the rest of her life.

> Bob and Mary got divorced 20 years ago. As part of the divorce, Mary was given a separate interest QDRO on Bob's pension with the ABC Corp. Bob, always a workaholic, recently told Mary he is not going to retire until he is 70. Bob is now 64. Under the ABC Corp. pension plan Bob can retire at 62. Mary needs more income now. She notifies the pension plan that she would like to start receiving her monthly pension benefits.

Accordingly, to give the former spouse a separate interest, the denominator "B" of the Majauskas formula would be adjusted to state as "the total number of months of credited service the member spouse had in the pension plan at the time of his retirement, ***or at the time the former spouse elects to begin to receive her pension share, whichever first occurs***" (emphasis added). Alternatively, the parties' agreement or court judgment would have to specifically state that the former spouse gets a ***separate interest*** in the member spouse's pension. Some private plans require that the award to the former spouse always be in the form of a separate interest, and the former spouse's share is split off immediately and paid for his/her lifetime.

> Many pension plans provide for annual or other periodic increases in a retiree's monthly pension. This is so that the pension payments keep up with inflation. These are called **COLA**s. Typically the former spouse will receive the same COLA, calculated on his/her share, under the plan, as the member spouse.

When distribution of a pension is done by the QDRO method, there are certain other issues that may be a subject for negotiation/agreement by the parties, or determination by the court. These issues include, but are not limited to, survivor benefits, treatment of early retirement incentives or enhancements, and ***Cost of Living Allowances*** ("COLAs"). The most important of these issues is protection for the former spouse if the member spouse dies before the former spouse.

Survivor Benefits-Protecting the Former Spouse

If the member spouse dies ***before retirement***, then his/her pension never gets paid, and the former spouse will receive nothing. To protect the former spouse, the member spouse could be required in the settlement agreement, or court decision, to designate and maintain the former spouse as beneficiary of all or part of the ***pre-retirement pension death benefit*** in a governmental plan. In an ERISA plan, the parties can agree or the court can direct, that the former spouse will be entitled to all or part of the ***pre-retirement surviving spouse annuity*** should the member spouse die prior to retirement. The QDRO would then include these provisions. Alternatively, the member spouse could be required to maintain a life insurance policy with the former spouse as beneficiary.

There is also the related but separate issue, of what happens if the former spouse is already collecting his/her share of the pension under the QDRO and then the member spouse dies. This contingency is entirely different. It must be specifically provided for in the parties' agreement, or court's decision, if protection of the former spouse's interest is intended. The manner in which this can be accomplished depends upon the whether it is a governmental plan or an ERISA private plan.

In any of the state or local governmental pension plans, the member's pension payments will always terminate when he/she dies and the former spouse's pension payments under the QDRO will thus stop as well. (Recall, they are a "carve-out" of the member spouse's payments.) Therefore, to protect the former spouse, the member spouse must be required to elect an "option" at the time of his/her retirement, that provides a survivor benefit; the former spouse must be designated as the beneficiary under that option. Each of the pension plans has a variety of options, and the specific option that must be chosen would be stated in the settlement agreement or by the court. Conveniently, the ***NYS Employees Retirement System*** and the ***NYC Police Pension Fund*** have a ***"special" option*** which will give the former spouse the same amount for the rest of his/her life that s/he receives under the QDRO while the member is alive. However, most of the other governmental pension plans do not have this "special" option. The option required under the settlement agreement or by the court, has to be one that is available under the member's particular pension plan; this is a subject for negotiation as the monthly pension is reduced based upon the survivor option selected. Notably, the reduction can be quite considerable, depending upon the particular option and the age of the former spouse-beneficiary. As a reminder, life insurance for the benefit of the former spouse, remains a possible alternative.

Under these governmental plans, once an ***option*** is selected by the member, it ***can never be changed.*** Therefore, in a case where the member spouse is about to retire, the non-employee spouse's attorney may make an emergency application to the divorce court, for a ***restraining order.*** A restraining order will prevent the member spouse from retiring unless s/he elects an appropriate survivor option for the beneficiary spouse.

In the ***Federal pension systems***, protection of the former spouse both pre-retirement and post-retirement can be provided as a "***former spouse survivor annuity***" either in the maximum (default) amount of 55%, or a lesser amount, which can be tailored to be the amount of the Majauskas share. The Federal pension system protects spouses, so that if parties are married at the time of retirement, the pension is automatically paid in form of a joint and surviving spouse annuity, unless it is waived.

One hallmark of ERISA pensions, is that if an employee is married at the time of retirement, s/he must take their pension in the form of a "***joint and survivor annuity.***" A joint and survivor annuity will give the surviving spouse 50% of the amount of the member spouse's pension (actuarially reduced for age) for the remainder of the surviving spouse's lifetime. The only way that the married employee can get their "single" full pension is if the spouse executes a very specific written spousal waiver. The spouse will be entitled to this survivor annuity in all cases, as long as the parties were married for a year. It does not matter if they have been separated for 20 years, or if they never were an economic partnership. A subsequent divorce after retirement, does not affect the right of the former spouse to receive this surviving spouse annuity if the member spouse is already retired at the time of divorce. However, the equitable distribution of the pension payment *during the employee-spouse's lifetime*, still must be determined and provided for in the agreement or divorce judgment and in the QDRO.

In an ERISA pension, if the former spouse is given a "***separate interest,***" then the subsequent death of the member spouse after the former spouse has begun receipt of his/ her share does not affect the payments. The former spouse will receive his/her pension share for his/her own lifetime.

Executive Benefits and Compensation

In addition to the retirement assets discussed, there are certain executive benefits and compensation, part or all of which may constitute marital assets subject to equitable distribution. These benefits and types of compensation are very prevalent among upper level management, and for both executives and lower level employees in the technology industry. These assets include, but are not limited to:

- **Incentive Bonuses**, which may be paid in stock or through contributions to a deferred compensation plan;
- **Other non-cash equity compensation**, such as employee stock options, restricted stock units, restricted stock awards, performance shares and stock appreciation rights; and
- **Non-qualified deferred compensation plans**.

While these forms of compensation/benefits are not necessarily all "retirement assets," they have certain characteristics and attributes in common with retirement assets

The assets ***must be valued***. Then the value of the marital portion must be determined. The rules for valuation of the different benefits, and for calculation of the marital share, can be very complicated. There is a separate body of case law which may be applicable. Some of these assets can be transferred to a spouse and some cannot. Some assets are divisible by QDRO and some are not. Usually an expert (e.g. a certified financial analyst or a CPA), who has particular experience in the valuation of these assets as part of a divorce, will be retained. There may be additional obstacles in identifying the assets and obtaining the information necessary for their valuation. This is a very complex area, which is well beyond the purview of this chapter. They are mentioned here only so that a person in a divorce situation is aware of their existence as potential marital assets, or depending upon the type of compensation/benefit, as income for the purposes of maintenance and/or child support.

Final Thoughts

Retirement assets, along with the marital home, often comprise the bulk of the marital estate in divorce involving middle class people.

They are also the assets that have the largest emotional component. It is important for parties in a divorce to be aware of all of the aspects and issues involved in the equitable division of these assets. With a modicum of good will and creative lawyering, options can be often be crafted that will satisfy the needs of both parties.

Karen Greenberg, Esq.

Karen Greenberg received her BA from Cornell University College of Arts and Sciences and her JD from Brooklyn Law School. After graduation, she served as a hearing officer ("Administrative Law Judge") at the N.Y.S Department of Social Services conducting administrative hearings involving public assistance, foster care and Medicaid provider fraud and abuse. Karen then joined DC 37 Municipal Employees Legal Services ("MELS") which provides legal services in a wide range of civil matters to employees and retirees of the City of New York, as part of their union health and security package of benefits. There she practiced in the areas of matrimonial/family law, government benefits, housing, consumer law, bankruptcy and wills. She practiced matrimonial law exclusively for 30 years, including all aspects of custody, child support, maintenance, and equitable distribution of marital property from inception through trial. For the last 26 years, Karen was a supervising attorney of the Matrimonial Department at MELS. As a matrimonial attorney, she developed a special interest and expertise in the area of the distribution of pensions and retirement benefits in divorce. As a result of her recognized expertise in this area, Karen frequently lectured at numerous continuing legal education programs for attorneys, sponsored by among other organizations, Legal Services of New York, In Motion, the Brooklyn Bar Association and the Staten Island Bar Association.

In March 2015, Karen opened an office for the private practice of matrimonial and family law, doing both litigation and mediation. She also serves as a consulting/reviewing attorney for parties in divorce mediation. She acts as consultant to matrimonial attorneys on the issues of equitable distribution of retirement benefits and QDROs. For more information about Karen's practice, visit www.kgreenberglaw.com.

SECTION D: PROPERTY DIVISION

CHAPTER 30

EQUITABLE DIVISION OF MARITAL PROPERTY

SUBPART F: ENHANCED EARNING CAPACITY & PROFESSIONAL LICENSES

By Robyn Myler Mann, Esq.

People generally understand that having an advanced degree or license will likely increase one's earnings. Since 1985,[34] the New York Courts have codified this understanding in divorce cases by analyzing the ***enhanced earning capacity*** ("EEC") of a spouse who holds ***an advanced degree or license*** and determining whether and to what extent this EEC is a marital asset to be equitably distributed between the spouses. As of September 25, 2015,[35] however, a new law was enacted that directs that EEC is no longer marital property subject to distribution. The potential impact on the line of cases that resulted in the rulings related to EEC and its distribution as a marital asset is yet to be determined, but at the end of this chapter, I will discuss how the law may affect the practice with regard to EEC.

New York Courts consider a marriage to be an ***economic partnership*** within which there are marital assets that should be fairly divided between the spouses. Within this context, the concept of EEC, was often used by the Courts to value the degrees or licenses that were earned by one spouse during the marriage and to distribute this as a marital asset. The ***degree or license is not technically a marital asset*** (since it cannot be distributed equitably), but the EEC that results from that degree or license is a marital asset if the degree or license was earned during the marriage. Also within this context, the courts have analyzed

---

[34] See, O'Brien v. O'Brien, 66 N.Y.2d 576 (1985) (where the New York Court of Appeals adopted the concept of enhanced earning capacity as a marital asset to be equitably distributed between the spouses).

[35] See, ***Maintenance Reform Legislation of 2015.***

the non-degreed spouse's contributions to the attainment of the degree or license in order to fairly distribute its value between the spouses.

Types of Degrees/Licenses that Confer EEC

Some degrees are obvious to all of us as contributing to EEC, including medical degrees and law degrees. However, the courts have extended the concept fairly broadly to include nursing degrees, master's degrees (e.g., business or psychology), and accounting degrees.

In fact, ***anything that contributes to the enhanced earning capacity*** of a spouse and that was obtained during the marriage can be considered a marital asset that can be equitably distributed in a divorce. Thus, it has been held that a stockbroker's "***book of business***"[36] is such an asset and that the celebrity status of a spouse is such an asset.[37] In general, if the other spouse's attorney can successfully argue that the 'license' or 'degree' confers professional career potential and a special skill set upon the spouse, that attorney is likely to be successful demonstrating to a court that the EEC be valued and equitably distributed.

Valuing EEC

Valuing EEC should be done by a ***forensic evaluator*** with special skills. Basically, though, the valuation formula looks like this:

EEC=
Actual current earnings of spouse
– Earnings of spouse if he/she didn't have the 'degree/license'
(i.e. the average college graduate earnings in the locality)
(a/k/a *earnings differential*)

× mortality discount until age 65 (an actuarial figure to reflect how likely the spouse is to be alive in a given year up to retirement age)
× an adjustment percentage to reflect the present value of the discounted earnings differential in that year (a/k/a the 'real' rate of interest).

---

[36] See, Moll v. Moll, 18 Misc.2d 770 (2001).
[37] See, Elkus v. Elkus, 179 A.D. 2d 134 (1st Dept., 1991).

Due to the complexity of an EEC valuation, forensic evaluators must be utilized.

Equitably Distributing EEC

This valuation process is not the end of the question: in order to distribute the EEC among the spouses equitably, the courts will ***deduct the value of any outstanding loans*** that were obtained by the spouse to obtain the necessary training and expertise for the degree, and it will also examine the contributions of the non-degreed spouse to the attainment of the degree, both monetary contributions and non-monetary contributions. Thus, if the non-degreed spouse worked outside the home, was primarily responsible for rearing the children while the degreed spouse pursued the degree, and if the duration of the marriage was long, that spouse could be entitled to 50% of the EEC less any outstanding loans.[38] The non-degreed spouse bears the burden of demonstrating to the Court that his or her contributions to the attainment of the degree or license were more than *de minimus* in order to receive a distributive share of EEC from that degree or license.

Personal Sidebar:

In representing a client who had a nursing degree that she earned during the marriage, the spouse was seeking equitable distribution of EEC as a result of that degree. The client began her training and education in nursing prior to their marriage, but she obtained her license during the marriage and had realized 5 years of enhanced earnings as a result of the degree as an emergency room nurse. The spouse had contributed financially to her support and the support of their son during the time that the client was receiving nursing training. The Court referred the valuation of the nursing degree and EEC therefrom to an expert forensic evaluator. The evaluator advised that loans that the client had already paid off would not be deducted from EEC. The evaluator advised that valuation would be based upon the formula noted herein. The evaluator's opinion has not been rendered as of the date of this publication.

---

[38] See, Jones v. Jones, 144 Misc.2d 295 (1989).

Permutations to Consider

1. Which is distributed equitably, the degree or the business?

Where the degreed spouse has ***established and maintained a valuable business practice***, the courts have struggled with determining how to separate the EEC from the value of the business that has been established, since that business is also marital property. In these instances, courts will declare the degree/license to have ***merged with the business*** practice and not separately valuable. Similarly, if the divorce action is initiated before the business practice has had a chance to realize its full enhanced earning potential, or if the degreed spouse sells the business practice or moves it to a new location (thus temporarily reducing actual earnings), the courts will ***value the EEC from the degree*** instead of the business for equitable distributions purposes.

2. What contributions of the non-degreed spouse are considered for equitable distribution purposes?

The non-degreed spouse will be credited with ***direct contributions***, like the funds he or she spent to help the degreed spouse obtain the degree or to support the parties during the time that the degreed spouse was obtaining the necessary training. Also, the non-degreed spouse's indirect contributions, such as caring for the home and kids during that period will be considered by the court in determining how to fairly distribute the EEC.

New Maintenance Law and its Impact on EEC

Although technically EEC is no longer a marital asset in a divorce action, the new maintenance law[39] still provides that the court ***shall*** consider the ***direct or indirect contributions*** to the development during the marriage of the enhanced earning capacity of the other spouse in arriving at equitable distribution of marital property. Thus, as a practical matter, valuation of EEC may ***still be relevant*** in a

[39] The new maintenance law was passed by the New York State Legislature in July 2015, and was signed into law by Governor Cuomo on September 25, 2015. More information on this law can be found in Wendy Harris's chapter on Spousal Maintenance in Section III(B).

divorce case where one spouse has a license, advanced degree, celebrity status or career enhancement.

Some matrimonial lawyers may argue that without making a threshold determination that there has been EEC developed during the marriage, a court cannot analyze what, if any, contributions the other spouse made to the development of that EEC. There is no better way to determine whether there is EEC than a valuation analysis by a forensic expert, and it is likely that the New York courts will continue to rely upon such valuations in making equitable distribution decisions in the future.

Robyn Myler Mann, Esq.

Robyn Myler Mann is an experienced litigator dedicated to representing clients during some of their most challenging times: in family disputes and elder matters involving loss and grief. Using careful legal and practical analysis, creative thinking and a deep insight into each family's needs, offers individualized and workable solutions for clients in a divorce and elder law practice in New York City focused on Manhattan, Brooklyn and the Bronx. Admitted to the Bar in New York, Connecticut and Colorado, Robyn serves the needs of clients in Supreme Court, Civil Court, Family Court and Surrogate Courts, guiding them through complicated and difficult divorces, child custody disputes, child support enforcement matters, and elder law matters to successful conclusions.

A graduate of Emory University and Benjamin N. Cardozo School of Law, Robyn is also a trained mediator in family disputes, helping couples to resolve parenting plans and financial matters during separation and divorce.

SECTION D: PROPERTY DIVISION

CHAPTER 30

EQUITABLE DIVISION OF MARITAL PROPERTY

SUBPART G: INTELLECTUAL PROPERTY

By Ravi Cattry, Esq.

Hank is a baker and owns multiple bakeries throughout New York, all of which are open using the same name, Hank's Heavenly Hot Buns. Hank is also going through a divorce from his wife, Whitney. During the course of his divorce Hank learns that the bakeries that he owns are subject to division where Whitney could be entitled to earnings from these bakeries or possibly even some of the bakeries as a whole. Aside from the physical locations of the bakeries themselves, the name of the bakeries and recipes of the food made there, amongst other aspects of the bakeries, are considered ***intellectual property*** ("IP") and similar to other property are subject to distribution during a divorce. There are three primary types of IP: ***copyrights***, ***trademarks***, and ***patents***. Trade secrets and website domains are other forms of IP.

> **Intellectual Property**. Intellectual Property ("IP") refers to the intangible, legal right to protect your ownership rights as the creator of a unique invention, expression of an idea or business mark.

Types of IP

Copyrights

A ***copyright*** is designed to protect "***original works of authorship***," such as literary, dramatic, musical, and artistic works that are both published and unpublished. Copyright protection arises when an expression is recorded in some manner, such as a writing, audio recording, or video. The copyright protects the form in which the subject matter appears rather than the subject matter itself. In some cases, the expression can be filed with the ***U.S Copyright Office*** which gives the owner of the copyright the exclusive right to reproduce the copyrighted work, to prepare derivative works, to distribute copies of the work, or to publically perform or display the work.

> For example, in Hank's case, if Hank designed a machine that he used to knead dough in the bakery more quickly and using less energy and then published a description of it on his website, that specific description and any pictures he used would be copyrighted and could not be used by someone else. If Hank did not register the copyright, common law copyright would only help him in determining when and where to make the first publication of the description. Further, the copyright, even if registered, would not protect Hank from someone who decided to build a machine using that description.

Even if an expression is not registered with the U.S. Copyright Office, it can still be protected under a ***common law copyright***. The common law copyright gives an author of an original work the right to determine when and where to publish the work. This does not give an author the protection from subsequent copying of their work once it is published. Common law copyright only protects instances of first time publication.

Trademarks

A ***trademark*** is an identifying mark for consumers in connection with a particular good or service. A trademark can be a word, name, symbol, device, sound, or packaging of food product that distinguishes it so that the origin of the product is known by that trademark. In the instance of Hank's bakeries, the name of the bakeries, Hank's Heavenly Hot Buns, would be considered a trademark. If a business operates in interstate commerce, then it may file a trademark at the federal level with the ***U.S. Patent and Trademark Office*** ("USPTO"); otherwise, it may register the trademark at the state level. Even if Hank does not register his mark, he has ***common law*** trademark rights over the following:

- The word mark of "Hank's Heavenly Hot Buns"
- The design mark for the logo that he uses
- A mark for the slogan that he uses ("Hank Likes 'Em Hot!")

Further, if Hank uses a specialized packaging used to identify his product (fire shaped foil, for example) then Hank would also have a trademark claim to the packaging of his food product.

Patents

A ***patent*** grants "the right to exclude others from making, using, offering for sale, or selling" an invention that you made. There are three types of patents: (1) ***utility patent***, (2) ***design patent***, and (3) ***plant patents***. A ***utility patent*** may be granted to a person who invents or discovers a new or useful process, machine, article of manufacture, or composition of matter, or any new and useful improvement thereof. A ***design patent*** is granted to a person who invents a new, original, and ornamental design for an article of manufacture. A ***plant patent*** is granted to a person who invents or discovers and asexually produces any distinct and new variety of plant.

A patent can be filed at the federal level with the ***U.S. Patent and Trademark Office*** ("USPTO") (if the mark enters interstate commerce) under the ***Latham Act*** or it can be filed at the state level with the ***NYS Department of State*** ("DOS" or "NYDOS"). Similar to a filed copyright, the filed patent will provide the owner with more protection than a common law patent will. Registering a patent allows others to learn whether or not the invention they created has already been registered and prevent litigation.

In Hank's situation, Hank could file a patent for his special machine that kneads dough faster and uses less energy than those currently available in the market. The patent would now protect others from making, using, offering for sale, and selling the special kneading machine. The registration would also give another inventor notice that this product exists and Hank owns the sole right to make, use, and sell this machine.

Trade Secrets

Another common topic that comes up with intellectual property is trade secrets. A ***trade secret*** is a formula, practice, process, design, instrument, pattern, commercial method, or compilation of information, which is not generally known, and can be used by a business to gain an economic advantage. A trade secret generally does not need to be registered to be protected from others trying to copy it or learn it. It does require that the person with the information about the trade secret take reasonable steps to keep it secret, such as having employees ***sign non-disclosure agreements*** or other agreements requiring that the confidential information not be shared with anyone. However, a trade secret cannot be protected if someone else is able to determine it through reverse engineering.

The recipe for Hank's hot buns can be considered a trade secret because he is using the recipe to gain a commercial benefit. Further the recipe is not known to the public and Hank also requires anyone who works at his bakeries to sign non-disclosure agreements to prevent them from telling his recipe to others.

Website Domains

An intellectual property topic that is becoming more relevant today is ***website domains***. A website domain is the root web address for a website, including the ".com" and may only be registered to one person or entity. The website domain is registered with the ***Internet Corporation for Assigned Names and Numbers*** ("ICANN"). The registration generally lasts for one year and must be renewed annually. Upon registration the person or entity that registered the domain name will have sole right to use that website name for his or her website until the registration expires. If it expires and the owner does not renew it, another person can claim that domain name.

> Hank has a website for his bakeries, www.HotBunsByHank.com, which he has registered in his name. As long as Hank keeps the registration of the website up to date by timely renewing it, he will be the sole owner of this website address.

Intellectual Property and Divorces

Now that Hank is going through a divorce, his spouse may be entitled to ownership and revenue from the bakeries, including ownership and revenue derived from its intellectual property. The main decider in whether or not intellectual property will be considered during distribution in a divorce is if it is considered ***separate property*** or ***marital property***. Separate property is any property that was owned prior to the marriage, which was not co-mingled with the spouse after marriage. Marital property is any property that is acquired during the marriage, regardless of which spouse owns the property or if it is titled only in the name of one spouse.

> **Equitable Distribution**. Divisions in property based on equitable distribution are based on fairness rather than dividing the property equally. Some factors that are considered are length of marriage, age and health of parties, income, and future earning capacities.

The general rule for intellectual property and how it is divided is that any value created during the marriage must be divided. In New York, Domestic Relations Law §236B governs how property is divided in a divorce, which is via ***equitable distribution***. It is used to decide which spouse gets what percentage of the value of the intellectual property. The first thing to look at in figuring out how intellectual property is divided is when the intellectual property was (1) ***first used***, (2) first used in ***interstate commerce*** (if applicable) or in ***intrastate commerce***, and (3) when copyrights, trademarks and patents were ***registered*** (if applicable). The intellectual property may be premarital if there was no enhanced value during the marriage.

> For example, if Hank wrote a book using some of the recipes from his bakery before the marriage and he did not sell any copies during the marriage nor updated the book in any way, he would most likely be entitled to sole possession of the copyright of the book. However, if Hank wrote a second edition to that book during the marriage, his spouse would be entitled to her equitable share of the copyright from the second book.

Another aspect in considering whether or not something is marital property is when the spouse that owns the intellectual property expended the energy in procuring it. For example, in the case of Hank's patent for a special dough kneading machine, if Hank started the process of getting the patent and all of his effort put into getting it was done before the marriage, his spouse may not be entitled to it even if the patent was received after the marriage. Since all of the work to get it was done before marriage, the act of simply receiving it while married does not make it marital property. However, if there was any enhanced value to the intellectual property during the marriage, the spouse would be entitled to it, no matter how small the value was. Similarly, if Hank applied for the patent while married, but did not receive the patent until after the divorce, Whitney will still be entitled to own a part of the patent because the time spent in order to get it was during the marriage.

Equitable Division of Intellectual Property

Once the determination is made about whether or not the intellectual property is marital or separate property, the next step is dividing the IP bucket. Intellectual property is then treated like any other type of asset and the ***value of the IP must be determined***. The parties can agree on a value themselves or hire an appraiser who deals specifically in IP valuations. Like any other marital assets being divided, the parties choose to negotiate outside of court or let a judge ultimately decide on the issues of IP.

One spouse may choose to ***buy the other spouse out*** of his or her ownership rights to the IP; however, the issue of valuation remains challenging. Another option would be to allow the other spouse to have a license to the IP. For example, if Hank had three bakeries, and in the divorce the parties decided that Hank would keep ownership to two bakeries while his spouse kept the third, the brand name "Hank Heavenly Hot Buns" could be licensed to the other spouse to use on the third bakery for $X/year for X years.

Another solution might be for one spouse to have complete ownership of the IP, but for both spouses to ***share revenue*** derived from the IP. Hank and Whitney could decide that Hank should have complete ownership of the copyright of books he wrote and that Whitney will get a percentage of the income that comes from the sale of the books. The percentage can be agreed upon as they see fit or can be equitably distributed based on factors mentioned before. Sharing the ownership of the IP is also an option for the spouses, but dividing ownership can bring up the issue of depreciation in value of the IP because it creates difficulties in selling the IP or licensing it.

A ***divorce settlement agreement*** should properly address the issue of intellectual property. It should discuss any changes in ownership, profit sharing from future revenues, or licenses Also, if any claims arise regarding the IP, the agreement should detail which spouse would be responsible for taking care of the litigation and how much each spouse would contribute in terms of time and money to deal with the litigation.

Restraining Orders. One other issue that might arise during divorce or after divorce is where the ex-spouse tries to use the intellectual property to benefit him or herself or hurt the ex-spouse. For instance, the judge might award Hank with sole rights to the trademark of Hank's Heavenly Hot Buns. If Hank is worried that Whitney might try to open a similar bakery nearby, he can ask the court for a restraining order preventing Whitney from doing that. Also, if Whitney has information regarding Hank's baking trade secrets, a court could grant a restraining order that prevents Whitney from disclosing that information.

During the process of dividing the IP, it is pertinent that the division complies with any and all legal formalities associated with the IP. Laws concerning transfers, reversions, and renewals should be reviewed. Additionally, please note that if the title owner of a copyright, trademark or patent changes, then the U.S. Copyright Office or U.S. Patent and Trademark Office requires an amendment.

Ravi Cattry, Esq.

Ravi Cattry is an associate attorney and is licensed to practice in New York and New Jersey and admitted into the Eastern and Southern District Courts of New York. She completed a Bachelor of Science at Fordham University in Manhattan where she was a double major in psychology and economics. She received a Juris Doctor from Pace University School of Law in White Plains, New York.

Before joining Rincker Law, PLLC, Ravi worked at a general practice firm located in Kew Gardens, New York. While working there her practice areas included landlord and tenant disputes, matrimonial and family law issues, commercial law, and immigration law. Ravi also worked with a boutique law firm specializing in bankruptcy law in Manhattan. During law school she interned with the Integrated Domestic Violence Court in White Plains, New York, where she assisted in handling divorce cases intertwined with domestic violence cases.

Ravi is fluent in Hindi and Punjabi, and conversational in Spanish. In her free time Ravi enjoys reading, watching movies, playing tennis, and keeping up with her favorite soccer teams. For more information about Rincker Law, PLLC, visit www.rinckerlaw.com.

SECTION D: PROPERTY DIVISION

CHAPTER 30

EQUITABLE DIVISION OF MARITAL PROPERTY

SUBPART H: ANIMALS

(1) MEDIATION AND CONFLICTS OVER THE FAMILY PET

By Debra Vey Voda-Hamilton, Esq.

> *We can work it out. Life is very short, and there's no time for fussing and fighting, my friend.*
>
> *– John Lennon and Paul McCartney*

Mediation, as discussed in Chapter 4(a), is a process in which a neutral facilitator helps two or more disputing parties address and resolve their disagreements to their mutual satisfaction. The mediator is not a party in the matter, does not make a decision or suggest a solution to the conflict like an arbitrator. Nor does the mediator impose a ruling upon the parties based on the law like a judge. To the contrary, a mediator ***facilitates agreement*** between disputing parties, using specialized skills to help the parties come together, address their conflict, communicate their feelings and points of view, listen to each other respectfully, and ultimately resolve the disagreement between themselves. This process will never be more usefully applied than to disputes between ***people over animals***.

It has been a long-standing tradition in many cultures to consider mediation preferable to litigation. However, here in the United States (especially in disputes involving animals) mediation is not as popular as litigation. Oftentimes, those with animal ownership disputes suffer in silence without recognizing they could go down a less difficult path. People going through divorce are often unaware there is another option, mediation, which can help them resolve their emotional issues concerning who gets the pets. Instead, parties in a divorce or separation add the pet dispute to their litigation. However, court is not an ideal place to discuss the placement of their pet.

Shift in Viewpoint about Animals

In the 1960-70s family pets were just that – pets. A shift in pet owners' opinions about their animals started in the 1980s and continues today, when these animals are seen as family members and companions. According to ***American Pet Products 2014 survey***, people spent $58 billion dollars on these beloved companions that year. For many, pets are like children. Disputes involving animals in the divorce or separation context usually become emotional. Most matrimonial litigators are comfortable with equitable distribution of property or custody of children, but are ill equipped to handle the emotional question of "***Who gets the pet?***"

Courts are no better equipped to answer this question because they still view pets as personal property. Courts try to keep it simple. In Travis vs. Murray, NY Slip Op 23405, 42 Misc 3d 447 (Supreme Court, New York 2013) the decision in a matrimonial action allowed the parties to have a one-day hearing where they would decide who was the sole owner of their dog based on the "***best for all concerned***" standard. The Court would entertain no other outcome – i.e., no shared ownership arrangement, only sole ownership to one spouse or the other. The judge expressed his hope that the parties would be able to share the pet down the road but stopped short of involving the Court in a "joint ownership agreement" over the dog.

Mediation: Best Method for Resolving Pet Ownership Disputes

Where the family pet is concerned, only the disputing parties know what the best resolution for all involved is – not a judge who has never even met the beloved animal. Separating or divorcing couples with a pet ownership dispute have a difficult time reaching a resolution in a way that satisfies their deeper emotional needs by using negotiation or litigation. Their respective attorneys represent one side in the disagreement and are one-side solution oriented. Only a mediator can provide the venue, skills and assistance the parties need to implement this time-tested process to resolve their dispute over their family member the cat, dog, bird or horse! Mediators are in a much better position to bring people together, validate their emotions and points of view, and help them find ways to reconcile the question about the family pet in a divorce.

The primary reason to choose mediation in a conflict over an animal is simple: mediation addresses the conflict itself, not just the facts. If the disputing parties are given a chance to come together in mediation to discuss who gets the pet they will have a better chance of speaking about and understanding each other's underlying emotions, which continue to drive the conflict. This will give them the best chance of coming to a mutually satisfying agreement for themselves and their pets.

When divorcing or separating couples come to a mediator, oftentimes, they are so upset that they cannot think about anything but getting their pound of flesh. They are in the middle of a divorce. When the question of who gets the pet comes up it can often set them off and make them very angry. A mediator can sit down with both parties and hear them out.

The best time to start a mediation about the pets of divorce is as soon as possible after the divorce proceedings begin. Think about it: when a conflict arises between two people, isn't it best to meet ASAP when the parties can still speak civilly to each other? In some cases, the pet itself created some acrimony between the parties; thus, settling the issue of pet custody first in a divorce can make negotiations of other issues go more smoothly. Mediation can help preserve the relationship between both of the divorcing or separating parties and their pet(s).

In some cases, the pet mediator will ***conflict coach each party***, helping him or her become a better listener so that together they can directly resolve the situation without litigation. Mediation is always one of the best venues in which to resolve pet ownership disputes because it allows the parties to feel heard and keeps their mindset focused on what is in the best interest of the pet.

What Happens in Mediation?

Chapter 4(a) goes into more detail about the mediation process; however, as a brief overview, mediation oftentimes includes:

- Confidential conversation
- Listening

- Clarification and resolution of the facts and perceptions
- Preservation of the relationship
- Reality check

Each will be discussed briefly below in the context of pet mediation in a divorce or separation.

Confidential Conversation

As you may remember, conversations in mediation are confidential. What is said about the pet or the pet's role in the parties' lives or break up of their marriage stays within the mediation room. People often feel they can speak more freely about controversies surrounding their marriage and the pet because the discussion cannot be used against them if future litigation proceedings were to occur. This is one of the strongest arguments for working within the mediation framework. People feel a sense of safety held in place by the mediator and the rules of mediation.

Listening

People in conflict have a hard time listening to each other. This is especially true in divorce and the endings of relationships. The parties are so entrenched in their own ideas, points of view and what they are going to say next that they are not listening to the other side. In these cases, mediation can be a more logical approach to resolving the conflict. The mediator is there not to render a decision but rather to help people keep talking until they feel heard, respected, and understood. From there, the parties can address the actions that will enable them to go forward more peacefully to resolve their pet ownership dispute.

Clarification and Resolution

In mediation, the parties can focus on the issues involving their pet. Their focus on the needs surrounding the pet helps them gain a clearer understanding of their own issues, the other party's issues and how best to resolve them all. Facts are clarified and perceptions dispelled. In some divorces, one spouse will state a position and then the other party will counter with an opposite view simply out of spite.

Neither focuses on the underlying issues or pet welfare. Focusing on the pet helps them reach a common ground.

Preservation of the Relationship

During a mediation which addresses pet issues, divorcing and separating parties are helped to recognize the sometimes destructive language they are using to discuss the pet ownership dispute. The idea in mediation is to help people resolve their pet conflict in a way that may help them keep the pet in their life. It is also hoped the parties will be encouraged to resolve other problems using this same process. This is not always possible. An inability of the parties to speak civilly to one another should not mean that one party no longer sees their beloved pet. This companion animal is usually the last best thing the parties did together. Keeping it open and available to each going forward can be very meaningful.

Working out terms that keep the pet in both their lives is possible. Working this out after litigation is difficult to achieve. Litigation is a process in which relationships may be destroyed and any hope of working out a collaborative solution dissolves with the marriage. Often, litigation attorneys think people who want to pursue ownership of their beloved pet via litigation are crazy – but they are not. This pet was an integral part of the fabric of their lives, and an attorney who ignores that fact does so at his/her peril. Divorce attorneys who have worked with mediators on pet issues can be heard saying say, "Boy, I wish I had known before that mediation worked so beautifully. I've had a few divorce settlements that almost went down the toilet once we got to the pet. There was no agreement and it became ugly."

Reality Check

"Reality testing" is an important part of pet mediation. Pet mediators might hear "I deserve 50 percent of this pet because I have paid half of this dog's bills!" This party might need to reflect on the experiences he or she had with the dog (e.g., hiking, road-trips, long walks, dog parks). The pet mediator might ask a party to visualize his or her life with the dog going forward or discuss the reality of having the dog live with him/her when the party now lives alone and works full-time.

During the reality check segment of the mediation, a couple might decide that it is better for the dog to live primarily with one spouse. Then the parties need to work out when they will exchange the dog; for example, one weekend a month and/or while the primary caregiver is on vacation. Ideally, this divorcing couple will discuss the drop-off and pick-up of the dog as well as payment for this service, food costs and veterinary care. Reality testing in mediation helps the parties think creatively so they can determine a win-win scenario for both parties and the pet.

Overview of Pet Mediation Process

The Function of the Pet Mediator

So how does a pet mediator work her magic in a conflict involving the family pet? She brings the parties involved in a divorce or relationship breakup together, gets them communicating and helps them find the path of least resistance to work out a solution in the best interest of all.

A clue as to what makes a good pet mediator comes from the wisdom of the ancient Chinese philosopher Lao Tzu:

The great leader speaks little.
He never speaks carelessly.
He works without self-interest
and leaves no trace.
When all is finished, the people say,
"We did it ourselves."

The goal of good animal conflict mediation is that in the end the disputing parties feel and believe they have created their own solution about their beloved companion. If parties depend on a court to decide their issue of pet ownership, their emotions will not be validated; they will not have meaningful closure. Divorcing and separating couples with a pet ownership dispute should choose a pet mediator who is, as Lao Tzu says, a great leader who speaks carefully, listens, and works without self-interest, encouraging the parties to develop their own solution.

How Long Does Mediation of a Pet Issue in Divorce Take?

Put simply, pet mediation is almost always quicker than litigation. While court cases can drag on for months or even years, some mediations that focus on pet disagreements are typically resolved in a session or two. Divorcing couples may choose to intermingle their pet ownership dispute with other issues ancillary to the matrimonial action (e.g., child custody, equitable distribution); doing so can elongate the divorce process. It is suggested that the parties focus on the ownership of the pet early on in the divorce process using mediation.

How Much Does Pet Mediation Cost?

In almost every case, pet mediation is unquestionably cheaper than litigation. The hourly rate for pet mediators varies based on geographic region and experience. Here are a few reasons why mediation is significantly cheaper than litigation for resolving pet ownership disputes:

- In litigation, each party has to pay their divorce lawyer's fees. In mediation, both parties hire the same mediator and usually split the mediator's fees between them equally (50/50).
- If a separating couple is not already involved in a court proceeding, then they can save the cost of filing fees and other court costs.

By itself, the cost savings of mediating a pet custody issue in divorce should be enough to steer someone away from litigation. But there's more. The emotional nature of disputes over animals can cause hurt feelings to become monetized to the tune of thousands of dollars. For example, if someone's pet has been a wedge in their relationship, the other party can hold the pet at ransom to "get even" for past misdeeds. Both love their animal and the animal loves both people. Courts will make them choose who will own the dog outright, which ultimately hurts the dog. Mediation works out the best solution for all.

Putting It All Together

During pet mediation, divorcing people may come up with original and even bizarre solutions to their conflicts. No matter how strange the idea might seem, the mediator will put everyone's proposed solutions up on a board and hear them out. The mediator does this because everyone needs to be acknowledged and respected. Once this is done the parties are usually surprised at how many of the other party's solutions are similar to their own. In fact, to appreciate each and every one of the solutions that the parties have in common is tantamount to resolution of their conflict. Through this brainstorming, the parties can avoid litigation.

Many divorcing and separating couples that start mediation "knowing" they are going into litigation because there is no way they are going to find a solution walk out of pet mediation with a resolution that meets all of their needs in far less time, for far less money, while keeping their relationship with their beloved pet alive. In this way parties can use mediation to come to a mutually satisfactory solution, keep their relationship with their animal, and maybe improve their human relationship.

If when you started this chapter you thought there were only two ways to deal with a conflict over animals – ignoring the conflict or litigation – now you have been provided with a third option: mediation, which will help a person resolve the conflict about the family pet in divorce, by letting everyone be heard, respected, and understood.

Debra Vey Voda-Hamilton, Esq.

Debra Vey Voda-Hamilton is the principal of Hamilton Law and Mediation (HLM). She is an attorney mediator who works with pet people and pet service providers who want to pursue their passion of helping people, their pets and all animals in general, while reducing exposure to litigation. She presents her programs, which teach people how to communicate without resorting to litigation, all over the country. She has been mentioned or featured in Forbes, US News and World Report, The Wall Street Journal, The New York Times and the Chicago Sun Times.

Debra graduated from Benjamin N. Cardozo Law School in 1983, was admitted to practice in New York in 1984. For more information about Debra and her practice, visit www.hamiltonlawandmediation.com or Debra's blog at hamiltonlawandmediation.blogspot.com.

SECTION D: PROPERTY DIVISION

CHAPTER 30

EQUITABLE DIVISION OF MARITAL PROPERTY

SUBPART H: ANIMALS

(2) COMPANION ANIMALS

By Kymberly A. Robinson, Esq. and Cari B. Rincker, Esq.

For many, companion animals are a part of their family. When people think of the term "companion animals," typically people think about dogs and cats; however, horses can be considered a companion animal in certain cases. A companion animal is defined by Agriculture & Markets Law § 350(5) as "any dog or cat, and shall also mean any other domesticated animal **normally maintained in or near the household** of the owner or person who cares for such other domesticated animal"[40] (emphasis added).

Matrimonial vs. Non-Matrimonial Cases

It is not unusual for a "break-up" to be between people with a shared companion animal. In a non-matrimonial case, ***replevin*** is the proper and only cause of action to recover a pet. See Travis v. Murray, 42 Misc. 3d 447, 461 (New York Co. Sup. Ct, 2013); Hennet v. Allan, 981 N.Y.S.2d 293 (Albany Co. Sup. Ct., 2014); and Ramseur v. Askins,

[40] See People v. Lohnes, 112 A.D.3d 1148 (3rd Dept., 2013) ("horses are excluded from the statutory definition of companion animals only when they are '[f]arm animal[s]' ...raised for commercial or subsistence purposes" (Agric. & Mkts Law § 350[4]). Any domesticated animal, including a horse, may be a companion animal where, as here, it is not kept for such purposes and is "normally maintained in or near the household of the owner or person who cares for [it]" (internal citations omitted).

44 Misc.3d 1209(A) (2014). Replevin means a ***superior right to possession*** in chattel. In a divorce action, possession of pets should be addressed in equitable distribution. Furthermore, a ***prenuptial agreement*** or ***postnuptial agreement*** can also address the disposition of a shared pet.

While pets technically still fall into the category of ***chattel*** (which is why replevin is the proper cause of action in non-matrimonial disputes), New York courts first recognized that pets have a special status as something somewhere "***in between a person and a personal piece of property***" in 1979. See Corso v. Crawford Dog and Cat Hospital, Inc., 97 Misc.2d 530 (Civ. Ct. Queens 1979) (where the veterinarian was found to have wrongfully disposed of a pet's remains) (emphasis added). Subsequently, in Feger v. Warwick Animal Shelter, 59 A.D.3d 68 (2nd Dept. 2008), the court acknowledged that companion animals are a "**special category of property**" that should be "treated differently than other forms of property" (emphasis added). This case carried more weight than Corso in influencing future decisions because it was an Appellate Division decision.

How Do Courts Handle Companion Animal Disputes

Now having discussed a brief background of companion animal law, it is important to look at some examples of how courts have dealt with disputes regarding companion animals in the context of ***family members, cohabitants, and divorce***.

Travis v. Murray – Best of All Concerned Standard

The most notable New York divorce case centering on a companion animal is a case dealing with a dog named "Joey." See Travis v. Murray, 42 Misc.3d 447 (New York Co. Sup. Ct., 2013). In that case, the plaintiff purchased Joey from a pet store in 2011, while the couple was living together (but not yet married). The couple subsequently got married in 2012. In 2013, while the plaintiff was away on business, the defendant took the dog and moved out. She lied and told the plaintiff that she lost Joey, but later admitted that she took Joey and relocated to her mother's house in Maine. The plaintiff filed for divorce from her partner one month later and requested the return of Joey, and ultimately sole custody of him.

The plaintiff's claim for Joey was based on a strict property analysis and, therefore, she stressed the facts that she *purchased Joey with her own money*, she "*financially supported*" Joey, and was the *primary caretaker* of Joey. The defendant's claim for Joey was based on an almost child custody/best interest of the child analysis; therefore, she argued that Joey was a gift to her from the plaintiff in exchange for her giving up her cat at the plaintiff's request, that she was the *best caretaker* for Joey, that Joey *slept on her side of the bed*, that she "*attended to all of Joey's emotional, practical, and logistical needs*," and that Joey should live with her at her mother's home in Maine (although the defendant would not be relocating to Maine).

The court struggled with what to do with Joey, and in its decision looked to how other states (such as Vermont, Wisconsin, Alaska, and Texas) had interpreted companion animal disputes, which is as somewhere in between a property case and a custody case. See Goodby v. Vetpharm, Inc., 182 Vt. 648 (2007); Rabideau v. City of Racine, 243 Wis.2d 486 (2001); Juelfs v. Gough, 41 P.3d 593 (Alaska 2002); and Bueckner v. Hamel, 886 S.W.2d 368 (Tex.App.-Houston (1st Dist.) 1994. In Juelfs (where the husband was granted sole custody of the chocolate laboardor) and in a Connecticut case, Van Arsdale v. Can Arsdale, 2013 WL 1365358, (2013), 2013 Conn Super LEXIS 574 (where the parties were granted joint custody of the dogs with primary residential custody to the plaintiff, and ordered to equally divide all reasonable costs of veterinary care and grooming) the courts **even use the word "*custody*"** in rendering their decision.

Although New York courts recognized that pets have a higher status than mere personal property, the Travis decision emphasized that a pet was still not entitled to the same standard as a child in awarding custody. So what did this court do? The court determined that there should be a hearing to determine what was "***best for all concerned.***" See Raymond v. Lachmann, 264 A.D.2d 340 (1st Dept., 1999) (where what was best for all parties, including the cat, trumped ownership in a dispute over a cat named Lovey who had already been living with one party for 4 years at the time the case reached the court and the cat was already 10 years old). At such hearing each party would be given an opportunity to prove not only why she would benefit from having Joey in her life, but why Joey has a better chance of living, prospering, loving, and being loved in the care of one spouse as opposed to the other.

Questions to be considered in determining the best for all concerned include whether one party received the pet as a gift. See e.g., C.R.S. v. T.K.S., 192 Misc.2d 547 (Sup. Ct. N.Y. Co., 2002) (where the wife was awarded temporary possession of a chocolate Labrador retriever since he was an "interspousal gift" to her by the husband). The court in Travis also noted other important factors such as:

- Who bore the major responsibility for meeting Joey's needs (i.e., feeding, walking, grooming and taking him to the veterinarian) when the parties lived together?
- Who spent more time with Joey on a regular basis?
- Why did plaintiff leave Joey with defendant, as defendant alleges, at the time the couple separated?
- And perhaps most importantly, why has defendant chosen to have Joey live with her mother in Maine, rather than with her, or with plaintiff for that matter, in New York?"

Until recently, the standard established in Travis, the best for all concerned, was the standard for pet ownership disputes in New York between people who are married or cohabitate. In the past year, courts have started to move away from the Travis standard, though, and have declined to adopt the "best for all concerned" standard. See Gellenbeck v. Whitton, (N.Y. Sup. Ct., N.Y. County, Oct. 26, 2015). Based on Szubski v. Conrad, Sup. Ct., NY County, July 13, 2015), a prior case concerning a companion animal dispute between an ex-boyfriend and ex-girlfriend where the Court used a strict property analysis, in Gellenbeck, the Judge decided that questions of ownership should be decided by reference to property law, and not to the family law principle of "best interest of the child". The Judge further stated, "the correct law is the law of property, and this court will determine and award possession of [the dog] according to that law, and no other."

As the Travis court explained, this is not nearly as involved as a child custody dispute where there are experts testifying, the child's wishes being considered, and the like, but will give the parties a chance to explain how a pet would be better off with one party versus the other. This is the case for replevin actions as well, where parties are usually given only a one-day hearing, at most. Importantly, a pet ownership dispute between a divorcing or separating couple results in ownership of the pet by one person only. As the Travis court reasoned, to determine a visitation schedule or joint custody arrangement would simply take up too much of the court's time.

Factors Courts Consider

Factors that the courts often consider in these cases include:

1) Whose ***money*** was used to purchase the pet?

2) Was the pet a ***gift***?

3) Who chose (or "***picked out***") the pet?

4) Who ***named*** the pet?

5) Who bore the responsibility of ***caring for the animal*** (e.g., feed, water, exercise, veterinary care)?

6) Who has an ***emotional connection***/attachment to the dog?

7) To whom does the companion animal have an emotional connection/attachment?

8) Are there any other factors (such as illness or anxiety experienced by the pet) that would make one party more favorable as the pet's caretaker?

> As a hypothetical, a cat that has diabetes and requires daily injections and monitoring would probably not be awarded to the spouse hates needles, travels often, and who has never given the injections in the past 5 years of the animal being diagnosed.

In evaluating these factors, proof such as the following would probably be helpful to the court in deciding ownership of a companion animal between separating or divorcing parties:

1) ***Purchase records*** (receipt, bill of sale, etc.) for the pet;
2) Documentation or correspondence referring to the ***decision*** to get the pet;
3) Documents or correspondence referring to the pet being a ***gift***;
4) Records regarding title and/or ***ownership*** or title of the pet;

5) Receipts, invoices or proof of payment for veterinary, doggie day care, cat-sitting, dog walking, food, grooming and any other ***expenses*** relating to the companion animal;;
6) ***Veterinary records*** (including vaccination or neutering certificates);
7) ***Microchip*** or other identification records;
8) ***Registration*** any breed organizations; and,
9) ***Licenses*** for city/town/parks.

Companion animal disputes are a growing point of contention. The law will likely develop even more as this issue becomes more frequently discussed in reported cases. In light of the cases that have reached the courts so far, it would seem wise to be extremely organized and succinct in one's presentation of arguments and evidence to the court since it is unlikely that the court will devote more than one day to these disputes.

Kymberly A. Robinson, Esq.

Kymberly is an associate attorney with Rincker Law, PLLC and is admitted to practice law in New York and Florida. She attended Union College in Schenectady, New York for her undergraduate studies, where she graduated with high honors as a psychology major. She then obtained her J.D. from Pace University School of Law in White Plains, New York and, subsequently, her L.L.M. (with a concentration in family law) from the Benjamin N. Cardozo School of Law in Manhattan. Kymberly entered the field of matrimonial and family law as a way to couple her interest in psychology and personal relationships with her legal education.

Cari B. Rincker, Esq.

Cari Rincker is the principal attorney at Rincker Law, PLLC, a national law practice focusing on "Food, Farm & Family." She is licensed to practice law in New York, New Jersey, Connecticut, Illinois and Washington, D.C. Cari was named as a Rising Star for Metro New York in 2015 by "Super Lawyers" and is an award-winning blogger. Cari is involved in several professional organizations including the Association for the Bar of the City of New York's Matrimonial Law Committee.

SECTION D: PROPERTY DIVISION

CHAPTER 30

EQUITABLE DIVISION OF MARITAL PROPERTY

SUBPART H: ANIMALS

(3) HORSES & LIVESTOCK

By Kymberly A. Robinson and Cari B. Rincker

Livestock and horses can be source of dispute (both financially and emotionally) in some divorces. When people think about marital assets they most commonly think about dividing any real estate, bank accounts, cars, businesses, retirement assets, etc. They seldom think about the equitable division of livestock and horses.

Equine Issues with Equitable Distribution

Valuation of Marital Asset

Valuation of animals, especially horses, is very complex and requires an appraiser with great expertise. The ***American Society of Equine Appraisers*** ("ASEA") is the nation's only appraisal association exclusively for horse appraisers. The ASEA is a division of ***The American Society of Agricultural Appraisers.***

In Kennedy v. Kennedy, 256 A.D.2d 1048 (3rd Dept., 1998), the court ordered the equitable division of a horse operation including the residence, trucks, a horse trailer, farm machinery, and several horses. One such horse was "Ima Flashy Zipper." Plaintiff-wife tried to assert that that Ima Flashy Zipper was not a marital asset ***because***

she gifted the horse to the parties' daughter. However, the record reflected that this horse was not a gift at all and, in fact, title to the horse remained in the ***wife's name*** and she continued to ride the horse. The Court in Kennedy then had to entertain valuation experts' reports on the ***value of the horse***, which was also disputed by the parties. In the end, the wife's expert's valuation was accepted by the Court, and the husband was granted one-half of that value, or $2,750, as a distributive award based on the court's intention to divide marital property equally.

As ***another valuation example***, in Rich v. Rich, 282 A.D.2d 952 (3rd Dept., 2001), in ordering equitable distribution of marital assets and liquidation of a thoroughbred horse boarding, breeding, and racing business, the court took in consideration the horses' purse earnings and expenses associated with training and boarding offset against their sale price when making a value determination.

Horses as Separate Property

In the prior case examples, the horses were deemed marital property and, thus, subject to equitable distribution. In other cases, horses (like any other type of property) can be found to be separate property, in which case they are not subject to equitable distribution. As discussed in Chapter 29, separate property is not typically distributed during equitable distribution; however, the ***appreciation in that separate asset*** due to the contributions or efforts of the non-titled spouse is subject to equitable distribution.

For instance, in Jones v. Jones, 92 A.D.3d 845 (2nd Dept., 2012), a ***horse farm*** was considered separate property. However, the appreciation of that separate property was subject to equitable distribution and the court awarded 40% of said appreciation to the wife due to her joint efforts and contributions to the horse farm by ***working on the farm***. In another case, the husband purchased a horse farm before the marriage (i.e., premarital property). He then purchased an adjourning farm with a horse barn after the marriage (i.e., marital property). The wife was awarded 50% of the increase in the value of the farm purchased before the marriage as a result of the added horse barn during the marriage. See Zelnik v. Zelnik, 169 A.D.2d 317 (1st Dept., 1991).

On the other hand, sometimes the appreciation of separate property is not subject to equitable distribution. In Brennan v. Brennan, 103 A.D.2d 48 (3rd Dept., 1984), the husband purchased a farm before the marriage. He had horses, cattle, equipment and machinery purchased and used before the marriage, which he brought onto the farm. The wife helped in the farm business for the first two years of their almost 30 year marriage. Upon dissolution of the marriage, the court held that the horses and related equipment were the separate property of the husband since they "were purchased by defendant and almost exclusively under his control as a type of hobby." Id. at 51.

Livestock and Horse Leases

Horses and livestock also can come into a divorce dispute in the context of a ***leasehold***. Unfortunately, the New York Domestic Relations Law ("DRL") ***does not regard leases as either marital or separate property***. See Cudar v. Cudar, 98 A.D.3d 27, 35 (2nd Dept., 2012) (discussing a rental lease, stating that a leasehold is "neither marital nor separate property as defined in [DRL]"). Instead, the court looks at a myriad of factors when determining title or occupancy of a leasehold. In Cudar, the court turned to DRL § 234, which discusses title, occupancy, and possession of a property.

> DRL § 234 states in relevant part:
>
> In any action for divorce * * * the court may (1) determine any question as to the title to property arising between the parties, and (2) make such direction, between the parties, concerning the possession of property, as in the court's discretion justice requires having regard to the circumstances of the case and of the respective parties. Such direction may be made in the final judgment, or by one or more orders from time to time ***before or subsequent to final judgment*** [such as *pendente lite* relief during litigation], or by both such order or orders and final judgment. * * * (Emphasis added). Neither the statute nor relevant case law enumerates a list of factors that the court looks at, leaving it up to the discretion of the court to make an equitable award.

With regard to leases of horses, bulls, cows, stallions, mares, and other livestock, factors to be considered in determining how a court would distribute the leasehold would include:

1) Who has ***title*** to the animal?
2) How long is the ***term*** on the lease?
3) How long has the lease already been in effect?
4) Did the lease start ***before or after the marriage***? (I.e., is the lease premarital?)
5) Who, if anyone, has any emotional attachment to the animal?

6) Who is ***taking care*** of the animal? If the leasehold concerns a horse, who rides the horse, grooms it, exercises it? Similarly, if the leasehold concerns a show animal (e.g., show heifer), who is showing the animal?
7) Who arranges for ***veterinary*** visits?

People develop relationships with domestic animals as well as farm animals, ***especially in the case of children*** who were raised on a farm. It is recommended that parties ***mediate*** these disputes.

The Commingling of Livestock and Horse Assets

A basic tenet of matrimonial law is that when separate property is ***commingled*** with marital property, the entire asset (typically) ***transmutes into marital property***. When separate property is merely ***exchanged***, it remains ***separate property***. So, a blue car purchased before the marriage exchanged for a red car purchased after the marriage is still separate property, as long as no marital funds were used to pay any additional cost or fee.

Livestock is different than other assets for many reasons, but specifically because it is an asset that ***regenerates***. Two situations arise with classification of livestock during a divorce:

- classifying offspring who are born during the marriage of separate property livestock; and
- herd regeneration or cattle that was originally purchased by one spouse prior to the marriage, but increases or changes due to the mortality of cattle and livestock.

These issues require distinguishing separate and marital property, and then deciding if there was appreciation of a separate asset and, if so, whether that appreciation was passive or active.

Example No. 1

Jane grew up on a farm and brings her favorite cows to the farm on which the couple now live. Joe and Jane think it would be nice to breed their favorite animals together. Although the cattle that came from Jane and the cattle that came from Joe are separate property, the calves the cattle produced together would be marital property.

As this hypothetical illustrates, livestock is difficult to define as marital or separate where there is commingling (or breeding of separate property) because animals reproduce and, therefore, the population fluctuates and regenerates. This asset is unlike other assets in that it is essentially self-replacing.

Example No. 2

The next example centers around an Oregon case, In re Marriage of Mallorie, 200 Or. App. 204 (2005). In Mallorie, the husband ran a dairy farm for which he leased cows to produce milk. Here are some key facts:

- He leased them for $8 per cow, per day.
- If a cow died, he was required to pay $900 for a new cow.
- The life of production for a dairy cow was three years and after three years the cow was replaced with a substitute cow.
- On the date of the marriage the husband had 362 milk producing cattle.
- On the date of commencement of the divorce the herd was up to 493 cows.

The trial court held that 362 were acquired prior to the marriage, and were the separate property of the husband, and that 131 were acquired during the marriage, and were marital property. The wife appealed, arguing that 362 of the now living cattle were marital property because the original 362 cattle the husband brought into the marriage are gone and were replaced during the marriage.

Here the replacement of the cow was not exactly like exchanging the blue car for the red car. The appellate court had to decide when the 362 cows were acquired – before the marriage or during the marriage. Since most states, like New York, distinguish between ***passive and active income*** in deciding whether separate assets' appreciation has become marital, the wife could not argue that the 362 cattle now was not separate property merely because they are 362 different cattle than those that existed as of the date of the marriage. She would have to show that the appreciation was due to ***active appreciation***. The husband argued that he did not bring 362 specific cows into the marriage, but brought 362 income-producing assets which were going to be regularly replaced. In essence, he argued that his 362 cows brought into the marriage were perpetual.

However, the court in Mallorie determined that cows are ***not perpetual, but are mortal***. Furthermore, old cows sold for $500, but a replacement cow was $900. So, the husband would sell the old cow for $500 and then add the $400 difference from his profits from the dairy farm to purchase a new cow for $900. Old cows cannot be merely replaced or exchanged for the new cows since new cows cost more money. Since the dairy farm belonged to the husband during the marriage, the income produced was ***active*** (from marital funds) and ***not passive*** (and, therefore, not separate property).

Thus, the cows had ***no residual value*** once they died despite the fact that the lease replenished the cow population. The court in Mallorie ultimately ***dismissed the portion of appreciation*** due to the husband's separate contribution, for which some people criticize this decision, but reaches the same conclusion – that the ***cows are marital property because of commingling and active appreciation***, since the husband did not meet his burden of demonstrating the tracing back to his original separate asset to show why the current herd was not marital.

> In other cases, courts do take into account the separate contribution in a commingled asset (even other Oregon cases do).

Tracing Funds

Likewise, if a spouse wants to claim separate property in a commingled asset, he or she must ***trace the funds back to the separate property***. That is what the husband did in an Ohio case, Blickel v. Blickel, 1996 Ohio App. LEXIS 2468 (Ohio App. 1996). In that case, the husband owned a herd of cattle at the time of the marriage. By the time of the divorce, none of the cattle remaining were the actual animals alive at the time of the marriage. However, the husband was able to "trace" the separate claim and show that 24 of the 30 cattle in the herd were descendants of the cattle he had on the date of the marriage. The court awarded him these animals as separate property.

Example No. 3

To sum up the difference between separate and marital property and the appreciation, let's look at one last hypothetical: Julie gets married to Benjamin. Julie ***owns one horse***, Lacey, that she received as a child. Lacey is now 12 years old. Julie rides Lacey for fun, grooms her, and considers her a ***pet***. Pepper is a thoroughbred jumper that Julie bought before the marriage. During the marriage, she spends half of her time working as a nurse and half of her time is dedicated to Pepper and retaining Pepper as a jumper. Also during the marriage, Julie buys a third horse, Lex. Over the course of the 10 year marriage, Pepper's value increased $25,000. One day Julie meets Bill, someone that shares her love of horses, and files for divorce. Pepper is appraised at that time and her value is confirmed.

Using this example, in a divorce, it is likely that the court would find Lacey to be a separate asset, Pepper to be a separate asset, and Lex to be a marital asset. However, the court would analyze whether the appreciation in value of Pepper from the date Julie bought her until the date of commencement of the divorce was ***passive appreciation or active appreciation***. Judging by the amount of time Julie spends on Pepper, in lieu of working more hours as a nurse, and the marital assets (money) she pays to enroll Pepper in competitions, professional grooming fees, and any equipment (bridle, saddle and halters) needed, it is likely the court would consider the appreciation in Pepper marital property, and Benjamin would be awarded a portion of that value.

Kymberly A. Robinson, Esq.

Kymberly is an associate attorney with Rincker Law, PLLC. Kymberly is admitted to practice law in New York and Florida. She attended Union College in Schenectady, New York for her undergraduate studies, where she graduated with high honors as a psychology major. She then obtained her J.D. from Pace University School of Law in White Plains, New York and, subsequently, her L.L.M. (with a concentration in family law) from the Benjamin N. Cardozo School of Law in Manhattan. Kymberly entered the field of matrimonial and family law as a way to couple her interest in psychology and personal relationships with her legal education.

Before joining Rincker Law, PLLC, Kymberly was an associate at boutique matrimonial law firms in Westchester County, Manhattan, and Florida. She was also a volunteer at the New York County Access to Justice Program-Uncontested Divorce Clinic where she assisted self-represented litigants in the divorce process. During law school Kymberly also participated in two legal clinics: one at the Pace Women's Justice Center, where she represented clients in obtaining orders of protection and another at the Brooklyn Family Defense Project, where she assisted in defending families in child abuse and neglect proceedings.

Kymberly likes to spend her free time with her family and also enjoys working out, cooking healthy meals, and getting together with friends. She lives in Westchester County, New York with her husband and daughter.

For more information about Rincker Law, PLLC, visit www.rinckerlaw.com.

Cari B. Rincker, Esq.

Cari Rincker is the principal attorney at Rincker Law, PLLC, a national law practice focusing on "Food, Farm & Family." She is licensed to practice law in New York, New Jersey, Connecticut, Illinois and Washington, D.C. Cari was named as a Rising Star for Metro New York in 2015 by "Super Lawyers" and is an award-winning blogger. Cari is involved in several professional organizations including the Association for the Bar of the City of New York's Matrimonial Law Committee.

In addition to her litigation practice, Cari is also a trained mediator for divorces, child custody and visitation, and commercial disputes. She was also an adjunct professor at New York University, College of Steinhardt (2013-2014), where she taught an undergraduate food law class.

On the food and agriculture side of her practice, Cari is the Chair of the American Bar Association, General Practice, Solo & Small Firm Division's Agriculture Law Committee and won the 2014 Excellence in Agriculture Law Award by the American Agriculture Law Association.

Cari is a distinguished alumni from Lake Land College in Mattoon, Illinois and Texas A & M University. Before attending law school at Pace University School of Law in White Plains, New York, Cari obtained a Master of Science from the University of Illinois. Cari's practice is family-centered and counsels clients on a myriad of family law and matrimonial law issues.

For more information about Rincker Law, PLLC, visit www.rinckerlaw.com. Cari is also active on social media. You can follow her on Twitter @CariRincker @RinckerLaw and Instagram and Facebook.

SECTION E: RELIGIOUS ISSUES

CHAPTER 31

THE GET AND RABBINICAL PRE-NUPS

By Deborah E. Kaminetzky, Esq.

For people of the ***Jewish faith***, there are additional issues regarding matrimonial law, both with divorces and prenuptial agreements.

The Get

First of all there is a Jewish divorce, otherwise known as a "***Get***." To explain, the husband has to voluntarily ***give the get*** to the wife for the divorce. Procedurally, the two parties go before a ***Bet Din*** (i.e., a ***rabbinical panel***) where a scribe writes up the divorce document and two witnesses sign it. The husband then hands the papers to the wife and if she accepts it, they are divorced under Jewish law.

New York has a law regarding ***removal of barriers to remarriage*** and the ***get*** is one of those barriers. The plaintiff in a divorce proceeding must remove the barriers to the defendant's getting remarried within the faith. Also in a negotiated divorce both parties attest in an affidavit that they will or have already removed said barriers. A problem arises when a female plaintiff in a contested divorce wants a ***get*** and the husband refuses to willingly give one. Under New York law, the Defendant is not required to remove the barriers to remarriage.

Therefore, the female plaintiff may be left in a precarious situation where she is divorced under civil law but not under Jewish law. This conundrum allows only the husband to get remarried within the faith. There is a term for this in the Hebrew language: "***Agunah***," or a chained woman. To circumvent this problem, some Rabbis draft what is known as a "***Rabbinical Pre-Nup***," discussed below.

Rabbinical Pre-Nup & the Bet Din

There is a difference between ***an attorney drafted*** pre-nuptial agreement and a ***Rabbinical*** "***Pre-Nup***." Attorney drafted agreements are not to be taken lightly, most attorneys will not even agree to draft one unless the couple is at least two to three months away from the wedding date (i.e., *before* the invitations have gone out). Civil pre-nuptial agreements generally at a minimum deal with financial issues such as ***maintenance*** (formerly known as alimony) and the division of property in case of a divorce. The closer the parties get to the wedding date, the more at risk the parties are that a court will say that one the parties was under duress.

Rabbinical prenuptial agreements usually have several sections. The first section has to do with ***agreeing to give the wife a "Get"*** (i.e., the Jewish divorce) should the couple get divorced civilly. The Rabbinical Pre-Nup specifies a compounded ***monetary fine*** for each day the couple is ***separated and a get is not given*** which is supposed to ***incentivize the husband*** to give the get instead of paying the fine. There are also optional sections, which have to do with financial obligations and child custody and visitation issues, respectively. However, as a caveat, the parties may not receive what they have bargained for in the Rabbinical Pre-Nup.

In New York, the ***Bet Din***, which is a ***Jewish Rabbinical Court*** (or any ***arbitration panel***) is not empowered to render decisions on child custody and welfare of children because New York courts have ruled that it is against public policy. There have been cases when a Bet Din's ruling has been overturned by New York Courts if the Child Support Standards Act was not properly addressed. In fact, in one case the court threw out the entire award made by the Bet Din because even though there were portions of the award which would normally have been upheld, the issues were so intertwined with child support that the court felt the global decision on economic issues could not stand.

However, New York Courts have repeatedly held up arbitration awards by a Bet Din which have to do with the economic issues of equitable distribution and maintenance. Should someone enter into a Rabbinical Pre-Nup, it will also ***require arbitration by the Bet Din***.

Civil prenups may also have a clause requiring the husband to give the Get. Jewish couples should consider having this language included in their prenuptial agreement instead of signing the Rabbinical Pre-Nup.

Deborah E. Kaminetzky, Esq.

Deborah E. Kaminetzky is the founding member of Kaminetzky & Associates, P.C. located in Cedarhurst, New York. Prior to starting the firm Deborah worked at a Long Island firm where she learned the practice of Matrimonial and Family law. Deborah has also worked at the New York Department of Consumer Affairs where she was responsible for prosecuting unlicensed home improvement contractors and negotiating settlements for consumers. Prior to practicing law, Ms. Kaminetzky served on the Architectural Control Committee of a Home Owners Association in Boca Raton while living in Florida, and was the president of a commercial property management corporation in the New York Metro area.

Ms. Kaminetzky is a member of the American Bar Association (General Practice, Solo and Small firm Division and Law Practice Management Sections), New York State Bar Association (Estate, Family Law and General Practice Sections), Nassau County Bar Association (where she serves as Chair of the Technology and Practice Management Committee, and is active in the Community Relations and Education Committee, Women in the Law committees and General and Solo Committee) Great Neck Lawyers Association, and The Nassau County Women's Bar Association.

Ms. Kaminetzky was recently appointed to the Committee on Law Practice Management of the New York State Bar Association. Ms. Kaminetzky serves on the Board of Directors of the Yashar Attorney and Judges Chapter of Hadassah as a Vice President, and was their Woman of the Year 2012. Deborah graduated from New York Law School in 1991 and the University of Michigan, Ann Arbor in 1986.

Ms. Kaminetzky was admitted to the First Department in 1991 and the United States Supreme Court Bar in February of 2015.

Deborah is on the Matrimonial fee dispute arbitration panel for Nassau County. She expanded her alternative dispute resolution practice by completing a Mediation certificate program in December of 2013 from The New York Peace Institute.

Ms. Kaminetzky has spoken to various groups on topics including matrimonial law, technology and social media use, and disaster preparedness for business including cybersecurity.

For more information about Ms. Kaminetzky and her practice, visit www.kaminetzkylaw.com

SECTION E: RELIGIOUS ISSUES

CHAPTER 32

CATHOLIC ANNULMENT

By Veronica Escobar, Esq.

Within the Roman Catholic Church, there is no such thing as divorce because "***Canonical Law***" – which is Church law – does not permit divorce. However, there are Roman Catholics who do divorce pursuant to the laws of the State of New York (or wherever they happen to live). Once a Roman Catholic divorces they will be unable to re-marry ***within the Roman Catholic faith***. This precept is governed by the tenets of the religion and will not be addressed here, since it is beyond the scope of the book (and the author's knowledge).

The only viable way for a Roman Catholic to remarry within the Church would be if he or she were granted an ***annulment***. This type of annulment is to be distinguished from the annulments that occur within the Supreme Courts of the State of New York. These two types of annulments are not the same.

Within the Roman Catholic Church, an annulment does not make the marriage a nullity; actually an ***annulment within a Church tribunal*** (i.e., a Church Court) could find that the marriage, which was thought "valid, actually fell short of one of the elements required for a 'binding union.'" The elements are as follows:

1) the spouses are free to marry;
2) they freely exchange their consent;
3) in consenting to marry, they have the intention to marry for life, to be faithful to one another and be open to children;
4) they intend the good of each other; and
5) their consent is given in the presence of two witnesses and before a properly authorized Church minister.

Exceptions to this last requirement must be approved by church authority.[41] The name of the instrument, which must be filed with the ***Archdiocese*** or ***Diocese*** located where the petitioner lives, is called a "***Petition for a Declaration of a Nullity of a Marriage***," an approximately twenty-five page document (which does not include the additional documentation that the application requests) including the Judgment of Divorce from Supreme Court (or whatever court wherein the divorce was granted, if not in New York State).

> For those who may be unfamiliar with the term "Archdiocese," it is a district or a territory under a Roman Catholic Archbishop's responsibility. It is the "head" diocese in a region and usually very large in terms of its Catholic population. A "diocese," is smaller but is still a district under a Roman Catholic bishop's responsibility.

New York State has eight dioceses:

1) The Archdiocese of New York[42];
2) Diocese of Albany[43] ;
3) Diocese of Brooklyn[44];
4) Diocese of Buffalo[45];
5) Diocese of Ogdensburg[46];
6) Diocese of Rochester[47];
7) Diocese of Rockville Centre[48];
8) Diocese of Syracuse[49]; and
9) Two other dioceses belonging to the "Eastern Rite" of the Catholic Church: a) Ukranian Eparchy of Stamford[50] and b) Eparchy of St. Maron of Brooklyn[51] (Maronite Catholics mostly hail from Lebanon).

Each of these dioceses has their own tribunal and inquiries should be made to them directly.

---

[41] The Archdiocese of New York, http://archny.org/faq-annulments (last visited August 29, 2015).

[42] Archdiocese of New York, http://archny.org/our-bishops (last visited Aug. 29, 2015).

[43] Roman Catholic Diocese of Albany, http://www.rcda.org/ (last visited Aug. 29, 2015).

[44] The Diocese of Brooklyn (serving Brooklyn and Queens), http://dioceseofbrooklyn.org/ (last visited Aug. 29, 2015).

[45] The Diocese of Buffalo, http://www.buffalodiocese.org/ (last visited August 29, 2015).

[46] The Diocese of Ogdensburg (Northern New York), http://www.rcdony.org/m (last visited Aug. 29, 2015).

[47] The Diocese of Rochester, http://www.dor.org (last visited Aug. 29, 2015).

[48] The Diocese of Rockville Centre, http://www.drvc.org/ (last visited Aug. 29, 2015).

[49] The Diocese of Syracuse, http://www.syracusediocese.org/ (last visited Aug. 29, 2015).

[50] Ukranian Eparchy of Stamford, http://stamforddio.org/ (last visited Aug. 29, 2015).

[51] Eparchy of St. Maron of Brooklyn, http://www.stmaron.org/ (last visited Aug. 29, 2015).

Depending on the diocese, the process of seeking an annulment to possibly being granted one can take anywhere from ***12 to 18 months***, if not longer. It should be noted that an annulment is not a guaranteed outcome.

For a more in depth treatment of the subject of annulment as well as the official position on divorce, interested parties should consult with the ***United States Conference of Catholic Bishops***.[52]

Veronica Escobar, Esq.

Veronica Escobar is the Principal and Founder of The Law Offices of Veronica Escobar, a practice focusing exclusively in the areas of Elder Law, Special Needs Planning and Trusts and Estates. Prior to forming her own law practice, Veronica worked as an attorney representing the City of New York, Administration for Children's Services (ACS) in child abuse and neglect matters (commonly referred to as an "Article 10") ranging from educational neglect to serious forms of abuse.

Veronica is admitted to practice in the state of New York. She is also admitted to practice before the U.S. District Courts for the Eastern and Southern Districts of New York and the United States Supreme Court. She graduated summa cum laude from Fordham College at Rose Hill, Fordham University, where she was also elected to Phi Beta Kappa, with a degree in American Studies and a minor in Latin American/Latino Studies. She also received her law degree from Fordham, where she was a Notes and Articles Editor of the Fordham International Law Journal.

52 United States Conference of Catholic Bishops, http://www.usccb.org/issues-and-action/marriage-and-family/marriage/annulment/, (last visited Aug. 29, 2015).

SECTION E: RELIGIOUS ISSUES

CHAPTER 33

ISLAMIC MAHR

By Bonnie L. Mohr, Esq.

A Mahr is a ***wedding contract*** the parties sign during an Islamic marriage. At the time of marriage, the groom promises to pay the bride money or its equivalent. The Mahr can also be paid up front, paid partially up front or deferred until divorce or the husband's death. The Mahr payment is the separate property of the wife.

> To be enforceable, the Mahr must meet all contractual requirements such as RPL section 301 and 301-a for proof of authentication and Domestic Relations Law Section 236.

New York courts do not recognize the religious elements of a contract. However, New York courts will recognize the non-religious or secular elements of a religious contract. This means the New York courts will likely recognize and enforce the financial obligations of a Mahr as a contract obligation even though the parties enter into the Mahr during a religious ceremony. In Aziz v. Aziz, in the divorce action, the court upheld the husband's Mahr obligation of a $5,000 payment to the wife. See Aziz v. Aziz, 127 Misc. 2d 1013 (1985).

Even where the Mahr is recognized as a "postmarital agreement" (see Section V(B) for more information on postnuptial agreements), it does not control the division of the marital assets between the spouses in the divorce action. In Farag v. Farag, the husband argued his obligation to his wife in the divorce action was limited to the $20,000 payment promised in the Mahr and nothing else – no spousal support and no division of marital assets. The wife argued she was entitled to spousal support and her share of the marital assets. The court found that the Mahr did not waive the husband's spousal support obligation and did not govern the division of marital assets. See Farag v. Farag, 4 A.D.3d 502 (2004).

Bonnie L. Mohr, Esq.

Bonnie L. Mohr, managing member of the Law Offices of Bonnie L. Mohr, PLLC, started the firm in 2008 to create a practice that educates and guides clients through life-altering and stressful family situations utilizing a comprehensive, holistic and strategic approach.

The firm's practice focuses on matrimonial law including contested and uncontested divorces, prenuptial and postnuptial agreements, and post-judgment enforcements. Bonnie also practices in the family courts on such matters as child support, parenting time (custody and visitation), paternity and family offense matters.

Bonnie L. Mohr is licensed to practice law in the states of New York (2004), New Jersey (2004), and Pennsylvania (2008). She is also licensed to practice in the district courts of the Eastern District of New York, the Southern District of New York and the District of New Jersey.

Bonnie's memberships include the matrimonial and family law committees for the Women's Bar Association, New York County Lawyer's Association and New York State Bar Association. Bonnie is also a member of the New York City Bar Association, where she was leader of the matrimonial mentoring circle. For more information about Bonnie's practice, visit www.mohresq.com.

SECTION F: USE OF PROFESSIONALS THROUGH DIVORCE & SEPARATION

CHAPTER 34

THE BENEFITS OF WORKING WITH A DIVORCE COACH

by Cheryl Lazarus, CLC, CRC, CDC

"My husband threatened to cut back on the money he's giving us!!" Ellen's voice caught on the other end of the line. It was her first consultation with Cheryl, her divorce coach, and Ellen explained that she and he ex-spouse had been separated for two years. He continued to support her and their son generously without a separation agreement in place.

"What just happened?" Cheryl the divorce coach asked.

"He emailed and asked about the large charges that were on the credit card that I use for our son's expenses," Ellen said.

"And then what?" Cheryl asked.

"I wrote that they were for dental expenses and then he threatened to cut back on our financial support!" Ellen explained.

This didn't make sense so Cheryl inquired, "Did you write anything else in that email?"

"Yes," said Ellen. She continue to tell Cheryl everything else she wrote in the email to her husband.

"Ellen, may I be direct with you even though it's our very first session?" Cheryl, asked.

"Yes," Ellen replied.

Cheryl told her that several of her statements were provocative and asked what she was trying to accomplish by writing them. Ellen explained the emotions behind the statements. Cheryl further asked, "And how long have you been doing this? Have you gotten the result that you want?"

"Two years and no!" Ellen answered. "I haven't not gotten what I want by saying it. Things are now getting worse as of today!" After explaining to Ellen

how her anger was affecting her communication and also her financial stability, Cheryl taught her a powerful anger release technique and recommended that she practice it two times a day for the next week. Then Ellen and the divorce coach went over the email line by line. Cheryl also taught Ellen how to write a non-emotional neutral reply.

At their next session, Ellen exclaimed, "After doing the anger release techniques for only five days, I felt more relief and peace that I have in the two years since he left! I followed your guidelines and wrote only neutral replies to his subsequent emails. He is now continuing to give us the financial support and is not cutting back. Everything is even better than before!"

Divorce coaching helped Ellen to release her anger and to become of aware of how it had been affecting her separation and upcoming divorce. Her divorce coach also redirected Ellen's priorities when interacting with her ex-spouse, from provoking him in an attempt to receive a response that she would never get, to staying focused on her goals. By learning new written communication skills Ellen avoided financial repercussions and improved their strained relationship.

The Role of a Divorce Coach

A divorce coach is a skilled professional who helps women and men to manage their lives and to take positive actionable steps as they go through the divorce process. Divorce coaches emphasize present situations and help clients to be accountable so that a person going through a divorce can more forward more quickly.

A divorce coach helps clients have laser focus on concrete actions that can provide support from a practical and emotional standpoint. For example, divorce coaches might encourage clients to become proactive in taking care of themselves or redesigning their life to become happier and more well-rounded.

While a divorce coach's services may vary based on their additional training and expertise, there are five core areas that most divorce coaches focus on:

1. Exploring and managing emotions so that the person can make rationally based divorce decisions;

2. Strategies for interacting and creating boundaries with a (soon-to-be) ex-spouse;

3. Developing priorities, focus and action plans;

4. Education and brainstorming so that the divorcing person can make knowledge-based decisions about the divorce process, parenting, lifestyle choices, social and family interactions; and/or

5. Adjusting to the changes, one's new identity and redesigning one's life.

How a Divorce Coach Can Help With the Five Core Areas

A divorce coach is a skilled professional who understands the pitfalls and process of divorce and can see the larger picture. The divorce coach can help a person going through a divorce by focusing on these Five Core Areas:

Managing Emotions to Help Make More Rational Decisions

It is not uncommon for a person going through a divorce or separation to experience a depth of feelings that they haven't felt before (e.g., anger, grief, guilt, fear). Experiencing these emotions during a divorce or separation may be one of the most difficult experiences that a person will ever go through.

A divorce coach can recognize when a person's emotions are becoming detrimental to the divorce process and help that person become aware and understand what is happening. Additionally, the divorce coach can create a safe environment for a person to express these vivid emotions so that clear decisions can be made.

Example: Giving it All Away

Stacy was a woman in her late 30s who had been married for over fifteen years. She had two school age children, a beautiful home in Philadelphia, was financially secure and had a lifestyle that many people would envy. She and her husband had originally decided that she would stay home and raise the kids.

As time went on, Stacy felt that she was losing herself in the marriage. She wanted to go back to work part-time and establish an identity outside of the home. Her husband blocked her attempts. He was also controlling and belittling. He humiliated her continually both in front of the kids and when they were alone.

Her confidence was at an all-time low and her enthusiasm for life had disappeared. Stacy didn't want to spend the rest of her life this way. In addition, her husband didn't want to work on their relationship. After a year-long internal struggle, Stacy asked for a divorce. Her husband was angry; he liked his life the way it was. He traveled a lot, worked long hours, came home to a cooked dinner, and his kids. He didn't want to change anything.

As soon as she asked for a divorce, her husband distanced himself and moved out. Within months he had a girlfriend. He wouldn't have anything to do with Stacy. She was devastated. Despite not wanting to stay married, she had envisioned a friendship with her soon-to-be ex-husband because they had known each other for most of their adult lives.

In her attempt to "remain friendly" with her husband and to assuage her guilt at initiating the divorce, Stacy agreed to whatever terms he wanted.

She wanted to sign papers that he shoved in front of her at the breakfast table; papers that could have detrimentally affected her custody of the kids and the dollar amounts that she received for child support. She was willing to reduce her entitled amount of maintenance and her share of material assets because she wanted to "keep the peace," in the hopes that he would act nice to her in front of the kids.

Stacy said that her lawyer almost fired her three times. Unfortunately, Stacy was one and a half years into her divorce process by the same she hired Cheryl the divorce coach. She was dealing with grief, guilt, and pleasing behaviors in spite of being in therapy for several years.

Through divorce coaching, she and her divorce coach addressed Stacy's guilt, her desire to please, and her grief over having to give up the dream of any kind of relationship with her ex-spouse. This was very hard for her. Once they worked with these issues, Stacy started making healthier decisions for her future and that of her kids.

Examples: Anger Spiraling out of Control

Here are a few stories of people's anger getting out of control during a divorce:

- A woman who was so enraged at her husband's affair that she spent $20,000 in attorney fees to prevent her spouse from acquiring a family heirloom that was valued at $1,200.
- A German man was so angry at his wife that he cut everything in half – including their car and a stuffed teddy bear. He posted the photos online and then attempted to sell the items on Ebay!

Divorce coaches can help people manage emotions while going through the divorce process and dealing with their (soon-to-be) ex-spouse.

Priorities, Focus and Action Plans

Laura stays focused during attorney meetings and accomplishes what she wants! Laura became intimidated, angry or tearful during her attorney meetings. It was hard to get issues resolved or decided upon. She also felt so overwhelmed and distracted that she often forgot what was discussed. This caused the meetings to be lengthy and she called additional meetings because she didn't accomplish what she needed to.

Adding to her stress, was the pressure that her ex-husband put on both Laura and her attorney to accept a settlement that was far below the norm for a 25 year marriage with their substantial financial situation.

Laura started working with Cheryl, a divorce coach. To prepare for attorney meetings, Cheryl and Laura brainstormed priorities and clarified goals. Cheryl gave Laura specific techniques for keeping her emotions in check, and methods for staying focused and on task during the meetings.

After applying these strategies, Laura called Cheryl and exclaimed, "The meeting was fantastic! We accomplished more in less time! And I stayed focused and unemotional the whole time!"

Laura followed the same formula for subsequent meetings, thus saving time, money and aggravation.

A divorce coach sees the larger picture and how the pieces fit together. People going through a divorce may be forgetful and easily distracted. This is natural because trauma can actually cause changes in the hippocampus, the memory part of the brain, so that it is harder to stay focused and remember.

A divorce coach can provide someone going through a divorce with strategies for handling stress and staying focused. A divorce coach can help to set priorities; and then break the tasks down into manageable steps.

Interacting and Setting Boundaries with the Ex-spouse

The stress, fear and uncertainty during a divorce can bring out the worst in both divorcing parties. For example, it can bring out aggressive or withdrawing behaviors, unkind words, provocations, manipulations. These dangerous emotions can escalate an already difficult situation and result in more time and money in costs and attorneys' fees.

A person going through a divorce or separation can be intimidated by his or her ex-spouse. Everyone becomes dependent on relationships being a certain way and when that changes or needs to change, it throws other aspects of life off balance. Divorce coaches can help people become more aware of this and better deal with manipulations and emotional triggers.

Manipulation

Manipulations may occur during your divorce or separation for the following reasons:

- The relationship may already have a pattern of manipulation.
- One party may be giving in to manipulation to keep the peace and doesn't want to "rock the boat."
- One party may not feel comfortable making his or her own decisions.
- One party feels intimidated or afraid of the other party.

Manipulation and Procrastination Hurts Tanya Financially. Tanya, a smart and accomplished woman in her 40s, worried about telling her teenagers that she and her husband were splitting up. Her husband, who knew of her fears regarding the kids, asked Tanya to wait until there was a "good time" to tell them. She put off filing the initial divorce papers even when urged to by many people to do so.

During that time her husband began positioning himself. Instead of continuing to pay their mortgage out of his salary, he borrowed from their credit line. He did this until he reached the limit. This ended up creating joint debt which Tanya had to share.

Since her spouse was a savvy entrepreneur, he also began hiding assets from his business and shifting their investments. His actions were influencing her financial security. Tanya was aware of his dealings and became so emotionally distraught that it affected her day to day interactions, her relationship with her children, and her work.

Tanya realized that she needed help that was beyond therapy, so she began working with Cheryl, a divorce coach. Through specific questions Cheryl discovered all of the above. In addition, Tanya had not told her attorney of her husband's financial maneuvers.

Cheryl recommended that Tanya tell her attorney immediately and that she file the divorce papers. They also set up a practical plan for gathering and filling out the net worth statement for her attorney so that temporary maintenance and child support could be set up.

As Tanya's finances were being affected they developed an assertive follow-up plan for working with her attorney so that the divorce process could move along more swiftly. Since Tanya felt scared and anxious when talking with her husband, Cheryl taught her effective communication techniques and quick methods for staying centered and calm when interacting with him.

People going through a divorce are more susceptible to manipulation because it is a confusing and scary time. However, despite that fact, it is important for people in this situation to learn how to stand up for themselves and avoid being manipulated. Divorce coaches are trained to help identify manipulations and teach clients skills to interact differently. It's easy to get intimidated or manipulated by an ex-spouse, so it is important to be forgiving of oneself and seek help. A divorce coach can help to teach a person to be assertive in a positive way.

Triggers

Tom's Triggers. Tom's wife was angry that he asked for a divorce and the process was becoming laborious. Their divorce was in its third year before Tom started working with a divorce coach. The costs were escalating and he had become exasperated.

Tom was triggered by his wife's non-responsiveness to his emails/correspondence and her stalling tactics during conversations and meetings. His tolerance level was becoming short. Tom was experiencing severe repercussions as a result of provoking his ex-spouse.

At one point, Cheryl, his divorce coach, became firm with him and said, "You need to stop raising your voice when you talk with her no matter how frustrated and angry you feel. Stop saying those specific statements that you know get her angry."

She continued, "Your ex is reacting to your tone and your words and even a slightly raised voice is setting her off. She is withdrawing because of the hurtful things that you are saying. This is hurting you, too! If you need to vent do it with me or with a friend but not to her. It's costing you!"

He finally listened and maintained his cool even when frustrated. As a result, the last issue of their settlement was quickly resolved.

It's crucial to become aware of triggers, both one's own and those of one's spouse. Triggers are the "hot buttons," and no one can push them better than people going through a divorce. However, this "button pushing" can make or break an important negotiation during a divorce. This can end up costing both parties unnecessary time, energy and money.

When a person is provoked, he or she may say things or act in ways he or she might later regret. This can create a rebound effect in the other person, causing a strong reaction or strong withdrawal or disappearing act. This can cause even more anxiety if one of the parties is wanting responses to open issues.

Sometimes a person can be so scared, angry or frustrated, that the need to take it out on their ex becomes greater than their ability for self-control or to keep their goals in mind. A divorce coach can help a person become cognizant of their triggers and teach alternate behaviors.

Education and Making Knowledge-Based Decisions

A person going through a divorce or separation can brainstorm with a divorce coach about the decisions that are made throughout the divorce process. The divorce coach can also provide emotional support and provide guidance on lifestyle and parenting choices.

Emotional Support Team

People recover from trauma faster when they have an emotional support team in place. A divorce coach and a therapist can help a person going through a divorce or separation in different ways. A therapist can help someone to explore their feelings as they relate to a current experience as well as to tie them into his/her past.

A divorce coach helps people going through a divorce to manage their feelings, understand the impact, and see the bigger picture. The divorce coach provides strategies for managing emotions. Furthermore, a divorce coach can teach someone how to avoid being overwhelmed and burned out. He/she can teach how to ask family and friends for emotional support through the divorce process.

In addition to using a therapist and a divorce coach, people going through a divorce or separation also encouraged to participate in support groups. Most people may not have a close relationship with someone who has gone through a divorce, or their friends and family become overwhelmed by ongoing divorce discussion. It can be helpful for people going through a divorce or separation to talk to other people going through a similar situation.

Lifestyle Choices and Social Interactions

A divorce coach may provide guidance on lifestyle choices and social interactions for people going through a divorce. This person can help someone brainstorm about financial decisions. Additionally, when a person is experiencing singleness for the first time in many years, social experiences inherently change. A divorce coach can help guide people through these transitions.

Parenting Options

A divorce coach can provide methods on how to listen and support children. He/she may discuss creative parenting options to present to an ex-spouse, attorney, or in mediation for the betterment of the children.

Adjusting to Change and a New Identity

The loss of structure, change and uncertainty during a divorce can feel overwhelming and challenging. A divorce coach can help someone going through that transition to adjust to these changes and see opportunities that he or she may not be aware of.

A divorce is a major life change – like a death. It's a loss of life, relationship and structure for a person. It is not unusual for some people to feel like they no longer know who they are without their spouse. Even the person who "leaves" or "divorces" his or her spouse is usually surprised at the emotions he or she experiences (e.g., guilt, fear, confusion). These emotions are only natural during a major life event such as a divorce.

The First Stage

In the initial stages of a divorce, it is not unusual for one or both parties to be in shock. The parties may be feeling a myriad of emotions – anger, grief, guilt, or relief. These conflicting emotions can be confusing.

In this first stage, people often miss the "relationship" but not the spouse. That person may yearn for a connection again with the spouse despite the fact that it may not be in that person's best interest. Sometimes, it takes time for heart and head to align. People become emotionally attuned to those they are close to; therefore, it is common for people going through a divorce to still want to connect with their spouse.

Free Time

Often during the first stage, people do not know what to do with their newly found free time that used to go to the spouse (and in some cases, the children). This extra free time can lead to loneliness.

Therefore, a divorce coach might help someone plan activities to provide something to look forward to.

Here are a few examples:

- Lewis had a challenging time on the weekends. His ex-spouse had their two boys on alternate weekends. He missed being with them and also had difficulty being alone with his upsetting thoughts. His divorce coach helped him brainstorm about activities and people that Lewis could spend time with to help fill his emotional needs.
- Nancy, a separated woman, adopted two cats. Rob, a divorcing man, rescued a dog from a shelter. Having care, love and connection with their pets helped to soothe an emotional void and give a different meaning to their lives.

Forgetful and Easily Distracted

People going through the first stage may be forgetful and easily distracted. As mentioned above, shock and trauma can affect the hippocampus part of the brain, and as this may make it more difficult to record short term memory; it is harder to remember and to stay focused. Therefore, a divorce coach may urge clients to write everything down – both smaller and greater tasks – and calendar appointments. It is more important than ever for people to get in this habit during the first stage. Additionally, divorce coaches may encourage taking copious notes during meetings with attorneys, coaches, therapists, accountants, or spouse.

Constancy and Routines

Even in this time of change, it's helpful to remember that there are some aspects of a person's life that remain constant. For example, if there are children involved then it is important that they continue to have the love and respect of both parents. Additionally, pets need to continue to be cared for.

During the first stage, certain friends and family members will be supportive. People going through a divorce should focus on their career, exercise routine, and their work in the home. Many find comfort in their spiritual or religious beliefs. Over time, people that go through a divorce can develop an amazing and improved version of themselves!

The Second Stage

During stage two, people begin to settle into a routine. During this stage, a person may be tap-dancing – two steps forward and one step back. As he or she gains skills for coping and being proactive during the divorce, he or she will eventually experience many steps forward.

People in the second stage have discovered friends and family members who are supportive and have become closer with them; however, they may be disappointed in the people who are not there for them as they hoped. This is a good time to reach out to support groups, as well.

Emotions

It is common for people in the second stage to still be experiencing a roller coaster of emotions. It's important to be patient with oneself. Some wonder, when will the pain stop?

The answer is that each person's experience is different. It depends on their current situation, support system, background and childhood experiences. A divorce coach can help guide them through these emotions. Receiving professional divorce support is instrumental in healing, getting through a divorce more easily, and moving on sooner.

If the separation and divorce is the result of an affair, then there is another level of healing that needs to take place, in order to recover and to trust again. Please see Chapter 48 on "Healing and Becoming Emotionally Available Again."

Practical Issues

For some people who are taking on new responsibilities (e.g., cooking, house repairs, paying bills), it may feel like they are working twice as hard after losing their other half. Additionally, both parents are likely spending less time with the children due to the parenting time schedule. These are great issues to discuss with a divorce coach, who can help brainstorm practical issues relating to the change in life responsibilities and routine.

Legal Process

Usually, the divorce process will be underway during stage two. A divorce coach can help a client prepare for meetings with his or her attorney.

Discovering Strengths and Independence

The second stage is usually a scary and exciting time. A divorcing person is usually starting to enjoy life again while dealing with the challenges of divorce. Even if he or she feels bogged down by the complexity of it all, a sense of freedom and independence can prevail.

During this second stage, people are making decisions for themselves. They no longer have to answer to a spouse. They can do what they want, when they want, and with whom they want. Life suddenly has fewer compromises.

People in stage two may be spending more quality time with their children than during stage one. There is typically less tension in the home, as one person has moved out. A divorce coach during the second stage may continue to encourage healing and letting go to help make room for new experiences and to help people become a better, stronger version of themselves.

The Third Stage

Typically, certain issues have been resolved in the divorce by the time people enter stage three. There is light at the end of the tunnel! People in this stage feel more certainty about their future.

In this stage, people have established friendships and a new routine. Children have been adjusting. Perhaps the children are receiving professional help during this period to help heal the wounds from the divorce or separation. People in this stage are excited to have found a new life for themselves and are having fun again.

People in stage three may begin dating again. This can be both intimidating and exciting, especially if a person hasn't dated in several years. Sex becomes an option again.

During the third stage, it is recommended that people explore their marriage and see their own part in its deterioration, even if it is a small percentage. Nothing happens "in a vacuum" and both people contribute to the demise of a marriage. This reflection helps people move forward empowered instead of seeing themselves as a victim. It is important to take responsibility and forgive oneself. One can feel remorse and learn skills to do better the next time around.

> **Martin Becomes Proactive.** Martin had only spoken to his divorce attorney three times in the last nine months. Martin came to see Cheryl the divorce coach. During their first consultation and she asked him why he spoke to his lawyer so infrequently. He responded, "I don't want to bother him or pile up attorney fees."
>
> Cheryl explained to him that attorneys are busy with many clients and that he needs to be proactive and to be on his attorney's mind. The divorce coach taught him how to do this while keeping the legal fees down.
>
> Martin also wanted to make decisions about moving to a new apartment, timelines, financial considerations, and scheduling so that he could spend more time with his son. Martin and Cheryl brainstormed and set up an action plan that took all this into consideration.

This "new identity" third stage offers an opportunity to become even more independent, empowered and confident again. Please see Chapter 48 on "Healing and Becoming Emotionally Available Again.")

When to Hire a Divorce Coach

Divorce coaching can help someone who is experiencing one of the following:

- Anger, fear, grief or guilt that is interfering with that person's ability to make decisions that are in his or her best interest or the children's best interest;
- Strong feelings that make him or her feel overwhelmed, forgetful, or distracted;
- Inability to focus on goals during a divorce process;
- Feelings of intimidation, anxiety and being manipulated when interacting with his or her (soon-to-be) ex-spouse;

- Need to brainstorm about legal options, finances, living arrangements, parenting options, social interaction, or other practical matters;
- Desire to gain emotional support from family and friends;
- Difficulty adjusting to the major life change;
- Stressful and challenging communication issues with his or her (soon-to-be) ex-spouse; and,
- Exhaustion from an elongated divorce process.

Cheryl Lazarus, CLC, CRC, CDC

Cheryl Lazarus, CLC, CRC, CDC is a Certified Divorce and Relationship Coach, Speaker, and NLP Master Practitioner with therapeutic training. Having gone through her own divorce successfully, Cheryl understands the practical and emotional challenges of the divorce process and the opportunities in redesigning one's life.

When working with clients, Cheryl provides actionable steps, strategies and resources which help clients to save time, money and have less aggravation during the divorce process. In addition, Cheryl includes heart-centered energetic and spiritual practices which helps women and men to heal and move forward on a profound level which positively affects all areas of their lives.

Cheryl has presented at the United Nations, to professional organizations, and has been on expert panels. She also holds workshops and support groups on topics ranging from "The Integrated Divorce," "Healing and Letting Go," to "Dating, Relationships and Becoming Emotionally Available Again."

Cheryl also coaches privately in person and globally through Skype and via phone consultations. For more information about Cheryl visit www.zengalove.com, www.easiertransitions.com.

SECTION F: USE OF PROFESSIONALS THROUGH DIVORCE & SEPARATION

CHAPTER 35

DIVORCE AND STRESS: HOW A DIVORCE COACH CAN HELP

With a Special Note to Women

By Kimberly Mishkin, CDC, and Liza Caldwell, CPC

Divorce is a major life-altering event, and for some, it is the ***most stressful event*** they will ever experience. When stressed, a person is not able to process information or problem-solve effectively. And yet, divorce is a process that specifically requires ***important decision-making***, especially in regard to children and finances. Poor decision-making during this period can have real and long-lasting consequences.

How Stress Impacts Our Ability to Think and Problem-Solve

Brain research shows that as we take in information, the ***thalamus region*** of our brain first assesses whether or not the input is threatening. If it is not threatening, the information is processed and we are able to recall the information later. On the other hand, if the information is deemed risky (real or perceived) the message is sent to the *amygdala region* of the brain. This region, dedicated to survival, causes our ***emotions and physical reactions*** to be heightened while our cognitive processes are bypassed until the danger is past.

What this means in terms of everyday life is that when navigating a crisis or feeling alarmed, people are unable to access the part of the brain that employs logic, problem solving, and memory. Stress causes that part of the brain ***to literally shut off.***

For someone dealing with the pain, grief and problematic challenges of divorce, this is especially hard. S/he must simultaneously contend with ongoing stressors and navigate a complex legal process, which, for many, is *also* a first experience with an attorney or the law. Combining these factors with the reality that *when stressed*, it is difficult to process information as effectively as usual, presents a dilemma for the client. It's very easy to walk away from a meeting forgetting half of what the attorney said and to feel flustered. To top it off, the ***sheer amount of information*** presented is often overwhelming, complicated, and in a language that is completely new and alien to the client.

How Divorce Coaches Can Help

Among many things, a divorce coach supports clients before, during, and after attorney meetings so time is managed more effectively, ***information is retained***, and clients are able to follow through with instructions so ultimately the best possible outcomes are achieved.

Trained and certified, a divorce coach will have both knowledge about the legal process and insight to what someone goes through (emotionally, psychologically, and physically) during a divorce. A good coach will give the client an overview of the divorce process and also help him/her:

- Organize thoughts and questions before, during, and after professional meetings;
- Focus and stay on track during the meetings;
- Listen closely and take notes;
- Communicate effectively;
- Control his/her emotions;
- Manage expectations and keep things in perspective; and,
- Maintain clear goals for desired outcomes.

If the client is considering or just starting a divorce, an ideal scenario is for the client to hire a divorce coach first. After hearing the client's story, the coach can make recommendations for various vetted attorneys or mediators who might be a good fit. The coach may also ***accompany the client to meetings***. The first meeting with an attorney is very valuable, for the attorney will often provide insight into what one can expect from the divorce process and how the attorney works. To ensure that everyone starts off on the right foot, it's recommended to have the coach attend the meetings from the very start. However, at any point during the process, having a coach attend meetings is a valuable strategy.

If this sounds expensive, understand that working with a coach actually helps to control attorney costs. Attorneys bill by the hour, if not by the minute. If a client has to ask the attorney to go over things repeatedly because s/he can't recall or doesn't understand, or if the attorney has to take time to send multiple emails and make multiple calls in order to obtain the information needed to proceed with the case, those minutes add up rapidly. A coach can help a client ***cut down on these costs*** because a coach typically bills at a lower rate and rarely charges extra for calls or emails.

A Divorce Coach May Be Especially Beneficial or Appealing to Women

While both men and women experience ***heightened emotional symptoms*** when stressed, men tend to react more aggressively (think "fight or flight") and will take action immediately. Conversely, research[53] indicates that women are more likely to address the situation differently. Australian researchers have uncovered a male gene known as SRY, which directs male development and drives aggression. Not having this gene, and governed by estrogen and other pain controlling hormones, ***women enduring stress*** tend to seek support and the input of others. This alternative response to "fight or flight" is referred to by some social scientists as the female tendency to "***tend and befriend.***[54]" Partnering with a trusted and respected coach who provides both emotional and practical support, helping women understand "all that they don't know," can be the comprehensive support system many women need and appreciate during their divorce.

A Case Study

Susan walked into her divorce coach Libby's office, very upset. She felt her attorney was not listening to her and that "after months of

[53] Wiley-Blackwell. (2012, March 8). Men respond more aggressively than women to stress and it's all down to a single gene. *ScienceDaily*. Retrieved August 10, 2015 from www.sciencedaily.com/releases/2012/03/120308071058.htm.

[54] Azar, Beth. (July/August 2000). A new stress paradigm for women. Retrieved August 14, 2015 from http://www.apa.org/monitor/julaug00/stress.aspx.

meetings, they had gotten nowhere." She didn't understand what her attorney was doing all this time. Susan was alarmed at how fast the bills were racking up and yet, it seemed as if no decisions had been made. She was convinced "***it just wasn't working***," and that she would have to start all over with a new attorney.

Coaches often hear a client say, "it's not working" with an attorney, but rarely is it because the attorney is incompetent. More often, it's a signal that the client is too stressed to hear and think clearly. This was true in Susan's case. Susan was in such a state of distress that she could not take in what her attorney was saying during their meetings, let alone follow through on what the attorney needed her to do to prepare for court. Alarmed and reacting emotionally, Susan was unable to think about things objectively.

This is understandable, as things had become untenable at home. The couple was still living together until their apartment could be sold, and between Susan and her husband, the conflict was escalating, with their young son caught in the middle. Miserable, panicked, and finding it increasingly difficult to remain calm, Susan told her story over and over again. She could not believe divorce was happening to her and her mind kept dwelling on worst-case scenarios – that her attorney would not listen to her, her husband was out to destroy her, that her son would forever hate her, and that she'd be penniless in the end. The fact that she was told she would "ultimately be okay" was something Susan could not even consider, take solace in, or entertain.

Libby, her ***newly hired divorce coach***, suggested that she join Susan and her attorney at their next meeting – with the attorney's permission. The three of them sat down together to sort things out. It became evident to Libby, early on, that Susan was not familiar with the vocabulary the attorney was using, nor did she have an overall sense of how the courts worked but she was afraid to ask any questions. Periodically Libby would stop to ask Susan, "Do you understand what that means?" and if she did not, Libby would translate for her, putting it in terms Susan could grasp easily. When Susan got sidetracked and started telling her story over again, Libby gently guided her back on topic so that the meeting did not go longer than needed.

Libby, Susan, and the attorney ***continued to meet regularly*** in order to prepare for trial. At one point, the attorney asked Susan to create a budget and to draft a plan for how she intended to support herself post-divorce. Answers to questions like, "Will you need to return to school or receive training?" "What kind of job will you seek after you are trained?" "In the meantime, how much money do you need to live?" needed to be addressed in order for the attorney to draft a proposal. Susan didn't know where to start. Together, however, Libby and Susan were able to work on these questions, and ultimately, develop a budget and a plan for Susan's future.

As part of Susan's divorce team, Libby saved Susan a lot of money in attorney's fees and helped her achieve the following:

- Assisted Susan in ***gathering and organizing*** important documentation regarding finances;
- ***Co-created a budget*** with Susan, as well as a plan for going back to school and work;
- Helped Susan remember ***what next steps*** were in her legal case, as well as in other areas of her life; and,
- Prepped Susan for her ***court appearances*** by providing strategies for remaining calm and communicating clearly and when needed, providing emotional support by attending court with Susan.

These were very practical ways in which Libby partnered with the attorney and client to ensure things went as smoothly as possible with the legal process. However, it was apparent that there were many additional challenges that Susan needed help with, things that were well ***outside the purview of her attorney***.

Susan's confidence was at an all-time low as a result of the demise of her long-term marriage. Now navigating divorce, she was unable to trust herself with decision-making of any kind. She didn't know how to tell her son about the divorce, and was anxious about whether or not she should tell her son's teachers about what was going on. She'd have to move, too, and she didn't know how to go about finding an apartment, especially when, for now, she didn't hold the purse strings. ***Susan wasn't taking care of herself*** either, and the lack of food and sleep was starting to catch up. She avoided looking in the mirror; unable to face herself or to imagine anything would ever be good again.

Given her circumstances, Susan's focus on the negative was not unusual. In fact, given brain research, it was utterly predictable. We are all hardwired to default to negative thoughts. While *any* kind of thought causes the brain to experience electrical and chemical reactions, "good" and "bad" thoughts don't elicit the same response. Negative thoughts

invoke a greater response[55] in the brain. This means "bad" thoughts come to us more readily. But with intention and practice, it is possible to train your brain to respond otherwise.

As Jeffrey Schwartz, author of The Mind and the Brain, explains, brain research reveals why change is so difficult for us, and it also suggests what approaches work best[56] to overcome our resistance to it. According to Schwartz, "***[f]ocusing our attention on solutions*** or new thinking is a better strategy than focusing or analyzing problems from the past, because the latter will only reinforce problems" (emphasis added). A good coach recognizes this and knows that it is possible to train the brain to circumvent the survival instinct. The coach's job is to help a client learn how to take in information by labeling certain messages as "harmless," and to move through and beyond it to take the right action.

Libby worked to bolster Susan's confidence and ***strengthen her resilience***, which little by little gave Susan the courage and strength to tackle practical matters. Susan learned to shut down the "negative replay" she had going on in her head, and she began to look at things in a new, more positive light. Together they worked on a plan for Susan to not only put her life back together, but to look ahead and become excited about her future.

Conclusion

Understanding how humans are biologically wired to deal with stress is *especially important* when it comes to divorce. Would Susan have been able to navigate her divorce without the assistance of a coach? Yes, of course. Eventually the anxiety would have subsided and her brain would have accessed the cognitive processes she needed to see more clearly. However, partnering with a divorce coach enabled Susan to shorten that timeline with ***less risk of making poor decisions***.

Libby helped Susan improve her ***ability to communicate*** with her attorney, helped her to feel grounded and centered for court; which

---

[55] Marano, Hara Estroff. (2010, October 29) Our Brian's Negative Bias. Retrieved August 11, 2015 from https://www.psychologytoday.com/articles/200306/our-brains-negative-bias.

[56] Williams, Ray. (2010, February 17). How Brain Science Can Change Coaching. *Psychology Today*. Retrieved August 10, 2015 from https://www.psychologytoday.com/blog/wired-success/201002/how-brain-science-can-change-coaching.

in turn, improved Susan's chances for a better custody outcome and financial settlement. Beyond the legal challenges, Libby helped Susan feel more in control of the many life decisions facing her. Susan learned to respond to stressful triggers from a more positive place and was finally able to enjoy her newfound independence.

For men and women navigating one of life's greatest stressors – the complex legal process, the emotional turbulence, and the logistical challenges of divorce – working with a certified coach can be *the strategic means* to overriding stress and making better decisions to achieve better outcomes. For women in particular, a divorce coach can play a pivotal role. Providing much needed emotional, practical, and logistical support, a coach can be the seasoned partner, advisor, and ally a divorcing woman needs to secure a more positive independent future.

Kimberly Mishkin CDC, and Liza Caldwell, CPC

Kimberly Mishkin and Liza Caldwell are cofounders of SAS for Women®, New York City's first comprehensive resource that provides strategic information, action-oriented coaching, and expert resources and tools to women navigating separation, divorce, empty-nesting, and widowhood. For more information visit www.sasforwomen.com.

SECTION F: USE OF PROFESSIONALS THROUGH DIVORCE & SEPARATION

CHAPTER 36

PSYCHOTHERAPISTS

by Diane Spear, LCSW-R

When a relationship is not mutually satisfying, it is advisable to work with a psychotherapist, both ***individually and as a couple***, to understand the problems. This Chapter describes how therapy can be helpful to couples and individuals in unsatisfying relationships; what to expect from a therapist; what to look for in a therapist; types of therapy and therapists; the role of therapy for children of unhappy parents; what couples, individual, and child therapy are like; and how to find a good therapist.

Reframing "Couples Therapy"

Is couples therapy only for couples who are committed to staying together, and is individual therapy only for people who are single? Absolutely not! Couples treatment can be valuable for sorting out differences, exploring whether both partners want to stay together and under what conditions, "recasting" the relationship if recommitting to it, separating ***without acrimony and blame*** if staying together is not a satisfying option, working together to lessen the impact on the children, and learning to be cooperative co-parents. Individual treatment is for understanding oneself and what one "brings to the table" in relationships and the rest of one's life, as will be explained in more detail later.

How Therapy Helps Couples, Individuals, and Children

Couples

For couples therapy it is crucial to have a therapist who does not have a stay-together agenda. Why? Some couples and families are happier and function better separately than together. When children are involved, the parents may be more effective as co-parents than they were as coupled parents, and the children may be relieved to be living with less tension and conflict. If there is eventually a more successful new relationship for one or both of the former partners, the children will have a better model of relationships and love than if the partners remained unhappily together "for the sake of the children." So a couples' therapist who has a bias toward "saving" a relationship may close off a reasonable option. Couples calling to schedule an appointment should ask the question: "Are you committed to the two of us staying together?" If the therapist says yes, the couple should continue their search.

Couples may hope that the therapist will tell them whether they should remain together or divorce, but that is not the therapist's job. The therapist is there to help the partners explore what ***they want in a relationship*** and what they find satisfying. The partners will be living with the consequences of their decision, so they have to make it, not try to have the therapist do that for them. Some areas of exploration include how they think about love, money, partnership, compromise and differences, family, and whether or not to have children. The individuals – ***not the therapist*** – will have to decide whether their goals and values are compatible enough to be mutually satisfying.

Partners may hope that a psychotherapist will ***referee their fights*** or change the other partner. A good therapist will not serve as referee, and will point out that each partner has the right to be as he or she is or to decide to change ***if he or she wants***, and that each partner has choices.

Couples or individuals may hope to make the therapist a part of their divorce case. Most therapists do not want to be part of that, and many will state this at the beginning of treatment. There are specially-trained therapists who work as coaches in collaborative divorces, which is vastly different from doing therapy with the couple or individuals. A therapist who helps individuals and couples separate without blame, get through the ups and downs of the divorce process, and heal and move on from the breakup is not part of the divorce process itself.

Individuals

Individual treatment is important for people in an unsatisfying relationship, whether or not they choose to remain in the relationship. It is said that those who do not learn from history are doomed to repeat it, so it is helpful to explore the models for relationship and marriage that an individual had growing up, and to understand the factors that led to being in the current relationship. Working on oneself can lead to ***rebuilding one's life*** in a satisfying way – in the relationship, alone, or eventually in a new and healthier relationship. Individual treatment with a skilled therapist can help a person learn, heal, and move on from an unsuccessful relationship and the anger, blame, and disappointment that often accompany it.

Children

Children are ***negatively affected by tension*** and fighting between their parents, and whether the parents decide to stay together or to separate, the children would benefit from therapy. Children often believe they are responsible for the conflict between their parents and may feel responsible for a separation and divorce. They can greatly benefit from the help of an outside professional to work through their feelings, cope with the lingering effects of the tension and fighting in the family, and avoid re-enacting their parents' relationship when they reach adulthood.

The Therapy Process

In couples' treatment, a therapist may do a ***combination of individual and couples sessions***. The couples sessions give the therapist a chance to observe how the partners interact with each other and to gauge the level of the couple's ***volatility and reactivity***. Individual sessions allow the therapist to learn what each partner brings to the relationship as an individual, and gives each individual the chance to express what he or she may feel uncomfortable saying in the partner's presence, such as revealing an affair, history of domestic violence, past or current alcohol or drug abuse, or that the individual is just going through the motions in coming to therapy and has already given up on the relationship. Because of the confidentiality required of licensed therapists, the therapist is not allowed to reveal anything one partner says in an individual session to the other partner.

The therapist will work with separating parents to ***lessen the negative impact*** on the children by suggesting that they agree not to do the following: argue in front of the children, badmouth the other parent when they are with the children, ask the children to choose sides, pump the children for information about the other parent, and discuss the issues in the failed relationship with the children. The therapist will also help the parents formulate the conversations they will have with the children to tell them about the upcoming separation, explain that it is not the children's fault, let them know which things will change and which will stay the same, etc.

A particularly effective approach to couples work is to start with four sessions:

- couple together;
- one partner individually;
- the other partner individually; and
- couple together to discuss the therapist's observations and treatment recommendations.

There will likely be an exploration of the history of the relationship and the individuals, as well as work on current issues that have brought the partners to treatment.

Therapy should be a ***time to de-escalate*** things, to try to turn down the volume and volatility. If partners are too reactive to use couples sessions productively, the therapist may opt to work on the relationship only through individual sessions until the partners can manage their impulses and interact in a more mature, calm way.

In effective individual therapy, the therapist will take a detailed history of the patient's life, and, over time, help the person understand the connections between past experiences and influences and current strengths and challenges, building on the strengths and learning to deal with the challenges in more productive, satisfying ways.

Mary and Ted came to their couples session prepared to rehash their latest fight. As soon as they began to raise their voices and call each other names, the therapist stopped them. "I'm not going to referee your fight. Cut it out."

"But we thought we'd fight, and you'd help us, and tell us who's right and who's wrong," they said, interrupting their argument with each other long enough to argue now with the therapist.

"You're already highly skilled at fighting. I'm not going to be your audience," the therapist said. "You don't need my help to fight. You need my help to calm down, warm up to each other, and start relating to each other in a reasonable, respectful way, whether or not you decide to stay together."

"But the only reason I raise my voice is because she's such a nag," Ted said.

"Are you telling me that your good behavior depends on Mary's good behavior? That doesn't make sense. And what do you think it's like for your kids when you yell?"

"See what I put up with every day? Ted, you're a jerk!" Mary said.

"Mary, please don't pile on. Ted, you're blaming Mary for your yelling. You need to take responsibility for your own behavior, just as Mary needs to. The name-calling and blame are destructive. If you separate, you're still going to need to deal with each other for many years to co-parent your kids. This anger and infantile behavior leaves your kids feeling scared and insecure. This needs to stop! I'm going to help you deal with your concerns in a productive way."

Parents may wonder what therapy is like with children. Therapists who work with very young children will use ***play therapy*** to understand what the child is going through and to help them. Older children and adolescents may engage with the therapist in an activity as well as talk therapy. With older adolescents the treatment will likely be all talk therapy.

Types of Psychotherapists

What kind of psychotherapists are there? Many different kinds, ***categorized by the type of training*** they have undergone and license they hold (e.g., clinical psychologist, clinical social worker, etc.), the age range or type of patients they treat (very young children, adolescents, adults, children or adults with special needs, etc.), the theoretical orientation underpinning the treatment they provide (e.g., psychodynamic, cognitive-behavioral, bioenergetic, etc.), and the kind of treatment offered (individual, couples, family, group therapy). Licensed clinical psychologists, licensed clinical social workers, licensed marriage and family counselors, and licensed mental health counselors have completed graduate programs in their field and are qualified to do the psychotherapy mentioned here. They do ***not prescribe medication***, though some clinical psychologists have received special training and are allowed to prescribe. If medication is warranted, the therapist will refer the patient to a psychiatrist (i.e., a medical doctor) for the medication, and will continue to do the ***talk therapy***, conferring with the psychiatrist as needed for the medication piece of the case. Because most psychiatrists are not interested in doing psychotherapy, the focus of their training is not in psychotherapy, and they are exponentially more expensive than psychotherapists, it is advisable to split the psychotherapy and the medication management (if needed).

What to Look for in a Therapist

Personality Fit

Couples and individuals should look for a therapist who is warm, compassionate, empathic, engaging, and licensed. An effective therapist does not indulge or infantilize a couple or individual, nor does he or she take sides. Some therapists make this clear by saying, "I'm only on the side of mental health." Couples should look for a skilled couples' therapist who approaches treatment by asking the partners to list their individual contributions to their relationship difficulties. Beware of a therapist who allows partners to use the sessions to fight, blame, or to list their partner's shortcomings – all of which are completely unproductive. Change happens when partners learn to take responsibility for their own behavior.

Also be leery of a therapist, individual or couples, who promises quick solutions, because 45 to 60 minutes per week cannot quickly "undo" the effects of years of misinformation, bad habits, poor problem-solving skills, faulty thinking and communication, and less-than-stellar role models. There's no such thing as a quick fix. The "chemistry" with a therapist is important, so a person should try another therapist if the first one does not feel like a good fit.

Theoretical Orientation

How does someone without a background in psychology choose which theoretical orientation will be most helpful? Everyone will have a different opinion, but it can be particularly helpful to find a treatment provider who has a psychodynamic orientation and incorporates some cognitive elements. ***Psychodynamic therapy*** is a mouthful that means that the therapy is focused on understanding how an individual's upbringing has shaped his or her views and outlook on things as an adult in the present: love, money, work, marriage, children, leisure, sex, etc. ***Cognitive therapy*** means that there is an emphasis on the quality of the thinking. People learn to look at their thoughts and how they affect their feelings, and learn to evaluate whether their thoughts make sense: are they rooted in logic and reality, or in fantasy and wishing?

Locating the Right Therapist

So how does a person find a therapist for couples, individual, or child therapy? A recommendation from a trusted professional or friend is an ideal way to find a therapist. Another way is to look through ***Psychology Today's "Find a Therapist"*** online search tool and read about a number of therapists. Many of the listings will include a link to the therapist's website, where there will be more information about the therapist's training, type of treatment offered, theoretical orientation, etc.

People often want a therapist who accepts insurance, but this is tricky in the mental health field, especially in New York City, where overhead is high, payment from insurance companies is low, the insurance companies are committed to limiting treatment and steering it toward pharmaceutical "solutions," and the in-network treatment provider is required to talk about the issues discussed in session in order to try to justify continuing treatment. All of which is to say that if people can afford to see an out-of-network provider, they may have more options to protect their and their children's confidentiality and to have the treatment provider – rather than someone administering a formula – determine the most effective treatment plan. Those who have a flexible spending account or health savings account through their employer may be reimbursed for the cost of psychotherapy with an out-of-network provider. If going out of network or paying out of pocket is not financially feasible, an individual, couple, or child should still go to an in-network provider or a clinic to receive the help and support they need.

Final Thoughts

Conflict, separation, and divorce are stressful to everyone, including the person initiating the change. Psychotherapy is an invaluable resource to everyone involved to get through this challenging time and work toward a more satisfying future.

Diane Spear, LSCW-R

Diane Spear is a psychotherapist and licensed clinical social worker in private practice in New York City since 1995, with a Master's Degree in Clinical Social Work from New York University and a certificate from the Institute of Developmental Psychotherapy. She treats older adolescents up through older adults – couples, former couples, and individuals – helping them deal with their problems so they can live more satisfying lives. She works with patients in person, and through phone and Skype sessions, so her practice includes people in the tristate area and throughout the world. She has written about couples counseling with high conflict people as a guest blogger for Psychology Today's website blog "Stop Walking on Eggshells" (https://www.psychologytoday.com/blog/stop-walking-eggshells/201307/couples-counseling-high-conflict-people), aspects of relationships for the online women's magazine Your Tango, and relationships and general topics in her own blog (dianespeartherapy.com/blog.html). Diane is committed to helping people find the joy in everyday life.

SECTION F: USE OF PROFESSIONALS THROUGH DIVORCE & SEPARATION

CHAPTER 37

LIFE COACHES

By Carol Dacey-Charles, ACC, CPCC

A life coach can be an invaluable resource for someone going through a divorce or separation. A ***certified life coach*** has been trained to partner with their clients to create a fresh perspective on an issue, to look at assumptions and expectations, create a safe place to process emotions, and to develop systems of accountability so a client actually takes positive steps toward the life s/he wants to be living now.

Whether you have been married 6 months or 30 years, going through a divorce is a ***major life change***. Divorce, and the conflicts that lead up to divorce, can take a toll ***emotionally, mentally, and physically***. A life coach is a ***partner through this journey*** – helping clients emerge stronger, with more clarity and focus. This chapter briefly defines life coaching, asks some life coaching questions, considers the challenges of divorce/separation, and illustrates how coaching can be of service during these challenges.

Overview of Life Coaching

A life coach is an ***unattached and confidential sounding board*** so clients can work through challenges, get clarity on goals and desires, and can start taking positive action. When considering life coaching, keep the following in mind:

- **While therapeutic, life coaching is not therapy.** Coaching takes a hard look at what a fulfilling life looks like, and then identifies specific plans, ***actions steps***, and ways of thinking that will move someone toward achieving his/her desired goals. Coaching takes the stand that people are not broken, so it does not focus specifically on healing. And yet, coaching can heal. It looks more at the present and the future, rather than the past.

- **While consultative, coaching is not consulting.** Traditional consulting offers answers and expertise. Coaching assists people to find ***their own unique answers***. A life coach's primary role is to listen, question, observe, re-frame, and articulate what is going on. The client is fully empowered to create and execute his/her goals and plans.

Coaching is about ***transformational change***. Clients learn to approach life from an empowered and positive perspective.

Defining Goals and Desires

> "When I found out my husband cheated, I felt like I was at sea, drowning in overwhelming emotions and betrayal. Having someone separate the emotions from the actions I could take to be pro-active and make myself feel better was vital in my process." - J.A.

During times of ***change and upheaval***, people shift into survival mode. Divorce and separation bring up many emotions – anger, sadness, relief, betrayal, and overwhelming feelings that can shift day-to-day, hour-to-hour and sometimes minute-to-minute. When emotions are volatile, ***people tend to be reactive*** – lashing out when feeling attacked, imploding when feeling out of control.

> Create a **What I Want list:**
>
> - What do I want for myself now?
> - What do I want for my children and family?
> - What do I want for my future?
> - What will give me peace of mind?

The first step toward clarity and regaining a sense of control is defining "***what we want.***" This list is not written in stone, it is just for now. From defining what is wanted, then it is possible to create a plan, break it down into discernable steps, and take one step at a time.

Notice the word "should" is not included in these questions. ***Should, have to, must*** are all rule words – rules made up because family, society, or "they" say so. If ***want or desire*** is not part of the equation, then maybe it is not vital right now.

Identifying Values

Reflect on these questions to help define your values:

- What is important for my peace of mind?
- Who do I admire? What are the qualities in them that I want to emulate?
- In a perfect relationship, what qualities are non-negotiable?
- What is important for me to create the best life I can imagine?
- What is non-negotiable for me now?

The next step after defining "What I Want" is defining "What is Important." A person's ***values*** are the core principles that define what is important for creating a fulfilled life.

For many people, their values are ***financial security, family, health, adventure, community, teamwork, peace or spirituality*** among many other things. There are no right or wrong values. No value is better to have than any other. Values are a person's guideposts to direct his or her life in a positive and growing direction.

Gaining clarity around values offers powerful insight into where and how clients want to spend their time and energy. ***Taking action based on values*** offers more joy, peace of mind and balance day-to-day.

How Coaching Can Help

Conflict and Change

"We cannot solve our problems with the same thinking we used when we created them." - Albert Einstein

Conflict – whether it is around ***communication, finances, expectations, values or sex*** – is a large part of divorce. How a person views and handles conflict can help determine that person's peace of mind in the process.

Conflict is not good or bad – it is merely a sign that ***change wants to happen***. That change may be in a long-held point of view or perspective that is no longer useful. A relationship may need to shift to accommodate the growth of its participants. Or the relationship is no longer serving the well-being of those involved, and it needs to dissolve.

A life coach creates the opportunity to step back from the details of the conflict to be able to get a bigger view of what is going on. What is really wanted by both parties? Is this ongoing conflict helping or harming the relationship? What new thing wants to take the place of the disharmony?

In order to change the habits created to deal with conflict, first the patterns and assumptions need to be acknowledged. Most people do not listen to the words that s/he perpetually repeats about their relationships or themselves. A life coach ***listens and reflects back*** the statements, actions and intentions of their clients so change can start to happen.

Change is not a quick or easy process, but it can be a friend and guide. The support of a life coach makes change a ***positive and manageable journey*** through awareness, actions, and ongoing accountability, to assist a client's transition into the life s/he wants.

From Conflict to Harmony

> "The advice I'd give to others going through divorce is to try not to be enemies. Try to work together one more time without war wounds. It is going to be hard, so make it as easy as you can." - C.R.

Through life coaching, a client can make a choice to work toward harmony even in the midst of a divorce or separation process. Many people going through divorce or separation need to make the process a war and make a once loved partner the enemy. Life coaching can help find a way to ***lay down the weapons*** and stop the bombardment.

The goal may be to create a ***positive environment*** for the children. The goal may be to find peace of mind. Arguments, verbal or legal, take a toll and life coaching can help diffuse the post-traumatic stress and find a new mode of communication.

> The **hard questions to consider** on the road to harmony:
>
> - Am I willing to ***be vulnerable*** and ask for what I want?
> - Am I willing to see a different perspective on the conflict for the sake of harmony?
> - What is more import—being right or having peace?
> - What do I really want instead of this conflict?

There are amazing ***opportunities for growth*** when a person embraces conflict as a teacher instead of an enemy.

Processing Feelings

Many people going through a divorce or separation are surprised that life coaching deals with ***processing feelings and emotions***. Emotions are part of the human experience and life coaching supports the whole person.

> "What helped me the most was having someone help me clarify the Big Picture. Then from there, we discovered what my priorities were. Next it was helping me break that down into smaller, manageable actions steps. I was in such overwhelm, that I couldn't see the forest from the trees on my own."
>
> - B. L.

It is normal for people going through a divorce to be filled with anger, fear, relief, and/or grief. People who ***love deeply*** often ***hurt deeply*** when that love is challenged or goes away. Pushing feelings down and trying to "be okay" is one of the least successful approaches to resolving overwhelming emotions. Many people do not have a safe place to "fall apart" with others. Life coaching can be that safe place of non-judgment, ***confidentiality and support*** that is so vital for healing. Processing feelings though life coaching is a ***transformational process through action***.

Some of the most successful methods that clients use to move through feelings are writing in a journal, screaming into pillows, dancing it out in the kitchen, and exercise. Some clients find a 5-minute pity party helpful, for others it may be creating art.

There is no one right way to handle the emotional journey of divorce and separation. A life coach can help a client find her or his best way to ***process feelings as they arise***. Learning how to not get overwhelmed is a great gift life coaching offers.

Acceptance & Getting Present

Acceptance is being able to be fully present with the facts of what is happening in a person's life right now. ***Acceptance is not approving*** or even liking what is happening. But until there is acceptance, a person is either re-living the past and trying to change it, or worrying about the future and trying to control it. Acceptance allows for clarity. With clarity, a plan can be made.

To illustrate, Dan's spouse had an affair. Those are the facts – Dan wished it never happened but he ***cannot change it***. In part, Dan blames himself for not seeing it and for being deceived. Naturally, part of Dan wants his spouse to suffer like he is suffering. However, until Dan can accept the facts (without blame or judgment), it will be difficult for him to have full clarity on the situation and what it means for his life and his relationship with his spouse.

A life coach helps people ***look at the facts***. Life coaching can help a person get beyond the blame, the shame, and the stories so she or he can get the clarity to take even one positive next step.

Accountability

> "The accountability I received, needing to check in with my progress, helped me move forward. There was always the temptation to blow off my homework in the busyness of work and dealing with the divorce. But the accountability gave me permission to do things that were focused on my well-being and empowerment that I wouldn't have done otherwise." - B.M.

Life coaching is a great way for someone to learn ***accountability for the commitments*** they are making in their life during the divorce or separation process.

Most people can relate to a New Year's resolution that was blown off and discarded by February. Life coaches can act as cheerleaders or drill sergeants to help someone keep on track with their goals.

Having a deadline and that sense of accomplishment when the task is done is a great motivator to keep moving forward during even the most chaotic of times. Accountability is the ***corner stone*** of a life coaching commitment.

Self-Care-The Secret Weapon

> **Self-care reflection:**
>
> List at least 20 things that bring you joy, refresh your spirit, relax your mind or body. These do not have to cost anything – a walk in the park or a hot bath. Self-care can also be splurges – a spa day or a weekend babysitter.
>
> Choose at least 2 things on your list to do every week. Do more if you like. Doing one thing a day that puts you first on your list is a great way to nurture yourself.

The divorce process can suck up time, energy, finances, mental focus, and psychological well-being. Going through a divorce can ***just plain suck*** at times. For health, clarity and stress-reduction, self-care is non-negotiable.

Self-care is like the importance of a ***pit stop in car racing***. If a racecar driver does not take the time to stop, refill the tank, check the gauges and put on some new tires, he runs the risk of not only a blow-out but putting his life, and the life of others, in danger if there is a failure at high speeds.

Self-care is more than massages and bubble baths. Self-care is whatever nurtures the body, mind, and spirit. Taking time to consciously "refill the tank" aids concentration and reduces stress.

New Yorkers live at high speeds. The stress and chaos of everyday life, combined with a divorce or separation, lead to a toxic situation. Self-care is vital to have the focus, energy and reserves that this kind of change demands. ***Even a simple divorce is stressful*** – everyone going through a divorce deserves to run on a ***full tank***.

Final Wrap

A life coach can be a great addition to a divorce support team. A person's lawyer, CPA, and financial planner are experts who give clarity to the legal and financial parts of life. A life coach is a partner to keep clients centered on values, focused on goals, and accountable to actions and commitments.

A life coach can help every person see his or her brilliance and wisdom, even when that person is having a hard time seeing it for him or herself. That can be a great asset during times of change and stress. There are ***no extra points for suffering***. Why not choose to thrive?

Carol Dacey-Charles, ACC, CPCC

Carol is unconventional with a wicked smile, quirky wit and the keenest BS-detector around. Carol is direct, and engaging, putting her powerful sense of spirituality and clarity towards working from the inside out.

She takes risks while being light; she cares while pushing hard, all with a grace, warmth and deftness that ease the way. Carol has a grounded presence that creates safety and trust for everyone around her.

In 2011, Carol founded Why Not Thrive?, an international coaching and training business. With a career spanning 25 years of management, training, and human development in the arts, non-profits, retail and ministry, Carol is working with clients around the world to help them transform their personal and professional lives. For more information about Carol or Why Not Thrive? Visit www.ynotthrive.com and Carol's blog at www.wordforgood.com.

SECTION F: USE OF PROFESSIONALS THROUGH DIVORCE & SEPARATION

CHAPTER 38

ACCOUNTANTS AND FORENSIC ACCOUNTANTS

By Meredith Verona, CPA/AVB/CFF

After ten years of marriage, Jenny and Keith decided it was time to acknowledge their once happy marriage turned into a daily struggle and tension between them. Divorce was inevitable. Keith had become a successful entrepreneur in the real estate industry. When Jenny and Keith met, he owned a handful of commercial and residential properties which grew to over fifty properties during the course of their marriage. Prior to the marriage, Jenny worked as a hygienist at a dental practice. After the marriage, she stopped working and became a homemaker. Jenny had not worked outside the home during the course of the marriage, and her primary responsibilities were caring for their son, Jeffrey, and maintaining their home.

With divorce imminent, Jenny was confronted with a dilemma. After years of allowing her husband to control the personal finances, her attorney was now asking her to provide information she had never been tasked with maintaining. Her attorney wanted to know:

- What accounts were in her possession?
- What were the account balances at the date of divorce?
- Which accounts were held jointly and held individually?
- How many properties did her husband own?
- How much did they spend on their son's school tuition?
- How much did her husband make in compensation that year?

Her attorney went on to describe what is known as the law of equitable distribution and why she needed to supply this information. Jenny stopped listening. She was overwhelmed and anxious because she did not know the answers.

An accountant that specializes in divorce can greatly assist a person in this situation. This chapter will answer ***the 5 W's –*** **<u>W</u>ho,**

What, Where, When and Why when using a forensic/divorce accountant.

WHO are the Divorcing Parties?

Typically there are two parties in a divorce: the ***moneyed spouse*** (or monied spouse) (i.e., the spouse who is the higher earner), and the ***non-moneyed spouse*** (or non-monied spouse) (i.e., the spouse who is the lower earner). What it boils down to is who is capable of paying the vast fees that may be associated with impending litigation. This becomes particularly important when dealing with legal fees or spousal maintenance fees. In certain circumstances, a divorcing couple may be able to proceed with retaining a ***neutral accountant*** or ***court appointed accountant*** where the fees are paid by the moneyed spouse or split between the parties at a specified percentage.

WHAT do Forensic Accountants Do?

Forensic accountants can greatly assist your team of legal professionals in divorce. Below is a brief description of some of the services that they can provide, including but not limited to a lifestyle analysis, tracing analysis, and business evaluations.

Lifestyle Analysis

Each party must draft a sworn document that shows a snapshot of their current financial situation. The actual name of the document varies by state. For example, in the state of New York, this document is known as the ***Statement of Net Worth***. In the state of New Jersey, it is known as a Case Information Statement. This document becomes important as the court may rely on this to determine spousal maintenance and child support.

Remember the story above about Keith and Jenny? Jenny would be considered the non-moneyed spouse. A non-moneyed spouse may not have had access or responsibility as to the financial situation during the marriage, and speculating about their financial situation could prove harmful to the non-moneyed spouse. A lifestyle analysis will quantify the spending the parties made during a specified period. A forensic accountant can perform this analysis over an agreed period. This analysis can get expensive especially if many years are being analyzed and a lot of activity existed. One way to minimize the cost is to obtain electronic credit card statements, bank statements, and brokerage statements for analysis. However, if a party intends to obtain this information, he/she should communicate with his/her attorney to ensure that this particular information would be useful to the individual situation.

Tracing Analysis

If a party going through a divorce suspects that there are ***hidden assets***, there may be a need for a tracing analysis. Essentially, this analysis is an examination of all banking activity at a specified time period. Again, this can get expensive – especially when a lot of activity exists. Before a party decides to perform this analysis, this person should speak to his or her attorney and discuss the likelihood of success. Simply put, parties should run a cost-benefit analysis.

Business Valuations

> Andrew and Beth were married for almost thirty years. They met and married while they were still in their teens. However, they have been separated for the past five years, partially due to Andrew's confession that he was gay. Although Andrew and Beth were technically separated years before their divorce, Beth still had a hard time ending their long marriage. She had continued to work harmoniously with Andrew as the office manager for his veterinary office, which was started after their marriage. She knew it was time to let him go after Andrew begged her for a divorce so that he could remarry. But she questioned as to the value of the business.

A business can be considered a marital asset, subject to equitable distribution. It should be noted that the non-business owner is entitled to a portion of the business's worth during the course of the marriage. If the moneyed spouse owned the business prior to the marriage, then there may be what is called ***appreciation***. In these particular cases, the valuator has to determine the business value both at the date of marriage and at the date of divorce (commencement). The difference is what is considered the marital portion. In other words, the law considers that the non-moneyed spouse contributed to [or, had some role to play in] any increased value of the business in intangible ways, such as by supporting the moneyed spouse during their marriage, emotionally and/or professionally, and helping to raise children if applicable. In the example above, Andrew established the business during the marriage so appreciation is not applicable.

Valuing a business can be subjective. This can result in two or more valuators developing different figures. Some significant factors that can impact the business valuation are the following:

- **<u>Experience Level of the Valuator</u>** – As valuation issues can become complex, it is important to find someone who regularly does business valuations and has the experience and the "know how" to address the issues. Currently, there are no requirements that an accountant or CPA have sufficient experience to perform a business valuation. An example would be hiring a criminal attorney to handle a divorce matter. Similar to the legal world, many accountants are specialized and it is generally preferred that you use the talents of a ***certified valuator*** rather than selecting a "jack of all trades."

- **<u>Qualifications of the Valuator</u>** – It is also important that the person who does the valuation be qualified. There are three designations to look for – the ***Accredited in Business Valuation*** ("ABV"), ***Certified Valuation Analyst*** ("CVA"), and ***Accredited Senior Appraiser*** ("ASA"). It is not required to be credentialed to perform a business valuation. Having the designation shows that that the valuator is committed to their specialty. In each particular designation, an individual is tested on their basic knowledge and experience.

- **<u>The Condition of Financial Records</u>** – There may be a need to ***make adjustments*** based upon the information indicated in the company's accounting records. Many times certain issues arise:

    1. There is a ***lack of detail*** that is needed to understand particular transactions.
    2. The accounting records may have ***inconsistencies*** – i.e., bookkeeper or external accountant had changed over the years.
    3. In smaller companies, sometimes accounting records just ***do not exist***.

- **<u>Cooperation from Key Member(s) of the Business and/or Their Accountant</u>** – A valuator has to understand the business risks to prepare a proper valuation of the business. The professional needs to recognize the company's internal ***strengths and weaknesses*** and external ***opportunities and threats***. In the business world, this is known as a ***SWOT*** analysis. These items can give the valuator an understanding of the risks of that particular business, which in part can impact the value of the business.

- **<u>Timing</u>** – Just like most things, the more time the valuator directs toward understanding the business, the greater likelihood the work product will be of higher quality.

In some instances, the business valuators can be court appointed by the judge. This means that the expert is not an expert for one side but acts as an impartial extension of the court and is considered more as the financial eyes of the court. In some cases, there can be a ***court appointed appraiser*** and an appraiser for ***each of the parties*** (i.e., three in total). If your case goes to court, the judge will mostly like decide what type of valuation(s) should be utilized.

Enhanced Earnings Capacity ("EEC")

> Jean and John met in their freshman year in college. Jean obtained her Bachelors of Arts in Political Science. Ever since she was a little girl, Jean wanted to become a lawyer. Prior to Jean starting law school, the couple decided to get married. After law school, Jean started working at a prestigious law firm in the Manhattan area. After five years of marriage Jean and John mutually decided to end it. When John met with his divorce attorney – he was told that his wife's law degree was considered an asset. John was surprised and then wondered, what is it worth?

A forensic accountant can perform calculation(s) to determine the ***value of the license or degree***. The underlying thought process is considering what the license or degree holder would have been compensated if he or she had not obtained the said license or degree. Going back to the example of Jean and John – Jean had her undergraduate degree in political science. If Jean decided to forgo law school, financial consideration is given to the type of career she would have had with a bachelor's degree. This is what is called a "baseline" in the calculation. Jean's current earnings at the law firm is considered her "topline." The difference between the topline earnings and baseline earnings is considered the marital component. There are more components to the calculation, such as extending it to the estimated date of retirement. A forensic accountant will be familiar with the components and apply the relevant factors.

Recently, the New York legislature moved to change how enhanced earning capacity is viewed during a divorce. Previously, New York was the only jurisdiction in the United States that considered the enhancement from a license/degree to be a marital asset. The new law, signed by Governor Andrew Cuomo on September 25, 2015, considers enhanced earning capacity only in terms of equitable distribution and support rather than an asset to be divided between the spouses during the dissolution of a marriage. The effective date of the new law is on January 25, 2016. For more information on EEC, please read Chapter 30 by Robyn Mann, Esq.

Valuing Stock Options

A forensic accountant can assist in valuing existing stock options and determining what portions are considered marital. As a general rule, the stock is analyzed to the date of divorce. This can become tricky especially if the options vest over a certain period. That period may well be beyond the date of divorce.

The Prenuptial (or Postnuptial) Agreement

Even with prenuptial (or postnuptial) agreements, there may be circumstances that have changed and could render the documents subject to possible loopholes in the wording. A forensic accountant can review and compare all the accounts in the party's possession to assist and aid in clarifying what is identified in the agreements. It should be noted that the attorney should first review the agreement, as it is a legal contract, to determine if it is necessary to then have a forensic accountant review for loopholes.

Separate Property

> Jack was on his second marriage, with Julie. He had purchased an apartment with Julie with proceeds he received from the sale of his prior home with his first wife (now ex-wife), Abigail. He is now divorcing Julie – can she really claim the apartment as a marital asset? Or is it separate property?

A party can claim separate property if they can establish an asset existed prior to the marriage (e.g., gift, inheritance, etc.) This can become difficult especially if ***funds are co-mingled*** with marital funds. A forensic accountant can help distinguish between the two. More information on the identification of separate property can be found in Chapter 29 by Sheera Gefen.

WHERE should I find a Forensic Accountant?

Someone going through a divorce and seeking to hire a forensic accountant should keep the following in mind:

- **Geographic Proximity** – Each state may have nuances that only someone working in the area may be aware of. It is also easier to have a forensic accountant available to meet with someone's team and opposing side without having travel restrictions and expenses.

- **Experience** – It important to look for someone who has the experience specifically in divorce accounting. It is a niche area. When looking for someone, make sure to ask for the CVs of the expert and any of their colleagues that will work on the matter.

- **Accountant and Attorney Relationship** – A person's legal team is only as strong as his or her weakest link. It is vital that the accountant and attorney effectively communicate with one another. Both need to be on the same page – the attorney should understand and advise whether taking the risk (and cost) of a trial will benefit this person. The accountant has to convey to the attorney the financial status of that particular matter – whether good or bad for the client.

WHEN is the Best Time to Involve a Forensic Accountant?

It best to get the accountant involved ***earlier in the process*** – it allows the accountant to better grasp the issues. If you are concerned about fees, tell your attorney of your concern so he/she can relay this to the forensic accountant to potentially avoid unexpected fees.

WHY should I Hire a Forensic Accountant?

People going through a divorce want to make sure that he or she is not being taken advantage of and that the division of assets is fair. Having a forensic accountant can assist this person in this goal. Remember that the decision someone makes with their divorce can impact his or her life choices going forward. More information on equitable distribution can be found in Chapter 30.

Meredith Verona, CPA/ABV/CFF

Meredith Verona is a Manager in the Litigation Services Group at Mark S Gottlieb CPA PC. She has over ten years of experience, working exclusively on litigation related matters. Specifically, Meredith specializes in business valuation and forensics for varied purposes including matrimonial, gift and estate, and shareholder disputes. She has worked on cases in multiple industries including medical, professional firms, retail and restaurant services for small to mid-size companies predominately located in the New York area. Her previous experience includes calculating/auditing business interruption claims and litigation support.

Ms. Verona is a member of the American Institute of Certified Public Accountants (AICPA), National Association of Certified Valuation Analysts (NACVA). She received her B.A. in Economics from Rutgers University and her M.B.A. with a concentration in Accounting from Monmouth University.

She is an Accredited Business Valuator (ABV) and a Certified in Financial Forensics (CFF) from the American Institute of Certified Public Accountants. She also received the designation of Certified Valuation Analyst (CVA) from the National Association of Certified Valuation Analysts.

SECTION F: USE OF PROFESSIONALS THROUGH DIVORCE & SEPARATION

CHAPTER 39

CERTIFIED DIVORCE FINANCIAL ANALYST

By Kymberly A. Robinson, Esq.

As one can imagine, financial issues and assets play a large role in divorces. ***Financial advisers*** ("FAs"), especially FAs who are ***Certified Divorce Financial Analysts*** ("CDFAs"), can play an instrumental role through the divorce transition in someone's life. CDFAs can help guide people going through a divorce on the division of assets, social security, evaluation of settlement offers and financial planning.

Using a Certified Divorce Financial Analyst

What is a CDFA?

A Certified Divorce Financial Analyst ("CDFA") is a ***type of financial planner*** who has been educated on financial issues pivotal in the divorce process. Two things that set these professionals apart from other financial professionals are: their unique focus on financial issues surrounding divorces and their role in projecting future financial outcomes after a divorce is finalized.

According to the ***Financial Industry Regulatory Authority*** ("FINRA"), a CDFA is someone with at least three (3) years of experience in the financial services, accounting or family law fields. In order to become a CDFA, the applicant must have taken a self-study course compete with a computer exam. Finally, this person must complete 15 hours of continuing education in the divorce arena every two years. Furthermore, usually a CDFA has an educational background and commitment for helping people through a divorce.

Role of CDFA

A financial planner helps people achieve financial goals (both short-term and long-term goals). An FA helps manage money and investments to maximize financial stability. For example, if you are trying to save to buy a house, a financial advisor will help you budget and save up appropriately for a house in your price range within the desired timeframe you wish to purchase.

A CDFA can be useful to hire at the ***inception of the divorce***. Couples can spend precious time ascertaining the financial picture of the marriage. Obtaining a CDFA at the beginning of the divorce process can establish a clear view of the financial present and future. This professional can help address the needs and capabilities of both parties as well.

During the divorce process, a CDFA can inform clients of financial ramifications of settlement offers keeping the client's short and long-term goals in mind. A CDFA can present an analysis and visual aids such as graphs and charts to show how a certain split of particular assets now can result in a large discrepancy in financial stability among the parties in 5 years. This type of information can be invaluable during the divorce settlement process.

Part of the Team of Professionals

A CDFA is an invaluable part of the team of professionals that helps someone through the divorce process. A good CDFA will work with a Certified Public Accountant ("CPA"), a matrimonial attorney and other types of financial professionals guiding the client through the divorce process. Each of these different types of professionals play a unique role in the process. It is recommended that each party consult with his or her own independent CDFA.

A CDFA in a particular geographic area can be located via the Institute for Divorce Financial Analysis at https://www.institutedfa.com/find-a-cdfa or (800) 875-1760.

Kymberly A. Robinson, Esq.

Kymberly is an associate attorney with Rincker Law, PLLC and is admitted to practice law in New York and Florida. She attended Union College in Schenectady, New York for her undergraduate studies, where she graduated with high honors as a psychology major. She then obtained her J.D. from Pace University School of Law in White Plains, New York and, subsequently, her L.L.M. (with a concentration in family law) from the Benjamin N. Cardozo School of Law in Manhattan. Kymberly entered the field of matrimonial and family law as a way to couple her interest in psychology and personal relationships with her legal education.

Before joining Rincker Law, PLLC, Kymberly was an associate at boutique matrimonial law firms in Westchester County, Manhattan, and Florida. She was also a volunteer at the New York County Access to Justice Program-Uncontested Divorce Clinic where she assisted self-represented litigants in the divorce process. During law school Kymberly also participated in two legal clinics: one at the Pace Women's Justice Center, where she represented clients in obtaining orders of protection and another at the Brooklyn Family Defense Project, where she assisted in defending families in child abuse and neglect proceedings.

Kymberly likes to spend her free time with her family and also enjoys working out, cooking healthy meals, and getting together with friends. She lives in Westchester County, New York with her husband and daughter.

For more information about Rincker Law, PLLC, visit www.rinckerlaw.com.

SECTION F: USE OF PROFESSIONALS THROUGH DIVORCE & SEPARATION

CHAPTER 40

CERTIFIED REAL ESTATE DIVORCE SPECIALIST

By David Perry

We have all heard the statistics, approximately 50% of all American marriages end in divorce, this may have been true years ago, but now people are getting married later. Fortunately, New York has one of the lowest divorce rates in the US. The divorce rate according to the NY State Census is 7 per 1000 per year.[57] But if you are reading this book, chances are you are either getting divorced or separated. Working with a certified real estate divorce specialist can be an invaluable professional resource to help these couples maneuver through the real estate industry and address important issues.

Evaluating the Choices with the Marital Home

During a divorce or separation, there are limited choices with their marital home:

- Parties sell the marital home;
- One spouse buys out the other spouse; and,
- One spouse could stay in the marital home for an agreed upon period of time (e.g., until children graduate from high school, 5 years).

---

[57] New York State Library, "New York State Census Records" available at http://www.nysl.nysed.gov/genealogy/nyscens.htm (last visited September 9, 2015).

When evaluating these three options, selling it is the easiest because buying a spouse out can be complicated (financially and emotionally). If the divorcing or separating couple decides to "buy" the other person out, then the fair market value (FMV) of the property must be agreed upon. The divorcing or separating parties could use a ***broker opinion letter***, an ***appraiser***, or an average of the two.

> Experienced brokers will have a more immediate ***relevant experience*** of what the market is; however, some believe that view may be inflated. On the flip side, appraisers use ***past sales*** as market data. Neither method is perfect.

If the divorcing or separating couple decides to sell the marital residence, it is ***highly recommended*** that they hire a real estate broker who is a ***certified real estate divorce specialist*** with a unique understanding of the legal and emotional issues affecting the transaction.

Additionally, if the divorcing or separating couple opts to keep the marital home for a certain time period, they should still consult with a real estate broker to help forecast the current market that they would potentially sell in. Now is a good time to be a seller with interest rates at an all-time low and inventory being scarce. Good properties are hard to find in today's market. Today there are scores of people on the sideline looking to purchase the right place. If interest rates rise the cost of owning the same home will increase and this will decrease the number of available purchasers.

Tax Considerations for Divorces

If you are a divorcing or separating couple considering selling the marital home, or holding on to the home for a disposition at a future date. It is important to ask your accountant questions about the exclusion allowed under the ***Tax Relief Act of 1997***. In sum, a tax exclusion for gain of ***up to $250,000*** is available to individuals. Married couples filing a joint return can claim a tax exclusion of ***as much as $500,000***. To qualify for the exclusion, an owner must use the property as the principal residence for a ***total of two years*** (does not need to be consecutive) ***out of the five years preceding the sale***. Only one sale every two years is permitted for each individual or couple. In theory an individual or couple could sell their home every two years for a gain of up to $500,000 and not have to pay any capital gains tax.

All or part of the gain from the sale of a principal residence ***may be excluded from income*** if certain ***ownership*** and ***use tests*** are met. Any gain in excess of these amounts is taxed at the ***capital gains tax rates***.

> Example: Frank and Susan buy a home for $1,000,000 cash. They then divorce. They agree to sell the home at a later date. In this example Susan stays in the marital home with the children until the youngest turns 18 and she remarries before they sell the home. The home is sold for a $2,000,0000. Both Frank and Susan have a long term gain of $1M, $500,000 each if they agreed to split the asset in half. Normally they would each get a $250,000 exemption from capital gains tax. In this example Frank gets a $250,000 exemption from capital gains, (capital gains tax varies based upon income. It could range between 0% and 28%). If Frank was an upper income tax bracket he could be faced with a tax of 28% or $70,000. Susan gets a $500,000 exemption from capital gains because she is married. If Frank were married he would also qualify for the $500,000 exemption and not have to pay a capital gains tax.

The Tax Relief Act requires that ***only one spouse*** needs to own the home; however, the statute requires that ***both spouses to have lived in the marital home two years*** to qualify for the joint filing $500,000 exclusions. For divorced or separated spouses, if either meets the two-of-five test (even if one lives there by court order), both spouses can exclude $250,000. If the divorcing couple remarries then they each ***can exclude $500,000 from the sale of the property***.

Case Studies

Real estate brokers can be instrumental in helping divorcing and separating parties through the process. Below are a few examples.

Case Study#1: Consider the Risks

John and Jane were going through a divorce and decided to sell their marital home. They listened to their real estate broker and listed the marital residence at a price that was ***higher than any other apartment*** in their building. Buildings in NYC can act as its own neighborhood; thus, the building itself can offer the best comparisons to determine value. The apartment next door to the subject apartment was sold just six months prior. The adjacent apartment was comparable in size but offered a clearer view of the New York Harbor.

As a caveat, an appraisal on John and Jane's property might have come in lower than the listed price. Fortunately for the divorcing couple, the marital residence received multiple offers at the first open house. Immediately, John & Jane began negotiating and vetting the finances of the interested parties to identify bona fide candidates. With the help of their real estate broker who was a ***certified real estate divorce specialist,*** John & Jane received some offers above the list price.

Needless to say, John and Jane were very happy with the sales price until it came time to sign the contract. This was the last piece left in the divorce and the finality of the relationship was presented to them in the form of a real estate contract which they both had to sign.

"***Comps***" are comparisons and oftentimes used by real estate brokers to determine sale or purchasing price.

At this point John felt that the home was being undersold by almost 40%. John provided addresses to other apartments that were larger, in better locations, with nicer views and were recently renovated. Importantly, these apartments were ***not direct "comps"*** to the subject apartment. This spouse did not want to sign the contract and wished that the home be relisted at 50% more.

During a teleconference, the real estate broker explained in great detail that the sales of these other homes were not directly relevant to their home. The real estate broker presented the divorcing couple with two options:

- Accept the contract; and,
- Relist the home at a new, unachievable list price.

The real estate market in New York is **surprisingly efficient**. If a property is priced too high, potential buyers will walk away from bidding. Therefore, an overpriced marital property could sit on the market for an extended period of time with price drops occurring every few months, even below its correct value. However, if a property is priced right then people will pay full price, sometimes encouraging a bidding war.

John and Jane decided to deliberate over the weekend. After considering the inherent risks, John and Jane both signed the contract on Monday. By giving them the option to think about what a re-listing could do they came to the choice that made the most sense for them at the time.

Case Study #2: Accepting Change in a Relationship

Jane and John were was divorcing and Jane was purchasing an apartment for the first time.

Many women in the United States have relied on their husband for all matters financial including the final decision to purchase a home they liked together. Jane had trouble making this financial decision on her own.

> "Two-thirds of divorces are initiated by women," says William Doherty, a marriage therapist and professor of family social science at University of Minnesota (NY Times Dec 2 2014).

Conflict resolution is an important skill of a good broker. Emotions and attitudes that accompany conflict keep the individuals trapped. Brokers filter comments from both sides of a transaction as part of normal business. This skill is used in dealing with conflict between divorcing or separating couples. It is important for the broker to establish a trusting relationship between the client and the broker. This is best done through understanding the client's needs. The client needs to know that the broker is listening. This can be established by asking what the client wants to accomplish and repeating back those needs to the client. They should be repeated until the client says yes that is what I am looking to accomplish in my search for a new home.

During the showing, the real estate broker should repeat those wish list items back to the client that meet their needs. For example saying something like "Jane, remember how you wanted a quiet 4 bedroom home on a good block, an apartment that gets good light and is in a full service building?" Repeating back her needs shows not only that the broker understood her but it established that the real estate broker was listening and this technique builds trust.

In this case study Jane was represented by Sally who brought her to Broker Donald's listing. Sally said that she has been working with this client for a long time and she cannot get her to commit to an apartment and has continued to show her apartments. Donald asked Sally if he could speak to Jane and asked her what she was looking for in an apartment – what her must-haves were, and what were the items that were unacceptable to Jane. At first Jane was slow to open up, but through Donald's patient demeanor – he was more interested in hearing

Jane's wants and objections than listing the virtues of the apartment – he established trust with the buyer. Broker Donald then reviewed all of Jane's wish list items until she said "yes, that is what I am looking for."

This is when the broker started the sales presentation for the apartment that Jane was looking for. It had all of the things that Jane wanted and none of the items that were deal killers. Donald asked her to think about this apartment. She scheduled another appointment with her parents. Her father pulled Donald aside and said this is the best apartment for her but she can't pull the trigger and pleaded for help.

Before the second appointment was over Donald had Jane review with him what she liked about the apartment and he was able to remind her that it sounded like it had all of the items that she was looking for. He knew that it had to be her decision to move forward. She, not her father, her broker or her friends saying that she should buy this would help with her decision. Donald knew that and asked her if this was the apartment that solved her apartment search. Sally was very smart and allowed Donald to take the lead with her buyer. She trusted him because they had done more than a few deals together. Jane found the perfect home. She lives there now with her two daughters. Maybe she will call Broker Donald when it is time to sell her home?

Final Thoughts

It is important for people going through a divorce or separation to work with a real estate broker who is aware of the unique issues affecting divorce and separation. It is ***highly recommended*** that they hire a real estate broker who is a ***certified real estate divorce specialist*** with a unique understanding of the legal and emotional issues affecting the transaction.

David Perry

David began his career in real estate 1987, working in finance and commercial leasing for Olympia and York, the largest NYC developer at the time. In 1998, he was part of the team that sold the Woolworth Building. For eleven years he was the Director of Sales and an executive for The Clarett Group, one of the city's largest residential developers. In those eleven years he sold over a billion dollars of residential real estate and leased more than one thousand apartments. During that time, he managed the leasing of The Montrose, Post Luminaria, Post Toscana and the Brooklyner, and was responsible for sales at 272 West 107th Street, Place 57, Chelsea House, Sky House, Forte, and 200 West End Avenue.

During the course of his career he was also involved in more than $1 billion in investment sales including such notable addresses as: 320 Park Avenue, 175 Water Street, 99 John Street, 233 Broadway, 308 East 38th Street, 385 First Avenue, 389 East 89th Street, and 111 Lawrence Street.

In 2011 he was the Director of Sales for Brown Harris Stevens Select's The Laureate, where he sold over $120 million of apartments in less than one year. David is leveraging this experience to market and sell exceptional residential properties and provide expert negotiation skills for purchasers.

David was the co-chair for the Real Estate Board of New York's Downtown Residential Division from 2005-2010. He served on the board of Community Access, a non-profit that built supportive low income housing from 2004 to 2010. He now serves as A Parent At Large for the PTA at P.S. 199 where his daughter is attending grammar school. He maintains a 15 handicap on the golf course and practices yoga up to five times per week. A Manhattan resident since 1988, David resides in the Upper West Side. Visit www.bhsusa.com/davideperry

SECTION F: USE OF PROFESSIONALS THROUGH DIVORCE & SEPARATION

CHAPTER 41

MORTGAGE PLANNERS

By Michael A. Mills, CMPS

This Chapter will address the most important aspects related to residential mortgages to help direct someone going through a divorce. It will give invaluable insights into the best way to interview and choose a ***mortgage professional***[58] ***("MP")*** as well as the criteria considered when determining what someone might qualify for.

The decisions and options about real estate – whether it is the marital home, a vacation retreat in the Hamptons, or a portfolio of income producing properties – can be some of the most daunting when going through a divorce. Divorcing parties need to consider who will live where as well as a host of other factors unique to real estate decisions.

Real estate is illiquid, meaning there are major costs and time factors involved in turning a property into cash. There can be concerns about maintaining stability for children, both in terms of their primary residence and school districts. When one spouse was the ***sole or primary income earner***, qualifying for a mortgage may seem impossible for the other. Selling properties that have significantly

---

[58] The term "***mortgage professional***" ("MP") is used ubiquitously throughout this Chapter. MPs come in three flavors: banker, mortgage banker, and mortgage broker, all of whom can be MPs as described in this chapter. "Loan Officer" usually refers to MPs who work at retail or mortgage banks and are also referred to as "bankers" or "mortgage bankers." "Mortgage Brokers" specifically refer to those MPs that act only as an intermediary between lenders and applicants but have no affiliation with any lender. A panacea term like MP is "loan originator" which can refer to any of these MPs who are actually engaged in the work typically associated with helping applicants apply for a mortgage. Underlying lenders are the end mortgage holders for a loan that is originated with a mortgage bank or broker. In the case of mortgage banks in particular, the guidelines provided by each of the underlying lenders they are able to originate loans for, comprise the breadth of their various programs.

appreciated in value since they were purchased can trigger tax consequences.

People going through a divorce or separation ***should not be overwhelmed***. Instead, they should hire a professional who, if chosen using the criteria below, can help them to successfully navigate all of the aforementioned concerns. In fact, this qualified professional should be sought after early on in the divorce process to accurately assess the objectives and outline a plan to achieve them.

Selecting a Mortgage Professional

When selecting a mortgage professional during a divorce, the criteria should not necessarily be the same as it would be for a person looking to save money with a routine refinance. The professional who quotes the lowest rate may not necessarily be the right choice. Unique qualifying circumstances, *e.g.*, the personal needs for communication and detailed explanations, or special program options that either minimize the negative income impact of ***spousal maintenance and child support*** or others that count it as valid qualifying income months earlier than the typical loan, are all important factors to consider. People going through a divorce or separation should ask his or her matrimonial attorney for a recommendation. A MP knowledgeable with the nuances of divorce can make the entire process go much more smoothly and eliminate work for an applicant.

Interview Questions

It is a good idea to speak with two or three MPs before making a final decision. When interviewing, a few questions to ask at minimum, along with details, are listed below.

1. "How are you compensated?"

People going through a divorce should work with somebody who can quickly and clearly answer this question. MPs who are paid based ONLY on the volume (i.e., total dollar amount) of all loans closed in a month are typically going to have the most reliable fiduciary relationship with their clients. They get paid the same commission on a $400,000 mortgage regardless of the rate, loan program, points, or closing costs. In a more complex scenario, the peace of mind and automatic trust that can be inferred by knowing that a MP's advice is truly unbiased and without self-motivation can be invaluable.

2. **"Do you only offer mortgage products from a single bank/lender or do you have access to a broad range of options to help me analyze and select the optimal mortgage program for my situation and goals?"**

Big retail banks can be a great place to get a mortgage, particularly when qualifying an applicant is simple and the transaction straight-forward. However, access to a variety of underlying lenders' underwriting guidelines and programs will make the need to switch lenders to find products that allow/enhance/ignore information in a borrower's profile, very unlikely – resulting in a more seamless process. Mortgage banks, mortgage brokers, and banks that have open-platforms that allow its loan officers to place loans in-house or act as a mortgage banker and broker will be the best bet.

3. **"What type of additional training, continuing education, or specialization curriculum do you participate in?**

Having training BEYOND the mandatory compliance courses and required continuing education signifies a professional dedicated to being an expert in his/her field, who will be able to provide clients relevant and helpful insights. One widely recognized program for training and certification of MPs to look for is the ***Certified Mortgage Planning Specialist*** designation. Mortgage Planning Specialists must complete 20 hours of training and pass a comprehensive exam to earn the CMPS® designation. For more information about the certification and education curriculum a CMPS® designated MP undertakes, visit https://cmpsinstitute.org/about.

4. **"How and when are you reachable?"**

For people that are working from 9am to 7pm or otherwise unavailable during business hours, it might be helpful to know that he or she can reach the MP at 8pm either for a pre-scheduled call or to answer a time sensitive question. People going through a divorce or separation should make sure meeting his or her schedule is something the MP will not have any issues with.

What Lenders Consider to Determine if You Qualify

Every lender has slightly different criteria when determining what their minimum acceptable borrower profile looks like. Some niche lenders use wildly ***different guidelines*** than others and many jumbo and super jumbo lenders offer looser or more restrictive underwriting in various areas, depending on program and loan amount. Therefore, this section will not seek to provide information regarding specific guidelines, but rather to educate on what the basic criteria categories are and how certain ***qualifying ratios*** are calculated.

A few qualifying categories will not be addressed but should be noted. The guidelines surrounding ***assets*** are as much about compliance with ***Anti-Money-Laundering*** and ***Patriot Act*** regulations as they are about the qualifying assets; hence these will not be covered. Property types for residential mortgages have different guidelines by lender, loan program, loan amount, and percentage of financing, and can only really be addressed on a case by case basis.

To determine whether someone going through a divorce is seeking a residential mortgage, commercial mortgage, or specialized real estate financing, the following list includes the generally accepted types of residences that fall under residential:

- 1-4 Unit Houses
- Single Condominium or Cooperative Units
- Houses in Planned or Gated Communities.

More specialized lenders are required for mobile, modular or pre-fabricated homes, properties with working farms, log-cabins, or other rustic vacation structures. When considering real estate assets as part of a portfolio, buildings with 5+ units fall under "Multifamily" which is similar to Commercial. A well-rounded lending institution should be able to help somebody going through a divorce with all residential, multifamily, and commercial real estate financing.

Credit and "Red Flags"

Almost 100% of mortgage lenders set a ***minimum qualifying credit score*** for each program, but they can vary by over 100 points. That said, there are a few "red flag" items on a credit report that are a major issue and can derail an applicant regardless of how strong other factors may be. The key to an applicant saving a lot of time, money, and stress is for him/her to be as forthcoming as possible with the MP about any of these items. If an applicant knows and shares this information in advance, then the MP can look to find this person a program that either allows him or her to ***qualify despite the red flag*** or ***disregards*** it with less time having passed since it occurred, compared to traditional guidelines.

The MP may refer to the amount of time between, for example, the date a foreclosure was finalized and when that person submits an application as "***seasoning***." The more seasoning, or the further in the past the derogatory event was resolved, the less impact it will have on qualifying. Below are some of the ***major red flags*** as they would be listed on credit reports and how much seasoning is required before most lenders will no longer treat it as an automatic disqualifier.

Red Flag	Time
Foreclosure	7 Years
Deed-in-Lieu of Foreclosure, Pre-foreclosure sale, or Charge off of Mortgage Account	4 Years
Chapter 7 or 11 Bankruptcy	4 Years from Discharge Date
Chapter 13 Bankruptcy	2 Years from Discharge or 4 Years from Dismissal Date
Multiple Bankruptcy Filings	5 Years if More than One Filing in Past 7 Years
Late Payment on Mortgage in Prior 12 Months	12 Months from Most Recent Late Payment
Foreclosure in Bankruptcy	4 Years with Proper Documentation

There is still hope for someone with these red flags. Loan programs that will allow applicants with one of these to still get a mortgage, even with a recent foreclosure or bankruptcy, do exist. These programs typically have significantly ***higher interest rates*** and should be viewed as ***temporary solutions***, allowing an applicant to achieve his/her housing objective within a preset time frame. That applicant should look to either undergo professional credit repair or simply prepare to apply for traditional mortgage financing as soon as the prescribed seasoning for a given red flag has passed.

Debt to Income Ratio

Lenders do not look at outstanding debt or the monthly income of an applicant in abstract. Instead, the applicant is given a calculated ***Debt to Income Ratio***, often referred to as ***DTI***. The lower an applicant's DTI, the stronger their borrower profile appears to lenders. Spousal maintenance and child support related considerations will be addressed at the end of the section, since they pose special issues to consider.

The D in the DTI ratio is calculated using the sum of all of an applicant's minimum monthly payments for servicing their debt as populated from their credit report, added to the proposed new housing payment [**Principal + Interest + Property Taxes + Homeowner's Insurance + Mortgage Insurance (when applicable) + Homeowner's Association or Condo Dues = Monthly Housing Payment**]. Monthly Housing Payment + Minimum Liability Payments = the top half of the DTI Ratio or the D.

> A borrower has only a $500/month car payment on credit, a new proposed mortgage of $2,500/month, $12,000/year in property taxes and a $1,200/year homeowner's insurance premium. Assume he earns $120,000/year in base salary. The calculation would be as follows:
> 500 + 2,500 + 1,000 (12,000/12) + 100 (1,200/12) = $4,100 / $10,000 (120,000/12) = 0.41 or a 41 DTI.

Income is calculated using the ***Gross Monthly Income*** of an applicant. In order for lenders to use specific income, the guidelines typically require that:

- there is some history of the income being received;
- the applicant is currently receiving it; and,
- there is a likelihood of continuation of that income.

When all acceptable and verifiable forms of income are calculated to a monthly figure and added together, this will form the bottom half of the DTI Ratio or the "I".

For a person receiving (or potentially receiving) spousal maintenance or child support, the timing of this DTI is critical. Some lenders require as many as six months' worth of received payments, supported by cancelled checks from the deposits and one's settlement agreement, divorce decree, or stipulation agreement. Other lenders will accept as few as two months' history for it to be used as additional income. Something critical to ask a MP about is whether child support income, which is not taxable, is counted at face-value or if it is given an upward adjustment to account for the tax treatment. Many lenders' guidelines allow child support to be counted at 1.25X the actual monthly amount received.

Borrower with $500,000 in Gross W2 income ($41,666.67/month) is responsible for a total of $7,000/month in support payments. He has $3,500 in monthly liabilities and a proposed housing payment of $7,500/month.

- **Traditional:** 3,500 + 7,000 + 7,500 = 18,000 / 41,666.67 = 43.20 DTI
- **Enhanced**: 3,500 + 7,500 = 11,000 / 34,666.67 (41,666.67 – 7,000) = 31.73 DTI

For the person paying (or potentially paying) spousal maintenance or child support, the majority of lenders will add these monthly payments to the liabilities or the top half of DTI, counting them the same way a lease payment is. This can make qualifying a challenge, which is why it is crucial to select a lender who has access to a broad range of products. If an applicant discloses his/her spousal and child support obligations upfront, a MP who specializes in working with individuals going through a divorce can guide this person towards the small handful of products that give more preferential treatment to these obligations. These products' guidelines dictate that they will subtract your monthly support payments from your gross income, instead of adding them to liabilities.

It is worth noting that for many loan products a 43 DTI is the upper threshold, and a jumbo loan could be capped between 36 – 42 DTI. This niche mortgage solution is something a borrower should specifically ask about if he/she is or will be paying alimony, child support, or durational maintenance.

Getting Started

The key to surviving the mortgage process and coming out with results that not only achieve the desired objective, but also make an applicant financially stronger than when they began, relies on these three things.

Prepare

> Professionals at FedEx, Kinkos, or UPS may be able to help scan the documents. Alternatively, your matrimonial attorney may be able to assist with this task since he or she may have a lot of the financial documents.

A tremendous amount of documentation will be required for the submission of an application. People going through a divorce should arm the chosen MP with all of that documentation upfront. These documents should be collected and ***scanned into one, clear, legible PDF***:

- ***2 Forms of Identification***, including at least 1 photo ID (license, passport, global entry card, social security card, or birth certificate);
- 2 consecutive, complete (all pages) statements from all ***checking, savings***, brokerage, retirement, and managed money accounts;
- The last ***2 years' federal tax returns***, all schedules plus all W2, 1099 and K1 forms from each year;
- If someone owns 20% or more of a business, include the prior 2 years' business tax returns for each company;
- If ***real estate*** is owned, including the property being refinanced, include all that apply:
    - most recent mortgage statement,
    - homeowner's insurance declaration page,
    - most recent property tax bill, and
    - a recent bill from any HOA or Coop maintenance;
- Records of paying or receiving ***child support or spousal maintenance*** for the last six (6) months or as many months as you have received; and,

- ***Divorce judgment***, applicable court orders (e.g., child support order from Family Court), and all stipulations OR filed and dually executed separation agreement.

Select a Mortgage Professional

A MP should be selected as early on in the divorce process as possible. A person going through a divorce or separation should provide the MP with all of the above documentation (or anything else requested). Furthermore, it is important to give this person permission to ***run his or her credit***. Additionally, a refinance applicant should not be shy about discussing various options for their divorce scenario and request analysis on said scenarios. A ***face-to-face*** meeting with the MP is paramount.

At a minimum, a mortgage refinance applicant should have the MP provide a copy of his or her credit report and walk this person through it, ***pointing out and explaining any potential pitfalls***, what easy steps this person can take to improve his/her score or protect it during the divorce, and if necessary recommend a reputable, pay-for-performance credit repair agency. For more information on credit repair, please read Chapter 47. Next, the MP should show the mortgagor how things look as a borrower on paper, reviewing anything that the mortgagor can improve either proactively or through the passage of additional time. Finally, the mortgage applicant should have the MP walk him or her through the details of any loan scenarios prepared based on his or her profile at present. The mortgagor should ask this person to follow up with a projection for what this person's loans would look like if that person successfully executes any discussed strategies to improve his or her borrowing profile before that person needs to submit the application.

Regular Communication

The MP should discuss the proposed scenarios with the divorce attorney and financial advisor. If someone going through a divorce does not have his or her own financial advisor, the mortgage professional and attorney should both be able to recommend people they have worked with in the past. Everyone going through a divorce should make sure his/her team of professionals ***communicates periodically with one another*** throughout the mortgage process, especially if any terms of the settlement are going to potentially change. This communication will continue to ensure they keep one another in the loop, enabling them to ***collaborate on any material changes*** that might impact one's mortgage options or borrower profile.

An early start, organization, and preparation will help make the process less stressful and reduce surprises that may arise. It is a mistake to ***put off the mortgage discussion*** merely because it is overwhelming or outside of someone's comfort zone. Instead, get a head start with a MP knowledgeable with divorce cases who will handhold applicants during the mortgage process, helping parties reach their goals.

Michael A. Mills, CMPS

Michael A. Mills is a Loan Officer in the Residential Mortgage Division of Sterling National Bank (Sterling Bancorp), a Certified Mortgage Planning Specialist® and an active member of the CMPS® Institute. The CMPS® Institute is a national organization that certifies mortgage bankers and brokers, with a stated mission, "...to help homeowners and homebuyers improve their lives by using the right mortgage strategies."

Before choosing to advise and educate homebuyers and current owners about mortgage planning, helping them to achieve their financial goals; Michael worked to obtain the same results in other areas of personal finance and banking. His experience spans multiple disciplines within the umbrella of financial planning, with a core focus on estate planning, retirement planning, education funding, investment management and family risk management through insurance.

Michael's aptitude and interest in asset management ultimately led him to accept a position as an investment wholesaler for Deutsche Bank. In this role he become a respected resource in tax-free fixed income, short-term bond, managed commodity, and mortgage-back security based investing.

In 2011 Michael joined Sterling National Bank with a lending practice centered around helping individuals and families reach their financial goals, now utilizing optimal mortgage financing and planning discussions instead of mutual funds and insurance. With a holistic approach to mortgage planning and its diverse applications, he continues to draw on his prior experience and insight to add greater depth to his consultative approach. Michael often identifying opportunities outside of the mortgage world, helping clients achieve other aspects of their financial goals by pointing them in the direction of other respected and vetted professionals.

SECTION F: USE OF PROFESSIONALS THROUGH DIVORCE & SEPARATION

CHAPTER 42

DAILY MONEY MANAGERS

By Peter Gordon, CSA

When Jane's divorce was finalized, the reality of her new life hit her smack in the face. While she would now be able to put many negative things behind her, a new world opened up ahead. One thing she was not prepared for was managing her daily finances. Unlike many of her friends, she had not been responsible for the billing and banking in her marriage – but this was a new beginning, with new responsibilities.

What are Daily Money Managers?

Jane was determined to take control of her spending and saving but had no idea where to start. At the suggestion of a friend, she took a look at the ***American Association of Daily Money Managers*** ("AADMM") website at www.aadmm.com. There she read that ***Daily Money Managers*** ("DMM") (a/k/a "financial organizers") help their clients organize their financial lives. Specifically, DMMs "provide personal business assistance to clients who have difficulty in managing their personal monetary affairs. The services meet a continuum of needs, from organizing and keeping track of financial and medical insurance papers, to assisting with check writing and maintaining bank accounts."

But What Do They Do?

She read that DMMs handle a broad range of tasks such as:

- Bill paying, including calls to payees regarding incorrect bills and preparation of checks for clients to sign.

- Balancing checkbooks and maintaining organization of bank records.
- Organizing tax documents and other paperwork.
- Negotiating with creditors.
- Deciphering medical insurance papers and verifying proper processing of claims.
- General organization assistance.
- Providing referrals to legal, tax, and investment professionals.

Jane was impressed by the AADMM's commitment to ensuring the highest quality interaction between its members and their clients, plus the fact that member DMMs are held accountable to the ***AADMM Board of Standards*** to resolve client concerns.

Interviewing a Daily Money Manager

Jane did not know what to ask a DMM during a consultation so she did some more investigation. She also found the "Questions to Ask" section of the website very handy. Some of these questions are:

- What is the scope of your work? Do you only do bookkeeping, or are there other ways that you can be of assistance?
- How long have you been working as a daily money manager?
- What are the ways in which you have assisted your clients?
- What kinds of professional insurance do you have? Do you have Errors & Omissions insurance and, if so, how much?
- To what professional organizations do you belong?
- Are there industry standards and code of ethics to which you adhere?
- Do you have any professional certifications or designations? Are you certified as a ***Professional Daily Money Manager*** ("PDMM")?
- With what professionals in other fields do you collaborate regarding your clients' issues?
- What are the costs of your services and what are the common billing methods?
- Do you have a letter of engagement? Does it include a confidentiality clause?
- With which local organizations are you affiliated?

- Can you provide a reference list?

Locating a DMM

Armed with this information, Jane decided to look for a DMM in her area. By entering her zip code into the "***Find a DMM***" page on the AADMM website, Jane was able to locate a number of DMMs near her. She called a few and, prepared with the "Questions to Ask," she decided to meet with Jack. He is an experienced DMM with excellent references and he quoted hourly rates charges that she felt she could afford.

Meeting with a DMM

At their meeting Jack revisited the role of a DMM and asked some basic questions including:

- How many bank accounts do you have?
- How many credit cards do you have?
- Do you own or rent?
- What is your monthly income?
- Do you own or lease an automobile?
- What insurance coverage do you have (e.g., life, health, long term care, disability, Medicare)?
- Do you have a will or a trust?
- Are you working with other financial/legal professionals?

Responsibilities

Cash Flow

Jack pointed out that DMMs do not ***manage investments***, but that they ***focus on the flow of funds***, what comes in and what goes out. In addition, he reiterated that DDMs are not accountants, brokers, insurance sales people or attorneys; however, DMMs often work closely with these professionals.

Mail

In order to provide an overview of the services he offers, Jack felt it would be worthwhile to review the typical steps that are taken when he begins working with a new client.

The first thing he does is ask clients to show him how they ***handle the mail*** in their home. This is critical since most of his clients still receive their bills and statements via the United States Postal Service ("USPS").

Filing System

The next step is to a look at the client's ***filing system***. Optimally, clients have their paid bills in manila folders, filed by month or payee, in a file cabinet. However, he is accustomed to seeing many other more challenging systems.

Then he sits down and sorts through the bills and statements. These are divided into specific categories. These may include, but are not limited to:

A. **Bank Accounts**

B. **Credit Card Accounts**

C. **Brokerage and Investment Accounts**

D. **Household Expenses**
   (1) Rent/maintenance
   (2) Cable/TV/Internet/Phone
   (3) Cell Phones
   (4) Gas & Electric
   (5) Home Repairs
   (6) Cleaning
   (7) Groceries
   (8) Entertainment

E. **Auto**
   (1) Registration, license, etc.
   (2) Insurance
   (3) Repairs

(4) Fuel

F. Insurance

(1) Life
(2) Home
(3) Long Term Care
(4) Disability

G. Medical

(1) Health Insurance
(2) Medicare (if applicable)
(3) Claims

H. Taxes

(1) Real Estate
(2) Charitable Deductions
(3) Estimated Payments
(4) Income Tax Returns

Looking at Finances

Once the bills are sorted out it is time to look at the checking account. Most people work with a check register and manually enter checks and bills paid. Jack sits with his client and reviews the current bills and their history. The clients' input is critical here. It is their responsibility to determine what should get paid and when.

Credit card bills and payments are also reviewed. Close attention is paid to all charges, balances, interest rates and due dates, to insure that unnecessary fees are not incurred. Together, Jack and Jane get a good sense of the transactions that ***flow through her credit cards***.

Many bills can be paid with automatic debits to bank accounts and credit cards. This is a great convenience but must be monitored closely. It is easy to lose track of these charges, resulting in ***unwanted expenses***. Jack and Jane do an inventory of these charges to insure that all of them are for services and products that she is currently using.

Ready for Financial Organization

The above actions can take a few hours so Jack schedules a ***second appointment*** to begin the payment of bills. At this meeting he will come armed with manila folders that match the categories established when the original bills were sorted. When each bill is paid, the amount, date, and check number (or confirmation number, if paid online) is written on the bill and filed in the appropriate labeled manila folder. The folders will be put into a file cabinet that has hanging folders labeled to match the categories for all of the expenses. The result is an organized, ***easy to reference***, collection of payment records.

Use of Computer Technology

As opposed to a paper register, Jack prefers to use a popular PC program, ***Quicken***, to enter all of the bills. Jack explains to Jane that there are a number of reasons for this:

- It allows income and expenses to be categorized, enabling the user to easily track payments and deposits. This in turn makes it easy to see where money is being spent and to create a budget.
- Transactions from checking and credit card accounts can be imported into the program, speeding up the bookkeeping process.
- Entries are memorized and simple to create from month to month and checks can be printed from the program. This saves a great deal of time over use of manual checks and registers.
- At tax time, reports detailing all tax related expenses can be provided to accountants, saving time and money.

Final Steps Toward a New Financial Future

As a result of this conversation, Jane had an excellent sense of what it would be like to work with Jack. She decided to request a letter of engagement so they could move forward. After a few months of working with Jack, Jane felt empowered by having the knowledge of where her money was being spent. Together with Jack, and the reports created in Quicken, they were able to create a monthly budget allowing her to make educated spending decisions. In retrospect, she was thrilled with her decision to hire a Daily Money Manager.

Final Thoughts

Some people might think that getting help to pay their bills is a sign of vulnerability. However, in today's economy, the many moving pieces of a household budget can be difficult to navigate. This is only compounded by the personal upheaval of a divorce or separation.

Clients gain a new sense of calm and security after only a few weeks of working with a Daily Money Manager. They no longer have piles of papers, mysterious unopened envelopes, and threats of unpaid bills hanging over them. They become empowered with the knowledge of what funds are coming in, where their money is being spent, and what is left over for savings. This provides them with more time to handle the many intricacies of their day-to-day life. It is very rewarding for the Daily Money Manager to be part of this new beginning of their clients' lives.

Peter Gordon, CSA

Peter Gordon is a partner at New York Financial Organizers, Inc. (www.nyfo.nyc). His focus is on client service and marketing. After learning to navigate the tricky waters of Medicare, Medicaid, community trusts and estate planning for his own parents, Peter began NYFO with the goal of helping others gain peace of mind and security with their families', or their own, financial affairs.

Peter earned a BA in Political Science from the University of Buffalo and an MBA in Finance from Baruch College. After spending three years at Sanford Bernstein & Co. in marketing services, he began his own computer graphic design business, Gordon Associates Inc., in 1990. In 1997 Peter teamed with Harvey Appelbaum, an award winning creative director, and formed inc3. In 2005, inc3 was sold to Kay Printing, a Clifton, New Jersey company, and re-branded as Kay Multimedia (KMM). In 2011, Peter became the Director of New Business Development for Dorian Orange, a Motion Design firm dedicated to producing captivating, innovative, and memorable brand messages.

Peter is a member of the American Association of Daily Money Managers; a Certified Senior Advisor (CSA); a member of the Orion Resource Group, and is pursuing Geriatric Care Management education at the Brookdale Center for Healthy Aging. He lives in Forest Hills, NY, is married, and has two sons.

SECTION F: USE OF PROFESSIONALS THROUGH DIVORCE & SEPARATION

CHAPTER 43

PROFESSIONAL ORGANIZERS

By Amy Neiman & Carrie Gravenson

Professional organizers help individuals create systems and processes using organizing principles. This Chapter explains how someone going through a divorce or separation can utilize a professional organizer to make their life and the divorce process easier, less stressful, and more organized.

A professional organizer is a neutral third party who helps eliminate the ***overwhelming feelings*** from the information overload and develops systems to prepare the client for life during the separation period and after the divorce. Going through a divorce is an emotional time, even in the best of circumstances. An organizer is focused solely on personal items and helps a divorcing client jumpstart into his or her new life, whether by staying in an existing home, moving to a new place, dealing with paperwork, or sorting through personal possessions.

Background

How Can a Professional Organizer Help Through a Difficult Life Change?

A professional organizer is someone who provides assistance, information, and resources to individuals who want to create a simpler life, a more efficient living space, or even a more productive working space. An organizer also helps clients with specific goals and challenges such as organizing paperwork and personal items associated with the dissolution of a marriage.

An organizer will focus on efficiency and reducing clutter when organizing important papers, helping to prepare for a move to a new home, or creating a useful home/work office. These professionals have the resources to conquer and divide a person's possessions, whether it involves keeping it, donating it, selling it, or simply discarding it.

Think of a professional organizer like a personal trainer for someone's items. Yes, a person could get in shape on his or her own; when working with a personal trainer, that trainer provides ***guidance***, ***inspiration***, and ***accountability*** to help a client achieve goals faster. Professional organizers offer the same kinds of services and tools. Some people can stay in shape on his or her own, and some find it more of a challenge. An upcoming event can inspire some, where as other individuals need a bigger push. The same is true with getting and staying organized.

Many people hire a professional organizer when they are going through a transition of some kind: moving, getting married, having a baby, selling a home, renovating a room, building a home office, or going through a divorce or separation. They want the guidance and focus to get it professionally done the first time.

Like other professionals, organizers offer a wide variety of specialties. Some professional organizers specialize only in the residential market, while some focus on businesses. There are some who specialize in working with clients who have been diagnosed with Attention Deficit Hyperactive Disorder ("ADHD"), some who work with the chronically disorganized, and some who work with hoarding disorders or tendencies. There are professional organizers who help clients prepare for a move or relocation; some create custom closets or filing systems. There are virtual assistants, tech and electronic organizers, photo organizers, and time management specialists just to name a few.

What *Doesn't* a Professional Organizer Do?

Because there are so many different kinds of professional organizers, there is often some overlap into other areas. In general, a professional organizer is not a therapist, designer, cleaner, realtor, nurse, informational technology ("IT") support person, babysitter, or personal assistant. The best advice is to talk with the potential organizer to determine if he/she can meet the needs of the divorcing or separating person.

Professional organizing has been getting more attention lately through new reality-like television programming. These programs can create some myths about the profession. Please keep these things in mind when hiring a professional organizer to ensure expectations are adequately met:

- **Manpower** – major networks can afford to hire 100 branded interns to unload and remodel an entire house in 6 hours. This will not be the case for an individual professional organizer.
- **Money** – organizers can vary in cost. Take the time to meet with the organizer, discuss the needs, identify a budget, and then figure out which organizer will offer the most value.
- **Time** – some clients' projects might take longer than others. There are no quick edits. Getting organized can be challenging work, yet the important thing to remember is the end results will be worth it. Discuss any deadlines or timeframes that must be met during the initial conversations with the professional organizer.

Divorce and Professional Organizing

Divorce definitely qualifies as one of life's ***major transitions***. Even an amicable divorce is a period of ***adjustment***. There are many details to work out and much to be done. A professional organizer can help lift the burden.

Hiring a professional organizer to help with paperwork can be a relief for many individuals working through a divorce. Professional organizers help manage and systemize required paperwork for professionals (e.g., divorce attorney, accountant, financial advisor, mortgage broker). Organizers can help mitigate chaos and stress. An organizer can save time, energy and money for a client going through a divorce or separation. Having a professional organizer guide working parents to create a system can be vital.

Case Study: Sara's Divorce

Sara has been going through a divorce for the past four years. She has two teenage sons and recently started a new job. She needed help gathering financial paperwork for her lawyer and accountant. There are seemingly endless forms to complete and data to collect. It has been overwhelming for her to sort through the files on her own and to decide what was needed and where to look for the files in her home office. In addition, there was so much communication with her soon-to-be ex that Sara felt the need to print out and keep track of everything. It all seemed like too much.

The organizer started with setting up a *filing system* for Sara. A file-cabinet was purchased and properly labeled hanging folders were created. Each member of her household was assigned a color (blue, red, green, yellow). Together, they sorted through all the paperwork and bills and medical claims. Sara and her organizer labeled all the files using very detailed and specific language. They also applied a set of rules for each document. She was able to find exactly what was needed for the past five years so she was prepared for her lawyer. What seemed like an overwhelming project became a simple matter of retrieving the right files when the time came.

To illustrate, a professional organizer helped Sara create and maintain a system for the following financial records for her divorce:

- Tax returns and W-2s
- Pay stubs
- Bank statements
- Business records
- Loan statements
- Credit card statements
- Deposit slips, canceled checks, and check registers
- Mortgage applications
- Retirement account statements
- Trademark certificates or other types of intellectual property
- Partnership agreements, limited liability operating agreements
- Personal finance statements
- Receipts of previous home repairs
- Last Will and Testaments
- Trusts
- Life insurance certificates
- Employment contracts
- Bankruptcy proceedings
- Motor vehicle registrations
- Receipts for living expenses
- Medical records
- Documents regarding the children

- Copies of calendars
- Running list of questions

In Sara's case, it was important to make sure her and her ex's documents were in order. Having an organizer available helps the divorcing couple have a third party present while dealing with sensitive paperwork. In some cases, having ***two independent organizers*** available might be best (a "his/hers" type scenario).

Organizing Paperwork

Organizing paperwork can be daunting during a divorce or separation. Creating space for a centralized system (i.e., file folders) for *new paperwork* or incoming mail will enable the party to find important papers quickly. This can include:

- **Action: Urgent** – items that require action (or reply) ASAP
- **Action: Non-Urgent** – items that still need action yet are not as pressing
- **Bills to Pay** – bills that need to be paid
- **Rainy Day Projects and/or Research** – items that might be interesting to learn more about, or a project to get to on a "rainy day"
- **For the lawyer** – items collected to be shared with his/her divorce/family lawyer

In addition, to ensure both online and offline filing systems are in-sync, all computer files and emails should be labeled the same as paper files. Utilizing the same system and the same file-labeling scheme will enable one to easily find the folders both digitally and via hard copy.

Take time every day to eliminate clutter and get organized.

Division of Property and Moving

As paperwork management is important during a divorce, so is *dividing households* into two physical spaces and relocating one or both parties. If children are involved, creating multiple spaces (one in each home) may also be necessary.

Where to start is a frequent question. If a couple has been married for many years, most of the belongings are mixed together: his yearbooks and her childhood memorabilia; his sports equipment and her kitchen gadgets; books and family photos. A professional organizer can help separate these items and create a plan of what goes where, what can be sold, and where unwanted items can be donated.

An organizer can also help with the *moving process* by being the liaison between the moving company, the new home, the client, and sometimes the realtor. Organizers use teams to pack and unpack a new home. This creates a space the client is familiar with and reduces the anxiety of negotiating too many details.

Case Study: Jack's Separation

Jack and his wife Melissa decided to separate after 11 years of marriage. They have 2 children and had lived together in a lovely house. When the couple decided to separate, they jointly decided to move into two new homes (and in a different state from where the family was currently living). A home was purchased for Melissa and the children, while Jack rented an apartment nearby. An organizer spent time dividing the household belongings. The best method was to use color-coded post-its or stickers: red stickers to her home and blue to his home. The majority of the children's items went to Melissa's house. It was mutually decided that the most important detail was to set up the home that would be the children's primary residence.

A moving company was hired and the organizer orchestrated moving day with one day dedicated to Melissa and another day dedicated to Jack. Luckily, the homes were close by, so if an item needed to be shifted it could happen seamlessly. An additional organizer was hired (in the new state) to assist with the unpacking and setting up the primary home. When children are involved, additional stress can occur; having the second organizer and team available ***eliminated tantrums*** and made the day more manageable. Jack's move, too, went smoothly as tension was already alleviated with the two moves happening on separate days.

An important note: an organizer was consulted early on in the separation process for this couple. It was decided to move the family before a divorce was filed as the couple considered the children's needs for their upcoming school term. It was also helpful that the separation was amicable.

Some Moving Tips

- ***Purge first.*** During packing, have an organizer help to decide which items to keep. If there is an item that is not used or loved, pass it on to someone who might appreciate the item.
- ***When packing,*** make sure to label boxes clearly; if not the exact contents, then at least the room wherein the items will reside in the new place.
- ***Start the packing weeks ahead*** of the move with items that are not essential to daily life: art work, memorabilia, off-season clothing, etc.
- ***Maximize empty space.*** One organizer saw an empty suitcase packed in a moving box. Clothing and soft items can be packed in suitcases. Do not pay to move air.
- ***Books go in small boxes.*** Even paperbacks can weigh down a larger box and make it difficult to move.
- When available, ***use old towels, linens, and blankets*** to pack fragile possessions; this saves money on bubble wrap and reduces waste.
- ***Unpack quickly.*** Make a point to get out of cardboard within a few days. Do not get comfortable living amongst boxes. Find a place for everything.

Case Study: Victoria's Divorce

Victoria hired a professional organizer when she was just starting the divorce paperwork. She was generally very organized but still felt overwhelmed. The organizer helped her get all of her paperwork in order. After the divorce was finalized and her now ex-husband Dennis moved out, she had to gather up all the things he left behind and donate them to Goodwill. It was not a particularly vicious divorce but he had taken the opportunity to de-clutter as he packed up so when he moved out, he left a lot of belongings behind, which he told her were now hers. Victoria, not needing 14 ties, donated them.

The organizer helped her set aside furniture to sell or give away to friends. A fresh start meant getting rid of everything from toiletries to golf clubs to books. The purge was very therapeutic as well as practical. Having an organizer there to help her sort without judgment was key for setting up her new life.

A happy side effect: new closet space! Suddenly, out-of-season clothing and accessories had a more comfortable place to be. It offered Victoria's other closet much needed breathing room. She could not be happier with the results.

Final Thoughts

An organizer will work to ease the transition to a new space and a new life. Divorce can be messy, stressful, and long. Divorce can also be a positive experience. An organizer can be a lifeline out of the chaos. Having support from an independent guide who is knowledgeable about systems and transitional times can be a blessing. Creating a new space, organizing the present home and handling paperwork is just a start of what an organizer can do to help during a difficult life change. Once the transition is complete, being able to maintain the new systems and continuing to live an organized and more simplified life is the ultimate goal.

Amy Neiman

Amy Neiman, M.A., is the Founder and CEO of *a simplified life*, providing organizing services to empower professionals to be more profitable and productive through simplifying their workspace. Her proven, disciplined approach allows individuals to establish an easy-to-follow process which helps organize their time, space, paper, and possessions more effectively. By de-cluttering and building structure, Amy has helped countless professionals better focus on their businesses and their lives.

With a Masters in Psychology and spending 15 years in the entertainment industry, Amy's organizing skills were well honed before launching her business. She firmly believes that organizing can be pain-free and consume a minimal amount of time during the day.

Amy is a contributor to the book, THE HAPPY LAW PRACTICE: EXPERT STRATEGIES TO BUILD BUSINESS WHILE MAINTAINING PEACE OF MIND. Her chapter is titled, Maximize Productivity: Tips for Organizing Your Office. Amy is also a member of the National Association of Professional Organizers (NAPO). For more information, visit www.amyneiman.com.

Carrie Gravenson

Unjumbler Professional Organizing was created in 2007 when Carrie Gravenson was hired as a temp for a boring and messy office. Left with nothing to do, she volunteered to organize the desk where she was sitting. Satisfied and energized by the results, she then asked to organize the supply closet. Then the kitchen, the storage room and the file room. A passion was discovered and an obsession was born.

Since 2007, Unjumbler has organized countless spaces for all walks of life. The home, the office and everything in between. From a messy drawer to a complete apartment renovation, Unjumbler has the skills and resources to create functional and beautiful order. As a native New Yorker and avid traveler, Carrie instinctively knows how to use space efficiently, even in small quarters. For more information about Unjumbler, visit www.unjumbleronline.com.

SECTION F: USE OF PROFESSIONALS THROUGH DIVORCE & SEPARATION

CHAPTER 44

LIFE INSURANCE BROKERS

By Joseph Wexler

Do you feel really good about the financial plan you have in place, or are you ***unsure whether your plan will cover*** everything you need? It's never too late to set up a plan you feel better about and can go a long way on the road to whatever is next. This Chapter was written for anyone who finds him or herself in the ***middle of a transition***, especially with divorce or separation. These transitions can be lengthy, challenging, and will have a lasting impact on our future depending on how we react.

This Chapter is intended to help with one specific piece of financial planning – ***life insurance*** – that may be helpful through a divorce or separation. Life insurance should be a well thought out purchase to ensure it will protect what is most important to you. Since the price of life insurance is based on age and health, delaying action can be costly and paralyzing.

What is Life Insurance?

Life insurance at its basics is simple. It is one of the best tools to ensure that someone you love or owe is taken care of should you no longer be around. In the divorce or separation context, life insurance can be a helpful mechanism with financial obligations, including child support or spousal maintenance.

How Much Coverage Do I Need?

With life insurance there are three questions that need to be answered:

- How much do you need?
- How do you own it?
- What is important to you to provide if you were to pass away tomorrow?

The third question is the first step in determining ***how much coverage you need***. For example, do you have any child support and/or spousal maintenance obligations under your settlement agreement, divorce judgment or court order? If so, then consider the following questions:

- How long is your financial obligation?
- Does this include private school, post-secondary education, graduate school or professional school (e.g., law school, medical school, dental school)?

Additionally, life insurance can be a useful mechanism with the payment of debts. Do you or your dependents have debts that you would like to be paid upon your death (e.g., mortgage, student loans)? If you did not live long enough would you want to provide income for your dependents to ensure their lifestyle remained the same? By figuring out how much income would be needed today to replace your total lifetime income you can secure enough life insurance to provide your entire lifetime earnings to your family.

Life insurance products differ in type length, and features. And so after determining the amount of coverage the next question is "What type of insurance do I need?" Different products are used for different needs. For instance only permanent life insurance has cash value that can be used while the person is living. While the cash value does offer you the flexibility while alive, any use of it may reduce the death benefit. You should have a discussion with your insurance agent about using the cash value to make sure that it does not undermine other planning based on the death benefit.

Some Things to Consider

Consider Your Blind Spots

It's hard to protect yourself from your blind spots – things you're not expecting. Today outliving your income in retirement can be more of an obstacle than not living long enough. What happens when retirement funds run out? Or long term care expenses eat into your hard-earned retirement funds? A permanent life insurance policy could help supplement a retirement at death, can reimburse costs for long term care, or be used to cover your unsettled debts which would otherwise be inherited by those who survive you.

Regular Life Insurance "Check-Ups"

Once you have considered what you want to occur you want to look at what has changed in regards to what you have. Often many changes have occurred since you last looked at your life insurance policy. Life insurance should be seen as a part of your financial plan that should be updated (ideally) on a yearly basis. When reviewing your plan, you should ask yourself, "***What is new or has changed in my life?***" Since you last looked at your life insurance, has your child graduated from middle school, high school, or college? Have you had an addition to the family? Has your salary increased or decreased? Have your assets increased or decreased? Have any of your goals for the life insurance changed or been accomplished?

> Some people review their insurance policies and estate plan each May after filing taxes in April. Alternatively, some make a "check-up" appointment after Thanksgiving or another major holiday when the family was together and able to discuss important financial matters.

Life insurance is like a bridge that is laid over the gap between what you want accomplished when you die and where are today. The larger the gap the more coverage you need. Each year as changes occur this gap will widen or close, but in general the gap will close as you get closer you your goals. Like most successful planners you should choose a ***specific time of the year*** to review all of your plans with a professional to ensure everything is up to date. This will help you stay on top of this very important plan, and remain confident that the amount of coverage you have is appropriate for the goals you want to accomplish.

Using a Life Insurance Agent

It is important to remember that you are not alone in the process of reaching your goals or determining the right amount of life insurance protection. A life insurance professional can help you determine the right amount of coverage by guiding you with good questions. Often the only cost of this type of consultation is your time. From this process a professional can put together a plan, which can show you an accurate estimate of the financial gap that needs to be filled. This will usually include finer details like an assumed inflation, rate of return, and savings strategies for other goals like retirement or education savings.

Term vs. Permanent Insurance

Once you have determined how much life insurance is needed an advisor can help you with how to own it. In general you can either rent insurance, known as ***term insurance***, for a period of time (10yrs, 20yrs, or to age 80) or it can be purchased permanently, known as ***permanent life insurance***. Neither is better than the other; the choice depends on your goals and objectives for the life insurance.

Rented or term insurance can be inexpensive, and good for goals that are only needed for a specific period of time, like education. Permanent insurance, on the other hand, lasts for your entire life as long as premiums are paid, builds a cash value that is often conceptually compared to equity that builds in a home and is accessible to the owner, and can be structured for flexibility. Permanent can be appropriate for any goals that occur after retirement such as outliving your savings or on the flip side maximizing your estate.

It is important you understand that utilizing the cash values through policy loans, surrenders of dividend values, or cash withdrawals could: reduce the death benefit, necessitate greater outlay than anticipated, or result in an unexpected taxable event. Briefly explained, over time a permanent life insurance will gain cash value, which the owner of the policy can access.

This is mentioned to highlight how important it is to work with an insurance agent who can help you understand how to structure a permanent insurance policy so that it can be used at the optimal time, living or dead, in the right way to minimize or negate tax consequences or increased outlay.

Is your coverage currently all rented through term insurance or is some of it owned through permanent coverage? A professional can help you make a determination on how much of each type you should have. Most term insurance has the capability to be converted to permanent coverage giving you options down the road.

Looking at the Structure

In regards to structuring a policy there are a few other important considerations. Depending on the goal of the insurance the owner, payer, insured, and beneficiary of a life insurance policy can be different from one another.

- For instance do you want the policy to ***be paid to your children***?
- Does a *trust* need to be set up on behalf of them?
- Will a trust be set up for a spouse due to ***estate planning*** issues, now or in the future?
- Who should own or have ***control*** over the policy?
- Who should ***pay*** for the policy?

These are all great questions to consider when structuring a policy. Incorrectly structured policies could lead to unfortunate results that are not simple to fix. This is why working with an advisor can make all the difference.

Divorce and Separation Context

Life insurance can play a significant role in protecting against a sudden loss of income in either divorce settlement agreement/judgment or child support agreement/order for financial issues including child support and spousal support, or can be used to equalize property distribution. Think about the following scenarios where life and disability insurance can be used in the ***divorce and separation context***:

- There is a ***child support agreement*** for the non-custodial parent to pay the custodial parent $X in basic child support plus 50% of unreimbursed medical expenses, necessary child care, and extracurricular (up to a certain cap). Additionally, the parents agreed to split the cost of four years of college education for the two children up to the State University of New York-Buffalo cap equally. Five years later, the non-custodial parent dies in a car accident. Fortunately, the child support agreement had a requirement for the non-custodial parent to have life insurance with a face value of the child support obligation under the agreement, including college education. In this case, the parents used a life insurance trust for the proceeds requiring that the life insurance proceeds be used for the health, education, housing, and extra-curricular activities of the children.

- In Joe and Jane's divorce settlement agreement, Joe agreed to pay Jane rehabilitative ***spousal maintenance*** for five (5) years to allow Jane time to go back to school and obtain employment. Joe gets in a car accident and becomes disabled. He is unable to earn income to pay for his spousal maintenance obligation. In the divorce settlement, Joe had agreed to purchase a disability insurance policy for the five (5) years while he had said spousal maintenance obligation.

- Spouses own a child care business together. Pursuant to the divorce settlement agreement, the spouses shall continue to own the ***small, closely held business together*** in equal shares. Over time, each ex-spouse remarries. The divorce settlement agreement required a life insurance policy to be purchased along with a buy-sell agreement so that if one owner dies the other business owner will have the cash to buy the ownership units instead of owning the child care business with his or her ex-spouse's widow(er).

Here are a few additional issues to address with life insurance policies in the context of a divorce or separation:

- As far as structuring the policy ***who should be the owner***? As a general rule, life insurance companies can only distribute information to the policy owner; however, with consent by the owner the company will be able to provide information to the former spouse.

- Will there be a ***change of ownership*** upon a future event such as remarriage or beneficiary reaching age of majority?

- Will there be any ***restrictions on access*** to the policy cash (e.g., loan dividends in cash, full surrender, partial surrender, exercise of settlement options)?

- Who will pay the ***premiums***? Should proof of payment be provided to the former spouse or require that one spouse pays premiums on the other spouse's policy?

- Will the policy qualify for spousal maintenance ***tax deductibility***?

- Who will be the beneficiary? For example, will the beneficiary be the children until they are at the age ***majority*** (18) or ***emancipation*** (21)? What happens when one reaches the age of majority or emancipation but the other has not? Does the minor have to be named the beneficiary of an entire policy? If the children are to be beneficiaries consider including a trust for their benefit to create the opportunity for flexible planning.

- Will the beneficiary designation be irrevocable? If not, should ***proof of the designation*** be provided to the former spouse?

You may also want to think about whether other types of risk management insurance is important to include in the plan. A financial advisor and attorney can make a great team in a divorce to ensure that not only are you taking the right steps for yourself and your family but also that the finances you are settling are being structured in the most beneficial way for your future.

Joseph Wexler

Joseph has cultivated a practice as a financial advisor working alongside goal oriented people who know that the ripple effect of their financial decisions (good and bad) will impact those that they love. Wexler works with his clients to provide options in growing, protecting, and distributing wealth in the right way and at the right time. Joseph also guides his clients to a better financial future through taking a consultative approach to systematically prioritizing mid to long term savings goals.

SECTION F: USE OF PROFESSIONALS THROUGH DIVORCE & SEPARATION

CHAPTER 45

PARENTING CLASSES

By Sabra R. Sasson, Esq.

People who have been parenting for a while, or even if just a beginner, may have come to realize that their children did not come with an instruction manual. Sometimes they may even wish that they had! In the seventies there was "***Doctor Spock***" whose ideas might seem controversial today. Maybe there is a sort of "***Cliff's Notes***" that could just give parents an inkling of an idea of what's to come.

As soon as parents feel as though they have figured out this parenting stuff, their child changes or moves out of a certain phase and is into something new that challenges a parent's patience, flexibility and acuity. Children seem to be one step ahead of the parents who are struggling to juggle jobs, the household, and themselves as well as trying to raise their children. While parents may receive "advice" from friends or other parents or even their own parents, sometimes it may feel like those friends or parents "just don't understand" or "they don't know the particular child." This can feel so frustrating to parents, making them feel alone or at their wit's end.

All the challenges of parenting are ***magnified when there is strife between the parents***, particularly in the context of a divorce. Fortunately, there are resources and parenting classes available to help parents through these challenging times.

Different Types of Parenting Classes

There are different types of parenting classes: (1) private parenting coaching classes, (2) classes through community organizations and community centers, (3) online courses, or (4) New York State Parent Education & Awareness Program offered through the New York State Unified Court System. For more information on parenting coaches, please review Chapter 23 in this book authored by Susan Nason. This Chapter will focus on parenting classes offered through the other three methods.

Parenting Classes at the Community Center

There are community organizations offering parenting classes that can help parents learn new techniques and skills and build their "arsenal" of tactics to aid in the development of their child. While every child is different and may have different communication and learning styles, there are some commonalities and generalities that have been identified and "summarized" and culled together in an organized way to be shared with parents in an interesting and fun way.

1. **What can a parent expect? Will these courses evaluate whether a parent is a "good" parent or a "bad" parent?**

No. While it may be nice to be told or to have it affirmed that you are being a good parent, that is not the purpose of these classes. They are simply classes and courses which show parents ***new techniques*** for aiding in the development of their child(ren) and transitioning through a divorce or separation. Learning and getting introduced to many different techniques, is a great way for parents to become aware of the possibilities of parenting styles and to pick and choose the best ones for their family. It is common that a parent may feel that some of the techniques seem useful and they may want to use them right away, while the same parent may feel skeptical and unsure of other techniques but may be willing to try them (and even be happily surprised of their effectiveness), while other approaches just may not be appropriate for the parent or his/her family. The idea is to learn with an open mind and be exposed to a variety of possibilities beyond one's circle of friends, family, and community – and be open to the possibility of learning and using effective parenting techniques.

2. **Where can someone find a community organization that offers parenting classes?**

To find a community organization that offers parenting classes, one can search online or visit local community centers such as the Young Men's Christian Association ("YMCA"), Jewish Community

Center ("JCC"), local libraries and other community centers. It is always smart to ask people in the community for referrals for parenting classes.

3. **Are there special parenting classes at community centers that help divorcing or separating parents?**

Additionally, parenting classes specific for the divorcing or separated parent can usually be located by visiting local community and religious organizations. For more information on parenting classes and other types of resources available through community organizations to help separating and divorcing parents, please read Chapter 45 authored by FamilyKind.

Online Courses

1. **What are the advantages or disadvantages in taking an online course vs. a course in person?**

When taking an ***online course***, one can learn techniques on his or her own time and convenience. It can be beneficial to learn the techniques and try them as they are learned from the online course and then the class may be watched again for clarification after trying the techniques. The downside is that if there are any questions, it may be difficult to get them answered or addressed by the instructor.

In contrast, at an ***in-person program***, one can learn all of the techniques at once and hear about all of the available options. If there are questions, the participants can ask them during the program. Sometimes, others in the class may have questions that all of the participants can benefit from. However, once the class is over, it may be difficult to make additional inquiries.

2. **Where is the best place to find quality online courses?**

Someone interested in looking for an online parenting class should search online. Additionally, attorneys, mediators, friends, colleagues, and family members may also offer helpful suggestions. Here is a link to some more information that can be used as a starting point:
http://www.parentingclassonline.net/parenting-class-newyork.html
(last visited October 3, 2015).

3. Are there special online courses for divorcing or separating parents?

Many of the classes may likely be appropriate for parents regardless of marital status. Parents who are co-parenting and have challenges in communicating with one another or in scheduling visitation and parenting time may benefit from an online resource called Family Wizard which is an online family management tool where email communication and schedules can be stored in one convenient place. The website address is: www.ourfamilywizard.com.

New York State Parent Education & Awareness Program

Finally, the New York State managed program is specifically designed for divorcing or separating parents to educate parents about the impact of their breakup on their children and ways in which to reduce stress and negative effects of their conflict on their children. For more information on the New York State Parent Education & Awareness Program visit https://www.nycourts.gov/ip/parent-ed/ or email nyparent-ed@courts.state.ny.us.

Sabra R. Sasson, Esq.

Sabra R. Sasson is an attorney and mediator practicing in New York City. She is the founder and Principal of Sabra Law Group, PLLC, a mediation and law practice in midtown Manhattan that offers legal and mediation services to its clients. Sabra handles the legal aspects of major transitions – buying or selling property, planning for marriage or getting divorced – and protects her clients' interests so they can focus on their evolution into this new life change. She employs her skills and experience to help her clients focus on life post-divorce and guide them through the process to get there. For couples embarking on marriage, she helps them protect accumulated assets and create a plan for building assets, wealth and valuables in the future.

Sabra is currently writing a book to guide and empower couples through the process of "uncoupling," THE HARMONIOUS DIVORCE: THE FOUR STEP PROCESS TO UNCOUPLING. She is also the author of a chapter in the best-selling book SUCCESS FROM THE HEART. Connect with her at www.sabralawgroup.com.

SECTION F: USE OF PROFESSIONALS THROUGH DIVORCE & SEPARATION

CHAPTER 46

PRIVATE INVESTIGATORS

By Thomas Ruskin

During the 1920s private investigators became accessible to the average American. Since then the demand for private investigation has increased and has changed the needs of corporations, law firms, their clients, and individuals. Today, private investigators are used more for surveillances, background and due diligence investigations, social media issues for employment verifications, infidelity and fraud research, and for litigation purposes. Private investigation firms create a comforting bond and build a trust with the client so there is no false hope or misunderstanding about what is going to happen during an investigation.

How Investigative Firms Work

A private investigative firm in New York is not only ***licensed, bonded, and insured***, but maintains its standards no matter what the investigation is, and maintains their accreditations as per legal and New York state regulations. Licensing restrictions are dictated by each state and most states now require that an investigative firm be properly licensed. An investigative firm employs former law enforcement investigators as employees of the investigative firm and does not hire subcontractors. A firm has a sense of quality control where all investigations and reports are maintained in a similar fashion. Investigative firms are reliable, professional, and reachable 24 hours a day, 7 days a week, and 365 days a year. This availability is for the clients who have a problem talking during a regular 9-5 work day or have investigative concerns during off hours. Confidentiality is the number one rule of a private investigation firm, and all files are stored accurately and in accordance to state laws.

Being fully equipped with an investigative and clerical staff, an investigative firm can perform any type of investigation for any family law or matrimonial law dispute. Some examples include, but are not limited to, high-tech surveillances, latent print forensics, background or due diligence investigations, impeachment material for a litigation, computer forensics, ***GPS vehicle tracking***, executive protection, ***bug sweeps*** ("TSCM"), and polygraph examinations. For investigations involving family and matrimonial law cases, the investigator can dig up sufficient evidence of cheating, financial information, hidden accounts, possible impeachment materials with which to cross examine a potential witness, and civil case information; the investigator can also review relevant case documents, criminal evidence, police reports, accident reports or investigations, or find witnesses that could potentially testify.

Investigative Methods

Computer Forensics

Computer forensics is used on work or family computers to determine what may exist on a computer or what may have been purposely deleted, maybe in violation of a previous court order (*i.e.*, spoliation). A proper computer forensic examination by an experienced investigative firm can reveal unknown financial accounts and statements, business and personal relationships, unknown business deals, criminal activity, and other information that might be helpful in the investigation or case. A private investigative firm's computer forensic expert can testify to the materials that are found to allow for their proper submission into evidence.

GPS Vehicle Tracking

GPS vehicle tracking can be used where it is permissible by law. GPS vehicle tracking can determine a car's specific location, where the car is traveling to or from, the specific routes that were traveled, the speed of the car, and if the car made stops along the way to its destination. Using a GPS vehicle tracking device during a private investigation can allow the private investigator to know the location of the suspect's vehicle at all times and its travel history.

If being utilized during a surveillance, GPS vehicle tracking allows the investigative team to follow the subject from a distance, and if the subject beats a yellow light, the surveillance team does not lose the subject. It can also save the client money, as it still notifies the investigator where the subject has been, even when he/she is not under constant surveillance.

This form of investigation can be useful in child custody cases where the supervision of visitation of a parent may be in question. An example of this is a case where the husband's driving with his children was of issue, because he had previously been convicted of reckless driving and speeding. The covert installation of the GPS on the family car proved unequivocally through GPS records that the husband exceeded the speed limit, driving in excess of 90+ mph, countless times over a two hour drive and this in conjunction with a surveillance documenting the reckless driving and crossing in and out of a designated HOV lane. This led to the husband being court ordered to have parenting time with the children only with court ordered supervision.

Executive Protection

Executive protection can be utilized to ensure the safety of a well-known celebrity, individual, a corporate executive, or other individuals who may be exposed to a personal risk due to their current situation, litigation, association, relationship, etc. Bug sweeps, also known as a ***technical surveillance counter measure*** ("TSCM"), are used in the detection of eavesdropping equipment, hidden cameras, or transmitting devices within a home, office, car, or cell phone.

Polygraphs

Polygraphs are administered by a licensed experienced technician. Polygraphs are used to determine the truth, e.g., origin of theft or the validity of a witness and his/her potential testimony. Polygraph tests may be admitted into court evidence, depending on the jurisdiction and nature of the case.

Evidence

An investigative firm knows how to gather evidence legally so that it may be admitted in a court and used to prove the case. Before investigative evidence can be used in court, it must be formally presented to a judge who will then determine if it is admissible or not. Just like a credible witness whose testimony is used as evidence, an investigative firm provides the court with written investigative reports, time and date stamped videos and photos, and professional courtroom testimony. The firm always keeps the original, unedited videos for the duration of the case and for the statutory number of years thereafter.

Surveillances

Surveillances are conducted for many different reasons, such as:

- custody and visitation disputes;
- unreported income and business activity;
- determinations of negligence, abuse or substance abuse problems;
- marital issues (e.g., infidelity); or
- Alleged violation of court orders.

> Surveillances can sometimes be done remotely through CCTV systems, GPS, and other methods.

Surveillances can also substantiate unlawful behavior. It can help the party make intelligent decisions of how to legally proceed.

In the family law context, a surveillance can also determine if the children are being left alone, especially during scheduled visitation. It can likewise determine if a parent is working when representing to the court that he/she has no form of income. By surveilling that parent the other party can see what form of employment the other party has and the method of payment (e.g., off the books for cash).

Closed-Circuit Television

Closed-circuit Television ("CCTV") installations can be installed in common areas of the house used by the family excluding bedrooms and bathrooms. Cameras can take the shape of working electrical outlets, iPod docking stations, fire alarms, and any other common object found around the home. Depending on the state in which the parties reside, audio recording is not permitted unless one of two of the parties consents.

The CCTV system can be monitored from laptops, desktops, tablets, and smart phones in real time. Footage can be downloaded and memorialized, encompassing an entire day or a particular segment. "***A picture is worth a thousand words***," and evidence should always be prepared to be court admissible.

In a recent case, evidence was observed through the covert CCTV system that the wife in a pending divorce case was using cocaine and other drugs when she was home alone with her children. The husband requested the investigative firm utilize narcotic canines to locate and seize the drugs that existed in their residence. The investigators located the illegal narcotics, but legally vouchered them with the local police department. All was later entered into evidence at the child custody portion of the case.

Investigative Forensic Accounting might be used to determine whether or not a party is hiding or spending marital funds, has hidden accounts, or is laundering money. This, combined with a computer forensics investigation, can assist a party in a matrimonial case in getting his/her fair share of the marital assets.

Final Thoughts

A private investigation firm can provide their clients going through family or matrimonial issues with a more reliable and professional way of determining or discovering information. The investigative firm can reassure their clients that they are in good hands and whatever problem may arise, it will be thoroughly investigated and all relevant information will be uncovered.

If a case requires more than one investigator for a surveillance, a private investigative firm can provide the additional coverage, as well as accommodate any other client need. Investigators who are employed at an investigative firm are generally former law enforcement investigators, giving them the edge in conducting proper investigations, obtaining evidence that can be used by the attorneys in court, revealing unknown facts to allow the clients to make intelligent decisions, and supporting their clients who require investigative services.

Thomas Ruskin

Thomas Ruskin has been the President of the CMP Protective and Investigative Group, Inc. for over the past decade. The CMP Group is an internationally recognized investigative and security firm with clients and corporations from around the world.

Thomas Ruskin is a highly decorated former New York City Police Detective Investigator. He was responsible for Crisis Management for the Mayor, Police Commissioner and Deputy Commissioners of Operations and Crime Control Strategies for New York City. He has been involved in cases that have received worldwide attention, including the 1993 terrorist attack on the World Trade Center, the NYC subway system bombing, airline crashes, police shootings, hostage situations and major organized crime and narcotic cases.

The majority of Mr. Ruskin's background ranging over two decades in law enforcement, has been spent in the field of investigation. He began his career with the Department of Investigations Inspector General offices of the Department of Environmental Protection and Fire Department, rising to the position of Senior Investigator. In the NYPD Mr. Ruskin was assigned to the Burglary Latent Print Unit, Anti-Crime Squad, and the Organized Control Bureau-Narcotics Division's Special Projects Unit. He was responsible for cases that lead to arrests of individuals who committed Federal and State crimes and was responsible for a 3 million dollar federally subsidized undercover program.

Mr. Ruskin's background includes responsibility for the protection of President Bill Clinton, Vice-President Al Gore, Mrs. Hillary Clinton, Mrs. Tipper Gore, 1998 Presidential candidate Senator Robert Dole and other national and international dignitaries and Heads of State. Mr. Ruskin has received specialized training from the NYPD Intelligence Division and the United States Secret Service in Dignitary Protection.

Mr. Ruskin is recognized as an international investigative, security and crisis management expert by various news organizations including NBC, ABC, The Today Show, Good Morning America, CNN, Fox News, Channel,Sky News and 1010 WINS News. He has made frequent appearances on various TV and radio shows.

SECTION F: USE OF PROFESSIONALS THROUGH DIVORCE & SEPARATION

CHAPTER 47

CREDIT REPAIR PROFESSIONALS

By Andrea Kent

Going through a divorce is very difficult. Financial issues, particularly credit, make it even harder. Sadly, a vindictive or irresponsible spouse can make it worse by trying to hurt their soon-to-be former wife or husband by making large credit purchases on joint accounts with the intent of punishing the other person with huge debts or wrecking their credit history.

What they usually do not understand is that by doing so they are also likely to destroy their own credit history at the same time. It's a bad situation to be in if someone has control over a person's credit. Credit repair specialists can help people pre- and post-divorce to provide guidance on protecting their credit.

Getting Control of Financial Life

Create a Post-Divorce Budget

Someone recovering from a divorce should not take on more obligations than they can handle under the divorce agreement or that person's credit could suffer. For most people going through a divorce, they are moving from a dual-income household to a single income budget, and as a result, both people will need to make tough choices. Housing costs should take top consideration in the new budget. This could include a mortgage payment, along with the property taxes, insurance, and maintenance or rent. Don't forget the security deposit and renters insurance. Utilities and phone bills are often extra and fall into the housing category.

Then factor in the other obligations, credit cards, auto payments, personal loans, and any other insurance costs. If someone is close to his or her limit, consider what can be cut, such as cable, a premium cell phone plan or other luxuries.

Take Stock of Debts and Credit lines

If someone was married for a number of years, that person may have forgotten about all of the accounts that he or she shared with their spouse such as an unused ***home equity line of credit*** or a Sears's credit card that person opened seven Christmases ago. To help jog this person's memory, it is recommended to pull a credit report to see the accounts that person has. That person should note the ones listed as individual, joint, or authorized user accounts. An individual account in that person's name means that person is solely responsible for the debt, unless that person lives in a ***community property state*** (e.g., California, Texas, Arizona) or have agreed otherwise in the divorce settlement agreement. A joint account means both people share responsibility for paying off any debt on that account. An authorized user means the account is held individually by one person who allows another to use the card, but not be responsible for the balance.

> In community property states, any debts acquired during the marriage and within those states are considered jointly owned. New York is not a community property state.

Not every lender or creditor reports to the credit bureaus, so that person may miss some accounts. Therefore, it is also recommended to look at that stack of unused credit cards in your desk drawer.

Remove Ex-Spouse as Authorized User

A person going through a divorce should note every credit card that lists his or her (ex) spouse as an authorized user. Unless your separation or divorce settlement agreement says differently, taking this step will help ensure that you are not responsible for repaying any debts incurred by your (ex) spouse. It is easy to remove an authorized user from a credit card. That person simply needs to call the credit card issuer and ask for the spouse's name to be removed.

> While a divorce is pending in court, neither party should remove his or her spouse on their credit cards as it might violate the automatic orders. Consult your matrimonial attorney before doing this if you are currently involved in litigation.

Similarly, it's just as important that a person that went through a divorce remove him or herself as an authorized user from the (ex) spouse's credit card accounts too because this accounts can still be included on that person's credit report and factored into the credit score. However, Experian says that they only include authorized user accounts on its credit reports if the history is positive.

Anyone should be able to ***contact the credit card issuer*** and have his or her name removed if the spouse refuses to do it. An attorney should not be necessary to do this. If the credit card issuer doesn't allow it, then that person should contact the credit reporting agencies and dispute the inclusion of the account on the credit report.

Untangle Joint Accounts, if Possible

The task of separating joint accounts where both spouses are responsible is more complicated. Ideally, a married couple should pay any existing balances and close any joint accounts before going into a divorce. However, each person may want to keep an account or two in his or her name only. It is important to continue using credit so that a current credit history can be maintained.

The important thing to understand is that the judgment of divorce does not change the contracts that you have with each lender. The decree is only an agreement between the court and the divorcing couple with regard to who will make the debt payments on each account.

Only the lender can change the contract, and as long this person's name is on the contract, the account will be reported to this person's credit history. In order to separate responsibility, each lender should be contacted to request that it change the credit contract so that one party is made responsible for the debt.

It's worth trying to ***refinance a mortgage*** into one spouse's name if that is possible. More information on mortgage refinancing is found in Chapter 41. In some cases, the lender may not agree to do so because often times an account is made joint because only one party cannot demonstrate an ability to repay the debt alone. If the person who wants to keep his or her name on the account cannot qualify for the debt based on their individual income and credit history, the lender may require that the balance be paid in full before removing one party form the contract.

If the parties can't split the accounts, divide the responsibilities of the joint debt. For example, the person who lives in the house takes on the mortgage. The spouse who gets the car gets the auto loan, too. Spell out the arrangements in the divorce agreement. The divorce settlement agreement should also spell out "what-if" scenarios. For instance, if a spouse is going to miss a payment on a joint debt, he or she must notify the other spouse in advance, so that person has the option to make the payment and avoid denting his or her credit.

Keep Tabs on Joint Accounts

Someone going through a divorce should ask his or her lender to send that person a copy of the joint account's statement each month, even if his or her spouse is responsible for making payments on that account. Some may do it automatically while others may allow access to account records online.

Otherwise, that person should pull his or her free credit report from a different credit reporting agency every four months to make sure all accounts are being paid on time. Everyone is entitled to a free credit report from each of the three major credit reporting agencies every 12 months under the federal law through AnnualCreditReport.com.

If a spouse isn't making the payments on the agreed accounts, then contact a matrimonial attorney right away. The court likely will make the spouse pay any legal fees if the creditor comes after this person along with reimbursement of any other out-of-pocket expenses.

Although it might be difficult, it is recommended for couples to try to continue communicating about finances as they go through the divorce process. Working together to separate financial lives will help smooth the transition for both people.

Working with a Credit Repair Specialist

There are a number of advantages of working with a credit repair specialist while going through a challenging divorce when the damage that can be done if finances aren't handled correctly is usually not on someone's mind. The best time to consult a credit repair specialist is before the actual divorce because they will provide a free credit consultation and advice on what to do in each individual's situation. If someone's credit has been damaged by a divorce, a credit repair specialist can help to remove negative items that may have been caused by the situation including any liens, judgments, collections, charge-offs and late payments that may have appeared on the individual's credit report. A credit repair specialist will work to remove the negative items which help to improve the person's credit score. The credit repair service is based on the amount of work each individual would need. Hiring a credit repair specialist can be a great resource to help getting anyone's finances back on track before, during, or after going through a difficult divorce.

Andrea Kent

Andrea's professional background includes over 30 years in Financial Services working 4.5 years as the VP of Mortgage Lending for Guaranteed Rate and prior to that Andrea spent 27 years as a payments expert for American Express and Visa Inc. Her extensive experience in mortgage lending and credit cards is a valuable asset for her clients at Prime National. With Andrea's long history of working with banks and credit card companies, she really understands credit which is so misunderstood.

Andrea knows that having a good credit score is critical to one's financial success. Without it you can't get a good rate on a mortgage, credit card or car loan, rent an apartment, or even apply for a job. Her company, Prime National Credit Repair offers industry-leading credit repair services backed with a 100% money-back guarantee. They have an excellent reputation with an A+ rating with the BBB.

For more information about Prime National, visit www.primenational.com.

SECTION IV: SPECIAL COURT PROCEEDINGS

SECTION A: FAMILY OFFENSE PROCEDINGS

By Joseph Nivin, Esq.

To obtain an ***Order of Protection*** in Family Court, a litigant must file a family offense petition. Because people's journeys through the Family Court and Supreme Court-Matrimonial systems often begin with family offense proceedings, discussion of this area of Family Court practice is essential for a party's understanding of court processes.

Does the Case Belong in Family Court?

Jurisdiction

Someone involved in a Family Court or matrimonial proceeding will likely hear attorneys and judges talk about "jurisdiction." "***Jurisdiction***" is, simply put, the court's authority to hear the case.

There are two types of jurisdiction: "***personal***" jurisdiction and "***subject matter***" jurisdiction. The Court obtains "personal jurisdiction" over a person when that individual is duly served with the proper paperwork. It is rare that people in family and matrimonial proceedings challenge personal jurisdiction. However, family offense cases are often dismissed on the ground that the Family Court lacks ***subject matter jurisdiction***.

When a court has subject matter jurisdiction, then the case is in the correct court. Subject matter jurisdiction in family offense proceedings is governed by N.Y. Family Court § 812(1), which states that Family Court can hear cases involving (1) family offenses committed between (2) members of the same family or household.

"Members of the Same Family or Household"

Pursuant to N.Y. Family Court Act § 812(1), "members of the same family or household" include:

- people who are ***related biologically***,
- people who ***are married*** to each other,
- people who ***used to be married*** to each other,

- people who have a ***child in common***, and
- people who are or used to be in an "***intimate relationship***."

The Family Court will decide whether the parties are or used to be in an "intimate relationship." The Family Court Act explicitly states that an "intimate relationship" does not include relationships between "casual acquaintance[s]," or "ordinary fraternization between two individuals in business or social contexts." In determining whether two people are in an "intimate relationship," the Court will consider "the nature or type of relationship. . .[,] the ***frequency of interaction*** between the persons[,] and the ***duration of the relationship***" (Emphasis added).

The Court will almost always find that two people are, or were, in an "intimate relationship" when the parties were in a long-term romantic relationship. This includes teenagers who are, or were formerly, dating. The Court will generally not find that the parties were in an intimate relationship in cases where a person files a petition against his or her ex-lover's new romantic partner, where the person files a petition against his or her ***stepchild's parent***, or where a person files a petition against someone whose romantic advances he or she rejected.

If someone cannot proceed with a case in Family Court because that person does not have a relationship with the other party, then that person can still seek an order of protection by filing a ***police report***. Criminal Court has the same ***power to issue*** orders of protection as Family Court.

What is a "Family Offense?"

N.Y. Family Court Act § 812(1) provides a ***list of crimes*** and ***violations*** which constitute "family offenses." Family offenses include:

- disorderly conduct,
- harassment (first and second degree),
- aggravated harassment in the second degree,
- sexual misconduct,
- forcible touching,

- sexual abuse in the third degree or second degree[59],
- stalking (first, second, third, and fourth degrees),
- criminal mischief,
- menacing (second and third degrees),
- reckless endangerment,
- criminal obstruction of breathing or blood circulation,
- strangulation (first and second degrees),
- assault (second and third degrees),
- attempted assault,
- identity theft (first, second, and third degrees),
- grand larceny (third and fourth degrees), and
- coercion in the second degree[60].

Petitions for Orders of Protection on Behalf of Children

Parents can file for orders of protection on behalf of their children. Parents who file these types of petitions must have a ***relationship with the respondent*** that would put the case within the Family Court's jurisdiction. For example, parents can file for orders of protection on behalf of their own children against the other parent (i.e., they have a child-in-common), against their own parents or siblings (i.e., related by blood), and against their current or former romantic partners (i.e., intimate relationship). However, they cannot file petitions for orders of protection in Family Court, for example, against the other parent's ***new romantic partner***.

A parent who feels that his or her child's safety is being endangered, and cannot pursue a Family Court order of protection against that person, can still pursue criminal charges by filing a police report, and can contact the local child welfare agency.

---

[59] Only pursuant to N.Y. Penal Law § 130.60(1), meaning that the perpetrator subjected the victim to sexual contact, where the victim was incapable of consent by reason of a factor other than being less than seventeen years old.

[60] Only pursuant to N.Y. Penal Law §§ 135.60(1), (2) and (3), meaning that the perpetrator compelled or induced the victim to engage in conduct which the victim had a legal right not to engage in, or compelled the victim not to engage in conduct which the victim had a legal right to engage in, by making the victim fear that the perpetrator would (1) cause physical injury to the victim, (2) cause damage to property, or (3) engage in other criminal conduct.

Intersection Between Criminal Court Cases and Family Court Cases

Concurrent Jurisdiction

Family Court has "concurrent jurisdiction" over family offense cases with Criminal Court, except where the ***respondent is less than sixteen years of age***. This means that both Family Court and Criminal Court can hear family offense allegations. However, where a person seeks an order of protection against someone who is under sixteen years old, then only Family Court can hear the case.

If the respondent is arrested, and the petitioner files for an order of protection in Family Court, the criminal case will continue even while the Family Court case is ongoing. Similarly, while the respondent is in Criminal Court, the petitioner can still proceed with his or her Family Court case. The Criminal Court will generally issue its own order of protection even if the Family Court has already issued one.

A significant difference between Family Court cases and Criminal Court cases is that Family Court cases are prosecuted by the ***petitioners themselves*** and/or their attorneys, whereas Criminal Court cases are prosecuted by the ***District Attorney's Office***. In the Family Court case, the respondent does not face criminal penalties unless the Family Court finds that the respondent violated an order of protection.

The Petitioner's Perspective

If the Criminal Court issues a final order of protection in the middle of the family offense proceeding, then the petitioner may consider withdrawing the Family Court case, based upon the existence of the Criminal Court order of protection. Below is a discussion of the factors for the petitioner to consider when making that decision.

If the respondent violates the order of protection, and there is an order of protection only in Criminal Court, then the petitioner can ***only seek sanctions*** against the respondent in Criminal Court. The sanctions for violating an order of protection are more severe in Criminal Court than in Family Court. However, the petitioner has to rely upon the District Attorney's Office to prosecute the respondent in Criminal Court. In contrast, in Family Court, the petitioner, or petitioner's counsel, is in charge of prosecuting the respondent. The petitioner cannot prosecute a petition for sanctions in Family Court after withdrawing the Family Court petition.

The petitioner should keep in mind that if the respondent is convicted in Criminal Court of committing the acts alleged in the family offense petition, then the petitioner can seek "***summary judgment***" in Family Court. That means that the petitioner can say that it is no longer necessary to prove the case in Family Court, because it was already proven in Criminal Court, and the petition should be granted based upon the criminal conviction.

The Respondent's Perspective

The existence of a criminal case has serious repercussions for the respondent. Where the respondent has a pending criminal case, it is critical for the respondent not to speak about the allegations to anybody, especially not in the courtroom in Family Court. Family Court proceedings are recorded, and any statements by the respondent in Family Court are easily ***accessible to the prosecutor***. These statements can be used against the respondent in Criminal Court. The respondent should exercise extreme caution about testifying in his or her own defense in Family Court if there is a pending criminal case based upon the same allegations.

Family Offense Procedure

Initial Filing

When the petitioner files for an order of protection in Family Court, he or she will be given a form to fill out describing both the respondent's ***biographical information*** (e.g., name, address, date of birth, etc.), and the ***incident(s)*** which led to the need for an order of protection. The Clerk's office will convert the information into a formal petition. The allegations must include illegal conduct that was committed by the respondent which constitutes a family offense. If the petitioner does not allege sufficient facts, then the petition will be dismissed.

This stage of the case is critical, as the Court may preclude the petitioner from offering evidence that is ***not in the petition***. The petitioner can, and should, include information regarding the most serious instances of domestic violence, even if they took place a long time ago. The Court cannot deny an application for an order of protection simply because the acts of domestic violence took place a long time ago, but the Court can consider the passage of time when determining the length and terms of the order of protection.

The petitioner will notice that there is very limited space in the form that the clerk provides. The petitioner can write the allegations on a ***separate sheet of paper***.

After the Clerk creates the petition, the petitioner will be called to appear before a judge or a referee. The purpose of this appearance, known as the initial appearance, is to determine whether to grant a temporary order of protection, which will last until the next court appearance. The Court will ask ***questions about the allegations*** in the petition.

> A referee is not a judge, but rather an attorney who works for the court.

While it is not definite, the final order of protection is likely to include the same terms as the ***temporary order of protection***, if the petitioner prevails in the case. It is even more likely that the terms of the temporary order of protection will continue until the end of the case, when the Court decides whether, and under which terms, to issue a final order of protection.

After appearing before the judge or referee, the petitioner will get a ***summons***, which is a paper directing the respondent to appear in court. The petitioner will also receive a copy of the petition that was created by the Clerk's office.

The Court may issue a ***warrant for the respondent's arrest*** if it finds that:

- the summons ***cannot be served***,
- the respondent is likely to ***leave the jurisdiction***,
- the summons would be ***ineffectual***,
- the ***safety of the petitioner*** is endangered,
- the ***safety of the child*** is endangered, or
- ***aggravating circumstances exist*** which require the respondent's immediate arrest, including (a) physical injury to the petitioner caused by the respondent, (b) the use of a dangerous instrument against the petitioner by the respondent, (c) a history of repeated violations of prior orders of protection by the respondent, (d) prior convictions for crimes against the petitioner by the respondent, or (e) exposure of any family or household

member to physical injury by the respondent which causes immediate and ongoing danger to the petitioner or any member of the petitioner's family or household.

Service of the Summons and Petition

The petitioner will need to make sure that the respondent is ***served with the summons, petition, and temporary order of protection***. The petitioner should have the respondent served as quickly as possible, as the temporary order of protection is not effective until the respondent is served with it. That means that the respondent cannot be arrested for violating the order of protection until service is completed.

> Some courts also provide the documents to the Sheriff's Department to serve upon the respondent.

The ***police will serve*** the respondent with the petition, but will not serve him or her with a petition for custody. If the parties live together, and the temporary order of protection excludes the respondent from the home, then the petitioner should have the police complete service. The police will make sure that the respondent leaves the home. For the petitioner's safety, it is advisable to ***not be in the home*** when the respondent is served if the respondent is being excluded. Anybody over the age of eighteen years who is not a party to the case can serve the respondent. The respondent must be served at least ***twenty-four hours*** before the next court date, cannot be served on a Sunday, and cannot be served on a federal holiday. If there is also a custody petition, that must be served at least ***eight days*** before the court date. Therefore, the petitioner should have the papers served at least eight days in advance if there is an intention to have the respondent served with the custody petition at the same time as the family offense petition.

After the respondent is served, the petitioner will receive an "affidavit of service," which is a sworn statement completed by the person who served the respondent. The petitioner should make sure that the affidavit is completed properly, and that it is notarized, or else the next court date may be unnecessarily adjourned. If the police served the respondent, the petitioner should make sure to get the ***affidavit of service***. If you are the petitioner, do not listen to them if they tell you that you do not need it! If you do not bring the affidavit to the next court appearance, then the court date may be adjourned for a proper affidavit.

If the person serving the respondent is unable to effectuate service, then that person should go to the respondent's home and/or place of employment three times at three different times of day. That person should then complete an "***affidavit of attempted service***," which should detail the efforts to have the respondent served. The petitioner must bring the affidavit to court on the adjourn date.

Return of Service

The next court date will be for return of service, also known as ***return of process***. The purpose of this court appearance is for the petitioner to provide the affidavit of service to the Court. If you are the respondent, this will be the first time that you appear.

Return of service is the first time that the parties are in court together. Therefore, the parties are often very eager to discuss the allegations in the petition. However, the litigants will not be permitted to speak much, as the only purpose of this appearance is to make sure that the respondent was served.

There are ***three scenarios*** that can transpire at return of service:

1. **<u>The respondent was served and appears in court</u>.**

If the respondent was served and appears, then the Court will first advise both parties of their right to be represented by attorneys (unless, of course, they show up with attorneys). The Court will advise both parties that if they cannot afford counsel, then the Court can appoint attorneys to represent them free of charge. Both parties may ask for time to retain counsel, which is likely to be granted. If a party requests ***assignment of counsel***, the Court may ask questions regarding the party's financial status, or adjourn the case for financial documents, such as tax returns, W2s, and paystubs. The Court may also appoint counsel on that same day after asking questions about the party's financial status.

If a party waives counsel, and asks to represent him or herself, the Court will advise the party of the disadvantages of self-representation. The parties may make different choices, e.g. the petitioner may retain an attorney, the respondent may represent him or herself, and vice versa.

If the petitioner is seeking an order of protection on behalf of the child or children, and/or there are custody petitions filed, then the Court will likely assign an attorney to represent the child or children.

Unless the case is adjourned for purposes of counsel, then the Court will inquire of the respondent whether he or she wishes to consent to the order of protection. If the respondent agrees for an order of protection to be entered against him or her, and both parties agree to the period that the order of protection will run for, then the case will end on that day. The Court will "***allocute***" the respondent. This means that the Court will ask questions of the respondent to make sure that he or she is agreeing to the order of protection knowingly and voluntarily. After the allocution, the Court will issue an order of protection against the respondent.

If the respondent does not agree to the order of protection, and the petitioner still wants the order, then the case will be adjourned for a hearing. There will be a new court date within three business days if the parties lived together, the temporary order of protection excludes the respondent from the home, and the respondent wishes to be allowed back into the home.

2. **The respondent was not served and does not appear in court.**

If the petitioner was unable to have the respondent served, then the petitioner should come to court with an affidavit of attempted service, completed by the person who was attempting to serve the respondent. The Court will likely authorize ***substituted service***, also known as "nail and mail." That means that someone who is not a party will have to mail a copy of the summons, petition, and order of protection to the respondent, and also affix a copy to the door.

The Court may also issue a warrant for the respondent upon a finding that the summons cannot be served.

3. **The respondent was served and does not appear**.

If the respondent is served, and does not appear in court, then the Court will likely permit the petitioner to proceed to "***inquest***." This means that the Court will permit the petitioner to present his or her case without the respondent being present. The Court will only allow the petitioner to proceed to inquest if he or she brings a completed affidavit of service. Otherwise, even if the petitioner tells the Court that the respondent was served, the case will be adjourned for new service.

At an inquest, either the Court, or counsel, will ask the petitioner questions about the allegations in the petition. The petitioner may also submit items such as police reports, medical records, and text messages. After testimony is completed, the petitioner should ask for an "***adverse inference***" against the respondent for his or her failure to appear in court and testify. That means that the respondent's nonappearance is itself evidence that the allegations are true.

If the petitioner presents sufficient evidence that the respondent committed a family offense, then the Court will issue an order of protection against the respondent. The petitioner will have to arrange for the respondent to be served with a copy of the order of protection, or else the respondent cannot be arrested for violating it. The petitioner should always carry a copy of the order of protection, with the affidavit of service, and keep another copy in a safe place at home.

As an alternative to an inquest, the Court can also issue a ***warrant for the respondent***.

The Attorney for the Child

The Court may appoint an attorney to represent the child or children, if there are custody petitions, and/or the petition seeks an order restricting the respondent's contact with the child or children. Attorneys for children all undergo specialized training on interviewing and representing children.

The attorney for the child will ask the custodial parent to bring the child or children to the attorney's office, to conduct an interview outside of the presence of the parents. The attorney will have to determine whether the child is capable of "***knowing, voluntary, and considered judgment***." If the attorney determines that the child is indeed capable of such judgment, then the attorney will advocate a position in court which is consistent with the child's wishes. If the attorney determines that the child is not capable of such judgment, then the attorney should conduct an independent investigation to determine a position which is consistent with the child's best interests, and advocate that position to the Court.

Information which children present to their attorneys is subject to attorney-client privilege, which means that attorneys for children cannot share the children's statements with the parents. However, the attorney for the child should state his or her client's position in court, especially the child's wishes regarding custody and visitation. The attorney for the child is also likely to state in court whether the child confirmed or denied the allegations in the family offense petition.

The Exclusion Hearing

If the parties ***previously lived together***, and the temporary order of protection excludes the respondent from the home over his or her objection, then the respondent has the right to an exclusion hearing within ***three business days***. The Court will have to determine whether there is "***good cause***" to exclude the respondent from the home, which is effectively a determination of whether the petitioner would be in danger with the respondent in the home.

During what is called "***direct examination***," the petitioner will tell the Court why he or she needs the order. The petitioner should focus on the most recent events causing the need for an order of protection. The petitioner should tell the Court about instances of physical violence, substance abuse issues, access to weapons, mental illness, and the effects of domestic violence upon the children.

If the petitioner has an attorney, then the attorney will ask questions to elicit this information. Either the petitioner or the petitioner's attorney can present evidence to the Court, such as police reports and medical records.

Either the respondent or the respondent's attorney will conduct "cross-examination," and ask questions to show either that the petitioner is not telling the truth, or that there is more to what happened than what was stated during direct examination.

After cross-examination, the petitioner or petitioner's attorney will have the opportunity to do "re-direct," and explain certain information which came out during cross-examination. Then, the respondent or the respondent's attorney will do "re-cross," and ask questions about the information elicited during re-direct examination.

The petitioner may then call additional witnesses, who will also be subject to cross-examination.

The respondent will be able to ***present his or her version***. The respondent, and his or her witnesses, will also be subject to cross-examination.

After both parties present their cases, the Court will decide whether to continue the order excluding the respondent from the home. If the Court decides not to continue the order, then the Court may issue a "limited," or "***usual terms***," order of protection, which is an order that permits the respondent to live with the petitioner, but directs the respondent to only act in a lawful manner.

The Family Offense Trial

Fact-Finding Hearing

If the respondent does not consent to an order of protection, and the petitioner still wishes to have one, then there will be a trial, also called ***fact-finding***. Before the case goes to trial, the Court may adjourn the case one or more times for a "settlement conference," to determine whether the parties can agree to an appropriate disposition, e.g. an order of protection on consent, or withdrawal of the petition.

At trial, the petitioner will have to prove that the respondent committed one or more of the family offenses alleged in the petition. If the respondent disputes whether the parties have the necessary relationship to bring the case within the Family Court's jurisdiction (generally, whether the parties are or were in an intimate relationship), then the petitioner will also have to prove that. However, most trials center on the issue of whether the respondent committed family offenses against the petitioner.

Either the petitioner or petitioner's attorney will present evidence to the Court, including but not limited to photographs, text messages, and medical and police records. The petitioner will testify about the incidents described in the petition. If the petitioner is represented by an attorney, then petitioner's counsel will ask questions to elicit that information.

The petitioner will be subject to cross-examination, by the respondent or his/her attorney. The respondent or respondent's counsel will ask questions, to show that the petitioner's direct testimony is not true, and/or that there is more to what happened than what is presented by the petitioner.

After cross-examination, the petitioner will conduct "***re-direct***," and present testimony designed to explain the information that was elicited during cross-examination. Then, the respondent will testify about the information elicited during re-direct, which is called "***re-cross***."

The petitioner can present other witnesses, who will be cross-examined. The witnesses must be people who actually saw and/or heard the events which constituted family offenses, not just people who know the respondent's "character," or who the petitioner spoke to about the allegations.

At the conclusion of the petitioner's case, the respondent may ask to dismiss the petition due to the failure of the petitioner to present a "***prima facie***" case. For the Court to dismiss the case at this stage, the Court will have to find that even if all of the testimony and evidence presented was true, it would not be enough for the petitioner to get an order of protection.

If the Court grants the motion to dismiss, then the petition will be dismissed, and there will be no order of protection. If the Court finds that the petitioner presented sufficient evidence of a family offense, then the respondent will present his or her case.

The respondent will present evidence, such as police records, photographs, text messages, and medical records. The respondent can testify on his or her own behalf, and will be subject to cross-examination. The respondent can also call other witnesses, who will also be cross-examined.

It is generally not sufficient for the respondent to say that the petitioner's allegations are false. In order for the respondent to prevail, the respondent should present evidence of a motive for the petitioner to fabricate the allegations. For example, it is common for parties who have a child in common to also have other cases taking place at the same time, such as a divorce proceeding, a custody case, and/or a child support case. The respondent may allege that the petitioner is using the family offense proceeding to pressure the respondent to agree to a resolution of those cases. The respondent may also argue that the petitioner is trying to get him or her out of the marital home, in order to gain an advantage in the divorce proceeding.

If the respondent fails to testify, then the petitioner can ask for an "***adverse inference***," which means that the respondent's failure to testify is evidence that the allegations in the petition are true.

After both parties present their cases, then the Court will have to decide whether the petitioner proved the allegations in the petition by a standard called a "***preponderance of the evidence***." That means that the Court will have to decide whether more than fifty percent of the evidence that it heard, and believed, showed that the respondent committed family offenses against the petitioner.

If the Court decides that the petitioner failed to prove his or her case, then the case will be dismissed and there will be no order of protection.

If the Court decides that the petitioner proved his or her case by a preponderance of the evidence, then the Court will issue an "order of fact finding," which is a court order stating that the respondent committed acts of domestic violence against the petitioner. If there is an existing custody case, then the Court has to consider those acts of domestic violence when it decides custody.

The Court will then proceed to disposition, which may or may not require a new court date.

Dispositional Hearing

If the petitioner wins at trial, then the Court will proceed to disposition, which is where the Court decides ***what to do about the acts*** of domestic violence committed by the respondent.

If the Court finds that the petitioner proved "aggravated circumstances," then the Court can issue an order of protection for up to five years. "***Aggravated circumstances***" include:

- ***physical injury*** or serious physical injury to the petitioner caused by the respondent,
- the use of a ***dangerous instrument*** against the petitioner by the respondent,
- a history of ***repeated violations*** of prior orders of protection by the respondent,
- ***prior convictions*** for crimes against the petitioner by the respondent, or
- exposure of any family or household member to physical injury by the respondent and like incidents, behaviors, and occurrences which to the Court constitute an immediate and ***ongoing danger*** to the petitioner, or any member of the petitioner's family or household.

In the absence of aggravated circumstances, the Court can issue an order of protection for up to ***two years***. The Court can also place the respondent on probation, which is rarely done. Furthermore, the Court can issue a suspended judgment, which is an order that the respondent would have to abide by certain conditions, but does not include an order of protection. If the Court finds that the respondent violated the suspended judgment, then the Court can issue an order of protection.

Orders of Protection on Consent

If the parties wish to avoid a trial, then a common resolution is a "consent" order of protection. The respondent's consent to an order of protection is not an admission that he or she committed the acts alleged in the petition.

The parties may seek to avoid a trial if they have retained counsel, and wish to avoid the expense of a trial. Additionally, the parties may have children in common, and understand that a trial would sabotage their ability to co-parent their children. The parties may also wish to avoid the ***emotional strain of a trial***. Furthermore, the respondent may consider that a judge could be less favorable to his or her side during the custody case after hearing detailed testimony about acts of domestic violence.

Unlike after a trial, if an order of protection is issued on consent, then there will be no court order stating that the respondent committed acts of domestic violence against the petitioner. Therefore, if the petitioner wishes for the Court to consider the acts of domestic violence in the custody context, then the allegations would have to be proven at a custody trial.

Most parties will agree that the order of protection will run for a period ***shorter than two years***, e.g. six months or one year. The petitioner guarantees that he or she will receive an order of protection, but avoids the need to prove the allegations at trial. The respondent avoids the risk that the Court may issue an order of protection for a lengthier period of time.

Types of Orders of Protection

An order of protection may direct the respondent to abide by the following conditions of behavior:

- To ***stay away*** from the home, school, business, or place of employment of the petitioner and/or the child (e.g., day care, place of worship) (usually called a "stay away" order),
- To refrain from committing a family offense or criminal offense against the petitioner and/or the child, and to refrain from ***harassing, intimidating, or threatening*** them (called a "limited" or "usual terms" order),
- To refrain from any acts of commission or omission that create an ***unreasonable risk*** to the health, safety, or welfare of a child,

- To pay the petitioner's ***reasonable costs and counsel*** fees,
- To participate in ***services***, such as a batterer's program and/or drug and alcohol counseling,
- To pay for the petitioner's ***medical expenses*** arising from the domestic violence,
- To refrain from injuring or killing the petitioner's ***pet***,
- To return ***identification documents*** (e.g., social security card or birth certificate), or
- To observe such ***other conditions*** as are necessary to protect the petitioner.

When Children Are Involved

If the order of protection directs that the respondent stay away from his or her child, then the respondent should ask that the order be "***subject to orders of custody and visitation***." That means that if the Court grants visitation to the respondent, then the respondent will not be in violation of the order for exercising that visitation.

If the order of protection directs that the respondent refrain from communicating with the child, then the respondent should seek a specific order of telephone, mail, and electronic contact. That avoids any possibility that the respondent will be in violation of the order by sending birthday and holiday cards, calling the children, or communicating with them via e-mail and social media. Many judges and referees require that the respondent file a petition for visitation to have these orders granted.

It is prudent for a respondent, who has children in common with the petitioner, to file a petition for custody and/or visitation. Parties are rarely granted visitation orders on the day that they file their petitions, so filing a petition early in the process can save the respondent from going a significant period of time without contact with the children.

Many courts will also issue orders of protection which permit parties who have children in common to communicate with each other only for purposes of discussing the children's health and well-being. In those cases, it is advisable that the parties only communicate with each other in writing, to avoid allegations that the respondent committed a violation.

Collateral Consequences of Orders of Protection

Intersection with Child Custody and Divorce Cases

Some of the most serious collateral consequences of orders of protection include their impact upon pending custody cases and divorce cases. If the Court issues the order of protection after a hearing, then there will be a court order stating that the respondent committed acts of domestic violence against the petitioner, which the Court has to consider when determining custody. If the Court issues an order of protection which restricts the respondent's contact with the children, then it is very unlikely that the respondent will have ***residential custody***, even if the order is subject to orders of custody and visitation.

If a petitioner receives a temporary order of protection at the very beginning of the case, before the respondent has been served, which directs the respondent to stay away from the children, then the petitioner has already gained an advantage in the custody case. The petitioner will already be established as the custodial parent on a "temporary" basis. The petitioner may "drag out" the family offense proceeding, while having a temporary order of protection which restricts the respondent's contact with the children. By the time that the family offense case is over, no matter the outcome, the petitioner will already have an argument in the custody case that the children have been in the petitioner's care for a ***lengthy period of time***, and that the children's stability requires that the petitioner have a final order of custody.

In divorce cases, attorneys commonly instruct their clients not to leave the marital home. It is well-known that the party who is in the marital home will likely get the house, residential custody of the children, and child support. The conventional means to get the other party out of the marital home is via an application for "***exclusive use and occupancy***." However, this will lead to a significant expense for attorney's fees, in addition to the filing fee in Supreme Court. Some people file family offense petitions because there are no filing fees in Family Court, and they can be done without an attorney. In some cases, they can get an order excluding the respondent from the marital home in one day, without spending money on attorney's fees, and therefore gain a significant advantage in the matrimonial proceeding.

Even if the petitioner only obtains a "limited" order of protection, it can be used to ultimately get the respondent excluded from the home. There are cases where the petitioner obtains a limited order of protection, and provokes the respondent until he or she violates the limited order of protection. Then, the petitioner can call the police, and have the respondent arrested for violating the order. In that case, it is likely that the Criminal Court will exclude the respondent from the marital home, and thereby give the petitioner an advantage in the matrimonial proceeding.

The Domestic Violence Registry

Anyone who has an order of protection issued against him or her is listed on the "domestic violence registry." That registry is available to court personnel. Therefore, if someone has an order of protection issued against him or her, then that information will be available in any future custody proceedings, including proceedings involving children who are not involved in the case that resulted in the issuance of the order of protection.

Furthermore, some employers search the domestic violence registry when making employment decisions, particularly employers in the field of law enforcement. Additionally, orders of protection may negatively impact upon applications for permanent residence and/or citizenship.

Firearms

It is a federal offense for anyone to possess a firearm while being the restricted party on an order of protection. There is a limited exception for military and law enforcement officers, but only when they are on duty. Additionally, the Court has the authority in family offense proceedings to revoke a license to possess a firearm, order the respondent ineligible for such a license, and order the immediate surrender of any firearms.

Mandatory Arrest

New York is a "mandatory arrest" state. Therefore, a police officer must arrest someone where there is probable cause to believe that the person violated an order of protection. As a result, someone who obtains an order of protection has the ability to have the restricted party ***arrested almost at will***.

IMPORTANT: If there is an allegation that someone violated an order of protection by having contact with the protected party, then the person who is accused of the violation will be arrested, even if the protected party ***invited the contact***. Therefore, if the wife has an order of protection directing the husband to stay away from her, and the wife invites the husband to have contact with her, the husband can still be arrested. The wife will not get in trouble unless there is also an order of protection against her which restricts her contact with the husband.

Post-Disposition Proceedings

Extensions of the Order of Protection

If the petitioner believes that there is a need to extend the order of protection after it expires, then he or she can file a petition to extend it "for good cause shown." The petitioner will file the petition for the extension in the same manner that he or she filed the original petition. There will likely be a temporary extension until the date for return of service. The petitioner will receive a summons, and the respondent will have to be served. Both parties will have the opportunity to be heard on the issue of whether there is "good cause" to extend the order of protection. The Court is not permitted to deny the extension solely on the basis that there were no violations of the order.

Violation Proceedings

If the petitioner alleges that the respondent violated the order of protection, then the petitioner can seek sanctions in Criminal Court or in Family Court. However, the respondent cannot be ***incarcerated*** in both courts for the same violation.

In Criminal Court, the respondent faces up to seven years in prison for each violation, depending upon the level of the violation, for contempt of court. Criminal Court violation proceedings are prosecuted by the District Attorney's office.

Family Court violation proceedings are prosecuted by the petitioners themselves, or their attorneys. The petitioner, or the petitioner's attorney, will file a petition for enforcement of the order of protection. The Court may issue a summons for the respondent to appear, and the petitioner will have to arrange for the respondent to be served with the summons and the petition. The Court may also issue a warrant for the respondent's arrest.

If the petitioner is seeking the respondent's incarceration, then the petitioner will have to prove beyond a reasonable doubt that the respondent violated the order of protection. The Family Court has the authority to incarcerate the respondent for up to six months for each violation. The Court may also issue a suspended sentence, which is an order that the respondent comply with certain conditions of behavior, with the provision that the respondent will be incarcerated if the orders are violated.

The petitioner may also file a violation petition while the family offense proceeding is pending, alleging that the respondent violated a temporary order of protection. It is common in these scenarios for the respondent to consent to a final order of protection, in exchange for withdrawal of the violation petition.

Conclusion

Family offense proceedings have a significant impact upon litigation in Family Court and matrimonial cases. Orders of protection can provide safety and peace of mind to victims of domestic violence, and can protect children from abuse and neglect. They also have significant impact upon custody and divorce proceedings.

With an understanding of the route of family offense proceedings, litigants can utilize the Family Court to protect themselves from abuse, keep their children safe, and maintain a positive role in their children's lives.

Joseph Nivin, Esq.

Joseph Nivin is a solo practitioner at The Law Offices of Joseph H. Nivin, P.C., a law firm focusing on family and matrimonial law, with offices in Jamaica, Queens and in Manhattan. He graduated from Brooklyn Law School in 2007, and received his undergraduate degree at the University of Pennsylvania in 2004. Prior to opening his practice, Mr. Nivin was an agency attorney at the Administration for Children's Services of the City of New York, where he represented the New York City government in child abuse and neglect proceedings. More information regarding Mr. Nivin's office is available on the web at www.nivinlaw.com.

SECTION B: CONCILIATION PROCEEDINGS

By Ravi Cattry, Esq.

If a family is going through difficulties, divorce is not always the right answer in resolving those issues. Albeit rare, New York Family Courts offer ***conciliation proceedings***, which is an informal proceeding to try to resolve difficulties for those whose marriages are in trouble. Families can use these conferences to resolve issues that are creating challenges in the marriage.

Procedure

Any spouse can file a petition in Family Court to start this proceeding. The proceeding is sent to a ***probation service***, which arranges for ***conferences*** between the petitioner and the petitioner's spouse to attempt to resolve the familial issues. The probation service can also ask for the attendance of ***any other party*** at the conferences that may help facilitate the conciliation between the spouses, such as ***children, parents, friends, or siblings***.

What if My Spouse Doesn't Appear in Court?

If the petitioner's spouse chooses ***not to attend the conference***, the petitioner can have a court order ***directing the spouse*** to attend the conference. The Family Court will require the petitioner's spouse to appear in court to determine whether he or she should attend the conference. If the court concludes that the conference will help in facilitating conciliation, then the spouse will be ordered to attend the conference. If court finds that conciliation proceedings will not be of help in this matter, the conciliation proceeding ***will be terminated***. If the spouse attends one conference but not any others, a similar hearing will be held to decide whether or not conciliation proceedings should continue.

Possible Referrals

The purpose of the conciliation proceedings is to open a dialogue between the spouses to help them resolve issues that are creating problems in their marriage. One way this can be done is by having the couple speak with ***social service agencies*** or ***religious agencies*** in their communities. By referring the couple to these agencies, the conciliation can be directed towards a method that is more consistent with the values of the marriage. For example, a couple that is heavily involved in their church might ***benefit more from speaking*** with their priest about their marriage and how to resolve it through their faith rather than trying to resolve the issues through other means.

Family Court Issues

The conciliation proceedings only resolve issues ***that would arise in Family Court***. Therefore, the probation service cannot issue any orders that would have an effect on marital status because that is an area governed by Supreme Court and not Family Court. These proceedings do allow for ***orders of support petitions*** and ***family offense petitions*** to be issued. Therefore, a couple attending conciliation conferences may hope to resolve issues of child support or scheduled visitation, but will not be provided with a resolution about the division of property.

How Long Will It Last?

The conferences for conciliation ***will occur as long as both spouses agree to continue coming to the conferences***. If one of the spouses does not agree, then the proceedings will end ***90 days after the petition was filed***. Upon the termination of the proceedings, the probation service may refer the couple to other social or religious services. The couple may seek to continue the conciliation with these services or if conciliation is not possible, a legal proceeding may be initiated to seek final judgment from the court.

Confidentiality

All of the statements made during the conciliation proceedings are considered ***confidential***. These statements cannot be admitted into evidence at subsequent proceedings or actions. Therefore, if the proceeding does not help in reconciling the familial issues and the parties end up in court, one party cannot use any admissions during the conciliation proceedings in court as evidence of what they are trying to prove.

Ravi Cattry, Esq.

Ravi Cattry is an associate attorney at Rincker Law, PLLC and is licensed to practice in New York and New Jersey and admitted into the Eastern and Southern District Courts of New York. She completed a Bachelor of Science at Fordham University in Manhattan where she was a double major in psychology and economics. She received a Juris Doctor from Pace University School of Law in White Plains, New York.

Before joining Rincker Law, PLLC, Ravi worked at a general practice firm located in Kew Gardens, New York. While working there her practice areas included landlord and tenant disputes, matrimonial and family law issues, commercial law, and immigration law. Ravi also worked with a boutique law firm specializing in bankruptcy law in Manhattan. During law school she interned with the Integrated Domestic Violence Court in White Plains, New York, where she assisted in handling divorce cases intertwined with domestic violence cases.

Ravi is fluent in Hindi and Punjabi, and conversational in Spanish. In her free time Ravi enjoys reading, watching movies, playing tennis, and keeping up with her favorite soccer teams.

For more information on Rincker Law, PLLC visit www.rinckerlaw.com.

SECTION V: SPECIAL CONTRACTS

SECTION A: COHABITATION AGREEMENTS

By Kymberly A. Robinson, Esq.

Most people do not begin relationships thinking: "what if we break up?" This is true for couples contemplating marriage and those never planning to marry. However, ***breaking up may be a reality*** for many (or even most) couples. Married people in New York are afforded some protection that unmarried people cohabitating together do not have if the relationship deteriorates. Married people who subsequently divorce may, for example, have their assets and debts divided by equitable distribution, may receive spousal maintenance, and may continue to be covered by health insurance. New York does not, however, provide any laws or rules governing unmarried people's rights and obligations when their relationship ends. For obvious reasons, this is particularly awkward and difficult when the separating couple cohabitates.

New York does not recognize common law marriages no matter how long a couple cohabitates, but *will* recognize a common law marriage that was valid in another state. However, domestic partnerships (close, committed relationships between two people) are legal in New York. These relationships are not the same as marriage in the eyes of New York law, and couples in a domestic partnership have fewer rights than married people. Likewise, the process for termination of the relationship differs from divorce. For more information of domestic partnerships in New York City (and generally), please visit the Office of the New York City Clerk website on "***Domestic Partnership Registration***" available online at http://www.cityclerk.nyc.gov/html/marriage/domestic_partnership_reg.shtml. Please check with your local County Clerk if you are in another area in New York.

Examples When Cohabitation Agreements May Apply Be Helpful

Cohabitation, with no marriage and no domestic partnership status is the focus of this Chapter. There are many situations where couples might cohabitate. Let's look at a few:

- Example #1: A couple in their late-twenties has been dating for two years and frequently discusses marriage. They decide to cohabitate as a "trial period" before an engagement. One person decides to make a career change and is accepted to medical school. The couple agrees that pursuing this career will be good for their future. The other partner works full time and supports the partner through medical school. What happens to the supporting partner if the other never proposes even though he/she had been supporting the other for 4 years?
- Example #2: A previously divorced couple in their mid-fifties purchases a home together, but has not discussed marriage and probably never will for whatever reason. One partner has been out of the work force for 20 years. If they break up, will he/she receive any sort of financial support? Since they were not married, he/she would be ineligible for spousal maintenance.
- Example #3: Business partners work closely for years and then become romantically involved. They eventually decide to cohabitate. Over time, the stress of the business wears on them and the relationship goes sour and the couple decides to go their separate ways. What happens to the business?
- Example#4: A couple decides to move into one person's apartment. The lessee continues to be the sole name on the lease and is responsible for paying rent. It is assumed between them that they will share expenses "equally." What does that mean for rent? Will one partner pay the other partner rent? Will one partner pay his/her share to the landlord directly? Will they both put their names on the lease (if that is even an option)? Are they splitting utilities and other household

expenses? Whose name will be on the utilities? What if there is late payment? For example, if someone does not pay the cable bill on time, what happens and who is responsible?

- Example #5: A woman moves into the townhouse that her boyfriend has owned for three years. She gives up her prior residence and considers this townhouse her home. There is no lease agreement with her boyfriend. What happens if they break up? Does she have any rights to the townhouse?
- Example #6: A couple purchases a dog in the house in which they cohabitate. If they break up, how is possession of the dog decided? (See also Debra Hamilton's Chapter on pet ownership disputes too in Chapter 30(h).)

All of these couples will face uncertainty if and when their relationships end, unless they have a cohabitation agreement. This agreement would outline the rights and responsibilities for both parties should the relationship end. As illustrated in the examples above, unmarried couples who cohabitate oftentimes find themselves in situations where they may share expenses for their residence (either equally or unequally), share a bank account, share a pet, share a business, purchase real estate together, move into his or her partner's residence, or be in a situation where one party supports the other while he or she is in school.

Cohabitation happens among people of all ages, but is most common with younger people in their twenties and thirties who are living together as a "trial" period for engagement and subsequent marriage.

New York Courts Will Typically Uphold Cohabitation Agreements

New York law regards cohabitation agreements as akin to any other contract, and both parties should have independent legal counsel. It behooves the couple to be represented by separate counsel and to sign the agreement before a notary. Most clauses will be upheld, as long as they are not unconscionable and have adequate consideration. The issue of adequate consideration has led to much case law in the context of cohabitation agreements. Consideration in a cohabitation agreement is the mutual promises made in the agreement. For example, in Dee v. Rakower, 112 A.D.3d 204 (2nd Dept., 2013), a same-sex couple with two children had an oral cohabitation agreement whereby one would give up her career to raise the children, but if the relationship ended, she would share in the other party's assets including retirement. The Court held that the agreement was supported by consideration, which was specifically defined by the Court as:

> [E]ither a benefit to the promisor or a detriment to the promisee. It is enough that something is promised, done, forborne, or suffered by the party to whom the promise is made as consideration for the promise made to him… [t]he consideration here for the alleged contract is the forbearance of the plaintiff's career, the inability to continue to save toward her retirement during that forbearance, and her maintenance of the household in return for a share in the defendant's retirement benefits and other assets earned during the period of forbearance.

Dee at 210 (internal citations omitted).

Cohabitation agreements are enforceable so long as the consideration is not based upon sexual relations. See Morone v. Morone, 50 N.Y.2d 481 (1980). For example, in Pizzo v. Goor, 50 A.D.3d 586 (1st Dept., 2008), a cohabitation agreement was determined to be invalid for lack of consideration where the consideration was the other party's sexual and platonic companionship in exchange for money when the relationship ended.

> For example, Mike and Courtney purchased a dog together while cohabitating in Costa Rica. Mike purchased the dog, Taylor, and took her to the veterinarian regularly. When the couple relocated to Queens, New York together, Mike coordinated the international transfer. The couple continued to cohabitate together for several years. Although Mike took on the primary responsibility for Taylor the couple viewed her as a joint pet. When they split, Mike and Courtney had a visitation arrangement with Taylor. However, one day, Mike wanted to relocate to Florida for a job and Courtney refused to give Mike the dog. This dispute over pet possession could have been prevented with a cohabitation agreement.

Top Ten Issues to Think About With Cohabitation Agreements

Now let's see what should be included in a cohabitation agreement, keeping in mind couples #1 through #6 in the examples at the beginning of this Chapter.

1. <u>**Expenses**</u>: A couple might decide to split all living expenses equally or they might each have certain expenses assigned to them (*i.e.* one person pays the utilities and the other pays for food and groceries). The cohabitation agreement may also state that each partner is going to put a certain percentage of their income into a joint bank account to pay these expenses. This can be particularly useful if, for example, the cohabitants receive a past-due notice for utilities because there is no argument as to who is responsible for correcting the problem. This provision would be important to couples #1, #2, #3, #4, #5, and #6 because everyone living together should have an understanding of what financial obligations he or she will incur and how expenses will be shared.

2. <u>**Estate Planning**</u>: Couples might specifically waive the right to each other's estates, especially where there are children from a prior marriage. On the other hand, other couples might make arrangements for their significant other to receive part of the estate if one of them dies during the relationship. In addition, when having advanced directive drafted, couples should decide if they want their significant other to be their health care agent and have authority under their power of attorney. Estate planning issues typically apply to older couples (couple #2); however, couples cohabitating at all age groups should consider having advance directives drafted.

3. Pet Custody/Possession: Shared pets is a growing problem with cohabitating couples when they are breaking up, especially when both persons want to live with the pet after the split. New York courts do not regard pets as children, but do not consider them simply chattel either. Pet custody disputes concerning couples who cohabitate will usually be resolved on the "best for all concerned" standard, with ownership being an important factor. Pet ownership disputes can be emotionally charged and expensive; therefore, as Debra Hamilton notes in her chapter, mediation is a preferred way to handle any pet custody/possession disputes. Couple #6 shares a dog, so this would be particularly important for them.

> Brandi's boyfriend, James, moves into her apartment. Brandi is on the lease and pays the rent. She assumes that James will pay the cable, electric, and gym membership for the condominium's gym. One night they return home to a notice from the cable company saying that the account is past due. If there is a cohabitation agreement, there is no need for arguments regarding whose responsibility the cable bill was. The couple can just look at the agreement and Brandi can say "Oh, see James, the cable and all other utilities are your responsibility."

4. Debt: Some cohabitating couples may not be getting married for fear of assuming the other's debt. Although this can be addressed in a pre-nuptial agreement, couples that were previously married and not looking to remarry (like Couple #2) might want to include provisions in their cohabitation agreement that make each individual solely and wholly responsible for his or her own debt. Couples #1, #2, #3, #4, #5, and #6 should all provide for debt responsibility in their cohabitation agreements.

5. Infidelity: Like with pre-nuptial agreements, a cohabitation agreement may have a clause whereby one party receives support or assets in the case of the other party's infidelity. This is more common in longer term relationships.

6. Assets: A cohabitation agreement could divide all of the couple's joint assets. It may also provide for how the less wealthy party will be taken care of by the monied partner. Taking care of a less wealthy partner would probably be more common among older people or couples who have been together for many years as if they were married. In any event, Couples #1, #2, #3, #4, #5, and #6 should all provide for how assets will be divided, but couple #2 might be more likely to include a provision whereby the less wealthy partner is awarded support (similar to spousal support in a divorce), especially if they are together for a number of years since the less-wealthy partner may have been out of the work force for a long time.

> Amanda's parent purchase a designer couch for the home Amanda and her boyfriend Jack live in. They are dating for three years and then the relationship ends. There is a dispute as to whether the couch was a gift to both Amanda and Jack or whether it belongs to Amanda and should stay with her. A cohabitation agreement can specify the disposition of certain important property upon break-up.

7. Separate or Joint Property: Cohabitants can expressly provide that their separate property shall remain separate, joint property be shared upon termination of the relationship, and discuss how to handle comingled property. Typically, comingled property will convert to joint property, but cohabitants can handle this either way. As with assets, couples #1, #2, and #3 should all include provisions outlining what property is separate and what property in joint at the outset of the cohabitation arrangement.

8. Businesses: If the cohabitants are also business partners, they might decide that they cannot maintain a professional, business relationship when their romantic relationship ends. A cohabitation agreement should provide for whether the couple plans to continue working together or not. After a break-up, the couple's decision whether or not to remain business partners might depend on the reason for the split. For example, infidelity and untruthfulness might change the situation versus simply ending a relationship because of incompatibility as living partners or boyfriend and girlfriend. A cohabitation agreement for couples with a joint business might provide for different outcomes based on the reason for the break-up. When considering businesses, business assets, client contacts, accounts receivable, accounts payable, rent and/or property, etc. should all be addressed. A provision like this would apply to couple #3.

9. **Housing**: More commonly in places outside of New York City, one party might own a residence that his/her significant other moves into. In that case, the New York State Bar Association ("NYSBA") recommends that the party owning the residence provide for a way to oust the cohabitant should the relationship end and the cohabitant refuses to leave. Per the NYSBA's recommendation, the party who does not own the residence should acknowledge in the Cohabitation Agreement that he or she is granted a license to live in the residence, which can be terminated by the owner at any time, whereby the non-owning party must vacate the residence immediately and may only return to retrieve his or her belongings upon reasonable notice to the owning party. Furthermore, NSYBA suggests that the Cohabitation Agreement should explicitly state that the license "shall not create any landlord-tenant relationship" and if the party fails to vacate upon the owner's request, the owner shall "have the right…to treat [him or her] as a 'squatter' and a trespasser… ".[61] Provisions concerning housing in the context of someone owning a residence would definitely apply to couple #5.

10. **Children**: Of course, children ALWAYS have protection in terms of receiving financial support from both parents under the Child Support Standards Act. However, couples who are not married, but cohabitating when their child is born, might have a clause in their cohabitation agreement regarding finances, roles and/or responsibilities once a child is born (especially for the woman giving birth). However, it is recommended if children are involved that the parents consider having a separate parenting agreement regarding child custody and child support (if agreed upon).

Cohabitation Agreements Can Help With Transitions

When going through an emotional break up, it is usually best to make the process as quick and easy as possible. A Cohabitation Agreement can streamline the break up process and make moving forward a quicker process for both parties. On the other (more

[61] New York State Bar Association, "Appendix E: Sample Cohabitation Agreement to be Tailored to Specific Facts" available at http://www.nysba.org/WorkArea/DownloadAsset.aspx?id=24079 (last visited May 14, 2015).

optimistic) hand, in the event that the cohabitating parties subsequently marry, the cohabitation agreement they previously agreed to can become the basis for a later executed pre-nuptial agreement.

When a couple lives together, there are inevitable issues that arise such as the residence, assets, debts, living expenses, pets and duties/chores. A Cohabitation Agreement should not be viewed as taboo; to the contrary, it can be a valuable tool utilized to help crystalize the agreement between the parties and prevent emotional and expensive litigation in the event a dispute arises.

Kymberly A. Robinson, Esq.

Kymberly is an associate attorney with Rincker Law, PLLC and is admitted to practice law in New York and Florida. She attended Union College in Schenectady, New York for her undergraduate studies, where she graduated with high honors as a psychology major. She then obtained her J.D. from Pace University School of Law in White Plains, New York and, subsequently, her L.L.M. (with a concentration in family law) from the Benjamin N. Cardozo School of Law in Manhattan. Kymberly entered the field of matrimonial and family law as a way to couple her interest in psychology and personal relationships with her legal education.

Before joining Rincker Law, PLLC, Kymberly was an associate at boutique matrimonial law firms in Westchester County, Manhattan, and Florida. She was also a volunteer at the New York County Access to Justice Program-Uncontested Divorce Clinic where she assisted self-represented litigants in the divorce process. During law school Kymberly also participated in two legal clinics: one at the Pace Women's Justice Center, where she represented clients in obtaining orders of protection and another at the Brooklyn Family Defense Project, where she assisted in defending families in child abuse and neglect proceedings.

Kymberly likes to spend her free time with her family and also enjoys working out, cooking healthy meals, and getting together with friends. She lives in Westchester County, New York with her husband and daughter.

SECTION B: NUPTIAL AGREEMENTS

PRENUPTIAL AND POSTNUPTIAL AGREEMENTS

by Sabra R. Sasson, Esq.

When a person gets engaged to be married, that person usually thinks of the wedding dress, the flowers, invitations, music and the venue. However, with the high prevalence of divorce, more couples are considering prenuptial agreements as a form of protection or insurance. A ***prenuptial agreement*** is also a way for two people to consider both the financial partnership and romantic bonding in the marriage.

In the absence of a prenuptial or postnuptial agreement, state law applies in a divorce or death. Prenuptial agreements are ***empowering*** and allow for parties to take the law into their own hands. Furthermore, laws can change during a marriage. A prenuptial or postnuptial agreement allows the couple to decide on financial rules in the event the marriage is dissolved.

Why Prenuptial Agreements Are Used

Prenuptial agreements ("prenups") have been used for many, many years (it may even date back to ancient Egyptians) to protect the assets of a wealthy man to ensure that his wife was not marrying him for his money. While prenups have been traditionally used to protect the assets of the wealthy partner, couples marrying later in life with accumulated assets are using them for their own reasons to protect the assets they worked hard to create. Other considerations: children from a prior marriage or relationship, protection from each other's debts, and clarity regarding financial rights and responsibilities during marriage.

The bottom line is that when a couple decides to create a prenuptial agreement, the couple is deciding, rather than the state, how they want property to be treated ***during marriage***, upon death, or in the event of a divorce. Prenuptial agreements give a couple an opportunity to decide what is fair, rather than leaving those decisions to the court.

Issues Covered in a Prenuptial (or Postnuptial) Agreement

Under New York law, prenuptial agreements cannot cover issues involving unborn children, including custody, visitation, relocation and child support. Instead, prenuptial agreements focus on the financial issues of the marriage, namely:

- Identification of ***Separate Property***;
- Identification of ***Marital Property***;
- How Separate and or Marital Property ***will be divided*** in a divorce; and,
- ***Spousal maintenance*** (both temporary and durational maintenance) or a waiver of maintenance.

Additionally, prenuptial agreements can memorialize **"*break-up*" *procedures*** including:

- When the prenuptial agreement comes into play (e.g., 30 days after a certified letter is sent or upon filing an action dissolving the marriage);
- Who will be ***moving out*** of the marital home and under what time frame;
- Procedures for selling marital property, including a marital residence; and
- Decisions to resolve issues with the divorce in ***mediation*** or a collaborative divorce setting.

Parties also can discuss issues involving the ***estate*** or ***confidentiality*** including:

- Whether to consent to the right of ***spousal election***, waive it, or make their own rules regarding distribution of wealth upon death; and
- Whether to restrict discussing the contents of the prenuptial agreement to others, such as financial advisors and attorneys.

Let us break a few of these issues down.

Identification of Separate Property

When parties agree to enter into a prenuptial agreement, they also agree to full financial disclosure of all assets and debts. Typically, a ***schedule is attached*** to the agreement which sets forth the assets and debts of the parties, such as the following, which is not intended to be a full and comprehensive list:

- Bank accounts, including savings and checking;
- Investment accounts, including stocks, bonds, mutual funds, and commodities;
- Retirement accounts, including IRAs, Roth IRAs, 401Ks, pensions, Keoghs, and stock options;
- Property, both real, including residential, commercial, and investment, and personal, including jewelry, gold, vehicles, boats, and airplanes;
- Income from all sources, such as salary, dividends, rental income, and capital gains;
- Insurance, including type, i.e., life, disability, and health, coverage limits, and beneficiaries;
- Business interests in corporations, partnerships, and limited liability companies;
- Trusts;
- Loans, including personal, school, and judgments;
- Credit card debt; and
- Mortgages.

Understanding what each partner has in terms of assets and debts will enable the parties to talk about the possibilities of building a financial future together; knowing where they are starting from in order to discuss what could be. After the parties understand the assets and debts of the other, they can decide what will be defined as separate property and marital property after marriage.

In New York, all property and debt that the parties bring into the marriage is deemed to be separate property of the parties and therefore not ***subject to division in the event of divorce***. And so long as such property is maintained separate during the marriage, it will maintain its identity as separate. However, it is possible to convert such property to marital property (as described in the next section) subject to division in the event of divorce.

For example, what happens with the value of property brought into the marriage? If one has an investment or retirement account that increases in value during the marriage, those would ordinarily be considered separate and not subject to division in divorce. Gifts to one partner and inheritances are considered to be separate. However, if one adds money to an investment or retirement account during the marriage, the sums added during the marriage are marital property subject to division in the event of divorce.

In New York, without a prenuptial agreement, the following property is treated as separate property:

- Property that a spouse owns before marriage
- Property that a spouse receives after marriage by gift or inheritance
- Property that a spouse purchases with separate property
- Property that a spouse earns or accumulates after an event of marital dissolution

A prenuptial agreement contains provisions defining what property is separate and what can happen to that property during the marriage such as whether the property will maintain its identity or whether it can be converted and in what instances. This is an opportunity for a couple to decide whether to opt out of New York's current presumptions and make their own rules. The prenup can clarify or override state law.

Identification of Marital Property

Marital property, generally, is any property acquired from the date of marriage including income earned, assets and debts acquired, and any property titled in both parties' names after marriage. Any property that is acquired after marriage whether or not it is titled in both parties' names is deemed marital property. Marital property belongs to both parties equally and is subject to equitable division in the event of divorce pursuant to state law or as described in the parties' prenuptial agreement. Equitable distribution does not necessarily mean 50/50 or equally.

Some couples decide to define marital property in their prenuptial agreement (or postnuptial agreement) as only that property or debt that is titled in both parties' names. So, for example, if income earned during the marriage is deposited into a bank account or invested in property or accounts that are titled only in one spouse's name, it will be treated as separate property not subject to division in the event of divorce even though it was earned or acquired during the marriage.

Again, in the prenuptial agreement, parties can create their own definitions and effectively "opt out" of their state's statutes. Without a prenup, in the event of a divorce in New York, the couple's marital property will be subject to equitable distribution. Where the couple has a prenup or postnup, they can determine how such property will be divided between them in the event of divorce.

Division of Marital Property

As described in the prior section, marital property is subject to equitable distribution in the event of divorce. In New York that means that the Court will evaluate each asset and debt of the marriage against the factors set forth in Domestic Relations Law Section 236(B). A list of the thirteen (13) factors is here:

(1) The ***income and property*** of each party at the time of marriage, and at the time of the commencement of the action;

(2) The ***duration of the parties' marriage*** and the age and health of both parties;

(3) The need of either party to ***occupy or own the marital residence*** and the use and ownership of its household effects;

(4) The ***loss of either party of inheritance*** and pension rights upon dissolution of the marriage as of the date of dissolution;

(5) Any ***award of maintenance*** under Domestic Relations Law Section 236(B)(6);

(6) Any ***equitable claim*** to, interest in, or direct or indirect contribution made to the acquisition of marital property by the party not having title, including joint efforts or expenditures and contributions and services as a spouse, parent, wage earner and homemaker, and to the career or career potential of the other party;

(7) The ***liquid or non-liquid character*** of all marital property;
(8) The ***probable future financial circumstances*** of each party;
(9) The ***impossibility or difficulty of evaluating*** any component asset or any interest in a business, corporation or profession, and the economic desirability of retaining such asset or interest intact and free from any claim or interference by any other party;
(10) The ***tax consequences*** of each party;
(11) The ***wasteful dissipation*** of marital property by either party;
(12) Any ***transfer or encumbrance*** made in contemplation of a matrimonial action without fair consideration; and
(13) Any other factor which the parties expressly find just and proper.

In a prenup or postnup, a couple can create their own set of factors or other "rule" relating to division of their marital property. For example, the couple may decide that any marital property acquired, whether titled in either spouse's name or jointly, will be divided equally.

Another common example involves real estate. Where the spouses purchase real estate together and one of them uses separate property toward the acquisition of such property, then, upon the sale of the real estate in the event of divorce, the sale proceeds (after closing costs and expenses) will be used first to reimburse the separate contribution from such spouse, and the balance left over would be divided equally between them.

<u>Example #1</u>:

- Couple purchases property for $500,000.
- Spouse 1 contributes $100,000 of separate property toward the purchase.
- Spouse 2 does not make any contribution.
- Property is sold for $900,000.
- Spouse 1 receives $100,000 plus $400,000
- Spouse 2 receives $400,000.

Another common way in which couples may decide to divide such property is based upon the percentage of the separate property contributed toward the purchase.

<u>Example #2</u>:

- Couple purchases property for $500,000.
- Spouse 1 contributes $100,000 of separate property toward the purchase.
- Spouse 2 does not make any contribution.
- Property is sold for $900,000.
- Spouse 1 receives 20% plus 40%of the proceeds, or $180,000 plus $360,000.
- Spouse 2 receives 40% of the proceeds, or $360,000.

Spousal Maintenance

Spousal maintenance, also referred to as alimony or spousal support, is monetary support paid by one spouse to another during or after divorce. A court can, after considering a list of factors, order one spouse to pay the other spouse a certain sum for a certain period of time.

It used to be that courts would order ex-husbands to pay ex-wives alimony in divorce cases. However, today, either spouse may be ordered to pay support to the other, for a limited period of time. The concept behind spousal maintenance is to obligate one spouse to pay the other until they become self-supporting. It is rare to have an order of permanent support or lifetime support, except in the event of illness or other factors.

In New York, the ***temporary spousal support*** statute provides a 2-step formula that the courts will apply during a contested divorce where the incomes of the spouses are disparate. The higher earning spouse pays support to the lower earning spouse during the pendency of the divorce. There is also a presumption that the higher earning spouse also pays counsel fees to the lower earning spouse. The obligation to pay temporary support terminates upon a final order of divorce by the court. The purpose of the temporary spousal support statute is to "equalize" the spouse's financial status so that one spouse will have less incentive to drag out the divorce because he/she has the financial wherewithal to do so. Where the spouse's incomes are similar, no temporary spousal support will be awarded. More information on temporary spousal maintenance is found in Section III(B) by Wendy Harris.

In a prenuptial agreement, the parties can agree to ***waive any claims of spousal support*** from the other, or they can provide and ***create their own formula*** for determining spousal support, taking into account that such support has two parts – the financial number and duration.

Another important factor to consider in deciding whether support or maintenance will be awarded to either spouse in the event of divorce, is the following default: spousal support is deductible to the payor spouse and includable as income to the payee spouse.

Estate Rights

A provision relating to estate rights is an optional provision in a prenuptial agreement. This provision addresses what happens if one of the spouses passes away during the marriage, while the prenup is in effect.

Without a prenuptial agreement, certain estate rights arise automatically upon marriage that may or may not be consistent with the desires of the parties getting married. For instance, in New York, spouses have a marital ***right of election***. In other words, neither spouse can disinherit the other. There is a "minimum" that each spouse is entitled to from the other's estate in the event of death. In New York, the marital right of election the surviving spouse is entitled to is the greater of 1/3 or $50,000 of the estate of the deceased spouse's estate.

While spouses can agree in a prenup how they want their property to be distributed upon their death, it is still advisable to create an estate plan after getting married. They can also decide whether to waive their right to be the executor of the other's estate.

In a prenuptial agreement, the spouses can waive all or some of their inheritance rights of the surviving spouse. For instance, it may be important to the spouses to provide for children from a prior relationship or to ensure that certain property stays in their family when they die.

"Break-Up" Procedures

The parties may include a provision describing the procedure for ending the marriage relationship. For instance, the parties may decide that the date of the termination of their marriage is the date of the filing for divorce, the filing of a separation agreement, or the date of a written declaration that the marriage is void or annulled. Other ways in which a relationship may be declared terminated is by delivering a notice to the other of the intent to terminate the marriage or by signing a written separation agreement.

A prenuptial agreement can provide that the parties go to mediation to resolve their divorce before proceeding to court. More information on mediation is found in Chapter 4(a) by Cari B. Rincker.

Confidentiality

Some couples prefer to keep their financial decisions private; even the decision to have a prenuptial agreement is a private matter. If one wants to be clear with their partner regarding confidentiality, it may be a good idea to include a provision in the prenuptial agreement that specifically provides that the agreement is confidential. The decision whether to specifically provide for confidentiality is a choice, a decision to be made between the parties. Often such confidentiality provisions will provide for exceptions such that either party can discuss the contents of the prenuptial agreement with attorneys, financial advisors or CPAs.

Another issue relating to confidentiality is that involving attorney-client privilege. While each party will be represented by separate counsel, most couples maintain communications with each other throughout the process to discuss the various issues within the agreement. They may discuss with one another about the advice received from their own attorneys and then make decisions together relating to those issues. Note, that while conversations between attorney and client are private and the attorney cannot disclose details later, unless the client consents – if the client tells somebody else about the communications with the attorney, then the rule of confidentiality no longer applies to that conversation. While confidentiality is valuable, ironing out the details of the prenuptial agreement jointly may outweigh preserving the coveted attorney-client confidentiality.

Miscellaneous Issues

Parties can decide the Choice of Law (e.g., New York, New Jersey, Connecticut) or Choice of Forum (i.e., in which court the divorce litigation will take place). Some couples may choose to have a sunset provision stating after a certain number of years, the prenup will be ineffective.

Unenforceable Clauses in a Prenup

Children Issues

Generally speaking, prenuptial agreements cannot discuss issues regarding unborn children, including but not limited to child custody, visitation/parenting time, relocation, or child support (including add-ons, such as college expenses). That said, prenuptial or postnuptial agreements can discuss children that have been born.

A provision requiring that any children born of the marriage be raised in the Catholic religion is an enforceable provision. See Ramon v. Ramon, 34 N.Y.S.2d 100 (NY Dom. Rel. Ct. 1942). Additionally, a provision stating that upon marriage the two children born to wife prior to marriage were not to reside in the household was not binding as it was against public policy and threatened the relationship between parent and child. See Mengal v. Mengal, 201 Misc. 104, 103 N.Y.S.2d 992 (NY Dom. Rel. Ct. 1951).

Lifestyle Clauses

Sometimes parties may have certain requests that they would like to include in an agreement. Generally speaking, only provisions that are illegal or against public policy will not be enforced by the courts. It is not advisable to try to list all of the aspects of your personal lives together in a prenuptial agreement such as tasks or household chores (e.g., cleaning, cooking, taking out the trash, etc.).

Validity of Prenuptial Agreements

Courts generally uphold prenuptial agreements so long as the following three things are satisfied:

- Both parties are represented by separate counsel;
- The terms of the prenuptial agreement are reasonable;
- Neither party signed the agreement under duress or undue influence.

Separate Counsel and Duress

In order prove coercion or duress, a party must establish that he or she was somehow pressured into signing the agreement. Threatening to call off the marriage unless an agreement is signed is not duress according to numerous court decisions. Where both parties are represented by counsel and the agreement is the result of arm's length negotiations, it may be nearly impossible to prove duress.

Each party being ***represented by counsel*** usually prevents claims of duress. See Barocas v. Barocas, 94 A.D.3d 551, 552, 942 N.Y.S.2d 491, 193 (2012), wherein the Defendant's claim that she believed that there would be no wedding if she did not sign the agreement where the wedding date was only two weeks away and the wedding plans had already been made, was *insufficient* to demonstrate duress. However, in certain circumstances and even where a party consults with counsel on the very date that the agreement is signed, being represented by counsel does not necessarily negate a duress claim. See Chait v. Chait, 256 A.D.2d 121, 681 N.Y.S.2d 269, 269-270 (1998).

There are even some instances where an agreement will still be enforceable even if one party is not represented by counsel where that party was given the opportunity to consult with an attorney, and was capable of making an informed decision even without counsel. See Hoffman v. Hoffman, 100 A.D.2d 704, 704-05, 474 N.Y.S.2d 621, 622 (1984), where the wife was given the opportunity to consult with counsel prior to signing the agreement, she was a real estate agent, and had two years of college credits, the court held that she was capable of making an informed decision even if she did not have counsel.

Reasonableness and Unconscionability

An agreement between spouses or prospective spouses that is fair on its face will be enforced according to its terms unless there is proof of fraud, duress, overreaching, or unconscionability. See Christian v. Christian, 42 N.Y.2d 63, 72-73 (1977). "Duly executed prenuptial agreements are accorded the same presumption of legality as any other contract." Barocas v. Barocas at 493 citing Bloomfield v. Bloomfield, 97 N.Y.2d 188, 193, 738 N.Y.S.2d 650, 764 N.E.2d 950 (2001) … An unconscionable contract is one "which is so grossly unreasonable as to be unenforceable because of an absence of meaningful choice on part of one of the parties together with contract terms which are unreasonably favorable to the other party." Barocas v. Barocas at 493 citing King v. Fox, 7 N.Y3d 181, 191, 818 N.Y.S2d 833, 851 N.E.2d 1184 (2006).

Proper Execution

It is crucial that the acknowledgment relating to the signatures of the parties include the phrase indicating that the notary public confirmed the identity of the person executing the agreement. Without that phrase, the entire agreement can be invalidated. Galetta v. Galetta, 2013 NY Slip Op 03871.

Changing the Stigma – Why Prenups Are Romantic

At the beginning of this chapter we discussed how prenups originally came about – to protect the husband from marrying a woman who was marrying him for his money. So many things have changed since then. We are more aware of the benefits of understanding our finances. We have financial advisors and trust and estates attorneys to advise us on how to manage our financial affairs. Getting married is part of that picture as well. Getting married is romantic and is also a financial decision.

How is a Prenuptial Agreement Romantic?

A prenuptial agreement is a way for both parties to let the other know that no matter what, they will take care of each other. Just as one purchases car insurance for protection in the event of a car accident, a prenuptial agreement is a way to provide the terms by which one will provide for the other in the event of a breakup. It is an opportunity, while the couple is very much in love, to declare how they will provide for the other if the unimaginable were to occur.

Another reason that prenups are romantic is because it allows the parties to get closer and more ***intimate*** by discussing what is often considered to be a "taboo" topic – money and finances. By discovering and learning how each party manages his/her finances, earns money, and manages debt, the couple can become closer as they discuss how to incorporate their money management styles when they begin their life together as a single married unit. It can be exciting to learn what opportunities become available when the two parties join forces.

The agreement and its terms are created "***cooperatively***." It is a "co-creation" consisting of terms and agreements reached by the couple in discussions together. And when agreements are reached, even if they are difficult, as they typically are, what often results is not only an agreement that they both can live with, but the couple also learns to communicate with one another on such difficult subjects as money, death, and disability.

So you see, a prenuptial agreement is not just for the rich and the famous, but it is truly for anyone who wants a greater assurance of their love for one another and the life they intend to create together.

Postnuptial Agreements

Put simply, a postnuptial agreement is just like a prenuptial agreement but it is entered into after a couple is married. Typically, this is entered into to amend a prenuptial agreement that may have been entered into prior to the marriage. Or, in some instances, a couple may not have had the time to enter into an agreement prior to marriage, and instead, one is signed after marriage.

Postnuptial agreements are typically more strictly scrutinized by the courts for enforceability since they are between spouses, which inherently carries with it a fiduciary responsibility. To illustrate, the Court in Petracca v. Petracca, 101 A.D. 3d. 695, 956 N.Y.S2d 77, 79 (2012) stated it succinctly as follows:

> In general, a postnuptial agreement "which is regular on its face will be recognized and enforced by the courts in much the same manner as an ordinary contract. . ." However, "[a]greements between spouses, unlike ordinary business contracts, involve a fiduciary relationship requiring the **utmost of good faith**" . . . Accordingly, "courts have thrown their cloak of protection" over postnuptial agreements, "and made

> it their business, when confronted, to see to it that they are arrived at fairly and equitably, in a manner so as to be **free from the taint of fraud and duress**, and to set aside or refuse to enforce those born of and subsisting in inequity . . ."
>
> Because of the fiduciary relationship between spouses, postnuptial agreements "are closely scrutinized by the courts, and such agreements are more readily set aside in equity under circumstances that would be insufficient to nullify an ordinary contract. . . ." "To warrant equity's intervention, **no actual fraud need be shown**, for relief will be granted if the [agreement] is manifestly unfair to a spouse because of the other's overreaching . . ."

(Emphasis added).

While one may not have time before the wedding date to sign a prenuptial agreement, the agreement can be signed after the wedding. However, the disadvantage is that the agreement will be more ***closely scrutinized*** by the court if it is later challenged. And, even where a prenuptial agreement was entered into, if circumstances change such that the couple seeks to revise the agreement, it can be done by amendment or an addendum to the agreement. Because it will be signed after marriage, it will still fall under the laws that apply to postnuptial or post marital agreements. Again, as stated by the Petracca court, spouses are inherently held to a higher standard due to the fiduciary relationship. Each spouse is expected to deal fairly with one another in matters affecting finances. If an agreement appears to favor one spouse over the other, it can be set aside.

Sabra R. Sasson, Esq.

Sabra R. Sasson is an attorney and mediator practicing in New York City. She is the founder and Principal of Sabra Law Group, PLLC, a mediation and law practice in midtown Manhattan that offers legal and mediation services to its clients. Sabra handles the legal aspects of major transitions – buying or selling property, planning for marriage or getting divorced – and protects her clients' interests so they can focus on their evolution into this new life change. She employs her skills and experience to help her clients focus on life post-divorce and guide them through the process to get there. For couples embarking on marriage, she helps them protect accumulated assets and create a plan for building assets, wealth and valuables in the future.

Sabra graduated from Brandeis University in 1995 with a Bachelor's in Mathematics and minor in Education, whereafter she enrolled in law school and graduated from Hofstra University School of Law in 1998 with her Juris Doctorate. She sat for the bar exam in three states and was thereafter admitted to practice law in New York, New Jersey and Connecticut, and has been practicing law ever since.

Sabra is currently writing a book to guide and empower couples through the process of "uncoupling," THE HARMONIOUS DIVORCE: THE FOUR STEP PROCESS TO UNCOUPLING. She is also the author of a chapter in the best-selling book SUCCESS FROM THE HEART. Connect with her at www.sabralawgroup.com.

SECTION C: MEDICALLY ASSISTED REPRODUCTION & SURROGACY

By Denise E. Seidelman, Esq., Nina E. Rumbold, Esq., and Ravi Cattry, Esq.

For some, ***Assisted Reproductive Technology*** provides a wonderful alternative way to build or expand their family. However, this is an area where science has outpaced the law and the law is in many instances still evolving and uncertain. ***Collaborative Reproduction***, including gamete donation (*i.e.*, sperm and egg donation), embryo donation, and surrogacy implicates important legal rights and relationships. Before anyone participates in Collaborative Reproduction, whether to become a parent, to gestate a child for another, or to donate gametes or embryos, all participants should seek the advice of knowledgeable legal counsel.

Surrogacy

Surrogacy involves the assistance of a woman who gestates a child for intended parent(s) who will be the child's legal parent(s). There are two types of surrogacy: ***gestational surrogacy*** and ***traditional surrogacy***. In a gestational surrogacy, the egg, which comes from a woman other than the surrogate (either the intended mother or an egg donor), is fertilized through ***in vitro fertilization*** ("IVF") and then the embryo is transferred to the surrogate. The child in this type of surrogacy is not genetically related to the surrogate. In a traditional surrogacy, the surrogate's own egg is used. The pregnancy is achieved through artificial insemination of the surrogate or IVF and embryo transfer. Traditional surrogacies are, for the most part, discouraged by professionals because of the legal and emotional risks which arise when the surrogate is genetically related to the child.

> IVF is the joining of a woman's egg and a man's sperm in a laboratory dish outside of the body.

New York Domestic Relations Law ("DRL") § 122 declares surrogate parenting contracts to be against the public policy of New York State. Accordingly, any agreement in New York which compels a surrogate to relinquish parental rights is void and unenforceable. In these situations, the woman who gives birth to the child is presumed to be the legal mother until a court order issues declaring the intended mother to be the legal mother. In addition, New York law makes it illegal for a surrogate to receive a fee or compensation in connection with a surrogate parenting contract. The participants to such a prohibited agreement can incur civil penalties while those who assisted or arranged the agreement are subject to criminal penalties.

While New York law imposes significant restrictions on the surrogacy process, there is no legal prohibition against a woman carrying a child for intended parents so long as she does not receive compensation for doing so. Because of this, there are many heartwarming examples of successful surrogacy arrangements between close relatives or friends where the surrogate has received no compensation beyond legally permissible expenses which typically include the cost of the medical procedures and legal counsel for the surrogate.

The participants in an ***uncompensated surrogacy arrangement*** (which is often called an ***altruistic or compassionate surrogacy***) are well advised to consult with legal counsel before the carrier becomes pregnant. Although surrogate parenting contracts are unenforceable, most attorneys working in this area advise the participants to enter into a "Memorandum of Understanding." The purpose of this memorandum is to allow the participants to address the complicated social and legal landscape of gestational surrogacy. Critical issues such as the number of embryos to transfer, whether to terminate a pregnancy, or whether to reduce the number of fetuses should be addressed to insure that the participants are consistent in their intentions. Even though this document is not legally enforceable, and cannot be used to establish parental rights, it is valuable because it sets forth the parties' understandings and expectations and gives them the security to undertake the surrogacy process.

Important legal issues must be confronted in every case where surrogacy is contemplated. Establishing the child's legal parentage is critical. While there have been some advances in New York law relating to gestational surrogacy arrangements, the parental rights of a traditional surrogate can only be terminated in an adoption proceeding instituted by the ***Intended Parents***.

The legal rights of an intended father who is genetically related to the child can be established in two ways:

- through an ***acknowledgment of paternity*** at the hospital (if the gestational carrier is not married); or
- through a ***paternity proceeding*** (if the gestational carrier is married).

A court paternity proceeding is required when the gestational carrier is married because, by law, the husband of the woman who gives birth to the child is presumed to be the legal father. That presumption can only be defeated by a court finding that someone, other than the carrier's husband, is the child's genetic parent.

Until 2011, the genetic mother of a child gestated by a gestational carrier was required to adopt her child. As stated above, a genetic father could be declared the legal father without undertaking an adoption but a genetic mother was not given this same opportunity. This apparent inequality was successfully challenged in the landmark case of T.V. v. NY State Department of Health, 88 AD3d 290, 929 N.Y.S.2d 139 (App Div 2d, 2011). In that case, a New York appellate court ruled, for the first time, that where the gestational carrier has no objection to the genetic mother being declared the legal mother, the genetic mother and genetic father have an equal right to a judicial declaration that they are the parents following the child's birth.[62] Unfortunately, the reasoning of this case has not been extended to include a child created through donor gametes. As a result, where the intended parents are not both genetically related to the child, adoption is presently the only way for them to establish a legal relationship between them and their child.

Because of the severe restrictions imposed on surrogacy arrangements undertaken within New York State, many New York families undertake these arrangements outside of the state. In fact there are many states where gestational carriers are entitled to be compensated for their valuable service and where the intended parents are recognized as the legal parents of the child from birth. While this provides a wonderful opportunity for many families, there is no doubt that New York families are burdened and disadvantaged by New York's archaic laws. At the time of this writing (2015) there is legislation pending before the New York Legislature (The ***Child Parent Security***

---

[62] New York City has been allowing genetic mothers to be legally recognized as a parent, without adoption, since another landmark case, Doe v. New York City Bd. of Health, 5 Misc. 3rd. 424, 782 N.Y.S.2d 180 (2004).

Act, or "CPSA") which would allow New Yorkers to enter into enforceable and compensated surrogacy agreements. If the CPSA is enacted, it would allow New York intended parents to remain in New York and to be securely recognized as the parents of their child from the moment of birth.

Sperm/Embryo/Egg Donation

DRL Section 73 provides that any child born to a married woman by means of artificial insemination performed by a physician, with the consent of the "woman and her husband" is the legal child of the "husband and his wife." Now that same sex couples are permitted to marry, the female spouse of a woman conceiving through donor insemination is entitled to the same recognition of parentage previously reserved for husbands. However, for reasons beyond the scope of this Chapter, same sex couples conceiving through artificial insemination are well advised to undertake an adoption proceeding to secure the legal rights of the non-gestating mother in the event her parentage is challenged in a state hostile to same sex parenting.

Other than the very limited protection afforded by ***New York's Donor Insemination Statute***, there is no New York law addressing the legal rights and obligations of sperm, egg, or embryo donors. In short, there is no specific New York law which declares that the donors of gametes used for procreation ***lack a legal relationship to the child*** conceived as a result of their donation. The failure of New York law to address the parentage of children conceived from donor gametes creates legal uncertainty for the intended parents, donors, and the children themselves.

Because of the lack of protection afforded by New York State law, people seeking to build their families with the use of donor gametes should retain experienced legal counsel who can help them understand the legal ramifications of entering into these arrangements. Many participants in egg, sperm, and embryo donation arrangements enter into written agreements outlining the mutual understandings and intentions of the parties. While there is no guarantee that such an agreement would be legally enforceable in the event of a contest between a donor and intended parent, the formal written agreement of the participants may guide the court to the right outcome.

Denise E. Seidelman, Esq.

Denise Seidelman is a partner in Rumbold & Seidelman, LLP, a firm devoted exclusively to adoption and reproductive law since 1996. Denise's practice includes the full gamut of adoption services ranging from private placement and agency adoptions to second and second parent adoptions. She also provides legal counsel to those building their families through egg, sperm, and embryo donation as well as those needing the assistance of a gestational surrogate. She is actively involved in the legislative effort to reform New York law so that those building their families with the assistance of reproductive technology will be recognized under New York law.

Nina E. Rumbold, Esq.

Nina E. Rumbold, Esq., is a Partner in the firm of Rumbold & Seidelman, LLP, practicing exclusively in the areas of adoption and reproductive law. Ms. Rumbold is a fellow the American Academy of Adoption Attorneys, the American Academy of Assisted Reproductive Technology Attorneys and a member of the National LGBT Bar Association Family Law Institute. Ms. Rumbold has lectured on Adoption Law and Reproductive Law. She is the past President of New York Attorneys for Adoption and Family Formation (NYAAFF).

Ravi Cattry, Esq.

Ravi Cattry is an associate attorney and is an associate attorney for Rincker Law, PLLC and is licensed to practice in New York and New Jersey. She completed a Bachelor of Science at Fordham University in Manhattan where she was a double major in psychology and economics. She received a Juris Doctor from Pace University School of Law in White Plains, New York. During law school she interned with the Integrated Domestic Violence Court in White Plains, New York, where she assisted in handling divorce cases intertwined with domestic violence cases.

PART VI: ESTATE PLANNING CONSIDERATIONS AND ACTIONS THROUGH VARIOUS LIFE STAGES & TRANSITIONS

By Veronica Escobar, Esq.

As children we became ***accustomed to having our parents*** (or our guardians) take care of every need and want that we had. We needed to eat? They cooked for us or took us out for a meal. We became sick? They would tend to us at home or take us to the doctor. We needed money? They would give us an allowance or make us do chores in order to earn it. We truly had no cares in the world because our families shouldered that responsibility.

However, the carefree "good times" of youth are not meant to last. With the age of majority, which is eighteen years old, come responsibility and big decisions. Some we are prepared for, like pursuing higher education or entering the workforce, and others that we'd prefer to hold off on – mainly contemplating our financial security, illness, aging and dying. And as we become older and add people, or subtract them, from our lives, these latter issues will require even more openness, thoughtfulness, honesty – and action.

The problem is that many of us do not take the time to think about these important issues at all, much less act on them, seemingly finding a way to make excuses; i.e. life "gets in the way," "I cannot afford it (to plan)" or "I have other things I need to do first." In the end, if certain actions are not taken to safeguard financial, medical and personal interests, there are likely to be very real financial, legal, and not to mention emotional, consequences.

This Chapter will attempt to outline estate planning considerations through different life stages. Each of us are in these life stages themselves or know someone who is going through these transitions, with a focus on family and matrimonial transitions.

The Emancipation Year

Once a person turns eighteen, he or she is an adult in the eyes of the law and the parent(s) no longer have control over their person – or any legal responsibility. Parent(s) can no longer make health or medical decisions. Parents can no longer control their child(ren) finances. An emancipated young person can live independently from his or her parents, without having to answer to them – whether they are emotionally mature enough to do so or not.

> In New York, emancipation for child support purposes is 21. More information on emancipation for child support is in Chapter 19.

But with this freedom, also comes the possibility of ***incapacity, illness as well as death*** – very adult subjects. The latter three do not discriminate; it is not just a reality for elder people. Legally speaking, parents can no longer intervene in these matters. And while it seems unlikely, a young adult may have assets even if they have never worked a day in their life, mainly through inheritance, the proceeds of lawsuit settlement or an outright gift from a family member.

At a bare minimum, a newly emancipated adult should have the first two of the following documents as part of their estate planning; however a complete estate plan is always recommended for full protection.

A Power of Attorney ("POA")

This is a legal document where a person, referred to as "principal," delegates to another person, referred to as "agent," the responsibility to manage his or her personal, financial and legal affairs should they become incapacitated. The types of matters handled range from opening or closing bank accounts, managing investments, making financial gifts, representing the principal in the event of a lawsuit, paying medical bills, and selling or buying real estate, just to name a few. The "POA" as it called in the practice area, is a very powerful document that is, unfortunately, prone to abuse.

That is why a person should take great care in naming an agent. The agent need not be a family member, but should be someone the principal trusts to carry out his or her wishes and who is fiscally responsible. And the principal should have a sincere discussion with the intended agent prior to executing the document to a) explain their wishes and b) ascertain if the individual wishes to be an agent.

Health Proxy

This is a legal document, which, in other states, is often referred to as a "***Medical Power of Attorney***." It is the health/medical equivalent of a POA, in that the principal names an agent to follow his or her wishes regarding medical care in the event of incapacity. Incapacity, in this context, means the principal's inability to communicate his or her wishes- either due to an unconscious or comatose state, injury that prevents verbal communication in an emergency situation, neurological issues that may prevent comprehension and/or communication, advanced Alzheimer's disease or dementia – just to list a few examples.

The common misconception is that a Health Proxy is an end-of-life document – and it is not. However, it does address "artificial nutrition and hydration" which does directly impact the end of life, should that be the situation at hand. And for the same reasons as stated for the POA, a principal should have a sincere discussion with their intended agent prior to executing the Health Proxy to a) explain their wishes and b) ascertain if the individual wishes to be an agent.

Living Will

This document is not statutory in the State of New York, which means it is not legally enforceable. However, it is oftentimes executed with a health care proxy. Opinion is mixed about the benefit of a Living Will; however the one benefit is that it allows the writer to go in to further detail about their medical care and end of life wishes. The above three documents are collectively known as "advance directives."

Last Will and Testament

This is commonly referred to as a "will." It is the legal document where a person, named the "testator," states who will inherit their belongings, property or "assets," whether personal or what is referred to as "real property" or real estate. The person who inherits is referred to as a "beneficiary." A single person can leave their belongings to family, friends, or ***even a charity*** – to whomever they want.

Once a person passes away, the Last Will and Testament goes through a court process called "***probate***" which will allow for the person's assets to be disposed of properly. There are some assets that are considered "***non probate***," in that they can "pass" outside of a Last Will and Testament to the named beneficiary. For example, a life insurance policy with a named beneficiary, real estate held in name with another person, jointly held bank account(s), retirement accounts with a named beneficiary, accounts "***In Trust For***" someone else, or property held in the name of a Trust.

Depending on the type of assets and their total monetary value, a will can be a relatively straightforward to complex document. As an introductory chapter, there is much detail that cannot be further elaborated on. Rest assured that no one should die without one.

Trust

A trust is a legal entity created by an individual, who is known as the "***settlor***," regarding the distribution of his or her property for the benefit of their person, or another, usually a spouse or children – or a charity. A trust can be created for use during life (*i.e.*, "***inter vivos***") or for disposition at death (*i.e.*, ***testamentary***). The person who controls the trust is named a "***trustee***," and the person who benefits from the trust is called a "***beneficiary***." The settlor creates the rules of the trust and the trustee enforces them.

What can be "placed" in a trust? While not an exhaustive list, these are some of the items: cash (in the form of any type of bank account), collectibles (like a coin collection), art work, antiques, stocks, bonds and other types of investment accounts (but not retirement accounts), life insurance, a home or other type of real estate, an interest in a small business, or patents or copyrights. When appropriate, a "***Transfer on Death***," or "***Payable on Death***" designation should be utilized when available for certain accounts, as this eases the transfer of the asset – even if already in a trust.

Trusts, of which there are quite a few types, can be complicated documents since they are utilized for various purposes, namely asset and tax protection. Every person's situation is unique and if trusts are to be utilized, they need to be specifically tailored to those assets.

Single in the City

Is someone who has been out "in the real world" for a few years… or decades, and has held a job, or two, or maybe changed careers once or twice… or more. They may rent or own a home… or own more than one. They may like riding their bicycle to get around town, or may prefer driving a four-wheeler. They may just be starting to invest in the stock market… or they may be sophisticated investors. And remember, you can be a home owner at the age of twenty-five and have never owned a car at the age of fifty. It is relative to lifestyle, priorities, as well as socio-economics.

At this point, the "single adult" should have a Last Will and Testament as well as a Health Proxy and Power of Attorney – and if his or her particular circumstances necessitate it or it confers a benefit – some type of trust or trusts. At this life stage there is likely the accumulation of assets – of some type – and their disposition becomes even more important regardless of the "single" status, as does health care decision-making. In fact, in the older single person the execution of these documents is crucial. Lack of planning could affect their financial security as well as future medical care. In older single adults there is a lack of a support network and the lack of estate planning leaves them without a safety net and especially vulnerable.

The Single Adult Who's a Package Deal

The above is an adult who is not married but may be rearing a child on his or her own or with the child's parent (but not married to him or her). A basic estate plan is still as applicable here, but once someone has children then there are other considerations. What happens if either parent dies? Who will care for the child(ren) then? Can a nest egg be created for the child(ren)'s future? What happens if the parents separate without hope of reconciliation? There are many questions that arise once someone becomes a parent. This is not an exhaustive list as numerous other issues may surface.

If there is no other parent in the picture, then a Last Will and Testament is a necessary document, particularly because of the "***guardianship***" provision. In the event of a parent's death, a suitable person must be left to care and raise the child(ren). Who is considered "suitable" really depends on the parent's beliefs and how he or she wishes for the child(ren) to be raised.

The guardian(s) are typically someone very well known to the parent and who reflects the same or similar values, or, minimally, is someone who can and will carry out the parent's wishes. A "Standby Guardianship" is another document that should be executed, as it allows for a person to care for a child in the event of the parent(s) incapacity; and in the event of death, it is a "placeholder" while the will is probated.

If there is another parent in the picture, both must be on board as to who the guardian(s) of the child(ren) will be. If one parent dies, the other parent automatically raises the child. There are exceptions to this that will not be addressed here, but mainly center on the surviving parent's general fitness (as a parent).

One or both parents can set up a trust for child's benefit, either testamentary or during life (*inter vivos*). Since the child's parents may not reside together or be a couple, they may want to each provide for the child. The parent may or may not designate the other as the trustee of the trust. Both parents should execute advance directives, for their sake, the child's overall welfare and to also alleviate stress from the caretaker parent in the event the other is incapacitated for a certain or indefinite period of time.

Party of Two

The uniting of two lives under the laws of the State of New York or the laws of God is a definite life change. This union also brings with it the "marrying" of finances, as well as the ups and downs of life- which can include job promotions, career changes, increases or decreases in income, home purchase, illness, incapacity and death. When two people act as a unit, most of their decisions must be made in the same way because the consequences will affect them both.

If either person entering a marriage has a Last Will and Testament, then he or she should amend it or draft a new one and add his or her spouse as a beneficiary. And even if you have a will and do not name your spouse, he or she has the right to inherit a part of your estate- unless he or she disclaims it. You cannot disinherit a spouse. Generally, spouses' wills tend to be almost identical, and are commonly referred to as "reciprocal" or "mirror" wills.

In terms of ***advance directives*** (i.e., the POA, Health Proxy and a Living Will), there is a belief that a spouse is automatically the agent under a POA or Health Proxy – even when neither exists. There is also the presumption that a spouse should be named the agent under both documents since there is an existing marriage. And if the spouse is not so named, then something is awry. Is it the norm for a spouse to be named? Yes. Are there exceptions? Of course there are. And it doesn't mean the marriage is "bad." It could be that the spouse is not very good with money, may not be the best decision maker or "too emotional" in certain situations. Life is not black and white and the same can be said for marriage.

In terms of a trust, a spouse may consider setting up one for the spouse's benefit, especially if she is a non U.S. citizen but one should also remember that there is an unlimited amount of transfers of assets between spouses (the "unlimited marital deduction") – which is also an effective planning tool.

And Baby Makes "Three"

There's a country song titled "A baby changes everything" and this is true, not only in life perspective, priorities, mindset and, yes, worries, but also in how a family now plans for the future. Before the baby… or babies… there were just two people. But now almost every decision made by the couple will affect their offspring and that carries, at times, enormous weight.

In terms of a will, in the event of the simultaneous death of both parents (or deaths close in time), a provision will need to be made in both parents wills (*both* parents should have executed wills) regarding the guardian or guardians of their child(ren). And both wills must name the same person or people as guardian(s). A "***Stand by Guardianship***," as mentioned previously, should also be executed so that the person named can immediately care for the child, in the event of both parents incapacity, or in the event of death, until the will(s) are probated

And now with the addition of children, testamentary bequests (in a will) need to be more thought out and provision should be made to provide for a minor child(ren) in the event of the death of either parent.

Testamentary bequests for a minor child are accomplished through trusts- that are established in a will – and are specifically designed to deal with minors, and usually have provisions that regulate when the minor child can inherit – and it does not necessarily mean the age of majority. It is whenever the parent believes he or she is emotionally ready to handle an inheritance – and that is completely subjective decision.

In addition to testamentary bequests, parents can also set up a trust(s) for the benefit of a child's education and/or general maintenance-outside of a last will and testament. Again, the trust determines if and when the child can access the trust as well as who controls it and how the money is to be utilized. And the settlor may or may not name the spouse (other parent of the child) as the trustee of the trust.

When "Happily Ever After"... Isn't

In a relationship, people either grow together or apart. Marriage is work and if a couple grows apart and the rift cannot be mended, a divorce is for many the next step. It is a difficult step for sure, which requires not only the severing of the legal relationship defined as marriage but also financial and emotional ties. If there are children of the marriage it can make the process more challenging as well as uncomfortable; children are truly the ties that bind.

Once a divorce is finalized and even if a Last Will and Testament is not modified or re-executed, the former spouse is automatically disinherited. Nevertheless, a new Last Will and Testament should be executed as a divorce also offers another opportunity to reconsider bequests and maybe our thoughts have changed since then. In terms of advance directives, the aforementioned disqualification in a last will and testament does not translate here. New ***advanced directives*** must be executed and actual notice must be provided to the prior agent (ex-spouse or not) of the revocation of the power of agent.

If there were any trusts set up for the benefit of a spouse, those will also need to be addressed and, if possible, done away with. And new ***trusts may need to be executed*** to benefit children or grandchildren – or even the self.

"Till Death Do Us Part"

The death of a spouse is devastating; no matter the length of the marriage. However, the longer the marriage the deeper the ties – punctuated by life's many changes. In addition to the personal and emotional tidal wave that person is confronting, he or she is also encountering years' worth of financial and, perhaps, legal history. Hopefully, any loose ends that may have existed were tied up during the marriage with proper legal and financial planning. And now that that person is facing the world without a spouse, what to do?

Most, if not all, of the testamentary documents and advanced directives will need to be re-drafted and executed anew. And again, the death of a spouse allows the widowed spouse to re-examine their testamentary objectives and perhaps make modifications to reflect their current and foreseeable life situation. Again, it is quite possible that completely new legal documents, like trusts, will be executed for the benefit of children or grandchildren – or even the self – in the ***wake of the death*** of a spouse and as a way to protect assets or confer benefits to the settlor/grantor.

Love the Second Time Around (or Maybe a Third)

Maybe a first marriage did not work out; or maybe that person is widowed. But he or she got back into the dating game and found love anew and are ready to profess wedding vows once more. This person already lived one life prior to meeting the new love; he or she may have children (and they may be adults), and/or that person may already own a home or other assets. This person may have inherited assets from a spouse upon his or her death or may have been awarded them pursuant to a divorce settlement. Life is good but not necessarily uncomplicated.

There may be children of the second or third marriage – as well as the children from the first, so attention must be paid when planning for them. Every family presents with a different dynamic and children may also present with different needs (or a lack thereof). Need could be based on age, education level, special needs, and/or family financial circumstances, just to name a few. Care and thought should be taken to provide for children in a way that is equitable without necessarily being equal – and without leaving the bitter taste of resentment.

The above would necessitate a re-execution of a Last Will and Testament. Also, since a spouse cannot be disinherited, a parent, again, could establish a trust in the name of the child(ren) in order to provide for them-even as adults – as a way to equitably distribute assets, provide for the future or to confer a benefit for themselves. Life insurance policies and other financial investments could also be utilized to provide for children – and this is applicable here and in every other life stage mentioned in this Chapter.

Final Thoughts

Change is never easy; while some life transitions bring great joy, others bring sadness. But even in the latter moments, there is always the hope and promise of new beginnings. Effective and comprehensive estate planning can actually help to make them more than possible.

Veronica Escobar, Esq.

Veronica Escobar is the Principal and Founder of The Law Offices of Veronica Escobar, a practice focusing exclusively in the areas of Elder Law, Special Needs Planning and Trusts and Estates. Prior to forming her own law practice, Veronica worked as an attorney representing the City of New York, Administration for Children's Services (ACS) in child abuse and neglect matters (commonly referred to as an "Article 10") ranging from educational neglect to serious forms of abuse.

Veronica is admitted to practice in the State of New York. She is also admitted to practice before the U.S. District Courts for the Eastern and Southern Districts of New York and the United States Supreme Court. She graduated summa cum laude from Fordham College at Rose Hill, Fordham University, where she was also elected to Phi Beta Kappa, with a degree in American Studies and a minor in Latin American/Latino Studies. She also received her law degree from Fordham, where she was a Notes and Articles Editor of the Fordham International Law Journal.

Currently, she is the Co-Chair of the Diversity Committee of the Elder Law and Special Needs Section of the New York State Bar, a member of the Elder Law and Special Needs and Trusts and Estates Sections of the New York State Bar Association, and is a Deputy Regional President for the Hispanic National Bar Association (HNBA) New York Region. She is a past member of the Legal Problems of the Aging and the Family Court and Family Law Committees of the New York City Bar.

She is also an avid reader of everything, a music lover, concertgoer, museum fan, and burgeoning world traveler, as well as an information sponge.

To learn more about Veronica, you can connect to her website www.veronicaescobarlaw.com, on Twitter @EscobarLawNY or on Facebook at www.facebook.com/VeronicaEscobarLawNewYork.

PART VII: MOVING ON

SECTION A: GETTING READY FOR THE NEXT CHAPTER

CHAPTER 48

HEALING AND BECOMING EMOTIONALLY AVAILABLE AGAIN

by Cheryl Lazarus, CLC, CRC, CDC

Relationships after a separation or divorce are very different than before marriage. The structure of life has changed. Dreams have shattered, perspectives have shifted from the experience of a long term commitment, in some cases having had children, and having experienced the dashed hopes of "***happily ever after.***"

As a result of this ***life-change***, a person recovering from a divorce or separation may:

- feel exhausted and need time to recover;
- wonder if he or she will ever find love again;
- have lost his or her self-confidence or sense of self;
- feel afraid to trust again; and/or
- be excited to finally create a fulfilling relationship.

Each one of these thoughts and feelings are valid for someone that has gone through a separation and divorce.

The following steps can help someone to heal and become emotionally available again. A ***relationship coach*** can provide help in all these areas.

Intentions Create Outcomes

Intentions are critically important as they create thoughts, feelings, behaviors and actions. It is that simple *and* that difficult! Most people do not create intentions; then they experience repetition of the same frustrating results.

The good news – we all play an ***important role in the outcome of relationships***. Each person has the ability to create better relationships. It takes being aware, being equipped with new tools and being willing to do something different.

Someone who recently went through a divorce or separation may have the following intentions:

- to heal and let go of the past;
- to uncover hidden barriers to love;
- to date causally and learn new skills; and/or
- to eventually be in a long term relationship or remarry.

Steps for Healing

Dealing with Shattered Hopes and Dreams

A person recovering from a divorce or separation may be experiencing heartbreak, oftentimes rooted in a commitment to spend a life with another person in "***good times and bad***." He or she may have said at some point, "I wasn't happy but I made a commitment and was going to stick it out," or "I know I didn't pay enough attention to her, but I never thought she would leave." Or, "How could he do this to the kids?"

These thoughts and feelings are natural after the trauma of a divorce. They will usually subside through the passage of time and by receiving support. However, sometimes a person is unable to let go and move forward. At these times, it can be even more critical to work with a relationship coach, particularly one who works with people who have gone through a divorce. The steps discussed below can help in healing and letting go, and creating new hopes and dreams.

Really Feel the Emotions – Don't Ignore Them

During and after a divorce, one may feel angry, sad, or scared. These emotions can be triggered when a person thinks of dating again or is in a new relationship. It is natural to experience a ***roller coaster ride of emotions***, yet it is necessary to express them and to keep energy flowing. If the emotions are ignored and not fully experienced, then:

- anger can become depression,

- unhealed grief can close your heart, and
- fear that runs rampant can turn into chronic anxiety.

There are ***healthy ways*** to express all three.

Write in a journal, cry and talk with people who support you, get professional help. This will help the healing process.

Grief

Maggie had been divorced for two years. Her 20-year marriage ended after her husband had an affair. Maggie said, "I'm ready to date again." At least she thought she was ready. The issue was that each time Maggie planned to log onto Match.com, go on a date, or attend a singles party, Maggie stopped herself with excuses.

In talking with Cheryl, her relationship coach, Maggie said, "I understand why he had an affair. We were unhappy for a long time and couples counseling didn't help. I still feel betrayed, though." Cheryl asked if she has allowed her to grieve. "Oh, yes," Maggie replied, "For a year I cried."

That's great," Cheryl said. "And what about anger? Have you allowed yourself to process anger?" Maggie thought about it and said, "But I understand why he did it even though I feel really betrayed and am upset that he broke up our marriage that way."

"That's on an intellectual level, which is good," Cheryl replied. She continued, "However, if you're still feeling betrayed and unable to trust men, then it's important to process your anger. The anger energy is stuck in your body and needs to move. This will help you to heal and move forward."

Her divorce coach helped Maggie get in touch with and release her anger. Maggie felt like a huge burden was lifted and was excited to meet new men.

There is ***no timetable for grief*** – everyone heals at their own pace. Someone recovering from a divorce or separation should be careful not to allow "well meaning" friends to cause them to feel that the process is taking too long.

Feng Shui the Home

Objects hold energy and are reminders of the person and what has been lost. To heal it is important

Janet worked with Cheryl, a relationship and divorce coach. Cheryl suggested that Janet put away all photos and objects that reminded her of her spouse Jeff. Janet took off her wedding ring and other jewelry that Jeff had given to her. Cheryl and Janet created a "letting go" ritual which was very emotional yet necessary. Janet also put Jeff's clothes and belongings into bags and placed them into a closet until he could pick them up. She then filled up the additional new closet space.

to lessen the conscious and unconscious "zings" that you get when looking at these objects.

Someone transitioning from a divorce or separation should take a look around the home and really make it their own. This can be done as simply as buying a few objects or dishes that represent his or her individual taste. Alternatively, it could include larger purchases such as new furniture. One might buy new drapes, linens, dishes and a new bed.

Remove Reminders

> It had been two years and Jeremy was having difficulty healing. Cheryl, his relationship coach, noticed Jeremy's watch. He said that his ex had given it to him and that he really liked it.
>
> The relationship coach said, "Yes, it is a very nice watch. How many times a day do you look at it?"
>
> He replied, "At least every hour."
>
> Cheryl commented, "Even though you really like your watch, on an unconscious level you are thinking of your ex at least every hour as you look at that watch. You never get away from it at work or at home. I recommend that you take the watch off. You can put it in your closet or donate it."
>
> He felt uncomfortable with this idea because he felt very attached to the watch and to the woman who gave it to him. Cheryl suggested that he take it off for one week and notice if there was a difference.
>
> Jeremy took it off and after a week he said, "I'm keeping it off and buying a new one!"

Steps for Uncovering and Letting Go

Limiting Love Beliefs

Limiting love beliefs are deeply rooted and influence how people see and experience the world. Limiting love beliefs are ***created in childhood***. These beliefs are a result of one's parents' relationship and of experiences with significant persons in one's life (e.g., teachers, friends and family). For example, if a child feels neglected, abandoned, criticized, not heard, humiliated, unloved or abused then he/she could create a limited love belief such as "I'm unlovable," "I'll be abandoned," or "I'm not good enough." The important thing with limiting love beliefs is to recognize them.

Since these limiting beliefs are created in childhood, this negative filter causes people to draw experiences supporting those negative thoughts, thereby enforcing this negative vision of the world. However, by releasing the structure of the belief and then by changing ***thoughts, feelings and taking conscious actions***, a person can create more positive beliefs and decisions about the world. Those positive decisions attract more positive experiences, people and relationships.

> Jan and her husband Ted had been drifting apart. She had been giving her time and attention to their three children, while he spent more and more time at the office. Their communication had eroded along with their intimacy. Jan was unwilling to bring this up as she was afraid of confrontation. She also enjoyed her home and their lifestyle so chose to ignore the dissolving nature of their marriage.
>
> As Jan and her relationship coach Cheryl explored these issues, Jan could see her part in the situation. Jan realized several ways that she had neglected Ted. She had not listened to his needs for attention nor communicated her dissatisfaction with their marriage. As Cheryl and Jan examined the patterns of complacency and avoidance, Jan's feeling of victimization lifted.
>
> In addition, Cheryl taught Jan new communication and listening skills which Jan practiced with significant people in her life. Over time, all Jan's relationships improved through use of these skills.

Holding Oneself Accountable

A divorce or broken relationship does not happen in a vacuum. Small infringements or deteriorations usually lead to the breakdown of the relationship. It is easier, however, to deny what is occurring or ignore red flags along the way.

Discovering even a small part of the failure in a relationship or trust can transform someone from feeling powerless to feeling empowered.

Self-Forgiveness

Susan felt devastated when her husband Jack left the marriage. She still loved him. At first she felt victimized; she blamed him totally and reinforced her despair by retelling her story to anyone who would listen.

Her relationship coach, Cheryl, helped Susan to explore her contribution to the difficulties in her marriage. Susan discovered that her marriage was similar to her parents' marriage. Susan realized that she treated Jack the same way that her mom had treated her dad. Like her mom, she criticized her husband continually; she found fault with everything he did.

In addition, Jack had requested twenty five minutes of "downtime" when he came home from the office. This could help him to transition and unwind from a tough day. Instead of providing it, Susan would meet him at the door with a list of things that she wanted him to do. She complained about the kids and followed him from room to room when she was trying to get his attention.

Jack got angry and withdrew behind his computer. Susan got frustrated and verbally attacked him. They were caught in a vicious cycle. Their resentment grew until Jack decided to leave the marriage.

After their separation, Susan got a job to bring in extra income. When she got home from work, she wanted to relax before spending time with the kids. She also appreciated it when her oldest daughter greeted her with a hug and got upset when her youngest made demands on her the moment she walked through the door.
She understood Jack's needs and his impatience with her demands. She felt guilty and sad for her behavior during the marriage. "If only I had given him space when he came home!" she exclaimed. "Why did I have to criticize him so much! I wish that I knew how to communicate better."

Through the process of understanding and forgiving herself for her behavior, Susan was able to heal. She moved forward from feeling victimized to empowered as she learned new skills to create more positive relationships in the future.

In time she forgave Jack. Forgiveness helps free one's heart as resentment and anger are released. Forgiving Jack was an act of compassion for herself.

Exploring one's contribution to the deterioration of a relationship can be a ***humbling experience***. It can bring up remorse and regret for what one has or has not done, has said or not said. One may criticize oneself for not knowing better, for having stayed in a bad marriage for so long, or for not speaking up or setting boundaries. Many women and men also feel guilty for hurting their spouse or leaving the marriage.

While this self-exploration is painful, it also ***provides an opportunity for growth***. It can help someone to understand what he or she needs to heal and the skills to learn. It is important for everyone to be compassionate with oneself, because everyone makes mistakes.

Self-forgiveness is crucial for healing and letting go. There are powerful processes that can help with this necessary step. After a person has self-forgiveness, he or she can learn new skills and develop more positive relationships.

Forgiveness of Others

Once a person has forgiven him or herself, it is easier to understand another person's perceived transgression. After a person has seen their contribution to the problems in the marriage, he or she may feel less victimized and be able to forgive a spouse. Forgiveness is an act of compassion for oneself, as it helps to heal one's heart. Forgiveness is not condoning another's behavior, it is resolving the hold of anger and resentment so one can feel free.

Self-Love and Renewal

Regaining Trust

Regaining trust after a separation or divorce ***can be challenging***. When people marry they expect the marriage to last "until death do us part." A person saying "I do" puts their ***trust in love***, in their spouse and in marriage itself.

Betrayals of trust can be devastating, especially if one's spouse has an affair. ***Betrayal sears the heart*** and creates a more complex level of healing, letting go, and renewal. When the marriage has ended through the catalyst of an affair, then it is especially important that the relationship be explored. While it can be difficult to experience the depth of the hurt and pain, it also creates an opportunity for more honesty with oneself and to develop more healthy relationship patterns in the future.

> Sunny's husband cheated on her twice. She stayed because of their three children and because she loved him. They moved across the country for his new job which uprooted her from friends and family.
>
> Two years later, she discovered sexy texts on Tom's cell phone. Devastated that he started a new affair, Sunny filed for a divorce.
>
> During their separation, she started dating John. He was kind and generous to both her and her children. He was also an understanding, attentive man.
>
> However, every time Sunny saw John writing a text, her stomach churned and her "trust antennae" went off. Logically, she knew that her new man was loyal, but her unhealed trust issues were in the way.
>
> Sunny worked with Cheryl, a relationship coach. They addressed Sunny's unresolved emotions, challenged her beliefs about men and created new internal conversations, Sunny made strides in her ability to trust herself, her choices and John. She realized that it is a process and that the time it takes is well worth it because she wants a fulfilling trusting connection with John.

It is also important to consider that the breakdown of the marriage through an affair may be the catalyst for a change that needed to come. People often avoid change out of fear; are comfortable with the *status quo*, since they do not know what the future will bring. Because of this, they stay in unhappy marriages.

Trusting Yourself

How much do you ***trust yourself***? How much do you ***trust your choices***? How a person answers these questions about him or herself affects how much he or she trusts other people, because one can only trust another based on how much one can trust oneself. Bolstering trust in oneself comes first.

People should be aware of their own choices and decisions. They should notice the effects on themselves, other people, and on their circumstances. One's choices may be on automatic or because it is "always done that way." However, a person can gain new tools to create other choices or behaviors.

When a person makes better choices, then he or she builds confidence in his or her ability to discern and create more positive outcomes. In turn, this builds trust within oneself.

Trust in a Partner and in Relationship

If someone is having trouble trusting a partner, then this person should ask two things: (1) is it them or (2) is it their partner?

Someone who has been hurt or betrayed in the past may experience distrust in relationships. For some, their parents may have been divorced, or perhaps their parents or loved ones died at an early age. For others, a partner may have cheated on them. These experiences can create a conscious or unconscious belief that men or women ***cannot be trusted***. It is important explore these beliefs and to take steps to heal and transform them.

In addition, people can build trust in a powerful way through their words. When a person makes a commitment, he or she should follow through with actions. This follow-through helps build confidence and trust in oneself and one's partner.

Trust issues will need to be explored, emotions felt and the heart healed. He or she may need to learn new skills for communicating, setting boundaries and making better choices.

Creating Healthy Love Patterns

When two people come together, they each bring their limiting love beliefs, and these create a love pattern. Thus a love pattern is the dynamic that one ***creates with a partner***. This love pattern involves how two people interact, react to one another, and respond to conflict and experiences. It is how one interacts, reacts or responds when one is in a relationship. This includes friends, family and intimate romantic relationships.

Patterns are developed out of necessity, to help a person to ***adapt and survive***. Some people have had childhoods that included abuse, emotionally unavailable parents, divorce or death. Certain patterns are created in order to help a person make it through difficult experiences. Although necessary at one time, such patterns can became automatic and habitual. Many people are not aware that they have fallen into a pattern or know how to change it.

> Kelley's mother had abandoned her when she was very young. Years later, her husband did the same. When she started relationship coaching with Cheryl, it was several years after her divorce. Kelley was in a relationship with a caring man named Sam, yet she had not healed from the past.
>
> When Kelley and Sam became close, she got scared. She provoked fights or criticized him. Sam then pulled away. This caused Kelley even more pain and reinforced her belief that she could not trust men.
>
> Cheryl helped Kelley to heal her heart from the unresolved abandonment by her mother. Cheryl also helped Kelley explore sabotaging behaviors with Sam and provided her with new responses to her fears of intimacy.
>
> Kelley was determined to change her love patterns and to move through her fears. She consciously made choices which supported this and created a trusting, close relationship with Sam.

Unhealthy love patterns can be roadblocks to happiness and fulfilling relationships. Someone recovering from a divorce or separation should thoughtfully explore his or her love patterns. New beliefs and behaviors can be learned, and healthier love patterns created.

Effectively Expressing Needs

Lack of communication during a relationship causes anger, resentment and distance. People can be afraid to speak-up for themselves because:

- Their parents fought a lot; therefore, "speaking up" equates to confrontation and conflict.
- He or she is afraid that the partner would leave.
- As a child, they did not feel "heard" so why should they feel "heard" now as an adult?

People can learn to separate their past experiences from their current relationships and gain important communication skills. Communication is not about the argument – it is about how issues are resolved. Communication can create connection and intimacy. One learns more about the needs of one's partner. Creating solutions together builds closeness.

There are several effective communication methods that combine assertiveness with sensitivity. When a person speaks from the heart, listens with curiosity, and aims for resolution then he or she can have more positive, fulling relationships!

Dating Again

Dating again can be both exciting and scary, especially for someone who had been married for a long time. The dating world is different than it was 10 or 20 years ago. Dating now requires new skills and flexibility.

When dating, a person should think about what he or she is looking for. For example, are casual relationships or long-term relationships the goal? To avoid the rebound effect, it is important to heal and become emotionally available before entering back into a long term serious relationship.

Dating provides an opportunity to know oneself better. Dating allows a person to analyze love patterns. By keeping a journal about these dating experiences one can discover more about oneself and how one relates to new dating partners. The self-discovery includes realizing issues that need to be healed and new skills one needs to learn.

> Carol had been married for 20 years. She did not want to jump back into a relationship or become sexually involved too soon. This gave her more flexibility in dating because she did not need to think about a man matching her "list" of ideal qualities.
>
> Since Carol loved jazz, classical music, and going to art shows, she dated men who enjoyed these things as well. This was a change from her husband, who had been more of a sports guy and who was not interested in music or art.

Loving Oneself

Self-love is the deeper inner work that rewires a person's view of him or herself. Most people need a ***huge dose of self-love***.

Self-love is about talking kindly to oneself and accepting oneself. Many have had a critical parent growing up and have internalized a critical voice. Those critical messages are ***continually***

repeated and are believed. This behavior is unhealthy and disempowering.

Once a person learns how to stop the negative messages, and to accept and speak compassionately to him or herself, *then* he or she will feel confident and empowered. When one accepts oneself, instead of seeking approval from a partner, one can feel complete and loved from the inside out.

Cheryl Lazarus, CLC, CRC, CDC

Cheryl Lazarus, CLC, CRC, CDC is a Certified Divorce and Relationship Coach, Speaker, and NLP Master Practitioner with therapeutic training. Having gone through her own divorce successfully, Cheryl understands the practical and emotional challenges of the divorce process and the opportunities in redesigning one's life.

When working with clients, Cheryl provides actionable steps, strategies and resources which help clients to save time, money and have less aggravation during the divorce process. In addition, Cheryl includes heart-centered energetic and spiritual practices which helps women and men to heal and move forward on a profound level which positively affects all areas of their lives.

Cheryl has presented at the United Nations, to professional organizations, and has been on expert panels. She also holds workshops and support groups on topics ranging from "The Integrated Divorce," "Healing and Letting Go," to "Dating, Relationships and Becoming Emotionally Available Again."

Cheryl also coaches privately in person and globally through Skype and via phone consultations. www.zengalove.com, www.easiertransitions.com.

CHAPTER 49

THE HERO'S JOURNEY—HOW MEN CAN LEARN TO REFRAME RECOVERY

By Scott A. Mills, DC

Men have a special path to recovery during and after a divorce and separation. This is largely due to the specific response common to many men facing divorce and traversing divorce recovery. This stems from the fact that in heterosexual marriages, about three quarters of divorces are initiated by the woman. This leaves many men feeling as though the proverbial rug has been pulled out from under them. Many men recognized that the signs of trouble were present, but they didn't think it would come to this.

This is a very typical divorce archetype, ***initiator and reactor***; based on the statistics, men are most likely going to be the latter.

Whether they realize it or not, people are constantly telling themselves a story. It's a dynamic process, constantly evolving with the ***ebb and flow of life***. And commonly in this stage of life, it can feel like a stormy tidal wave pummeling them into a rocky shore.

The Hero's Journey Defined

Enter "***The Hero's Journey***." For those unfamiliar with this concept, it is the explanation of what makes a story compelling and relatable originally proposed by author and psychologist Joseph Campbell in his book THE HERO WITH A THOUSAND FACES.[63] The general concept is that throughout human history, people have tried to ***use story to communicate and understand the world around them***. Think of it as a template for myths, stories, and religions that become repeated throughout humanity; this is often referred to as the

---

[63] Joseph Campbell, THE HERO WITH A THOUSAND FACES. Princeton: Princeton University Press, 1968, p. 30 / Novato, California: New World Library, 2008, p. 23.

"***monomyth.***" Campbell's influence has grown popular amongst those seeking to understand the universe as well as entertainers wishing to tell a more compelling story.

Campbell's full explanation has 17 parts, but for the purposes of this chapter, it can be distilled into 4 simple stages.

- An inciting event ***disrupts and displaces*** one from one's "normal" life.
- This results in a "***forced adventure.***"
- A boon of ***new knowledge*** and/or understanding is acquired.
- There is an ***edification of others*** with this new knowledge (i.e., passing it on).

Put simply, people love a story about someone who ***has been down and out***, only to come out on top. No one loves a story about a guy who is awesome, keeps being great, wins a bunch of things, and continues having success after success forever. People inherently need the struggle to ***appreciate the victory.*** Otherwise the story falls flat. It doesn't stick. It isn't retold.

The Hero's Journey in Pop Culture

Whether it's Luke Skywalker from STAR WARS, Neo in THE MATRIX, or Paulo Coehlo's Santiago in THE ALCHEMIST, The Hero's Journey is the underlying template found throughout our most notable and memorable narratives. It's the silver thread woven though the lining of the human struggle. It is pulling people toward something more meaningful.

It helps make sense out of one's trials and make peace with one's demons. And it can help speed up recovery by giving focus and meaning to the process.

The Hero's Journey and Divorce Recovery

One might wonder, "What does this concept have to do with divorce and divorce recovery?" To answer that, let's look back at the ***4 basic stages of The Hero's Journey*** through the perspective of divorce.

1. **An inciting event that disrupts and displaces our normal life.**

Clearly divorce can be defined as an event that forces one out of one's normal life and routine. For many men, it means a physical displacement as they look for new residence. For others it is a disruption of routine. Oftentimes it means both of these things. As divorce forces people from what they considered "normal," they often struggle to find a new normal.

2. A forced adventure.

Surely not all would call divorce recovery an adventure! Many are more likely to describe it as a nightmare. But one of the things that time affords is perspective. If you ask people who have recovered from their divorce and moved forward with their lives, you will find they often recount their divorce as one of the best things that ever happened to them. Reading this in a time of struggle, that will probably sound completely ridiculous. However, often in life, to progress one must be forced out of one's comfort zone.

3. A boon of new knowledge and /or understanding.

If one learns nothing from one's struggle and adventure, what's the point? The ultimate sign of recovery is new understanding. Without this, one is left in an existential vacuum, constantly wondering, "Why me? Why this?" With no answers, people are stuck. They must strive to find the purpose, the meaning to their suffering.

4. Edification of others with the new knowledge (e.g.: passing it on).

The goal of divorce recovery then, is to utilize what one has learned in order to help others in a similar predicament. What better way to realize recovery than to walk a brother through his? One should ask oneself, what part of my experience is relatable? Who could benefit from the things my divorce has taught me? In this way one takes a life experience and turns it into a learning experience for the betterment of mankind.

That might sound like a lofty goal, but reframing recovery in this manner helps shift the focus away from one's own suffering. It gives men a goal, a task to be completed. This feels right to men. Give men seeking a better life a task to accomplish and it will get done.

Final Thoughts

To reiterate, people are drawn to stories about men who have been down and out and have come back to be successful. Men should ***reframe their divorce*** as a new beginning in the story of themselves. Men are not defined by this singular event, rather they are stimulated into action, understanding and new success.

A man is tasked with recovery in order to help the man struggling next to him. Like brothers in arms, he takes up the challenge of recovery. Men need to tell and live a better story, for their own sake and for the sake of others.

In the end, this may help men to see that divorce is not the final chapter of their story, but the beginning of new book along their Hero's Journey. A divorce coach can help men find ***their very own story*** to enter into the next chapter. For more information on this topic and additional help, see the recommended reading for "The 7 Step Reboot" from DivorceWingman.com.

Scott A. Mills

Dr. Scott A. Mills is a chiropractor with a passion for empowering others with the knowledge and tools needed to optimize health and life.

While going through a divorce he became dismayed at the lack of authentic, modern feeling resources for men recovering from divorce. He noticed the best help he received was from guys who had already been through the process and moved forward with their own successful lives.

In 2015 Scott launched DivorceWingman.com to encourage, support and give hope to guys in the recovery process. The idea is to pay forward the help he received and bring guys through the post-divorce funk into a new and better chapter of life.

SECTION B: USE OF PROFESSIONALS

CHAPTER 50

DATING AFTER DIVORCE: A NEW BEGINNING

By Suzanne K. Oshima

Going through a divorce is never easy, even if both parties amicably agree to part ways. As you start a new part of your life, it can be scary, exciting and challenging all at the same time. As you go through this process, it is important to remember to not tackle this new adventure until you are fully ready.

But wait, don't let that scare you, because I'm here to help guide you through the entire process. This chapter is aimed to help you navigate the dating game with complete confidence when you get back out there.

So, are you ready? Take a deep breath. And get ready to jump in!

Before You Start Dating

Let's face it – you are going through a very challenging time in your life. It's something you didn't plan on happening, so it's going to feel like an emotional rollercoaster ride. One minute, you're feeling fine and the next minute you're crying, and you feel like you don't want to get out of bed. But at some point, you will feel like you are finally ready to let go of your ex-spouse and move on. And when you do, you will need to go through a pre-dating process, before you actually get out there and date.

Letting Go!

Release the Heartbreak

The first step in the letting go process is to ***release the heartbreak***. And what that means is, you have to accept where you are at in your life right now. That means accepting that you are not going to be "happily ever after" with your ex-spouse, as you had originally thought.

Healing Traumas

It is important to allow yourself to grieve. While your ex-spouse has not passed away, the fact remains – a loss is a loss. You have to allow yourself to ***grieve your loss***. And that includes allowing yourself to cry, talk about it, get angry and scream about it… whatever it takes to heal the trauma. The worst thing you can do is to keep it bottled up inside, because the pressure will build up until you eventually explode.

Make a Decision: Do I Want to Be Happy or Unhappy?

Ask yourself, "***Do I want to be happy or unhappy?***" It is a decision you have to consciously make, as some people would rather wallow in their sorrow and remain depressed about their current situation for an indefinite period of time. If you are not ready to be happy, then you need to ask yourself a couple of questions and answer them honestly:

- **What's keeping me stuck here?**
- **What am I really afraid of?**

These are important questions to ask yourself because the truth of the matter is, all too often there are some people who would rather stay within their comfort zone of misery than to move on. Why, you ask? Because they are too afraid to venture out into a world of uncertainty and the unknown. However, if you have made the decision to move forward and be happy, then you are clearing the way to find a new love and a new life!

Moving Forward

> "You can't drive forward looking in the rear view mirror."

In order to move on with your life, you have to ***stop dwelling*** on the past. So, if you are really ready to move forward then it is time to truly "let go," so you can find the ***real love of your life*** for the long term.

Spring Cleaning

There is one last step that you need to take before you start dating post-divorce: you first have to "***spring clean***" your love life. Here are the steps:

- **Physical Cleanse.** First, you have to let go of physical items in your home that remind you of him/her. If you just cannot bring yourself to throw the things away or give them back to your ex-spouse, then you need to at least put those things in storage so they are "***out of sight, out mind.***" The last thing you need is a daily reminder of your ex-spouse; this will hold you back from moving forward.

- **Social Media Cleanse.** Next, you need to remove all photos of you and your ex-spouse on social media (Facebook, Twitter, Instagram, etc.)[64]. Then you need to disconnect from your ex-spouse on social media. When an ex is connected on social media then there is a temptation to *cyber snoop* to see what he/she is doing, who he/she is dating, etc. Even if you have moved on and are in another relationship, it can still be hurtful to see your ex-spouse with a new boyfriend/girlfriend (e.g., holding hands, being affectionate). It will just be hurtful

---

[64] This is only recommended if the divorce ended badly. If you have an amicable relationship with your ex-spouse, there's no need to do this, unless you feel the need to.

to you and create anxiety. So, why would you knowingly do that to yourself? It's time to move on and disconnect!

When Is the Right Time to Start Dating?

There isn't a right answer as to when the right time is to start dating again after divorce. It really depends on you and how you are feeling. If you have gone through the above process of "letting go," then you will know if you are really ready to date again. Don't just jump in with two feet and your eyes closed. You've been through a lot, so it's important to first test the waters. You have to ***be gentle on yourself and start out slow***.

Time for Self-Reflection

Getting a divorce is not uncommon anymore, nor is it the end of the world. So, try not to look at yourself as "damaged goods." In fact, some men and women ***prefer to date*** people that have been married before because it shows his/her ability to make a commitment to someone for the long term.

This is a great time in your life. It is a chance to really ***focus on you*** and ***take the time to re-discover who you are*** and what you have to offer another person. Now is the time to figure out what it is that you want in a new partner and relationship.

Take the time to analyze why your marriage didn't work and what was missing, because the last thing you want to do is to jump into a relationship/marriage just like the last one.

When you do this exercise, just make sure you are being realistic. The worst thing you can do is to have a list so long that no one could ever live up to it…which could actually end up keeping you single!

You're Ready! Have a Plan to Get Back Out There & Date

Now you are *finally* ready to get back out there and date! And here's the good news: there are many new ways to date and meet the right person.

Online Dating Sites & Apps

If you haven't dated for a decade or two, then welcome to the world of online dating! While it can seem a little scary to put yourself out there so publicly, online dating is actually one of the best ways to meet someone.

> **Focus on:**
>
> - What qualities do I want in a man/woman?
> - What common values must he/she have?
> - What are my "must haves"?
> - What are my deal breakers?

It is recommended to join at least ***two online dating websites*** – one paid and one unpaid. This will help maximize your chances of meeting the right person. You can go mainstream on one of the big sites, or you can choose a site that caters to a specific interest or demographic, like religion, ethnicity, or activity/interest.

Alternatively, many prefer to use the dating apps, which are growing in popularity. Just ask your single friends which websites and apps they use, as they will be able to recommend the best ones based on your age, preferences, lifestyle and interests.

Friends & Family

Friends and family are great sources to help you meet the right man/woman, so put the word out to them that you're ready to start dating. They are only going to want the best for you; thus, they will only chose someone who gets their ***stamp of approval***. More importantly, it will give you a sense of security knowing that he/she came recommended.

Matchmaking

Are you a busy professional who doesn't have a lot of time for dating? Or is online dating or bar hopping not your scene? If so, then consider ***hiring a matchmaker***.

Hiring a matchmaker is like hiring a real estate broker. A matchmaker will do all the work for you and will find you the best women/men who meet your specifications and don't have any of your deal breakers.

However, you should be aware that hiring a matchmaker is not going to be cheap. Matchmakers will spend a significant amount of time searching and weeding out men/women in order to find the one that could be your next husband/wife. Therefore, for something that important in your life, be prepared to make a financial investment to find the right one for you.

That being said, be careful about hiring a matchmaker ***too soon after you get divorced.*** You need some time to just get out there and date as many people as you can so you can discover more about yourself and what you want in the future.

Dating Coaches

Dating is not as organic or easy as it once used to be. So, if you have been out of the dating scene for a while, are really afraid to "get back out there" and don't know which way to turn, then you don't have to go it alone. A dating coach is the right way to go.

A dating coach will help you guide you through the ins and outs of dating process with ease:

- The ***best places to meet the right person*** based on your lifestyle and interests;
- How to ***meet someone organically*** without being too forward or desperate;
- Key ***flirting*** techniques in the early stages of dating and beyond;
- Understanding how the ***texting game*** is a push, pull dynamic;
- How to turn ***a first date*** into a second date and many more thereafter;
- What the real keys are to ***attracting*** the right man/woman;
- How to succeed at ***online dating*** and meet the right man/woman;
- What ***turns a man/woman off;***
- What you may be doing to ***scare him/her away;***
- Why he/she will ***disappear*** without a trace;
- How to ***deal with rejection*** so it doesn't break you;
- How to ***demolish your insecurities*** with dating;

- The right time to ***sleep with*** a new partner;
- What men/women want in a ***girlfriend/boyfriend***;
- How to go from just dating to an ***exclusive relationship***;
- ***Effective communication*** methods to a strong healthy relationship that lasts; and,
- How to go from an exclusive relationship to ***married again***!

For more information on dating advice and date coaching for both men and women, visit www.dreambachelor.com and for dating tips & advice exclusively for women, visit www.singleinstilettos.com.

Some Dating Pointers

How to Answer: "Why Did You Get Divorced?"

No matter what the reason is for your divorce, it is important on a first date to just keep it to ***top line info***. Nobody wants to hear you rant about your ex-spouse on a date and how he/she did you wrong and what a horrible person he/she is. If you do that on a first date, you will come across as bitter and not ready to date. And more importantly, you probably won't get a second date. Details about your divorce and marriage will come out naturally in the early stages of dating.

Don't Compare Your Date to Your Ex

It is completely normal at times to miss your ex-spouse and wish that your current date possess some of his/her qualities (the good ones, that is!). However, don't fall into the comparison trap. Remember: this is a ***whole new ballgame*** with ***different players*** and ***different dynamics***. Embrace getting to know someone new and what he/she has to offer in a relationship, because it just might be better than the last one.

Dating With Kids

How to Tell Your Date You Have Kids

You should never be afraid to tell your date that you have kids, for fear that it will scare him/her away. The fact of the matter is, your kids come as a package deal with you. If someone you are interested in dating is scared off by the fact that you have children, then he/she is not the right person for you.

As a rule of thumb, don't go into too much detail about your kids on the first few dates, as you want to focus the attention on getting to know each other first. Extensive details about your kids can come later in the dating process.

How to Tell Your Kids That You Are Dating Again

It is important to not hide that you're dating again from your children. Kids are smart and they will figure out that you are dating. And the last thing you want to happen is for your kids to think that you are being dishonest or hiding something from them.

Just tell them you are slowly getting back out there and that you are going to start dating again. Make sure they understand that it is not going to affect their relationship with you, which will always remain secure.

When Should You Introduce Your Kids to Someone New?

You should consider introducing your children to the person you are dating when you both are on the same page about wanting to take the relationship to the next level. When there is a certain level of commitment between you and your new boyfriend/girlfriend, it's important to see if she/he can handle being around your kids and if it's going to work for the long term.

How to Balance Dating & Kids

As a single parent, you no longer have a spouse to help you balance your career and kids. Adding dating into the mix can add a lot of stress in your life. So, it's important to just take a deep breath and realize that it's not impossible to balance all these things in your life; determine your priorities and make time for what's most important. Focus on what makes you happy. ***Kids usually want to see their parents happy,*** so do not feel guilty about dating again, as it will take the responsibility and pressure away from them to make you happy.

Embrace Dating & the Future with Someone New!

If you truly want to meet the right man/woman and find your "***happily ever after,***" then it is going to take putting in a real effort into dating. No one ever said dating was going to be easy, but it's important to look at this as an exciting time to start a new life and embrace the future with someone new.

Your real happily ever after is just right around the corner!

Suzanne K. Oshima

Suzanne K. Oshima is a Matchmaker, Dating Coach & Founder at Dream Bachelor & Bachelorette

Suzanne has worked with thousands of single men and women to help them uncover the core issues of what may be preventing or blocking them from finding love. Suzanne has helped them transform and elevate their dating lives to meet, attract & keep the right one.

Suzanne is also the Founder of Single in Stilettos. Single in Stilettos gives women the best dating advice from all the top dating experts to help you meet, attract & keep the right man… so they can go from Single in Stilettos to Engaged in Stilettos!

Suzanne has been seen in the media on Bravo TV, The Today Show, Good Afternoon America, ABC News, Inside Edition, BBC Radio, Men's Health, Glamour, and much more! For more information, visit www.dreambachelor.com or www.singleinstilettos.com.

CHAPTER 51

GUIDE TO WARDROBE PLANNING

By Mona Sharaf

So now you are divorced and you are looking to ***create a new identity***. You are not the married wife or husband you used to be. You are single. You are your own entity. Your current wardrobe is a reminder of the person you used to be as part of set package. You are trying to learn how to come into your own and discover the new you. The easiest way to do that is to start with your wardrobe. This is the perfect time for a closet cleanse!

Closet Cleanse

A closet cleanse ***assists your mind, body and spirit*** to lose attachments to old possessions and leave room for a new life in which to create new memories. Start by going through each piece of clothing, shoes and accessories and ask yourself these questions:

- Where did I used to wear this to? And will I still continue to go to these types of places?
- Does this piece of clothing make me sad or do I associate it with negative feelings?
- When was the last time I wore this?
- Does this look good on me and suit my body shape?
- What can I wear this with?
- Is this outdated?
- Is this age appropriate?

Do this with ***each*** piece of clothing. On average it should take about a day. But think of it this way: you have a whole lifetime ahead of you with your new life and new memories you will be creating – what's one day?

Now see what you have left. Likely it's a lot of the clothes you love, that look great on you, that serve a lot of different purposes, are multi-functional and a real staple in your wardrobe. Now look at it again, what's missing? Can't think of it?

Go to ***Pinterest.com*** and ***Polyvore.com*** for ideas. Put in some key phrases of clothing styles, genres, designers, or even celebrity styles you would like to emulate. Pin them and make a board. Now you have your inspiration. Look at your board before you venture out shopping. Take a friend with you that is NOT critical of you but also really honest and that you trust. Make a fun day out of it.

Updating the Closet

Now Let's Talk Shopping

A lot of new divorcees make the mistake of going on a "shopping spree" after their divorce. It's their way of opening a new door, creating a fresh new look and detaching themselves from old memories. However, a shopping spree that is not well thought out can be a very ***costly mistake***. There should be a plan and questions you must ask yourself first:

- Who do I want to be? What do I want to communicate through my new wardrobe?
- What colors look good on me?
- Is this right for my body type?
- Is this age appropriate?
- Do I have places to wear this to?
- Is this worth the cost?

Let's take these questions one by one.

Who Do You Want to Be and How Can Your Wardrobe Best Communicate That?

This takes some thought and research. Do you want to look powerful and authoritative or friendly and approachable? Sophisticated and sexy or eclectic and worldly? Feminine and romantic or simplistic and natural? It may be easiest to start by picking a celebrity style you really like and start by trying to emulate their style in a way that best flatters your particular shape.

When ***communicating your personality*** through your wardrobe there are lot elements that are important – textures, colors, the movement and lines of the fabric and fit of the garment all should be considered. Usually a particular designer will stick to representing a certain style or aesthetic. Choose a few designers/stores that you like and try to look for the cohesive theme in the items that you think best represent who you want people to see you as.

What Colors Look Good on Me?

Aside from having certain groups of colors that make you look more youthful, brighter, awake and more vibrant, wearing the right colors can dictate your mood. Try to stay away from black and gray for now and discover new colors that complement you and make you feel happy and refreshed when you wear them. There are also connotations that every color evokes, for example:

- <u>Red</u> – enthusiastic, exciting, stimulating, passionate.
- <u>Orange</u> – lively, active, happy.
- <u>Yellow</u> – warm, cheery, optimistic and creative.
- <u>Blue</u> – serene, thoughtful, honest, patient.
- <u>Brown</u> – simple, comfortable, responsible, secure, earthy.
- <u>Green</u> – harmonious, natural, prosperous, growing.
- <u>Pink</u> – feminine, approachable, sensitive, loving.
- <u>Purple</u> – regal, mystical, artistic, unique.

Is this Right for My Body Type?

There are 5 basic body shapes for women:

- Pear,
- Inverted Triangle,
- Rectangle,
- Round, and
- Hourglass.

The ultimate goal of most women is for their body shape to reflect that of an hourglass. An hourglass is even from top to bottom and draws in at the middle. The ideal shape for women are shoulders that are in line and same width as hips with a well-defined, narrow waistline. Try best to create this same silhouette with your clothing.

- Pear shape – build up your shoulders to match the width of your hips, e.g. wide/draping sleeves, structured jackets, horizontal stripes.
- Inverted triangle – look for clothing to build up the lower the part of your body, e.g. draping or fuller skirts, wider leg pants, peplum jackets, patterns and textured pants.
- Rectangle – look for items with pleating and details that create the illusion of pulling your waist in.
- Round – look for clothes that have straight lines up or down to move the eye up and down and take attention away from the roundness at your center.
- Hourglass – are freer to experiment with different shapes and styles of clothing.

For men the goal is create a V shape, or inverted triangle shape silhouette. The ideal is broadest at the shoulders with a defined waist that draws in.

Is this Age Appropriate?

When it comes to buying pieces that are age appropriate the best way to judge is think about whom you have seen wearing similar pieces. If it's something your teenage daughter/son wear, put it down! It's not for you. If it's something your mother/father would wear put it down! As we get older, for women, hemlines generally tend to get lower and lower. Women over the age of 35-40 should retire their mini-skirts. There are other ways to show off your legs without baring it all. Try skirts with high slits, skinny jeans, or fitted pencil skirts to the knee. These are all more age appropriate ways to show a little leg. Usually highly trendy items skew younger. Try to stick to pieces that are more classic and timeless, and that you know will not go out of style in a year.

Do I Have Places to Wear This?

Most of the clothing we purchase is worn to work or to wherever else we are from 9am-5pm Monday through Friday. When shopping, there should be ***70% focus on a daytime/work wardrobe***. Try to pick up pieces that will carry you into the evening. Layering or accessorizing is the best way to do this. For instance, sleeveless dresses and slinky tops that you can layer over with a smart jacket are great ways to carry your wardrobe from desk to dinner. The use of accessories such as a bold necklace or earrings, high heeled shoes/boots, belt, or any really great statement piece like a colorful scarf will help carry your outfit into the evening.

Is this Worth the Cost?

It's really easy to fall in love with a particular piece and purchase it at whatever cost. But there are certain items we call "***investment pieces.***" These are the pieces we wear consistently and are worth their price because of the amount of times they are worn. Here is the mathematical formula. Sorry in advance for making you do math, but it's a simple formula, I promise!

Calculate the amount of times you are going to wear the piece over its lifetime. For instance if it's a black pair of slacks let's assume you will wear its once a week for 2 years. That's about 100 times. Divide that number by its cost. Let's say they are $400. That comes to $4 cost per wear. The magic number is ***$10 or under***; you want to keep it to a $10 cost per wear to make it worth its cost.

Hiring a Personal Shopper to Help

A ***personal shopper***, ***image consultant*** or ***wardrobe consultant*** can help through this process. Not only will most of them do a full closet makeover for you, this professional will also help you discover the image you would like to project. He/she will help you build a wardrobe that best suits you, your lifestyle and your specific body shape. It's hard to look at yourself with an objective eye; that's why people seek help such as this during a major life change like a divorce. You can find these types of professionals simply by doing a Google search and visiting sites like Yelp.com to read reviews. It should be someone that can travel to where you are, because an at-home consultation is an important step in the process. Most personal shoppers "pre-shop" for their clients. The client walks into a fitting room all prepared with composed outfits to try on specifically chosen for them, making the process easy, stress-free, luxurious and most of all fun!

Fresh Start, Fresh Look

If you follow this basic guide your shopping adventure will be a huge success. Remember, your new life is more sociable, looking to date, build new relationships, and go to different places. Let the clothing inspire you to live the life you want to live.

Put a little less focus on your staple wardrobe for now. You've done that all your life. Reach for something you never would have before. Have the guts to try it on and come out of the fitting room. Let your friends see it on you. Let the other people in the store see it – not just the sales people, because most of the time they have a different motivation for telling you something looks good on you.

Ask yourself how it makes you feel. This is easy to tell. How's your posture in it? Are you smiling? Dancing? Trust your body language when you have it on. Are you slumped over, shying away from the mirror, covering yourself with your hands? If so, realize it's not for you and move on. Don't be fooled by items that are trendy, in style or carry a big label. Focus on what looks good on you.

Shopping is another form of therapy, it releases endorphins that you can't from working out, or even having sex. So go do it, but first be prepared and knowledgeable before you set out to shop.
A great wardrobe builds confidence and when you're confident your mind is clear to work and grow in other aspects of your life. Now is your time to grow and discover the new you. Start with a great wardrobe and the rest should come just a little bit easier. Happy Shopping!

Mona Sharaf

Mona Sharaf is a New York City based, personal shopper and image consultant for both men and women. Her mission is to help her clients create the image they are looking to portray all while making them feel more beautiful, confident and educated on how to shop.

She studied image consulting at the Fashion Institute of Technology. She has worked for very reputable clothing designers such as Norma Kamali, where she worked as a personal shopper developing wardrobes for her client base all around the country.

CHAPTER 52

UTILIZING HEALTH COACHES TO BECOME A BETTER YOU

By Andrea Moss

It is not uncommon for people to start a nutritional program and quickly announce that they're getting divorced. Or leaving their job. Or moving across the country. It might sound like a funny and unlikely result of working with a nutrition coach, but nutritionists have become pretty used to these kinds of occurrences. In fact, we have come to really appreciate (and celebrate) a client when they make those ***giant decisions***.

When we take the time to ***focus on ourselves*** and the nourishment we really need and want in our lives, we can begin to see what no longer serves us. As we deepen our connection to what truly supports us, and what *doesn't*, we can see what is keeping us back from being as healthy as we want to be (physically, and mentally). We begin to cultivate more of what feels good, balanced, and supportive – from healthier food choices to overall lifestyle decisions. We also begin to explore ways of deeply "feeding" ourselves that don't come solely from our food; and hence, big life decisions get made more easily, and lifelong addictive/destructive food behavior gets broken.

> Mel was an incredibly sweet, loving, single mother of two boys. She had recently gotten divorced, and came to see us to begin taking care of herself for the first time in years. Mel found that when she focused on healthy nourishment for the whole family, everyone felt better. The boys performed better in school. Mel was losing weight and feeling more confident than ever. And her long-standing aches and pains (caused by years of food "neglect" and inflammation) began to disappear.

Food Affects Everything

The foods that we eat have ***an effect on everything***. It is easy to see the connection between our dietary choices and our waistline (eat too many French fries and candy bars, and suddenly our pants feel pretty snug). But we coach our clients to learn how food has an impact on mood, focus, and productivity, too. Have you ever tried to make a big decision when you were starving? Or to focus on a really big project at work around 4 o'clock in the afternoon – after a morning of donuts and mega-doses of caffeine? It usually does not work out all that well...

A balanced, healthy diet means balanced blood sugar levels – which is key to maintaining a positive attitude and moving forward with perseverance and grace. When we go too long between meals, or focus solely on carbs, sugar, and caffeine to fuel us, we are left depleted.

As most anyone can tell you, after a divorce (or any traumatic life experience), diet is usually the last thing to get our focus. We are so busy just trying to get through the day – who has the energy to focus on the meals we are cooking or the food we are ordering? Ironically, the time when we most need our diet to support us is when we feel we have the least attention to give it. But I am here to make a case for the importance (the necessity!) of taking the most beautiful, the deepest, most loving care of yourself right now. Perhaps more than you ever have before. And it starts with how you feed yourself.

Healing from trauma – and moving towards new potential and possibility – takes profound nourishment. And it is not only about bringing in the emotional support you need to move forward, but the physical support you need to fuel your body. It doesn't have to be hard or complicated. In fact, I encourage you to be easy with yourself right now and find easy, simple ways of feeding yourself a healthy diet.

Three Meals of Balanced Nutrition

Start with breakfast. It truly is the most important meal of the day. What you eat in the morning sets you up for the rest of the day. By starting your day with balanced blood sugar levels, you will feel more calm, focused, and productive. Seven breakfasts can be downloaded at www.mosswellness.com that only take five minutes to prepare (healthy eating doesn't have to mean a ton of time in the kitchen!).

For lunches and dinners, focus on eating balancing, grounding protein and veggies. If spending time in the kitchen feels like the last thing you can handle right now, pick up rotisserie chicken, canned beans and canned fish, and eggs for quick, easy sources of healthy protein. You have my total permission to use frozen veggies, too!

We often use food to comfort us in times of stress, but again, ironically, this can leave us feeling more stressed out than before. When you find yourself craving sweets, try opting for dark chocolate, fruit, and healthy smoothies to satisfy your sweet tooth in a cleaner way.

One way of getting support is to use the daily check-list included below. Use this list every day to remind yourself to take care of *you*. You can download this check-list for free on my website at http://mosswellness.com/ (in the 3-Day Jumpstart Guide to Feel Good Every Day):

"Feel Good Every Day" Daily Check-List

Date: ________________________

What is your intention for today? (Examples: I want to deeply nourish my body, I want to eat less sugar, I want to increase my veggie intake, I want to slow down with my eating, I want to do exercise that I enjoy, I want to drink more water, etc.)

My Intention for Today:

____

____

____

Do you need any support to make this happen? (This can be anything from letting a friend know your intention, looking into local fitness classes, buying a new water bottle, starting your day with meditation/breath work to help you stay focused and grounded, etc.)

Support:

____

____

____

___Water (aim for 6-8 glasses, or around 64 ounces per day, potentially more if you are very physically active.)

___Minimum of 5 servings of fruits or vegetables (bonus points for leafy greens like kale, collards, arugula, bok choy, spinach, etc!)

___Self-Care (meditation, massage, breath work, inspirational reading, acupuncture, journaling, etc.)

___30 minutes of enjoyable movement (walking, stretching, yoga, jogging, group fitness class, etc.)

End of day check-out:

What felt good today? (Examples: I enjoyed my Pilates class, I felt more energized with more water, I loved how I felt eating leafy greens, I liked trying a new recipe, I enjoyed being able to pass up those donuts at work, I feel more committed to nourishing my body, etc.)

Did anything feel challenging? Do you need to bring in more support/approach things differently?

Final Thoughts

I ask you to be gentle with yourself right now. This isn't necessarily the time to force yourself through a hardcore cleanse program or juice fast – unless that really feels like what you're called to do! Rather, this is about finding a way of feeding yourself that helps you feel healthy, grounded, and supported.

We can use food as a way of showing love to ourselves. Every morning upon waking, you have the opportunity to start fresh. It's time to focus on *you* – on what you need to heal, feel supported, and nourished.

Take a holistic approach to nourishment. You can eat all the kale in the world, but if you hate your job or your spouse, you will still feel depleted. Food is one very big piece of the puzzle, for sure. But beyond food, see where you can bring comfort and support into your life. From getting a massage to having a coffee date with a friend to joining a new exercise class to buying yourself flowers, look for ways to bring love, joy, and fun into your life.

Most importantly, know that you don't have to go it alone. Whether it's a nutrition coach, a therapist, or a dear friend, bring support into your life so that you can heal, take loving care of yourself, and begin anew.

Andrea Moss

Andrea Moss is the founder of Moss Wellness, a holistic nutrition team devoted to supporting their clients learn how to finally feel confident about what to eat. The nutrition coaches at Moss Wellness will help you make enjoyable changes based on your individual lifestyle, personal preferences, and body type.

Andrea and her team work with you to naturally deconstruct food cravings, skyrocket energy levels, balance out your digestive system, and reach an ideal weight – without torturous dieting!

The Moss Wellness team works with clients and corporations around the globe to make healthy eating and healthy living easy, pleasurable, and lots of fun! For more information about Moss Wellness, visit www.mosswellness.com.

CHAPTER 53

USING PERSONAL TRAINERS

By Anthony Gittens, CPT

Going through a divorce is one of life's most difficult challenges. Whether divorce comes as a complete surprise or has been a long time in the making, it ***can damage one's physical as well as mental well-being***. Divorce means different things to different people. However, it comes with the certainty that one's life will not be the same. The companionship and support of a spouse, the joint rearing of children, and their role in the community as a couple – all of these will never be the same again. When faced with this situation there are two choices: fold, or ***aggressively take charge of one's life***. One can and should take positive action to regain a healthy lifestyle while addressing the difficult emotional, legal and other issues of the divorce.

Physical Fitness is One Element of Taking Charge of One's Life

One of the best things one can do to take charge of one's life is to ensure that one is at – or is working toward – a ***high level of physical fitness***. Physical fitness brings with it ***confidence, discipline, endurance, purpose, optimism***, and a general sense of well-being. Do not, however, think that achieving a high level of physical fitness is easy. It is not. That is why professional guidance is indispensable. Not only will one substantially increase one's chances for success but, more importantly, chances of injury will substantially decrease. This chapter will focus on the specific steps one should take to avoid letting divorce affect one's health adversely. One ***need not do it alone***!

Using a Personal Trainer

A personal trainer can be the invaluable piece of the puzzle that links together various efforts to cope with divorce. Let's start with ***stress management***. There are numerous approaches to managing stress: the first is exercise, including boxing, ***high intensity interval training*** ("HIIT"), ***resistance training*** and, of course, ***pure muscle exhaustion***. The correct training regime results in regular sleep patterns, dietary changes, and improvements in metabolism. Together these can set one on the path to improved health and a more positive disposition.

Experienced personal trainers have broad experience and expertise in many areas, such as ***diet, massage therapy, and human physiology***. They also understand the differences that result from each age, gender and occupation, and they create programs that are as unique as the individual being trained. Good personal trainers are also ***good listeners***. And it is essential that the personal trainer develop a bond of trust and mutual respect with the person receiving training.

Positive Effects

Let us talk about the issue of stress. The effects of stress manifest themselves in many ways, but a common reaction is retreating into oneself. The physical exertion that results from training can help one come out of one's shell. This release may come in many forms – tears, shouting, etc. What matters is that the ***emotions "come out."*** An experienced personal trainer provides the right environment for release of stress.

For many women, personal training is a way to ***increase self-esteem and self-worth***. Being ***strong is empowering*** and will promote better interactions with others. This will become a positive self-fulfilling cycle. Moreover, the focus, discipline and self-control involved in getting into excellent physical condition will create values that have extensive non-physical benefits. As she considers herself more appealing to the opposite sex, she becomes more approachable, and this self-confidence will show. This process may also be helpful in finding another long-term spouse or companion, if that is desired. A woman who looks and feels better, exudes ***more self-confidence*** and can better express what is important to her in a relationship.

For many men, personal training is a way to reduce stress and achieve a more positive outlook through improved physical strength and a more ***attractive appearance***. However, an unexpected benefit may be the ability to harness and express one's emotions. Interestingly, most men tend to internalize stress more than women. Being able to get the stress out is an important benefit of using a personal trainer. In addition, being muscular often makes a man feel more physically desirable and more emotionally secure.

Conclusion

Trainers do not utilize psychological tactics to improve motivation or to attain desired goals. Trainers do not manipulate their clients' thoughts or emotions. Rather, ***they encourage openness*** by straightforwardly addressing their clients' need for physical achievement and increased strength which, in turn, have a positive effect on their self-image. The ultimate goal is that the client will look, feel and simply ***be better and more confident*** as they navigate the murky territory of divorce and prepare to carve out a new path for themselves, and, if desired, to seek possible new outcomes with a different partner.

Anthony Gittens, CPT

Anthony Gittens has worked as a fitness professional in the New York metropolitan area for over nineteen years since his honorable discharge from the Marine Corps after eight years of service. Gittens earned a bachelor's degree in business management before completing a six-month, 1000-hour, intensive massage therapy course at Finger Lakes School of Massage and gaining NY state licensure as a massage therapist. It is goal for him and his team as fitness professionals to bring appropriate and effective training to everyone they can, regardless of body type, ability, age, or weight. He believes in listening closely to what people want to accomplish – and why, and derives great satisfaction from helping people grow in strength, serenity and competence.

CHAPTER 54

MINDFULNESS AND LIFESTYLE COACHING

By Tina Paymaster, HHC, AADP

When overcoming a breakup, divorce or separation, two of the most common responses people may have are worrying about what is to come in the future or dwelling on and overanalyzing what could have been different in the past. Mindfulness and lifestyle coaches can help people "move on" into the next chapter of their life.

Be Present

Get "Unstuck"

Fear, worry and anxiety can lead to more intense feelings of anger, resentment and hopelessness. When these negative emotions arise, the underlying reason is that the person has emotionally and mentally left the present moment and is now living in the past or the future. Allowing the mind to continuously time travel will cause that person to relive or anticipate painful experiences. When this occurs, that person may feel trapped by his or her emotions and experiences and may have the ***feeling of being "stuck,"*** finding it difficult to move on.

For people going through a divorce or separation, stress and other negative emotions are oftentimes rooted in thoughts about what has occurred in the past or anxiety about what may occur in the future. In the past and future, change and outcomes are not in their control, which causes uneasiness. Because they are preoccupied with negative emotions and experiences, they will also be less likely to notice any positive opportunities and aspects of their lives.

Mindfulness practices are an effective way to overcome these negative emotions because they bring one back to the present moment, a place where there is nothing to fear. This ***calmer state of mind*** provides the ideal space for healing to occur; it will help the overcome pain and suffering and move on.

Operating on Auto-Pilot

Not being able to mindfully manage life's daily demands and endless to-do lists may cause people to lack focus, clarity, awareness and ***pleasure in the present moment***. Trying to juggle work, family, finances, health and socializing has them in a constant state of action and stress, always thinking about the next thing that has to get done, never being able to fully experience or appreciate what is currently happening. Society, media and culture often perpetuate this behavior by rewarding people that work harder and longer hours, viewing it as a sign of their dedication, worthiness and ability to succeed. This type of continuous ***"mindless" living*** often leads to making choices without thinking about their consequences.

Most of us can relate to the feeling of eating a whole bag of chips and only remembering the first few handfuls, reading an entire chapter of a book without remembering word or arriving at a destination without recalling the journey getting there. These are just some examples of "mindless" actions.

Operating on autopilot is not all that unusual. Studies show that 95% of what we do on a daily basis is controlled by the subconscious mind. Only 5% of our actions are from a conscious behavior. The subconscious mind is programmed from birth to about age 7. Most beliefs and behaviors that we have are ones that we picked up through observing our parents, community, environment and culture. That is why many people find themselves in relationships that closely resemble those of their parents.

The downside to subconscious programming is that people often lose their sense of self and live their lives according to what their parents or culture may expect, instead of one that is aligned with their true desires. This will often lead to feelings of dissatisfaction, regret and resentment.

In addition, when people are rushing through life on auto-pilot, they rarely take the time to assess how they are truly feeling physically and emotionally. They only notice this when their situations get so extreme and symptoms get so noticeable that there is an undeniable need for some type of intervention.

All of this naturally causes people to focus more time and energy on everything that is going wrong in their lives, feeling like nothing is in their control, instead of noticing all the opportunities they have to create the lives they truly want to be living. However, with regular mindfulness practices, the quality of a person's life can dramatically improve, even if the situations around them do not.

In fact, numerous studies have shown the vast amount of benefits a person can experience as a result of practicing mindfulness including increasing ***positive emotions, decreasing stress,*** improving focus, increasing compassion of self and others, increasing optimism, deepening understanding and acceptance in relationships, increasing gray matter in the brain (responsible for learning, memory and emotional balance), reducing symptoms of depression and ***Post-Traumatic Stress Disorder*** ("PTSD"), boosting the immune system and aiding with weight loss through mindful eating.

Most people have experienced mindfulness without even knowing it. For example, slowly savoring a decadent piece of chocolate cake or noticing the warm breeze on a sailboat. In moments like these, the person was fully present – not worrying about what happened the day before or what could happen tomorrow. They were ***fully engaged*** in what they were doing with all of their senses activated and therefore able to also feel the true pleasure and rewards of the experience. That is mindfulness!

What is Mindfulness?

Jon Kabat-Zinn, founder of ***Mindfulness Based Stress Reduction*** ("MBSR") defines mindfulness as "paying attention in a particular way; on purpose, in the present moment, and non-judgmentally." Although mindfulness won't eliminate all challenges from a person's life, it will help them respond to challenges in a calmer and more rational way, which will reduce the emotional and physical impacts it can have on their mind, body and soul. Being able to react to life's often unpredictable circumstances in this way will enable the person to bounce back from hardships faster and with more clarity and allow them to continue moving forward, focusing on their goals and desires.

Mindfulness techniques include ***simple breathing techniques***, sitting meditations, walking meditations, mindful eating, body scanning, gratitude, object focus and sound awareness exercises. Qualified mindfulness coaches, life coaches and holistic healers can help educate someone going through or recovering from a divorce or separation on these various techniques.

> When Tina began going to Buddhist meditation classes, one of the first lessons she learned was "**it's not what happens to you, it's how you react to it.**" Essentially, it's how we choose to respond to a situation that creates our experience of it and the emotions we feel. Through practicing daily meditation, Tina was able to view challenging situations from a calmer perspective and have the opportunity to react in a way that led to her experiencing less pain and suffering, and therefore more joy.

When a person practices mindfulness, that person will be less likely to have the same negative habitual responses to stressful situations and instead approach them with more ***insight, rationale and understanding***. That person will be more likely to have compassion towards oneself and others, helping to disengage the often turbulent cycle of blame that can result from a failed relationship.

For a person who is going through a separation, divorce or any other life-changing situation, oftentimes sadness, anger, worry and fear will cause the mind to think irrationally, create disempowering beliefs and lead to unhealthy or harmful behaviors. ***Mindfulness brings awareness*** and clarity to one's thoughts, emotions and behaviors, allowing the person to feel what he or she is feeling without judgment, safely disassociate him or herself from the negative emotions and enable them to release the emotions in a healthy way.

Subconscious programming causes a person to *feel* certain ways about what they are experiencing, either in the present moment or when thinking about the past or future. These feelings or emotions are what then drive his or her actions. Mindfulness can help in releasing self-sabotaging beliefs and reprogramming the subconscious mind to react in a more beneficial way. When negative emotions fade, more ***positive emotions naturally arise***, leading to more positive behaviors. So through mindfulness techniques, instead of drowning one's sorrows in a pint of ice cream, bottle of wine, arguing or violence, one will be more likely to move forward through the pain, while still honoring one's health and happiness. Qualified mindfulness coaches, life coaches and holistic healers can help a person step forward to create a more beautiful life through these techniques.

Using Mindfulness to Reduce Negative Emotions

Pain and Withdrawal

Studies have shown that brains respond to breakups in a ***similar way to actual physical pain.*** The function of pain is to alert our bodies that there is danger and protective measures need to be taken to survive. Long ago, if a member ***was rejected from the tribe***, his or her chances of being attacked by a predator increased – thus rejection may have felt like an actual threat to physical survival. So pain from a breakup may very well be an evolutionary human reaction passed down through generations that is more a part of our basic need for survival, rather than a self-destructive reaction.

The natural progression of many breakups are ***first intense pain***, then periods where emotional pain is avoided through distractions such as other activities, food or alcohol, ***followed by periods where memories***, thoughts and intense feelings come rushing back in again, causing craving-like emotions for the ex-partner. Many people try to suppress their negative emotions too quickly instead of fully processing them. This can lead to intense emotions arising at unexpected times and repetitive patterns of negative experiences.

The truth is, breakups take time to fully recover from. To expect to not feel the pain is unrealistic. It's important to allow oneself to feel the pain and work through it in a healthy manner. Through mindfulness techniques, a person can safely ***feel their emotions without judgment*** or blame, gradually connect to that space within themselves that is the source of true happiness, feel pleasure in activities again and regain their sense of self – all of which is essential in being able to move on to healthier and happier future relationships and experiences.

Forgiveness

Forgiveness can be a difficult topic when it comes to divorce or separation. During a divorce or separation, it is not unusual for there to be intense feelings ***of betrayal, blame and resentment*** (on both sides). We may think not forgiving the other person is punishment to him or her. However, lack of forgiveness is only hurting is the person that cannot forgive, because it keeps him or her trapped by negative emotions. Forgiveness is not saying that what has been done is okay of acceptable. Rather, it's about releasing oneself from the shackles that unforgiving has around one's life.

Although it may seem that negative thoughts about an ex are the truth, it's important to remember that a thought is simply a ***point of view***. Everyone experiences the world in their own unique way even if they are in the same exact situation. The filters through which a person sees the world will create his or her own unique experience of it. One person may see a particular situation as terrible, while another sees it as a ***blessing***. Who is right? A person's viewpoints are always partly true and partly untrue.

Through daily meditation, a person can create a safe internal space for forgiveness to occur. Qualified mindfulness coaches, life coaches and healers can help guide a person through various forgiveness meditations and practices to help them move on.

Mindfulness practices will help a person experience a sense of security and peace within him or herself, enabling him or her to see the ***situation more objectively***, lower his or her defenses and create the space for forgiveness to be given and accepted. When a person can forgive, that person can move on.

Fear in Moving On

Fear is natural when it comes to any sort of change. Fear's job is to prevent a person from getting hurt, so it usually stops him or her from moving forward to avoid any type of danger or negative outcome. However, when fear comes up, it's more a call to action than a call to inaction. It's important to note that when a ***person can feel fear***, it means that he or she is ready to release the emotions causing it. If he or she were unable to feel the fear, it would mean that his or her body does not feel safe enough to release the emotions.

The other important point to remember about fear is that it is caused by not staying in the present moment. Fear occurs by ***reliving the past*** or anticipating the future. However, through mindfulness practices, such as meditation, when one can bring oneself back to the present moment, fear can be dramatically reduced and help bring one back to a place where one feels safe, calm and able to move forward.

A simple meditation technique to help reduce fear is to ***close one's eyes and focus on one's breath***. Focus on how it feels when breathing in and out, in and out. This will help bring oneself back to the present moment.

Another technique is to bring one's attention to the space around oneself and start identifying what one sees in detail. While doing this, one will be bringing one's focus from fear about the past or future, to a feeling of safety in the present moment.

Sadness

Sadness is another natural emotion after any sort of loss. Some studies show that breakups, to some can actually feel as intense as ***experiencing the death of a loved one***. This is common when a person identifies his or her sense of worth so deeply with the relationship that he or she forgets who he or she is outside of the relationship. Therefore, once the relationship ends, it feels as though the person he or she used to know does not exist either.

However, a person recovering from a divorce or separation should not judge him or herself for feeling sad or angry. Mindfulness practices can help this process along by encouraging acceptance of all emotions, including sadness. Mindfulness does not focus on ***what one should feel***. Every person has his or her own path to and from painful experiences. Mindfulness allows a person to accept his or her emotions and gain control over them rather than allowing emotions to control them.

When a person feels sadness, that person shouldn't try to force the sadness away. If that person feels the need to cry then they should cry. They should let it out, then move on to more mindful practices to help them move through the pain.

A common mindfulness practice when experiencing sadness or other overwhelming emotions is first becoming aware of the emotion when it arises, then asking without judgment, "**Why am I *choosing* this emotion**?" Next, the person should then ask, "**Is this choice helping me get to where I want to be or preventing me from getting there**?" Lastly, "**What other emotion would I rather choose**?" This gives the person the control and option of being in a more positive state of mind, rather than feeling helpless in the state he or she is in.

Another effective technique to use when a particular negative thought arises is responding to it with "***I notice that I'm having this thought about…***" This will help the person disassociate themselves from the thought or emotion instead of defining him or herself by it.

For example, "I am angry" versus "I notice that I am feeling angry about..."

When a person can disassociate him or herself from a negative thought, then he or she can make more sense of where it came from and why, instead of continuously becoming a victim of it.

Other Important Techniques

After a person practices mindfulness techniques and once he or she begins to experience some emotional relief, then and only then is it recommended to try doing something else. If a person distracts him or herself too early, this will simply suppress the negative emotions. Once the person begins to feel some relief, he or she should focus on doing things that bring joy or that once brought joy, or create new memories by taking on a new hobby. It's important to identify oneself in new ways outside of a past relationship.

Compassion is another key part of mindfulness. It teaches one to respond to oneself the way one may respond to a friend going through a heartbreak, acknowledging that it is okay to feel sadness and that there are better days ahead. Research shows that people who relate to themselves with self-compassion heal more quickly than those who are hard on themselves. A person can simply ***repeat loving and compassionate statements*** towards him or herself throughout the day as if he or she were responding to a close friend.

Practicing ***daily gratitude*** for all the things one has in one's life is also incredibly powerful. This will help one not to focus so much time and energy on one's negative emotions and see the blessings and opportunities in one's life. In time, a person may even be able to feel gratitude for all the good times that person had in the relationship. A mindfulness coach can help someone learn these techniques.

Tina Paymaster, HHC, AADP

Tina Paymaster is a Certified Health & Lifestyle Coach, recipe developer and inspirational speaker.

Combining nutritional guidance with spirituality and psychological techniques, Tina helps her clients gain the energy, confidence and clarity they need to break through their self-defeating habits so they can create the bodies and lives they truly desire.

Her approach focuses on aligning the mind, body and soul so results are achieved with less resistance and more sustainability.

Tina's mission is to inspire others around the world to rise above their fears, reclaim their health and happiness, create their own path in life, stop settling and start living!

Tina currently works with private clients around the country, develops recipes for her blog and top health food companies and holds frequent speaking events and workshops. She has been featured on Shape, MindBodyGreen, SheKnows, Live Science, Elephant Journal and other digital publications. Email tina.paymaster@gmail.com or visit www.tinapaymaster.com for more information.

SECTION C: OTHER RESOURCES

Family

THOMAS ATWOOD & JAYNE SCHOOLER, THE WHOLE LIFE ADOPTION BOOK: REALISTIC ADVICE FOR BUILDING A HEALTHY ADOPTIVE FAMILY (2008).

SUSAN PHILLIPS, STEPCHILDREN SPEAK: 10 GROWN-UP STEPCHILDREN TEACH US HOW TO BUILD HEALTHY STEPFAMILIES (2004).

Divorce

CHRISTINE AHRONS, THE GOOD DIVORCE: KEEPING YOUR FAMILY TOGETHER WHEN YOUR MARRIAGE FALLS APART (1998).

CALISTOGA PRESS, DIVORCE SURVIVAL GUIDE: THE ROADMAP FOR EVERYTHING FROM DIVORCE FINANCE TO CHILD CUSTODY (2014).

LOIS GOLD, THE HEALTHY DIVORCE: KEYS TO ENDING YOUR MARRIAGE WHILE PRESERVING YOUR EMOTIONAL WELL-BEING (2009).

LINDA GUNSBERG & PAUL HYMOWITZ, A HANDBOOK OF DIVORCE AND CUSTODY: FORENSIC, DEVELOPMENTAL, AND CLINICAL PERSPECTIVES (2013).

GAYLE ROSENWALD SMITH & SALLY ABRAHMS, WHAT EVERY WOMAN SHOULD KNOW ABOUT DIVORCE AND CUSTODY: JUDGES, LAWYERS AND THERAPISTS SHARE WINNING STRATEGIES ON HOW TO KEEP THE KIDS, THE CASH, AND YOUR SANITY (2007).

Relationships and Dating

GARY CHAPMAN, THE 5 LOVE LANGUAGES: THE SECRET TO LOVE THAT LASTS (2015).

DAVID FRISBIE & LISA FRISBIE, DATING AFTER DIVORCE: PREPARING FOR A NEW RELATIONSHIP (2012).

Children and Parenting

KIMBERLY KING, WHEN YOUR PARENTS DIVORCE: A KID-TO-KID GUIDE TO DEALING WITH DIVORCE (2013).

VICKI LANSKY, IT'S NOT YOUR FAULT, KOKO BEAR: A READ-TOGETHER BOOK FOR PARENTS AND YOUNG CHILDREN DURING DIVORCE (1997).

WENDY MOGEL, THE BLESSING OF A SKINNED KNEE: USING JEWISH TEACHINGS TO RAISE A SELF-RELIANT CHILDREN (2008).

CATHERINE STEINER-ADAIR & TERESA H. BARKER, THE BIG DISCONNECT: PROTECTING CHILDHOOD AND FAMILY RELATIONSHIPS IN THE DIGITAL AGE (2014).

ELIZABETH THAYER & JEFFREY ZIMMERMAN, THE CO-PARENTING SURVIVAL GUIDE: LETTING GO OF CONFLICT AFTER A DIFFICULT DIVORCE (2001).

ANTHONY W. WOLF, WHY DID YOU GET A DIVORCE? AND WHEN CAN I GET A HAMSTER?: A GUIDE TO PARENTING THROUGH DIVORCE (1998).

Marriage

ARLENE DUBIN, PRENUPS FOR LOVERS: A ROMANTIC GUIDE TO PRENUPTIAL AGREEMENTS (2001).

RABBI YIRMIYOHU & TEHILLA ABRAMOV, TWO HALVES OF A WHOLE; TORAH GUIDELINES FOR MARRIAGE (2006).

Moving On

Scott A. Mills, "The 7-Step Reboot" available at http://divorcewingman.com/support-center/free-ebook-7-day-reset/ (last visited November 23, 2015).
JUDITH RUSKAY RABINOR, BEFRIENDING YOUR EX AFTER DIVORCE: MAKING LIFE BETTER FOR YOU, YOUR KIDS, AND YES, YOUR EX (2013).

ABIGAIL TRAFFORD, CRAZY TIME: SURVIVING DIVORCE AND BUILDING A NEW LIFE (1992).

Pets

DEBRA VEY VODA-HAMILTON, NIPPED IN THE BUD, NOT IN THE BUTT: HOW TO USE MEDIATION TO RESOLVE CONFLICTS OVER ANIMALS (2015).

ABOUT THE AUTHORS

Maxine S. Broderick, Esq.

A lifelong resident of Long Island, New York, Ms. Broderick concentrates her practice on matrimonial and family law. She is experienced in handling uncontested and contested divorces, legal separation, child support, child custody, visitation, spousal support, orders of protection and modification of Family Court orders.

Committed to community service, Ms. Broderick has provided pro bono legal assistance to low income New Yorkers with respect to personal bankruptcy, uncontested and contested divorces, consumer debt, foreclosure prevention and housing disputes.

Ms. Broderick was named an "Access to Justice Champion" by the Nassau County Bar Association for pro bono service in 2013, was the recipient of an Outstanding Service certificate from the Nassau County Coalition Against Domestic Violence (NCCADV) in 2012, and was recognized by the New York State Courts Access to Justice Program for outstanding work and dedicated service in the uncontested divorce Volunteer Lawyers Program in 2010.

She is a member of the New York State Bar Association, the Association of Black Women Attorneys (ABWA), the Nassau County Bar Association, the Nassau County Women's Bar Association, the Hempstead Branch of the NAACP and is President-elect of the Amistad Long Island Black Bar Association.

Ms. Broderick is a proud graduate of Sacred Heart Academy in Hempstead, New York, earned a bachelor degree from Fordham University and a juris doctor from Brooklyn Law School in 2003.

She is admitted to practice law in New York State, The United States District Court, Eastern District of New York (EDNY), The United States District Court, Southern District of New York (SDNY), and was admitted to The U.S. Supreme Court in 2014. For more information about Ms. Broderick's practice, visit www.brodericklawny.com.

Liza Caldwell, CPC

Liza Caldwell, cofounder and director of SAS for Women®, is a graduate of Fordham University and holds an MA in education from Columbia University's Teachers College where she studied gender and leadership development. Trained in transformational coaching with the faculty of Leadership That Works, she is a certified professional coach (CPC) recognized by the International Coach Federation (ICF). Divorced after 17 years of marriage, Liza is a single parent to two young women in college.

SAS for Women® is New York City's first comprehensive resource that provides strategic information, action-oriented coaching, and expert resources and tools to women navigating separation, divorce, empty-nesting, and widowhood. For more information, visit sasforwomen.com.

Ravi Cattry, Esq.

Ravi Cattry is an associate attorney with Rincker Law, PLLC and is licensed to practice in New York and New Jersey and admitted into the Eastern and Southern District Courts of New York. She completed a Bachelor of Science at Fordham University in Manhattan where she was a double major in psychology and economics. She received a Juris Doctor from Pace University School of Law in White Plains, New York.

Before joining Rincker Law, PLLC, Ravi worked at a general practice firm located in Kew Gardens, New York. While working there her practice areas included landlord and tenant disputes, matrimonial and family law issues, commercial law, and immigration law. Ravi also worked with a boutique law firm specializing in bankruptcy law in Manhattan. During law school she interned with the Integrated Domestic Violence Court in White Plains, New York, where she assisted in handling divorce cases intertwined with domestic violence cases.

Ravi is fluent in Hindi and Punjabi, and conversational in Spanish. In her free time Ravi enjoys reading, watching movies, playing tennis, and keeping up with her favorite soccer teams. For more information about Rincker Law, PLLC, visit www.rinckerlaw.com.

Daniel Clement, Esq.

Daniel Clement is a dedicated, hands-on New York divorce and family law attorney with more than 25 years' experience. He takes a pragmatic, individualized and realistic approach to helping his clients through the often thorny path of divorce.

Daniel graduated from Brooklyn Law School and the State University of New York at Albany. He is a member of the New York City Bar Assoc., and has served as a member of the Matrimonial Committee. He has also worked as an Arbitrator in the Small Claims Court of the City of New York.

In addition to practicing, Daniel has extensively written and lectured on a range of family law issues. Daniel writes and maintains a blog, the New York Divorce Report, which explores current topics in New York family law and matrimonial practice.

For more information about Daniel and his practice, visit clementlaw.com.

Carol Dacey-Charles, ACC, CPCC

Carol is unconventional with a wicked smile, quirky wit and the keenest BS-detector around. Carol is direct, and engaging, putting her powerful sense of spirituality and clarity towards working from the inside out.

She takes risks while being light; she cares while pushing hard, all with a grace, warmth and deftness that ease the way. Carol has a grounded presence that creates safety and trust for everyone around her.

In 2011, Carol founded Why Not Thrive?, an international coaching and training business. With a career spanning 25 years of management, training, and human development in the arts, non-profits, retail and ministry, Carol is working with clients around the world to help them transform their personal and professional lives. For more information about Carol or Why Not Thrive? Visit www.ynotthrive.com and Carol's blog at www.wordforgood.com

Briana Denney, Esq.

Briana Denney, a partner in the law firm of Newman & Denney P.C., represents clients in all aspects of matrimonial and family law matters, including prenuptial and postnuptial agreements, divorce, child custody and visitation, and enforcement of divorce agreements and judgments. Prior to private practice, she was a court attorney for Justice Rosalyn Richer. Briana is an active member of several bar associations and committees. She grew up in Arizona and attended the University of Arizona, where she earned her B.A. in Psychology with honors. She moved from Boston to attend the City University of New York where she earned her J.D. For more information about Briana and Newman & Denney P.C., visit www.newmandenney.com.

Veronica Escobar, Esq.

Veronica Escobar is the Principal and Founder of The Law Offices of Veronica Escobar, a practice focusing exclusively in the areas of Elder Law, Special Needs Planning and Trusts and Estates, as well as Family Law. Prior to forming her own law practice, Veronica worked as an attorney representing the City of New York, Administration for Children's Services (ACS) in child abuse and neglect matters (commonly referred to as an "Article 10") ranging from educational neglect to serious forms of abuse.

Veronica is admitted to practice in the State of New York. She is also admitted to practice before the U.S. District Courts for the Eastern and Southern Districts of New York and the United States Supreme Court. She graduated summa cum laude from Fordham College at Rose Hill, Fordham University, where she was also elected to Phi Beta Kappa, with a degree in American Studies and a minor in Latin American/Latino Studies. She also received her law degree from Fordham, where she was a Notes and Articles Editor of the Fordham International Law Journal.

Currently, she is the Co-Chair of the Diversity Committee of the Elder Law and Special Needs Section of the New York State Bar, a member of the Elder Law and Special Needs and Trusts and Estates Sections of the New York State Bar Association, and is a Deputy Regional President for the Hispanic National Bar Association (HNBA) New York Region. She is an adjunct member of the Legal

Problems of the Aging Committee and a past member of The Family Court and Family Law Committee at the New York City Bar.

She is also an avid reader of everything, a music lover, concertgoer, museum fan, and burgeoning world traveler, as well as an information sponge.

To learn more about Veronica, you can connect to her website www.veronicaescobarlaw.com, or on Facebook at www.facebook.com/VeronicaEscobarLawNewYork.

Lesley Ann Friedland, Esq.

Lesley Ann Friedland is FamilyKind's Executive Director. Prior to her work at FamilyKind, Ms. Friedland was employed by the New York State Family Court for over 25 years as a Court Attorney Referee hearing cases concerning visitation, custody, neglect, abuse and domestic violence and as a Court Attorney assisting Judges. While at the the Family Court, Ms. Friedland also oversaw the Kings County NYS Certified Parent Education Program and also served as the Court liaison to the Mediation program. There Ms. Friedland realized the benefits these services held for families in transition. Unfortunately, in 2008/9 both programs along with other valuable resources were no longer funded. Knowing that supportive services were vital to the health of transitioning families, in 2012 Ms. Friedland left her job and founded FamilyKind, a 501(C) (3) public charity. With the support of accomplished and altruistic mediators, parenting coordinators, lawyers and educators, FamilyKind seeks to fulfill two missions: provide high quality services for divorcing and separating families without regard to their financial resources and to change the way our society views the transitioning family. Friedland graduated with a BA from Sarah Lawrence College and a JD from Antioch School of Law.

Frank Galchus, Esq.

Frank Galchus began his legal career more than 30 years ago with the Criminal Defense Division of the Legal Aid Society. Since then he has represented clients in criminal matters and family matters in Criminal Court, Supreme Court, and Family Court. His Family Court representation includes children who have been arrested and are facing charges in Family Court.

Sheera Gefen, Esq.

Sheera Gefen, Esq. graduated *phi beta kappa*, *magna cum laud*, with a B.A. in psychology from Barnard College, Columbia University and earned her J.D. from Fordham Law School. She has been a practicing attorney for 14 years and has gained expertise exclusively in matrimonial law for most of her career, working for District Council 37's Municipal Employees Legal Services. She has extensive experience representing clients in custody, child support, maintenance and equitable distribution matters as well as resolving disputes pertaining to the distribution of governmental and ERISA pensions. For the past 10 years, Sheera has been an instructor of Business Law at Touro College. Her research on the psychological implications of procedural justice has been presented at various psychology and law conferences including the European Conference on Psychology and Law in Krakow, Poland, the annual meeting of the International Congress of Applied Psychology in San Francisco, CA, and the annual meeting of the American Psychological Society in Washington, D.C. She often appears as a guest-lecturer at universities, speaking on topics related to the interplay between psychology and law. Sheera is also a Certified Divorce Mediator and a member of the Academy of Professional Family Mediators. She resides with her husband and children in Long Island, NY.

Carrie Gravenson

Unjumbler Professional Organizing was created in 2007 when Carrie Gravenson was hired as a temp for a boring and messy office. Left with nothing to do, she volunteered to organize the desk where she was sitting. Satisfied and energized by the results, she then asked to organize the supply closet. Then the kitchen, the storage room and the file room. A passion was discovered and an obsession was born.

Since 2007, Unjumbler has organized countless spaces for all walks of life. The home, the office and everything in between. From a messy drawer to a complete apartment renovation, Unjumbler has the skills and resources to create functional and beautiful order. As a native New Yorker and avid traveler, Carrie instinctively knows how to use space efficiently, even in small quarters. For more information about Unjumbler, visit www.unjumbleronline.com.

Anthony Gittens, CPT

Anthony Gittens has worked as a fitness professional in the New York metropolitan area for over nineteen years since his honorable discharge from the Marine Corps after eight years of service. Gittens earned a bachelor's degree in business management before completing a six-month, 1000-hour, intensive massage therapy course at Finger Lakes School of Massage and gaining NY state licensure as a massage therapist. It is a goal for Anthony and his team as fitness professionals to bring appropriate and effective training to everyone they can, regardless of body type, ability, age, or weight. Anthony believes in listening closely to what people want to accomplish and why, and he derives great satisfaction from helping people grow in strength, serenity and competence.

For more information about Element Fitness, visit www.elementfitness.net.

Ronna Gordon-Galchus, Esq.

Ronna Gordon-Galchus has been practicing law for more than 25 years. She began her career as an attorney with the Criminal Defense Division of the Legal Aid Society representing indigent individuals charged with crimes. Throughout the years she has devoted her practice to representing people facing various levels of felonies and misdemeanors and has tried numerous jury and non-jury trials. A large part of her practice is dedicated to those who are involved with cases in Family Court, including representing juveniles who have been arrested and charged with delinquency. She has also have authored numerous appellate briefs and has argued both in the Appellate Division and the New York State Court of Appeals.

Peter Gordon, CSA

Peter Gordon is a partner at New York Financial Organizers, Inc. (www.nyfo.nyc). His focus is on client service and marketing. After learning to navigate the tricky waters of Medicare, Medicaid, community trusts and estate planning for his own parents, Peter began NYFO with the goal of helping others gain peace of mind and security with their families', or their own, financial affairs.

Peter earned a BA in Political Science from the University of Buffalo and an MBA in Finance from Baruch College. After spending three years at Sanford Bernstein & Co. in marketing services, he began his own computer graphic design business, Gordon Associates Inc., in 1990. In 1997 Peter teamed with Harvey Appelbaum, an award winning creative director, and formed inc3. In 2005, inc3 was sold to Kay Printing, a Clifton, New Jersey company, and re-branded as Kay Multimedia (KMM). In 2011, Peter became the Director of New Business Development for Dorian Orange, a Motion Design firm dedicated to producing captivating, innovative, and memorable brand messages.

Peter is a member of the American Association of Daily Money Managers; a Certified Senior Advisor (CSA); a member of the Orion Resource Group, and is pursuing Geriatric Care Management education at the Brookdale Center for Healthy Aging. He lives in Forest Hills, NY, is married, and has two sons.

Karen Greenberg, Esq.

Karen Greenberg received her BA from Cornell University College of Arts and Sciences and her JD from Brooklyn Law School. After graduation, she served as a hearing officer ("Administrative Law Judge") at the N.Y.S Department of Social Services conducting administrative hearings involving public assistance, foster care and Medicaid provider fraud and abuse. Karen then joined DC 37 Municipal Employees Legal Services ("MELS") which provides legal services in a wide range of civil matters to employees and retirees of the City of New York, as part of their union health and security package of benefits. There she practiced in the areas of matrimonial/family law, government benefits, housing, consumer law, bankruptcy and wills. She practiced matrimonial law exclusively for 30 years, including all aspects of custody, child support, maintenance, and equitable distribution of marital property from inception through trial. For the last 26 years, Karen was a supervising attorney of the Matrimonial Department at MELS. As a matrimonial attorney, she developed a special interest and expertise in the area of the distribution of pensions and retirement benefits in divorce. As a result of her recognized expertise in this area, Karen frequently lectured at numerous continuing legal education programs for attorneys, sponsored by among other organizations, Legal Services of New York, In Motion, the Brooklyn Bar Association and the Staten Island Bar Association.

In March 2015, Karen opened an office for the private practice of matrimonial and family law, doing both litigation and mediation. She also serves as a consulting/reviewing attorney for parties in divorce mediation. She acts as consultant to matrimonial attorneys on the issues of equitable distribution of retirement benefits and QDROs. For more information about Karen's practice, visit www.kgreenberglaw.com.

Wendy A. Harris, Esq.

Wendy Harris is the founding member of Wendy Harris Law, PLLC, a law firm dedicated to providing quality services to individuals, families and small businesses. Wendy has over 14 years of experience representing a diverse range of clients in civil litigations, regulatory investigations, estate planning, and matrimonial and family law matters.

After receiving her JD, cum laude, from Cornell Law School, Wendy began her legal career clerking for Judge Kollar-Kotelly and Judge Oberdorfer, both of the United States District Court for the District of Columbia.

She then went on to practice with the New York offices of WilmerHale (formerly Wilmer Cutler & Pickering), and Richards Kibbe & Orbe LLP, before founding WHL, representing both Fortune 500 companies and professionals in high profile litigations and civil and criminal investigations. Wendy also has had an active pro bono practice and has represented clients in family law and matrimonial matters, and has drafted an amicus brief for the Second Circuit on behalf of Children's Rights, Inc. In 2008, she received the "Above and Beyond Pro Bono Achievement" award from Sanctuary for Families for her representation of a victim of domestic violence in order of protection, custody and divorce proceedings.

Wendy is a member of the New York Bar, and is admitted to practice before both federal and state courts in New York. She is also an active member of the New York State Bar Association and the New York Women's Bar Association. For more information about Wendy's practice, visit www.wendyharrislaw.com.

Paul Hymowitz, Ph.D.

Paul Hymowitz, Ph.D. has been practicing psychology for over 30 years. Specializing in divorce and custody work, he previously co-edited one book on the matter, entitled *A Handbook of Divorce and Custody*.

Paul Hymowitz is on the faculties of New York Medical College, Yeshiva University and IPTAR (Institute for Psychoanalytic Training and Research). For more information, visit paulhymowitzphd.com.

Deborah E. Kaminetzky, Esq.

Deborah E. Kaminetzky is the founding member of Kaminetzky & Associates, P.C. located in Cedarhurst, New York. Prior to starting the firm Deborah worked at a Long Island firm where she learned the practice of Matrimonial and Family law. Deborah has also worked at the New York Department of Consumer Affairs where she was responsible for prosecuting unlicensed home improvement contractors and negotiating settlements for consumers. Prior to practicing law, Ms. Kaminetzky served on the Architectural Control Committee of a Home Owners Association in Boca Raton while living in Florida, and was the president of a commercial property management corporation in the New York Metro area.

Ms. Kaminetzky is a member of the American Bar Association (General Practice, Solo and Small firm Division and Law Practice Management Sections), New

York State Bar Association (Estate, Family Law and General Practice Sections), Nassau County Bar Association (where she serves as Chair of the Technology and Practice Management Committee, and is active in the Community Relations and Education Committee, Women in the Law committees and General and Solo Committee) Great Neck Lawyers Association, and The Nassau County Women's Bar Association.

Ms. Kaminetzky was recently appointed to the Committee on Law Practice Management of the New York State Bar Association. Ms. Kaminetzky serves on the Board of Directors of the Yashar Attorney and Judges Chapter of Hadassah as a Vice President, and was their Woman of the Year 2012. Deborah graduated from New York Law School in 1991 and the University of Michigan, Ann Arbor in 1986.

Ms. Kaminetzky was admitted to the First Department in 1991 and the United States Supreme Court Bar in February of 2015.

Deborah is on the Matrimonial fee dispute arbitration panel for Nassau County. She expanded her alternative dispute resolution practice by completing a Mediation certificate program in December of 2013 from The New York Peace Institute.

Ms. Kaminetzky has spoken to various groups on topics including matrimonial law, technology and social media use, and disaster preparedness for business including cybersecurity.

For more information about Ms. Kaminetzky and her practice, visit www.kaminetzkylaw.com.

Andrea Kent

Andrea Kent is a franchise owner of Prime National Credit Repair. Andrea's professional background includes over 30 years in Financial Services working 4.5 years as the VP of Mortgage Lending for Guaranteed Rate and prior to that Andrea spent 27 years as a payments expert for American Express and Visa Inc. Her extensive experience in mortgage lending and credit cards is a valuable asset for her clients at Prime National. With Andrea's long history of working with banks and credit card companies, she really understands credit which is so misunderstood.

Andrea knows that having a good credit score is critical to one's financial success. Without it you can't get a good rate on a mortgage, credit card or car loan, rent an apartment, or even apply for a job. Prime National Credit Repair offers industry-leading credit repair services backed with a 100% money-back guarantee. They have an excellent reputation with an A+ rating with the BBB.

Andrea is active both in NYC and the community of Southampton where she has owned a home for the past 17 years; Andrea is a runner and triathlete. She has participated in the New York City Triathlon four times (yes, that's swimming in the Hudson River) and Andrea has run 9 marathons including the New York City

Marathon four times. Andrea was nominated in 2013 as the NYRR Runner of the Year. Andrea is also on the Board as Secretary for NAWBO-NYC (The National Association of Women Business Owners)

For more information contact Andrea Kent at:
akent@primenationalny.com; call 212-889-0613, or visit http://pncr.us/andreakent.

Cheryl Lazarus, CLC, CRC, CDC

Cheryl Lazarus, CLC, CRC, CDC is a Certified Divorce and Relationship Coach, Speaker, and NLP Master Practitioner with therapeutic training. Having gone through her own divorce successfully, Cheryl understands the practical and emotional challenges of the divorce process and the opportunities in redesigning one's life.

When working with clients, Cheryl provides actionable steps, strategies and resources which help clients to save time, money and have less aggravation during the divorce process. In addition, Cheryl includes heart-centered energetic and spiritual practices which helps women and men to heal and move forward on a profound level which positively affects all areas of their lives.

Cheryl has presented at the United Nations, to professional organizations, and has been on expert panels. She also holds workshops and support groups on topics ranging from "The Integrated Divorce," "Healing and Letting Go," to "Dating, Relationships and Becoming Emotionally Available Again."

Cheryl also coaches privately in person and globally through Skype and via phone consultations. For more information, visit www.zengalove.com, www.easiertransitions.com.

Robyn Myler Mann, Esq.

clients during some of their most challenging times: in family disputes and elder matters involving loss and grief. Using careful legal and practical analysis, creative thinking and a deep insight into each family's needs, offers individualized and workable solutions for clients in a divorce and elder law practice in New York City focused on Manhattan, Brooklyn and the Bronx. Admitted to the Bar in New York, Connecticut and Colorado, Robyn serves the needs of clients in Supreme Court, Civil Court, Family Court and Surrogate Courts, guiding them through complicated and difficult divorces, child custody disputes, child support enforcement matters, and elder law matters to successful conclusions.

A graduate of Emory University and Benjamin N. Cardozo School of Law, Robyn is also a trained mediator in family disputes, helping couples to resolve parenting plans and financial matters during separation and divorce.

Donna Manvich MA, JD

Donna Manvich holds a J.D. from Touro Law Center and a master's degree in Philosophy from SUNY Stony Brook. She is president of Jurissistance Inc., a company dedicated to legal research and writing. Ms. Manvich is also passionate in her advocacy regarding such matters as International Parental Child Abduction and children's rights. Her collaboration by way of support with Ms. Marquez is a natural fit and the two have worked together for many years.

Ann Marquez, Esq.

Ann Marquez, Esq. is admitted to practice law in the State of New York, as well as the United States District Courts for the Eastern and Southern Districts of New York. Ms. Marquez is a passionate advocate of a child's best interests and possesses extensive experience advocating issues relating to child welfare (child abuse, neglect) international parental child abduction, and all custody/visitation matters. Ms. Marquez is on the attorney list of the US Department of State for cases involving international parental child abductions under the Hague Convention.

Ms. Marquez began her career as an agency attorney for the City of New York's Child Protective Services, representing the agency in over 1500 various child welfare proceedings. As a result, she gained significant insight into the "best interests" of the child, and now dedicates her practice to the advocacy of children and parents in domestic and international cases.

Ms. Marquez represented the prevailing party in a complex case of international parental child abduction in federal district court that distinguished a recent U.S. Supreme Court ruling. See Buenaver v. Vasquez (In re R.V.B), 13-CV-4354 (E.D.N.Y. 2014).

Michael A. Mills, CMPS

Michael A. Mills is a Loan Officer in the Residential Mortgage Division of Sterling National Bank (Sterling Bancorp), a Certified Mortgage Planning Specialist® and an active member of the CMPS® Institute. The CMPS® Institute is a national organization that certifies mortgage bankers and brokers, with a stated mission, "...to help homeowners and homebuyers improve their lives by using the right mortgage strategies."

Before choosing to advise and educate homebuyers and current owners about mortgage planning, helping them to achieve their financial goals; Michael worked to obtain the same results in other areas of personal finance and banking. His experience spans multiple disciplines within the umbrella of financial planning, with a core focus on estate planning, retirement planning, education funding, investment management and family risk management through insurance.

Michael's aptitude and interest in asset management ultimately led him to accept a position as an investment wholesaler for Deutsche Bank. In this role he become a respected resource in tax-free fixed income, short-term bond, managed commodity, and mortgage-back security based investing.

In 2011 Michael joined Sterling National Bank with a lending practice centered around helping individuals and families reach their financial goals, now utilizing optimal mortgage financing and planning discussions instead of mutual funds and insurance. With a holistic approach to mortgage planning and its diverse applications, he continues to draw on his prior experience and insight to add greater depth to his consultative approach. Michael often identifying opportunities outside of the mortgage world, helping clients achieve other aspects of their financial goals by pointing them in the direction of other respected and vetted professionals.

Scott A. Mills, DC

Dr. Scott A. Mills is a chiropractor with a passion for empowering others with the knowledge and tools needed to optimize health and life.

While going through a divorce he became dismayed at the lack of authentic, modern feeling resources for men recovering from divorce. He noticed the best help he received was from guys who had already been through the process and moved forward with their own successful lives.

In 2015 Scott launched DivorceWingman.com to encourage, support and give hope to guys in the recovery process. The idea is to pay forward the help he received and bring guys through the post-divorce funk into a new and better chapter of life. For more information, visit www.DivorceWingman.com.

Kimberly Mishkin, CDC

Kimberly Mishkin, cofounder and director of SAS for Women®, is an educator of 21 years and former administrator for The Spence School. Kim holds a BA in Education from Miami University, a MS in Science Education from Wright State University, and is licensed in Educational Leadership through The Ohio State University. She is a CDC Certified Divorce Coach® and a Grief Recovery Specialist® with The Grief Recovery Institute®. Kim was divorced after 13 years of marriage and is now happily remarried and a new mother to a beautiful baby boy.

SAS for Women® is New York City's first comprehensive resource that provides strategic information, action-oriented coaching, and expert resources and tools to women navigating separation, divorce, empty-nesting, and widowhood. For more information, visit sasforwomen.com.

Bonnie L. Mohr, Esq.

Bonnie L. Mohr, managing member of the Law Offices of Bonnie L. Mohr, PLLC, started the firm in 2008 to create a practice that educates and guides clients through life-altering and stressful family situations utilizing a comprehensive, holistic and strategic approach.

The firm's practice focuses on matrimonial law including contested and uncontested divorces, prenuptial and postnuptial agreements, and post-judgment enforcements. Bonnie also practices in the family courts on such matters as child support, parenting time (custody and visitation), paternity and family offense matters.

Bonnie L. Mohr is licensed to practice law in the states of New York (2004), New Jersey (2004), and Pennsylvania (2008). She is also licensed to practice in the district courts of the Eastern District of New York, the Southern District of New York and the District of New Jersey.

Bonnie's memberships include the matrimonial and family law committees for the Women's Bar Association, New York County Lawyer's Association and New York State Bar Association. Bonnie is also a member of the New York City Bar Association, where she was leader of the matrimonial mentoring circle. For more information about Bonnie's practice, visit www.mohresq.com.

Andrea Moss

Andrea Moss is the founder of Moss Wellness, a holistic nutrition team devoted to supporting their clients learn how to finally feel confident about what to eat. The nutrition coaches at Moss Wellness will help you make enjoyable changes based on your individual lifestyle, personal preferences, and body type.

Andrea and her team work with you to naturally deconstruct food cravings, skyrocket energy levels, balance out your digestive system, and reach an ideal weight – without torturous dieting!

The Moss Wellness team works with clients and corporations around the globe to make healthy eating and healthy living easy, pleasurable, and lots of fun! For more information about Moss Wellness, visit www.mosswellness.com.

Susan Nason

Susan Nason was trained by her aunt, author Adele Faber and co-author Elaine Mazlish and has been a facilitator of their "How To Talk So Kids Will Listen, How To Listen So Kids Will Talk" and "Siblings Without Rivalry" workshops for over 35 years. She recently retired from her position as Assistant to the Director of The First Presbyterian Church Nursery School where she worked for 35 years; her position included working with parents as the school's Parent Educator and working with teachers to facilitate a harmonious atmosphere in their classrooms. Susan has a thriving domestic and international Parent Counseling practice specializing in exploring conscious parenting employing therapeutic, spiritual and practical approaches to the challenges of raising children. Susan teaches concrete and effective communication skills to parents of children of all ages.

She has facilitated workshops at the Ackerman Institute for the Family, Seleni Institute, All Souls Church School, The Brick Church School, First Presbyterian Church Nursery School, Barrow Street Nursery School, Rockefeller Children's School, Ross Global Academy, Girl's Prep, Chelsea Day, Bowery Babes and Beit Rabban. She conducts teacher trainings in and around the tri-state area. She has been a speaker for the Parents' League, the Junior League, Hudson River Park Mamas, Bowery Babes and other organizations and schools.

Most importantly, she brings her love and compassion of being a proud mother and ecstatic grandmother to her work with parents and children.

Susan is available for private sessions or to facilitate parenting workshops.

Amy Neiman

Amy Neiman, M.A., is the Founder and CEO of *a simplified life*, providing organizing services to empower professionals to be more profitable and productive through simplifying their workspace. Her proven, disciplined approach allows individuals to establish an easy-to-follow process which helps organize their time, space, paper, and possessions more effectively. By de-cluttering and building structure, Amy has helped countless professionals better focus on their businesses and their lives.

With a Masters in Psychology and spending 15 years in the entertainment industry, Amy's organizing skills were well honed before launching her business. She firmly believes that organizing can be pain-free and consume a minimal amount of time during the day.

Amy is a contributor to the book, THE HAPPY LAW PRACTICE: EXPERT STRATEGIES TO BUILD BUSINESS WHILE MAINTAINING PEACE OF MIND. Her chapter is titled, Maximize Productivity: Tips for Organizing Your Office. Amy is also a member of the National Association of Professional Organizers (NAPO). For more information, visit www.amyneiman.com.

Joseph Nivin, Esq.

Joseph Nivin is a solo practitioner at The Law Offices of Joseph H. Nivin, P.C., a law firm focusing on family and matrimonial law, with offices in Jamaica, Queens and in Manhattan. He graduated from Brooklyn Law School in 2007, and received his undergraduate degree at the University of Pennsylvania in 2004. Prior to opening his practice, Mr. Nivin was an agency attorney at the Administration for Children's Services of the City of New York, where he represented the New York City government in child abuse and neglect proceedings. Mr. Nivin is a member of the New York State Bar Association, the New York City Bar Association, the Queens County Bar Association, and the Brandeis Association of Queens County. He serves on the Queens County Bar Association Juvenile Justice Committee and on the Committee on Lawyer Assistance. Mr. Nivin is a member of the Assigned Counsel/Attorneys for Children Panel for the Second Judicial Department, and is certified to represent indigent litigants, as well as children, in Family Court proceedings at both the trial and appellate levels. He was selected as a 2015 Rising Star in Super Lawyers magazine. More information regarding Mr. Nivin's office is available on the web at www.nivinlaw.com.

Suzanne K. Oshima

Suzanne K. Oshima is a Matchmaker, Dating Coach & Founder at Dream Bachelor & Bachelorette

Suzanne has worked with thousands of single men and women to help them uncover the core issues of what may be preventing or blocking them from finding love. Suzanne has helped them transform and elevate their dating lives to meet, attract & keep the right one.

Suzanne is also the Founder of Single in Stilettos. Single in Stilettos gives you the best dating advice from all the top dating experts to help you meet, attract & keep the right man… so you can go from Single in Stilettos to Engaged in Stilettos!

Suzanne has been seen in the media on Bravo TV, The Today Show, Good Afternoon America, ABC News, Inside Edition, BBC Radio, Men's Health, Glamour, and much more! For more information, visit www.dreambachelor.com or www.singleinstilettos.com.

Tina Paymaster, HHC, AADP

Tina Paymaster is a Certified Health & Lifestyle Coach, recipe developer and inspirational speaker.

Combining nutritional guidance with spirituality and psychological techniques, Tina helps her clients gain the energy, confidence and clarity they need to break through their self-defeating habits so they can create the bodies and lives they truly desire.

Her approach focuses on aligning the mind, body and soul so results are achieved with less resistance and more sustainability.

Tina's mission is to inspire others around the world to rise above their fears, reclaim their health and happiness, create their own path in life, stop settling and start living!

Tina currently works with private clients around the country, develops recipes for her blog and top health food companies and holds frequent speaking events and workshops. She has been featured on Shape, MindBodyGreen, SheKnows, Live Science, Elephant Journal and other digital publications. Email tina.paymaster@gmail.com or visit www.tinapaymaster.com for more information.

David Perry

David began his career in real estate 1987, working in finance and commercial leasing for Olympia and York, the largest NYC developer at the time. In 1998, he was part of the team that sold the Woolworth Building. For eleven years he was the Director of Sales and an executive for The Clarett Group, one of the city's largest residential developers. In those eleven years he sold over a billion dollars of residential real estate and leased more than one thousand apartments. During that time, he managed the leasing of The Montrose, Post Luminaria, Post Toscana and the Brooklyner, and was responsible for sales at 272 West 107th Street, Place 57, Chelsea House, Sky House, Forte, and 200 West End Avenue.

During the course of his career he was also involved in more than $1 billion in investment sales including such notable addresses as: 320 Park Avenue, 175 Water Street, 99 John Street, 233 Broadway, 308 East 38th Street, 385 First Avenue, 389 East 89th Street, and 111 Lawrence Street.

In 2011 he was the Director of Sales for Brown Harris Stevens Select's The Laureate, where he sold over $120 million of apartments in less than one year. David is leveraging this experience to market and sell exceptional residential properties and provide expert negotiation skills for purchasers.

David was the co-chair for the Real Estate Board of New York's Downtown Residential Division from 2005-2010. He served on the board of Community Access, a non-profit that built supportive low income housing from 2004 to 2010. He now serves as A Parent At Large for the PTA at P.S. 199 where his daughter is attending grammar school. He maintains a 15 handicap on the golf course and practices yoga up to five times per week. A Manhattan resident since 1988, David resides in the Upper West Side. Visit www.bhsusa.com/davideperry for more information.

Kymberly A. Robinson, Esq.

Kymberly is an associate attorney with Rincker Law, PLLC. Kymberly is admitted to practice law in New York and Florida. She attended Union College in Schenectady, New York for her undergraduate studies, where she graduated with high honors as a psychology major. She then obtained her J.D. from Pace University School of Law in White Plains, New York and, subsequently, her L.L.M. (with a concentration in family law) from the Benjamin N. Cardozo School of Law in Manhattan. Kymberly entered the field of matrimonial and family law as a way to couple her interest in psychology and personal relationships with her legal education.

Before joining Rincker Law, PLLC, Kymberly was an associate at boutique matrimonial law firms in Westchester County, Manhattan, and Florida. She was also a volunteer at the New York County Access to Justice Program-Uncontested Divorce Clinic where she assisted self-represented litigants in the divorce process. During law school Kymberly also participated in two legal clinics: one at the Pace Women's Justice Center, where she represented clients in obtaining orders of protection and another at the Brooklyn Family Defense Project, where she assisted in defending families in child abuse and neglect proceedings.

Kymberly likes to spend her free time with her family and also enjoys working out, cooking healthy meals, and getting together with friends. She lives in Westchester County, New York with her husband and daughter.

For more information about Rincker Law, PLLC, visit www.rinckerlaw.com.

Cari B. Rincker, Esq.

Cari Rincker is the principal attorney at Rincker Law, PLLC, a national law practice focusing on "Food, Farm & Family." She is licensed to practice law in New York, New Jersey, Connecticut, Illinois and Washington, D.C. Cari was named as a Rising Star for Metro New York in 2015 by "Super Lawyers" and is an award-winning blogger. Cari is involved in several professional organizations including the Association for the Bar of the City of New York's Matrimonial Law Committee.

In addition to her litigation practice, Cari is also a trained mediator for divorces, child custody and visitation, and commercial disputes. She was also an adjunct professor at New York University, College of Steinhardt (2013-2014), where she taught an undergraduate food law class.

On the food and agriculture side of her practice, Cari is the Chair of the American Bar Association, General Practice, Solo & Small Firm Division's Agriculture Law Committee and won the 2014 Excellence in Agriculture Law Award by the American Agriculture Law Association.

Cari is a distinguished alumni from Lake Land College in Mattoon, Illinois and Texas A & M University. Before attending law school at Pace University School of Law in White Plains, New York, Cari obtained a Master of Science from the University of Illinois. Cari's practice is family-centered and counsels clients on a myriad of family law and matrimonial law issues.

For more information about Rincker Law, PLLC, visit www.rinckerlaw.com. Cari is also active on social media. You can follow her on Twitter @CariRincker @RinckerLaw and Instagram and Facebook.

Nina E. Rumbold, Esq.

Nina E. Rumbold, Esq., is a Partner in the firm of Rumbold & Seidelman, LLP, practicing exclusively in the areas of adoption and reproductive law. Ms. Rumbold is a fellow the American Academy of Adoption Attorneys, the American Academy of Assisted Reproductive Technology Attorneys and a member of the National LGBT Bar Association Family Law Institute. She received her Juris Doctor degree from New York University Law School and is admitted to practice in New York and New Jersey. Ms. Rumbold has lectured on Adoption Law and Reproductive Law as a member of the faculties of the ABA Family Law Section, Practicing Law Institute, the New York Judicial Institute and the New York City Bar Center for Continuing Legal Education. She is the past President of New York Attorneys for Adoption and Family Formation (NYAAFF), an organization of New York attorneys which advocates for legislative reform in the areas of adoption and reproductive law. She is also a regular speaker at the Adoptive Parents Committee annual conference. For more information, visit www.adoptionlawny.com.

Thomas Ruskin

Thomas Ruskin has been the President of the CMP Protective and Investigative Group, Inc. for over the past decade. The CMP Group is an internationally recognized investigative and security firm with clients and corporations from around the world.

Thomas Ruskin is a highly decorated former New York City Police Detective Investigator. He was responsible for Crisis Management for the Mayor, Police Commissioner and Deputy Commissioners of Operations and Crime Control Strategies for New York City. He has been involved in cases that have received worldwide attention, including the 1993 terrorist attack on the World Trade Center, the NYC subway system bombing, airline crashes, police shootings, hostage situations and major organized crime and narcotic cases.

The majority of Mr. Ruskin's background ranging over two decades in law enforcement, has been spent in the field of investigation. He began his career with the Department of Investigations Inspector General offices of the Department of Environmental Protection and Fire Department, rising to the position of Senior Investigator. In the NYPD Mr. Ruskin was assigned to the Burglary Latent Print Unit, Anti-Crime Squad, and the Organized Control Bureau-Narcotics Division's Special Projects Unit. He was responsible for cases that lead to arrests of individuals who committed Federal and State crimes and was responsible for a 3 million dollar federally subsidized undercover program.

Mr. Ruskin's background includes responsibility for the protection of President Bill Clinton, Vice-President Al Gore, Mrs. Hillary Clinton, Mrs. Tipper Gore, 1998 Presidential candidate Senator Robert Dole and other national and international dignitaries and Heads of State. Mr. Ruskin has received specialized training from the NYPD Intelligence Division and the United States Secret Service in Dignitary Protection.

Mr. Ruskin is recognized as an international investigative, security and crisis management expert by various news organizations including NBC, ABC, The Today Show, Good Morning America, CNN, Fox News, Channel,Sky News and 1010 WINS News. He has made frequent appearances on various TV and radio shows.

Sabra R. Sasson, Esq.

Sabra R. Sasson is an attorney and mediator practicing in New York City. She is the founder and Principal of Sabra Law Group, PLLC, a mediation and law practice in midtown Manhattan that offers legal and mediation services to its clients. Sabra handles the legal aspects of major transitions – buying or selling property, planning for marriage or getting divorced – and protects her clients' interests so they can focus on their evolution into this new life change. She employs her skills and experience to help her clients focus on life post-divorce and guide them through the process to get there. For couples embarking on marriage, she helps them protect accumulated assets and create a plan for building assets, wealth and valuables in the future.

Sabra graduated from Brandeis University in 1995 with a Bachelor's in Mathematics and minor in Education, whereafter she enrolled in law school and graduated from Hofstra University School of Law in 1998 with her Juris Doctorate. She sat for the bar exam in three states and was thereafter admitted to practice law in New York, New Jersey and Connecticut, and has been practicing law ever since.

Sabra is currently writing a book to guide and empower couples through the process of "uncoupling," THE HARMONIOUS DIVORCE: THE FOUR STEP PROCESS TO UNCOUPLING. She is also the author of a chapter in the best-selling book SUCCESS FROM THE HEART. Connect with her at www.sabralawgroup.com.

Stefany Schaefer

Stefany Schaefer assists with special projects at FamilyKind and also serves as the FamilyKind Meetup Group organizer. She has worked with children and families in a variety of roles including private tutor, nanny, and a Court Appointed Special Advocate. Through her work, she has gained experience in family dynamics, family court proceedings in abuse and neglect cases, child development, and family conflict. Ms. Schaefer earned her B.A. in Forensic Psychology and Certificate in Dispute Resolution from John Jay College of Criminal Justice. She is committed to continue to empower families both through her work with FamilyKind and with her aspiration to pursue a career in family law.

Denise E. Seidelman, Esq.

Denise Seidelman is a partner in Rumbold & Seidelman, LLP, a firm devoted exclusively to adoption and reproductive law since 1996. Denise's practice includes the full gamut of adoption services ranging from private placement and agency adoptions to second and second parent adoptions. She also provides legal counsel to those building their families through egg, sperm, and embryo donation as well as those needing the assistance of a gestational surrogate. She is actively involved in the legislative effort to reform New York law so that those building their families with the assistance of reproductive technology will be recognized under New York law. Denise is licensed to practice law in New York and New Jersey. She is on the Board of Path2Parenthood, a Fellow of the American Academy of Adoption Attorneys, the American Academy of Assisted Reproductive Technology Attorneys, and a member of the National LGBT Bar Association Family Law Institute. Denise has lectured frequently on the legal aspects of the adoption process and on reproductive law before the New York State and New York City Bar Associations as well as before the New York Judicial Institute. Denise is a graduate of the University of Pennsylvania and the Washington College of Law. She was admitted to practice in New York in 1980 and in New Jersey in 2006. She began her legal career as a trial attorney for the Criminal Defense Division of the New York City Legal Aid Society. For more information visit www.adoptionlawny.com.

Mona Sharaf

Mona Sharaf is a New York City based, personal shopper and image consultant for both men and women. Her mission is to help her clients create the image they are looking to portray all while making them feel more beautiful, confident and educated on how to shop.

She studied image consulting at the Fashion Institute of Technology. She has worked for very reputable clothing designers such as Norma Kamali, where she worked as a personal shopper developing wardrobes for her client base all around the country.

Mona is committed to working very closely with her clients to develop their personal style. She listens carefully to their needs, goals and lifestyles and incorporates current and diverse pieces into a wardrobe that already exists.

Diane Spear, LCSW-R

Diane Spear is a psychotherapist and licensed clinical social worker in private practice in New York City since 1995, with a Master's Degree in Clinical Social Work from New York University and a certificate from the Institute of Developmental Psychotherapy. She treats older adolescents up through older adults – couples, former couples, and individuals – helping them deal with their problems so they can live more satisfying lives. She works with patients in person, and through phone and Skype sessions, so her practice includes people in the tristate area and throughout the world. She has written about couples counseling with high conflict people as a guest blogger for Psychology Today's website blog "Stop Walking on Eggshells" (https://www.psychologytoday.com/blog/stop-walking-eggshells/201307/couples-counseling-high-conflict-people), aspects of relationships for the online women's magazine Your Tango, and relationships and general topics in her own blog (dianespeartherapy.com/blog.html). Diane is committed to helping people find the joy in everyday life.

Nicole Trivlis, Esq.

Nicole Trivlis began her legal career in matrimonial law as a paralegal upon her graduation from the Catholic University of America (BA - 2004). She is a graduate of Pace University School of Law (JD - 2008). Nicole is currently an associate with the Silva Thomas PC law firm (www.silvathomas.com) in New York, New York where she focuses her practice on matrimonial law. Nicole is admitted to practice law in New York, Connecticut, the District of Columbia, the Southern District of New York, and the Eastern District of New York. She has represented high-net worth individuals in contested and uncontested matrimonial actions, paternity proceedings, and custody matters. Nicole has negotiated and drafted various prenuptial, postnuptial, settlement, and separation agreements.

Nicole also has significant experience with national and international courts. While in law school, she interned for Trial Chambers III at the International Criminal Tribunal for the Former Yugoslavia in The Hague, The Netherlands and The United States Court of International Trade. Additionally, she was a student attorney for John Jay Legal Services Immigration Justice Clinic at Pace Law School where she actively represented immigration clients before the Immigration Courts.

Following her graduation from law school, Nicole gained extensive experience with the New York State Courts and the Federal Courts as an attorney in private practice in New York and as a legal consultant for private and government agencies in Washington, D.C. Nicole is an active member of the New York Women's Bar Association, and was the Chair of the New Lawyer's Section of the Westchester County Bar Association (2010-2012) and was elected to the Board of Directors of the Putnam County Bar Association (2011-2012). Nicole has been instrumental in organizing several CLE programs and events through her active participation in these professional associations.

Andrea Vacca, Esq.

Andrea Vacca is the founder of Vacca Law and Mediation, a law firm in Manhattan that focuses exclusively on non-adversarial divorce and family law matters. Ms. Vacca regularly lectures and writes on the topics of collaborative law, mediation, and topics related to non-adversarial family law. She blogs at www.creativeresolutionsblog.com.

After practicing traditional litigation-focused family law for many years, Andrea became certified as a family and divorce mediator and later as a collaborative divorce attorney. Andrea's firm now works only with clients who want to keep their divorces out of court and want their prenuptial and postnuptial agreements negotiated in a non-adversarial manner. Andrea uses collaborative and cooperative divorce processes as well as mediation to achieve these goals.

She serves as Vice President of the New York Women's Bar Association; Secretary of the New York Association of Collaborative Professionals; is on the Editorial Board of Matrimonial Strategist; on the Advisory Council of FamilyKind; is a member of the Family and Divorce Mediation Council of Greater New York; a member of New York County Lawyers; and a member of the New York State Bar Association. Andrea received her B.A. in Journalism from SUNY College at Buffalo and her J.D. from Albany Law School of Union University. She also has a certificate in Positive Psychology.

Andrea can be reached through her website www.vaccalaw.com, through her email avacca@vaccalaw.com, or by calling 212-768-1115.

Meredith Verona, CPA/ABV/CFF

Meredith Verona is a Manager in the Litigation Services Group at Mark S Gottlieb CPA PC. She has over ten years of experience, working exclusively on litigation related matters. Specifically, Meredith specializes in business valuation and forensics for varied purposes including matrimonial, gift and estate, and shareholder disputes. She has worked on cases in multiple industries including medical, professional firms, retail and restaurant services for small to mid-size companies predominately located in the New York area. Her previous experience includes calculating/auditing business interruption claims and litigation support.

Ms. Verona is a member of the American Institute of Certified Public Accountants (AICPA), National Association of Certified Valuation Analysts (NACVA). She received her B.A. in Economics from Rutgers University and her M.B.A. with a concentration in Accounting from Monmouth University.

She is an Accredited Business Valuator (ABV) and a Certified in Financial Forensics (CFF) from the American Institute of Certified Public Accountants. She also received the designation of Certified Valuation Analyst (CVA) from the National Association of Certified Valuation Analysts.

Debra Vey Voda-Hamilton, Esq.

Debra Vey Voda-Hamilton is the principal of Hamilton Law and Mediation (HLM). She is an attorney mediator who works with pet people and pet service providers who want to pursue their passion of helping people, their pets and all animals in general, while reducing exposure to litigation. She presents her programs, which teach people how to communicate without resorting to litigation, all over the country. She has been mentioned or featured in Forbes, US News and World Report, The Wall Street Journal, The New York Times and the Chicago Sun Times.

Debra graduated from Benjamin N. Cardozo Law School in 1983, was admitted to practice in New York in 1984. For more information about Debra and her practice, visit www.hamiltonlawandmediation.com or Debra's blog at hamiltonlawandmediation.blogspot.com.

Joseph Wexler

Joseph has cultivated a practice as a financial advisor working alongside goal oriented people who know that the ripple effect of their financial decisions (good and bad) will impact those that they love. Wexler has a knack for navigating his clients to the best options in growing, protecting, and distributing wealth in the right way and at the right time. Joseph also guides his clients to a better financial future through taking a consultative approach to systematically prioritizing mid to long term savings goals.

27,99 ✓

44937508R00377

Made in the USA
Middletown, DE
20 June 2017